The Sundance Writer

A Rhetoric, Reader, and Research Guide

BRIEF FIFTH EDITION

The Sundance Writer

A Rhetoric, Reader, and Research Guide

BRIEF FIFTH EDITION

Mark Connelly
Milwaukee Area Technical College

WADSWORTH
CENGAGE Learning™

Australia • Brazil • Japan • Korea • Mexico • Singapore • Spain • United Kingdom • United States

WADSWORTH
CENGAGE Learning™

The Sundance Writer: A Rhetoric, Reader, and Research Guide, Brief Fifth Edition
Mark Connelly

Senior Publisher: Lyn Uhl

Publisher: Monica Eckman

Acquisitions Editor: Margaret Leslie

Senior Development Editor: Judith Fifer

Assistant Editor: Amy Haines

Editorial Assistant: Danielle Warchol

Associate Media Editor: Janine Tangney

Managing Media Editor: Cara Douglass-Graff

Executive Marketing Manager: Stacey Purviance

Marketing Coordinator: Brittany Blais

Marketing Communications Manager: Courtney Morris

Content Project Manager: Aimee Bear

Senior Art Director: Jill Ort

Senior Rights Specialist: Dean Dauphinais

Cover Designer: Sarah Bishins

Cover Image: gettyimages.com

For product information and technology assistance, contact us at
Cengage Learning Customer & Sales Support, 1-800-354-9706

For permission to use material from this text or product, submit all requests online at **www.cengage.com/permissions**. Further permissions questions can be e-mailed to **permissionrequest@cengage.com**.

Library of Congress Control Number: 2011936487

ISBN-13: 978-1-111-84137-9

ISBN-10: 1-111-84137-3

Wadsworth
20 Channel Center Street
Boston, MA 02210
USA

Cengage Learning is a leading provider of customized learning solutions with office locations around the globe, including Singapore, the United Kingdom, Australia, Mexico, Brazil and Japan. Locate your local office at **international.cengage.com/region**

Cengage Learning products are represented in Canada by Nelson Education, Ltd.

For your course and learning solutions, visit **www.cengage.com.**

Purchase any of our products at your local college store or at our preferred online store **www.cengagebrain.com.**

Instructors: Please visit **login.cengage.com** and log in to access instructor-specific resources.

Printed in the United States of America
1 2 3 4 5 6 7 15 14 13 12 11

For Larry Riley

TEACHER · MENTOR · FRIEND

CONTENTS

EXPANDED CONTENTS

Part Three THE RESEARCH PAPER

23 Conducting Research 513

Part Four   WRITING IN COLLEGE

PREFACE

Valued for its real-world emphasis and focus on critical thinking, *The Sundance Writer* is the complete textbook for composition courses. Going beyond the standard presentation of readings, grammar, and the writing process, *The Sundance Writer* presents strategies for professional writing, conducting research, analyzing and using images, and interpreting literature. *The Sundance Writer's* balance of theory and strategy, blend of readability and intellectual rigor, critical thinking focus, and practical emphasis on writing for the "real world" make it a flexible teaching and learning tool.

New to This Edition

The fifth edition was thoroughly reviewed by composition instructors from across the country, who called it "unparalleled to comparable texts" and praised its "impressive" readings and assignments. The new *Sundance Writer* builds on the proven success of previous editions, maintaining its readable style and easy-to-navigate format while offering innovative new features for the ever-evolving needs of today's classroom.

Updated MLA and APA Styles

The documentation in this text has been thoroughly updated to reflect current MLA and APA styles. The updates are based on the seventh edition of the *MLA Handbook for Writers of Research Papers* and the sixth edition of the *Publication Manual of the American Psychological Association.*

New Readings

The fifth edition features fourteen new readings, including classic pieces, such as Martin Gansberg's "Thirty-Eight Who Saw Murder and Didn't Call the Police," as well as new essays, such as Sharon Begley's "What's in a Word?" and Christopher Jencks's "Reinventing the American Dream."

New Critical Issues Online Readings with Research Assignments

Organized by mode, the reader portion of *The Sundance Writer* includes a thematic anthology of ninety-nine electronic readings that students can access through the Cengage CourseMate for this text. The new edition offers expanded commentary and critical thinking questions. E-readings can be used as controlled resources units for writing research papers, allowing instructors to monitor documentation and plagiarism on nine critical issues:

1. Immigration
2. The Health Care Crisis
3. Debtor Nation
4. The War on Terrorism
5. The Environment
6. The Job Market
7. The Criminal Justice System
8. Privacy in the Electronic Age
9. Public Schools

E-Sources

Throughout *The Sundance Writer,* students are referred to reliable online resources that will assist them in every step of the writing process.

Key Features

The Sundance Writer is divided into five sections: The Rhetoric, The Reader, The Research Paper, Writing in College, and Writing in the Information Age.

The Rhetoric

The Sundance Writer focuses on critical stages in the writing process, providing students with techniques to improve their writing and overcome common problems. *The Sundance Writer* encourages students to see English as a highly practical course giving them skills they need in future classes and in any field or occupation they pursue—the ability to reason logically, organize ideas, and communicate effectively.

Writing does not occur in a vacuum but in a context that consists of the writer's objective, the reader, the discourse community, and the nature of the document. After introducing strategies for establishing context and enhancing critical thinking, *The Sundance Writer* guides students in developing and supporting a thesis. Students also are given practical directions for revising and editing.

The Reader

Organized by rhetorical mode, this section presents fifty entries, including classic essays by George Orwell, Martin Luther King Jr., and Bruce Catton, as well as recent works by John Taylor Gatto, Sharon Begley, and Anna Quindlen. Women, African

Americans, Asians, and Hispanics are all well represented. The subjects cover a range of issues: public schools, American Muslims, getting a job, privacy, and the homeless.

The wide variety of topics on science, law, culture, business, and social issues make *The Sundance Writer* suitable for thematic courses. In addition, this textbook has several features that make it a useful teaching tool for college instructors:

A range of readings Each chapter opens with brief, easy-to-read entries that clearly demonstrate the rhetorical mode, followed by longer, more challenging essays. Instructors have the flexibility to assign readings best suited to their student populations.

Brief entries suitable for in-class reading Many of the essays are short enough to be read in class and used as writing prompts, thus reducing the need for handouts.

An emphasis on critical thinking *The Sundance Writer* stresses critical thinking by including essays such as Samuel Scudder's "Take This Fish and Look at It," which dramatizes the importance of detailed observation.

SPECIAL FEATURES

Writing beyond the classroom *The Sundance Writer* places a unique emphasis on the practical value of writing skills. Each chapter ends with a sample of "real-world" writing that illustrates how professionals use the modes in different fields.

Blending the modes Each chapter highlights an essay that demonstrates how writers use different modes to relate a narrative, make a comparison, or outline a definition.

Opposing viewpoints Paired essays present different opinions on four critical issues: legalizing drugs, ethnic identity, bankruptcy, and nuclear energy.

Student papers in annotated and final draft for each mode Samples of student writing offer models of common assignments and demonstrate the revision process.

Collaborative writing Each reading concludes with directions for group writing.

Responding to images Classic and contemporary photographs prompt student writing, class discussion, and collaborative analysis.

The Research Paper

The Sundance Writer offers students a complete discussion of writing research papers, initially addressing common student misconceptions. Defining *what a research paper is not* is very effective in preventing students from embarking on misguided, time-consuming endeavors. Updated to focus on using Internet sources, *The Sundance Writer* gives guidelines to help students locate, evaluate, and document electronic material.

SPECIAL FEATURES

- Strategies for selecting and evaluating sources
- Strategies for overcoming problems with research
- Strategies for evaluating Internet sources
- Strategies for conducting interviews and surveys
- Strategies for locating and documenting visual images
- Separate MLA and APA research papers

Writing in College

The Sundance Writer includes chapters on writing essay examinations and writing about literature.

SPECIAL FEATURES

- Sample essay examination questions and responses
- An introduction to major literary terms
- A complete short story, two poems, and a dramatic scene
- Sample literary essays

Writing in the Information Age

The Sundance Writer includes chapters on analyzing and using photographs, graphs, tables, and charts in both academic and business writing. In addition, *The Sundance Writer* provides strategies for writing effective e-mail, résumés, letters, and business reports. Strategies are also presented to communicate in a range of special writing contexts:

- collaborative writing
- online writing groups
- writing as the representative of others
- writing to mass audiences
- writing to multiple readers
- giving multimedia and oral presentations
- writing portfolios

English CourseMate

Cengage Learning's **English CourseMate** brings concepts to life with interactive learning, study, and exam preparation tools that support the printed textbook. **CourseMate** includes

- An interactive eBook
- Interactive teaching and learning tools, such as

- Quizzes, flashcards and videos
- An online study guide devoted to the writing process, modes of exposition, research and the research paper, special kinds of writing, and grammar/ sentence skills
- Engagement Tracker, a first-of-its kind tool that monitors student engagement in the course.

Learn more at **www.cengage.com/coursemate.**

Enhanced InSite for *The Sundance Writer, Fifth Edition*

Insightful, effective writing begins with **Enhanced InSite™**. From a single, easy-to-navigate site, you can manage the flow of papers online, check for originality, access electronic grade-marking tools, and conduct peer reviews. Students can also access an interactive eBook, private tutoring options, anti-plagiarism tutorials, and down-loadable grammar podcasts. Learn more at **cengage.com/insite.**

Interactive eBook

Students can do all of their reading online or use the eBook as a handy reference while they're completing their other coursework. The eBook includes the full text of the print version with user-friendly navigation, search and highlight tools, and more.

Online Instructor's Manual

Available for download on the instructor companion site, accessed at **login.cengage .com,** this manual offers resources such as teaching tips, syllabus planning, and lesson organization that help instructors prepare for class more quickly and effectively.

Acknowledgments

This book and previous editions have benefited tremendously from the critiques and recommendations of the following instructors:

Booker Anthony, *Fayetteville State University*

Janet Bland, *Marietta College*

Patricia Bostian, *Central Piedmont Community College*

Suzane Bricker, *DeVry University*

Linda Caine, *Prairie State College*

Shery Chisamore, *SUNY Ulster*

Nandan Choksi, *American InterContinental University*

Kathryn Cid, *Gibbs College*

Lynn Coleman, *DeVry University*

Karen Compton, *Emmanuel College*

David Cooper, *Northwestern Business College*
Everett Corum, *American Public University System*
Jennifer Dahlen, *Northland Community and Technical College*
Jonathan Dewberry, *New Jersey City University*
William Donovan, *Idaho State University*
Robert Dunne, *Central Connecticut State University*
Daniel Fitzstephens, *University of Colorado*
Luisa Forrest, *El Centro College*
Leanne Frost, *Montana State University–Billings*
Sharon George, *College of Charleston*
Paul Goodin, *Northern Kentucky University*
Rima Gulshan, *Northern Virginia Community College*
John Hardecke, *East Central College*
Shannah Hogue, *Cedarville University*
Marjanna Hulet, *Idaho State University*
Parmita Kapadia, *Northern Kentucky University*
Roba Kribs, *Ancilla College*
Jane Lasarenko, *Slippery Rock University of Pennsylvania*
Chad Littleton, *University of Tennessee–Chattanooga*
Keming Liu, *Medgar Evers College*
Brad Marcum, *Pikeville College*
Laura McCullough, *Vance-Granville Community College*
Jim McKeown, *McLennan Community College*
Karen Miller, *University of Minnesota–Crookston*
Amy Minervini-Dodson, *Arizona Western College*
Dorothy Minor, *Tulsa Community College, NEC*
Adrielle Mitchell, *Nazareth College*
Torria Norman, *Black Hawk College*
Ben Railton, *Fitchburg State College*
Marsha Rutter, *Southwestern College*
Shawn Schumacher, *DeVry University*
Jennifer Swartz, *Lake Erie College*
Susan Swetnam, *Idaho State University*
Mary Trent, *Oral Roberts University*
Ben Varner, *University of Northern Colorado*
Paul Vasquez, *El Paso Community College*
Kymberli Ward, *Southwestern Oklahoma State University*
Vernetta Williams, *Southwest Florida College*

All books are a collaborative effort. My special thanks goes to PJ Boardman, editor-in-chief; Lyn Uhl, senior publisher; Monica Eckman, publisher; Margaret Leslie, acquisitions editor; Judith Fifer, senior development editor; Amy Haines, assistant editor; Janine Tangney, associate media editor; Danielle Warchol, editorial assistant; Jason Sakos, marketing director; Stacey Purviance, executive marketing manager; Brittany Blais, marketing coordinator; Jill Ort, senior art director; Aimee Bear, content project manager; Samantha Ross, production manager; and Dean Dauphinais, senior rights specialist.

The Sundance Writer

A Rhetoric, Reader, and Research Guide

BRIEF FIFTH EDITION

Why Write?

A writer is someone who writes, that's all.

—Gore Vidal

Few students intend to become writers. You probably think of writers as people who write for a living—reporters, playwrights, and novelists. But all professionals—all educated men and women, in fact—write to achieve their goals. Police officers and nurses document their daily activities in reports and charts, knowing that whatever they write may be introduced in court as evidence months or years in the future. Salespeople send streams of e-mail to announce new products, introduce themselves to new accounts, respond to buyers' questions, and inform management of their progress. A young couple opening a bed-and-breakfast will find themselves writing to secure financing, develop brochures, create a website, answer guests' e-mail, and train employees. Men and women entering any profession soon realize that they depend on writing to share ideas, express opinions, and influence people.

Thinking about your future career, you probably envision yourself in action—a doctor treating patients, an architect walking through a construction site, a choreographer directing a rehearsal. But whether your goal is Wall Street or the Peace Corps, writing will be critical to your success.

WRITERS AT WORK

I don't know any writer who thinks that writing is fun. It's hard work, and the way I do it is just as if I'm doing any other job. I get up in the morning and I have breakfast and read the newspapers and shave and shower and get dressed. But [then] I go down in my cellar, where I have my study, and work. I try to get to my machine by eight or nine o'clock in the morning. Sometimes I'll run out of steam in the afternoon, but sometimes I'll go until midnight. But you have to treat it as a job; you have to be disciplined. You don't sit around waiting for inspiration. If you do, you're never going to get anything done because it's much more fun taking the dog out for a walk along the canal than sitting down there and writing. But the thing that keeps you going, I think, is that you have these peaks in which you really do begin to feel that you're getting the story told and this chapter looks pretty good. Very often it looks good, and you put it aside; you look at it two weeks later and it looks terrible. So you go back and work on it again.

Stanley Karnow, journalist
SOURCE: *Booknotes*

As a college student you will be judged by the papers, essay examinations, research papers, and lab reports you produce. After graduation you will have to write a convincing letter and résumé to secure job interviews. Throughout your career you will encounter challenges and problems that demand a written response.

Learning to write well sharpens your critical thinking skills, improving your ability to communicate. The strategies you learn in a writing course can also enhance your performance in oral arguments, presentations, job interviews, and meetings. By learning to think more clearly, analyze your audience, and organize your ideas, you will be a more effective communicator in any situation.

THE GOALS OF THIS BOOK

The Sundance Writer **has been created to**

✔ increase your awareness of the importance of writing

✔ help you appreciate the way context shapes writing

✔ improve your critical thinking skills

✔ provide practical tips in overcoming common writing problems

✔ increase your ability to analyze and use visual images

✔ introduce you to writing research papers, business documents, and literary criticism

Above all, *The Sundance Writer* was created to help you develop the skills needed to succeed in composition, other courses, and your future career. Because no single text can fully address every aspect of writing, *The Sundance Writer* provides links to online support.

Using *The Sundance Writer*

The Sundance Writer is divided into five parts: the Rhetoric, the Reader, the Research Paper, Writing in College, and Writing in the Information Age.

I. The Rhetoric

Rhetoric is the art of communicating effectively. The twelve chapters in Part 1 of *The Sundance Writer* explain stages in the writing process, providing practical strategies to help you develop ideas, overcome writer's block, and avoid common problems.

In addition to guiding you in writing a thesis, supporting your ideas, and improving sentence and paragraph structure, *The Sundance Writer* emphasizes the importance of context and critical thinking. **E-Writing** activities help you explore writing resources on the Internet.

II. The Reader

The Sundance Writer includes more than fifty examples of professional and student writing, each illustrating one of nine modes of writing: description, narration, example, definition, comparison/contrast, process, division/classification, cause and effect, and argument and persuasion. These chapters feature works by George Orwell, Malcolm X, Julianne Malveaux, Anna Quindlen, and Martin Luther King, Jr. The subjects cover a range of issues: cell phones, reading, the job search, homelessness, terrorism, and student loans.

Chapters open with a discussion of the mode, pointing out strategies you can use to improve your writing and avoid errors. Sample writings illustrate how writers in different fields or professions use a particular mode to develop their ideas.

Readings are followed by questions focusing on key aspects of good writing.

- *Understanding Context*   Analyze the writer's thesis, purpose, and interpretation of events or ideas.
- *Evaluating Strategy*   Review the writer's methods, use of support, and appeals to readers.
- *Appreciating Language*   Study the writer's choice of words, tone, and style.

Each entry includes writing suggestions, allowing you to use essays as starting points for your own assignments.

Special Features

Blending the Modes.   Each chapter highlights an essay demonstrating how writers use different modes to relate a narrative, establish a comparison, or outline a definition.

Writing Beyond the Classroom. All chapters conclude with a brief example of how writers use the modes in real-world writing such as ads, web pages, and business documents.

Responding to Images. Each chapter includes an image to analyze and discuss or write about.

Opposing Viewpoints. Paired essays present differing opinions on four critical issues: legalizing drugs, ethnic identity, bankruptcy, and nuclear power.

Student Papers. Each chapter includes an instructor-annotated and revised version of a student essay that serves as a model for the kind of paper you may be expected to write.

Critical Issues. Each chapter offers a summary of articles available online through your English CourseMate. This site, which can be accessed at **www.cengagebrain.com**, provides additional readings on nine key issues: immigration, health care, the national debt, the war on terrorism, the environment, the job market, criminal justice, privacy in the electronic age, and public schools.

English CourseMate, accessed at **www.cengagebrain.com**, also provides support for each mode and supplies additional assignments, exercises, checklists, and sample papers. Throughout *The Sundance Writer,* CourseMate icons and descriptions guide you to this online support.

Enhanced InSite for Composition™, available through **www.cengagebrain.com**, provides tools for composition such as anti-plagiarism tutorials, grammar podcasts, exercises, private tutoring options, peer review, online paper management, and more.

III. The Research Paper

The Sundance Writer provides a full discussion of the research paper, including strategies to overcome common misconceptions and problems that often frustrate students. Useful research guides include

- two complete research papers in MLA and APA formats
- strategies for using Internet sources

IV. Writing in College

Writing the Essay Examination

Throughout your college career you may encounter essay examinations. *The Sundance Writer* includes sample questions and strategies for preparing for examinations and writing better responses.

Writing about Literature

Many courses require students to write about works of literature. This chapter defines common literary terms and includes strategies for reading and analyzing fiction, poetry, and drama.

V. Writing in the Information Age

Increasingly, we communicate in images as well as words. The Internet, camera phones, and desktop publishing allow people to attach photographs, charts, and graphs to e-mail, letters, and reports. Bloggers include images and videos on their web pages. Digital photography has made it possible for an image to be broadcast around the world instantly. The opening chapters in this part of the book explain how to analyze, interpret, and use images to enhance your critical thinking and writing.

Writing outside of college takes place in a special context. To be effective in your future career you need to appreciate the needs of writing in the workplace. *The Sundance Writer* provides strategies for writing e-mail, résumés, cover letters, and reports.

The final chapter of Part 5 provides advice on the following special writing situations you may encounter in college and your future career:

- writing in groups, in person, and online
- writing as the representative of others
- writing to a mass audience
- writing to multiple readers
- giving oral and multimedia presentations
- preparing portfolios

Strategies for Succeeding in Composition

1. **Study your course materials and syllabus carefully.** Become acquainted with the indexes, glossaries, and tables of contents in your textbooks to quickly locate information. Make sure you understand your instructor's policies on incompletes, late papers, and grading. *Record assignment due dates on a calendar.*

2. **Review *all* the assignments in the syllabus.** Reading all the assignments at the beginning of the course lets you think ahead and plan future papers.

3. **Read descriptions of assignments carefully.** Be sure you fully understand what your instructors expect before you begin writing. Review these instructions *after* completing the first draft to make sure you are headed in the right direction. Talk to instructors about topics you are considering and show them rough drafts to make sure your paper will meet the goals of the assignment.

4. **Write when you are focused.** Writing requires concentration. Write at the beginning of a study session when your energy level is high.

5. **Utilize down time.** Review drafts while riding the bus or waiting for a class to begin.

(Continued)

6. **Talk to other students about writing.** Bounce ideas off classmates. Ask for comments about your topic, your thesis, your approach, and the evidence you present.

7. **Read papers aloud before handing them in.** The easiest and fastest way to improve your grades is to read your papers aloud. It is easier to *hear* many errors than *see* them.

8. **Keep copies of all your papers.**

9. **Study returned papers to improve your grades.** If you do poorly on a paper, your first instinct may be to discard it or bury it under some books. But this paper holds the key to getting better grades in the future. Read your instructor's comments and list the mechanical errors you made. If you have a tendency to write run-ons or overlook needed commas, target these items when you edit future assignments. Refer to the handbook section of this book for further assistance.

10. **Read with a "writer's eye."** Whether reading for class or personal enjoyment, notice how other writers select details, choose words, and organize ideas. When you discover a passage you find interesting, study how it is constructed.

11. **Write as often as you can.** Like driving a car, writing improves with practice. The more you write, the more natural it will feel to express yourself on paper. Besides the common advice to keep a journal, there are many other strategies that can help you squeeze practice writing into your busy schedule.

    - *Take notes in other classes.* Even if you understand the material in lecture courses, take notes. You can easily get in hours of practice writing by listening to a professor's remarks and restating them in your own words.

    - *Text, e-mail, and instant message friends.* The liveliest chats on the Internet force you to express yourself in writing.

    - *Freewrite whenever you can.* Riding a bus or waiting for the dryer to switch off, scribble your thoughts in a notebook.

    - *Keep a daily journal.* Write at least a paragraph a day in a diary. Comment on political events, what you have seen on television, the latest gossip, or the way your job is affecting your ability to study.

    - *Blog.* Join the millions of people who post their thoughts, experiences, opinions, and feelings online. Ask readers to respond to you. Notice how people react to your ideas and your choice of words.

    - *Post comments on what you read online.* Become part of a discourse community by responding to opinions or news items. Read the comments of others and determine which writers make sensible arguments and which ones simply vent their emotions, convincing no one.

Avoid Plagiarism

In writing college papers, you often include ideas, facts, and information from outside sources. Whenever you copy material or restate the ideas of others in your own words, you must indicate the source. Presenting the words or ideas of others as your own is called *plagiarism,* which is a serious academic offense. Students who submit plagiarized papers are frequently failed or expelled.

Strategies for Avoiding Plagiarism

1. **When you copy a source word for word, indicate it as a direct quote with quotation marks:**

   Original source:

   > The airbag is not the most important automotive safety device. It is a sober driver.
   >
   > *William Harris, address before National Safety Council*

   Quotation used in student paper:

   > Speaking before the National Safety Council, William Harris said, "The airbag is not the most important safety device. It is a sober driver."

2. **When you state the ideas of others in your own words, you still must acknowledge their source:**

   Paraphrase used in student paper:

   > According to William Harris a sober driver is a better safety device than an airbag.

3. **When working on drafts, color-code quotations and paraphrases to distinguish them from your own words.** In writing a paper over several days, you may forget where you used outside sources. Whenever you cut and paste material into a paper, color-code it or place it in bold as a reminder that it needs to be treated as a quotation or a paraphrase in final editing.

4. **Always record the source of outside material.** When you cut and paste or paraphrase material, always copy the information needed to cite the source: the author, title, website or publication, dates, and page numbers.

   Refer to pages 547–553 for information on using and citing outside sources.

The Rhetoric

1

The Writing Process

An Overview

You learn how to write by writing.

—Stanley Weintraub

What Is Writing?

Writing is a process as well as a product. Writing requires creativity, concentration, and determination. Even professional writers struggle with the same problems you face in college—setting the right tone, explaining complicated ideas, sharing experiences that are difficult to put into words, deciding which details to add and which to delete, and, often toughest of all, just getting started.

Hollywood depicts writers as people who work in bursts of inspiration. Tough reporters rush to their typewriters and pound out flawless stories that they tear off and hand to copyboys without changing a line. Poets gaze dreamily at the portrait of a lost love and in a flash of creativity dash out a masterpiece, the soundtrack soaring in the background.

In reality, most writers don't have time to wait until inspiration strikes, and they rarely get it right the first time. Writing, like building a table or creating a computer program, takes effort. Although it helps to think about a topic, it rarely pays to wait, hoping for a sudden insight to automatically guide you. *The best way to begin writing is to write.*

Developing a Composing Style

Writing is highly personal. Many writers prefer to work at certain times of day, in specific rooms, or in a favorite coffee shop, and use pencils, an antique fountain pen, or a laptop. Some writers work in two- or three-hour blocks; others work in fits and starts, continually interrupting themselves to study for a quiz or run an errand.

If you have not been accustomed to writing, it may take you a while to discover when, where, and how you will be most productive. If you find writing difficult, consider changing the time, place, and conditions in which you work. Even if you achieve high grades, you may be able to improve your productivity and save time by examining the way you write.

WRITERS AT WORK

In the old days, when I used to write on a typewriter, I would start my drafts on that yellow paper. I just opened my mind and just kept going. I would never know exactly what I was going to say until my fingers were on the keyboard and I'd just type. And a lot of it would be junk, so I'd retype it, and then I'd put in more, and it would get better. These were called "zero minus drafts," and they were on the yellow paper. And then I would cut them up, and cut and paste, and I'd have these cut-and-paste yellow pie sheets. Then finally it would begin to look like it should, and then I'd start typing on white paper, and then I'd have white paper with yellow parts on it. By the time it got to all white paper, that was the first draft. Now I write on a computer, but I just do endless drafts.

Nell Irvin Painter, historian
SOURCE: *Booknotes*

Writing does not always occur in fixed stages. It is often a *recursive* process—writers repeat steps, often carrying out two or three simultaneously. Writing on a computer makes it easy to scroll up and down, jotting down ideas for the conclusion, then moving back to change a word or two to polish the introduction. Though they may not follow them in any particular order, most good writers follow six stages:

Prewrite	Explore topics and develop ideas.
Plan	Establish context and outline points.
Write	Get your ideas on paper.
Cool	Put your writing aside.
Revise	Review your draft and rewrite.
Edit	Check the final document.

At first glance, a six-step process may appear time-consuming, but mastering these strategies can improve the speed and quality of your writing. Follow these steps, altering them if needed, to create your own composing style.

1. **PREWRITE—Explore topics and develop ideas.** Good writing does not just express what you "feel" about a subject or repeat what you have read online or heard on talk radio—it explores issues, challenges commonly held beliefs, engages readers, and moves beyond first impressions and immediate responses. Effective prewriting begins with critical thinking strategies:

   - **observing details**
   - **asking questions**

- **checking facts**
- **distinguishing between fact and opinion**
- **looking for patterns or relationships between ideas**
- **searching for further evidence**

The goal of prewriting is to discover a subject, identify supporting details, and determine what you want to say.

2. **PLAN—Establish context and outline ideas.** Once you have established your subject, develop your thesis—your main idea—and supporting details in a context formed by four factors:

- **your goal as a writer**
- **the needs of your reader,**
- **the standards of the discourse community (a particular discipline, profession, community, culture, or situation)**
- **the conventions of the document**

If you are responding to a school assignment, for example, make sure your plan addresses the instructor's requirements. Develop an outline listing the items you need to achieve your goal and the best way to arrange them in a logical pattern:

- **the introduction—attracts attention, announces the subject, and prepares readers for what follows**
- **the body—organizes main ideas in a logical pattern**
- **the conclusion—presents a final fact, observation, quotation, or question to make a lasting impression**

An outline does not have to be a formal plan using Roman numerals and capital letters; it can be a simple list or a diagram that allows you to visualize the essay on a single sheet of paper. Outlining helps to organize ideas, spot missing information, and prevent writing in circles or going off topic.

Long projects should also include a budget or timeline. If you are working on a research paper that will take weeks to complete, consult a calendar to break the process into steps. Don't spend six weeks conducting research and expect to write and revise a twenty-page paper over a weekend. Make sure you devote enough time for *each* stage in the writing process.

3. **WRITE—Get your ideas on paper.** After reviewing your plan, write as much as possible without stopping, using the following guidelines:

- **Record *all* your thoughts.** It is easier to delete ideas later rather than try to remember something you forgot to include.
- **Do not break your concentration to look up a fact or check spelling.** Instead, make notes as you go. Underline words you think are misused or misspelled. Leave gaps for missing details. Write quick reminders in parentheses or the margins.

- **Place question marks next to passages that may be inaccurate, unclear, or ungrammatical.**
- **If writing on a computer, use color or bold font for passages needing further attention.**

Above all, keep writing!

4. **COOL—Put your writing aside.** This is the easiest but one of the most important steps in the writing process. It is difficult to evaluate your work immediately after writing because much of what you wish to say is still fresh in your mind. Set your draft aside. Work on other assignments, run an errand, watch television, or read a book to clear your mind. Afterward, you can return to your writing with more objectivity. Just ten minutes of "cooling" can help you gain a new perspective on your work, remember missing details, and eliminate errors you may have overlooked.

5. **REVISE—Review your draft and rewrite.** Before searching your paper for misspelled words or fragments, evaluate it holistically using these steps:
   - **Review your assignment and your plan.** Does your draft meet the needs of your audience? Does it follow the format expected of this document?
   - **Does the paper have a clear thesis or goal?**
   - **Did you include enough details to support your thesis?** If you have developed new ideas, are they relevant? What facts, ideas, or quotes do you need to add? Are there any passages that should be deleted?
   - **Is the paper logically organized?** Are there clear transitions between paragraphs? Can readers follow your train of thought?

6. **EDIT—Check the final document.** When you have completed your last revision, examine it for awkward sentences, grammatical errors, and misspelled words.
   - **Review your diction.** Have you used the right words?
   - **Revise sentences.** Are there wordy or repetitive phrases that could be shortened or deleted?
   - **Examine the format.** Does your writing meet the needs of the document? Should it be single- or double-spaced? Do you include required course information or list sources?

Reading a paper aloud can help you spot errors and awkward passages.

Finally, keep in mind that each writing assignment is unique. For example, a narrative requires attention to chronology, a comparison paper demands clear organization, and a persuasion essay depends on the skillful use of logic. You may find some papers more challenging than others. Because it is often difficult to determine how hard a particular assignment may be, start writing as soon as possible. Just ten minutes of prewriting will quickly reveal how much time and effort you need to devote to a paper.

CREATING A COMPOSING STYLE

✔ **Review your past writing.** Consider how you have written in the past. Which papers received the highest and lowest grades in high school? Why? What can you recall about writing them? What mistakes have you made? What comments have teachers made about your work?

✔ **Experiment with composing.** Write at different times and places, using pen and paper or a computer. See what conditions enhance your writing.

✔ **Study returned papers for clues.** Read your instructors' comments carefully. If your papers lack a clear thesis, devote more attention to prewriting and planning. If instructors fill your papers with red ink, circling misspelled words and underlining fragments, you should spend more time editing.

Writing on a Computer

Almost every business and profession today requires computer literacy. If you find yourself overwhelmed by technology, as many professional writers do, consider taking a computer course. Many colleges offer one-credit courses or free seminars. If nothing else, ask a friend or classmate to show you how he or she uses a computer to write.

Strategies for Writing on a Computer

1. **Appreciate the advantages and limitations of using a computer.** Computers can speed up the writing process and allow you to add ideas, correct spelling, and delete sentences without having to retype an entire page. Computers, however, will not automatically make you a better writer. They cannot refine a thesis, improve your logic, or enhance critical thinking. *Don't confuse the neatness of the finished product with good writing.* An attractively designed document must still achieve all the goals of good writing.

2. **Learn the features of your program.** If you are unfamiliar with writing on a computer, make sure you learn how to move blocks of text, change formats, check spelling, and, most importantly, master the print and save functions. *Find out if your program has an undo function. This can save the day if you accidentally delete or "lose" some of your text.* This function simply undoes your last action, restoring deleted text or eliminating what you just added.

3. **Write in single-spacing.** Most instructors require that papers be double-spaced, but you may find it easier to compose your various drafts in single-spacing so that you can see more of your essay on the screen. You can easily change to double-spacing when you are ready to print or e-mail the final version.

(Continued)

4. **Date and color-code your drafts.** To make sure you do not accidentally turn in an earlier, unedited draft of a paper, always put today's date in the header to identify the most recent version. In writing and editing a longer paper, highlight passages and change colors. You might highlight passages needing grammatical editing in red and those needing fact checking or additional details in blue. Marking up drafts like this can make final editing easier. When you complete editing a section, change the text color to black. When the entire document is free of red or blue paragraphs, you know you have fully edited the paper.

5. **Save your work.** If your program has an automatic save function, use it. Save your work to a flash drive or Internet-based space (such as DropBox). If you are writing on a college or library computer and do not have a flash drive, e-mail your work to yourself, or print a hard copy. Don't let a power shortage or a keystroke error make you lose your work!

6. **Print drafts of your work as you write.** Computer screens usually allow you to view less than a page of text at a time. Although it is easy to scroll up and down through the text, it can be difficult to revise on screen. You may find it easier to work with a hard copy of your paper. Consider double- or even triple-spacing before you print, so you will have room for handwritten notations.

7. **Make use of special features.** Most word-processing applications allow you to count the number of words, check spelling, and use a built-in thesaurus. Some programs will aid you with grammar and usage rules.

8. **Use spelling and grammar checkers but recognize their limitations.** A spell-checker will go through your document and flag words it does not recognize, quickly locating many mistakes you might overlook on your own. Spell-checkers do not locate missing words or recognize errors in usage, such as confusing *there* and *their* or *adopt* and *adapt*. Grammar checkers sometimes offer awkward suggestions and flag correct expressions as errors. **Reading your text aloud is still the best method of editing.**

Writer's Block

Almost everyone experiences writer's block—the inability to write. With a paper due in a few days, you may find yourself incapable of coming up with a single line, even unable to sit at a desk. You can feel frustrated, nervous, bored, tired, or anxious. The more time passes, and the more you think about the upcoming assignment, the more frustrated you can become. There is no magic cure for writer's block, but there are some tactics you can try.

Strategies for Overcoming Writer's Block

1. **Recognize that writer's block exists.** When you have the time to write, *write*. If you have two weeks to complete an assignment, don't assume that you will be able to write well for fourteen days. Get as much writing as possible done when you can. If you delay work, you may find yourself unable to write as the deadline nears.

2. **Review your assignment.** Sometimes the reason you feel that you have nothing to say is that you have not fully understood the assignment. Read it carefully and turn the instructions into a series of questions to spark critical thinking.

3. **If you are having trouble selecting a subject, review the assignment for key-words and search the Web.** If you don't have access to the Web, look up these words in a dictionary or encyclopedia. Even wholly unrelated references can spark your imagination and help you develop ideas.

4. **Write anything.** The longer you delay writing, the harder it will be to start. If you have trouble focusing on your assignment, get into the mood for writing by sending an e-mail to a friend. Use an online chat room to get into the rhythm of expressing yourself in writing.

5. **Discuss your assignment or goal with others.** Talking with a friend can often boost your confidence and reduce your anxiety about an assignment. A spirited discussion can generate free associations about your topic, helping you to view your subject from new angles.

6. **Force yourself to write for five minutes.** Sit down and write about your topic for five minutes nonstop. Let one idea run into another. If you have trouble writing about your topic, write about anything that comes to mind. Even writing nonsense can break the physical resistance you may have to sitting down and working with a pen or keyboard. Try to steer your experimental writing to the assigned task. If your draft is going nowhere, save your work and stop after five minutes. Take a walk or run some errands; then return to your writing. Sometimes seeing a word or phrase out of context will lead to significant associations.

7. **Lower your standards.** Don't be afraid to write poorly. Write as well as you can, making notes in the margin as you go along to remind yourself of areas that need revision. Remember that writing is recursive, so even badly written statements can form the foundation of a good paper.

8. **Don't feel obligated to start at the beginning.** If you find yourself unable to develop a convincing opening line or a satisfactory introduction, begin writing the body or conclusion of the paper. Get your ideas flowing.

9. **Switch subjects.** If you are bogged down on your English paper, start work on the history paper due next month. Writing well on a different subject may help you gain the confidence you need to return to a difficult assignment.

(Continued)

10. **Record your thoughts.** If you find writing frustrating, consider talking into a recorder or listing ideas on index cards. You may find working with different materials an effective method of getting started.

11. **Try writing in a different location.** If you can't work at home because of distractions, go to the library or a quiet room. If the library feels stifling and intimidating, move to a less formal environment. You may discover yourself doing your best work while drinking coffee in a noisy student union.

12. **If you still have problems with your assignment, talk to your instructor.** Try to identify what is giving you the most trouble. Is it the act of writing itself, finding a topic, organizing your thoughts, or developing a thesis?

WRITING ACTIVITIES

THE SIX STAGES OF THE WRITING PROCESS

1. Choose a topic from the list on pages 751–752 and use the six-step method described in this chapter to draft a short essay. As you write, note which stages of the process pose the greatest challenges. Alter your composing style in any way that improves your writing.

2. Select an upcoming assignment and write a rough draft. Use this experience to identify areas that require the most attention. Save your notes and draft for future use.

3. E-mail a friend about a recent experience. Before sending it, set the letter aside, letting it "cool." After two or three days, examine your draft for missing details, awkward or confusing phrases, misspelled words, or repetitious statements. Notice how revision and editing can improve your writing.

e-writing

Exploring Writing Resources Online

1. The Web offers an ever-growing variety of resources for student writers: dictionaries, encyclopedias, grammar drills, databases of periodicals, library catalogs, editing exercises, and research guides.

2. Review your library's electronic databases, links, and search engines. Locate online dictionaries and encyclopedias you can use as references while writing assignments.

3. Using a search engine, such as Yahoo! or Google, enter keywords, such as *prewriting, proofreading, narration, capitalization, thesis statement, comma exercises, editing strategies,* and other terms that appear throughout the book, the index, or your course syllabus. In addition to formal databases, many instructors and writing centers have constructed online tutorials that can help you improve your writing, overcome troubling grammar problems, and research specific assignments.

4. Ask your instructors for useful websites. Use your browser's bookmark function to keep track of these and other sources you find useful.

For Further Reading

Elbow, Peter. *Writing without Teachers.*

Flesch, Rudolf, and A. H. Lass. *The Classic Guide to Better Writing.*

Strunk, William, and E. B. White. *The Elements of Style.*

Zinsser, William. *On Writing Well: The Classic Guide to Writing Nonfiction.*

E-Sources

Writing in College: A Short Guide to College Writing
    http://writing-program.uchicago.edu/resources/collegewriting

Online Writing Lab at Purdue University
    http://owl.english.purdue.edu/handouts/general

The Nuts and Bolts of College Writing
    http://nutsandbolts.washcoll.edu/

 Access the English CourseMate for this text at **www.cengagebrain.com** for further information on the writing process.

The Writing Context

You don't write because you want to say something;
you write because you've got something to say.

—F. Scott Fitzgerald

What Is Good Writing?

No doubt you have read things that break the "rules" of good writing. Advertisements include slang. Novels contain fragments. Scientific journals run multisyllabic terms into paragraph-long sentences. Government reports are filled with indecipherable acronyms.

Writing can be judged only in context. Writing does not occur in a vacuum but in a context shaped by four factors:

- The writer's purpose and role
- The knowledge base, attitudes, needs, expectations, and biases of the reader
- The discipline or profession, community, culture, or situation in which the writing takes place
- The conventions of the document or publication

Another way of thinking of context is to think of a *genre*—a kind or type of writing. The genre a writer is working within takes into account all four factors. Genre explains why a story about an airplane crash in the *Chicago Tribune* differs from a National Transportation Safety Board (NTSB) report or the airline's condolence letter to the victims' families. Stated simply and printed in narrow columns for easy skimming, a newspaper account briefly describes current events for general readers. An NTSB investigation will produce multivolume reports, including extensive test results and testimony of survivors and witnesses. Directed to aviation safety experts, the report is presented in technical language largely incomprehensible to the average reader. In contrast, the airline's letter to victims' families addresses people experiencing confusion, grief, loss, and anger. Carefully drafted by crisis communications experts and reviewed by attorneys, it attempts to inform without admitting liability or appearing falsely sympathetic.

Writing that is successful in one context may not be acceptable in another. The lecture notes you write to prepare for an upcoming examination may be totally useless to other students. If you keep a diary, you may be reluctant to alter the context by allowing your roommate to read it. The essay about sexual harassment that impresses your instructor and classmates in English might be

WRITERS AT WORK

I sit at my computer and write, and then when I have a couple of sentences, I read them over aloud to see how they sound—not what they look like, but how they sound. Could a reader get the meaning of this? Could he follow the words and sound of it? . . . I talk to myself as I write in the hope of getting something of the spoken language into the written page because I think that's the way people read.

David Herbert Donald, Lincoln scholar
SOURCE: *Booknotes*

---

rejected by the editor of the college paper as "too wordy" for the editorial page. A psychology professor may find your essay's comments about male and female sexual behavior simplistic and unsupported by research. An attorney could dismiss your thesis, arguing the policies you urge the university to accept would be unconstitutional.

To be an effective writer, it is important to realize that there is no standard form of "good writing" that is suitable in all circumstances.

QUESTIONS

1. Can you recall situations in which you had difficulty expressing yourself because you were unsure how your reader would react? Did you have problems finding the right word or just getting your ideas on paper?

2. Have you found that professors have different attitudes about what constitutes good writing? How is writing a paper in English literature different from writing one in psychology or economics?

3. Have you noticed that magazines and websites have strikingly different writing styles? What do articles in the *Nation, Car and Driver, Cosmopolitan, Time, People,* and *Rolling Stone* reveal about their readers? How does The Huffington Post differ from TMZ?

The Writer

The Writer's Purpose

Everything you write has a goal. The note you scribble on a Post-it® and stick on your computer screen reminds you of an upcoming test. Research papers demonstrate your skills and knowledge in college courses. The résumé you submit to employers is designed to secure an interview.

Good writing has a clear goal—to inform, to entertain, or to persuade. Students and professionals in all fields face similar writing tasks. The way they present their ideas, the language they use, and even the physical appearance of the finished document are determined in part by their purpose. Although each writing assignment forms a unique context, most writing tasks can be divided into ten basic modes or types:

Description *creates a picture or impression of a person, place, object, or condition.* Description is an element in all writing and usually serves as support of the writer's main goal. Descriptions can be wholly factual and objective, as in an accident report, encyclopedia article, or parts catalog. In other instances, descriptions are highly subjective, offering readers a writer's personal impressions of a person or subject.

Narration *relates a series of events, usually in chronological order.* Biographies, histories, and novels use narration. Business and government reports often include sections called *narratives* that provide a historical overview of a problem, organization, or situation. Narration can be fictional or factual, and it can be related in first or third person.

Example *presents a specific person, place, object, event, or situation as representative or symbolic of a larger subject.* A writer may isolate a particular event and describe it in detail so readers can have a fuller appreciation of a larger or more abstract topic. The fate of a single business can illustrate an economic or technological trend.

Definition *explains a term, condition, topic, or issue.* In many instances definitions are precise and standard, such as a state's definition of second-degree murder. Other definitions, such as the statement of what makes a good teacher or parent, may be based on a writer's personal observation, values, experience, and opinion.

Comparison and Contrast *examines the similarities and differences between two or more subjects.* Textbooks often employ comparison or contrast to discuss different scientific methods, theories, or subjects. Comparisons may be made to distinguish items or to recommend one theory as superior to others. Comparison can also be used to present a "before and after" view of a single subject or contrast a myth with reality.

Process *explains how something occurs or demonstrates how to accomplish a specific task.* Writers can explain how nuclear power plants generate power, how the Internet works, or how the liver functions by breaking the process down into a series of events or stages. Writers also use process to provide directions. Recipes, operator's manuals, and first-aid books provide step-by-step instructions to accomplish specific tasks.

Division *names subgroups in a broad class.* Writers can make complex topics understandable or workable by dividing them into smaller units. Insurance can be divided into life, health, homeowner's, and auto policies. Writers can develop their own divisions, often creating names or labels for each category.

Classification *places subjects in different classes or levels according to a standard measurement.* Homicides are classified as first, second, or third degree according to circumstances and premeditation. Burns are classified first, second, and third degree based on their severity. As with division, writers often establish subjective classifications, creating a personal system to rate people, products, or ideas.

Cause and Effect *examines the reasons for an occurrence or explains the results of an event.* A writer can detail the *causes* of a decrease in crime, a rise in the stock market, or the extinction of a species. Similarly, he or she could describe the *effects* a decrease in crime will have on property values, how rising stock values will impact pension funds, or what effect the loss of a species will have on the environment.

Argument and Persuasion *influences opinion and motivates actions.* Writers persuade readers using logical appeals based on evidence and reasoning, ethical appeals based on values or beliefs, and emotional appeals that arouse feelings to support their views. Columnists and commentators try to influence readers to accept their views on issues ranging from abortion to casino gambling. Fund-raising letters motivate readers to donate to charities or political campaigns.

QUESTIONS

1. Consider how you have used these modes in the past. How often have you used them to achieve your goals in communicating with people? Can you think of essay questions that directed you to demonstrate your knowledge by writing comparison or cause and effect? Have you used comparison, division, or cause and effect to organize e-mails or business letters?

2. How often do you use modes such as comparison or classification in organizing your ideas and solving problems? Before you buy a product, do you compare it to others? Do you classify the courses you would like to take next semester by their difficulty or desirability? Do you seek solutions to problems by applying cause-and-effect reasoning?

A Note about Modes

Modes refer to a writer's basic goal. Few writing tasks, however, call for use of a single mode. In most instances, writers blend modes to achieve their goals. A biographer's main purpose is to tell a story, to *narrate* the events of a person's life. Within this narrative, the author may use *cause and effect* to explain the forces that molded a person's childhood, draw *comparisons* to illustrate how that person differed from his or her peers, and *persuade* readers to accept the subject as an *example* or role model.

When you write, select the mode or modes that best suit your purpose. Don't feel obligated to fit your paper into any single pattern.

The Writer's Role

The way writers create documents is shaped by their role. An independent blogger may spew out whatever comes into his or her head to amuse, influence, annoy, or infuriate nameless readers in cyberspace. A corporate attorney drafting a response to an angry customer demanding a refund is guided by company policy, the standards of the legal profession, and the peers and superiors he or she is representing.

In college your role is like that of a freelance writer. Your essays, reports, and research papers are expected to reflect only your own efforts. In general, your work is judged independently. The grades you receive in psychology have no effect on the way your English papers will be examined. In addition, college instructors are supposed to be objective. In a composition class, your papers are likely to be graded by *how* you state your views, not *what* they are. Your opinions on controversial topics are not likely to be raised in future courses or at job interviews.

Beyond the classroom, your role may be more complicated. First, you will be seeking more than an endorsement of your writing ability. Instead of working toward an A, you will be asking readers to invest money, buy a product, give you a job, accept your idea, or change their opinions on an important issue. In addition, you may have an ongoing relationship with your reader. If you give a client bad news in November, you cannot expect that he or she will read your December letter with much enthusiasm. It is important to consider how one message will affect the way future messages will be evaluated.

In many instances your profession dictates a role that greatly influences the kind of writing you will be expected to produce. Police officers and nurses, for example, are required to provide objective and impersonal records of their observations and actions. Fashion designers, decorators, and advertising copywriters, who are judged by their creativity and originality, are more likely to offer personal insights and write in the first person.

QUESTIONS

1. Consider the jobs you have had in the past and organizations you have worked for. What writing style would be considered appropriate for employees in these fields? Was objective reporting more important than personal opinion? Can you think of instances where an employee could jeopardize his or her job by making inappropriate statements to customers or clients? What image did the organization try to project in its memos, ads, websites?

2. What kind of writing would be effective in your future career? How does writing in engineering or medical malpractice law differ from writing in sales, hotel management, or charities? Does your future profession demand strict adherence to government or corporate regulations or allow for personal expression?

The Reader

Writing is more than an act of self-expression; it is an act of communication. To be effective, your message must be understood. The content, form, style, and tone of your writing are shaped by the needs, expectations, and attitudes of your readers. A medical researcher announcing a new treatment for AIDS would write an article for *Immunology* very differently from one for *Newsweek* or *Redbook*. Each magazine represents a different audience, knowledge base, and set of concerns. Doctors and scientists would be interested in the writer's research methods and demand detailed proof of his or her claims. Most readers of nonmedical publications would need definitions of scientific terms and explanations of data they would be unable to interpret on their own. Readers of *Newsweek* would be interested in a range of issues such as cost, government policy, and insurance coverage. Subscribers to a women's magazine might wonder if the treatment works equally well for both sexes or is suitable for pregnant women.

As a writer you have to determine how much knowledge your readers have about your subject. Are you writing to a general audience or specialized readers from the same discipline, profession, or area of interest? Do technical terms require definition? Are there common misunderstandings that should be explained? In addition to your reader's level of knowledge about your subject, you should consider your readers' goals, needs, and expectations. Is your audience reading for general interest or seeking information needed to make decisions or plan future actions?

It is also important to take into account how your readers will respond to your ideas. Who are your readers? Are they likely to be friendly, uninterested, or hostile to you, your ideas, or the organization you might represent? What are their interests and concerns? Environmentalists and real estate developers have conflicting philosophies of land use. Liberals and conservatives have opposing concepts of the role of government. When presenting ideas to audiences with undefined or differing attitudes, you will have to work hard to overcome their natural resistance, biases, and suspicions.

Individual Readers

The papers you write in college are usually read by a single instructor evaluating your work within the context of a specific course. Teachers and professors form a special audience because they generally provide clear instructions outlining requirements for each assignment. They are obligated to read your writing and are usually objective in their evaluations.

Beyond the classroom, however, you may have to persuade people to read your work. No one is required to read your résumé or proposal. Your readers will be expected to do more than evaluate how effective your writing is. You will be asking readers to give you a job, buy your product, or accept your opinions. You may ask readers to invest substantial resources on your behalf, conceivably placing their careers in your hands. When you write to individuals, you will have to carefully analyze their needs, concerns, and objections.

The more you learn about the individual you are writing to, the better equipped you will be to shape an effective message. If possible, speak with or e-mail this person to gain greater insight about his or her background, needs, interests, and concerns. Before submitting a long report, you may be able to test your ideas by sending a letter or preliminary draft for consideration and discussion before committing yourself to a final document.

Extended Audiences

In college your papers are graded and returned. Beyond the classroom, there are often two audiences: immediate readers who receive your documents and a second, extended audience. In most professional situations, letters and reports are retained for future reference. The angry e-mail you send to an irate customer may be passed on by the consumer to your supervisor, the Better Business Bureau, or an attorney. At a trial, it may be entered into evidence and read to a jury. The safety inspection report you write in March may be routinely skimmed and filed. But if a serious accident occurs in April, this report will be retrieved and closely examined by insurance investigators, state inspectors, and attorneys for the injured. Whenever you write beyond the classroom, realize that many people other than your immediate readers may see your documents. Avoid making remarks that may be misunderstood out of context.

The Perceptual World

To appreciate the way readers will respond to your ideas, it is useful to understand what communications experts call the *perceptual world*—the context in which people respond to new information and experiences. As individuals or as members of groups, readers base their responses on a variety of factors that have varying significance. Advertising and marketing executives analyze the perceptual world of consumers to design new products and commercials. Trial attorneys assess the perceptual world of juries to determine their most persuasive argument. Biographers and psychologists often construct the perceptual world of an individual to explain past actions or predict future behavior. Political candidates take polls, conduct interviews, and operate focus groups to establish the perceptual worlds of voters.

The perceptual world is often depicted as a circle to indicate that its elements are not ranked in any particular order and often operate simultaneously.

- *Social roles,* such as being a parent, civic leader, or homeowner, influence how people interpret new ideas. A thirty-year-old with two small children has concerns that differ from those of someone of the same age with no dependents.
- *Reference groups* include people or institutions readers respect and defer to in making judgments. A physician unsure about prescribing a new drug may base his or her decision on recommendations by the American Medical Association.
- *Past experiences* influence how people react to new information and situations. Readers who have lost money in the stock market will be more skeptical of an investment offer than those who have enjoyed substantial profits. People who have a history of conflict with law enforcement may view police officers differently from those who rely on their services to protect their property.

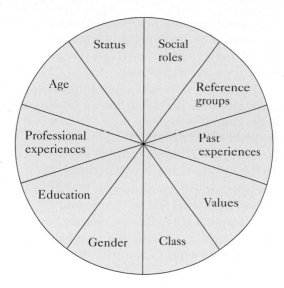

The Perceptual World

Values, whether religious, political, or cultural, shape how readers react to ideas. Although often unspoken, these values may be deeply held. People's attitudes about money, sexual behavior, drug use, politics, technology, and child rearing frequently stem from a core set of beliefs.

Class influences attitudes. Wealthier people may be more optimistic about the economic system that has worked for them, whereas poor people may feel pessimistic, seeing few examples of success among their peers.

Gender has proved to affect people's judgments. Polls about a president's popularity, for example, often show a gender gap between men and women. Although gender may have no impact on how people evaluate their pension plans or the introduction of computers in the workplace, it can influence how readers respond to issues such as child care, divorce laws, and sexual harassment.

Education, both formal and informal, shapes the intellectual background against which new ideas are examined and tested. Readers with greater academic training are in a stronger position to measure ideas, evaluate evidence, and analyze the validity of a writer's conclusions. Education in specific disciplines will influence how readers consider the evidence writers present. Scientists and mathematicians, for example, are more likely than the general public to question advertising claims that use statistics.

Professional experiences, along with training and career responsibilities, form people's attitudes about a number of issues. An economics professor with tenure may more easily embrace a new tax policy than does a struggling business owner worrying about meeting next week's payroll would. Occupations expose readers to a range of situations, problems, and people, leading them to develop distinct attitudes and values about the government, success, crime, relationships, money, and technology.

Age affects how people look at the world and interpret experiences. An eighteen-year-old naturally views life differently than a fifty-year-old does. In addition, people's attitudes are influenced by their experiences. People who came of age during the brief Gulf War of 1991 have different views about using military power than does the generation whose experience of war was shaped by the protracted conflict in Afghanistan a decade later.

Status influences people's responses, especially to change. A proposed modification in Social Security policies will be of little interest to high school students but of immediate importance to those collecting benefits. An entry-level employee with little invested in a corporation may feel less threatened by rumors of a merger than does a senior executive whose hard-won position may be eliminated.

Other aspects of the perceptual world can include physical stature, ethnic background, and geography. In determining your readers' perceptual world, it is important to realize that in some instances people will respond to your ideas based on their entire life experiences. In other circumstances, they may respond in solely a professional role or because your ideas trigger a specific reaction. In assessing perceptual worlds, avoid basing your assumptions on stereotypes. Not all older people are conservative, and not all minorities support affirmative action. Many elements of a reader's perceptual world are unconscious and cannot be easily ascertained. But by learning as much as you can about your readers, you can better determine which strategies will influence them to accept your ideas.

QUESTIONS

1. How would you describe your own perceptual world? Which factors most influence the way you respond to new ideas?

2. How would you describe the perceptual world of your parents, coworkers, and friends? Are there sharp individual differences? Are there shared values and experiences that might lead them to respond as a group in some circumstances? How would they respond to a letter urging them to donate money to a homeless shelter, support a handgun ban, or vote for a candidate? Which issues would be difficult to present to them? Why?

3. Have you ever tried to understand someone you hoped to influence? In practicing a presentation, preparing for a job interview, or seeking the right words to discuss a difficult issue with family or friends, do you consider how your audience will react? Is understanding people's perceptual worlds something we engage in every day?

4. Examine the photographs on pages 624, 626, 629, and 630. How do your attitudes, experiences, social roles, and values affect the way you perceive these images? Can you predict how other people might respond to them?

Evaluating Readers

In many situations you will be unable to learn much about your readers. A want ad may offer only a box number to respond to. Foundations and government agencies sometimes have strict policies that limit information given to applicants. In most cases, however, you can learn something about your reader or readers that can guide your writing.

General Readers

1. Envision your readers. Who are you writing to? What kind of person are you addressing? How do you want people to respond to your ideas?

2. Consider your purpose. What are you asking your readers to accept or do? What objections might they have to your thesis? How can you answer their questions or address their concerns? Play the devil's advocate and list all the possible objections people may have to your ideas, evidence, and word choice. How can you overcome these objections?

3. Test your writing. Before sending a mass e-mail, show it to a small group of people who represent your wider audience. Ask if they can detect errors, misleading statements, or inappropriate comments you may have overlooked.

Individual Readers

1. As a college student, ask instructors for further guidelines about upcoming assignments and request comments on an outline or rough draft.

2. For writing beyond the classroom, learn as much as you can about your reader. If you cannot obtain personal information, learn what you can about the organization he or she is associated with. What does your reader's profession suggest about his or her perceptual world?

3. Before submitting a résumé or proposal, call ahead and see whether you can speak to the person who will evaluate your work. Even a brief conversation with a receptionist or an assistant can provide insight about your reader.

Extended Readers

1. Determine who else may see your writing. How will the administration respond to an article you write for the student newspaper or a comment about the college you post on the Internet? Will your managers approve of the tone and style of the e-mails you send customers?

2. Review your writing to see if it reflects the kind of image your organization or professional peers feel is appropriate.

3. Realize that your writing may surface months or years later. Think how what you write today will affect your future options. Can anything you write today blemish your future?

The Discourse Community

The communication between writer and reader takes place in a particular environment, discipline, profession, community, culture, situation, or publication. A doctor responding to a reader's question for an advice column in a women's magazine has different concerns and responsibilities than one answering an e-mail from one of his or her patients. A lawyer discussing the first amendment in a law review article may use hypothetical examples and discuss abstract legal principles. The same lawyer drafting a motion for a judge about a specific case will have to limit his or her writing to evidence relevant to a single situation and a single defendant. Effective writers are sensitive to the role the discourse community has in how their ideas will be received and evaluated. Like the perceptual world of the reader, the discourse community may contain several elements operating simultaneously with varying degrees of influence.

Discipline.   Each discipline has a unique history that can dictate how writers collect information, evaluate evidence, measure results, and propose ideas. In the humanities, research usually involves an individual's interpretation of specific works. Such fields as physics, biology, and chemistry demand that a thesis result from experiments using standard methods that can be replicated by independent researchers.

Profession.   Each profession has its own context of historical experience, technical training, areas of concern, responsibilities, and political outlooks. Law enforcement officers approach a case of suspected child abuse with the goal of determining if there is enough evidence to file charges. Mental health professionals are more interested in the well-being of the child, regardless of whether the situation meets the legal definition of abuse.

Community.   People are influenced by those around them. A community may be a geographic region, organization, or collection of people with shared interests. Residents of midtown Manhattan have different interests, concerns, and challenges than Midwestern farmers. The U.S. Navy, IBM, the National Organization for Women, the Catholic Church, and NASA each form a distinct community with a unique history, values, problems, and philosophies. Communities form when people share a common interest. AIDS patients, Iraq War veterans, and adopted children have special concerns about government regulations and public policy.

Culture.   National, regional, religious, and ethnic groups have common histories and values that influence how ideas are expressed and evaluated. Although Americans generally respect individuality, other nationalities may value conformity. What may appear to Westerners as frank and honest writing may be viewed by others as brash and disrespectful.

Situation.   A discourse community can be altered by a specific event. The way a manager writes to employees will change during a strike. An international crisis will influence the way the president addresses senators opposed to his policies. A crisis may bring writer and reader together as they face a common threat, or it may heighten differences, creating mutual suspicion and hostility.

1. Examine textbooks from different courses. What do they indicate about the values, standards, and practices in each discipline? Do sociologists write differently from psychologists? What do the books' glossaries reveal about how terms are defined?

2. Consider your future career. What values, attitudes, and skills are important? How will they influence the way you would write to peers? What kind of writing would be considered unprofessional or inappropriate?

3. Think of jobs you have had. Did each workplace form a specific community or culture? Did one office, warehouse, or restaurant have a different atmosphere or spirit than others? Would you word an e-mail to employees in one business differently from those in another?

4. How can a dramatic event shape the way messages are written and evaluated? How would you word a statement announcing the death or injury of a fellow classmate, teammate, or employee?

The Document

The nature of the document influences reader expectations. Memos and e-mail may include informal abbreviations and slang that would be unacceptable in a formal report. Readers expect newspaper articles to be brief and simply stated. Because reporters must write quickly, their readers anticipate that factual errors or inaccurate quotes may appear in print. However, the same readers would have higher expectations of a scholarly journal or a book, because the writers have weeks or years to check their sources and verify facts.

Certain documents such as research papers, résumés, wills, legal briefs, military action reports, dissertations, and press releases have unique styles and formats. Writers who fail to follow the standard forms may alienate readers by appearing unprofessional.

Strategies for Writing Specialized Documents

1. **Make sure you understand the form, style, and rigor expected in the document.** Legal documents, grant proposals, and academic dissertations have distinct standards. If no formal directions or guidelines exist, review existing samples, or ask an instructor or manager what is expected.

2. **Determine if the document suits your purpose.** The importance of your message, the amount of information, and the style of writing should match the form. E-mail is suited for routine information and reminders. But announcing salary changes or job reclassifications in an informal document will strike readers as callous and impersonal.

3. **Use more than one document to achieve your goals.** If an accident prompts you to immediately alert employees of new safety regulations, you can state

(Continued)

them in a short e-mail. If, however, you find yourself producing pages of text, consider writing a formal report or set of guidelines. Use e-mail to quickly alert readers of the most important actions they should take and tell them to expect detailed regulations in the near future. Sometimes formal documents restrict your ability to highlight what you consider significant. Attach a cover letter or send a preliminary report that allows greater freedom of expression.

Strategies for Establishing Context

Whenever you write, consider the context.

Your Purpose and Role

1. What is your goal? To provide information, change opinions, or motivate action? Have you clearly determined what you want to express?

2. Are you presenting your own ideas or those of others? If you serve as a representative of a larger group, does your writing reflect the needs, style, attitudes, and philosophies of your peers or superiors? Do you avoid making statements that might jeopardize your position or expose the organization to liability? Will your peers and superiors approve of your ideas and the way you express them?

Your Reader

1. Define your readers. What is their perceptual world?

2. What objections might your readers have to your ideas?

3. Are there potential extended readers? Who else may see this writing? Have you made any statements that could be misunderstood out of context?

The Discourse Community

1. Are you operating in a general or specific discourse community? What is expected in this discipline, community, or profession?

2. Is your writing affected by a specific event or situation that could change in the future? Should you qualify your remarks so they will not be misunderstood if read out of context later?

The Document

1. Does the document have any special requirements? Do you fully understand what is required, what your readers expect?

2. Does the document suit your purpose? For example, are you using e-mail to transmit a message better stated in a personal letter?

3. Should you use more than one document? Would preliminary messages, attachments, or cover letters assist in communicating to your reader?

Strategies for College Writing

The College Writing Context

Each college course can constitute its own unique context. A literature professor may encourage original interpretations of a short story, while a physics instructor demands lab reports follow objective guidelines free of personal observations or opinions. There are, however, some general strategies for writing in college:

Write Objectively

Except for personal essays written for a composition class, college papers generally avoid first-person statements such as "I think" or "I feel."

Demonstrate Critical Thinking

College instructors expect papers to reflect intellectual rigor and accomplish more than simply repeat facts or summarize other sources. A literature professor requires a college paper to go beyond a plot summary of a novel to show original and thoughtful analysis that might examine a character's motivation, the author's use of symbols, or the book's depiction of a social problem. In the sciences, lab reports must reflect accuracy and objective reporting that can be verified by others.

Use Scholarly Sources for Support

In high school you may have relied on newspapers, newsmagazines, and popular websites to find support for research papers. College instructors expect students to obtain evidence from government documents, professional publications, and peer-reviewed academic journals.

Evaluate Sources

In addition to including evidence to support your thesis in college papers, it is important to comment on the quality and reliability of the sources you use.

Do not simply cut and paste quotations or statistics without explaining their significance and reliability.

Write in Standard Edited English

College instructors expect you to master the diction used by professionals in your intended field. Avoid slang and conventional phrases you might use in an e-mail to a friend such as "back in the day" or "way bad." Write in full sentences, avoiding texting shorthand such as "u" or "thru."

College instructors expect papers to be free of spelling and punctuation errors. Proofread your work carefully.

(Continued)

Use Words Precisely

In addition to learning specialized vocabulary used in a college course, make sure you know the difference between words like *continual* and *continuous* or *imply* and *infer*. Avoid awkward phrases that add little meaning to your sentences. Be aware of words that may reflect bias. Do not attempt to impress professors by cluttering your paper with big words that only obscure what you are trying to say. Read professional journals and your textbooks to determine the style of language used in your field.

WRITING ACTIVITIES

Choose one or more of the following situations and develop writing that addresses the needs of the writer, immediate and extended readers, the discourse community, and the document.

1. You serve on a student committee concerned with underage and binge drinking that was formed after a fraternity party erupted in violence and led to dozens of arrests and a serious drunk-driving accident. Write a brief statement to each of the following readers, urging greater responsibility. Consider their perceptual worlds and invent any needed details. Keep the extended audience in mind. How will other students, student organizations, the administration, and local media respond to your messages?

   - the president of the fraternity
   - the liquor distributor who promoted the event
   - incoming freshmen
   - a local disc jockey who had repeatedly urged listeners to "crash the party and get blasted"

2. Write a short letter asking for funds to support a shelter for homeless and battered women. Consider how each reader's perceptual world will influence responses.

   - the director of women's studies at a university
   - small-business owners in a neighborhood that has become a gathering place for homeless people
   - local ministers
   - the chamber of commerce
   - a local organization of women entrepreneurs

e-writing

Exploring Context Online

The Internet offers a quick lesson in the diversity of writing contexts: academic journals, corporate websites, commercial catalogs, political messages, and personal expressions.

1. Using InfoTrac College Edition (available through your English CourseMate at **www.cengagebrain.com**), find relevant articles by entering a search word, such as diabetes, racial profiling, terrorism, income tax, or any topic in the news. You may also search using one of your library's databases. Scan down the list of articles and select a variety to review. How do the style, format, vocabulary, and tone of a medical journal or law review differ from an article in a popular magazine? What does the language reveal about the intended audience? Can you determine the kinds of readers the writers were trying to reach?

2. If you use e-mail, review recent messages you have received. Do e-mails from friends reflect their personality, their way of speaking? Do personal e-mail messages have a different tone than promotional messages you might receive?

3. Analyze the language used in blogs, chat rooms, Facebook, or Twitter. Have these electronic communities produced their own slang or jargon? Do chat rooms of car enthusiasts differ from those dedicated to child care or investments? Do people with special interests bring their particular terminology and culture into cyberspace?

4. Using a search engine, such as Yahoo! or Google, enter the following search terms to locate current sites you might find helpful:

perception	*audience analysis*
persuasion	*perceptual world*
making presentations	*influencing readers*
reader analysis	*communications skills*
writing genres	

E-Sources

Paradigm Online Writing Assistant—The Writing Context
    http://www.powa.org
Online Writing Lab—Identifying an Audience
    http://owl.english.purdue.edu/owl/resource/658/04/
University of North Carolina Writing Center—Audience
    http://www.unc.edu/depts/wcweb/handouts/audience.html

 Access the English CourseMate for this text at **www.cengagebrain.com** for further information on context.

Critical Thinking

Seeing with a Writer's Eye

*It is part of the business of the writer . . . to examine
attitudes, to go beneath the surface, to tap the source.*

—James Baldwin

What Is Critical Thinking?

Good writing is not a repeat of what you have read online or seen on television, and it is more than a rush of thoughts and feelings. Too often we tend to respond to ideas and experiences based solely on our existing perceptual worlds. We allow our emotions to color our judgment and guide our decisions. We confuse opinions with facts, accept statistics without question, and allow stereotypes to influence our evaluations. In short, we let our perceptual world short-circuit our thinking, and we rush to judgment:,

> Pete Wilson was a great quarterback—he'll make a great coach.
>
> Nancy's driving a BMW—her new restaurant must be a success.
>
> Alabama improved reading scores 12 percent using this program—our schools should use it, too.
>
> Jersey Lube ruined my car—two days after I went there for an oil change my transmission went out.

All these statements make a kind of sense at first glance. But further analysis will lead you to question their validity.

> Does a skilled quarterback necessarily know how to coach—how to inspire, manage, and teach other players, especially those on defense?
>
> Does Nancy even own the BMW she was seen driving? Did she get it as a gift, pay for it with existing savings, borrow it from a friend, or lease it at a low rate? Does the car really prove anything about the success or failure of her restaurant?
>
> Alabama may have improved reading scores with a particular program, but does that really prove the program will work in Nevada or Minnesota? Could children in other states have low reading scores caused by reasons other than those in Alabama?
>
> Did Jersey Lube ruin your transmission? The technicians may have only changed the oil and never touched the transmission, which was due to fail in two days. Had you driven through a car wash the day before, could you just as easily blame them?

WRITERS AT WORK

There are difficult moments where you think you're never going to get a handle on it. You end up with a bulging computer with all these little disparate items of information. Some of them you got four years ago and you can't figure out where in the world they fit. They look like they belong to a different jigsaw puzzle, and [as if] you shouldn't be bothering with them at all. Until you get a handle on it, it can be very difficult. I always write a first draft that has everything in it, and it reads about as interesting as a laundry list—"first he did this, and then he did this." I just have a chronological laundry list of everything that happened to him and that he did on a given day. Only after dealing with that, and wrestling with that by just getting it down on the page, which is a chore, do murky shapes begin to appear. Then you just go with those, and you test them and make sure that they work before you finally decide to use them. It's really feeling in the dark for a while, and it can be discouraging. But I always knew he was there somewhere for me, and so I wasn't going to let him go.

Clare Brandt, biographer of Benedict Arnold
SOURCE: *Booknotes*

Errors like these are easy to make. Unless you develop critical thinking skills, you can be impressed by faulty evidence that at first glance seems reliable and convincing.

Critical thinking moves beyond casual observation and immediate reactions. Instead of simply responding with what you *feel* about a subject, critical thinking guides you to *think*—to examine issues fully and objectively, test your own assumptions for bias, seek additional information, consider alternative interpretations, ask questions, and delay judgment.

How to See with a Writer's Eye

Good writers are not passive; they don't simply record immediate responses. They *look closely, ask questions, analyze, make connections,* and *think*. Learning to see with a writer's eye benefits not just those who write for a living but all professionals. In any career you choose, success depends on keen observation and in-depth analysis. A skilled physician detects minor symptoms in a physical or follows up on a patient's complaint to ask questions that lead to a diagnosis others might miss. A successful stockbroker observes overlooked trends and conducts research to detect new investment opportunities. A passerby might assume a busy store must be successful, but a retail analyst would observe what merchandise people are purchasing and how they are paying for it. If all the shoppers are buying discount items and paying with credit cards, the store could be losing money on every sale.

Asking questions can help you become a critical consumer of information and a better writer as you test the validity of assumptions. Consider a passage from a freshman essay:

> America must restrict immigration. Millions of people are coming to this country, taking jobs and running businesses while Americans are out of work. A lot of these people don't even speak English. With a recession deepening, this country should promise jobs to people who have lived here and paid taxes, not to new arrivals who are willing to work cheap.

The thesis—that America must restrict immigration—is clearly stated. But where is the proof? The student mentions "millions" of immigrants—but is there a more precise number? Just how many people are we talking about? What evidence is there that immigrants are "taking jobs" from others? Could they work in jobs that others wouldn't take? Does the country "promise" jobs to anyone? What relationship is there between paying taxes and being qualified for a job? Do immigrants really "work cheap"? A thesis makes an assertion; it states a point of view. But without credible support, it remains only an opinion.

Critical thinking reveals that the student needs to conduct research and refine his or her arguments. Should the paper make a distinction between legal and illegal immigrants? In addition, the writer should consider what opponents will say. Can he or she call for restrictions on immigration without appearing to be racist? What proof can be offered to support the need for restrictions?

Strategies for Increasing Critical Thinking

There is no quick method of enhancing critical thinking, but you can challenge yourself to develop a writer's eye by asking questions to improve your prewriting, drafting, and editing skills.

1. **How much do you really know about this subject?** Do you fully understand the history, depth, and character of the topic? Are you basing your assumptions on objective facts or only on what you have read on blogs or heard on talk shows? Should you learn more by conducting research or interviewing people before making judgments?

2. **Have you looked at your topic closely?** First impressions can be striking but misleading. Examine your subject closely, ask questions, and probe beneath the surface. Look for patterns; measure similarities and differences.

3. **Have you rushed to judgment?** Collect evidence but avoid drawing conclusions until you have analyzed your findings and observations.

4. **Do you separate facts from opinions?** Don't confuse facts, evidence, and data with opinions, claims, and assertions. Opinions are judgments or inferences, not facts. Facts are reliable pieces of information that can be verified by studying other sources:

FACT: This semester a laptop, petty cash, and an iPod were taken from the tutoring lab while Sue Harper was on duty.

OPINION: Sue Harper is a thief.

The factual statement can be proved. Missing items can be documented. The assumption that Sue Harper is responsible remains to be proved.

5. **Are you aware of your assumptions?** Assumptions are ideas we accept or believe to be true. It is nearly impossible to divorce ourselves from what we have been taught, but you can sharpen your critical thinking skills if you acknowledge your assumptions. Avoid relying too heavily on a single assumption—that IQ tests measure intelligence, that poverty causes crime, that television has a bad influence on children.

6. **Have you collected enough evidence?** A few statistics and quotations taken out of context may seem convincing, but they cannot be viewed as adequate proof. Make sure you collect enough evidence from a variety of sources before making judgments.

7. **Do you evaluate evidence carefully?** Do you apply common standards to evaluate the data you collect? Do you question the source of statistics or the validity of an eyewitness? The fact that you can find dozens of books about alien abductions does not prove they occur.

Common Errors in Critical Thinking

When you attempt to understand problems, evaluate evidence, draw conclusions, and propose solutions, it is easy to make mistakes. These lapses in critical thinking include *logical fallacies*. In establishing your reader's perceptual world, developing your ideas, and interpreting information, avoid these common mistakes.

Avoiding Errors in Critical Thinking

In reading the works of others and developing your own arguments, avoid the following errors in reasoning:

- **Absolute statements.** Although it is important to convince readers by making strong assertions, avoid absolute claims that can be dismissed with a single exception. If you write, "All professional athletes are irresponsible," readers only need to think of a single exception to dismiss your argument. A qualified remark, however, is harder to disprove. The claim that "Many professional athletes are irresponsible" acknowledges that exceptions exist.

- *Non sequitur* **(it does not follow).** Avoid making assertions based on irrelevant evidence, such as "Jill Klein won an Oscar for best actress last year—she'll be great on Broadway." Although an actress might succeed on film, she may lack the ability to perform on stage before a live audience. The skills and style suited for film acting do not always translate well to the theater.

■ **Begging the question.** Do not assume what has to be proved. "These needless math classes should be dropped because no one uses algebra and geometry after they graduate." This statement makes an assertion, but it fails to prove that the courses are needless or that "no one" uses mathematics outside of academic settings.

■ **False dilemma.** Do not offer or accept only two alternatives to a problem; for example, "Either employees must take a 20 percent wage cut, or the company will go bankrupt." This statement ignores other possible solutions such as raising prices, lowering production costs, selling unused assets, or increasing sales. If a wage cut is needed, does it have to be 20 percent? Could it be 15 percent or 10 percent? Before choosing what appears to be the better of two bad choices, determine if there are other options.

■ **False analogy.** Comparisons make weak arguments. For example, if you write, "Marijuana should be legalized since Prohibition did not work," you are forgetting that marijuana and alcohol are different substances. Alcohol has been consumed by humans for thousands of years. Marijuana, however, has never had wide social acceptance. The fact that Prohibition failed could be used to justify legalizing anything that is banned, including assault weapons, child pornography, or crack cocaine.

■ **Red herring.** Resist the temptation to dodge the real issue by making emotionally charged or controversial statements, such as "How can you justify spending money on a new football stadium when homeless people are sleeping in the streets and terrorists are threatening to destroy us?" Homelessness and terrorism are genuine concerns but have little to do with the merits of a proposed stadium. The same argument could be used to attack building a park, a zoo, or an art gallery.

■ **Borrowed authority.** Avoid assuming that an expert in one field can be accepted as an authority in another. One example is "Senator Goode claims Italy will win the World Cup." A respected senator may have no more insight into soccer than a cabdriver or a hairdresser does. Celebrity endorsements are common examples of borrowed authority.

■ *Ad hominem* **(attacking the person).** Attack ideas, not the people who advocate them. "How can you accept the budget proposed by an alderman accused of domestic violence?" The merits of the budget have to be examined, not the person who proposed it.

Other errors in critical thinking can occur when writers conduct research, collect evidence, or make observations. Make sure that in collecting and evaluating evidence, you avoid making the following errors:

■ **Hasty generalizations.** If your dorm room is robbed, a friend's car stolen from the student union parking lot, and a classmate's purse snatched on her way to class, you might assume that the campus is experiencing a crime wave. The evidence is compelling because it is immediate and personal. But it does not prove there is an increase in campus crime. In fact, crime could be dropping, and you and your friends may simply have had the misfortune to fall into the declining pool of victims. Only a comparative review of police and security reports would prove if crime is increasing. *Resist jumping to conclusions.*

■ **"Filtering" data.** If you begin with a preconceived thesis, you may consciously or unconsciously select evidence that supports your view and omit evidence that contradicts it. Good analysis is objective; it does not consist of simply collecting facts to support a previously held conviction. A list of high school dropouts who became celebrities does not disprove the value of a diploma. Avoid selecting anecdotal examples that counter a general trend.

■ **Ignoring alternative interpretations.** Even objective facts can be misleading. If research shows that reports of child abuse have jumped 250 percent in the last ten years, does that mean that child abuse is on the rise? Could those numbers instead reflect stricter reporting methods or an expanded definition of abuse, so that previously unrecorded incidents are now counted?

■ **Mistaking a time relationship for a cause** *(post hoc, ergo propter hoc).* Can the president take credit for a drop in unemployment six months after signing a labor bill? Because events occur in time, it can be easy to assume an action that precedes another is a cause. A drop in unemployment could be caused by a decline in interest rates or an upsurge in exports and may have nothing to do with a labor bill. Do not assume events were caused by preceding events.

■ **Mistaking an effect for a cause.** If you observe that children with poor reading skills watch a lot of television, you might easily assume that television interferes with their reading. In fact, excessive viewing could be a symptom. Because they have trouble reading, they watch television instead.

■ **Assuming past events will predict the future.** The 2008 recession was caused, in part, because mortgage brokers believed that real estate prices would continue to rise 6 percent annually. When home values fell as much as 50 percent, millions of homeowners faced foreclosure and investors lost billions of dollars. Past trends cannot be assumed to continue into the future.

WRITING ACTIVITIES

1. Select a recent editorial and examine it for lapses in critical thinking. Does the writer make statements that rest on untested assumptions, false analogies, or insufficient data? Write a critique, commenting on the writer's use of logic to support his or her views.

2. Select a topic from the list on pages 751–752 and identify the types of errors in critical thinking you might face in addressing this issue.

3. Examine a session or two of cable news or radio talk shows. How many guests engage in arguments that are laced with errors in critical thinking? Can you identify people who use guilt by association, anecdotal evidence, and faulty comparisons? Do interviewers or guests try to persuade viewers by begging the question or creating false dilemmas?

CRITICAL THINKING CHECKLIST

✔ Examine your writing for evidence of critical thinking.

✔ Have you carefully examined your subject or relied solely on casual observation?

✔ Is your main idea clearly and logically stated?

✔ Have you collected enough information to make judgments?

✔ Are your sources reliable and unbiased?

✔ Have you considered alternative interpretations?

✔ Have you avoided errors in critical thinking such as hasty generalizations?

e-writing

Exploring Critical Thinking Online

You can find a range of sources on the Web dedicated to critical thinking, ranging from sites maintained by academic organizations to those created by individual teachers posting information for their students.

1. Using InfoTrac College Edition (available through your English CourseMate at **www.cengagebrain.com**) or one of your library's databases, enter *critical thinking* as a search term and locate articles that may assist you in your writing course and other classes.

2. Locate the online version of a national or local newspaper and review recent editorials. Can you detect any lapses in critical thinking? Do any editorials rely on hasty generalizations, anecdotal evidence, faulty comparisons, filtering data, or false authorities?

3. To learn more about critical thinking, enter *critical thinking* as a search term in a general search engine such as Yahoo! or Google, or enter one or more of the following terms:

coincidence	*anecdotal evidence*
post hoc	*circular reasoning*
red herrings	*guilt by association*
hasty generalizations	*fact and opinion*

For Further Reading

Barnet, Sylvan, and Hugo Bedau. *Critical Thinking: Reading and Writing.*
Dauer, Francis Watanabe. *Critical Thinking: An Introduction to Reasoning.*
Hirschberg, Stuart. *Essential Strategies of Argument.*

Packer, Nancy Huddleston, and John Timpane. *Writing Worth Reading: The Critical Process.*

Paulos, John Allen. *Innumeracy: Mathematical Illiteracy and Its Consequences.*

Rosenwasser, David, and Jill Stephens. *Writing Analytically.*

E-Sources

The Critical Thinking Community
http://www.criticalthinking.org

 Access the English CourseMate for this text at **www.cengagebrain.com** for additional information on critical thinking.

Prewriting Strategies
Getting Started

I think best with a pencil in my hand.

—Anne Morrow Lindbergh

What Is Prewriting?

Writing is more than a means to create a document; it can be a method to discover topics and explore ideas. *Prewriting* is practice or experimental writing—writing that helps you get started and measure what you know, identify new ideas, and indicate areas requiring further research. Prewriting can sharpen your skills of observation and evaluation. Like an artist making quick sketches before beginning a mural, you can test ideas, explore a range of topics, list points, and get a feel for your subject. Prewriting can help you save time by quickly determining which ideas are worth developing and which should be discarded. *Prewriting puts critical thinking into action.*

Prewriting Strategies

Writers use a number of strategies to discover and develop ideas. Prewriting can be highly focused or totally open. You may wish to target a specific assignment or explore ideas that might generate topics for a number of papers.

People think in different ways. Review these methods and experiment with them. Feel free to combine strategies to create your own method. If you are responding to a specific assignment, consider all the elements of the context:

- **the writer**—your goal and the demands of the assignment, especially your thesis or main idea
- **the reader**—the knowledge and attitudes of your audience and the kind of support needed to convince them
- **the discipline**—the culture, history, and methods used to express and support ideas
- **the document**—the purpose, rigor, style, length, and format of the finished product

Make sure you understand what your instructor expects and how your paper will be evaluated. If you are unsure, talk to your instructor or other students. Sometimes even a casual conversation about an upcoming assignment will reveal different perspectives and insights.

Sam Diephuis/Jupiterimages

Maria Toutoudaki/Jupiterimages

WRITERS AT WORK

I write by longhand. I like to see the words coming out of the pen. And once they distribute themselves, one has the stylistic struggle to try to turn that clumsy sentence on the page into something lucid. That can take a long time. I remember once spending seven hours on one sentence—seven hours. And I looked at it the next morning, it was a pretty banal sentence. That's writing. Writing is a reduction to essentials, elimination, and that takes time.

Edmund Morris, historian
SOURCE: *Booknotes*

Freewriting

Freewriting records your thoughts, ideas, impressions, and feelings without interruption and without any concern for spelling, grammar, punctuation, or even logic. Don't confuse freewriting with writing a rough draft of an essay; instead, it is a method of discovering ideas. Freewriting is like talking to yourself. It has no direction: it can skip from one topic to another without rational transitions; it may contain contradictory statements. Freewriting produces "running prose," like a recording of a rambling telephone conversation. The goal is to discover ideas. Here are some tips:

- **Write as fast as you can.**
- **Don't pause to correct spelling or check facts—but make notes as you go.**
- **Don't feel obligated to write in full sentences—list ideas and key words.**
- **Keep writing and record everything that comes to you—remember your goal is to explore ideas, not write a rough draft.**

Having spent the evening searching the Web for material for a paper, a student switched to a word processing program and rapidly recorded her thoughts on the information superhighway:

> The information superhighway links anyone to the world. A college student, sitting in a dorm or libary, can connect to sources in New York, London, or Tokio. Web pages link you to sources you would nevre find on your own or now about. Within fifteen minutes tonight I printed off twenty pages of infomation that would take hours to find in a conventional libary. The interent is the ultimate consumer guide. I could find online catalogs and read product descriptions and prices for things I thought about buying for xmas gifts and presents. I could even check sticker prices on new cars. Xxxxxxxxxxxxxxxx xxxxxxxxx.
>
> But switching from web page to web page, bieng hit with all kinds of data from around the owrld wears off after a while. The internet is exciting but like having cable TV, you get used to having 80 channels instead of four or five.
>
> Years ago Clinton promised to have every shcool in America wired to the interent.

But one wonders. If children have trouble reading, what does the internet provide books don't? The information super highway bombards us with statistics and facts. The real question is can people analyze it? Do we have the wisdom to know what to make of all this material. I see students in the lib. Get excited as they see the stacks of information slipping from the printers. But like students forty years ago who were the first to be able to use a Xerox machine and copy an article instead of haivng to take notes—I wonder what will they do with all this informaiton when they get home?

Wisdom vs. Knowledge. X xxxxxxxx x xxxx x Being able to synehisize data. xxxxxxxxxx

CNN tells us about a crisis in Iraq or a stock plunge in Korea in seconds. The TV screen flashes with images and numbers. We hear soundbites from experts. But do we know enough history of the Middle east to now what this crisis means? Do we know enough about international business and trading to know how the Korean markets effect ours? What does information mean if we dont appreciate what it means?

This freewriting is a loose, repetitive, and misspelled collection of ideas, switching from the Internet to cable television without connection. But within the text there are the germs of ideas that could lead to a good essay about the information super-highway and critical thinking.

Advantages

- **Freewriting can help overcome writer's block.** Giving yourself the freedom to write anything—even meaningless symbols—forces you to overcome the idea that every time you write you must come up with significant insights and flawless prose.

- **Freewriting is useful when you simply have no idea what to write about.** It can help you discover a subject by free association.

Disadvantages

- **Because of its unrestricted nature, freewriting can spin off a lot of interesting but inappropriate ideas.** You may find yourself writing off track, getting farther from the writing needed to meet the needs of your readers. You can focus your freewriting by considering the needs of your readers. Study your instructor's guidelines for the paper before starting to write. *Write with your reader in mind.*

- **Freewriting can be tiring.** Feel free to list or cluster ideas to save time. *Don't feel obligated to write in complete sentences.*

WRITING ACTIVITY

FREEWRITING

Select one of the following issues and write about it for at least five minutes without stopping. Don't worry about making sense, keeping on topic, or connecting ideas. Remember, this is not a rough draft, but an exploration of ideas. The topic is simply a catalyst, a jumping-off point. Let your free associations flow. If the topic of your hometown leads you to comment on your neighbors' divorce, go with it. *Keep writing!*

your hometown	campus child care	roommates	reality TV shows
job interviews	blind dates	student loans	unemployment
best friends	diets	mortgages	first day at work
gay rights	binge drinking	the Internet	outsourcing

Brainstorming

Brainstorming is another method of finding ideas to write about. Brainstorming can take different forms, the most simple being making lists. As in freewriting, do not attempt to be selective; just follow these guidelines:

- **Write down every idea you can come up with, whether it makes sense or not.**
- **Don't stop to check facts or spelling—list ideas.**
- **Cluster or group ideas to make connections if you can.**
- **Make notes or write short paragraphs to record important ideas you may forget.**

A psychology student searching for a subject for a term paper might begin listing the following thoughts and topics:

```
mental illness—schizophrenia
inability to function in society
insanity defense
mental illness/homelessness
mentally ill off medication
public disturbances by mental patients
institutions/group homes
commitment laws, decision to protect patients against their will
human rights versus incarceration without trial
committing the homeless to mental health institutions for their own safety
```

Through brainstorming the student moves from the general topic of mental illness and legal issues to a subject suitable for a research paper—institutionalizing homeless mentally ill patients. With further prewriting, the student can develop this topic to compare past and present practices, argue for more group homes, study the causes of homelessness, or debate the merits of a local ordinance.

Brainstorming can help you develop writing even when the topic is clearly defined and the context is fixed. Having observed a shoplifter race out of her store with a jacket, the owner of a dress shop who plans to write an incident report to the manager of the shopping mall jots down the following list:

```
time/date of incident
item(s) stolen—get values wholesale/retail
location of video cameras? (Check)
security guard took 6 minutes to respond
guards never at north end of mall
```

problems at other stores—check video & computer stores
need for security
lease expires in three months/may not renew

From this list, the store owner identifies the information needed to document the problem and comes up with the threat of leaving the mall to dramatize her position and prompt a response.

Advantages

- **Like freewriting, brainstorming can help you get started when you have no topic in mind.**
- **Brainstorming allows you to jot down rapid-fire ideas,** freeing you from the need to write complete sentences.
- **Brainstorming can quickly identify information needed to support your points.**

Disadvantages

- **Brainstorming sometimes produces nothing more than a shopping list of unrelated ideas.** Use other techniques, such as freewriting, to flesh out superficial ideas.
- **Because it rests on free associations, brainstorming can lead you far astray from an assigned topic.** If you are working on a specific assignment, keep your syllabus or instructor's guidelines in front of you to help focus your train of thought.

WRITING ACTIVITY

BRAINSTORMING

Select one column from the topics below and build on it, adding your own ideas. Jot down your thoughts as quickly as possible. Allow your thoughts to flow freely. Do not worry about changing direction or coming up with an entirely different subject.

men/women	success	campus housing
attitudes about relationships	careers	dorms/off campus
ending relationships	salaries	having your own apt.
how men and women cope with failed relationships	the perfect first job	advantages/disadvantages of living alone

---

Asking Questions

Asking questions is a method of exploring ideas that can focus your thoughts and identify not only a thesis but information you need. For over a century reporters, working under tight deadlines, have been trained to approach a news story by asking the Five Ws: *Who? What? Where? When? Why?* Asking questions can help you avoid writing in circles and can highlight important issues.

You can use the modes (see pages 22–23) to generate questions.

- **description:** What are the key details of your subject?
- **narration:** What happened? Can you explain the background or history of your subject? What events are significant? What do they mean?
- **example:** Does your subject illustrate a larger trend, issue, or problem?
- **definition:** Do key terms or the subject itself need to be precisely defined?
- **comparison:** How does your subject compare to another? Are there similarities or differences?
- **process:** Can you explain how your subject occurs or operates?
- **division/classification:** Can your subject be divided into types or ranked in varying degrees?
- **cause and effect:** Can you explain what caused your subject or describe its influence or results?
- **argument and persuasion:** What will you have to present to convince readers to accept your ideas?

A student in a literature class has chosen to write a research paper about Arthur Miller's play *Death of a Salesman*. Note the number of questions that stem from one of the modes:

Death of a Salesman
How can you describe Willy's values?
Is Willy a victim of society or of his own delusions?
What role does Uncle Ben play? Is he an example of Willy's dream?
Is Willy's suicide caused by despair or a last attempt at success?
What effect does Willy's infidelity have?
Biff steals a suit and a fountain pen. What do these objects symbolize?
Linda knows Willy has lost his salary but does not confront him about it. Why?
Why does Miller compare Willy and Biff to Uncle Charlie and Bernard?
Is the play an attack on the American dream?
Why causes Willy to reject Charlie's job offer?
This play is world famous but the hero is abusive, selfish, and short-tempered. Why is the play so popular?
What is the purpose of the requiem at the end? How would the play be different without it?

Asking questions can help target other forms of prewriting, giving direction to your freewriting and brainstorming. In addition, questions can help spark critical thinking. Exploring the whys and hows of people, places, and events can help you move beyond simply recording first impressions and superficial observations.

Advantages

- **Asking questions can help transform a topic into a thesis** by directing you to state an opinion or take a position.
- **Questions, if carefully worded, force you to think and test your preconceived notions and attitudes.**
- **Questions reveal needed information,** guiding you to conduct research.

Disadvantages

- **Questions in themselves are not necessarily effective in provoking thought.** Unless you are careful, you may find yourself simply creating pat questions that lead to simple answers. If your answers simply restate what you already know or believe, write tougher questions or try another prewriting method.
- **Asking too many questions, especially misdirected ones, can lead you on a scattered mission, finding unrelated or trivial information.** Edit your questions when you complete your list. Don't feel obligated to consider every question you jot down.

WRITING ACTIVITY

ASKING QUESTIONS

Select one of the topics below and develop as many questions as you can. If you find yourself blocked, choose another topic or create one of your own. List as many questions as you can and don't worry about repeating yourself. Consider using one or more of the modes to develop questions:

campus crime	credit cards	online shopping	drinking age
prisons	stalking laws	online dating	fashion
cell phone etiquette	health clubs	divorce	media images of women

Look over your questions and circle those that suggest interesting topics for papers.

Clustering

Clustering is a type of prewriting that helps people who are visually oriented. If you have an artistic or technical background, you may find it easier to explore ideas by blocking them out on a sheet of paper or computer screen. Clustering is a form of directed doodling or informal charting. Instead of listing ideas or writing paragraphs, sketch your ideas on paper, as if arranging index cards on a table. People who use clustering often develop unique visual markers—using rectangles, arrows, and circles to diagram their ideas.

Thinking about his sister's decision to adopt a baby from China, a student clustered a series of observations and questions:

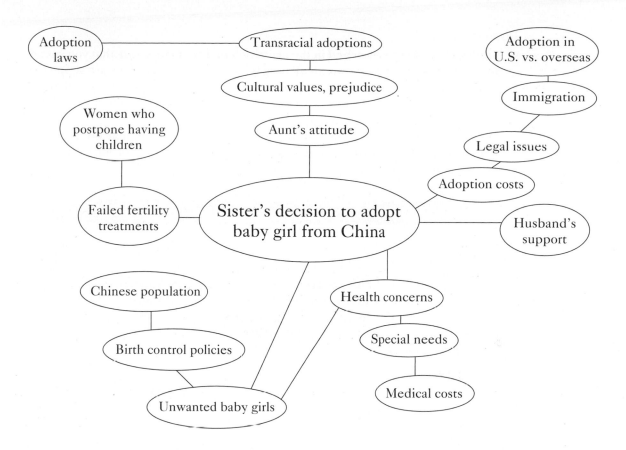

In this case, clustering helps chart the positive and negative elements of transracial adoptions.

Advantages

- **Clustering is suited to people who think spatially and find it easier to draw rather than write.**
- **Clustering is a good method to explore topics for comparison and classification papers.**
- **Clustering can save time.** Freewriting, brainstorming, and asking questions all list ideas in the order in which they occur to the writer rather than in relationship to each other. These ideas have to be examined and reorganized. Clustering allows you to create several lists or groupings, ranking ideas in importance and immediately showing links between related ideas.
- **Clustering can help place ideas in context.** You can group ideas in columns to contrast advantages and disadvantages or create a spectrum, showing the range of ideas.

Disadvantages

■ **You can become so absorbed in the artistic elements of clustering that you spend more time toying with geometrical designs than with the ideas they are supposed to organize.** Keep your artwork simple. Don't waste your time using rulers to draw arrows or make perfect squares and circles. If you prewrite on a computer, don't bother using clip art.

■ **Clustering can be an excellent device for organizing ideas but may not help you get started.** Use freewriting or ask questions to start the flow of ideas, then arrange them with clustering techniques.

WRITING ACTIVITY

CLUSTERING

Select one of the following topics. Use a blank sheet of paper to record and arrange your ideas. You may wish to list pros and cons in separate columns or use a simple pie chart to split up a complex or confusing topic. Connect related ideas with arrows. Use different shapes and colors to distinguish contrasting ideas. Remember, clustering is a means to an end. Don't allow your artwork to get in the way of your thinking or take too much time. Neatness does not count.

computer hackers	being laid off	worst/best jobs
role models	airport security	teen pregnancy
violence on TV	singles' bars	fast food
the stock market	poverty	eating disorders
racial profiling	having children	video games

Strategies for Prewriting

1. **Write as often as you can.**
2. **Get in the habit of asking questions and listing ideas and observations.**
3. **Make notes of interesting items you see on television, clip newspaper and magazine articles, and bookmark websites that could serve as writing prompts.**
4. **Review upcoming assignments and make lists of possible topics.**
5. **Experiment with different forms of prewriting and feel free to blend them to develop your own style.**
6. **Save your notes. Ideas that you might discard for one paper might aid you in developing a topic for a future assignment.**

e-writing

Exploring Prewriting Strategies Online

Websites with prewriting resources range from those maintained by academic organizations to those created by individual teachers posting information for their students.

1. Using InfoTrac College Edition (available through your English CourseMate at **www.cengagebrain.com**) or one of your library's databases, enter *prewriting strategies* as a search term to locate articles that may assist you in your writing course and other classes.
2. Using a search engine, such as Yahoo! or Google, enter such terms as *prewriting*, *freewriting*, and *brainstorming* to locate current websites.
3. Familiarize yourself with your library's online databases and resources, such as encyclopedias. Often checking a fact or reference can help trigger ideas for an assignment or prevent you from wasting time.

For Further Reading

Lamm, Kathryn. *10,000 Ideas for Term Papers, Projects, Reports, and Speeches.*

E-Sources

The University of Kansas Writing Center
   http://www.writing.ku.edu/guides
Online Writing Lab at Purdue University
   http://owl.english.purdue.edu/owl/

 Access the English CourseMate for this text at **www.cengagebrain.com** for further information on prewriting strategies.

Developing a Thesis

*I write because there is some lie I want to expose, some
fact to which I want to draw attention, and my initial
concern is to get a hearing.*

—George Orwell

What Is a Thesis?

Once you discover a topic through prewriting, your next step is developing a thesis.
Good writing has a clear purpose. An essay is never just *about* something. Whether
the topic is climate change, your first job, high school football, or *A Streetcar Named
Desire,* your writing should make a point or express an opinion. The *thesis* is a writer's
main or controlling idea. A *thesis statement* presents the writer's position in a sentence
or two and serves as the document's mission statement. *A thesis is more than a limited
or narrowed topic; it expresses a point of view. It is a declaration, summarizing your purpose.*

Topic	Narrowed Topic	Thesis Statement
gun control	handgun ban	*The city's proposed handgun ban will not prevent gang violence.*
campus housing	rehabbing dorms	*Given the demand for more on-campus housing, the men's dorm, which is fifty years old, should be rehabilitated.*
terrorism	cyber-terrorism	*Federal security agencies must take steps to protect the Internet from cyber-terrorism.*

WRITERS AT WORK

I write in my studio. I've got a little studio in Brooklyn, a couple of blocks from
my house—no telephone, nothing there.
When I go there, the only thing I ever do
there is work, so it's wonderful. I'm like
a dog with a conditioned reflex. There
is no television, no telephone, nothing. My wife wants me to get a portable
telephone. I refuse. I don't want to be
tempted. There's an old Jewish belief
that you build a fence around an impulse.
That's not good enough, you build a
fence around the fence, so no telephone.

Norman Mailer, novelist
SOURCE: *Booknotes*

WRITING ACTIVITIES

Develop a thesis statement for each of the following topics. Use prewriting techniques such as asking questions and clustering to explore ideas. Remember, your thesis should state a viewpoint, express an opinion, make an appeal, or suggest a solution, not simply make a factual statement or limit the subject.

1. Driver's licenses for illegal immigrants
2. Universal health care
3. Subprime mortgages
4. The Internet's impact on journalism
5. The aging baby boom generation
6. Welfare reform and child care
7. America's role in the twenty-first century
8. The current job market for college graduates
9. DNA testing and criminal investigations
10. Minimum wage jobs

Elements of a Thesis Statement

Effective thesis statements share the following common characteristics:

- **They are generally stated in a single sentence.** This statement forms the core of the paper, clearly presenting your point of view. Writing a thesis statement can be a critical part of the prewriting process, helping you move from a list or cluster of ideas to a specific paper. Even if the thesis statement does not appear in the final paper, writing this sentence can focus your ideas and direct your writing.
- **They express an opinion, not a topic.** What distinguishes a thesis statement from a topic is that it does not announce a subject but expresses a viewpoint. The statement "There is a serious shortage of campus parking" describes a problem, but it does not express an opinion. "Shuttle bus service should be expanded to alleviate the campus parking problem" serves as a thesis statement, clearly asserting a point of view.
- **They focus the topic.** Part of the job of a thesis statement is to direct the paper, limiting the scope of the writer's area of concentration. "Television is bad for

children" states an opinion, but the subject is so broad that any essay would probably just list superficial observations. A thesis such as "Television action heroes teach children that violence is an acceptable method of resolving conflicts" is limited enough to create a far more engaging paper.

- **They indicate the kind of support to follow.** Opinions require proof. "Because of declining enrollment, the cinema course should be canceled" indicates a clear cause-and-effect argument based on factual evidence, leading readers to expect a list of enrollment and budget figures.

- **They often organize supporting material.** The thesis statement "Exercise is essential to control weight, prevent disease, and maintain mental health" suggests that the body of the paper will be divided into three parts.

- **Effective thesis statements are precisely worded.** Because they express the writer's point of view in a single sentence, thesis statements must be accurately stated. General terms, such as *good, bad, serious,* and *important* weaken a thesis. Absolute statements can suggest that the writer is proposing a panacea. "Deadbolt locks should be installed in all dorm rooms to *prevent crime*" implies that a single mechanism is a foolproof method of totally eradicating all crime. "Deadbolt locks should be installed in all dorm rooms to *deter break-ins*" is far more accurate and easier to support.

WRITING ACTIVITIES

Revise the following thesis statements, increasing their precision.

1. The Internet provides students with a lot of educational opportunities.

2. Providing employee health insurance is a challenge for many businesses.

3. Employers should assist employees with small children.

4. Public schools must prepare students for the twenty-first century.

5. Attitudes about fatherhood have changed in the last twenty years.

6. Commercials mislead consumers.

7. Hollywood has given foreigners distorted views of American society.

8. Americans suffer from their lack of understanding of other cultures.

9. Illegal immigration remains a problem for many reasons.

10. Peer pressure can be negative.

Locating the Thesis

To be effective, thesis statements must be strategically placed. The thesis statement does not have to appear in the introduction but can be placed anywhere in the essay.

- **Placing the thesis at the opening starts the essay with a strong statement, providing a clear direction and an outline of the supporting evidence.** However, if the thesis is controversial, it may be more effective to open with supporting details and confront readers' objections before formally announcing the thesis. An essay that opens with the statement "We must legalize heroin" might easily be dismissed by people who would think the writer must be naive or insensitive to the pain of addiction, the spread of AIDS, and other social problems stemming from drug abuse. However, if the essay first demonstrates the failure of current policies and argues that addiction should be treated as a medical rather than a legal issue, more readers might be receptive to the writer's call for legalization.

- **Placing the thesis in the middle of the essay allows a writer to introduce the subject, provide support, raise questions, and guide the reader into accepting a thesis that is then explained or defended.** However, placing the thesis somewhere within the essay may weaken its impact because reader attention is strongest at the opening and closing paragraphs. Writers often highlight a thesis statement in the middle of an essay by placing it in a separate paragraph or using italics.

- **Placing the thesis at the end allows a writer to close the essay with a strong statement.** Delaying the thesis allows the writer to address reader objections and bias, providing narratives, examples, and statistics to support the conclusion. However, postponing the thesis will disappoint some readers who want a clear answer. Delaying the thesis can suggest to some readers that the writer's position cannot stand on its own and depends on a great deal of qualification.

Explicit, Evolving, and Implied Theses

Many textbooks suggest that every essay should have an easily identifiable thesis statement, a sentence you should be able to locate and underline, but this is not always the case. Most writers present explicit thesis statements, but others use a series of sentences to develop their opinions. In some instances, the writer's thesis is not formally stated but only implied or suggested.

Explicit Thesis Statements

Alan M. Dershowitz opens his essay "The 'Abuse Excuse' Is Detrimental to the Justice System" with a boldly stated, explicit thesis statement:

> The "abuse excuse"—the legal tactic by which criminal defendants claim a history of abuse as an excuse for violent retaliation—is quickly becoming a license to kill and maim.

Explicit theses are best used in writing in the modes of argument and persuasion, comparison, and division and classification.

Advantages

- **An explicit thesis statement is clear and concise.** The writer's purpose is stated directly so that readers are not confused.
- **An explicit thesis makes a strong opening or closing statement.**
- **A concise, strongly worded statement is easily understood so that even a casual reader will quickly grasp the writer's main idea.**

Disadvantages

- **Explicit thesis statements can present a narrow interpretation or solution to a complex situation or problem.** In many instances an evolving or implied thesis gives the writer greater freedom to discuss ideas and address possible objections.
- **Explicit theses can easily alienate readers with differing opinions.** An evolving thesis, on the other hand, allows the writer to explain or qualify opinions.

Evolving Thesis Statements

In "Grant and Lee," Bruce Catton compares the two Civil War generals meeting at Appomattox Court House to work out terms for the South's surrender. But instead of stating his thesis in a single sentence, he develops his controlling ideas in a series of statements:

> They were two strong men, these oddly different generals, and they represented the strengths of two conflicting currents that, through them, had come into final collision.

After describing the life and social background of each general, Catton expands his thesis:

> So Grant and Lee were in complete contrast, representing two diametrically opposed elements in American life. Grant was the modern man emerging; beyond him, ready to come on the stage, was the great age of steel and machinery, of crowded cities and a restless burgeoning vitality. Lee might have ridden down from the old age of chivalry, lance in hand, silken banner fluttering over his head. Each man was the perfect champion of his cause, drawing both his strengths and his weaknesses from the people he led.

Catton concludes his essay with a final controlling statement:

> Two great Americans, Grant and Lee—very different, yet under everything very much alike.

Evolving thesis statements are best suited for complex or controversial subjects. They allow you to address an issue piece by piece or present a series of arguments.

Advantages

- **An evolving thesis lets a writer present readers with a series of controlling ideas, allowing them to absorb a complex opinion point by point.**

- **An evolving thesis can be useful in presenting a controversial opinion by slowly convincing readers to accept less threatening ideas first.**

- **An evolving thesis can help a writer tailor ideas to suit different situations or contexts.** An evolving thesis can also be organized to address specific reader objections.

Disadvantages

- **Because the statements are distributed throughout an essay, they can appear scattered and have less impact than a single, direct sentence.**

- **Evolving theses can make writers appear unsure of their points, as if they are reluctant to state direct opinions.**

Implied Thesis Statements

In describing Holcomb, Kansas, Truman Capote supplies a number of facts and observations without stating a thesis. Although no single sentence can be isolated as presenting the controlling idea, the description is highly organized and is more than a random collection of details.

> The village of Holcomb stands on the high wheat plains of western Kansas, a lonesome area that other Kansans call "out there." Some seventy miles east of the Colorado border, the countryside, with its hard blue skies and desert-clear air, has an atmosphere that is rather more Far Western than Middle West. The local accent is barbed with a prairie twang, a ranch-hand nasalness, and the men, many of them, wear narrow frontier trousers, Stetsons, and high-heeled boots with pointed toes. The land is flat, and the views are awesomely extensive; horses, herds of cattle, a white cluster of grain elevators rising as gracefully as Greek temples are visible long before a traveler reaches them.

Having carefully assembled and arranged his observations, Capote allows the details to speak for themselves and give readers a clear impression of his subject.

Implied thesis statements work best when the writer's evidence is so compelling that it does not require an introduction or explanation. Writers also use an implied thesis to challenge readers by posing an idea or presenting a problem without suggesting an interpretation or solution. Although you may not state a clear thesis statement in writing a description or telling a story, your essay should have a clear purpose, a direction.

Advantages

- **An implied thesis allows the writer's images and observations to represent his or her ideas.** Implied thesis statements are common in descriptive and narrative writing.

- **An implied thesis does not dictate an opinion but allows readers to develop their own responses.**

- **An implied thesis does not confront readers with bold assertions but allows a writer to slowly unfold controlling ideas.**

Disadvantages

■ **Writing without an explicitly defined thesis can lead readers to assume ideas unintended by the writer.** Capote's description of a small town may provoke both positive and negative responses, depending on the readers' perceptual world.

■ **Writing that lacks a clear thesis statement requires careful reading and critical thinking to determine the writer's purpose.** A strong thesis sentence at the opening or closing of an essay makes the author's goal very clear.

Strategies for Developing Thesis Statements

1. **Develop a thesis statement while planning your essay.** If you cannot state your goal in a sentence or two, you may not have a clear focus regarding your purpose. Even if you decide to use an implied thesis, a clearly worded statement on your outline or top of the page can help keep your writing on track.

2. **Write your thesis statement with your reader in mind.** The goal of writing is not only to express your ideas—but also to share them with others. Choose your words carefully. Be sensitive to your readers' perceptual world. Avoid writing biased or highly opinionated statements that may alienate readers.

3. **Make sure that your thesis statement expresses an opinion.** Don't confuse making an announcement or a factual statement with establishing a thesis.

4. **Determine the best location for your thesis.** If you believe that most of your readers will be receptive to your views, placing the thesis at the opening may be appropriate. If your position is controversial or depends on establishing a clear context of support, delay your thesis by placing it in the middle or at the conclusion.

5. **Make sure your thesis matches your purpose.** Persuasive arguments demand a strongly worded thesis statement, perhaps one that is restated throughout the essay. If your position is complex, you may wish to develop it by making partial thesis statements throughout the essay. If you are not motivating your readers to take specific action, you may wish to use an implied thesis. State your observations or evidence and permit readers to develop their own conclusions.

6. **Test your thesis.** It is not always easy to find people willing to read a full draft of your essay, but you can usually find someone who will listen to a sentence or two. Ask a friend or acquaintance to consider your thesis statement. Is it precise? Does it seem logical? What kind of evidence would be needed to support it? Are there any words or phrases that seem awkward, unclear, or offensive? If your thesis statement seems weak, review your prewriting notes. You may need to further limit your topic or choose a new subject.

7. **Make sure your thesis does more than present a fact, announce a subject, or narrow a topic.** The most common errors writers make in developing thesis statements include simply stating what the paper is about or presenting a narrowed topic:

ANNOUNCEMENTS:	My paper is about racial profiling.
	Snowboarding is a popular sport.
NARROWED TOPICS:	Police departments have been accused of racial profiling.
	Snowboarders are regarded as outlaws by traditional skiers.
IMPROVED THESIS STATEMENTS:	Police departments must develop methods to combat crime and prevent terrorism without resorting to racial profiling.
	Snowboarders and traditional skiers must learn to respect each other on the slopes.

WRITING ACTIVITIES

1. Select three to five topics from pages 751–752 and write thesis statements to guide possible rough drafts. Make sure your statements are opinions, not merely narrowed topics.

2. Skim through the entries in the Reader section of the book and locate thesis statements. Note where they are located and whether they are explicit, implied, or evolving.

3. Select an issue you have thought about over a period of time and write a series of thesis statements illustrating your evolving viewpoints.

e-writing

Exploring Thesis Statements Online

You can use the Web to learn more about developing thesis statements.

1. Using a search engine such as Yahoo! or Google, enter *thesis statement* as a term and review the range of sources. You may wish to print out helpful web pages.

2. Locate one or more newspapers online and scan through a series of recent editorials. Select a few articles on topics you are familiar with and examine the thesis

statements. Which sentence summarizes the editorial's main point or assertion? Where is it placed? Are the thesis statements explicit, evolving, or implied? Are they carefully worded?

3. Using InfoTrac College Edition (available through your English CourseMate at **www.cengagebrain.com**) or one of your library's online databases, search for articles on gun control, abortion, capital punishment, or any other controversial topic. Can you identify the writers' thesis statements? Are they effective?

E-Sources

Indiana University Writing Tutorial Services: How to Write a Thesis Statement
    http://www.indiana.edu/~wts/pamphlets/thesis_statement.shtml

University of Toronto: Using Thesis Statements
    http://www.writing.utoronto.ca/advice/planning-and-organizing/thesis-statements

University of Wisconsin—Madison, Writing Center: Developing a Thesis Statement
    http://www.wisc.edu/writing/Handbook/Thesis.html

 Access the English CourseMate for this text at **www.cengagebrain.com** for further information on thesis statements.

Supporting a Thesis

By persuading others, we convince ourselves.

—Junius

What Is Support?

Whether your thesis is explicitly stated or only implied, it must be supported with evidence. Readers will share your views, appreciate your descriptions, understand your narratives, change their opinions, or alter their behavior only if you provide sufficient proof to convince them. Most people associate *evidence* with persuasive or argumentative writing, but all writers—even those composing personal essays or memoirs—provide supporting details for their ideas.

A student proposing a new computer system must provide factual support to create a convincing argument:

> *The college must improve its computer system.* This semester four hundred students did not receive mid-term grades because of a computer breakdown. The college e-mail system, which is critical to the distance learning department, malfunctioned for two weeks, preventing students from electronically submitting research papers. The eight-year-old system simply does not have the speed and capacity needed to serve the faculty, students, and administration. Students were told two years ago that online registration would save the college money and make it possible to sign up for courses from home. But this service has been postponed for another year because the computers can't support it. If the college is to attract students, maintain its programs, and offer new services, it must upgrade its computers.

The same student writing a personal narrative would use supporting details to paint a picture, set a mood, and express a feeling:

> *I spent two years in Paris and hated it!* Most people raise their eyebrows when I say that, but it is true.
>
> My Paris was not the Paris shown in the movies or the Paris seen by tourists. I lived with my mother in a cramped high-rise built for low-income workers. My Paris was a noisy, dark two-room apartment with bad heat, banging pipes, and broken elevators. The hallways were filled with trash and spattered with graffiti. Neighbors blasted us night and day with bad rock music. Punks and druggies harassed my mom every time she left for school. I could not wait for her to finish her degree so we could move back to New Jersey. I never even saw the Eiffel Tower.

One day I lost my fountain pen, and I could not find another decent fountain pen. Phyllis Wright has this wonderful store where I live . . . called East End Computers. She is a wonderful woman. I walked in there, and I said, "All right, it's time for me to change my life. I can't find a fountain pen in this town." She really not only taught me how to do it [use a computer], she helped me to do it. Every time I had a problem and I couldn't get my document up, I would call Phyllis Wright. She gave me her home number so I could call her day or night for that period of transition that drives writers crazy. Now I'm all plugged in. Now I have a computer everywhere and a laptop that I take everywhere. I still have a fountain pen. Someone bought me one, but the fountain pen era is over.

Blanche Wiesen Cook, biographer
SOURCE: *Booknotes*

Writers verify their theses using various types of evidence, ranging from personal observations to statistics. Because each type of evidence has limitations, writers usually present a blend of personal observations and testimony, statistics and examples, or facts and analogies. The evidence you select should reflect the writing context and accomplish four goals:

- **Support your thesis.**
- **Address readers' needs and concerns.**
- **Respect the history and values of the discipline or situation.**
- **Suit the nature of the document.**

Types of Evidence

Personal Observations

Personal observations are descriptive details and sensory impressions about a person, place, object, or condition. Writers can support a thesis by supplying readers with specific details. The thesis that "Westwood High School must be renovated" can be supported with observations about leaking roofs, faulty wiring, broken elevators, and defective plumbing.

Advantages

- **Personal observations can be powerful as long as they are carefully selected and well organized.** To be effective, writers must choose words carefully, being aware of their connotations.
- **Personal observations can balance objective facts by adding human interest.**

Disadvantages

- **Because they are chosen by the writer, personal observations are biased.** They often require outside evidence such as facts, statistics, or testimony to be convincing.

- **Personal observations may be inappropriate in objective reports.** Writers often avoid using first-person references such as *I* or *me* when including evidence they observed in formal documents.

Personal Experiences

Like personal observations, accounts of your own life can be persuasive support. As a college student, you have great authority in discussing higher education. A patient's account of battling a serious disease can be as persuasive as an article by a physician or medical researcher.

Advantages

- **Personal experiences can be emotionally powerful and commanding because the writer is the sole authority and expert.**
- **Personal experiences are effective support in descriptive and narrative writing.**
- **Individual accounts can humanize abstract issues and personalize objective facts and statistics.**

Disadvantages

- **Personal experience, no matter how compelling, is only one individual's story.** As with personal observations, personal experience can be supported with expert testimony, facts, and statistics.
- **Personal experience, unless presented carefully, can seem self-serving and can weaken a writer's argument.** Before including your own experiences, consider whether readers will think you are making a selfish appeal, asking readers to accept ideas or take actions that primarily benefit only you.

Examples

Examples are specific events, persons, or situations that represent a general trend, type, or condition. A writer supporting the right to die might relate the story of a single terminally ill patient to illustrate the need for euthanasia. The story of one small business could illustrate an economic trend.

Advantages

- **Specific cases or situations can dramatize a complex or abstract problem.** They often make effective introductions.
- **Examples can be used to demonstrate facts and statistics that tend to be static lists.**
- **Examples allow you to introduce narratives that can make a fact-filled paper more interesting and readable.**

Disadvantages

- **Examples can be misleading or misinterpreted.** Examples must be representative. Avoid selecting isolated incidents or exceptions to a general condition. For instance, a single mugging, no matter how violent, does not prove that a crime wave is sweeping a college campus.

- **Because they are highlighted, examples can sometimes be distorted into being viewed as major events instead of illustrations.** Another danger is that examples can create false generalizations and conceal complex subtleties. Examples can be placed in context with statistics or a disclaimer:

  > Mary Smith is one of five thousand teachers who participated in last year's strike. Though some of her views do not reflect the opinions of her colleagues, her experiences on the picket line were typical.

Facts

Facts are objective details that are either directly observed or gathered by the writer. The need to renovate a factory can be demonstrated by presenting evidence from inspection reports, maintenance records, and a manufacturer's repair recommendations.

Advantages

- **Facts provide independent support for a writer's thesis, suggesting that others share his or her conclusions.**
- **Facts are generally verifiable.** A reader who may doubt a writer's personal observations or experiences can check factual sources.
- **Because of their objectivity, facts can be used to add credibility to personal narratives.**

Disadvantages

- **Facts, like examples, can be misleading.** Don't assume that a few isolated pieces of information can support your thesis. You cannot disprove or dismiss a general trend by simply identifying a few exceptions.
- **Facts, in some cases, must be explained to readers.** Stating that "the elevator brakes are twenty years old" proves little unless readers understand that the manufacturer suggests replacing them after ten years. Lengthy or technical explanations of facts may distract or bore readers.

Testimony (Quotations)

Testimony, the observations or statements by witnesses, participants, or experts, allows writers to interject other voices into their documents, whether in the form of direct quotations or paraphrases.

Advantages

- **Testimony, like factual support, helps verify a writer's thesis by showing that others share his or her views and opinions.**

- **Testimony by witnesses or participants adds a human dimension to facts and statistics.** Comments by a victim of child abuse can dramatize the problem, compelling readers to learn more and be willing to study factual data.

- **Expert testimony, usually in the form of quotations, enhances writers' credibility by demonstrating that highly respected individuals agree with them.**

Disadvantages

- **Comments by people who observed or participated in an event are limited by the range of their experiences.** An eyewitness to a car accident sees the crash from one angle. Another person, standing across the street, may report events very differently.

- **Witnesses and participants interpret events based on their perceptual worlds and may be less than objective.**

- **Expert testimony can be misleading.** Don't take quotes out of context. Don't assume that you can impress readers by simply sprinkling a paper with quotations by famous people. *Statements by experts must be meaningful, relevant, and accurate.*

Strategies for Using Testimony

Testimony, the statements of others, can be included in your paper in two ways: direct quotes and paraphrases (indirect quotes). Make sure you avoid plagiarism (see pages 7–8) by clearly identifying which words are yours and which are the words of others.

Do not simply cut and paste material into your paper without acknowledging where it came from. Quotations of a few words to a few sentences should be placed in quotation marks. Longer quotations should be placed in indented blocks. These visual markers clearly separate your words from those you have copied from another source.

Original Quote:

> The Safe and Sober Program, initiated this year, has clearly worked. Eight students were arrested for drunk driving during the fall semester, compared to fifteen the year before. The number of disorderly conduct charges involving alcohol during Homecoming Week dropped from six last year to just two this year.
>
> *Nancy George,* The Campus Times Online, *editorial*

Student Paper Using Direct Quote:

> Efforts by college administrators and student organizations can reduce binge drinking. Writing in *The Campus Times Online*, Nancy George notes, "The number of disorderly conduct charges involving alcohol during Homecoming Week dropped from six last year to just two this year."

(Continued)

Student Paper Using Paraphrase:
Efforts by college administrators and student organizations can reduce binge drinking. At Pacific College, the Safe and Sober Program reduced alcohol-related disorderly conduct charges during Homecoming Week by two-thirds (George).

Even if your assignment does not require formal documentation, clearly indicate the source of material you quote or paraphrase.

Analogies (Comparisons)

Analogies compare similar situations, people, objects, or events to demonstrate the validity of the thesis. The thesis "AIDS prevention programs will reduce the incidence of infection" can be supported by pointing to the success of similar programs in combating other infectious diseases.

Advantages

- **Analogies can introduce new topics by comparing them to ones readers find familiar or understandable.**
- **Comparisons can counter alternative theses or solutions by showing their failures or deficiencies in contrast to the writer's ideas.**

Disadvantages

- **Analogy is a weak form of argument.** Because no two situations are exactly alike, analogy is rarely convincing in itself. Arguing that school uniforms reduced violence in one school does not prove it would work in another with different students, teachers, and social challenges.
- **Comparisons depend on readers' perceptual worlds.** Suggesting that an urban planner's design should be adopted because it will transform a city's business district into another Fifth Avenue assumes that readers find Fifth Avenue desirable.

Statistics

Statistics are factual data expressed in numbers and can validate a writer's thesis in dramatic terms readers can readily appreciate. However, you must be careful, because although statistics represent facts and not an opinion, they can be very deceptive. The statement "Last year the number of students apprehended for possessing cocaine tripled" sounds alarming until you learn the arrests went from one to three students at a university with an enrollment of 30,000. Numbers can be used to provide strikingly different perceptions. Suppose the state of California pays half a million welfare recipients $800 a month. A proposal to increase these benefits by 2 percent can be reported as representing $16 a month to the poor or $96 million a year to taxpayers. Both figures are accurate, and one can easily imagine which numbers politicians will use to support or reject the proposal.

Advantages

- **Statistics can distill a complex issue into a single dramatic statement:**

  One out of three American children grows up in poverty.

  Each cigarette takes seven minutes off a smoker's life.

  Twenty-one thousand instances of domestic violence are reported every week.

- **Statistics can be easily remembered and repeated to others.**

Disadvantages

- **Because they are often misused, statistics are often distrusted by readers.** Whenever you quote statistics, be prepared to explain where you obtained them and why they are reliable.

- **Although statistics can be dramatic, they can quickly bore readers.** Long lists of numbers can be difficult for readers to absorb. Statistics can be made easier to understand if presented in graphs, charts, and diagrams.

Strategies for Using Statistics

In gathering and presenting statistics, consider these questions:

1. **Where did the statistics come from?** Who produced the statistics? Is the source reliable? Statistics released by utility companies or antinuclear organizations about the safety of nuclear power plants may be suspect. If the source might be biased, search for information from additional sources.

2. **When were the statistics collected?** Information can become obsolete very quickly. Determine whether the numbers are still relevant. For example, surveys about such issues as capital punishment can be distorted if they are conducted after a violent crime occurs.

3. **How were the statistics collected?** Public opinion polls are commonly used to represent support or opposition to an issue. A statement such as "90 percent of the student body think Dean Miller should resign" means nothing unless you know how that figure was determined. How many students were polled—ten or a thousand? How were they chosen—at an anti-Miller rally or by random selection? How was the question worded? Was it objective or did it provoke a desired response? Did the polled students reflect the attitudes of the entire student body?

(Continued)

4. **Are the units being counted properly defined?** All statistics count some item—home foreclosures, student dropouts, teenage pregnancies, or AIDS patients. Confusion can occur if the items are not precisely defined. In polling students, for instance, the term *student* must be clearly delineated. Who will be counted? Only full-time students? Undergraduates? Senior citizens auditing an elective art history course? Without a clear definition of *alcoholic* or *juvenile delinquent,* comparing studies will be meaningless.

5. **Do the statistics measure what they claim to measure?** The units being counted may not be accurate indicators. Comparing graduates' SAT scores assumes that the tests accurately measure achievement. If one nation's air force is 500 percent larger than its neighbor's, does it mean that it is five times as powerful? Counting aircraft alone does not take quality, pilot skill, natural defenses, or a host of other factors into account.

6. **Are enough statistics presented?** A single statistic may be accurate but misleading. The statement that "80 percent of Amalgam workers own stock in the company" makes the firm sound employee owned—until you learn that the average worker has half a dozen shares. Ninety percent of the stock could be held by a single investor.

7. **How are the statistics being interpreted?** Numbers alone do not tell the whole story. If one teacher has a higher retention rate than another, does it mean he or she is a better instructor or an easy grader? If the number of people receiving services from a social welfare agency increases, does it signal a failing economy or greater effort and efficiency on the part of an agency charged with aiding the disadvantaged?

WRITING ACTIVITIES

List the types of evidence needed to support the following thesis statements:

1. The city's proposed handgun ban will not prevent gang violence.

2. Consumers will resist shopping on the Web until credit card security is assured.

3. Given the demand for more on-campus housing, the fifty-year-old dorm for men should be rehabilitated.

4. Women must learn to express intolerance toward sexual harassment without appearing humorless or fanatical.

5. Vote for Sandy Mendoza!

Using and Documenting Sources

No matter how dramatic, evidence is not likely to impress readers unless they know its source. Chapter 24 details methods of using academic documentation styles, such as MLA (Modern Language Association) and APA (American Psychological Association) formats. Documentation, usually mandatory in research papers, is useful even in short essays. Even informal notations can enhance your credibility:

> According to a recent *Newsweek* poll, 50 percent of today's first-year students plan to own their own business.

> Half of today's freshmen plan to open their own businesses someday (*Newsweek*, March 10, 2011).

In addition to identifying an outside source, it is important to explain its significance:

> A survey of five thousand heroin addicts conducted by the National Institute of Health revealed . . .

> Mario Perez, who coached teams to four state championships, has stated . . .

Strategies for Evaluating Evidence

Use these questions to evaluate the evidence you have collected to support your thesis.

1. **Does the evidence suit your thesis?** Review the writing context to determine what evidence is appropriate. Personal observations and experiences would support the thesis of an autobiographical essay. However, these subjective elements could weaken the thesis of a business report.

2. **Is the evidence accurate?** It may be possible to find evidence that supports your thesis—but are these quotations, facts, and statistics accurate? Are they current?

3. **Are the sources reliable?** Evidence can be gathered from innumerable sources, but not all proof is equally reliable or objective. Many sources of information have political biases or economic interests and only produce data that support their views. In gathering information about the minimum wage, balance data from labor unions and antipoverty groups with government statistics and testimony from business owners.

4. **Is sufficient evidence presented?** To convince readers, you must supply enough evidence to support your thesis. A few isolated facts or quotations

(Continued)

from experts are not likely to be persuasive. A single extended example might influence readers to accept your thesis about a close friend or relative but would not be likely to alter their views on such issues as immigration, recycling, divorce laws, or public schools. Such topics require facts, statistics, and expert testimony. *Examine your thesis carefully to see whether it can be separated into parts, and determine whether you have adequate proof for each section.*

5. **Is the evidence representative?** To be intellectually honest, writers have to use evidence that is representative. You can easily assemble isolated facts, quotations taken out of context, and exceptional events to support almost any thesis. Books about UFOs, the Bermuda Triangle, or assassination conspiracies are often filled with unsupported personal narratives, quotations from questionable experts, and isolated facts. If you can support your thesis only with isolated examples and atypical instances, you may wish to question your conclusions.

6. **Is the evidence presented clearly?** Although evidence is essential to support your thesis, long quotations and lists of statistics can be boring and counterproductive. Evidence should be readable. Outside sources should blend well with your own writing. *Read your paper out loud to identify awkward or difficult passages.*

7. **Does the evidence support the thesis?** Finally, ask yourself if the evidence you have selected really supports your thesis. You may have found interesting facts or quotations, but that does not mean they should be included in your paper. *If the evidence does not directly support your thesis, it should be deleted.*

WRITING ACTIVITIES

1. If you developed any thesis statements in the exercises on page 55, list the types of sources that would prove the best support.

2. Select a topic from pages 751–752 and list the kind of evidence readers would expect writers to use as support.

e-writing

Exploring Thesis Support Online

You can use the Web to learn more about supporting a thesis.

1. Locate resources about specific types of evidence online or in your library's data-bases by using *statistics* and *personal testimony* as search terms.
2. Search newspapers and journals online and select a few articles and editorials. After identifying the thesis, note how the authors presented supporting evidence.
3. Ask instructors in your various courses to help you locate useful websites in various disciplines.

E-Sources

Paradigm Online Writing Assistant: Supporting Your Thesis
    http://www.powa.org/thesissupport-essays/supporting-your-thesis.html
UC Berkeley Library: Evaluating Web Pages
    http://www.lib.berkeley.edu/TeachingLib/Guides/Internet/Evaluate.html
Johns Hopkins University Libraries: Evaluating Information Found on the Internet
    http://www.library.jhu.edu/researchhelp/general/evaluating/

 Access the English CourseMate for this text at **www.cengagebrain.com** for further information on supporting a thesis.

Organizing Ideas

Planning a work is like planning a journey.

—H. J. Tichy

What Is Organization?

Whenever you write, you take readers on a journey, presenting facts, relating stories, sharing ideas, and creating impressions. Readers can follow your train of thought only if you provide them with a clear road map that organizes your thesis and evidence. Even the most compelling ideas will fail to interest readers if placed in a random or chaotic manner. The way you arrange ideas depends on your purpose, the audience, and conventions of the discourse community. Some formal documents dictate a strict format that readers expect you to follow. But in most instances you are free to develop your own method of organization.

As you review the readings in this book, notice how writers organize their essays and provide transitions from one idea to another.

Once you have written a thesis statement and collected supporting material, create a plan for your paper. Prewriting techniques such as brainstorming, writing lists, and clustering can help establish ways to structure your essay. You do not have to develop an elaborate outline with Roman numerals and letters for every paper; a plan can be a simple list of reminders, much like a book's table of contents or a shopping list. A short narrative recalling a recent experience may require only a few notes to guide your first draft.

A complex research paper with numerous sources, however, usually demands a more detailed outline to keep you from getting lost. Sketching out your ideas can help you identify potential problems, spot missing information, reveal irrelevant material, and highlight passages that would make a good opening or final remark.

Informal and Formal Outlines

In most cases, no one sees your outline. It is a means to an end. If prewriting has clearly established the ideas in your mind, you may simply need a few notes to keep your writing on track. The student who worked for an insurance agency for a

WRITERS AT WORK

I had a tape recorder with me and also had a notebook. I'm scribbling furiously, but . . . what ended up being very beneficial . . . is that I had a little tape recorder with me. For example, the night that we were trapped in the mine field—it's pitch black. You can't see to write a note anywhere. I just turned on the tape recorder, and in doing the research for the book, I just listened to hours and hours of these tapes and could reconstruct entire conversations verbatim.

Molly Moore, Gulf War correspondent
SOURCE: *Booknotes*

number of years needs only a few reminders to draft the following comparison of two types of policies:

Whole Life and Term Insurance

Whole Life
— define premiums
— savings & loan options

Term (compare to whole life)
— no savings
— lower rates

Conclusion—last point

A formal outline, however, can serve to refine your prewriting so that your plan becomes a detailed framework for the first draft. Formal outlines organize details and can keep you from drifting off the topic. In addition, they provide a document an instructor or peer reviewer can work with. Few people may be able to decipher the rough notes you make for yourself, but a standard outline creates a clear picture of your topic, thesis, and evidence for others to review and critique. (See the complete essay—based on the following outline—on page 303).

Whole Life and Term Insurance

I.   Introduction: Whole life and term insurance
II. Whole life insurance
  A. General description
    1. History
    2. Purpose
      a. Protection against premature death
      b. Premium payments include savings
  B. Investment feature
    1. Cash value accrual
    2. Loans against cash value

    III. Term insurance
        A. General description
            1. History
            2. Purpose
                a. Protection against premature death
                b. Premium payments lower than whole life insurance
        B. Investment feature
            1. No cash value accrual
            2. No loans against cash value
        C. Cost advantage
            1. Lower premiums
            2. Affordability of greater coverage
    IV. Conclusion
        A. Insurance needs of consumer
            1. Income
            2. Family situation
            3. Investment goals & savings
            4. Obligations
        B. Investment counselors' advice about coverage

Whether your plan is a simple list or a formal outline, it serves as a road map for the first draft and should focus on three main elements:

Title and introduction
Body
Conclusion

Because new ideas can occur throughout the writing process, your plan does not have to detail each element perfectly. You may not come up with an appropriate title or introduction until final editing. In planning, however, consider the impact you want each part of your paper to make. Consider the qualities of an effective title, introduction, body, and conclusion. Develop as complete a plan as you can, leaving blank spaces for future changes. *Remember, place your most important ideas at the opening or ending of your paper. Do not bury the most important information in the middle of the document, which readers are most likely to skip or skim.*

Writing Titles and Introductions

Titles

Titles play a vital role in creating effective essays. A strong title attracts attention, prepares readers to accept your thesis, and helps focus the essay. If you find developing a title difficult, simply label the paper until you complete the first draft. As you write, you may discover an interesting word or phrase that captures the essence of your essay and would serve as an effective title.

Writers use a variety of types of titles—labels, thesis statements, questions, and creative statements.

Labels

Business reports, professional journals, student research papers, and government publications often have titles that clearly state the subject by means of a label:

> Italian Industrial Production—Milan Sector
>
> Bipolar Disorders: Alternative Drug Therapies
>
> Child Abuse Intervention Strategies

■ Labels should be as precisely worded as possible. Avoid general titles that simply announce a broad topic—"*Death of a Salesman*" or "Urban Crime." Titles should reflect your focus—"Willy Loman: Victim of the American Dream" or "Economic Impact of Urban Crime."

Thesis Statements

Titles can state or summarize the writer's thesis:

> We Must Stop Child Abuse
>
> Legalizing Drugs Will Not Deter Crime
>
> Why We Need to Understand Science

■ Thesis statements are frequently used in editorials and political commentaries to openly declare a writer's point of view.

■ Bold assertions attract attention but can also antagonize readers. If you sense that readers may not accept your thesis, it is better to first build your case by introducing background information or supporting details before stating a point of view.

Questions

Writers use questions to arouse interest without revealing their positions:

> Does Recycling Protect the Environment?
>
> Is There an Epidemic of Child Abuse?
>
> Should This Student Have Been Expelled?

■ Questions spark critical thinking and prompt readers to analyze their existing knowledge, values, and opinions.

■ Questions are useful for addressing controversial issues, because readers must evaluate the evidence before learning the writer's answer.

Creative Phrases

Writers sometimes use an attention-getting word or creative phrase to attract readers:

> Pink Mafia: Women and Organized Crime
>
> Sharks on the Web: Consumer Fraud on the Internet
>
> Climbing the Ebony Tower: Tenure in Black Colleges

- Creative titles, like questions, grab attention and motivate people to read items they might ignore. Magazine writers often use clever, humorous, or provocative titles to stimulate interest.
- Creative titles are usually unsuited to formal documents or reports. Creative wording may appear trivial, inappropriate, or biased and should be avoided in objective writing.

Introductions

Introductions should arouse attention, state what your essay is about, and prepare readers for what follows. In addition to stating the topic, the introduction can present background information and provide an overview of the entire essay. A student explaining the different types of Hispanic students on her campus uses the first paragraph to address a misconception and then describes how she will use classification to develop the rest of her essay.

> Students, faculty, and administrators tend to refer to "Hispanics" as if all Latino and Latina students belonged to a single homogeneous group. Actually, there are four distinct groups of Hispanic students. Outsiders may only see slight discrepancies in dress and behavior, but there are profound differences which occasionally border on suspicion and hostility. Their differences are best measured by their attitude toward and their degree of acceptance of mainstream American values and culture.

If you don't have a strong introduction in mind, use a thesis statement (see next section) to focus the first draft. In reviewing your initial version, look for quotes, facts, statements, or examples that would make a strong first impression. Avoid making general opening statements that serve as diluted titles: "This paper is about a dangerous trend happening in America today."

Writers use a number of methods to introduce their essays. You can begin with a thesis statement, a striking fact or statistic, or a quotation, among other possibilities.

Open with a Thesis Statement

> The "abuse excuse"—the legal tactic by which criminal defendants claim a history of abuse as an excuse for violent retaliation—is quickly becoming a license to kill and maim. More and more defense lawyers are employing this tactic and more and more jurors are buying it. It is a dangerous trend, with serious and widespread implications for the safety and liberty of every American.
>
> *Alan Dershowitz, "The 'Abuse Excuse' Is Detrimental to the Justice System"*

- Opening with a thesis creates a strong first impression so even a casual reader quickly understands the message.

■ Like a title summarizing the writer's thesis, however, introductions that make a clear assertion may alienate readers, particularly if your topic or position is controversial. You may wish to present evidence or explain reasons before openly announcing your thesis.

Begin with Facts or Statistics

One out of every five new recruits in the United States military is female. The Marines gave the Combat Action Ribbon for service in the Persian Gulf to 23 women. Two female soldiers were killed in the bombing of the USS Cole.

The Selective Service registers for the draft all male citizens between the ages of 18 and 25.

What's wrong with this picture?

Anna Quindlen, "Uncle Sam and Aunt Samantha:
It's Simple Fairness: Women as Well as Men Should Be Required to Register for the Draft"

■ The fact or statistic you select should be easy to comprehend and stimulate reader interest.

Use a Quotation

In 1773, on a tour of Scotland and the Hebrides Islands, Samuel Johnson visited a school for deaf children. Impressed by the students but daunted by their predicament, he proclaimed deafness "one of the most desperate of human calamities." More than a century later Helen Keller reflected on her own life and declared that deafness was a far greater hardship than blindness. "Blindness cuts people off from things," she observed. "Deafness cuts people off from people."

Edward Dolnick, "Deafness as Culture"

■ Quotations allow you to present another voice, giving a second viewpoint. You can introduce expert opinion, providing immediate support for the upcoming thesis.

■ Select relevant quotations. Avoid using famous sayings by such people as Shakespeare or Benjamin Franklin unless they directly relate to your subject.

Open with a Brief Narrative or Example

At first, Robert Maynard thought they were harmless—albeit crude—electronic postings. Most closed with the same poem: "Lord, grant me the serenity to accept the things I cannot change . . . and the wisdom to hide the bodies of the people I had to kill." One claimed that Maynard's employees were liars. Others that his wife, Teresa, was unfaithful. But when the messages, posted on an Internet newsgroup, did not stop, Maynard went to court.

Kevin Whitelaw, "Fear and Dread in Cyberspace"

■ A short narrative personalizes complex topics and helps introduce readers to subjects that they might not initially find interesting.

■ Narratives should be short and representative. An engaging example may distort readers' understanding and should be balanced with facts and statistics to place it in context.

Pose a Question

> Think for a minute. Who were you before this wave of feminism began?
>
> *Gloria Steinem, "Words and Change"*

- An opening question, like one posed in the title, arouses attention by challenging and engaging readers, prompting them to consider your topic.
- Questions can introduce a discussion of controversial topics without immediately revealing your opinion.

Organizing the Body of an Essay

Once you introduce the subject, there are three basic methods of organizing the body of the essay: *chronological, spatial,* and *emphatic.* Just as writers often have unique composing styles, they often have different ways of viewing and organizing their material. The way you organize the body of the essay should reflect your thesis and your train of thought. Within these general methods of organization, you may include portions using different modes. For example, a spatially organized essay may contain chronological sections.

Chronological: Organizing by Time

The simplest and often the most effective way of structuring an essay is to tell a story, relating events as they occurred. Narrative, process, cause-and-effect, and example essays commonly follow a chronological pattern, presenting evidence on a timeline. Biographies, history books, accident reports, and newspaper articles about current events are often arranged chronologically.

A student discussing the causes of the Civil War might explain the conflict as the result of a historical process, the outcome of a chain of events.

THESIS: The American Civil War resulted from a growing economic, cultural, and ideological division between North and South that could not be resolved through peaceful compromise.

Outline

I. 1776 historical background
   A. Jefferson's deleted anti-slavery statement in Declaration of Independence
   B. Seeds of eventual clash
II. 1820s economic conflict
   A. Growth of Northern commercial and industrial economy
   B. Growth of Southern agrarian economy
III. 1830–1840s political feuds stemming from conflicting interests
   A. Northern demand for tariffs to protect infant industries
   B. Southern desire for free trade for growing cotton exports

(Continued)

IV. 1850s ideological conflict
    A. Growing abolitionist movement in North
       1. John Brown
       2. Underground Railroad
    B. Southern defense of slavery
       1. Resentment of abolitionist actions in South
       2. Resistance to westward expansion and free states
V. 1860s movement to war
    A. Election of Lincoln
    B. Southern calls for secession
    C. Fort Sumter attack, start of Civil War

- Readers are accustomed to reading information placed in chronological order. Using a narrative form allows writers to demonstrate how a problem developed, relate an experience, or predict a future course of action.

- Chronological organization does not have to follow a strict timeline. Dramatic events can be highlighted by using flash-forwards and flashbacks (see pages 188–189).

- Arranging evidence in a chronological pattern can mislead readers by suggesting cause-and-effect relationships that do not exist.

Spatial: Organizing by Division

Writers frequently approach complex subjects by breaking them down into parts. Comparison, division, and classification essays are spatially arranged. Instead of using chronology, another student explaining the causes of the Civil War might address each cause separately.

THESIS: The American Civil War was caused by three major conflicts between the North and the South: economic, cultural, and ideological.

Outline

I. Economic conflict
    A. Northern commercial and industrial economy
       1. Demand for tariffs to protect infant industries
       2. Need for skilled labor
    B. Southern agrarian economy
       1. Desire for free trade for cotton exports
       2. Dependence on slave labor
II. Cultural conflict
    A. Northern urban business class
    B. Southern landed aristocracy

(Continued)

III. Ideological conflict
  A. Growing abolitionist movement in North
    1. John Brown
    2. Underground Railroad
  B. Southern defense of slavery
    1. Resentment of abolitionist actions in South
    2. Resistance to westward expansion and free states

- Spatial organization can simplify complex issues by dividing them into separate elements. By understanding the parts, readers can appreciate the nature of the whole.
- Spatial organization is useful if you are addressing multiple readers. Those with a special interest can quickly locate where a specific issue is discussed. In a chronological paper, this information would be distributed throughout the essay and require extensive searching.

Emphatic: Organizing by Importance

If you believe that some ideas are more significant than others, you can arrange information by importance. Because readers' attention is greatest at the beginning and end of an essay, open or conclude with the most important points. A writer could decide that simply enumerating the causes of the Civil War fails to demonstrate the importance of what he or she considers the driving reason for the conflict. The student who believes that slavery was the dominant cause of the war could organize a paper in either of two patterns.

Advantages: Most Important to Least Important

- **Starting with the most important idea places the most critical information in the first few paragraphs or pages.** This can be useful for long, detailed papers or documents that you suspect may not be read in their entirety.
- **You are likely to devote less space and detail to minor ideas, so the reading will become easier to follow and will counter reader fatigue.**

Disadvantages: Most Important to Least Important

- **The principal disadvantage of this method is that the paper loses emphasis and can trail off into insignificant details.** An effective conclusion that refers to the main idea can provide the paper with a strong final impression.
- **In some instances, important ideas cannot be fully appreciated without introductory information.**

THESIS: Although North and South were divided by cultural, economic, and ideological conflicts, slavery was the overwhelming issue that directly led to secession and war.

Outline (Most Important to Least Important)

I. Slavery, most important cause of Civil War
  A. Jefferson compromise in 1776
  B. Abolitionist movement in North
    1. Expansion of abolitionist newspapers
    2. Establishment of Underground Railroad
    3. Protests and riots over Fugitive Slave Act
    4. *Uncle Tom's Cabin* & popular culture
    5. International resentment over slavery
  C. Growing Southern dependence on slavery
    1. Growth of militant press
    2. Rise of King Cotton
    3. Intellectual defenses of slavery
    4. Need for cheap labor
    5. Resentment of Northern attacks on slavery

II. Economic Conflict
  A. Northern economy
    1. Commercial, financial, industrial interests
    2. Factory owners
    3. Rise of New York as financial center
  B. Southern economy
    1. Agricultural interests
    2. Landowners
    3. Resentment of Northern financial power

III. Ideological Conflict
  A. Northern philosophy
    1. Desire for Western expansion to add free states
    2. Need for stronger federal government
  B. Southern philosophy
    1. Desire for Southern expansion to add slave states
    2. Need to assert states' rights

IV. Foreign Trade
  A. Northern demand for tariffs
  B. Southern need for free trade

Outline (Least Important to Most Important)

I. Foreign Trade
  A. Northern demand for tariffs
  B. Southern demand for free trade

II. Ideological conflict
  A. Northern philosophy
    1. Desire for Western expansion to add free states
    2. Need for stronger federal government
  B. Southern philosophy
    1. Desire for Southern expansion to add slave states
    2. Need to assert states' rights

III. Economic conflict
  A. Northern economy
    1. Commercial, financial, industrial interests
    2. Factory owners
    3. Rise of New York as financial center
  B. Southern economy
    1. Agricultural interests
    2. Landowners
    3. Resentment of Northern financial power

IV. Slavery, most important cause of Civil War
  A. Jefferson compromise in 1776
  B. Abolitionist movement in North
    1. Expansion of abolitionist newspapers
    2. Establishment of Underground Railroad
    3. Protests and riots over Fugitive Slave Act
    4. *Uncle Tom's Cabin* & popular culture
    5. International resentment over slavery
  C. Growing Southern dependence on slavery
    1. Growth of militant press
    2. Rise of King Cotton
    3. Intellectual defenses of slavery
    4. Need for cheap labor
    5. Resentment of Northern attacks on slavery

Advantages: Least Important to Most Important

■ **Papers concluding with the most important idea create intensity, building a stronger and stronger case for the writer's thesis.**

■ **Concluding with the most important information leaves readers with a dominant final impression.**

Disadvantages: Least Important to Most Important

■ **Readers' attention diminishes over time, so that the ability to concentrate weakens as you present the most important ideas.** Because you are likely to devote more space to the significant points, the sentences become more complex and the paragraphs longer, making the essay more challenging to read toward the end. Subtitles, paragraph breaks, and transitional statements can alert readers to pay particular attention to your concluding remarks.

■ **Readers who are unable to finish the paper will miss the most important ideas.**

Writing Conclusions

Not all essays require a lengthy conclusion. A short essay does not need a separate paragraph that simply repeats the opening. But all writing should end with an emphatic point, final observation, or memorable comment.

Summarize the Thesis and Main Points

A long, complex essay can benefit from a summary that reminds readers of your thesis and principal considerations:

> Public understanding of science is more central to our national security than half a dozen strategic weapon systems. The sub-mediocre performance of American youngsters in science and math, and the widespread adult ignorance and apathy about science and math, should sound an urgent alarm.
>
> *Carl Sagan, "Why We Should Understand Science"*

■ Ending with a summary or restatement of the thesis leaves readers with your main point.

■ Summaries in short papers, however, can be redundant and weaken rather than strengthen an essay.

End with a Question

Just as an introductory question can arouse reader interest, so concluding with a question can prompt readers to consider the essay's main points or challenge readers to consider a future course of action:

> So the drumbeat goes on for more police, more prisons, more of the same failed policies. Ever see a dog chase its tail?
>
> *Wilbert Rideau, "Why Prisons Don't Work"*

Some writers pose a last question and provide an answer to reinforce their thesis:

> Can such principles be taught? Maybe not. But most of them can be learned.'
>
> *William Zinsser, "The Transaction"*

- Questions can be used to provoke readers to ponder the issues raised in the essay, guiding them to take action or reconsider their views.

- Questions lead readers to pause and consider the writer's points. Readers may be tempted to skim through an essay, but a final question provides a test—prompting them to think about what they have just read.

Conclude with a Quotation

A quotation allows writers to introduce a second opinion or conclude with remarks by a noted authority or compelling witness:

> I once had the opportunity to describe father's life to the late, great Jewish American writer Bernard Malamud. His only comment was, "Only in America!"
>
> *José Antonio Burciaga, "My Ecumenical Father"*

- Select quotations that are striking, relevant, and that emphasize the main points of the essay.

- Avoid irrelevant or generic quotations by famous people.

End with a Strong Image

Narrative and descriptive essays can have power if they leave readers with a compelling fact or scene:

> When the others went swimming, my son said he was going in, too. He pulled his dripping trunks from the line where they had hung all through the shower and wrung them out. Languidly, and with no thought of going in, I watched him, his hard little body, skinny and bare, saw him wince slightly as he pulled up around his vitals the small, soggy, icy garment. As he buckled the swollen belt, suddenly my groin felt the chill of death.
>
> *E. B. White, "Once More to the Lake"*

- Choose an image that will motivate readers to consider the essay's main points.

- Concluding images and statements should be suited to the conventions of the discourse community and the nature of the document.

Conclude with a Challenging Statement

Writers of persuasive essays frequently end with an appeal, prediction, warning, or challenge aimed directly at the reader:

> Ally yourself with us while you can—or don't be surprised if, one day, you're asking one of *us* for work.
>
> *Suneel Rataan, "Why Busters Hate Boomers"*

- Direct challenges are effective if you want readers to take action. Make sure that any appeal you use is suited to both your goal and your audience.

- Avoid making statements that are hostile or offensive. Consider possible extended audiences. If you are writing as the agent of others, determine if the remark you make reflects the attitudes, values, and tone of those you represent.

Moving from Prewriting to Planning

The plan you develop builds upon your prewriting, pulling the relevant ideas into meaningful order. Having read and discussed several essays concerning criminal justice, a student decided to write a short essay debating the merits of a current legal issue. At first she listed topics, then used clustering, freewriting, and questioning to narrow her topic and develop her thesis.

After reviewing her prewriting notes, the student created an outline organizing her essay spatially, presenting positive and then negative effects of victim impact statements. To give her paper a strong conclusion, she decided to end the paper with her thesis.

TOPICS:

Criminal justice (issues)
Capital punishment, pro/& con
Gun control
Court TV
Teenage shootings
Gangs
How does the media influence juries?
Jury nullification—moral or unjust?
Victims of crime—are they forgotten?
Who speaks for victims? (victims' rights movement)
Do prosecutors represent victims or the state?

Victims	TV coverage
Privacy issues	Rape cases
Addresses to the judge	Impact statements

Victim impact statements are increasingly a feature of modern trials as people are allowed to state their feelings about the crime and the criminal after he/she has been convicted. Judges can consider the impact of the crime on the victim in sentencing. Sometimes victims ask for harsh punishment and sometimes they even ask for leniency and give criminals, especially the young, a second chance.

Who is most impressive?
What about victims who can't speak well or don't know English?
What about families of homicide victims?
Victims without mourners? Less important?

Topic: Victim impact statements

Thesis: Although victim impact statements are designed to empower the victims of crime, they may serve only to further marginalize the most helpless among us.

OUTLINE

I. Introduction
    A. Background of victim impact statements
    B. Definition of victim impact statements
II. Goals of victim impact statements (pro)
    A. Victims granted a voice
    B. Therapeutic benefits for victims
    C. Recommendations for sentencing
III. Negative effects of victim impact statements (con)
    A. Inarticulate victims ignored
    B. Benefits limited to the affluent
IV. Conclusion

Thesis: Victim impact statements marginalize the poor and helpless.

WRITING ACTIVITIES

1. Write a brief plan for the following topics. Choose one of the three basic methods of organization for each.

    Topic: Television violence

    Chronological | Spatial | Emphatic

    Topic: Texting while driving

    Chronological | Spatial | Emphatic

    Topic: America's role in the twenty-first century

    Chronological | Spatial | Emphatic

2. Review the following prewriting notes and assemble the ideas into an effective outline. (You may use more than one organizational method.)

    Topic: Telemarketing Fraud

    Thesis: State and federal agencies must take greater steps to stem the rapid increase in telemarketing fraud.

NOTES

Thousands of victims defrauded of their life savings

Failure of police and DAs to investigate and prosecute

History of telemarketing fraud

Case of Nancy Sims—defrauded of $75,000 in investment scam

Statements by former telemarketer who admitted preying on the elderly

(Continued)

> Need to change attitudes that fraud is "nonviolent crime"
>
> Telemarketing scams use long distance to avoid local victims
>
> Failure of existing state and federal laws
>
> Telemarketing scams rarely lead to convictions or harsh sentences

PLANNING CHECKLIST

After you have completed your plan, consider these questions.

✔ **Does your plan fulfill the needs of the writing task?** Review notes, comments, or instructor's guidelines to make sure you have clearly understood the assignment. Are there standard formats that should be followed, or are you free to develop your own method of organization? Does your plan address the needs of readers?

✔ **Is your thesis clearly stated?** Does your thesis state a point of view, or is it simply a narrowed topic?

✔ **Have you developed enough evidence?** Is the thesis clearly supported by examples, details, facts, quotations, and examples? Is the evidence compelling and clearly stated? Are the sources accurate? Will readers accept your evidence? Should outside sources be documented?

✔ **Have you selected an appropriate method of organization?** Will readers be able to follow your train of thought? Are transitions clearly indicated?

✔ **Does your plan help overcome common problems?** Review previous assignments or comments instructors have made about your writing in the past. Does your plan provide guidelines for a stronger thesis or more organized support?

✔ **Does your opening arouse attention and introduce readers to your topic?**

✔ **Does your conclusion end the paper with a strong point or memorable image?**

✔ **Does your plan give you a workable guideline for writing your first draft?** Does it include reminders, references, and tips to make your job easier? Do you use a format that you can easily amend? *(Note: If writing on paper, leave space between points so you have room for new ideas.)*

Strategies for Overcoming Problems in Organization

If you have problems organizing your ideas and developing a plan for your paper, review your prewriting.

1. **Examine your thesis and goal.** The subject and purpose of your writing can suggest an organizational method. Would your ideas be best expressed by telling a story or categorizing them? Are some ideas more important than others?

2. **Use prewriting strategies to establish a pattern.** Make a list of your main ideas. Use clustering to draw relationships between points. What pattern best pulls these ideas together?

3. **Discuss your paper with your instructor or fellow students.** You may be so focused on details that you cannot obtain an overall view of your paper. Another person may be able to examine your notes and suggest a successful pattern.

4. **Start writing.** Although writing without a plan may make you feel like starting a journey without a map, plunging in and starting a draft may help you discover a way of organizing ideas. Although you are writing without a plan, try to stay on target. Focus on your goal. If the introduction gives you trouble, start with the body or conclusion. Developing connections between a few ideas may help you discover a method of organizing your entire essay.

e-writing

Exploring Organization Online

You can use the Web to learn more about organizing an essay.

1. Using a search engine, enter such terms as *organizing an essay, topic outline, sentence outline,* or *writing introductions* to locate current sites of interest.

2. Using InfoTrac College Edition (available through your English CourseMate at **www.cengagebrain.com**) or one of your library's databases, look up recent editorials or brief articles and notice how authors organized their ideas. Did the writers use a chronological or a spatial method? Where did they place the thesis and the most important evidence? How did they begin and end the article? Could any parts be improved to make the article easier to read or more effective?

E-Sources

Paradigm Online Writing Assistant: Introductions and Conclusions
   http://www.powa.org/thesissupport-essays/introductions-and-conclusions.html
Purdue Online Writing Lab: Four Main Components for Effective Outlines
   http://owl.english.purdue.edu/owl/resource/544/01/

 Access the English CourseMate for this text at **www.cengagebrain.com** for further information on organizing ideas.

Developing Paragraphs

Just as the sentence contains one idea in all its fullness,
so the paragraph should embrace a distinct episode; and
as sentences should follow one another in harmonious
sequence, so the paragraphs must fit on to one another like
the automatic couplings of railway carriages.

—Winston Churchill

What Are Paragraphs?

Most students can explain the goal of an essay and define the meaning of a sentence. But many are unsure how to describe paragraphs or even when to make them. In writing, they often fail to use paragraphs at all or impulsively indent every few sentences just to break up their essay.

A paragraph is more than a cluster of sentences or a random break in a block of text. **Paragraphs are groups of related sentences unified by a single idea. Like chapters in a book, they organize details and have a clear goal.** Paragraphs are used to introduce a subject, explain a point, tell a story, compare ideas, support a thesis, or summarize a writer's main points.

The importance of paragraphs can be demonstrated by removing them from a text. Printed without paragraphs, Walter Lord's foreword to *A Night to Remember* is difficult to comprehend and becomes an unimaginative jumble of facts and numbers:

WRITERS AT WORK

I don't allow anybody around while I'm writing. My wife manages to live with me, and my son and our dog, but I like to be let alone when I'm working. I see these Hollywood movies where the man gets up in the middle of the night and dashes off a few thousand words, and his little wife comes in to make sure he's comfortable and everything. That's all foolishness. It would never be anything like that. In fact, I'm privately convinced that most of the really bad writing the world's ever seen has been done under the influence of what's called inspiration.

Shelby Foote, historian
SOURCE: *Booknotes*

In 1898 a struggling author named Morgan Robertson concocted a novel about a fabulous Atlantic liner, far larger than any that had ever been built. Robertson loaded his ship with rich and complacent people and then wrecked it one cold April night on an iceberg. This somehow showed the futility of everything, and in fact, the book was called *Futility* when it appeared that year, published by the firm of M. F. Mansfield. Fourteen years later a British shipping company named the White Star Line built a steamer remarkably like the one in Robertson's novel. The new liner was 66,000 tons displacement; Robertson's was 70,000. The real ship was 882.5 feet long; the fictional one was 800 feet. Both vessels were triple screw and could make 24–25 knots. Both could carry about 3,000 people, and both had enough lifeboats for only a fraction of this number. But, then, this didn't seem to matter because both were labeled "unsinkable." On April 12, 1912, the real ship left Southampton on her maiden voyage to New York. Her cargo included a priceless copy of the *Rubaiyat of Omar Khayyam* and a list of passengers collectively worth two hundred fifty million dollars. On her way over she too struck an iceberg and went down on a cold April night. Robertson called his ship the *Titan;* the White Star Line called its ship the *Titanic.* This is the story of her last night.

Presented as Lord wrote it, the foreword is far more striking:

In 1898 a struggling author named Morgan Robertson concocted a novel about a fabulous Atlantic liner, far larger than any that had ever been built. Robertson loaded his ship with rich and complacent people and then wrecked it one cold April night on an iceberg. This somehow showed the futility of everything, and in fact, the book was called *Futility* when it appeared that year, published by the firm of M. F. Mansfield.

Fourteen years later a British shipping company named the White Star Line built a steamer remarkably like the one in Robertson's novel. The new liner was 66,000 tons displacement; Robertson's was 70,000. The real ship was 882.5 feet long; the fictional one was 800 feet. Both vessels were triple screw and could make 24–25 knots. Both could carry about 3,000 people, and both had enough lifeboats for only a fraction of this number. But, then, this didn't seem to matter because both were labeled "unsinkable."

On April 12, 1912, the real ship left Southampton on her maiden voyage to New York. Her cargo included a priceless copy of the *Rubaiyat of Omar Khayyam* and a list of passengers collectively worth two hundred fifty million dollars. On her way over she too struck an iceberg and went down on a cold April night.

Robertson called his ship the *Titan;* the White Star Line called its ship the *Titanic.* This is the story of her last night.

Each paragraph signals a shift, breaking up the text to highlight the parallels between the fictional ocean liner and the real one. The conclusion dramatizes the eerie similarity between the ships' names by placing the final two sentences in a separate paragraph.

Although it is important to provide breaks in your text, choppy and erratic paragraph breaks interrupt the flow of ideas and create a disorganized list of sentences:

I was born in New Orleans and grew up in a quiet section of Metairie. I had a lot of friends and enjoyed school a lot.

I played football for two seasons. In my sophomore year I won an award at the Louisiana Nationals.

The games are held in Baton Rouge and allow high school athletes from across the state to compete in a number of events.

I came in second out of over fifty high school quarterbacks.

The award guaranteed me a slot on my school's varsity team when I started my junior year. But that summer my Dad was transferred to Milwaukee.

In August we moved to Bayside, a north shore suburb. Our house was larger, and we had a wonderful view of Lake Michigan.

The move was devastating to me personally. I missed my friends. I found out that I would not even be allowed to try out for football until my senior year.

The coach was impressed with my ability, but he told me all positions had been filled.

Improved:

I was born in New Orleans and grew up in a quiet section of Metairie. I had a lot of friends and enjoyed school a lot. I played football for two seasons. In my sophomore year I won an award at the Louisiana Nationals. The games are held in Baton Rouge and allow high school athletes from across the state to compete in a number of events. I came in second out of over fifty high school quarterbacks. The award guaranteed me a slot on my school's varsity team when I started my junior year.

But that summer my Dad was transferred to Milwaukee. In August we moved to Bayside, a north shore suburb. Our house was larger, and we had a wonderful view of Lake Michigan.

The move was devastating to me personally. I missed my friends. I found out that I would not even be allowed to try out for football until my senior year. The coach was impressed with my ability, but he told me all positions had been filled.

WRITING ACTIVITY

Read this passage and indicate where you would make paragraph breaks. See page 359 for the original essay.

The car ahead of you stops suddenly. You hit the brakes, but you just can't stop in time. Your front bumper meets the rear end of the other car. *Ouch!* There doesn't seem to be any damage, and it must be your lucky day, because the driver you hit agrees that it's not worth hassling with insurance claims and risking a premium increase. So after exchanging addresses, you go your separate ways. Imagine your surprise when you open the mail a few weeks later only to discover a letter from your "victim's" lawyer demanding $10,000 to cover car repairs, pain, and suffering. Apparently the agreeable gentleman decided to disagree, then went ahead and filed a police report blaming you for the incident and for his damages. When automobiles meet by accident, do you know how to respond? Here are 10 practical tips that can help you avoid costly legal and insurance hassles.

Developing Paragraphs

Experiment with different ways to develop paragraphs to determine which way best fits your writing context.

Creating Topic Sentences

A topic sentence serves as the thesis statement of a paragraph, presenting the writer's main point or controlling idea. Like a thesis statement, the topic sentence announces the subject and indicates the writer's stance or opinion. The text of the paragraph explains and supports the topic sentence.

Writing about the status of France following the First World War, Anthony Kemp uses strong topic sentences to open each paragraph and organize supporting details:

> **The French won World War I—or so they thought.** In 1918, after four years of bitter conflict, the nation erupted in joyful celebration. The arch-enemy, Germany, had been defeated and the lost provinces of Alsace and Lorraine had been reunited with the homeland. The humiliation of 1870 had been avenged and, on the surface at least, France was the most powerful nation in Europe. Germany was prostrate, its autocratic monarchy tumbled and the country rent by internal dissension.
>
> *topic sentence*
> *supporting details*
>
> **The reality was different.** The northern provinces, as a result of the fighting, had been totally devastated and depopulated. The treasury was empty and saddled with a vast burden of war debt. The French diplomat, Jules Cambon, wrote prophetically at the time, "France victorious must grow accustomed to being a lesser power than France vanquished."
>
> *topic sentence*
> *supporting details*
>
> **The paradox was that Germany had emerged from the war far stronger.** France had a static population of some 40 million, but was confronted by 70 million Germans whose territory had not been ravaged and who had a higher birthrate. The Austro-Hungarian Empire had been split up into a number of smaller units, none of which could pose a serious threat to Germany. Russia, once the pillar to the Triple Entente, forcing Germany to fight on two fronts, had dissolved into internal chaos. The recreation of an independent Poland after the war produced a barrier between Russia and Germany that meant the old ally of France no longer directly threatened German territory.
>
> *topic sentence*
> *supporting details*

The topic sentence does not always open a paragraph. Like an essay's thesis statement, the topic sentence can appear in the middle or end. Often a writer will present supporting details, a narrative, or a description before stating the topic sentence, as in the following passage:

> The airline industry has suffered dramatic losses in the last two years. Lucrative business travel has ebbed, and overseas tourist bookings have dropped by a third. In addition, rising fuel prices and an inability to increase fares have eroded the profit margin on most domestic

flights. Reflecting the ongoing concern with terrorism, insurance costs have soared. Four of the largest airlines have announced plans to lay off thousands of employees. **The federal government must take steps to save airlines from bankruptcy.**

Not all paragraphs require an explicit topic sentence, but all paragraphs should have a controlling idea, a clear focus or purpose. By including enough details, Truman Capote lets the facts speak for themselves to create a clear impression about the lonely desolation of a small Kansas town:

> Down by the depot, the postmistress, a gaunt woman who wears a rawhide jacket and denims and cowboy boots, presides over a falling-apart post office. The depot itself, with its peeling sulphur-colored paint, is equally melancholy; the Chief, the Super Chief, the El Capitan go by every day, but these celebrated expresses never pause there. No passenger trains do—only an occasional freight. Up on the highway, there are two filling stations, one of which doubles as a meagerly supplied grocery store, while the other does extra duty as a café—Hartman's Café, where Mrs. Hartman, the proprietress, dispenses sandwiches, coffee, soft drinks, and 3.2 beer. (Holcomb, like all the rest of Kansas, is "dry.")
>
> *Truman Capote, "Out There," pages 167–168*

Using Modes

Just as writers organize essays using modes such as narration and definition, they can use the same patterns of development to unify paragraphs. In writing a comparison, you can use definition, cause and effect, or classification to organize individual paragraphs. You can also number points to make your train of thought easier to follow.

In *Race Matters*, Cornel West uses several modes to analyze views of African American society:

topic sentence division definition	**Recent discussions about the plight of African Americans—especially those at the bottom of the social ladder—tend to divide into two camps.** On the one hand, there are those who highlight the *structural* constraints on the life chances of black people. Their viewpoint involves a subtle historical and sociological analysis of slavery, Jim Crowism, job and residential discrimination, skewed unemployment rates, inadequate health care, and poor education. On the other hand, there are those
contrast definition	who stress the *behavioral* impediments on black upward mobility. They focus on the waning of the Protestant ethic—hard work, deferred gratification, frugality, and responsibility—in much of black America.
topic sentence transition examples contrast	**Those in the first camp—the liberal structuralists—call for full employment, health, education, and child-care programs, and broad affirmative action practices.** In short, a new, more sober version of the best of the New Deal and the Great Society: more government money, better bureaucrats, and an active citizenry. Those in the second camp—the conservative behaviorists—promote self-help programs, black business expansion, and nonpreferential job practices. They support vigorous "free market" strategies that depend on fundamental changes in how black people act and live. To put it bluntly, their projects rest largely upon a cultural revival of the Protestant ethic in black America.

(Continued)

Unfortunately, these two camps have nearly suffocated the crucial debate that should be taking place about the prospects for black America. This debate must go far beyond the liberal and conservative positions in three fundamental ways. First, we must acknowledge that structures and behavior are inseparable, that institutions and values go hand in hand. How people act and live are shaped—though in no way dictated or determined—by the larger circumstances in which they find themselves. These circumstances can be changed, their limits attenuated, by positive actions to elevate living conditions.

Second, we should reject the idea that structures are primarily economic and political creatures—an idea that sees culture as an ephemeral set of behavioral attitudes or politics; it is rooted in institutions such as families, schools, churches, synagogues, mosques, and communication industries (television, radio, video, music). Similarly, the economy and politics are not only influenced by values but also promote particular cultural ideals of the good life and good society.

Third, and most important, we must delve into the depths where neither liberals nor conservatives dare to tread, namely, into the murky waters of despair and dread that now flood the streets of black America. To talk about the depressing statistics of unemployment, infant mortality, incarceration, teenage pregnancy, and violent crime is one thing. But to face up to the monumental eclipse of hope, the unprecedented collapse of meaning, the incredible disregard for human (especially black) life and property in much of black America is something else.

The liberal/conservative discussion conceals the most basic issue now facing black America: the nihilistic threat to its very existence. This threat is not simply a matter of relative economic deprivation and political powerlessness—though economic well-being and political clout are requisites for meaningful black progress. It is primarily a question of speaking to the profound sense of psychological depression, personal worthlessness, and social despair so widespread in black America.

Annotations (right margin):
- topic sentence / transition
- use of numbered points
- topic sentence / supporting detail
- topic sentence / supporting detail
- thesis statement example

Emphasizing Transitions

Just as writers use exclamation points to dramatize a sentence, a paragraph break can serve to highlight a transition or isolate an important idea that might be buried or overshadowed if placed in a larger paragraph. In some instances writers will use a one- or two-sentence paragraph to dramatize a shift or emphasize an idea:

> He could remember a time in his early childhood when a large number of things were still known by his family name. There was a Zhivago factory, a Zhivago bank, Zhivago buildings, a Zhivago necktie pin, even a Zhivago cake which was a kind of *baba au rhum,* and at one time if you said "Zhivago" to your sleigh driver in Moscow, it was as if you had said: "Take me to Timbuctoo!" and he carried you off to a fairy-tale kingdom. You would find yourself transported to a vast, quiet park. Crows settled on the heavy branches of firs, scattering the hoarfrost; their cawing echoed and re-echoed like crackling wood. Pure-bred dogs came running across the road out of the clearing from the recently constructed house. Farther on, lights appeared in the gathering dusk.
>
> And then suddenly all that was gone. They were poor.
>
> *Boris Pasternak,* Doctor Zhivago

Organizing Dialogue

Dialogue can be difficult to follow unless paragraph breaks show the transition between speakers. Paragraph breaks make dialogue easier to follow and allow you to avoid repeating "he said" or "I said." In "The Fender-Bender," Ramón "Tianguis" Pérez reproduces a conversation that occurred after a minor traffic accident:

> I get out of the car. The white man comes over and stands right in front of me. He's almost two feet taller.
>
> "If you're going to drive, why don't you carry your license?" he asks in an accusatory tone.
>
> "I didn't bring it," I say, for lack of any other defense.
>
> I look at the damage to his car. It's minor, only a scratch on the paint and a pimple-sized dent.
>
> "I'm sorry," I say. "Tell me how much it will cost to fix, and I'll pay for it; that's no problem." I'm talking to him in English, and he seems to understand.
>
> "This car isn't mine," he says. "It belongs to the company I work for. I'm sorry, but I've got to report this to the police, so that I don't have to pay for the damage."
>
> "That's no problem," I tell him again. "I can pay for it."

Paragraph Style

A writer's style or the style of a particular document is shaped by the length of the paragraphs as well as the level of vocabulary. Newspaper articles, which are meant to be skimmed, use simple words, short sentences, and brief paragraphs. Often a paragraph in a newspaper article will contain only two or three sentences. E-mail and memos also use short paragraphs to communicate quickly. Longer and more detailed writing tends to have paragraphs containing 50 to 250 words. No matter what their length, however, paragraphs should be well organized and serve a clear purpose.

Strategies for Developing Paragraphs

1. **Use topic sentences to organize supporting details.**
2. **Use modes to unify paragraphs.**
3. **Use paragraphs to highlight transitions.**
4. **Use paragraphs to distinguish speakers in dialogue.**

WRITING ACTIVITIES

1. In the following excerpt, indicate paragraph breaks to distinguish speakers. See pages 245–246 for the original version.

   Both cops got out. The older one checked out the rental plates. The younger one wanted to see my driver's license. "Where's your hotel?" he asked. Right over there, I said, the Maria Cristina Hotel on Rio Lerma Street. "I don't know any hotel by that name," he said. "Prove it. Show me something from the hotel." I fumbled through my wallet, finally producing a card-key from the hotel. The dance between the cops and me had begun. "I see," the young policeman said. "What are you doing in Mexico?" I'm a journalist, I said. I'd been reporting in Queretaro state. "You know," he said, "for making that illegal turn, we're going to have to take away your driver's license and the plates from the car." I said, What? Why can't you just give me a ticket? He then walked away and asked the other, older, policeman, "How do you want to take care of this?" The veteran officer then took over. "The violation brings a fine of 471 pesos," he told me. "But we still have to take your plates and license. You can pick them up at police headquarters when you pay the fine. Or, I can deliver them to you tomorrow at your hotel, but only after you pay."

2. Select one or more of the subjects listed and write a paragraph about it. Your paragraph may or may not have a topic sentence—but it should have a controlling idea. It should have a clear purpose and focus and not simply contain a number of vaguely related ideas. After drafting your paragraph, review it for missing details or irrelevant material. Underline your topic sentence or list your controlling thought.

   - Describe your first car.
   - Compare high school and college instructors.
   - Explain with one or more reasons why you are attending college.
   - State one or more reasons why you admire a certain actor, singer, athlete, or politician.

3. Develop paragraphs using the topic sentences provided. Use each topic sentence as a controlling idea to guide your selection of supporting details and examples.

   Living off campus provides students with many opportunities.

   However, off-campus housing poses many challenges to young adults.

   Distractions and unexpected responsibilities can interfere with studying.

   Students who plan to live off campus should think carefully before signing a lease.

4. Write a paragraph supporting each of the following topic sentences:

   College students must develop self-discipline to succeed.

   The central problem in male–female relationships is a failure to communicate.

   Three steps must be taken to curb teenagers from smoking.

   Proper nutrition is essential for maintaining good health.

5. Develop a conversation between two people and use paragraphs to indicate shifts between the speakers.

e-writing

Exploring Paragraphs Online

You can use the Web to learn more about developing paragraphs.

1. Using a search engine, enter terms such as *paragraph structure* and *topic sentence* to locate current websites of interest.

2. Using InfoTrac College Edition (available through your English CoureMate at **www.cengagebrain.com**) or one of your library's databases, look up recent editorials or brief articles and notice how authors developed paragraphs. Did they use paragraph breaks to signal important transitions, group related ideas, and make the text easier to follow?

   Were individual paragraphs organized by specific modes such as comparison, process, or cause and effect? How many had topic sentences you could underline?

E-Sources

University of North Carolina–Chapel Hill, Writing Center: Paragraph Development
   http://www.unc.edu/depts/wcweb/handouts/paragraphs.html

Access the English CourseMate for this text at **www.cengagebrain.com** for further information on developing paragraphs.

Writing the First Draft

Try simply to steer your mind in the direction or general
vicinity of the thing you are trying to write about and start
writing and keep writing.

—Peter Elbow

What Is a First Draft?

The goal of a first draft is to capture your ideas on paper and produce a rough version of the final essay. A first draft is not likely to be perfect and will probably include awkward sentences, redundant passages, irrelevant ideas, and misspelled words—but it gives you something to build on and refine.

There is no single method of transforming your outline into a completed draft, but there are techniques that can improve your first efforts.

WRITERS AT WORK

The key to turning out good stuff is rewriting. The key to grinding it out is consistency. It sounds silly, but if you write four pages a day, you've written 1,200 pages in a year—or 1,400, whatever it is. You accumulate the stuff. So what I normally do is give myself quotas. They'll vary depending on the depth and complexity of the subject, but somewhere between three and five pages—that's my day's writing. I've got to do it every day. I can't go out and work on my farm until I've done my day's writing, and working on my farm is so pleasurable. So that's my incentive. I hold myself hostage, so to speak, and it gets done.

Forrest McDonald, historian
SOURCE: *Booknotes*

Strategies for Writing the First Draft

1. **Review your plan.** Examine your outline, prewriting notes, and any instructions to make sure your plan addresses the needs of the writing assignment. If you have developed a formal outline, use it as a road map to keep your writing on track.

2. **Focus on your goal.** As you write, keep your purpose in mind. What is your objective—to entertain, inform, or persuade?

3. **Write to your reader.** Consider the readers' perceptual world. What information do readers need to accept your thesis? How will they respond to your ideas? How can your paper arouse their interest, build on their current knowledge, or address their objections?

4. **Visualize the completed document.** Consider the writing context and what the final product should look like to guide decisions about word choice, sentence structure, and paragraph length.

5. **Support your thesis.** Include sufficient evidence that is accurate, relevant, and easily understood.

6. **Amend your plan if needed.** In some cases you will be able to follow a detailed outline point by point, turning words into sentences and adding supporting detail to transform a single line into a half page. In other instances, you will discover new ideas while writing. **Be willing to make changes, but keep your goal, your reader, and the nature of the document in mind to keep your writing on course.**

7. **Start writing.** The most important thing in writing a first draft is getting your ideas on paper.

   - Start with the easiest parts. Don't feel obligated to write the introduction first.
   - Give yourself room for changes. You can easily insert text on a computer, but if you are writing on paper, leave wide margins for last-minute additions.
   - Don't edit as you write. Pausing to look up facts or check spelling can interrupt your train of thought, but you can make notes as you write to identify items for future revisions. Underline words you think might be misspelled or misused. Make notes in parentheses to signal missing details.
   - Break the paper into manageable parts. Instead of attempting to write a complete draft, you may find it more effective to focus on one section, especially if your paper is long and complex.
   - If you get stuck, return to passages you have written and revise them. Keep writing.

8. **Read your work aloud.** Hearing your words can help you evaluate your writing and test the logic of your ideas.

9. **Lower your standards.** Keep writing even if your ideas seem clumsy or repetitive. Don't expect to write flawless copy; this is a rough draft.

10. **Save everything you write.** Ideas that may seem unrelated to your topic could prove to be valuable in future drafts or other assignments.
    - Make sure you save your work on a flash drive if working on a computer. If you print a hard copy, you may wish to double- or triple-space the text for easier editing.

11. **Avoid plagiarism.** If you insert material from other sources, highlight these passages in another color for future reference. Clearly distinguish your words and ideas from the words and ideas of others. **Record source information needed for documentation** (see pages 7–8).

Making Writing Decisions

In writing the first draft, you will make a series of decisions. In expressing your ideas, you will choose words, construct sentences, and develop paragraphs. The more thought you put into these decisions, the better your rough draft will reflect what you want to say and the less rewriting it will require.

Choosing the Right Words

Words have power. The impact of your writing greatly depends on the words you choose. In writing your first draft, select words that represent your stance and will influence readers. Because the goal of the first draft is to record your ideas, don't stop writing to look up words; instead, underline items for further review.

Use Words Precisely

Many words are easily confused. Should a patient's heart rate be monitored *continually* (meaning at regular intervals, such as once an hour) or *continuously* (meaning without interruption)? Is the city council planning to *adapt* or *adopt* a budget? Did the mayor make an *explicit* or *implicit* statement?

Your writing can influence readers only if you use words that accurately reflect your meaning. There are numerous pairs of frequently confused words:

allusion	an indirect reference
illusion	a false or imaginary impression
conscience (noun)	a sense of moral or ethical conduct
conscious (adjective)	awake or aware of something

principle	a basic law or concept
principal	something or someone important, as in a school *principal*
affect (verb)	to change or modify
effect (noun)	a result

See pages 746–748 for a list of commonly confused or misused words.

Use Specific Words

Specific words communicate more information and make clearer impressions than abstract words, which express only generalized concepts.

Abstract	**Specific**
motor vehicle	pickup truck
modest suburban home	three-bedroom colonial
individual	boy
protective headgear	helmet

Specific words make a greater impact on readers, as these examples show:

ABSTRACT: Wherever we went, malnourished individuals lined the road in serious need of assistance.

SPECIFIC: Wherever we walked, starving children lined the road like skeletons silently holding empty bowls with bony fingers.

As you write, try to think of effective images and specific details that will suit your purpose and your reader.

Use Verbs that Create Action and Strong Images

Linking verbs (such as *is* and *are*) join ideas but do not suggest action or present compelling images. Like abstract nouns, generalized verbs, such as *move, seem,* and *appear,* make only vague impressions. Use verbs that express action and create strong images.

Weak Verbs	**Strong Verbs**
The landlord *expressed* little interest in his tenants and *did not repair* the building.	The landlord *ignored* his tenants and *refused to repair* the building.
The firefighters *moved* quickly to the accident scene and then *moved* slowly through the debris *to look* for victims.	The firefighters *raced* to the accident scene and then *crept* slowly through the debris *searching* for victims.

Use an Appropriate Level of Diction

The style and tone of your writing are shaped by the words you choose. Your goal, your reader, the discourse community, and the document itself usually indicate the kind of language that is appropriate. Informal language that might be acceptable when texting a coworker may be unsuited to a formal report or article written for publication.

FORMAL: Sales representatives are required to maintain company vehicles at their own expense. (employee manual)

STANDARD: Salespeople must pay for routine maintenance of company cars. (business letter)

INFORMAL: Remind the reps to change their oil every 3,000 miles. (e-mail memo)

Slang expressions can be creative and attention-getting, but they may be inappropriate and detract from the credibility of formal documents.

Appreciate the Impact of Connotations

All words *denote,* or indicate, a particular meaning. The words *home, residence,* and *domicile* all refer to where someone lives. Each has the same basic meaning or *denotation,* but the word *home* evokes personal associations of family, friends, and favorite belongings. *Domicile,* on the other hand, has a legalistic and official tone devoid of personal associations.

Connotations are implied or suggested meanings. Connotations reflect a writer's values, views, and attitudes toward a subject. A resort cabin can be described as a *rustic cottage* or a *seedy shack.* The person who spends little money and shops for bargains can be praised for being *thrifty* or ridiculed for being *cheap.* The design of a skyscraper can be celebrated as being *clean* and *streamlined* or criticized for appearing *stark* and *sterile.*

The following pairs of words have the same *denotation* or basic meaning but their *connotations* create strikingly different impressions:

young	inexperienced
traditional	old-fashioned
brave	ruthless
casual	sloppy
the homeless	bums
residential care facility	nursing home
unintended landing	plane crash
uncompromising	stubborn
torture	enhanced interrogation
junkies	the chemically dependent

In selecting words, be sure that your connotations are suited to your task, role, and readers. *Avoid terms your readers may find inappropriate or offensive.*

Writing Effective Sentences

Writing well is more than a matter of avoiding grammatical errors such as fragments and run-ons. Sentences express thoughts. Your sentences should be clear, logical, and economical. There are several techniques that can increase the power of your sentences.

WRITING ACTIVITIES

1. Review papers you have written in previous classes and examine your use of words. Read passages out loud. How does your writing sound? Are there abstract terms that could be replaced by specific words? Are there connotations that detract from your goal? Does the level of diction fit the assignment?

2. Write a description of your hometown, using as many specific words as possible to provide sensual impressions. Avoid abstract words like *pleasant* or *noisy* and offer specific details.

3. Use connotations to write a positive and a negative description of a controversial personality such as a politician, celebrity, or sports figure.

4. Translate the following negative description into a positive one by substituting key words:

   Frank Kelso is a reckless, money-grubbing gossip who eagerly maligns celebrities. He is impulsive, stubborn, and insulting. He refuses to show restraint and will exploit anyone's personal misfortune to get ahead while claiming to serve his readers' desire for truth.

Emphasize Key Words

Words placed at the beginning and end of sentences receive more attention than those placed in the middle.

Cumulative sentences open with the main idea or key word:

Computer literacy is mandatory for today's high school students.

Alcoholism and drug addiction are contributing causes of child neglect.

Periodic sentences conclude with a key word or major idea:

For today's high school student, success demands *computer literacy*.

Child neglect often stems from two causes: *alcoholism and drug addiction*.

Both cumulative and periodic sentences are more effective than those that bury important words in the middle:

In today's world *computer literacy* is mandatory for high school students to succeed.

The problem of child neglect often has *alcoholism and drug addiction* as contributing causes.

Use Parallel Structures to Stress Equivalent Ideas

You can demonstrate that ideas have equal value by placing them in pairs and lists:

Coffee and tea are favorite beverages for dieters.

Wilson, Roosevelt, and Johnson managed domestic reform while waging war.

His doctor suggested that *diet and exercise* could *lower his blood pressure and reduce his risk of stroke*.

Subordinate Secondary Ideas

Secondary ideas that offer background information should be subordinated or merged into sentences that stress primary ideas. Combining ideas into single sentences allows writers to demonstrate which ideas they consider significant.

PRIMARY IDEA: *Nancy Chen was accepted into Yale Law School.*

SECONDARY IDEA: Nancy Chen did not learn English until she was twelve.

COMBINED VERSIONS: Although she did not learn English until she was twelve, *Nancy Chen was accepted into Yale Law School.*

Nancy Chen, who did not learn English until she was twelve, *was accepted into Yale Law School.*

Secondary ideas can be placed at the beginning, set off by commas in the middle, or attached to the end of a sentence:

PRIMARY IDEA: *Bayport College will close its doors.*

SECONDARY IDEAS: Bayport College has served this community for a hundred years.

Bayport College was forced to declare bankruptcy.

Bayport College will close on June 15.

COMBINED VERSIONS: On June 15, *Bayport College,* forced to declare bankruptcy, *will close its doors* after serving this community for a hundred years.

After serving this community for a hundred years, *Bayport College,* forced to declare bankruptcy, *will close its doors* on June 15.

Forced to declare bankruptcy, *Bayport College,* which served this community for a hundred years, *will close its doors* on June 15.

Stress the Relationship between Ideas

You can make your train of thought easier for readers to follow if your sentences stress how one idea affects another. **Coordinating conjunctions**—words that join ideas—demonstrate relationships:

and   joins ideas of equal importance:

> The president urged Americans to conserve oil, **and** he denounced Congress for failing to pass an energy bill.

or   indicates choice, suggesting that only one of two ideas is operative:

> The university will raise tuition **or** increase class size.

but   indicates a shift or contrast:

> The company lowered prices, **but** sales continued to slump.

yet   also demonstrates a contrast, often meaning *nevertheless:*

> He studied for hours **yet** failed the exam.

so   implies cause and effect:

> Drivers ignored the stop sign, **so** authorities installed a traffic light.

In addition to coordinating conjunctions, there are transitional expressions that establish the relationship between ideas.

TRANSITIONAL EXPRESSIONS

To establish time relationships:

before	*after*	*now*	*then*
today	*further*	*once*	*often*

To demonstrate place relationships:

above	*below*	*over*	*under*
around	*inside*	*outside*	*nearby*
next	*beyond*	*to the left*	

To indicate additions:

again	*also*	*moreover*	*too*
furthermore		*in addition*	

To express similarities:

alike	*likewise*	*in the same way*

To stress contrasts:

after all	*different*	*on the other hand*
although	*however*	*still*
unlike	*in contrast*	

To illustrate cause and effect:

as a result	*because*	*therefore*

To conclude or summarize:

finally	*in conclusion*	*in short*

When you write the first draft, try to stress the relationships between ideas as clearly as you can. If trying to determine the best way to link ideas slows your writing down, simply underline related items to flag them for future revision and move on to the next point.

Understand How Structure Affects Meaning

Just as the connotations of words you choose shape meaning, so does the structure of your sentences. The way you word sentences can create both dramatic effects and make subtle distinctions. Although the basic facts are the same in the following sentences, notice how altering the words that form the subject (in boldface) affects their meaning:

Dr. Green and a group of angry patients are protesting the closing of the East Side Clinic.

(*This sentence suggests the doctor and patients are of equal importance.*)

Dr. Green, flanked by angry patients, **is** protesting the closing of the East Side Clinic.

(*This sentence emphasizes the role of the doctor. The singular verb "is protesting" highlights the actions of a single person. Set off by commas, the "angry patients" are not even considered part of the subject.*)

Angry patients, supported by Dr. Green, **are** protesting the closing of the East Side Clinic.

(*In this version the angry patients are emphasized, and the doctor, set off by commas, is deemphasized, reduced to the status of a bystander.*)

Despite protests by Dr. Green and angry patients, **the East Side Clinic** is being closed.

(*This wording suggests the protests are futile and that the closing of the clinic is inevitable.*)

The closing of the East Side Clinic has sparked protests by Dr. Green and angry patients.

(*This sentence indicates a cause-and-effect relationship, implying that the final outcome may be uncertain.*)

WRITING ACTIVITIES

1. Combine the following sets of items into single sentences that emphasize what you consider the most important idea.
   a. Alcatraz is located on an island in San Francisco Bay.
      Alcatraz is one of the most famous prisons in American history.
      Alcatraz was closed in 1963.
      Alcatraz is now a tourist attraction.
   b. Arthur Conan Doyle created Sherlock Holmes.
      Arthur Conan Doyle modeled his detective after Dr. Bell.
      Dr. Bell was famous for his diagnostic ability.
      Arthur Conan Doyle was an eye specialist.
   c. Dr. James Naismith was born in Canada.
      He was a YMCA athletic director.
      He invented the game of basketball.
      Naismith wanted to develop a new recreation.

2. Combine the following sets of facts into a single sentence and write three versions for each, placing emphasis on different elements.
   a. The student council proposed a freeze on tuition.
      The faculty accepted the student proposal.
      The alumni accepted the student proposal.
   b. The city was devastated by an earthquake.
      The public responded with calm determination.
      The mayor urged citizens to help authorities.

(Continued)

c. Job interviews are stressful.
    Applicants fear rejection.
    Interviewers fear hiring the wrong employee.

3. Select a topic from the list on pages 751–752 and freewrite for ten minutes. Let the draft cool and then analyze your use of sentences. Do they emphasize primary ideas? Are minor ideas given too much significance? Are the relationships between ideas clearly expressed?

Writing Paragraphs

Paragraphs are the building blocks of an essay. If writing the entire paper seems like a confusing or overwhelming task, focus on writing one paragraph at a time.

Use Topic Sentences or Controlling Ideas to Maintain Focus

It is easy to become sidetracked when you write a first draft. You can keep your writing focused by using a topic sentence as a goal for each paragraph. If you have not created an outline, you might organize your paragraphs by writing down possible topic sentences:

The United States must reduce its national debt.

Cutting debt will require Americans to make painful sacrifices.

The solutions we select will change the way our government operates at home and abroad.

Let each topic sentence dictate the details you include in each paragraph. Even if you do not plan to include a topic sentence, make sure your paragraph has a controlling idea and a clear purpose.

Use the Modes to Organize Paragraphs

Generally, outlines and notes list *what* you want to write but not *how* to express or organize the ideas. As you develop paragraphs, consider using one or more of the modes. In writing a narrative about moving into your first apartment, for instance, you might use *cause and effect* in one paragraph to explain why you decided to get your own apartment and *comparison* in another paragraph to show how your initial expectations about living alone contrasted with the reality. Later paragraphs in this narrative might be organized by using *process* or *classification*.

Note New Ideas Separately

As you write a first draft, new ideas may come to you. If they do not directly relate to the paragraph you are writing, jot them down on a separate piece of paper or in a different computer file apart from your essay. This way they will not clutter up the paragraph you are working on but remain available for future versions. You might use different fonts or colors to distinguish ideas.

Note Possible Paragraph Breaks

Some people find it difficult to make paragraph breaks in the first draft. Narrative and descriptive essays, for example, often seem like a seamless stream of events or details. Because the main goal of the first draft is to get your thoughts on paper, don't agonize over making paragraph breaks. As you write, you might insert a paragraph symbol (¶) or even a pair of slashes (//) to indicate possible breaks.

Moving from Plan to First Draft

A writer's plan serves as a guide for the first draft, a framework or blueprint that is expanded into a rough version of the final essay. The student writing about victim impact statements used her outline as a guideline for her first draft. In writing her draft, she introduced new ideas, departing from the original plan. At this stage, she does not worry about spelling—the purpose of writing the first draft is not to produce flawless prose, but to get ideas down on paper.

Outline

I. Introduction
   A. Background of victim impact statements
   B. Definition of victim impact statements

II. Goals of victim impact statements (pro)
   A. Victims granted a voice
   B. Therapeutic benefits for victims
   C. Recommendations for sentencing

III. Negative effects of victim impact statements (con)
   A. Inarticulate victims ignored
   B. Benefits limited to the affluent

IV. Conclusion

Thesis: Victim impact statements marginalize the poor and helpless.

First Draft

Across America today more and more victims of crime are being allowed to address the court in terms of making what is called a victim impact statment. This written or oral presentation to the court allows victims to express their feelings to the judge after someone has been convicted of a crime.

Advocates of victim impact statements point to key advantages. First, these statements give victims' a voice. For years, victims have felt helpless. Prosecutors represent the state, not the crime victim. Victims have been dismayed when prosecutors have arranged pleas bargains without their knowledge. Some victims are still recovering from their injuries when they learn the person who hurt them has plead to a lesser charge and received probation.

Therapists who work with victims also say that being able to address the court helps with the healing process. Victims of violent crime can feel powerless and vulnerable. Instead of suffering in silence, they are given the chance to addres the criminal, to clear their chests, and get on with the rest of their lives.

(Continued)

Impact statements allows judges to consider what sentences are aproppriate. In one case a judge who planned to fine a teenager for shoplifting excepted the store owners suggestions to waive the fine if the defendent completed his GED.

But giving victims a change to speak raises some issues. What about the victim who is not articulate, who doesn't even speak English? In murder cases the victim's relatives are given a chance to speak? Does this mean that a middle class professional victim with a circle of grieving friends and family members will be granted more signifiacne than the homeless murder victim who leaves no one behind?

Victim impact statements may help empower victims who are educated, personally impressive, and socially promient. But they may also allow forgotten victims to remain voiceless.

Strategies for Overcoming Problems in the First Draft

In writing a first draft, you may encounter problems. Remember, your goal is to sketch out your main ideas, not to write flawless prose. Write as well as you can in the first draft—but keep in mind that your objective is to get your ideas on paper.

1. **Getting started.** You may find yourself unable to write. Perhaps the task seems imposing, your outline too complex, your thoughts unclear.
   - See pages 17–18 for overcoming writer's block.
   - Freewrite on your topic to loosen up and get in the mood to write.
   - Break your essay into parts and start with the easiest section.
   - Flesh out your plan. Write a new version, turning words into phrases and expanding them into full sentences. Let the draft emerge from the outline.

2. **Running out of time.** Often you will be writing well, discovering new thoughts as you go. If you cannot write fast enough to capture these ideas or if you run out of time, make notes. A rough draft does not have to be stated in complete sentences.

3. **Writing in circles.** Even with the best map, you can sometimes get lost and find yourself repeating ideas, discovering that on page 3 you are restating your introduction.
   - Stop writing and reread your introduction. Does it clearly set up the rest of the essay? Does it try to say too much? An introduction indicates upcoming ideas, but it does not have to summarize every point.
   - List your main ideas or use a diagram to create a pattern you can follow.

4. **Running out of ideas.** Sometimes you may find yourself running out of ideas on the first page of a five-page essay.
   - Review your goal and plan. Are there details that could be added to support your points? Do not add extra ideas just to increase the length of your paper. Whatever you write should relate to your thesis.

■ If you can't think of anything else, stop writing and put the draft aside. Do other work, read something about your topic, and let the draft cool. Return to it later and try adding more details. You may find it beneficial to start fresh with a new draft rather than working with an unsuccessful attempt.

Use key words from your essay as search terms for a quick Internet search. See if the results can stimulate additional ideas of your own.

5. **Your draft becomes too long.** You might find that the writing goes very well. One idea leads to another. Details and examples come easily. Then you discover that at this rate you will need fifteen pages to cover all the points you planned to discuss in a five-page paper.

■ Read your draft aloud. Are you recording interesting ideas, developing needed support, or merely summarizing the obvious or repeating yourself?

■ Continue writing, concentrating on capturing main points and realizing that much of what you write will be deleted.

■ Narrow the scope of your paper. You may have to limit your subject and refine your thesis. Look over what you have written and determine what section would make the best topic for a more sharply defined essay.

e-writing

Exploring Writing the First Draft Online

You can explore the Web to learn more about writing first drafts.

1. Using a search engine, enter such terms as *writing process* and *writing first drafts* to locate current sites of interest.

2. Write the draft of an e-mail to a friend. Relate an interesting story about something that happened recently at school or at work. Write a full draft if you can, but do not send it.

E-Sources

University of Chicago Writing Program: Preparing to Write and Drafting the Paper
http://writing-program.uchicago.edu/resources/collegewriting

Online Writing Lab at Purdue University: Avoiding Plagiarism
http://owl.english.purdue.edu/owl/resource/589/01/

Access the English CourseMate for this text at **www.cengagebrain.com** for further information on writing a first draft.

Revising and Rewriting

Rewriting is the essence of writing well . . .
—William Zinsser

What Is Revision?

After completing the first draft, you may be tempted to start rewriting immediately—to reword awkward sentences, add a quote or statistic, or look for missing commas. But revision is more than correcting mistakes and inserting missing details. *Revision* means "to see again." Before you begin to start rewriting, it is important to examine your draft the way your readers will.

Developing a Revising Style

Most writers follow a standard pattern for revising. They begin by examining the larger elements, reading through the draft for content and rewriting the paragraphs, before making corrections at the sentence and word levels. In revising, ask yourself key questions about the goals of your writing:

- **Is my thesis clear?**
- **Is my thesis adequately supported?**
- **Does my draft suit the writing context?**

    Does it meet the needs of the assignment and my reader?

    Does it reflect the methods, style, and approach expected in the discipline or situation?

    Does my essay follow the format expected in this kind of document?

WRITERS AT WORK

I sometimes write in bars in the afternoons. I go out and find a corner of a bar. If the noise is not directed at me—in other words, there's not a phone ringing or a baby crying or something—I quite like it if the jukebox is on and people are shouting the odds about a sports game. I just hunch over a bottle in the corner. I write in longhand anyway, so I can do it anywhere—sometimes in airport terminals. Then when I've got enough [written] down, I start to type it out, editing it as I go. I don't use any of the new technology stuff.

Christopher Hitchens, editor

SOURCE: *Booknotes*

Strategies for Revising

1. **Let your writing "cool."** Before you can look at your draft objectively, set it aside. Attempting to revise a text immediately after writing is difficult because many of your ideas are still fresh in your mind. Take a walk, check your e-mail, or work on other assignments before attempting to review the text.

2. **Print your draft.** Although some students are skilled at revising on a computer, many find it easier to work with hard copy. Printing the draft can allow you to spread out the pages and see the entire text. Double- or even triple-space the document to provide room for notes and corrections.

3. **Examine your draft globally.** Revising is not editing. Don't immediately start by correcting spelling and punctuation. Instead, focus on the larger elements of the draft.

   - **Is the thesis clearly stated?**
   - **Is the supporting evidence sufficient?**
   - **Is the paper logically organized?**
   - **Does the introduction arouse interest and prepare readers for what follows?**
   - **Does the conclusion leave readers with a strong final impression, question, or challenge?**
   - **Are sections off topic or redundant?**
   - **Does this draft meet the needs of the writing assignment?**
   - **What are the strong and weak points of the essay? What problems should be given priority?**

4. **Examine your paper with a reader's eye.** Consider your readers' perceptual world. What existing knowledge, experiences, values, or attitudes will shape their responses to your paper?

(Continued)

5. **Analyze your critical thinking.** In the rush of creating a first draft, it can be easy to make lapses in critical thinking. New ideas spring to mind, and you may make connections that lack logical foundation. Review "Common Errors in Critical Thinking" on pages 39–41.

6. **Consider the nature of the document.** Documents often dictate specific styles and formats. The brief sentences and short paragraphs expected in an e-mail are inappropriate for a research paper. The subjective impressions that add color to a personal essay are unsuited to a business report.

7. **Read your draft aloud.** Hearing how your draft sounds increases your ability to evaluate your draft for clarity, logic, and tone. Awkward sentences, illogical statements, redundant passages, and missing details are far easier to *hear* than see.

8. **Revise and rewrite.** If you are fortunate, your first attempt will be well written enough to require only minor revisions. But many writers, especially those working on complex or challenging assignments, usually discover enough flaws to require extensive revising.
   - If your first attempt is very unsatisfactory, it may be easier to return to your plan and start a fresh draft. Try writing from a different angle, starting with a new introduction, using different examples, selecting different words and images. Often it will take you less time to write a new draft than to repair an existing one.
   - If you placed images or visual aids in your draft, review their use. Do photographs support your points or simply supply illustrations? Avoid images that will distract or offend readers. Make sure that graphs, charts, and diagrams are accurate and do not oversimplify or distort data. Do you explain where they came from and their significance?
   - **Examine your use outside sources.** If you have included words, facts, numbers, or ideas from other sources, do you acknowledge them? Are direct quotes placed in quotation marks or indented blocks to distinguish them from your own writing? Are paraphrases—indirect quotes—identified?

Strategies for Peer Review

Writers can greatly benefit from editors, people who can offer a fresh perspective on their work and objective analysis of their writing. Professional writers receive reactions from editors and reviewers who analyze their work for factual errors, lapses in judgment, and mechanical mistakes. Many instructors encourage students to engage in peer review.

Your Role as Writer

1. **Let others read your work "cold."** If you preface their reading by telling them what you are trying to say, they will have a harder time evaluating your work objectively.

2. **If you ask people outside of your composition class to read your paper, however, explain the assignment first.** People cannot provide advice if they read your draft in a vacuum. The more they know about your goal and the intended audience, the more valuable their responses will be.

3. **Ask specific questions.** If you simply ask, "Do you like it?" or "Is my paper any good?" you are likely to receive polite compliments or vague assurances that your work is "okay." To get helpful advice, ask peers specific questions, such as "Is my thesis clear?" or "Do I need more evidence to make my point?"

4. **Ask your peers to identify the paper's strong and weak points.**

Your Role as Editor

1. **Understand the role of editors.** An editor is not a writer. Your job as an editor is not to tell others how you would write the paper but to help a writer craft his or her document. Work with the writer to identify errors and suggest improvements.

2. **Understand the writer's goal and the assignment.** If you are not familiar with the assignment, ask to see any directions the student received from his or her instructor. Does the paper meet the instructor's requirements?

3. **Review the document globally, and then look at specifics.**
   - Does the topic suit the assignment?
   - Does it need to be more clearly focused or limited?
   - Does the paper have a clear thesis?
   - Is the thesis effectively supported with details?
   - Are there irrelevant details that can be deleted?
   - Do paragraphs adequately organize the paper? Could the paragraph structure be more effective?
   - Can you detect sentences that are unclear, illogical, or awkward?
   - Does the paper need proofreading for spelling and grammar errors? As a peer editor, your job is not to correct mechanical errors but to indicate to the writer whether the paper needs proofreading.

4. **Be positive.** Make constructive, helpful comments. Don't simply point out errors, indicate how they might be corrected or avoided.

5. **Ask questions.** Instead of stating that a sentence or paragraph does not make sense, ask the writer what he or she was trying to say. Asking questions can prompt a writer to rethink what he or she wrote, remember missing details, or consider new alternatives.

Revising Elements of the First Draft

Although you can correct errors in spelling and punctuation at any point, your main objective in revising an essay is to study the larger elements, especially the paragraphs.

Look at the Big Picture

Review the Entire Essay

Read the paper aloud. How does it sound? What ideas or facts are missing, poorly stated, or repetitive? Highlight areas that need improvement and delete paragraphs that are off topic or redundant.

- How does your draft measure up against your goal?
- What prevents this draft from meeting the needs of the writing assignment?
- What are the most serious defects?
- Have you selected an appropriate method of organizing your essay? Would a chronological approach be better than division? Should you open with your strongest point or reserve it for the conclusion?

Examine the Thesis

Most important, focus on the thesis or controlling idea of the essay. Does your paper have a clear thesis, a controlling idea—or is it simply a collection of facts and observations? Does the essay have a point?

- If your paper has a thesis statement, read it aloud. Is it clearly stated? Is it too general? Can it be adequately supported?
- Where have you placed the thesis? Would it be better situated elsewhere in the essay? Remember, the thesis does not have to appear in the opening.
- If the thesis is implied rather than stated, does the essay have a controlling idea? Do details and your choice of words provide readers with a clear impression of your subject?

Review Topic Sentences and Controlling Ideas

Each paragraph should have a clear focus and support the thesis.

- Does each paragraph have a clear purpose?
- Do all the paragraphs support the thesis?
- Are there paragraphs that are off topic? You may have developed some interesting ideas, recalled an important fact or quote, or told a compelling story—but if these don't directly relate to the thesis, they do not belong in this essay.

Review the Sequence of Paragraphs

While writing, you may have discovered new ideas or diverted from your plan, altering the design of the essay. Study your topic sentences and determine whether their order serves your purpose.

- Should paragraphs be rearranged to maintain chronology or to create greater emphasis?
- Does the order of paragraphs follow your train of thought? Should some paragraphs be preceded by those offering definitions and background information?

Revise the Introduction

The opening sentences and paragraphs of any document are critical. Because you cannot always predict how you will change the body of the essay, you should always return to the introduction and examine it before writing a new draft.

INTRODUCTION CHECKLIST

✔ Does the introduction clearly announce the topic?

✔ Does the opening paragraph arouse interest?

✔ Does the opening paragraph limit the topic and prepare readers for what follows?

✔ If the thesis appears in the opening, is it clearly and precisely stated?

✔ Does the language of the opening paragraph set the proper tone for the paper?

✔ Does the introduction address reader concerns, correct misconceptions, and provide background information so that readers can understand and appreciate the evidence that follows?

Revise Supporting Paragraphs

The paragraphs in the body of the essay should support the thesis, develop ideas, or advance the chronology.

PARAGRAPH CHECKLIST

✔ Does the paragraph have a clear focus?

✔ Is the controlling idea supported with enough evidence?

✔ Is the evidence easy to follow? Does the paragraph follow a logical organization? Would a different mode be more effective in unifying the ideas?

✔ Are there irrelevant ideas that should be deleted?

✔ Are there clear transitions between ideas and between paragraphs?

✔ Do paragraph breaks signal major transitions? Should some paragraphs be combined and others broken up?

Revise the Conclusion

Not all essays require a separate paragraph or group of paragraphs to conclude the writing. A narrative may end with a final event. A comparison may conclude with the last point.

CONCLUSION CHECKLIST

✔ Does the conclusion end the paper on a strong note? Will it leave readers with a final image, question, quotation, or fact that will challenge them and lead them to continue thinking about your subject?

✔ Does the conclusion simply repeat the introduction or main ideas? Is it necessary? Should it be shortened or deleted?

✔ If your purpose is to motivate people to take action, does the conclusion give readers specific steps to follow?

Improving Paragraphs

First drafts often produce weak paragraphs that need stronger topic sentences and clearer support. Look at the following example of revising a first draft to create an improved version:

FIRST DRAFT

The automobile changed America. Development increased as distances were reduced. People moved outward from the city to live and work. Highways and bridges were built. Travel increased and greater mobility led to rapid population shifts, causing growth in some areas and declines in others. Cars created new industries and demands for new services.

REVISION NOTES

too vague, needs tighter topic sentence
The automobile changed America. Development increased as distances were reduced. People moved outward from the city to live and work. Highways and bridges were built.

lack of sentence variety *explain*
Travel increased and greater mobility led to rapid population shifts, causing growth in
which areas? *give examples*
some areas and declines in others. Cars created new industries and demands for new services.

REVISED DRAFT

The automobile reshaped the American landscape. As millions of cars jammed crowded streets and bogged down on unpaved roads, drivers demanded better highways. Soon great bridges spanned the Hudson, Delaware, and Mississippi to accommodate the flood of traffic. The cities pushed beyond rail and trolley lines, absorbing farms, meadows, and marshland. The middle class abandoned the polluted congestion of the city for the mushrooming suburbs that offered greater space and privacy. Gas stations, garages, parking structures, drive-ins appeared across the country. Motels, chain stores, and fast food restaurants catered to the mobile public. Shopping malls, office towers, factories, and schools appeared in the new communities, all of them surrounded by what the cities could not offer—free parking.

Other drafts contain overwritten paragraphs cluttered with redundant statements and irrelevant details. Although they may contain strong controlling statements and impressive evidence, these paragraphs are weakened by unnecessary detail:

FIRST DRAFT

One of Howard Hughes' early first ventures was the creation of a steam-powered sports-car. Hughes had just recently inherited his father's lucrative tool company, which produced the best oil drill bit of the day. Hughes' father wisely leased rather than sold his "rock eater" to maintain control and increase profits. At nineteen, Hughes could now easily afford to build his dream car. Steam cars, though considered obsolete in 1926, had one advantage over gasoline-powered automobiles. They had as much power at a standing start as they did at full power. But they required ten minutes or more to build up enough steam to run and had to stop for water every fifty miles. Hughes, who would later pour millions into the famed Spruce Goose which made only one test flight after World War II, wanted a state of the art steam car. He hired engineers from Caltech and challenged the engineers to build a steamer that would start in two minutes and be able to drive from Los Angeles to San Francisco on a single tank of water. Hughes went back to making movies and dating starlets as his crack team of Caltech engineers worked in a secret garage. The engineers worked for three years and spent $550,000 to develop a steam car that would start in two minutes and drive from Los Angeles to San Francisco on a single tank of water. Hughes was delighted with his new car and asked the engineers how they had achieved their goals. They explained that a network of radiators ran throughout the body of the car, including the doors. Realizing that even a minor accident could rupture a steam pipe and scald the driver, Hughes ordered his half million dollar dream car, the only one its kind, to be cut to pieces with blow torches.

REVISION NOTES

One of Howard Hughes' early first ventures was the creation of a steam-powered   *redundant*
sportscar. Hughes had just recently inherited his father's lucrative tool company, which
produced the best oil drill bit of the day. Hughes' father wisely leased rather than sold his   *delete*
"rock eater" to maintain control and increase profits. At nineteen, Hughes could now easily afford to build his dream car. Steam cars, though considered obsolete in 1926, had one advantage over gasoline-powered automobiles. They had as much power at a standing start as they did at full power. But they required ten minutes or more to build up enough steam to run and had to stop for water every fifty miles. Hughes, who would later pour millions into the famed Spruce Goose which made only one test flight after World War II,,   *delete*
wanted a state of the art steam car. He hired engineers from Caltech and challenged the engineers to build a steamer that would start in two minutes and be able to drive from Los Angeles to San Francisco on a single tank of water. Hughes went back to making movies

(Continued)

---

delete   ~~and dating starlets~~, and the engineers worked for three years and spent $550,000
to develop a steamcar ~~that would start in two minutes and drive from Los Angeles to San Fran-~~
delete   ~~cisco on a single tank of water.~~ Hughes was delighted with his new car and asked the engineers
how they had achieved their goals. They explained that a network of radiators ran throughout
the body of the car, including the doors. Realizing that even a minor accident could rupture a
steam pipe and scald the driver, Hughes ordered his half million dollar dream car, the only one
its kind, to be cut to pieces with blow torches.

REVISED DRAFT

One of Howard Hughes' first ventures was a steam-powered sports car. Having recently
inherited his father's lucrative tool company at nineteen, Hughes could easily afford to build
his dream car. Though considered obsolete in 1926, steam cars had one advantage over gasoline-powered automobiles. They had as much power at a standing start as they did at full
power, but required ten minutes to build up enough steam to run and had to stop for water
every fifty miles. Hughes wanted a state-of-the-art steam car, so he hired engineers from
Caltech and challenged them to build a steamer that would start in two minutes and drive
from Los Angeles to San Francisco on a single tank of water. The scientists worked for three
years and spent $550,000 to develop a steam car that met Hughes's demanding specifica-
tions. Hughes was delighted with his new car until the engineers explained that a network
of radiators ran throughout the body, including the doors. Realizing that even a minor accident could rupture a steam pipe and scald the driver, Hughes ordered his half-million-dollar
dream car cut to pieces with blow torches.

WRITING ACTIVITY

Revise the following paragraphs by restating topic sentences, deleting redundant or irrelevant statements, and adding ideas and observations of your own.

1. Students face a number of challenges in college. Many will have problems making the
    transition from high school to college. College presents students with new challenges
    and many new distractions that can lure them away from class work. Living away
    from home for the first time presents additional challenges to students who face new
    responsibilities. All of these problems can overwhelm students facing a number of
    troubles. Many colleges see as many as a third of freshmen drop out after the first
    year, wasting valuable public and private resources. Colleges need to do more to help
    students adjust to and succeed in college.

2. For more than one generation, parents have shown concern about the effects of television on children. Violent television programs expose children to violence, giving them the ideas that complex problems can be easily resolved with the employment of force. Even nonviolent programs grossly simplify complex human issues and suggest that almost any problem can be resolved in thirty or sixty minutes. Commercials brainwash children into seeking quick fixes to problems, seeing products as substitutes for rewards that come from hard work and effort. Television, above all, reduces children to viewers, passive receivers of messages rather than active participants in social interaction and social discussion.

Revising the First Draft

The student writing about victim impact statements reviewed her first draft and read it to several classmates who offered suggestions. As she listened to them, she added notes in the margins and developed a checklist to guide her second draft. At this point, the writer is focusing on the big picture, as well as making some adjustments at the level of word choice. Editing and proofreading will come later.

Revision of First Draft

Across America today more and more victims of crime are being allowed to address the court in terms of making what is called a victim impact statment. This written or oral presentation to the court allows victims to express their feelings to the judge after someone has been convicted of a crime.   *wordy/weak*

Advocates of victim impact statements point to key advantages. First, these statements give victim's a voice. For years, victims have felt helpless. Prosecutors represent the state, not the crime victim. Victim have been dismayed when prosecutors have arranged pleas bargains without their knowledge. Some victims are still recovering from their injuries when they learn the person who hurt them has plead to a lesser charge and received probation.

Therapists who work with victims also say that being able to address the court helps with the healing process. Victims of violent crime can feel powerless and vulnerable. Instead of suffering in silence, they are given the chance to address the criminal, to clear their chests, and get on with the rest of their lives.   *cliche*

Impact statements allows judges to consider what sentences are aproppriate. In one case a judge who planned to fine a teenager for shoplifting excepted the store owners suggestions to waive the fine if the defendent completed his GED.

But giving victims a change to speak raises some issues. What about the victim who is not articulate, who doesn't even speak English? In murder cases the victim's relatives are given a chance to speak. Does this mean that a middle class professional victim with

(Continued)

a circle of grieving friends and family members will be granted more significance than the homeless murder victim who leaves no one behind?

Victim impact statements may help empower victims who are educated, personally impressive, and socially prominent. But they may also allow forgotten victims to remain voiceless.

Revision Notes

Needs stronger opening—needs attention-getter
Sharper definition
Too short/superficial discussion
Clearer examples/Use real-life trials
Tighter conclusion

Second Draft

The courtroom scene was riveting. One by one, the survivors of a deadly commuter train shooting took the stand and addressed the man who had maimed them. Their voices quivering with emotion, they told the court how the gunman's actions changed their lives forever. Spouses and parents of the dead spoke of loss. There were tears, moments of intense anger, and quiet despair. Victim impact statements have become a common feature of criminal proceedings. Spoken in court or submitted in writing, these statements provide an opportunity for victims to be heard before sentencing.

Advocates of victims impact statements believe these declarations give victims a voice, an opportunity to be heard. Traditionally, victims have appeared in court only as witnesses subject to cross-examination. Prosecutors, victims soon learn, represent the state and not individuals. Still hospitalized after a brutal beating, a New Jersey restaurant owner learned from reading a newspaper that his assailants had plea-bargained to lesser charges and received probation. Joining with other victims, he became an advocate for victims' rights, including impact statements.

Therapists who counsel victims of crime believe that addressing the court and taking an active role in the legal process helps people recover from a sense of helplessness and regain a measure of self-respect.

Impact statements allow judges to consider appropriate sentences. In a Florida case, a judge who intended to fine a teenager for shoplifting agreed with the store owner's suggestion that the fine be waived if the defendant completed his GED.

But giving victims a chance to speak has led to ugly courtroom scenes that seem inappropriate in a democracy. In Milwaukee a sister of a young man murdered by Jeffrey Dahmer wailed and shrieked in contortions of pure rage. The relative of another murder victim shouted that he would execute the killer himself. Bailiffs had to restrain him as he begged the judge, "Just gimme five minutes with him!" Defense attorneys argue these harangues are unnecessary. What need is there to heap abuse upon a person about to lose his or her life or liberty? Can anger and harassment be considered healing?

(Continued)

But even restrained, well-reasoned impact statements raise troubling questions. What about the victim who is too impaired, too frightened, or too wounded to speak? Is his or her absence to be judged as indifference? What about those whose English is limited? What of those without friends or family? Should the drunk driver who kills a young professional missed by friends, family, and colleagues receive a tougher sentence than the drunk driver who kills a homeless man who dies unmourned, unmissed, and uncounted? Do we really want our courts and society to suggest that some lives are more significant than others?

Victim impact statements may help empower victims, especially the educated, the personally impressive, and the socially prominent. But these statements, unintentionally, may also further marginalize the most helpless among us, allowing forgotten victims to remain voiceless.

Strategies for Overcoming Problems in Revising

Revising a draft can be challenging. Writers encounter a range of common problems.

1. **The draft remains unfocused.** If your writing remains too general and seems to lack direction, review your thesis statement.
   - Does your thesis limit the scope of the paper?
   - Does your thesis provide a method of organizing the evidence?
   - Apply prewriting techniques such as lists and clustering to map out the ideas in the draft. Often a list will help you discover a new organizational method and identify ideas that are off topic.

2. **The draft remains too short.** If, after extensive reading, revising, and rewriting, your essay remains too short and superficial, return to your plan.
   - Review your thesis and return to prewriting to develop more evidence.
   - Use key words or phrases from your essay as search terms to locate online information that might provide additional evidence or introduce you to new points of view.

3. **The draft is too long and seems incomplete.** Examine your thesis. Have you attempted to cover too broad a topic given the limits of the assignment?
   - Review your goal and any instructor's guidelines for methods of limiting the paper.
   - An essay that offers an in-depth view of a narrow topic is far more interesting than a longer piece that provides a superficial examination of a broader subject.

e-writing

Exploring Revision Online

You can use the Web to learn more about revising first drafts.

1. Using a search engine, enter such terms as *writing process* and *revision* to locate current sites of interest.
2. If you wrote an e-mail to a friend at the end of the previous chapter, review and revise your draft. What ideas did you forget to add? Are there irrelevant details that could be deleted? Could paragraphs be stronger, better organized? Does your e-mail have the focus, the impact you intended?
3. Review past e-mails you have sent. What changes would you make now? Do you find awkward and wordy sentences? Are there missing details?

For Further Reading

Cook, Claire Kehrwald. *Line by Line: How to Improve Your Writing.*
Venolia, Jan. *Rewrite Right! Your Guide to Perfectly Polished Prose.*

E-Sources

University of Chicago Writing Program: A Strategy for Analyzing and Revising a First Draft
   http://writing-program.uchicago.edu/resources/collegewriting/
Online Writing Lab at Purdue University: Proofreading
   http://owl.english.purdue.edu/owl/resource/561/01/

 Access the English CourseMate for this text at **www.cengagebrain.com** for further information on revising your writing.

Editing and Proofreading

All good essays are not only fine-tuned but also waxed and polished—they are edited and proofread repeatedly for errors until they shine.

—Jean Wyrick

What Are Editing and Proofreading?

Editing and proofreading are the final steps in the writing process. In the *editing* stage, you focus on improving the impact of sentences, correcting errors, eliminating needless phrases, and enhancing the style and clarity of your writing. *Proofreading* checks the visual appearance of your document, reviewing the paper for spelling, proper format, pagination, margins, and accuracy of names, dates, and numbers.

Editing and proofreading, though often seen as final steps, can occur throughout the writing process. While writing and revising, you can fix mechanical errors, provided it does not distract you from focusing on the larger elements.

A number of tools can assist you in editing and proofreading:

- **a dictionary**—to check spelling and definitions
- **a thesaurus**—to find alternatives for overused or imprecise words
- **a handbook**—to check grammar, punctuation, mechanics, and documentation styles
- **an encyclopedia**—to check names, dates, facts, historical and biographical references

If you compose on a computer, you have easy access to online resources.

Editing

In editing, you have three key goals:

- **Eliminate grammar errors.**
- **Improve the precision, clarity, and readability of your sentences.**
- **Maintain a style suited to the needs of the writing context.**

WRITERS AT WORK

If I wake up and I've got a deadline looming, it's just awful.

To get through it, you just make coffee. You make a lot of coffee, and you sit down in front of the [computer] screen and you just type out a word. Then you go and talk on the telephone. You go get some more coffee, you come back, and you make yourself type out [a] sentence.

Then, if you're at home, you rearrange your ties or you clean off your dresser. Then you go back and do it again. You make another phone call. And pretty soon your editor's on the phone saying, "Where is my copy? I need your column." So then you sit down, and you just do it.

Andrew Ferguson, editor
SOURCE: *Booknotes*

Strategies for Editing

1. **Read your paper aloud.** Missing and misspelled words, awkward and redundant phrases, and illogical constructions are easier to hear than see.

2. **Use peer editing.** It is far easier to detect errors in someone else's writing. Switch papers with another student if you can. Read this student's paper aloud if possible, noting mistakes and areas needing revision.

3. **Use the spell-checker and other computer tools.** Most word-processing programs include a spell-checker, which detects items it does not recognize as words.
   - Spell-check systems have limitations. They will not find missing words or always distinguish between homonyms such as *their* and *there*. In addition, they will not be able to detect errors in unusual proper names such as *Kowalski* or *Aix-la-Chapelle*.

4. **Edit backward.** An effective way of spotting errors is to start with the last line and read backward, moving from the conclusion to the introduction. Working in reverse order isolates sentences so that you can evaluate them out of context.

5. **Focus on identifying and correcting habitual errors.** Students often have habitual errors. You may frequently make spelling errors, forget needed commas, or continually confuse *its* and *it's*.
   - Review previously written papers and instructor comments to identify errors you are likely to repeat.

Correcting Grammar

Common Grammar Errors

When editing drafts, look for these common grammar errors.

Fragments

Fragments are incomplete sentences. Sentences require a subject and a verb and must state a complete thought:

Tom works until midnight.	**sentence**
Tom working until midnight	**fragment** (incomplete verb)
Works until midnight.	**fragment** (subject missing)
Because Tom works until midnight.	**fragment** (incomplete thought)

Notice that even though the last item has a subject, *Tom,* and a verb, *works,* it does not state a complete thought.

See pages 698–700 for more on fragments.

Run-ons and Comma Splices

Run-ons and comma splices are incorrectly punctuated compound sentences. Simple sentences (independent clauses) can be joined correctly to create compound sentences in two ways:

1. Link with a **semicolon (;)**
2. Link with a **comma (,) + and, or, yet, but,** or **so**

I was born in Chicago, but I grew up in Dallas.	**correct**
I studied French; Jan took Italian.	**correct**
We have to take a cab my battery is dead.	**run-on**
Jim is sick, the game is canceled.	**comma splice**

See pages 700–702 for more about run-ons and comma splices.

Subject and Verb Agreement

Subjects and verbs must match in number. Singular subjects use singular verbs, and plural subjects use plural verbs.

The boy *walk*s to school.	**singular**
The boys *walk* to school.	**plural**
The cost of drugs *is* rising.	**singular** (the subject is *cost*)
Two weeks *is* not enough time.	**singular** (amounts of time and money are singular)
The jury *is* deliberating.	**singular** (group subjects are singular)
The teacher or the students *are* invited.	**plural** (when two subjects are joined with *or,* the subject nearer the verb determines whether it is singular or plural)

See pages 706–709 for more on subject and verb agreement.

Pronoun Agreement

Pronouns must agree or match the nouns they represent. Singular nouns require singular pronouns, and plural nouns require plural pronouns.

Everyone should cast *his* or *her* vote.	**singular**
The children want *their* parents to call.	**plural**

The most misused pronoun is *they*. *They* is a pronoun and should clearly refer to a noun. Avoid unclear use of pronouns as in "Crime is rising. Schools are failing. *They* just don't care." Who does *they* refer to? The citizens? City officials?

See pages 710–712 for more on pronoun agreement.

Dangling and Misplaced Modifiers

To prevent confusion, modifiers—words and phrases that add information about other words—should be placed near the words they modify.

Rowing across the lake, the moon rose over the water.	**dangling** (who was *rowing*? The *moon?*)
Rowing across the lake, *we* saw the moon rise over the water.	**correct**
She drove the car to the house which was rented.	**misplaced** (which was rented, the car or the house?)
She drove the car to the rented house.	**correct**

See pages 719–721 for more about dangling and misplaced modifiers.

Faulty Parallelism

Pairs and lists of words and phrases should match in form.

Jim is tall, handsome, and an athlete.	**not parallel** (list mixes adjectives and a noun)
Jim is tall, handsome, and athletic.	**parallel** (all adjectives)
We need to paint the bedroom, shovel the walk, and the basement must be cleaned.	**not parallel** (The last item does not match with *to paint* and *shovel*.)
We need to paint the bedroom, shovel the walk, and clean the basement.	**parallel** (all verb phrases)

See pages 703–705 for more on faulty parallelism.

Awkward Shifts in Person

Avoid illogical shifts in person.

We climbed the tower and you could see for miles.	**illogical shift from *we* to *you***
We climbed the tower and we could see for miles.	**correct**

If a student works hard, you can get an A.	**illogical shift from** *student* **to** *you*
If you work hard, you can get an A.	**correct**

Awkward Shifts in Tense

Avoid illogical shifts in tense (time).

Hamlet hears from a ghost; then he avenged his father.	**awkward shift from present to past**
Hamlet heard from a ghost; then he avenged his father.	**correct** (both past)
Hamlet hears from a ghost; then he avenges his father.	**correct** (both present)

Improving Sentence Structure

Editing Sentences

Along with editing the grammar of your draft, examine the sentences in each paragraph. Read each sentence separately to make sure it expresses the thoughts you intended.

SENTENCE CHECKLIST

✔ Does the sentence support the paragraph's controlling idea? Could it be eliminated?

✔ Are key ideas emphasized through specific words and active verbs (see pages 102–104)?

✔ Are secondary ideas subordinated (see page 105)?

✔ Are the relationships between ideas clearly expressed with transitional expressions (see page 106)?

✔ Do the tone and style of the sentence suit your reader and the nature of the document?

Be Brief

Sentences lose their power when cluttered with unnecessary words and phrases. When writing the rough draft, it is easy to slip in expressions that add nothing to the meaning of the sentence.

ORIGINAL: I was running late and went racing home to get ready to pack for our trip.

It was starting to get dark, so we went out and looked for a cab.

You have a lot of smokers out there who are desperate to quit.

IMPROVED: I was late and raced home to pack for our trip.

It was getting dark, so we looked for a cab.

A lot of smokers are desperate to quit.

Phrases that begin with *who is* or *which were* can often be shortened:

ORIGINAL: Viveca Scott, who was an ambitious business leader, doubled profits, which stunned her stockholders.

He sold tickets he got as premiums which was illegal.

IMPROVED: Viveca Scott, an ambitious business leader, stunned her stockholders by doubling profits.

He illegally sold premium tickets.

Delete Wordy Phrases

Even skilled writers use wordy phrases in trying to express themselves in a first draft. When editing, locate phrases that can be replaced with shorter phrases or single words:

Wordy	Improved
at that period of time	then
at the present time	now
in the near future	soon
winter months	winter
round in shape	round
blue colored	blue
for the purpose of informing	to inform
render an examination of	examine
make an analysis	analyze
in the event of	if

Delete Needless Detail and Superfluous Sentences

Unimportant details can be deleted. Avoid sentences that simply present a single detail.

ORIGINAL: It was October 24, 2011. It was the day I would learn if my football career was over. I had to have a CAT scan at Columbia. I got in my car and drove to Columbia Hospital. I found a place to park and went inside. I made it just in time, so I did not have to wait long.

IMPROVED: On October 24, 2011, I went to Columbia Hospital for a CAT scan that would determine if my football career was over.

Eliminate Redundancy

Repeating or restating words and ideas can have a dramatic effect, but it is a technique that should be used sparingly and only when you wish to emphasize a specific point.

REDUNDANT: The computer has revolutionized education, revolutionizing delivery systems, course content, and teaching methods.

He took his medicine, but poor nutrition, bad eating habits, his lack of exercise, and sedentary lifestyle hampered his recovery.

IMPROVED: The computer has revolutionized educational delivery systems, course content, and teaching methods.

He took his medicine, but his bad eating habits and sedentary lifestyle hampered his recovery.

Limit Use of Passive Voice

Most sentences state ideas in *active voice*: the subject performs the action of the verb. In *passive voice* the order is reversed and the sentence's subject is acted on:

Active	Passive
Mr. Smith towed the car.	The car was towed by Mr. Smith.
The hospital conducted several tests.	Several tests were conducted by the hospital.
The mayor's office announced a new round of budget cuts.	A new round of budget cuts was announced by the mayor's office.

Passive voice is used when the actor is unknown or less important than the object:

My car was stolen.
The door was locked.
His chest was crushed by a rock.

Passive voice, however, can leave out critical information:

After the plane crash, several photographs were taken.

(*Who took the photographs—investigators, reporters, the airline, survivors, bystanders?*) Use passive voice *only* when it emphasizes important elements in a sentence.

Vary Your Use of Sentence Types

You can keep your writing interesting and fresh by altering types of sentences. Repeating a single kind of sentence can give your writing a monotonous predictability. A short sentence isolates an idea and gives it emphasis, but a string of choppy sentences explaining minor details robs your essay of power. Long sentences can subordinate minor details and show the subtle relationships between ideas, but they can become tedious for readers to follow.

UNVARIED: Mary Sanchez was elected to the assembly. She worked hard on the budget committee. Her work won her respect. She was highly regarded by the mayor. People responded to her energy and drive. She became popular with voters. The mayor decided to run for governor. He asked Mary Sanchez to manage his campaign.

VARIED: Mary Sanchez was elected to the assembly. Her hard work on the budget committee won her respect, especially from the mayor. Voters were impressed by her drive and energy. When the mayor decided to run for governor, he asked Mary Sanchez to manage his campaign.

WRITING ACTIVITIES

Edit the following sentences to eliminate wordy and redundant phrases and emphasize main ideas.

1. In many ways students must learn to teach themselves to be successful.

2. American automobiles, once threatened by imports from Japan and other countries, are entering and competing in the global car market.

3. Illness and disease can be prevented through proper diet, appropriate exercise, and moderation in the consumption of alcohol.

4. In my personal opinion, the calculus course is too tough for the majority of freshmen students.

5. The exams were distributed by the professor after a brief introduction.

Edit the sentences in the following paragraph to reduce clutter and increase clarity and variety:

The English Department originally opened the writing lab three years ago. This lab was designed to aid and assist students taking freshman composition courses. The lab was at first staffed by four paraprofessionals with extensive experience in teaching writing and editing. The dean of liberal arts cut the lab budget, reducing funds. Now only two part-time graduate students are available in the lab to help students. Neither has teaching or editing experience. The students are no longer getting the assistance they need to improve their writing. The lab is no longer crowded and hardly used. Often students are found using the computers to send e-mail to friends. Some students with nothing to do drop in to play solitaire or minesweeper, killing time between classes. This should change.

Maintaining Style

Editing Words

Your writing will improve when you make careful decisions about *diction,* the choice of appropriate words.

DICTION CHECKLIST

✔ Are the words accurate? Have you chosen words that precisely reflect your thinking? (See pages 101–103.)

✔ Have you chosen the right word from easily confused pairs like *affect* and *effect, there* and *their,* and *weather* and *whether?* (See pages 746–748.)

✔ Is the level of diction appropriate? Do your words suit the tone and style of the document? (See pages 102–103.)

✔ Do connotations suit your purpose or do they detract from your message? (See page 103.)

✔ Are technical terms clearly defined?

✔ Do you use specific rather than abstract words?

Replace General or Abstract Words with Specific Ones

GENERAL: My grandmother was a very *special* person. Her death *affected* me *greatly.* I was sixteen years old at the time. Her loss made me *feel bad,* and I *acted out negatively.*

SPECIFIC: My grandmother was a *generous, caring, wise* person. When I was sixteen, she died suddenly, leaving me feeling *sad, lost,* and *angry.* I *skipped school, quit the basketball team,* and *failed three classes.*

Avoid Sexist Language

Sexist language either ignores the existence of one gender or promotes negative attitudes about men or women.

■ **Replace sexist words with neutral terms.**

Sexist	Nonsexist
mankind	humanity, people
policeman	police officer
Frenchmen	the French
manmade	synthetic
everyman	everyone
fireman	firefighter
chairman	chairperson, chair

■ **Avoid nouns with "female" endings or adjectives.** Although the words *actress* and *waitress* are still used, other words designating female professionals are largely considered obsolete:

Sexist	Nonsexist
poetess	poet
authoress	author
lady lawyer	lawyer
woman judge	judge

■ **Avoid using male pronouns when nouns refer to both genders.** The single noun *man* takes the single male pronoun *he.* If you are writing about a boys' school, it is appropriate to substitute "he" for the noun "student." But if the school includes both males and females, both should be represented:

Every student should try *his or her* best.
All students should try *their* best.

Plural nouns take the pronouns *they* and *their,* avoiding wordy *he or she* and *his or her* constructions.

Avoid Clichés

Clichés are worn-out phrases. Once creative or imaginative, these phrases, like jokes you have heard more than once, have lost their impact. In addition, clichés allow simplistic statements to substitute for genuine thought.

white as snow	light as a feather	acid test
perfect storm	in the thick of it	on pins and needles
evil as sin	dead heat	crushing blow
viable option	bottom line	all that jazz
crack of dawn	calm before the storm	dog-tired

WRITING ACTIVITY

Edit the diction in the following sentences to avoid sexism, clichés, awkward phrases, and misused words.

1. Every student should bring his books to class.

2. He jogged at the crack of dawn every morning.

3. The university has listed three mandatory requirements for future revision.

4. We had better get down to brass tacks if we want to get a fresh start.

5. Threatened by drug dealers, the witness required continual security.

6. This dispute must be settled by an uninterested judge.

7. He could manage to explain a difficult problem with childish simplicity.

8. The computer company began to flounder in debt.

9. The president's speech contained several illusions to the New Deal.

10. A voter should use his best judgment.

Proofreading

Proofreading examines writing for mechanical errors and evaluates the physical appearance—the *look*—of the finished document.

Strategies for Proofreading

1. **Make a last check for errors in the text.** Read the paper through to make last-minute corrections in grammar, spelling, usage, punctuation, and capitalization.
   - **Double-check details, such as names, dates, addresses, and prices, for accuracy.**

2. **Use the appropriate format.** College instructors often dictate specific styles and requirements about paging, margins, spacing, and cover sheets. Business, government, and professional documents may have precise guidelines.

3. **Use standard formats.** If you are not given specific instructions, follow these standard guidelines.
   - Use standard-size 8½- × 11-inch white paper.
   - Remove any perforated edges.
   - Use standard typeface or fonts. Avoid script or fonts smaller than ten point. Use fonts larger than fourteen point only for titles and headings.
   - Double-space your text, leaving ample margins.
   - Use a title page or header listing your name, instructor's name, course, date, and assignment.

4. **Keep copies of all your papers.** Papers do get lost. Always make a copy in case your instructor fails to get your assignment. Save documents on flash drives or e-mail them to yourself.

Fixing Common Mechanical Errors

Spelling and Usage Errors

Spell-checkers do not distinguish between words like *its* and *it's* or *affect* and *effect*. Get in the habit of using a dictionary and see pages 749–751 and 746–748.

Punctuation

Use **commas** to separate items in a list, set off introductory and nonrestrictive elements, and join clauses in complex and compound sentences:

> We bought pens, pencils, paper, and ink.
> After losing the game, we met with the coach to discuss strategy.
> My brother, who was born in Manhattan, took us to 21.
> Because it was hot, the game was canceled.
> We bought the plane tickets, but Hector paid for the hotel.

Use **semicolons** to separate independent clauses in compound sentences:

I flew to San Francisco; Juan took the train.

Use **apostrophes** to indicate contractions and possessives:

Don't let Carlo's truck leave the garage.

See pages 723–736 for more on punctuation.

Capitalization

Capitalize proper nouns such as names of products, organizations, geographical places, and people:

Buick   Yale University   Chicago   Rocky Mountains   Jim Wilson   Jane

Capitalize titles when used before a name:

We called for a doctor just as Dr. Green walked in.

Capitalize *East, North, West, South* when they refer to regions, not directions:

We drove south to the airport and grabbed a flight to the East.

See pages 737–739 for more about capitalization.

WRITING ACTIVITY

Edit and proofread the following essay, correcting errors in spelling, capitalization, and punctuation.

Most American Muslims are not Arab and most Americans of Arab decent are Christian not Muslim. People of south Asian decent—those with roots in Pakistan, India, Bangladesh, and Afghanistan—make up 34 percent of American Muslims, according to the polling organization Zogby international. Arab-Americans constitute only 26 percent while another 20 percent are native-born American blacks most of whom are converts. The remaining 20 percent come from Africa, Iran, Turkey, and elsewhere.

Muslims have no equivalent to the catholic pope and his cardinals. The faith is decentralized in the extreme and some beliefs and practices vary depending on region and sect. In America, Muslims do not think and act alike any more than Christians do. That said all observant Muslims acknowledge Islam's "five pillars": faith in one God, prayer, charity, fasting during Ramadan, and pilgrimage to Mecca. Muslims are also united in the way they pray. The basic choreography of crossing arms bowing kneeling and prostrating oneself is more or less the same in mosques everywhere.

The two major subgroups of Muslims, Sunni and Shiite, are found in the United States in roughly their global proportions: 85 percent Sunni, 15 percent Shiite. Ancient history still animates the rivalry, which began in the struggle for Muslim leadership after the Prophet Muhammad's death in 632. Shiites believe that Muhammad intended for only his blood descendents to succeed him. Muhammad's beloved cousin and son-in-law Ali was the only male relative who qualified. Ali's followers became known as Shiites, a derivation of the Arabic phrase for "partisans of Ali." Things did not go smoothly for them. The larger body of early Muslims known as Sunnis a word related to Sunnah, or way of the Prophet, had a more flexible nation of who should succed Muhammad. In 661, an extremist asassinated Ali near Najaf in what is now Iraq. Nineteen years later Sunnis killed his son, Hussein, not far away in Karbala. These deaths permanently divided the aggreved Shiite minority from the Sunni majority.

(See the proper text on page 178 to check your answers.)

Strategies for Overcoming Problems in Editing and Proofreading

1. **Sentences remain awkward.** Even after revising and editing, a sentence may still be awkward or garbled.
   - Think about the idea you were trying to express and write a new sentence without looking at your paper. Try restating your ideas with different words.
   - Use peer review if possible.
2. **Sentences contain redundant phrases and repeated words.**
   - Search a thesaurus for alternative words.
   - Examine your text to see whether subtitles or other devices could substitute for repeating phrases.
   - Read your paper aloud or use peer review to detect needless or awkward repetitions.
3. **You are unable to determine the final format of the document.** Even when your text is perfected, you may find yourself unable to decide whether your paper should be single- or double-spaced, whether diagrams or charts should be included, or whether citations should appear at the bottom of the page, within the text, or at the end.
   - Review instructions for guidelines or talk with your instructor.
   - Examine any existing examples for guidance.
   - Review official sources such as *The Chicago Manual of Style* or *The MLA Handbook*.

e-writing

Exploring Editing Online

You can use the Web to learn more about editing.

1. Using a search engine, enter such terms as *editing drafts* and *editing process* to locate current sites of interest.
2. If you wrote an e-mail to a friend in Chapter 10, review and edit your revised draft. Can you locate any grammar errors such as fragments, run-ons, or dangling modifiers? Have you used standard forms of punctuation and capitalization?

For Further Reading

Fulwiler, Toby, and Alan R. Hayakawa. *The College Writer's Reference.*

Sabin, William A. *The Gregg Reference Manual.*

Stilman, Anne. *Grammatically Correct: The Writer's Essential Guide to Punctuation, Spelling, Style, Usage, and Grammar.*

Sutcliffe, Andrea, ed. *The New York Public Library Writer's Guide to Style and Usage.*

Wilson, Kenneth G. *The Columbia Guide to Standard American English.*

E-Sources

Answers.com—online dictionary and encyclopedia

http://www.answers.com

Dictionary of Difficult Words

http://www.talktalk.co.uk/reference/dictionaries/difficultwords/

Thesaurus

http://thesaurus.com/

Capital Community College: Guide to Grammar and Writing

http://grammar.ccc.commnet.edu/grammar/index.htm

 Access the English CourseMate for this text at **www.cengagebrain.com** for further information about editing and proofreading.

Sam Diephuis/Jupiterimages

Becoming a Critical Reader
Reading with a Writer's Eye

If reading is to accomplish anything more than passing time, it must be active.

—Mortimer Adler

What Is Critical Reading?

As a student you are accustomed to reading for information. Studying for examinations, you review textbooks, highlighting facts, dates, statistics, quotations, and concepts that you expect to be tested on. Engrossed in a novel, you read for plot, paying little attention to the author's syntax and literary techniques as you follow the story.

As a composition student, however, you need to read critically; you need to read with a "writer's eye." Tourists in Rome marvel at the ancient ruins; an architectural student examines how the columns support the roof. Moviegoers gasp at car chases, but filmmakers study the director's use of camera angles and special effects. The audience in a comedy club laughs as a comic spins out a series of one-liners, while a would-be performer analyzes her timing and delivery.

To increase your skills as a writer, you need to read like a writer, examining *how* something is written. Reading gives you the opportunity to watch other writers at work. When you read, note the way other writers use words, form sentences, and develop paragraphs. Focus on techniques that you can use in your own assignments:

- **How did the author limit the subject?**
- **Where did the writer place the thesis statement?**
- **What kind of support is used?**
- **How did the writer organize ideas?**
- **What sentence opens the essay?**
- **What thought, image, question, or fact did the author choose for the conclusion?**

In short, learn to read like a writer.

How to Read with a Writer's Eye

When you pick up a magazine, you rarely read every article. Flipping through the pages, you allow your eyes to guide you. A headline, a photograph, a chart, or a famous name makes you pause and begin reading. If you become bored, you skip to

Maria Toutoudaki/jupiterimages

Sam Diephuis/jupiterimages

the next article. Reading textbooks, you skim over familiar material to concentrate on new information.

In a composition course, however, you should read *all* the assigned selections carefully. Reading as a writer, you examine familiar works differently than do readers seeking information. Even if you know a particular essay well, study it closely, observing how it is constructed. As a writer, you read to learn, seeing the writing as a model demonstrating strategies that you can use in your own work.

Like writing, critical reading occurs best in stages.

First Reading

1. **Look ahead and skim selections.** Do not wait until the night before a class discussion to tackle your assigned reading. Skim through upcoming readings to get a general impression. If you think about the authors and their topics, you can approach essays more critically.

2. **Study the headnote and introduction.** Consider the author, the issue, and the writing context. What readers does the writer seem to be addressing? What can you observe about the discourse community?

3. **Suspend judgment.** Try to put your personal views aside as you read. Even if you disagree with the author's choice of topic, tone, or opinion, read the essay objectively. You can still learn useful writing techniques even if you reject an author's thesis.

4. **Consider the title.** Titles often provide clues about the author's attitude toward his or her subject. Does the title label the essay, state a thesis, pose a question, or use a creative phrase to attract attention?

5. **Read the entire work.** Just as in writing the first draft, it is important to complete the entire selection in one sitting if possible. Do not pause to look up an unfamiliar word at this stage. Instead, try to get the big picture.

6. **Focus on understanding the writer's main point.** If possible, summarize the writer's thesis in your own words.

7. **Jot down your first impressions.** What do you think of this work? Do you like it? If so, why? If you find it dull, disturbing, or silly, ask yourself why. What is lacking? How did the author fail in your eyes?

Put the essay aside, allowing it to cool. If possible, let two or three days pass before returning to the assignment. If the assignment is due the next day, read the selection early in the day and then turn to other work or run an errand, so that you can come back to it with a fresh outlook.

Second Reading

1. **Review your first impressions.** Determine whether your attitudes are based on biases or personal preferences rather than the writer's ability. Realize that an essay that supports your views is not necessarily well written. If you disagree with

the author's thesis, try to put your opinions aside to objectively evaluate how well the writer presented his or her point of view. Don't allow your personal views to cloud your critical thinking. Appreciating an author's writing ability does not require you to accept his or her opinion.

2. **Read with a pen in your hand.** Make notes and underline passages that strike you as interesting, odd, offensive, or disturbing. Reading with a pen will prompt you to write, to be an active reader rather than a passive consumer of words.

3. **Look up unfamiliar words.** Paying attention to words can increase your vocabulary and enhance your appreciation of connotations.

4. **Analyze passages you found difficult or confusing during the first reading.** In many instances a second reading can help you understand complex passages. If you still have difficulty understanding the writer's point, ask why. Would other readers also have problems comprehending the meaning? Could ideas be stated more directly?

5. **Review the questions at the end of the selection.** When available, the questions can help you focus on a closer, more analytical reading of the work.

This book's questions are arranged in three groups:

- *Understanding Context*
  What is the writer's purpose?
  What is the thesis?
  What audience is the writer addressing?
  What is the author trying to share with his or her readers?

- *Evaluating Strategy*
  How effective is the title?
  How does the writer introduce the essay?
  What evidence supports the thesis?
  How does the writer organize ideas?
  Where does the author use paragraph breaks?
  Is the writer's approach subjective or objective?
  How does the writer address possible objections or differing opinions?
  How does the writer conclude the essay?
  Does the author use any special techniques?

- *Appreciating Language*
  How does the writer use words?
  What does the language reveal about the intended readers?
  What connotations do the words have?
  How do the words establish the writer's tone?

6. **Summarize your responses in a point or two for class discussion.** Consider how you will express your opinions of the essay to fellow students. Be prepared to back up your remarks by citing passages in the text.

7. **Most important, focus on what this essay can teach you about writing.** How can this writer's style, way of organizing ideas, or word choice enrich your own writing?

Though you may not wish to imitate everything you see, you can learn techniques to enhance your writing and overcome problems.

8. **Consider how writers resolve problems that you have encountered.** If you have trouble making an outline and organizing ideas, study how the essays in this book are arranged. If your instructor returns papers with comments about vague thesis statements and lack of focus, examine how the writers in this book generate controlling ideas.

Before Class Discussion

1. **Before class discussion of an assigned essay, review the reading and your notes.** Identify your main reactions to the piece. What do you consider the essay's strongest or weakest points?

2. **Ask fellow students about their reactions to the writing.** Determine whether their responses to the writer's thesis, tone, approach, and technique match yours. If their reactions differ from yours, review your notes to get a fresh perspective.

3. **Be prepared to ask questions.** Ask your instructor about unfamiliar techniques or passages that you find confusing.

Read the following essay by Emily Prager and study how it has been marked during a critical reading. Notice how the student used the essay to generate ideas for upcoming assignments.

Emily Prager (1952–) graduated from Barnard College with a degree in anthropology. She has written pieces for *National Lampoon* as well as several screenplays. Prager has also appeared in several films. For four years she was a star on *The Edge of Night,* a popular soap opera. She has published three books of fiction: *A Visit from the Foot-Binder and Other Stories, Clea and Zeus Divorce*, and *Eve's Tattoo*.

Our Barbies, Ourselves

Source: "Our Barbies, Ourselves" by Emily Prager. Copyright © 1991 by Emily Prager. By permission.

Notice how Prager uses a variety of modes, including comparison, description, narration, and cause and effect, to develop her essay about the Barbie doll. As you read the piece, consider her choice of topics. Is a popular toy a fitting subject to prompt thoughts about gender roles? Is it too trivial? Does Prager give a doll too much significance?

1 I read an astounding obituary in *The New York Times* not too long ago. It concerned the death of one Jack Ryan. A former husband of Zsa Zsa Gabor, it said, Mr. Ryan had been an inventor and designer during his lifetime. A man of eclectic creativity, he designed Sparrow and Hawk missiles when he worked for the Raytheon Company, and, the notice said, when he consulted for Mattel he designed Barbie. *[introduction (obituary as writing prompt)]*

2 If Barbie was designed by a man, suddenly a lot of things made sense to me, things I'd wondered about for years. I used to look at Barbie and wonder, What's wrong with this picture? What kind of woman designed this doll? Let's be honest: Barbie looks like someone who got her start at the Playboy Mansion. She could be a regular guest on *The Howard Stern Show*. It is a fact of Barbie's design that her breasts are so out of proportion to the rest of her body that if she were a human woman, she'd fall flat on her face. *[description WHY? female/feminist reaction?]*

3 If it's true that a woman didn't design Barbie, you don't know how much saner that makes me feel. Of course, that doesn't ameliorate the damage. There are millions of women who are subliminally sure that a thirty-nine-inch bust and a twenty-three-inch waist are the epitome of lovability. Could this account for the popularity of breast implant surgery? *[questions cause and effect]*

4 I don't mean to step on anyone's toes here. I loved my Barbie. Secretly, I still believe that neon pink and turquoise blue are the only colors in which to decorate a duplex condo. And like so many others of my generation, I've never married, simply because I cannot find a man who looks as good in clam diggers as Ken.

5 The question that comes to mind is, of course, Did Mr. Ryan design Barbie as a weapon? Because it *is* odd that Barbie appeared about the same time in my consciousness as the feminist movement—a time when women sought equality and small breasts were king. Or is Barbie the dream date of a weapons designer? Or perhaps it's simpler than that: Perhaps Barbie is Zsa Zsa if she were eleven inches tall. No matter *[Barbie as a weapon? cause and effect]*

Sam Diephuis/Jupiterimages

modern ideal
of a hard
body?

what, my discovery of Jack Ryan confirms what I have always felt: <u>There is something indescribably masculine about Barbie—dare I say it, phallic.</u> For all her giant breasts and high-heeled feet, she lacks a certain softness. If you asked a little girl what kind of doll she wanted for Christmas, I just don't think she'd reply, "Please, Santa, I want a hard-body."

Barbie as role
model?

6   On the other hand, you could say that Barbie, in feminist terms, is definitely her own person. With her condos and fashion plazas and pools and beauty salons, <u>she is definitely a liberated woman</u>, a gal on the move. And she has always been sexual, even totemic. Before Barbie, American dolls were flat-footed and breastless, and

Barbie = adult
not baby or
child doll

ineffably dignified. They were created in the image of little girls or babies. Madame Alexander was the queen of doll makers in the fifties, and her dollies looked like Elizabeth Taylor in *National Velvet*. They represented the kind of girls who looked perfect in jodhpurs, whose hair was never out of place, who grew up to be Jackie Kennedy—before she married Onassis. Her dolls' boyfriends were figments of the imagination, figments with large portfolios and three-piece suits and presidential aspirations, figments who could keep dolly in the style to which little girls of the fifties were programmed to become accustomed. . . . And perhaps what accounts for Barbie's vast popularity is that she was also a sixties woman: into free love and fun colors, anti-class, and possessed of real, molded boyfriend, Ken, with whom she could chant a mantra.

Ken sexless in
comparison to
Barbie

7   But there were problems with Ken. <u>I always felt weird about him</u>. He had no genitals, and, even at age ten, I found that ominous. I mean, here was Barbie with these humongous breasts, and that was OK with the toy company. And then, there was Ken, with that truncated, unidentifiable lump at his groin. I sensed injustice at work. Why, I wondered, was Barbie designed with such obvious sexual equipment and Ken not? Why was he treated as if it were more mysterious than hers? Did the fact that it was treated as such indicate that somehow his equipment, his essential maleness, was considered more powerful than hers, more

questions

worthy of the dignity of concealment? And if the issue in the mind of the toy company was obscenity and its possible damage to children, I still object. How do they think I felt, knowing that no matter how many water beds they slept in, or hot tubs they romped in, or swimming pools they lounged by under the stars, Barbie and Ken could never make love? No matter how much sexuality Barbie possessed, she would never turn Ken on. He would be forever withhold-

Barbie's fate

Conclusion
and final
observation

ing, forever detached. <u>There was a loneliness about Barbie's situation that was always disturbing.</u> And twenty-five years later, movies and videos are still filled with topless women and covered men. <u>As if we're all trapped in Barbie's world and can never escape.</u>

STUDENT NOTES

First Reading

Barbie as symbol of male domination?

What about G.I. Joe and boys?

Is Prager really serious about this?

Barbie as paradox—a toy that presents a sexist Playboy image of women but a toy that is independent and more "liberated" than traditional baby dolls.

Tone: witty but serious in spots, raises a lot of issues but doesn't really discuss many.

Second Reading

Thesis: The Barbie doll, the creation of a male weapons designer, has shaped the way a generation of women defined themselves. (Get other opinions.)

Body: spins off a number of topics and observations, a list of associations, suited for general readers

Approach: a mix of serious and witty commentary, writer appears to entertain as much as inform or persuade

Organization: use of modes critical to keeping the essay from becoming a rambling list of contradictory ideas. Good use of description, comparison, cause and effect

Conclusion: "trapped in Barbie's world," good ending

Prewriting—Possible Topics

Description—childhood toys—models of cars and planes? games—Monopoly (preparing kids for capitalism?)

Comparison/contrast—boy and girl toys and games, playing house vs. playing ball (social roles vs. competition, teamwork)

Cause and effect—we are socialized by our toys and games in childhood, affecting how men and women develop (needs support—Psych class notes)

Example—My daughter's old Beanie Baby?

Using the Reader

The Reader portion of *The Sundance Writer* is organized in nine modes focusing on writers' goals. The readings in each section illustrate how writers achieve their purpose in different contexts. Each chapter opens with an explanation of the goal or mode. The opening readings in each chapter are brief, clear-cut examples of the mode and can serve as models for many of your composition assignments. Later readings are longer and more complex and demonstrate writing tasks in a range of disciplines and writing situations. Chapters end with samples of applied writings taken from business, industry, and government to illustrate how the mode is used beyond the classroom.

In addition to reading entries assigned by your instructor, perhaps the best way to improve your writing is to flip through the Reader and review how different writers state a thesis, support an argument, open an essay, organize ideas, and present a conclusion. Focus on how other writers cope with the problems you encounter in your writing.

Strategies for Critical Reading

As you read entries in the reader, ask yourself these questions:

1. **What is the writer's purpose?** Even writers pursuing the same goal—to tell a story or explain a process—have slightly different intentions. What is the goal of the writing—to raise questions, motivate readers to take action, or change people's perceptions?

2. **What is the thesis?** What is the writer's main idea? Is the thesis explicitly stated, developed throughout the essay, or only implied? Can you state the thesis in your own words?

3. **What evidence does the writer provide to support the thesis?** Does the writer use personal observations, narratives, facts, statistics, or examples to support his or her conclusions?

4. **How does the writer organize the essay?** How does he or she introduce readers to the topic, develop ideas, arrange information, and conclude the essay? How does the writer use modes?

5. **Who are the intended readers?** What does the original source of the document tell you about its intended audience? Does the writer direct the essay to a particular group or a general readership? Are technical or uncommon terms defined? What knowledge does the writer seem to assume readers already possess?

6. **How successful is the writing—in context?** Does the writer achieve his or her goals while respecting the needs of the reader and the conventions of the discipline or situation? Are there particular considerations that cause the writer to break the "rules of good writing"? Why?

7. **What can you learn about writing?** What does this writer teach you about using words, writing sentences, developing paragraphs? Are there any techniques you can use in future assignments?

e-writing

Exploring Reading Online

The Web offers extensive opportunities to read a variety of articles and documents in a range of professions and disciplines and from different organizations.

1. Using InfoTrac College Edition (available through your English CourseMate at **www.cengagebrain.com**) or one of your library's databases, enter a search for the term *critical reading* to access current articles about the reading process.
2. Become familiar with library databases to locate reading material that can assist you not only in composition but also in all your college courses.

E-Sources

York University Counselling and Development Centre: Reading Skills for University
> **http://www.yorku.ca/cdc/lsp/skillbuilding/reading.html**

Study Guides and Strategies
> **http://www.studygs.net/**

Dartmouth Academic Skills Center: Reading Your Textbooks Effectively and Efficiently
> **http://www.dartmouth.edu/~acskills/success/reading.html**

 Access the English CourseMate for this text at **www.cengagebrain.com** for further information about critical reading.

Description

Presenting Impressions

What Is Description?

Description captures impressions of persons, places, objects, or ideas. It records what we see, hear, feel, taste, and smell. Description is probably the most basic task that writers encounter. Whether you are writing a short story or a sales proposal, your success depends on your ability to effectively share impressions. Good description not only provides information but brings subjects to life through sensory details. Almost all writing requires a skilled use of description. Before you can narrate events, establish a cause-and-effect relationship, or develop a persuasive argument, you must provide readers with a clear picture of your subject. Dramatists open plays with set descriptions. Homicide detectives begin reports with descriptions of the crime scene. Before proposing an airport expansion, the writers of a government study must first describe congestion in the existing facility.

The way writers select and present details depends on context, particularly their purpose and the needs of their readers.

Objective and Subjective Description

There are two basic types of description. **Objective description** attempts to create an accurate, factual record, free of personal interpretation or bias. In contrast, **subjective description** emphasizes a writer's personal reactions, opinions, and values.

Objective Description

Objective description focuses on facts and observable details. Textbooks, newspaper articles, business reports, and professional journals include objective description. Although objective description may avoid highly charged emotional appeals or creative imagery, it is not necessarily lifeless. Objective description is effective when the writer's purpose is to present readers with information required to make an evaluation or decision. In many instances objective description does not attempt to arouse interest or attract attention, because it is often written in response to reader demand. *The New Illustrated Columbia Encyclopedia*, for example, includes this description of Chicago:

> The third largest city in the country and the heart of a metropolitan area of almost 7 million people, it is the commercial, financial, industrial, and cultural center for a vast region and a great midcontinental shipping port. It is a port of entry; a major Great Lakes port, located at the junction of the St. Lawrence Seaway with the Mississippi River system; the busiest air center in the country; and an important rail and highway hub.

- Objective description is best suited for providing reference material for a diverse audience seeking reliable, factual information.

- Objective description avoids figurative language that is subject to interpretation. A personal essay or real-estate brochure might describe a home as being a "snug cottage" or "stylish condo." But an insurance underwriter would demand specific facts about its location, size, and construction.

- If you are writing as an employee or agent of others, objective description allows you to avoid personalizing a document that must express the views of others.

- Objective description is useful when you are writing to a critical or hostile audience that may demand explanations or justifications of subjective characterizations.

- Objective description is effective when the evidence you are presenting is compelling and dramatic. A description of a plane crash or a famine can be totally factual yet emotionally wrenching to readers. Objective description can be powerful and influential.

Subjective Description

In contrast to objective description, subjective description creates impressions through sensory details and imagery. Short stories, novels, personal essays, advertising copy, memoirs, and editorials use highly personal sensory details and responses to create an individual's sense of the subject. The writer's perceptual world guides the writing. Instead of photographic realism, subjective description paints scenes, creates moods, or generates emotional responses. Providing accurate information is less important than giving readers a feel for the subject. In a subjective description of a car, the color, shape, ride, and memories it evokes for the owner are more important than facts about horsepower, resale value, and fuel efficiency.

Attempting to capture his view of Chicago, John Rechy gives the city a personality, comparing it to an expectant mother:

> You get the impression that once Chicago was like a constantly pregnant woman, uneasy in her pregnancy because she has miscarried so often. After its rise as a frontier town, plush bigtime madams, adventurers, and soon the titanic rise of the millionaires, the city's subsequent soaring population—all gave more than a hint that Chicago might easily become America's First City. But that title went unquestionably to New York. Brazenly, its skyscrapers, twice as tall as any in the Midwest city, symbolically invaded the sky. Chicago, in squat self-consciousness, bowed out. It became the Second City.

Rechy uses imagery and unconventional syntax to create a highly personalized view of the city. In the context of his essay, written for a literary magazine, impression is more important than accuracy. Dates and statistics are irrelevant to his purpose. The goal in subjective description is to share a vision, not provide information.

- Subjective description emphasizes the writer's personal impressions rather than accurate reporting. It is best suited for writers who are acting independently, giving readers their personal insights.

- Subjective description relies heavily on the writer's selection and presentation of details. The choice of words and their connotations is critical in achieving the writer's goal.

- Subjective description is widely used when the goal is to entertain and persuade readers rather than to provide information. Humorists, columnists, political commentators, essayists, and advertising copywriters use subjective writing to shape readers' opinions of their subject.

Blended Description

Most description is not purely objective or subjective. Many writers blend subjective elements into objective reporting. Even when trying to be neutral and unbiased, reporters and historians generally cannot avoid being influenced by their personal values and attitudes. Popular nonfiction writers include subjective touches to humanize their writing and enhance the appeal of their work. Best-selling biographers, for instance, frequently employ subjective details to make remote historical figures and events more contemporary and more accessible to readers.

In his description of Chicago's State Street, Russell Miller blends elements of objective realism and subjective impressions to create a striking portrait:

> Summer 1983. State Street, "that great street," is a dirty, desolate, and depressing street for most of its length. It runs straight and potholed from the Chicago city line, up through the black ghettos of the South Side, an aching wasteland of derelict factories pitted with broken windows, instant slum apartment blocks, vandalized playgrounds encased in chain-link fencing, and vacant lots where weeds sprout gamely from the rubble and the rusting hulks of abandoned automobiles. Those shops that remain open are protected by barricades of steel mesh. One or two men occupy every doorway, staring sullenly onto the street, heedless of the taunting cluster of skyscrapers to the north.

In this description, objective details such as "vandalized playgrounds" are interwoven with expressions granting human emotions to inanimate objects so that wastelands are "aching" and skyscrapers "taunting." Blended descriptions such as this one are useful in strengthening subjective accounts with factual details.

- Blended descriptions are found in newsmagazines, literary criticism, and most nonfiction books. The degree and intensity of subjective elements depend on the context and may have to conform to stylistic guidelines established by editors.

- If you are writing as the agent of others or part of a larger organization, examine the use of subjective words carefully. Avoid connotations and characterizations that may offend or displease those you represent. Peer review can help you determine whether you have achieved the right blend of objective and subjective description.

Dominant Impressions

Whether their goal is to produce an objective, subjective, or blended description, writers generally strive to create a **dominant impression** that expresses their thesis or main point. A good description is not a collection of random facts or a list of everything you can remember about a subject, but a focused, organized presentation of key details that gives readers a specific, clear understanding or feeling.

The description of a room, for instance, can concentrate on one detail:

> Although I live three hundred miles from the ocean, my apartment has a seagoing motif. Beneath a sweeping seascape, a large antique aquarium dominates the living room, its colorful tropical fish flashing among rocks and shells I brought back from Florida. Miniature schooners, windjammers, and ketches line the windowsill. The ornate glass cabinet intended for china houses my collection of Hawaiian seashells.

By highlighting a single distinctive feature, the student creates a more memorable description of her apartment than one that lists all of its contents.

The Language of Description

Diction—the choice of words—is important in all writing, but it has a special role in description. Whether your description is objective, subjective, or a blend, the words you select should be accurate, appropriate, and effective. In choosing words, consider your purpose, readers, and discipline. *Review Chapter 10 to make sure that you have used words accurately and have been particularly sensitive to their connotations.*

WRITING ACTIVITY

Select sample descriptions from a variety of sources—readings from this chapter, other textbooks, magazine articles, brochures, mail-order catalogs, and newspaper advertisements—and review their use of objective and subjective details.

1. Can you detect subjective description in newsmagazines such as *Time or Newsweek?* Is there a difference between the news stories and personal essays and political commentary pieces?

2. Do you observe different blends of subjective elements in online sources such as CNN, Salon, TMZ, and The Huffington Post?

3. Circle the subjective details used in ads that describe products.

4. Can you detect subjective description in any of your textbooks?

5. How does the writer's stance affect the blend of objective and subjective elements?

6. What details and words do writers use to create dominant impressions? Do they serve as thesis statements?

WRITING ACTIVITIES

1. Read the following pair of descriptions of a village:

    The Yucca tribe lives in dire poverty. Their homes consist of rude shacks clustered around a rotting wooden platform that serves as a stage for primitive rituals. The village has no paved streets, no electricity, no running water. They subsist on fish and roots they dig from the ground with crude sticks. The village women spend their days fashioning coarse garments from tree bark and leaves. Their children wander aimlessly about the village without supervision. Their chief, an illiterate old man, resents the intrusion of outsiders who threaten his hold over his people.

    The Yucca tribe lives simply. Their homes consist of small cottages grouped around an altar that serves as the center of their religious worship. The village has no crime, pollution, or violence. They live on natural fish and vegetables they harvest using the tools of their ancestors. Their children play freely with no fear of traffic or molestation. Their chief, steeped in tradition, resents the intrusion of outsiders who threaten to erode their culture.

    - How do these passages differ? How does word choice affect your impression of the village and its inhabitants?
    - What do word choices reveal about the attitudes and values of the writer?
    - Do you consider these objective, subjective, or blended descriptions?

2. Review a number of advertisements in women's magazines. What words and images are used to sell products to women? Would these connotations appeal to men?

3. Consider words used by advocates on both sides of a controversial issue—abortion, capital punishment, affirmative action, or sexual harassment. Can you draw parallel lists of words and phrases that reflect the views of opposing groups? Why, for instance, do both pro-life and pro-choice groups talk about "rights"?

4. Analyze several popular television commercials. What connotations are used? Do they have any logical connection to the products or services being sold?

Strategies for Writing Description: Prewriting and Planning

Critical Thinking and Prewriting

1. **Use brainstorming and lists to generate possible topics.** Choose subjects you are familiar with—people you know, places you have visited, items you work with.
    - You may find it easier to write about a person you met once than a close friend, or a city you toured on vacation rather than your hometown. Sometimes a subject may have so many memories and complex associations that it is difficult to develop a clear focus for a short paper.

2. **Narrow your list of possible topics and generate details.** Use clustering and freewriting to develop details about your subject.

3. **Use senses other than sight.** Most writers immediately think of description as being visual. But descriptions can be enriched by including impressions of taste, touch, smell, and hearing.
   - Experiment by building a description based on nonvisual impressions. Describe your job or neighborhood, for instance, by sound rather than sight.

Planning

1. **Determine your purpose.** What is your goal—to entertain a general audience or provide information to colleagues, employees, your boss, or customers? What are the most important details needed to support your thesis?
   - Even if no formal thesis statement appears in the text, your description should have a controlling idea or focus. *Ask yourself what is the most important thing readers should know about your subject.*

2. **Define your role.** If you are expressing personal opinion or observations, you are free to add subjective details. You may include yourself in the description, referring to your actions and observations in the first person. If you are writing as a representative of others, however, an objective impersonal approach is more appropriate.

3. **Consider your reader.** Which type of description best suits your audience— subjective impressions or objective facts? What needs and expectations do your readers have? What details, facts, statistics, or observations will help them appreciate your topic and share your impression?

4. **Review the nature of the discourse community.** Determine whether you should use technical or specialized terminology. If you are writing within a profession, academic discipline, government agency, or corporation, use standard methods of presenting information, such as choosing an appropriate format.

5. **Select key details.** Having determined the context, choose points that will reflect your purpose and impress your readers, and follow any guidelines dictated by the assignment or discourse community. Descriptions should have focus.

6. **Organize details.** Good descriptions should be logically organized. You may arrange details spatially by describing a house room by room or a city neighborhood by neighborhood. You can present ideas in the order of their importance. If your essay includes both objective and subjective description, these can be blended or placed in separate paragraphs.
   - Use modes like comparison and contrast, narration, or process to organize details.

Strategies for Writing Description: Writing the First Draft

Writing the First Draft

1. **Describe people and objects in action.** Descriptions of people and objects can become stilted lists of facts. You can bring your subject to life by introducing short narratives or showing people in action. In writing description, follow the creative writer's advice to *show*, not *tell.*

Original

Mr. Bryant was the best boss I ever worked for. He supervised the payroll office. He was smart, generous, and patient. He knew the payroll office like the back of his hand. He had a fantastic eye for detail and a great memory. He appeared to have memorized the most complicated IRS regulations and could master any new accounting software in less than an hour. He was a great teacher and trainer. He was always available if anyone in the office had problems with a complex situation. He had excellent communications skills. I never saw him lose his temper no matter how mad employees got when the company made mistakes on their paychecks. He would simply and calmly explain policies and do his best to rectify any errors. He always gave his staff and the employees more than anyone expected. People came away from payroll usually wishing the rest of the company could be run the same way.

Improved

The payroll office came alive the moment Al Bryant stormed in, usually bearing a carton of donuts and a bag of carrot sticks for his employees. Unlike the other supervisors, he rarely used his private office but spent his day roving past our cubicles, answering our questions, showing us shortcuts, and tackling problems we couldn't figure out. Highly patient, he never lost his temper when an employee banged at the door, waving an incorrect check. Instead, he offered the employee a donut and grabbed the nearest computer. He punched in data like a speed typist while juggling a telephone receiver, checking pay schedules, consulting IRS guidelines, and asking the employee about his or her family. He worked with the precision of a surgeon and the speed of a race car driver, bobbing and weaving behind the computer as he sliced through a week of paperwork. Glancing at the clock, he would start to hum, going into overdrive, making it his personal mission to cut a new paycheck before the employee's break was over.

2. **Use dialogue to add action to descriptions involving people.** Allowing people to speak for themselves is more interesting and effective than simply describing their comments.

3. **Avoid unnecessary detail or static descriptions.** Avoid writing descriptions that are cluttered with unimportant facts like dates and addresses or place unnecessary emphasis on organizational arrangements:

On the left-hand wall is a bookcase. *To the right of the bookcase* is a stereo. *Around the corner of* the stereo stands an antique aquarium with tropical fish. *Above the aquarium* is a large seascape painting. Model ships line the windowsill. A cabinet *to the right of the window* is filled with seashells.

4. **Keep the length of your paper in mind as you write the first draft.** If you are writing a 500-word essay describing your hometown and discover that by the second page you have covered only two of a dozen items on your outline, you may wish to review your plan.
   - Revise your outline, expanding or limiting your topic. It is better to describe a single New York neighborhood in detail than to attempt to create an impression of the entire city that becomes only a bland list of generalities.

Strategies for Writing Description: Revising and Editing

Revising

1. **Review your plan and read your draft, focusing on its overall impact.**
   - Does it capture the true essence of your topic?
   - Is the draft too general, too vague? Should the topic be narrowed?
   - Does the paper generate interest by telling a story, highlighting details that would otherwise be overlooked, or does it read like a shopping list of facts?
2. **Examine the information you have included.**
   - Are there minor details that should be deleted?
   - Can the description be improved by adding essential or interesting details that you overlooked in the first draft?
   - Did you include impressions from senses other than sight?
3. **Does the paper create a dominant impression?**
   - Does your paper have a clear focus? Can you state a thesis?
   - Can ideas be rearranged to add emphasis, suspense, or interest?
4. **Is the description clearly organized?**
   - Does the paper's opening arouse interest?
   - Are details logically arranged? Do you use other modes to tell a story, create a pattern, or establish contrasts?
   - Does the paper end with a strong image, thought, or question that will leave a lasting impression on readers?
5. **Does your paper maintain a consistent point of view?** Avoid shifting from third to first person.
   - Determine whether you should change your role in the description. Would it be better stated from an objective or subjective viewpoint? Should you appear in the essay?
6. **Can you add action and dialogue to enliven the description?**

(Continued)

7. **Can you blend other modes into the description to make it more interesting or easier to follow?**
   - Could the description be revised by adding narrative elements to tell a story?
   - Would comparison and contrast or cause and effect help present the details?
8. **If possible, use peer review to gain an additional perspective.**
   - Ask a friend or fellow student to read your draft. Ask your readers whether your paper creates a vivid picture of your subject. Ask what elements could be added to make the essay more effective.

Editing and Proofreading

1. **Read the paper aloud.** Listen to your sentences.
   - Are there awkward or repetitive phrases that could be revised or deleted?
   - Are the sentences varied in length and complexity, or do they fall into a redundant, humdrum pattern?
2. **Examine your choice of words.**
   - Is your diction fresh and inventive or bland and general?
   - Do you use specific words?
   - Can clichés be replaced with original statements?
   - Do you use words accurately?
   - Do your connotations create the impressions you intend?
3. **Use a dictionary and thesaurus to examine word choice.**

STUDENT PAPER

This descriptive paper was written in response to the following assignment in a composition course:

> Briefly describe a current social or technological trend that is changing the way we live. Document the use of outside sources.

FIRST DRAFT WITH INSTRUCTOR'S COMMENTS

better title?
Using the Web to Build a Career

run-on   *Vague*
All over the country people are unemployed and new graduates cannot get jobs in the field

they want to enter. It is easy to get discouraged. After a year of looking for work, people

(Continued)

are afraid of their skills eroding or being so out of touch, that when the economy does turn

wordy

around and jobs come back that employers will look at these people and not consider them.

A lot of these people are using the Internet to not just look for jobs or post their résumés

Who?/slang

but demonstrate their skills online. A guy on TV last week said people are becoming blog-

sp

gers to stay current and build a network in there field. One guy was an unemployed quality

control engineer from GM. He used Facebook to connect with other quality control experts.

He created a blog, linking to current articles, and discussing technical problems. He got a

discourse going with other engineers, posting pictures and videos. He made up YouTube

awkward   *sp*

lectures that small companies used in training. Basically, he became like a free consulstant

slang

and the go-to guy in his field. He had factories in India and Canada asking for his advice. He

picked up a few consulting jobs. But the main thing when a job came up, he a lot more than a

résumé to show people what he could do.

which article?   *exact quote?*

People right out of college, an article online said, should retool their social networking

profile to create a credible professional package that demonstrates skills and abilities. In

wordy

looking for jobs, people right out of school should like continue to do research and build a

website that is like an ongoing class project showing their practical knowledge in their field.

They should cut and paste facts and become a source they email to people. In a way they

give away some of what they learned for free. A finance major, for example, did a whole

informal

website on how to invest for retirement and got 10,000 hits and then got a bunch of attor-

neys and accountants to contribute and link to her site. So when she interviewed for a job at

comma?

a bank/she didn't just have a résumé but thousands of potential customers.

(Continued)

People always complained you can't get a job without experience and you can't get

sp

<u>expeirence</u> without a job. But now people are using the Internet to build what people call

good word

<u>shadow jobs.</u> If you can't fix cars, sell insurance, plan weddings, or run a <u>restuarant</u> like you   *sp*

want for real to make money, you do it online to show off your skills, build a network, and

get experience you need to be an asset in a tough job market.

REVISION NOTES

You have identified an important and interesting topic and provide specific details. Your description needs to be refined through revision and editing:

* Document the outside sources you refer to. Make sure exact quotes are placed in quotation marks.
* Revise the introduction to be more direct and precise.
* Delete wordy phrases such as "look at these people and not consider them."
* Edit for spelling and run-ons.
*Delete informal and slang phrases unsuited for a college paper.

REVISED DRAFT

Hector Ruiz   September 15, 2011
English 201-038

Casting a Cyber Shadow

Job seekers have been using the Internet to locate jobs and email résumés for twenty years. Today, downsized executives and new graduates are using the Web to create a shadow career, a kind of virtual internship to demonstrate their skills, gain experience, and build a presence online they can sell to employers. When job searches during a recession can take years, professionals worry about losing skills, becoming out of touch, and appearing stale to employers. New graduates, unable to find entry level positions, fear being trapped in marginal jobs and losing out to the next graduating class. Without relevant experience, the class of '11 is less attractive than brand new graduates, untainted by a minimum wage track record.

Speaking last week on the *Today Show,* Brad Manning, a New York career consultant, pointed out that a lot of job seekers are creating "shadow careers" online. Instead of just posting their résumés on Facebook, they are demonstrating their skills online by blogging

(Continued)

about issues, posting videos, answering questions, proposing ideas, and often providing free consultation services. A quality control engineer laid off after fifteen years at General Motors created his own technical journal, posting pictures, articles, and videos about quality control issues. Factories in India and Canada began using his videos to train new employees. In applying for jobs, he could prove that he was an expert in his field and that his skills had not eroded.

New college graduates who cannot find jobs in their careers now use social networking sites and blogs to create their own shadow jobs, creating an imaginary internship in which they demonstrate their skills. "After graduation," Nancy Pearlman suggests, "it's time to clear your Facebook page of spring break photos and create a credible professional package that demonstrates your skills and abilities." She points out that a finance major who ended up working in retail sales to pay her rent created a website on investing for retirement. By taking her academic knowledge and putting it in plain language, she attracted over ten thousand hits. She answered questions and began a running discourse with attorneys and accountants, who contributed articles to her site. When she interviewed for a job at a bank, she did not arrive with just a résumé but a list of a two hundred potential clients and a proven ability to handle day-to-day problems. Pearlman, who teaches online networking, reminds students to make their websites polished and professional. "They can't be a scrapbook of cut and paste articles and blogger-ese," she notes, "but clearly unified, credible, formal presentations that resemble corporate websites."

Shadow careers sometimes turn into consulting businesses with their creators abandoning the job search to form their own companies. In most cases, however, these websites allow job seekers to actually work in their fields, link with professionals, demonstrate an ability to solve problems, gather information, and connect with potential customers. In a competitive job market employers want recent "real world" experience. The down-sized executive or college graduate waiting tables has to bring more to an interview than a résumé or a two-year-old degree to stand out. A well packaged blog can overshadow months of unemployment or unrelated entry level work to make an applicant the talented, proven professional organizations need in a challenging marketplace.

Works Cited

Manning, Brad. Interview with Matt Lauer. *The Today Show*. NBC. WNBC, New York. 28 Jan. 2011. Television.

Pearlman, Nancy. "Putting Facebook to Work." *Career News*. Career News, 21 May 2011. Web. 15 Sep. 2011.

QUESTIONS FOR REVIEW AND REVISION

1. How interesting do you find this essay? How successfully did the student describe his subject?

2. Can you describe a "shadow career" in your own words?

3. What is the student's goal in this essay? What does he want readers to know?

4. How effective is the ending? Does it sum up the point of the essay?

5. Descriptions do not always have an identifiable thesis statement. How would you state the student's thesis?

6. Where did the student use other modes, such as comparison or example, to build his description? Why are they important?

7. Did the student follow the instructor's comments? Could you suggest other improvements?

8. Did the student document the paper properly? (See pages 554–563.)

9. Read the paper aloud. Are there any sentences that could be revised for clarity?

WRITING SUGGESTIONS

1. Write a description of a social or technological trend you are familiar with. How has texting changed the way people communicate? Do you observe new types of friendships or communities emerging from social networking?

2. *Collaborative writing:* Discuss this essay with a group of students. Have each member volunteer opinions on its strengths and weaknesses. Do members suggest revisions or a need for added detail?

Suggested Topics for Writing Description

General Assignments

Write a description of any of the following topics. Your description may include other modes. Determine whether your description should rely on objective observations and factual detail or subjective impressions. When you select words to describe your topic, be conscious of their connotations. Above all, keep in mind what you are trying to share with your reader.

- Your first apartment
- The people who gather in a place you frequent—a coffee shop, store, nightclub, library, or student union
- Your best or worst boss or professor
- The most desirable or least desirable place to live in your community
- The most dangerous situation you have faced
- The worst day you have had in recent memory
- The type of man or woman you find attractive
- The most serious environmental problem in your region
- The best or worst party you have attended
- Holiday shopping at the mall
- Starting a new job

- Cramming for final exams
- Completing the chore you hate the most
- The most serious problem you face today
- Student attitudes about a specific subject: terrorism, racism, crime, jobs, television
- Violence in America

Writing in Context

1. Imagine that your college has asked you to write a description of the campus for a brochure designed to recruit students. Write a three- or four-paragraph description that is easy to read and creates a favorable impression. Consider what would appeal to high school seniors or adults returning to school.

2. Assume you are writing a column for an alternative student newspaper. Develop a short, satiric, or sarcastic description of the campus, the administration, or the student body. Draw witty comparisons to create humor and use inventive word choices.

3. Write an open letter to the graduating class of your high school describing college life. You may wish to compare college to high school to prepare students for the problems and challenges they will encounter.

4. Imagine you are trying to sell your car. Write two short ads, one designed for a campus flyer and the other for a newspaper.

Strategies for Reading Description

As you read the descriptions in this chapter, keep these questions in mind:

Context

1. **What is the author's goal—to inform, enlighten, share personal observations, or provide information demanded by others?** What is the writer's role? Is he or she writing from a personal or professional stance?

2. **What is the intended audience—general or specific readers?** How much knowledge does the author assume readers have? Are technical terms defined? Does the description appear to have a special focus?

3. **What is the nature of the discourse community?** What does the source of the document—newsmagazine, corporation, personal essay, or book—reveal about the context?

(Continued)

Strategy

1. **What details does the writer select?** Does he or she appear to be deliberately emphasizing some items while ignoring or minimizing others?
2. **Does the description establish a dominant impression?** What method does the writer use to create it?
3. **How much of the description is objective and how much is subjective?**
4. **How does the author organize details?** Is there any particular method of grouping observations?
5. **Does the writer include sensory impressions other than visual details?**

Language

1. **What level of language does the writer use?** Are technical terms explained?
2. **What role do connotations have in shaping the description?** How do they support the writer's goal?

READING TO LEARN

As you read the descriptions in this chapter, note techniques you can use in your own writing.

- **"The Bomb" by Lansing Lamont** blends objective and subjective details about the world's first atomic bomb, bringing a metallic object to life by describing it as a "bloated black squid" with "guts" and a "heart."

- **"Out There" by Truman Capote** creates a dominant impression about the lonesome isolation of a Kansas town that is so small the streets have no names.

- **"Border Story" by Luis Alberto Urrea** describes both the US–Mexican border and the illegals trying to cross it. By using the word "you" to describe the illegals, he puts his readers in their place.

- **"American Islam" by Paul M. Barrett** uses example, narration, and comparison to build a factual description of Muslims in America that dispels common misconceptions.

- **The job announcement by Bayou Printing** selects key words to describe both the company and the ideal candidate it seeks.

Lansing Lamont was born in New York City and was educated at Harvard College and the Columbia School of Journalism. He was a national political correspondent for *Time* magazine from 1961 to 1968. He became deputy chief of *Time*'s London bureau and later served as the magazine's Ottawa bureau chief. His best-selling book *Day of Trinity* (1965) told the story behind the development of the atom bomb during World War II. His second book *Campus Shock* (1979) examined American college life in the 1970s.

The Bomb

Source: "The Bomb" from *Day of Trinity* by Lansing Lamont, pp. 11–12. Copyright © 1985 by Lansing Lamont. By permission.

In this section from Day of Trinity *Lamont describes the first atomic bomb before its detonation in the New Mexico desert in July 1945. Note how Lamont includes both objective facts and subjective impressions of the bomb.*

1 The bomb rested in its cradle.

2   It <u>slept</u> upon a steel-supported oakwood platform, inside a sheet-metal shack 103 feet above the ground: a <u>bloated black squid girdled with cables and leechlike</u> <u>detonators</u>, each tamped with enough explosive to spark simultaneously, within a millionth of a second, the final conflagration. <u>Tentacles</u> emerged from the <u>squid</u> in a harness of wires connecting the detonators to a shiny aluminum tank, the firing unit.

subjective animal imagery

3   Stripped of its coils, the bomb weighed 10,000 pounds. Its teardrop dimensions were 4½ feet wide, 10½ feet long. Its guts contained two layers of wedge-shaped high-explosive blocks surrounding an inner core of precisely machined nuclear ingots that lay, as one scientist described them, like diamonds in an immense wad of cotton. These ingots were made from a metal called plutonium.

objective facts

4   At the <u>heart</u> of the bomb, buried inside the layers of explosive and plutonium, lay the ultimate key to its success or failure, a metallic sphere no bigger than a ping-pong ball that even twenty years later would still be regarded a state secret: the initiator.

5   Within five seconds the initiator would trigger the sequence that hundreds of shadows had gathered to watch that dawn. The bomb would either fizzle to a premature death or shatteringly christen a new era on earth.

6   Weeks, months, years of toil had gone into it.

7   The nation's finest brains and leadership, the cream of its scientific and engineering force, plus two billion dollars from the taxpayers, had built the squat monster on the tower for this very moment. Yet it had been no labor of love. There was not the mildest affection for it.

8   Other instruments of war bore dashing or maidenly names: Britain's "Spitfires"; the "Flying Tigers"; the "Gravel Gerties" and "Gypsy Rose Lees" that clanked across North Africa or blitzed bridgeheads on the Rhine; even the Germans' "Big Bertha" of World War I; and, soon, the Superfortress "Enola Gay" of Hiroshima, deliverer of an atomic bundle called "Little Boy."

9   The test bomb had no colorful nickname. One day its spawn would be known as "Fat Man" (after Churchill). But now its identity was cloaked in a welter of impersonal

terms: "the thing," "the beast," "the device," and its Washington pseudonym, "S-1." The scientists, most of whom called it simply "the gadget," had handled it gently and daintily, like the baby it was—but out of respect, not fondness. One wrong jolt of the volatile melon inside its Duralumin frame could precipitate the collision of radioactive masses and a slow, agonizing death from radiation. Or instant vaporization.

use of witness 10   The <u>monster</u> engendered the sort of fear that had caused one young scientist to
quotation   break down the evening before and be escorted promptly from the site to a psychiatric ward; and another, far older and wiser, a Nobel Prize winner, to murmur, as he waited in his trench, "I'm scared witless, absolutely witless."

UNDERSTANDING CONTEXT

1. What dominant impression does Lamont make?
2. How did the scientists feel about the bomb they created?
3. What impact does the final quotation have?
4. *Critical thinking:* Lamont notes that, unlike other weapons of WWII, the bomb was not given a colorful nickname. What does this imply? How does it set this weapon apart from the others that bore heroic or even whimsical names?

EVALUATING STRATEGY

1. How does Lamont blend objective details and subjective impressions?
2. How does Lamont demonstrate how the scientists felt about the weapon?

APPRECIATING LANGUAGE

1. What words create Lamont's dominant impression?
2. What role does animal imagery play in the description? How does it make the bomb appear as a "monster"?

WRITING SUGGESTIONS

1. Write a short description of an object like a car, house, or computer, and use subjective impressions to bring it to life by comparing it to a person or animal. You might describe an old car as a "beast" or a guitar as a "best friend."
2. *Collaborative writing:* Work with a group of students and write a short essay describing the threat of nuclear terrorism. What would happen if terrorists were able to place a nuclear weapon in a large American city? How would the nation and the public respond to a sudden, unexpected explosion that claimed a hundred thousand lives?

Truman Capote (1924–1985) was born in New Orleans and first gained prominence as a writer of short stories. At the age of twenty-four he produced his first novel, *Other Voices, Other Rooms,* which achieved international attention. His other works include *Breakfast at Tiffany's* and *A Tree of Night.* In 1965 he published *In Cold Blood,* which became an immediate best seller. Based on extensive research and interviews, *In Cold Blood* tells the story of a 1959 mass murder of a Kansas farm family and the fate of the killers. Although nonfiction, Capote's book reads much like a novel. *In Cold Blood* helped shape a new school of journalism that uses the stylistic touches of fiction to relate actual events.

Out There

Source: From *In Cold Blood* by Truman Capote. Copyright © 1965 by Truman Capote and renewed 1993 by Alan U. Schwartz. By permission.

The opening pages of In Cold Blood *describe the small town of Holcomb, Kansas, where the murders occurred. Capote spent a great deal of time in Holcomb and describes it almost as if it had been his own hometown. Notice how Capote blends objective facts with subjective impressions.*

1 The village of Holcomb stands on the high wheat plains of western Kansas, a lonesome area that other Kansans call "out there." Some seventy miles east of the Colorado border, the countryside, with its hard blue skies and desert-clear air, has an atmosphere that is rather more Far Western than Middle West. The local accent is barbed with a prairie twang, a ranch-hand nasalness, and the men, many of them, wear narrow frontier trousers, Stetsons, and high-heeled boots with pointed toes. The land is flat, and the views are awesomely extensive; horses, herds of cattle, a white cluster of grain elevators rising as gracefully as Greek temples are visible long before a traveler reaches them.

2 Holcomb, too, can be seen from great distances. Not that there is much to see—simply an aimless congregation of buildings divided in the center by the main-line tracks of the Santa Fe Railroad, a haphazard hamlet bounded on the south by a brown stretch of the Arkansas (pronounced "Arkan-sas") River, on the north by a highway, Route 50, and on the east and west by prairie lands and wheat fields. After rain, or when snowfalls thaw, the streets, unnamed, unshaded, unpaved, turn from the thickest dust into the direst mud. At one end of the town stands a stark old stucco structure, the roof of which supports an electric sign—Dance—but the dancing has ceased and the advertisement has been dark for several years. Nearby is another building with an irrelevant sign, this one in flaking gold on a dirty window—Holcomb Bank. The bank closed in 1933, and its former counting rooms have been converted into apartments. It is one of the town's two "apartment houses," the second being a ramshackle mansion known, because a good part of the local school's faculty lives there, as the Teacherage. But the majority of Holcomb's homes are one-story frame affairs, with front porches.

3 Down by the depot, the postmistress, a gaunt woman who wears a rawhide jacket and denims and cowboy boots, presides over a falling-apart post office. The depot

itself, with its peeling sulphur-colored paint, is equally melancholy; the Chief, the Super Chief, the El Capitan go by every day, but these celebrated expresses never pause there. No passenger trains do—only an occasional freight. Up on the highway, there are two filling stations, one of which doubles as a meagerly supplied grocery store, while the other does extra duty as a café—Hartman's Café, where Mrs. Hartman, the proprietress, dispenses sandwiches, coffee, soft drinks, and 3.2 beer. (Holcomb, like all the rest of Kansas, is "dry.")

4   And that, really, is all. Unless you include, as one must, the Holcomb School, a good-looking establishment, which reveals a circumstance that the appearance of the community otherwise camouflages: that the parents who send their children to this modern and ably staffed "consolidated" school—the grades go from kindergarten through senior high, and a fleet of buses transport the students, of which there are usually around three hundred and sixty, from as far as sixteen miles away—are, in general, a prosperous people. Farm ranchers, most of them, they are outdoor folk of very varied stock—German, Irish, Norwegian, Mexican, Japanese. They raise cattle and sheep, grow wheat, milo, grass seed, and sugar beets. Farming is always a chancy business, but in western Kansas its practitioners consider themselves "born gamblers," for they must contend with an extremely shallow precipitation (the annual average is eighteen inches) and anguishing irrigation problems. However, the last seven years have been years of droughtless beneficence. The farm ranchers in Finney County, of which Holcomb is a part, have done well; money has been made not from farming alone but also from the exploitation of plentiful natural-gas resources, and its acquisition is reflected in the new school, the comfortable interiors of the farmhouses, the steep and swollen grain elevators.

5   Until one morning in mid-November of 1959, few Americans—in fact, few Kansans—had ever heard of Holcomb. Like the waters of the river, like the motorists on the highway, and like the yellow trains streaking down the Santa Fe tracks, drama, in the shape of exceptional happenings, had never stopped there. The inhabitants of the village, numbering two hundred and seventy, were satisfied that this should be so, quite content to exist inside ordinary life—to work, to hunt, to watch television, to attend school socials, choir practice, meetings of the 4-H Club. But then, in the earliest hours of that morning in November, a Sunday morning, certain foreign sounds impinged on the normal nightly Holcomb noises—on the keening hysteria of coyotes, the dry scrape of scuttling tumbleweed, the racing, receding wail of locomotive whistles. At the time not a soul in sleeping Holcomb heard them—four shotgun blasts that, all told, ended six human lives. But afterward the townspeople, theretofore sufficiently unfearful of each other to seldom trouble to lock their doors, found fantasy re-creating them over and again—those somber explosions that stimulated fires of mistrust in the glare of which many old neighbors viewed each other strangely, and as strangers.

UNDERSTANDING CONTEXT

1. How much of Capote's description can be considered objective, how much subjective?
2. Capote includes a great deal of factual detail—the name of a highway, the number of students in the high school, and Holcomb's population. Why are these facts important in establishing an impression of the town?
3. What does Capote attempt to capture about this town?

EVALUATING STRATEGY

1. *Critical thinking:* A key element in the opening of any book is to get people's attention and motivate them to continue reading. How does Capote generate interest by describing a nondescript town?
2. What is the impact of the closing lines?

APPRECIATING LANGUAGE

1. How does the language of Capote's description differ from that of an encyclopedia or newspaper article?
2. *In Cold Blood* has sold millions of copies. What elements in Capote's style make his story about a crime in a small Kansas town so popular? What phrases strike you as being colorful or interesting?

WRITING SUGGESTIONS

1. Rewrite a recent article from the local newspaper, adding subjective details to arouse human interest for a national audience. Include observations about your community to give readers a feel for the location.
2. Using Capote's description as a resource, write a purely objective one-paragraph description of Holcomb, Kansas.
3. Write a one-line thesis statement for "Out There."

Luis Alberto Urrea

Luis Alberto Urrea was born in Tijuana to a Mexican father and American mother. He grew up in San Diego and attended the University of California. After graduation and a brief career as a movie extra, Urrea worked with a volunteer organization that provides food, clothing, and medical supplies to the poor of northern Mexico. In 1982 he taught writing at Harvard. His most recent novel, *Into the Beautiful North,* was published in 2010.

Border Story

Source: From *Across the Wire: Life and Hard Times on the Mexican Border* by Luis Alberto Urrea, copyright © 1993 by Luis Alberto Urrea. Photographs © 1993 by John Lueders-Booth. By permission.

In this description of the Mexican–American border from Across the Wire: Life and Hard Times on the Mexican Border *(1993), Urrea uses the device of second person to place his reader in the scene. By making "you" the "illegal," he seeks to dramatize and humanize the plight of the poor seeking a new life in the United States.*

1 At night, the Border Patrol helicopters swoop and churn in the air all along the line. You can sit in the Mexican hills and watch them herd humans on the dusty slopes across the valley. They look like science fiction crafts, their hard-focused lights raking the ground as they fly.

2 Borderlands locals are so jaded by the sight of nightly people-hunting that it doesn't even register in their minds. But take a stranger to the border, and she will *see* the spectacle: monstrous Dodge trucks speeding into and out of the landscape; uniformed men patrolling with flashlights, guns, and dogs; spotlights; running figures; lines of people hurried onto buses by armed guards; and the endless clatter of the helicopters with their harsh white beams. A Dutch woman once told me it seemed altogether "un-American."

3 But the Mexicans keep on coming—and the Guatemalans, the Salvadorans, the Panamanians, the Colombians. The seven-mile stretch of Interstate 5 nearest the Mexican border is, at times, so congested with Latin American pedestrians that it resembles a town square.

4 They stick to the center island. Running down the length of the island is a cement wall. If the "illegals" (currently, "undocumented workers"; formerly, "wetbacks") are walking north and a Border Patrol vehicle happens along, they simply hop over the wall and trot south. The officer will have to drive up to the 805 interchange, or Dairy Mart Road, swing over the overpasses, then drive south. Depending on where this pursuit begins, his detour could entail five to ten miles of driving. When the officer finally reaches the group, they hop over the wall and trot north. Furthermore, because freeway arrests would endanger traffic, the Border Patrol has effectively thrown up its hands in surrender.

5 It seems jolly on the page. But imagine poverty, violence, natural disasters, or political fear driving you away from everything you know. Imagine how bad things get to make you leave behind your family, your friends, your lovers; your home, as humble as it might be; your church, say. Let's take it further—you've said good-bye to the graveyard, the dog, the goat, the mountains where you first hunted, your

grade school, your state, your favorite spot on the river where you fished and took time to think.

6   Then you come hundreds—or thousands—of miles across territory utterly unknown to you. (Chances are, you have never traveled farther than a hundred miles in your life.) You have walked, run, hidden in the backs of trucks, spent part of your precious money on bus fare. There is no AAA or Travelers Aid Society available to you. Various features of your journey north might include police corruption; violence in the forms of beatings, rape, murder, torture, road accidents; theft; incarceration. Additionally, you might experience loneliness, fear, exhaustion, sorrow, cold, heat, diarrhea, thirst, hunger. There is no medical attention available to you. There isn't even Kotex.

7   Weeks or months later, you arrive in Tijuana. Along with other immigrants, you gravitate to the bad parts of town because there is nowhere for you to go in the glittery sections where the *gringos* flock. You stay in a rundown little hotel in the red-light district, or behind the bus terminal. Or you find your way to the garbage dumps, where you throw together a small cardboard nest and claim a few feet of dirt for yourself. The garbage-pickers working this dump might allow you to squat, or they might come and rob you or burn you out for breaking some local rule you cannot possibly know beforehand. Sometimes the dump is controlled by a syndicate, and goon squads might come to you within a day. They want money, and if you can't pay, you must leave or suffer the consequences.

8   In town, you face endless victimization if you aren't streetwise. The police come after you, street thugs come after you, petty criminals come after you; strangers try your door at night as you sleep. Many shady men offer to guide you across the border, and each one wants all your money now, and promises to meet you at a prearranged spot. Some of your fellow travelers end their journeys right here—relieved of their savings and left to wait on a dark corner until they realize they are going nowhere.

9   If you are not Mexican, and can't pass as *tijuanense,* a local, the tough guys find you out. Salvadorans and Guatemalans are routinely beaten up and robbed. Sometimes they are disfigured. Indians—Chinantecas, Mixtecas, Guasaves, Zapotecas, Mayas—are insulted and pushed around; often they are lucky—they are merely ignored. They use this to their advantage. Often they don't dream of crossing into the United States: a Mexican tribal person would never be able to blend in, and they know it. To them, the garbage dumps and street vending and begging in Tijuana are a vast improvement over their former lives. As Doña Paula, a Chinanteca friend of mine who lives at the Tijuana garbage dump, told me, "This is the garbage dump. Take all you need. There's plenty here for *everyone!*"

10   If you are a woman, the men come after you. You lock yourself in your room, and when you must leave it to use the pestilential public bathroom at the end of your floor, you hurry, and you check every corner. Sometimes the lights are out in the toilet room. Sometimes men listen at the door. They call you "good-looking" and "bitch" and "*mamacita,*" and they make kissing sounds at you when you pass.

11   You're in the worst part of town, but you can comfort yourself—at least there are no death squads here. There are no torturers here, or bandit land barons riding into

your house. This is the last barrier, you think, between you and the United States—*los Yunaites Estaites.*

12   You still face police corruption, violence, jail. You now also have a wide variety of new options available to you: drugs, prostitution, white slavery, crime. Tijuana is not easy on newcomers. It is a city that has always thrived on taking advantage of a sucker. And the innocent are the ultimate suckers in the Borderlands.

UNDERSTANDING CONTEXT

1. Urrea has called the border a "battlefield." How does his description illustrate this view?
2. What problems do the undocumented aliens face in their attempt to cross the border?
3. How are non-Mexican refugees treated in Tijuana?
4. What is the plight of refugee women on the border?
5. *Critical thinking:* Urrea quotes a Dutch woman who used the term "un-American" to describe the border patrols. What is un-American about fences and helicopter patrols? Does this response to immigration clash with the Statue of Liberty's promise to welcome the tired and poor?

EVALUATING STRATEGY

1. How effective is the use of the second person? Does it really put you in the scene? Does it help dramatize the plight of people many readers might choose to ignore?
2. What details does Urrea use to dramatize conditions along the border?

APPRECIATING LANGUAGE

1. Throughout the description, Urrea uses lists—"beatings, rape, murder, torture, road accidents . . ." How effective are they? Can listing words become tedious?
2. Select the words that create the most powerful images of the border. Why do they make strong impressions?

WRITING SUGGESTIONS

1. Write an essay describing a place that highlights a social problem. Select a location you have personal knowledge of, and try to convey the conditions residents face through lists of details.
2. *Collaborative writing:* Ask a group of fellow students to respond to Urrea's account. Consider the issues his description of the border raises. Ask members to suggest how conditions could be improved, and then draft a short *persuasion* essay outlining your ideas.

CRITICAL ISSUES

© Corbis Premium RF/Alamy

Immigration crossing sign

Immigration

Immigration reform is perhaps the most important challenge facing America. How America resolves this challenge will not only determine what kind of country America will be, but whether or not America will remain a country at all.

Tom Tancredo

I reject the idea that America has used herself up in the effort to help outsiders in, and that now she must sit back exhausted, watching people play the cards fate has dealt them . . . We have no right to be content, to close the door to others now that we are safely inside.

Mario M. Cuomo

America is a nation of immigrants. Since its founding, the United States has absorbed waves of new arrivals from around the world. Settled primarily by the English, French, and Dutch in the seventeenth century, America attracted large numbers of Germans in the early nineteenth century. During the potato famine of the 1840s and 1850s, 1,700,000 Irish emigrated to the United States. Near the end of the century, millions more arrived from Italy and Eastern Europe. By 1910, 15 percent of American residents were foreign born.

These immigrants filled American cities, adding to their commerce and diversity. European immigrants provided the labor for the country's rapid industrial expansion. Chinese workers laid the railroad tracks that unified the nation and opened the West to economic expansion.

But immigrants also met with resistance. Groups like the Know Nothings opposed the influx of Irish Catholics. As late as the 1920s, help-wanted ads in many newspapers contained the statement "No Irish Need Apply." California passed laws denying rights to the Chinese. Ivy League universities instituted quotas to limit the enrollment of Jewish students. Despite discrimination and hardships, these immigrants and their descendents entered mainstream American society and prospered. Today, some 40 percent of Americans can trace their roots to ancestors who passed through Ellis Island during the peak years of immigration a century ago.

The United States is experiencing the largest increase in immigration in its history. Between 1990 and 2000 the number of foreign-born residents increased 57 percent, reaching 31 million in 2000. Today's immigrants come primarily from Mexico, Asia, and the Middle East. This new wave of immigration is changing the nation's demographics, so that Hispanics, not African Americans, are the largest minority group. Within decades Muslims may outnumber Jews, making Islam America's second-largest religion.

This flow of immigrants, both legal and illegal, has fueled a debate about whether immigration benefits or hurts the United States. Supporters of immigration argue that immigrants offset a declining birthrate, adding new workers and consumers needed to expand the nation's economy. Critics argue that the United States has a limited capacity to absorb immigrants, especially the unskilled. Although immigrants provide employers with cheap labor, they tax the local governments that must provide them and their children with educational and health care services. Because of their numbers and historic ties to the land, Mexicans are changing the cultural fabric of the Southwest. In response, Americans concerned about national identity call for tighter border controls, restricted immigration, and the establishment of English as an official language.

Additionally, the terrorist attacks of September 11, 2001, led to new concerns about immigration, border controls, and national security. At the same time, economists are concerned that America is suffering a "brain drain" of talented foreign students who are compelled to leave the United States after graduating with advanced degrees.

Before reading the articles, consider the following questions:

1. *Where did your ancestors come from?* Were they immigrants? Did they encounter discrimination when they arrived? Did they struggle to maintain their own language and culture or seek to assimilate into American society?

2. *Should people who entered the country illegally be given legal status?* Should amnesty be given to illegal immigrants who have lived and worked in the United States for several years?

3. *Do wealthy countries like the United States have a moral obligation to accept immigrants?* The United States has historically accepted immigrants fleeing war and oppression. After Castro assumed power, 250,000 Cubans fled to the United States. Tens

of thousands of Vietnamese refugees entered the United States after the fall of South Vietnam. Does a prosperous nation also have an obligation to absorb some of the world's poor?

4. *How should the United States determine the number and type of immigrants allowed to enter the country each year?* Should talented immigrants be given priority over the un-skilled? Should the number of immigrants be limited during times of recession and high unemployment?

5. *Does admitting immigrants improve the country by adding consumers and workers or weaken it by draining resources and taxing public services?*

E-READINGS ONLINE

Use InfoTrac College Edition, available through your English CourseMate at **www.cengagebrain.com,** to find the full text of each article online.

Jon Meacham. "Who We Are Now."
The 1965 Immigration and Nationality Act signed by Lyndon Johnson will have pro-found consequences well into the twenty-first century, when whites will constitute only 47 percent of the population, making them the nation's largest minority group.

Robert J. Bresler. "Immigration: The Sleeping Time Bomb."
Although past waves of immigrants have enriched this country, Bresler argues that unless immigration is limited our population could swell to 500 million in less than fifty years, reducing the quality of life for all citizens.

Anna Quindlen. "Undocumented, Indispensable; We Like Our Cheap Houses and Our Fresh Fruit."
Our borders remain porous because, despite concerns about illegal immigrants, Americans benefit from people willing to work hard for little pay.

Robert Samuelson. "The Hard Truth of Immigration: No Society Has a Boundless Capacity to Accept Newcomers, Especially When Many of Them Are Poor and Un-skilled Workers."
Samuelson argues that immigration reform is needed to stem illegal immigration while granting legal status to illegal immigrants already living in the United States. "The stakes are simple," he argues. "Will immigration continue to foster national pride and strength or will it cause more and more weakness and anger?"

Peter Duignan. "Do Immigrants Benefit America?"
Duigan believes that most of today's immigrants "will be an integral part of a revised American community" but warns that "past success does not guarantee that history will repeat itself."

Arian Campo-Flores. "America's Divide. The Lawmakers See Legals and Illegals."
Americans tend to see immigrants as being illegal or legal, but many families are blended. Deporting an illegal immigrant may force American citizens to leave the country of their birth.

Charles Scaliger. "Double Standard on Immigration."
While Mexico calls for an open border with the United States, it maintains a tough policy on its own southern border, deporting more illegal immigrants than does the United States.

Steven Camarota. "Our New Immigration Predicament."
"Rather than changing our society to adapt to existing immigration," Camarota insists, "it would seem to make more sense to change the immigrant stream to fit our society."

Vivek Wadhwa. "A Reverse Brain Drain."
Having started 52 percent of Silicon Valley's technology companies and contributed 25 percent of America's global patents, highly skilled immigrants are vital to the nation's economy and their loss threatens our country's future.

Michael Elliott. "A Fresh Look at Immigration."
When the developed world attracts the best and brightest minds, it deprives poor nations of the talent they need to modernize.

Warren Mass. "Immigration as a Win-Win Affair."
Mass asserts that immigration has benefited the nation's culture and economy—when it has been properly regulated and controlled.

CRITICAL READING AND THINKING

1. What do authors see as the major costs and benefits of immigration?
2. What reasons do the authors give for the country's unwillingness to address illegal immigration?
3. What drives immigrants, both legal and illegal, to enter the United States?
4. How will the current wave of immigration change American society?
5. What motivates people to demand restrictions on immigration?

WRITING SUGGESTIONS

1. Write an essay about your own family history. Were you or your ancestors immigrants? When did they arrive? Did they encounter any discrimination or hardships? Did they assimilate into mainstream American society or seek to maintain ties to their native language, culture, and traditions?
2. *Collaborative writing:* Discuss immigration with other students and develop an essay presenting your group's views on one aspect of immigration—tightening border security, giving amnesty to illegal aliens, developing a guest-worker program, or prosecuting employers who hire illegal aliens. If members have differing opinions, consider developing opposing statements.
3. *Other modes:*
   - Write an essay that examines the *definitions* and terms used to discuss illegal immigrants, such as "undocumented workers," "illegal immigrants," and "illegal aliens." Note the role that connotation plays in shaping attitudes toward illegal immigrants.

- *Compare* current immigrants with those who entered Ellis Island a century ago.
- Use *process* to explain how immigrants can obtain citizenship.
- Write a *division* essay to outline the major problems that recent immigrants face in finding employment, housing, and health services in the United States.
- Use *classification* to rank suggestions for immigration reform from the most to the least restrictive, or from the most to the least acceptable to the public and politicians.

RESEARCH PAPER

You can develop a research paper about immigration by conducting further research to explore a range of issues.

- How effectively does law enforcement prosecute companies that hire illegal aliens?
- How has the concern about terrorism affected immigration policies? Do immigrants from Muslim countries face greater scrutiny? Has Homeland Security viewed the borders as potential weak spots?
- What does current research reveal about the status of Mexican Americans? Are immigrants from Mexico entering the middle class at a similar rate to immigrants from other countries?
- How will the new wave of immigrants influence American society, culture, economy, and foreign policy?
- Examine the impact immigration has had on other developed countries, such as Canada, Britain, France, Germany, and Italy. What problems, if any, have immigrant populations posed in these nations?

FOR FURTHER READING

To locate additional sources on immigration, enter *immigration policy* as a search term in InfoTrac College Edition, available through **CourseMate for *The Sundance Writer*,** or one of your college library's databases, and examine readings under the following key subdivisions:

analysis	economic aspects
cases	evaluation
comparative analysis	political aspects

ADDITIONAL SOURCES

Using a search engine such as Yahoo! or Google, enter one or more of the following terms to locate additional sources:

immigration	green cards
visa lotteries	Ellis Island
citizenship	bilingual education
Mexican Americans	English only

See the Evaluating Internet Source Checklist on page xxx. See Chapter 24 for using and documenting sources.

Paul M. Barrett has been a reporter and editor at the *Wall Street Journal* for over eighteen years and now directs the investigating reporting team at *Business Week*. His books include *The Good Black: A True Story of Race in America* (1999) and *American Islam: The Struggle for the Soul of a Religion* (2007).

American Islam

Source: Excerpt from "Muslims in America" from *American Islam* by Paul M. Barrett. Copyright © 2004 by Paul Barrett. By permission.

In this section from American Islam, *Barrett uses* example, narration, *and* comparison *to provide readers with a general description of American Muslims. Note how he presents objective details to counter commonly held misconceptions about Islam in the United States.*

1   Most American Muslims are not Arab, and most Americans of Arab descent are Christian, not Muslim. People of South Asian descent—those with roots in Pakistan, India, Bangladesh, and Afghanistan—make up 34 percent of American Muslims, according to the polling organization Zogby International. Arab-Americans constitute only 26 percent, while another 20 percent are native-born American blacks, most of whom are converts. The remaining 20 percent come from Africa, Iran, Turkey, and elsewhere.

2   Muslims have no equivalent to the Catholic pope and his cardinals. The faith is decentralized in the extreme, and some beliefs and practices vary depending on region and sect. In America, Muslims do not think and act alike any more than Christians do. That said, all observant Muslims acknowledge Islam's "five pillars": faith in one God, prayer, charity, fasting during Ramadan, and pilgrimage to Mecca. Muslims are also united in the way they pray. The basic choreography of crossing arms, bowing, kneeling, and prostrating oneself is more or less the same in mosques everywhere.

3   The two major subgroups of Muslims, Sunni and Shiite, are found in the United States in roughly their global proportions: 85 percent Sunni, 15 percent Shiite. Ancient history still animates the rivalry, which began in the struggle for Muslim leadership after the Prophet Muhammad's death in 632. Shiites believe that Muhammad intended for only his blood descendants to succeed him. Muhammad's beloved cousin and son-in-law Ali was the only male relative who qualified. Ali's followers became known as Shiites, a derivation of the Arabic phrase for "partisans of Ali." Things did not go smoothly for them. The larger body of early Muslims, known as Sunnis, a word related to Sunnah, or way of the Prophet, had a more flexible notion of who should succeed Muhammad. In 661, an extremist assassinated Ali near Najaf in what is now Iraq. Nineteen years later Sunnis killed his son, Hussein, not far away in Karbala. These deaths permanently divided the aggrieved Shiite minority from the Sunni majority.

4   Sunnis historically have afflicted the weaker Shiites, accusing them of shaping a blasphemous cult around Ali and Hussein. At the Karbala Islamic Education Center in Dearborn, Michigan, a large mural depicts mourning women who

have encountered the riderless horse of Hussein after his final battle. "You see our history and our situation in this," says Imam Husham al-Husainy, a Shiite Iraqi émigré who leads the center. In Dearborn, Shiite Iraqis initially backed the American invasion to depose Saddam Hussein, who persecuted Iraq's Shiite majority. Most Sunnis in Dearborn condemned the war as an exercise in American imperialism.

5   Sufism, another important strain of Islam, is also present in the United States. Sufis follow a spiritual, inward-looking path. Only a tiny percentage of American Muslims would identify themselves primarily as Sufis, in part because some more rigid Muslims condemn Sufism as heretical. But Sufi ideas crop up among the beliefs of many Muslims without being labeled as such. Sufism's emphasis on self-purification appeals to New Age seekers and has made it the most common avenue into Islam for white American converts such as Abdul Kabir Krambo of Yuba City, California. Krambo, an electrician who grew up in a conservative German Catholic family, helped build a mosque amidst the fruit arbors of the Sacramento Valley, only to see it burn down in a mysterious arson. Once rebuilt, the Islamic Center of Yuba City was engulfed again, this time by controversy over whether Krambo and his Sufi friends were trying to impose a "cult" on other worshipers.

6   Although there is a broad consensus that Islam is the fastest-growing religion in the country and the world, no one has provable numbers on just how many American Muslims there are. The Census Bureau doesn't count by religion, and private surveys of the Muslim population offer widely disparate conclusions. A study of four hundred mosques nationwide estimated that there are two million people in the United States "associated with" Islamic houses of worship. The authors of the survey, published in 2001 under the auspices of the Council on American-Islamic Relations (CAIR), a Muslim advocacy group, employed a common assumption that only one in three American Muslims associates with a mosque. In CAIR's view, that suggests there are at least six million Muslims in the country. (Perhaps not coincidentally the American Jewish population is estimated to be slightly below six million.) Other Muslim groups put the number higher, seeking to maximize the size and influence of their constituency.

7   Surveys conducted by non-Muslims have produced much lower estimates, some in the neighborhood of only two million or three million. These findings elicit anger from Muslim leaders, who claim that many immigrant and poor black Muslims are overlooked. On the basis of all the evidence, a very crude range of three million to six million seems reasonable. Rapid growth of the Muslim population is expected to continue, fueled mainly by immigration and high birthrates and, to a lesser extent, by conversion, overwhelmingly by African-Americans. In the next decade or two there probably will be more Muslims in the United States than Jews. Worldwide, the Muslim head count is estimated at 1.3 billion, second among religions only to the combined membership of Christian denominations.

8   American Muslims, like Americans generally, live mostly in cities and suburbs. Large concentrations are found in New York, Detroit, Chicago, and Los Angeles. But they also turn up in the Appalachian foothills and rural Idaho, among other

surprising places. Often the presence of several hundred Muslims in an out-of-the-way town can be explained by proximity to a large state university. Many of these schools have recruited foreign graduate students, including Muslims, since the 1960s. In the 1980s Washington doled out scholarships to Arab students as part of a campaign to counter the influence of the 1979 Iranian Revolution. Some of the Muslim beneficiaries have stayed and raised families.

9   In New York, Muslims are typecast as cab drivers; in Detroit, as owners of grocery stores and gas stations. The overall economic reality is very different. Surveys show that the majority of American Muslims are employed in technical, white-collar, and professional fields. These include information technology, corporate management, medicine, and education. An astounding 59 percent of Muslim adults in the United States have college degrees. That compares with only 27 percent of all American adults. Four out of five Muslim workers earn at least twenty-five thousand dollars a year; more than half earn fifty thousand or more. A 2004 survey by a University of Kentucky researcher found that median family income among Muslims is sixty thousand dollars a year; the national median is fifty thousand. Most Muslims own stock or mutual funds, either directly or through retirement plans. Four out of five are registered to vote.

10   Relative prosperity, high levels of education, and political participation are indications of a minority population successfully integrating into the larger society. By comparison, immigrant Muslims in countries such as Britain, France, Holland, and Spain have remained poorer, less well educated, and socially marginalized. Western European Muslim populations are much larger in percentage terms. Nearly 10 percent of French residents are Muslim; in the United Kingdom the figure is 3 percent. In the more populous United States the Muslim share is 1 to 2 percent, depending on which Muslim population estimate one assumes. It's unlikely that American cities will see the sort of densely packed, volatile Muslim slums that have cropped up on the outskirts of Paris, for example.

11   America's social safety net is stingy compared with those of Western Europe, but there is greater opportunity for new arrivals to get ahead in material terms. This may attract to the United States more ambitious immigrants willing to adjust to the customs of their new home and eager to acquire education that leads to better jobs. More generous welfare benefits in Europe allow Muslims and other immigrants to live indefinitely on the periphery of society, without steady jobs or social interaction with the majority. Europeans, who for decades encouraged Muslim immigration as a source of menial labor, have shown overt hostility toward the outsiders and little inclination to embrace them as full-fledged citizens. Partly as a result, violent Islamic extremism has found fertile ground in Western Europe.

UNDERSTANDING CONTEXT

1. What are some of the more striking facts Barrett presents about American Muslims? Would most Americans be surprised to learn that most Muslims in this country are not Arabs and have higher than average incomes?

2. How does Barrett explain the difference between Sunni and Shia Muslims? What percentage of American Muslims are Sunni?

3. Barrett states that Muslims have a faith that is "decentralized in the extreme." What basic beliefs do most Muslims share?

4. Why is it difficult to ascertain exactly how many Americans are Muslim?

5. *Critical thinking:* How is the Muslim American community different from those found in Western Europe? Does America's history of absorbing diverse immigrant groups create a different environment for Muslims? Why or why not?

EVALUATING STRATEGY

1. How difficult is it to objectively describe a religion? Do you think Barrett is successful? Why or why not?

2. Which facts about American Muslims do you consider the most significant? How can a writer determine which facts are important and which are trivial?

3. *Blending the modes:* How does Barrett use *comparison* to develop and organize his description?

APPRECIATING LANGUAGE

1. Do you think Barrett uses objective and neutral language in describing American Muslims? Can you detect any terms some readers might find insensitive or biased?

2. Barrett states that some Muslims condemn Sufi Muslims as "heretics" trying to impose a "cult" on other Muslims. Look up the words *heretic* and *cult* in a dictionary. What do these words mean? Are these terms objective or subjective?

WRITING SUGGESTIONS

1. Write a description essay that objectively describes a group of people. You might provide details about the residents of your apartment building, coworkers, or members of a sports team. Use neutral language and include factual details.

2. *Collaborative writing:* Working with a group of students, review Barrett's description and select three facts about American Muslims you think most significant. Which ones would surprise most Americans? Write a brief set of factual statements that might be used on billboards or blogs to educate the public.

WRITING BEYOND THE CLASSROOM

Want ads describe ideal job candidates. This want ad describes a print shop manager position in New Orleans.

Bayou Printing

1500 Magazine Street
New Orleans, LA 70130
(504) 555-7100
www.bayouprinting.com

JOB ANNOUNCEMENT

Join a winning team!

Bayou Printing, New Orleans's largest independent chain of print shops, needs a creative, dynamic store manager to join our team. Bayou offers successful managers unique opportunities unavailable in national firms:
- Performance bonuses
- Profit sharing
- Full medical and dental coverage
- Education benefits

Requirements:
- Experience in hiring, training, and supervising employees in a high-volume retail operation.
- Full knowledge of state-of-the-art printing technology.
- Strong leadership and communications skills.
- Proven ability to lower employee turnover and overhead costs.

To apply for this job and join our winning team, e-mail us at info@bayouprinting.com.

UNDERSTANDING CONTEXT

1. How does the ad describe the position at Bayou Printing?
2. What are the most important requirements for the job?
3. What kind of person does Bayou Printing want to attract?
4. *Critical thinking:* What are the limits of any want ad? Can a job be fully described in a few sentences? Why can't employers address all their interests and concerns? How much of anyone's success in a job depends on personality as well as skills and experience?

EVALUATING STRATEGY

1. Why does the ad first list the job's benefits, then its requirements?
2. How effective are the use of bulleted points? Would this ad be less successful if written in standard paragraphs?

APPRECIATING LANGUAGE

1. What impact does the phrase "winning team" have? Why would it appeal to job seekers?
2. What words does the ad use to describe the ideal candidate?

WRITING SUGGESTIONS

1. Write a want ad for a job you once had. Model yours after ones you have seen in newspapers or online. Remember to keep your ad as short and easy to read as possible.
2. *Collaborative writing:* Work with a group of students and create a want ad. Imagine you are hiring a part-time secretary for your writing group who would organize your communications, schedule meetings, and conduct online research. Determine the skills needed, major duties, and the wording of the ad. You might have each member create a draft, then compare versions to select the most effective want ad.

RESPONDING TO IMAGES

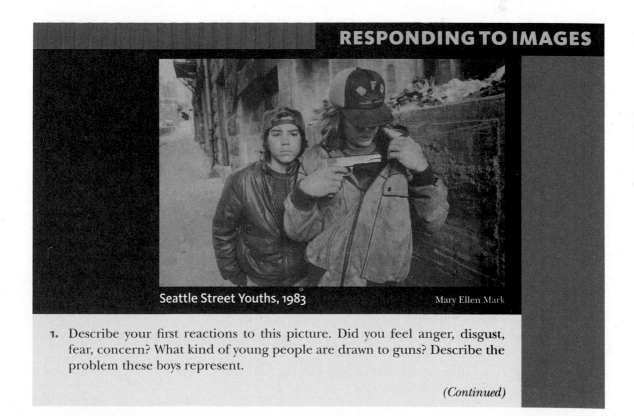

Seattle Street Youths, 1983

Mary Ellen Mark

1. Describe your first reactions to this picture. Did you feel anger, disgust, fear, concern? What kind of young people are drawn to guns? Describe the problem these boys represent.

(Continued)

RESPONDING TO IMAGES

2. This photograph was taken in 1983. What do you assume happened to the boys in the picture? Where might they be today? Describe what you think may have happened to them.

3. *Visual analysis:* What do the hats, clothing, and demeanor suggest about these two boys? What do you see in the face of the boy on the left—defiance, resignation, or anger? What does the position of the weapon imply?

4. *Collaborative writing:* Discuss this picture with a group of students and describe how it might be used in a political ad about gun control, juvenile programs, tougher laws, or improved social programs. Write the text to accompany the ad. Pay attention to word choice and connotation.

5. *Other modes:*
   - Write a *narrative* to accompany this picture. Invent dialogue for the two boys.
   - Write a *cause-and-effect* essay and outline the causes or effects of youth crime.
   - Develop a *process* paper detailing the steps it would take for a youth program to intervene in these boys' lives.
   - Write a *persuasive* letter to the editor clearly stating your views on gun control. Would handgun bans keep young people from obtaining firearms?

DESCRIPTION CHECKLIST

✔ Have you limited your topic?

✔ Does your support suit your context? Should it be objective, subjective, or a blend?

✔ Is your description focused and clearly organized, or is it only a random list of facts and observations?

✔ Have you avoided including unnecessary details and awkward constructions?

✔ Does sensory detail include more than sight? Can you add impressions of taste, touch, sound, or smell?

✔ Do you avoid overly general terms and focus on specific impressions? Have you created dominant impressions?

✔ Do you *show* rather than *tell*? Can you add action to your description to keep it from being static?

✔ Do you keep a consistent point of view?

✔ Read your paper aloud. How does it sound? Do any sections need expansion? Are there irrelevant details to delete or awkward expressions to revise?

 Access the English CourseMate for this text at **www.cengagebrain.com** for additional information on writing description.

Narration

Relating Events

What Is Narration?

Narration relates an event or tells a story. Short stories and novels form narratives, as do fables, legends, biographies, annual reports, and history books. Narratives can be imaginative or factual, fiction or nonfiction. Narrative writing includes most newspaper articles, magazine stories, blogs, and biographies. All narratives seek to answer a simple question—*what happened?*

Physicians write narratives when they record a patient's history or trace the course of a treatment schedule. Attorneys use narrative writing to relate the details of a crime or justify their client's actions in a civil matter. A store manager filing an accident report will summarize an incident, relating the chain of events preceding the accident.

The Writer's Purpose and Role

Writers tell stories to inform, entertain, enlighten, or persuade. In some instances the writer's goal is to reconstruct a chain of events as accurately as possible. The purpose of a brief news story or an accident report is to supply readers with an objective statement of facts. In other cases, writers relate a story in order to provide an insight, share an experience, or teach a lesson. The writer will be selective, highlighting key events and describing them in ways to shape readers' perceptions. Some writers prefer to let a story speak for itself, assuming people will understand their point without an actual thesis statement. James Dillard (page 211), however, provides a clear thesis, stating what he learned after he treated an accident victim. Realizing that a malpractice lawsuit could have ended his medical career, he looks back on the incident, explaining the lesson the accident taught him:

> I took an oath to serve the sick and the injured. I remembered truly believing I would be able to do just that. But I have found out it isn't so simple. I understand now what a foolish thing I did that day. Despite my oath, I know what I would do on that cold roadside near Gettysburg today. I would drive on.

The writer of a narrative can be the central character, an eyewitness, or a researcher who reconstructs a chain of events from remaining evidence or interviews. Narration can be *objective* or *subjective*, depending on the writer's goal and context. **Objective narration** is generally stated in the third person to give the writer's account a sense of neutrality. In objective narration, the author is not a participant but a collector

Sam Diephuis/jupiterimages

Maria Toutoudaki/jupiterimages

and presenter of facts. In "Thirty-Eight Who Saw Murder and Didn't Call the Police" (pages 207–208), Martin Gansberg chronicles a murder victim's last movements:

> Twenty-eight-year-old Catherine Genovese, who was called Kitty by almost everyone in the neighborhood, was returning home from her job as manager of a bar in Hollis. She parked her red Fiat in a lot adjacent to the Kew Gardens Long Island Rail Road Station, facing Mowbray Place. Like many residents of the neighborhood, she had parked there day after day since her arrival from Connecticut a year ago, although the railroad frowns on the practice.
>
> She turned off the lights of her car, locked the door, and started to walk the 100 feet to the entrance of her apartment at 82-70 Austin Street, which is in a Tudor building with stores on the first floor and apartments on the second.

In contrast, **subjective narration** highlights the role of the writer, either as an eyewitness to events or as a main participant. James Dillard provides a gripping personal account of trying to resuscitate his victim (page 211), focusing not only on the objective appearance of the injured driver but also his own subjective feelings and his role as a participant:

> He was still out cold, limp as a rag doll. His throat was crushed and blood from the jugular vein was running down my arms. He still couldn't breathe. He was deep blue-magenta now, his pulse was rapid and thready. The stench of alcohol turned my stomach, but I positioned his jaw and tried to blow air down into his lungs. It wouldn't go.

Focus

Related closely to the writer's purpose and role is the narrative's *focus*. A biography of Abraham Lincoln can be a general account of his entire life or a psychological study of his battle with depression during the Civil War. A book about World War II can provide an overview of events or a detailed account of the role of women in the defense industry. An article on recycling may provide a survey of national trends or an in-depth history of tire recycling in a single city. Focus determines the details the writer includes in the narrative and the kind of evidence he or she relies on. A narrative does not have to include each event and every detail as the following one does:

> For our tenth anniversary my husband and I planned a trip to Hawaii. The seven-hour flight was exhausting, but as soon as I saw the Easter egg blue of the sky and the bright yellows and reds of the flowers I was energized. We rented a car at the airport and drove to our hotel. On the first day we went to the mountains. The scenery was incredible. The following day it rained, so we took the opportunity to visit a local art museum and dine in a Chinese restaurant. The next day we went to the beach.

Attempting to capture a ten-day vacation in a five-hundred-word essay, the student produces only a catalog, a listing of events. Like a video in fast-forward, the narrative sweeps readers through brief scenes that offer only superficial impressions. It is more effective to concentrate on a single event, as if highlighting a single scene from a movie or chapter in a book.

In "The Fender-Bender" (page 203), Ramón "Tianguis" Pérez focuses on a single incident, a minor traffic accident. As an illegal alien without papers, he fears that any contact with law enforcement could lead to an investigation of his status and deportation. Pérez does not bother explaining how he immigrated to America, why he left Mexico, or even the date or location of the incident, but immediately plunges his reader into the event:

> One night after work, I drive Rolando's old car to visit some friends, and then head towards home. At a light, I come to a stop too late, leaving the front end of the car poking into the crosswalk. I shift into reverse, but as I am backing up, I strike the van behind me. Its driver immediately gets out to inspect the damage to his vehicle. He's a tall Anglo-Saxon, dressed in a deep blue work uniform. After looking at his car, he walks up to the window of the car I'm driving.
>
> "Your driver's license," he says, a little enraged.
>
> "I didn't bring it," I tell him.
>
> He scratches his head. He is breathing heavily with fury.
>
> "Okay," he says. "You park up ahead while I call a patrolman."
>
> The idea of calling the police doesn't sound good to me, but the accident is my fault. So I drive around the corner and park at the curb. I turn off the motor and hit the steering wheel with one fist. I don't have a driver's license. I've never applied for one. Nor do I have with me the identification card that I bought in San Antonio. Without immigration papers, without a driving permit, and having hit another car, I feel as if I'm just one step from Mexico.

This single, almost incidental, event reveals more about the status of an illegal alien than a three-page summary of the author's life history. By including dialogue, Perez creates an active narrative instead of a summary of events.

WRITING ACTIVITY

Select examples of narrative writing from your textbooks, readings from this chapter, online articles, brochures, short stories, or passages from novels.

1. Can you identify the writer's purpose? Are some narratives written solely to inform, while others also seek to persuade or entertain readers?

2. What role does the author play in these narratives? Are some written in the first person? Is the writer the main participant, a minor character, or a witness of the events?

3. How do the various writers focus their narratives? What details do they leave out? How do they introduce background material?

4. Do the writers include dialogue and action to advance the narratives?

Chronology

Chronology or time is a central organizing element in narrative writing. Writers do not always relate events in a straight timeline. A biography, for instance, does not have to open with birth and childhood. Writers often alter the time sequences of their stories to dramatize events or limit their topics. A biographer of Franklin Roosevelt might choose to highlight a key event or turning point in his life. The narrative could open with his polio attack, flash back to his childhood and early political career, then flash forward to his recovery and entry into national and international politics. Other writers find it more dramatic to open a narrative with a final event and explain what led up to it. The first chapter of a biography about Czar Nicholas II could describe his execution and then flash back to the events leading to his downfall and death.

Each method of organizing a narrative has distinct advantages and disadvantages:

- **Beginning at the beginning** creates an open-ended narrative, providing readers with few hints about later events. Writers who relate complex stories with many possible causes can use a straight chronology to avoid highlighting a single event. Using a direct beginning-to-end approach is the most traditional method of telling a story. One of the difficulties can be determining exactly when the narrative should start. Often the beginning of a story consists of incidental background information that readers may find uninteresting.

- **Beginning at the middle or turning point** can arouse reader interest by opening with a dramatic scene. This method of organizing plunges the reader directly into the narrative and can give the chain of events a clear focus. This is a commonly used pattern in popular biographies. Critics, however, may argue that altering the chronology can be distorting. Not all historians, for instance, might agree that Roosevelt's polio attack was the "turning point" of his life. Some biographers may feel that this approach overemphasizes his physical disability and overshadows the political significance of Roosevelt's career.

- **Beginning at the end** dramatizes the final event. Organizing a narrative in this way can suggest that the conclusion was inevitable. When everything is presented in flashback, readers see events, actions, and thoughts in hindsight. The elements of suspense and randomness are removed, providing a stronger sense of cause and effect. Some readers will object to this method because it implies the final outcome was unavoidable, when in fact events just as easily could have led to alternative endings.

WRITING ACTIVITY

Select sample narratives from this chapter or look at one of your favorite books—fiction or nonfiction—and examine how the writers organized the chronology of events.

1. What pattern appears to be the most common?

2. Do any of the authors use flashbacks or flash forwards? If so, what impact do they have? How do the authors blend these sections into the main narrative without confusing their readers?

3. How do the writers use transitional statements and paragraph breaks to move the narrative and signal changes in time?

4. How do the writers use chronology to establish meaning? Do they use time relationships to indicate cause and effect?

5. How do the writers slow or speed up the narrative to emphasize important events or skim through minor ones?

Strategies for Writing Narration: Prewriting and Planning

Critical Thinking and Prewriting

1. **List topics suitable to your goal.** Consider the nature of the narrative assignment. What subjects would best suit your purpose?

2. **Determine your purpose.** Does your narrative have a goal beyond telling a story? What details or evidence do readers need to accept your point of view?

3. **Define your role.** As a narrator you can write in the first person, as either the major participant or the witness to events. You can write in the third person to establish greater objectivity, inserting personal opinion if desired.

4. **Consider your readers.** Define your readers' perceptual world. How much background information will you have to supply for readers to appreciate the significance of events?

5. **Review the discourse community or writing situation.** If you are writing a narrative report as an employee, study samples to determine how you should present your story.

6. **Freewrite for a few minutes on the most likely two or three topics to generate ideas.**

Planning

1. **Develop a clear thesis.** A narrative usually has a goal of doing more than simply listing a chain of events.
   - What is the purpose of your narrative—to persuade, to entertain, or to teach readers a lesson?
   - Should the thesis be clearly stated or implied?

2. **Identify the beginning and end of your narrative.** You may find it helpful to place background information in a separate foreword or introduction and limit comments on the ending to an afterword or epilogue. This can allow the body of the work to focus on a specific chain of events.

3. **Select a chronological pattern.** After reviewing the context of the narrative, determine which pattern would be most effective for your purpose—using a straight chronology, opening with a mid- or turning point, or presenting the final event first.

4. **Select key details that support your thesis.** Focus on those impressions of sight, sound, smell, taste, and touch that will bring your narrative to life.
   - Avoid minor details about times, dates, and locations unless they serve a clear purpose.

5. **Draft a timeline, listing main events of the narrative to guide your draft.** Leave space between each item on the timeline for last-minute additions.

Strategies for Writing Narration: Writing the First Draft

Writing the First Draft

1. **Use your plan as a guide, but be open to new ideas.**

2. **Use dialogue to advance the narrative.** If your narrative contains interactions between people, reconstruct conversations in direct quotations rather than summaries. Allowing people to speak for themselves gives you the opportunity to use word choice to convey a person's level of education, attitude, and lifestyle.

3. **Use transitional statements.** To prevent readers from becoming confused, make clear transitional statements to move the narrative. Such statements as "two days later" or "later that afternoon" can help readers follow the passage of time. Clear transitions are important if you alter the chronology with flashbacks and flash-forwards.

   - Paragraph breaks can be very important in narratives. They can function like chapters in a book to signal changes, isolate events, and highlight incidents.

4. **Monitor your length as you write.** If your draft begins to run too long, make notes or list points, and try to complete a full version.

Strategies for Writing Narration: Revising and Editing

Revising

1. **Review your thesis, plan, and goal.** Examine your prewriting notes and outline to determine if changes are needed.

2. **Read the first draft to get an overall view of your narrative.**
   - Does the opening generate interest and plunge readers into the story, or does it simply announce the topic or state the time and location?
   - Does the narrative have a thesis, a clear point?
   - Is the narrative easy to follow? Do transitional statements and paragraph breaks help dramatize shifts between main points?
   - Does the narrative end with a memorable impression, thought, or question?

3. **Examine the draft and isolate the narrative's key events.**
   - Can these elements be heightened or expanded?
   - Should these elements be placed in a different order?

4. **Decide whether the narrative should be expanded or narrowed.** If the draft is too short or seems to stall on a minor point or uninteresting detail, consider expanding the scope of the narrative by lengthening the chain of events.
   - If the draft is too long or reads like a summary of events, tighten the focus by eliminating minor events. *Remember, your narrative does not have to record everything that happened.*

(Continued)

5. **Determine whether the narrative can be improved by adding details, including dialogue, or altering the chronological pattern.**

Editing and Proofreading

1. **Review subsequent drafts for content, style, and tone.** Make sure that your choice of words suits the subject matter, mood, and thesis of the narrative.
   - Review your choice of words to make sure their connotations are appropriate.

2. **Make sure the narrative does not shift tense without reason.** In relating a narrative, you can write in present or past tense. In some cases, you may shift from past to present to express different actions, but you will otherwise want to remain consistent with your choice of tense.

   Acceptable: I *drive* to work every day, but that morning I *took* the bus.
   Awkward: Smith *rushes* into the end zone and the game *was* won.

3. **Avoid shifts in person or stance.** Narratives can be related in first, second, or third person. In most instances, avoid shifts in person, unless there is a clear shift in focus.

   Acceptable: I found working on a farm fascinating, though *you* might find it tedious and boring.
   Awkward: I crossed the bridge where all *you* can see is desert.

STUDENT PAPER

This paper was written in response to the following assignment:

> Write a 300- to 500-word narrative essay based on a personal experience or observation. Limit your topic, select details, and use figurative language to recreate what you experienced.

FIRST DRAFT WITH INSTRUCTOR'S COMMENTS

weak intro *Add title open with stronger image*

This paper is about a trip I made last spring to San Diego to visit my aunt and uncle. I saw a

one-day

lot during that week but the most meaningful part I remember was a one day trip to Mexico.

it's

I think it really changed the whole way I think about things. Sometimes its the minor things

you remember as important.

(Continued)

run-on
I got off the San Diego Trolley and I knew that I was going to start an adventure.

sp   *Fragment*
Tijuana. As I neared the entrance to cross the boarder there is a priest with a plastic bowl.

Avoid shift from past to present/ delete "to myself"
With a picture of some kids saying "feed Tijuana's homeless children." Yeah, right, I think

to myself, just another scam, this guy probably isn't even a priest.

Tijuana. Just the name of the city brings back a special smell. A smell that you will only

know if you have been there. It only takes one time and you can relate to what I am trying to

                    Fragment
say to you. A smell that will permeate your olfactory senses forever. The smell was terrible.

        sp   *shift*
As I cross the boarder the first thing that hits you is the smell I just mentioned. Then you

witness the terrible suffering and horrible poverty. It makes you realize how terrible many

people have it in this world.

Once I get past the few blocks of poverty and handed out all I can, I wandered upon a

       Avoid shifts from past to present & "I" to "you"
busy little plaza where you could see all kinds of people having fun and partying.

                           Add detail
As I continued my journey, I reached a bridge. The bridge was horrible. Toward the mid-

span of the bridge, I experienced one of the most touching moments in my whole life, one of

              sp
those happy ones where it's not clear weather you should laugh or cry. There was this little
Add details about children
child playing the accordion and another one playing a guitar.

It was getting to be late, and I started to get ready to leave. But this time as I passed the

                    Good image
priest I filled his plastic bowl with the rest of my money.

Like I stated, this one afternoon is what I remember from my whole trip. I still think

            vague
about those people and the way they lived their lives. We as Americans take way too
Ending could be stronger, conclude with a strong image
much for granted and never realize how bad other people have it in this world today.

(Continued)

REVISION NOTES

This is a good topic for a narrative. There are changes you can make to create a stronger essay.

1. *Delete the first and last paragraphs; they are vague and general. Let the experience speak for itself. Focus on the event rather than telling readers how significant it was.*

2. *Add details to explain general terms such as "horrible" and "terrible."*

3. *Avoid illogical shifts in time. Describe your actions in the past tense: "I got off the trolley," "I walked," or "I saw." You can use present tense to explain general ideas or impressions not restricted to this specific event: "Tijuana is poor."*

4. *Avoid awkward shifts from "I" to "you." Write "I walked into the plaza where I could see" instead of "I walked into the plaza where you could see."*

5. *Edit for fragments and run-ons.*

REVISED DRAFT
Spare Change

   As I stepped off the San Diego Trolley, I knew I was going to embark on a great adventure. Tijuana. As I neared the entrance to cross the border, I saw a priest with a plastic bowl with a picture of some kids. The caption of the picture said, "Feed Tijuana's homeless children." Yeah, right, I thought, just another scam. This man, I was convinced, probably was not even a priest.

Tijuana   © Les Stone/Sygma/Corbis

(Continued)

Tijuana. Just the name of the city brings back a distinct smell, one that will permeate my olfactory senses forever. A thousand different scents compounded into one. A smell of fast food, sweat, sewage, and tears hung over the city.

As I crossed the border the first thing that hit me was the smell. Then I witnessed countless victims of unforgettable poverty and suffering. A man without legs begged for money from a makeshift wagon. A woman with her children huddled around her stared at me, waving an old grease-stained wax cup at me, asking for help. The children, dressed in Salvation Army hand-me-downs, ripped pants and mismatched shoes, surrounded me, begging for money. Their tiny hands plucked at jacket pockets, looking for change or something to eat.

Once I got past the few blocks of human suffering and handed out all I could, I wandered upon a busy little plaza. This place was reasonably clean and clear of trash, and I heard the deafening music coming from a row of flashy clubs and saw dozens of young Americans drinking and partying. Tourists, who had spent the day in the outlet stores, trudged past distressed and exhausted from a day of hard shopping. They lugged huge plastic bags jammed with discount jeans, shoes, purses, and blouses. A score of children held out little packs of colored Chicklets, a local gum they sold to Americans at whatever price the tourists could haggle them down to. It is pathetic to think tourists feel the need to haggle over the price of gum with a child, but this is Tijuana.

Americans and tourists come from all over the world to drink, to shop, to haggle with children. This is just the way it is, the way it will always be. As I continued my journey, I reached a bridge. The bridge was horrible. Along the sides there was trash and rubbish. Towards the midspan of the bridge, I experienced one of the most touching moments of my life, one of those happy ones where I didn't know if I should shed a tear from happiness or out of despair. A small boy played an accordion and another played a guitar. He was singing a Spanish song; well actually, it sounded like he was screaming as his compadre strummed a guitar. He had a little cup in front of him, and I threw a coin into it. He just smiled and kept singing. I turned around and left, but as I passed the priest at the border, I filled his plastic bowl with the rest of my change.

QUESTIONS FOR REVIEW AND REVISION

1. This student was assigned a 300- to 500-word narrative in a composition class. How successfully does this paper meet this goal?

2. How does the student open and close the narrative? Does the opening grab attention? Does the conclusion make a powerful statement?

3. What devices does the student use to advance the chronology?

4. Most writers focus on visual details. This student includes the senses of sound and smell as well. How effective is this approach?

5. Did the student follow the instructor's suggestions? Do you see any errors the student should identify to improve future assignments?

6. Read the paper aloud. What changes would you make? Can you detect passages that would benefit from revision or rewording?

7. In the final draft the student included a photograph. Does this add value to the essay? Why or why not? Would you suggest keeping or deleting this image? Why?

WRITING SUGGESTIONS

1. Using this essay as a model, write a short narrative about a trip that exposed you to another culture. Try to recapture the sights, sounds, and smells that characterized the experience.

2. *Collaborative writing:* Ask a group of students to assign a grade to this essay and then explain their evaluations. What strengths and weaknesses does the group identify?

Suggested Topics for Writing Narration

General Assignments

Write a narrative on any of the following topics. Your narrative may contain passages making use of other modes, such as *description* or *persuasion*. Choose your narrative structure carefully and avoid including minor details that add little to the story line. Use flashbacks and flash-forwards carefully. Transitional statements, paragraphing, and line breaks can help clarify changes in chronology.

- Your first job interview
- Moving into your first apartment
- The event or series of events that led to you take some action, such as quitting a job, ending a relationship, or joining an organization
- A sporting event you played in or observed, perhaps limiting the narrative to a single play
- A first date, using dialogue as much as possible to set the tone and advance the narrative
- An event that placed you in danger
- An experience that led you to change your opinion about a friend or coworker
- The events of the best or worst day you experienced in a job
- An accident or medical emergency, focusing on creating a clear, minute-by-minute chronology
- A telephone call that changed your life, using dialogue as much as possible

Writing in Context

1. Imagine you are participating in a psychological experiment measuring stressors students face: lack of sleep, deadlines, financial problems, scheduling conflicts,

decreased contact with family and friends. Write a diary for a week, detailing instances when you experience stress.

2. Write a letter to a friend relating the events of a typical day in college. Select details your friend may find interesting or humorous.

3. Preserve on paper for your children and grandchildren a favorite story told by your grandparents or other relatives. Include needed background details and identify characters. Consider what you want your descendants to know about their ancestors.

4. You have been accused of committing a crime last Tuesday. Create a detailed log to the best of your recollection of the day's events to establish an alibi.

Strategies for Reading Narration

When reading the narratives in this chapter, keep these questions in mind:

Context

1. What is the author's narrative purpose—to inform, entertain, enlighten, share a personal experience, or provide information required by the reader? Does the writer have a goal beyond simply telling a story?

2. Does the writer include a thesis statement? If so, where does it appear in the essay?

3. What is the writer's role? Is the writer a participant or a direct witness? Is he or she writing in a personal context, focusing on internal responses, or in a professional context, concentrating on external events?

4. What audience is the narrative directed toward—general or specific? How much knowledge does the author assume readers have?

5. What is the nature of the discourse community or writing situation? Is the narration subjective or objective? Does the original source of the narrative— newsmagazine, book, or professional publication—reveal anything about its context?

Strategy

1. How does the author open and close the narrative?

2. What details does the writer select? Are some items summarized or ignored? If so, why?

3. What kind of support does the writer use—personal observation or factual documentation?

(Continued)

4. Does the author use dialogue or special effects like flashbacks or flash-forwards to advance the narrative?

5. What transitional devices does the writer use to prevent confusion? Does the author use paragraph breaks or time references such as "two hours later" or "later that day"?

Language

1. What does the level of vocabulary, tone, and style suggest about the writing context?

2. How is the author's attitude toward the subject or intended readers reflected by his or her choice of words?

READING TO LEARN

As you read the narratives in this chapter, note techniques you can use in your own writing:

- **"Take This Fish and Look at It" by Samuel Scudder** uses repetition to drive home an experience that taught him a valuable lesson.

- **"The Fender-Bender" by Ramon "Tianguis" Perez** uses a single incident to demonstrate how precarious life can be for undocumented workers. Perez includes extensive dialogue to advance his narrative.

- **"Thirty-Eight Who Saw Murder and Didn't Call the Police" by Martin Gansberg** is a fact-driven objective newspaper account of a murder. The first sentence, which many critics view as misleading, helped transform this incident into a national controversy.

- **"A Doctor's Dilemma" by James Dillard** uses the story of an accident to demonstrate why many doctors, fearing lawsuits, refuse to administer first aid to victims.

- **"Shooting an Elephant" by George Orwell** relates an event where a police-man feels pressured by a crowd to act against his better judgment.

- **"Incident Report" by Roisin Reardon** objectively records a hotel employee's observations and actions during a disturbance.

Samuel Scudder (1837–1911) attended Williams College. In 1857 he entered Harvard, where he studied under the noted scientist Louis Agassiz. Scudder held various positions and helped found the Cambridge Entomological Club. He published hundreds of papers and developed a comprehensive catalog of three hundred years of scientific publications. While working for the United States Geological Survey, he named more than a thousand species of fossil insects. Much of Scudder's work is still admired for its attention to detail.

Take This Fish and Look at It

Today educators stress critical thinking, which begins with close observation. As you read this essay, consider how effective the professor's teaching method is. Does it rest on the age-old notion that "people learn by doing"?

1 It was more than fifteen years ago that I entered the laboratory of Professor Agassiz, and told him I had enrolled my name in the Scientific School as a student of natural history. He asked me a few questions about my object in coming, my antecedents generally, the mode in which I afterwards proposed to use the knowledge I might acquire, and, finally, whether I wished to study any special branch. To the latter I replied that, while I wished to be well grounded in all departments of zoology, I purposed to devote myself specially to insects. *Intro sets time*

brief summary

2 "When do you wish to begin?" he asked. *uses dialogue*

3 "Now," I replied.

4 This seemed to please him, and with an energetic "Very well!" he reached from a shelf a huge jar of specimens in yellow alcohol. "Take this fish," he said, "and look at it; we call it a haemulon; by and by I will ask what you have seen."

5 With that he left me, but in a moment returned with explicit instructions as to the care of the object entrusted to me.

6 "No man is fit to be a naturalist," said he, "who does not know how to take care of specimens."

7 I was to keep the fish before me in a tin tray, and occasionally moisten the surface with alcohol from the jar, always taking care to replace the stopper tightly. Those were not the days of ground-glass stoppers and elegantly shaped exhibition jars; all the old students will recall the huge neckless glass bottles with their leaky, wax-besmeared corks, half eaten by insects, and begrimed with cellar dust. Entomology was a cleaner science than ichthyology, but the example of the Professor, who had unhesitatingly plunged to the bottom of the jar to produce the fish, was infectious; and though this alcohol had a "very ancient and fishlike smell," I really dared not show any aversion within these sacred precincts, and treated the alcohol as though it were pure water. Still I was conscious of a passing feeling of disappointment, for gazing at a fish did not commend itself to an ardent entomologist. My friends at home, too, were annoyed when they discovered that no amount of eau-de-Cologne would drown the perfume which haunted me like a shadow. *gives direction*

8   In ten minutes I had seen all that could be seen in that fish, and started in search of the Professor—who had, however, left the Museum; and when I returned, after lingering over some of the odd animals stored in the upper apartment, my specimen was dry all over. I dashed the fluid over the fish as if to resuscitate the beast from a fainting fit, and looked with anxiety for a return of the normal sloppy appearance. This little excitement over, nothing was to be done but to return to a steadfast gaze at

my mute companion. Half an hour passed—an hour—another hour; the fish began to look loathsome. I turned it over and around; looked it in the face—ghastly; from behind, beneath, above, sideways, at three-quarters' view—just as ghastly. I was in despair; at an early hour I concluded that lunch was necessary; so, with infinite relief, the fish was carefully replaced in the jar, and for an hour I was free.

9   On my return, I learned that Professor Agassiz had been at the Museum, but had gone, and would not return for several hours. My fellow-students were too busy to be disturbed by continued conversation. Slowly I drew forth that hideous fish, and with a feeling of desperation again looked at it. I might not use a magnifying-glass; instruments of all kinds were interdicted. My two hands, my two eyes, and the fish: it seemed a most limited field. I pushed my finger down its throat to feel how sharp the teeth were. I began to count the scales in the different rows, until I was convinced

that was nonsense. At last a happy thought struck me—I would draw the fish; and now with surprise I began to discover new features in the creature. Just then the Professor returned.

10   "That is right," said he; "a pencil is one of the best of eyes. I am glad to notice, too, that you keep your specimen wet, and your bottle corked."

11   With these encouraging words, he added: "Well, what is it like?"

12   He listened attentively to my brief rehearsal of the structure of parts whose names were still unknown to me: the fringed gill-arches and movable operculum; the pores of the head, fleshy lips and lidless eyes; the lateral line, the spinous fins and forked tail; the compressed and arched body. When I finished, he waited as if expecting more, and then, with an air of disappointment:

13   "You have not looked very carefully; why," he continued more earnestly, "you haven't even seen one of the most conspicuous features of the animal, which is plainly before your eyes as the fish itself; look again, look again!" and he left me to my misery.

14   I was piqued; I was mortified. Still more of that wretched fish! But now I set myself to my task with a will, and discovered one new thing after another, until I saw how just the Professor's criticism had been. The afternoon passed quickly; and when, towards its close, the Professor inquired:

15   "Do you see it yet?"

16   "No," I replied, "I am certain I do not, but I see how little I saw before."

17   "That is next best," said he, earnestly, "but I won't hear you now; put away your fish and go home; perhaps you will be ready with a better answer in the morning. I will examine you before you look at the fish."

18   This was disconcerting. Not only must I think of my fish all night, studying, without the object before me, what this unknown but most visible feature might be; but

also, without reviewing my discoveries, I must give an exact account of them the next day. I had a bad memory; so I walked home by Charles River in a distracted state, with my two perplexities.

19   The cordial greeting from the Professor the next morning was reassuring; here was a man who seemed to be quite as anxious as I that I should see for myself what he saw.

20   "Do you perhaps mean," I asked, "that the fish has symmetrical sides with paired organs?"

21   His thoroughly pleased "Of course! of course!" repaid the wakeful hours of the previous night. After he had discoursed most happily and enthusiastically—as he always did—upon the importance of this point, I ventured to ask what I should do next.   *asks for help*

22   "Oh, look at your fish!" he said, and left me again to my own devices. In a little more than an hour he returned, and heard my new catalogue. "That is good, that is good!" he repeated; "but that is not all; go on"; and so for three long days he placed that fish before my eyes, forbidding me to look at anything else, or to use any artificial aid. "Look, look, look," was his repeated injunction.   *repeated command*

23   This was the best entomological lesson I ever had—a lesson whose influence has extended to the details of every subsequent study; a legacy the Professor has left to me, as he has left it to so many others, of inestimable value, which we could not buy, with which we cannot part.   *thesis/value of lesson*

24   A year afterward, some of us were amusing ourselves with chalking outlandish beasts on the Museum blackboard. We drew prancing starfishes; frogs in mortal combat; hydra-headed worms; stately crawfishes, standing on their tails, bearing aloft umbrellas; and grotesque fishes with gaping mouths and staring eyes. The Professor came in shortly after, and was as amused as any at our experiments. He looked at the fishes.   *flash-forward to humorous incident*

25   "Haemulons, every one of them," he said; "Mr. —— drew them."

26   True; and to this day, if I attempt a fish, I can draw nothing but haemulons.

27   The fourth day, a second fish of the same group was placed beside the first, and I was bidden to point out the resemblances and differences between the two; another and another followed, until the entire family lay before me, and a whole legion of jars covered the table and surrounding shelves; the odor had become a pleasant perfume; and even now, the sight of an old, six-inch, worm-eaten cork brings fragrant memories.

28   The whole group of haemulons was thus brought in review; and, whether engaged upon the dissection of the internal organs, the preparation and examination of the bony framework, or the description of the various parts, Agassiz's training in the method of observing facts and their orderly arrangement was ever accompanied by the urgent exhortation not to be content with them.

29   "Facts are stupid things," he would say, "until brought into connection with some general law."   *conclusion*

30   At the end of eight months, it was almost with reluctance that I left these friends and turned to insects; but what I had gained by this outside experience has been of greater value than years of later investigation in my favorite groups.

UNDERSTANDING CONTEXT

1. What is Scudder's purpose in this narrative? Why is this essay more than a typical "first day at school" story?

2. What did Professor Agassiz mean when he stated that "a pencil is one of the best of eyes"?

3. *Critical thinking:* How effective was Professor Agassiz's teaching method? By directing a new student to simply "look, look again," did he accomplish more than if he had required Scudder to attend a two-hour lecture on the importance of observation? Does this method assume that students have already acquired basic skills? Would this method work for all students? Why or why not?

4. What has this essay taught you about your future career? How can keen observation and attention to detail help you achieve your goals?

EVALUATING STRATEGY

1. How does Scudder give the narrative focus? What details does he leave out?

2. Scudder does not bother describing Professor Agassiz. Would that add or detract from the narrative?

3. *Other modes:* How does Scudder use *description* of the fish, specimen bottles, and smells to provide readers with a clear impression of the laboratory?

APPRECIATING LANGUAGE

1. How much scientific terminology does Scudder use in the narrative? What does this suggest about his intended audience?

2. This essay contains little action. Essentially it is a story about a man interacting with a dead fish. What words add drama and humor to the narrative?

WRITING SUGGESTIONS

1. Apply Professor Agassiz's technique to a common object you might use every day. Take your clock radio or a can of your favorite soft drink and study it for five minutes. Write a description of what you have observed. List the features you never noticed before.

2. Professor Agassiz gave his student little direction other than a simple command. Write a brief account about a time when a parent, teacher, coach, or boss left you to act on your own. What problems or challenges did you encounter? Did you feel frustrated, afraid, angry, or confident? What did you learn?

3. *Collaborative writing:* Working with three or four other students, select an object unfamiliar to the group. Allow each member to study the object and make notes. Compare your findings, and work to create a single description incorporating the findings of the group.

Ramón "Tianguis" Pérez is an undocumented immigrant and does not release biographical information.

The Fender-Bender

Source: "The Fender Bender" from *Diary of an Undocumented Immigrant* by Ramon "Tianguis" Perez. Copyright © 1991 by Arte Publico Press–University of Houston. By permission.

As you read the essay, notice how Pérez uses dialogue to advance the narrative. Pay attention to the role common documents such as a driver's license or a letter play in the drama.

1 One night after work, I drive Rolando's old car to visit some friends, and then head towards home. At a light, I come to a stop too late, leaving the front end of the car poking into the crosswalk. I shift into reverse, but as I am backing up, I strike the van behind me. Its driver immediately gets out to inspect the damage to his vehicle. He's a tall Anglo-Saxon, dressed in a deep blue work uni form. After looking at his car, he walks up to the window of the car I'm driving.

2 "Your driver's license," he says, a little enraged.

3 "I didn't bring it," I tell him.

4 He scratches his head. He is breathing heavily with fury.

5 "Okay," he says. "You park up ahead while I call a patrolman."

6 The idea of calling the police doesn't sound good to me, but the accident is my fault. So I drive around the corner and park at the curb. I turn off the motor and hit the steering wheel with one fist. I don't have a driver's license. I've never applied for one. Nor do I have with me the identification card that I bought in San Antonio. Without immigration papers, without a driving permit, and having hit another car, I feel as if I'm just one step away from Mexico.

7 I get out of the car. The white man comes over and stands right in front of me. He's almost two feet taller.

8 "If you're going to drive, why don't you carry your license?" he asks in an accusatory tone.

9 "I didn't bring it," I say, for lack of any other defense.

10 I look at the damage to his car. It's minor, only a scratch on the paint and a pimple-sized dent.

11 "I'm sorry," I say. "Tell me how much it will cost to fix, and I'll pay for it; that's no problem." I'm talking to him in English, and he seems to understand.

12 "This car isn't mine," he says. "It belongs to the company I work for. I'm sorry, but I've got to report this to the police, so that I don't have to pay for the damage."

13 "That's no problem," I tell him again. "I can pay for it."

14 After we've exchanged these words, he seems less irritated. But he says he'd prefer for the police to come, so that they can report that the dent wasn't his fault.

15 While we wait, he walks from one side to the other, looking down the avenue this way and that, hoping that the police will appear.

16 Then he goes over to the van to look at the dent.

17 "It's not much," he says. "If it was my car, there wouldn't be any problems, and you could go on."

18   After a few minutes, the long-awaited police car arrives. Only one officer is inside. He's a Chicano, short and of medium complexion, with short, curly hair. On getting out of the car, he walks straight towards the Anglo.

19   The two exchange a few words.

20   "Is that him?" he asks, pointing at me.

21   The Anglo nods his head.

22   Speaking in English, the policeman orders me to stand in front of the car and to put my hands on the hood. He searches me and finds only the car keys and my billfold with a few dollars in it. He asks for my driver's license.

23   "I don't have it," I answered in Spanish.

24   He wrinkles his face into a frown, and casting a glance at the Anglo, shakes his head in disapproval of me.

25   "That's the way these Mexicans are," he says.

26   He turns back towards me, asking for identification. I tell him I don't have that, either.

27   "You're an illegal, eh?" he says.

28   I won't answer.

29   "An illegal," he says to himself.

30   "Where do you live?" he continues. He's still speaking in English.

31   I tell him my address.

32   "Do you have anything with you to prove that you live at that address?" he asks.

33   I think for a minute, then realize that in the glove compartment is a letter that my parents sent to me several weeks earlier.

34   I show him the envelope and he immediately begins to write something in a little book that he carries in his back pocket. He walks to the back of my car and copies the license plate number. Then he goes over to his car and talks into his radio. After he talks, someone answers. Then he asks me for the name of the car's owner.

35   He goes over to where the Anglo is standing. I can't quite hear what they're saying. But when the two of them go over to look at the dent in the van, I hear the cop tell the Anglo that if he wants, he can file charges against me. The Anglo shakes his head and explains what he had earlier explained to me, about only needing for the police to certify that he wasn't responsible for the accident. The Anglo says that he doesn't want to accuse me of anything because the damage is light.

36   "If you want, I can take him to jail," the cop insists. The Anglo turns him down again.

37   "If you'd rather, we can report him to Immigration," the cop continues.

38   Just as at the first, I am now almost sure that I'll be making a forced trip to Tijuana. I find myself searching my memory for my uncle's telephone number, and to my relief, I remember it. I am waiting for the Anglo to say yes, confirming my expectations of the trip. But instead, he says no, and though I remain silent, I feel appreciation for him. I ask myself why the Chicano is determined to harm me. I didn't really expect him to favor me, just because we're of the same ancestry, but on the other hand, once I had admitted my guilt, I expected him to treat me at least fairly. But even against the white man's wishes, he's trying to make matters worse for me.

I've known several Chicanos with whom, joking around, I've reminded them that their roots are in Mexico. But very few of them see it that way. Several have told me how when they were children, their parents would take them to vacation in different states of Mexico, but their own feeling, they've said, is, "I am an American citizen!" Finally, the Anglo, with the justifying paper in his hands, says good-bye to the cop, thanks him for his services, gets into his van and drives away.

39   The cop stands in the street in a pensive mood. I imagine that he's trying to think of a way to punish me.

40   "Put the key in the ignition," he orders me.

41   I do as he says.

42   Then he orders me to roll up the windows and lock the doors.

43   "Now, go on, walking," he says.

44   I go off taking slow steps. The cop gets in his patrol car and stays there, waiting. I turn the corner after two blocks and look out for my car, but the cop is still parked beside it. I begin looking for a coat hanger, and after a good while, find one by a curb of the street. I keep walking, keeping about two blocks away from the car. While I walk, I bend the coat hanger into the form I'll need. As if I'd called for it, a speeding car goes past. When it comes to the avenue where my car is parked, it makes a turn. It is going so fast that its wheels screech as it rounds the corner. The cop turns on the blinking lights of his patrol car and leaving black marks on the pavement beneath it, shoots out to chase the speeder. I go up to my car and with my palms force a window open a crack. Then I insert the clothes hanger in the crack and raise the lock lever. It's a simple task, one that I'd already performed. This wasn't the first time that I'd been locked out of a car, though always before, it was because I'd forgotten to remove my keys.

UNDERSTANDING CONTEXT

1. What is the author's purpose in telling the story? What do we learn from this experience?

2. Pérez answers the Chicano patrolman in Spanish. Was this a mistake? What does their exchange reveal about cultural conflicts within the Hispanic community?

3. *Critical thinking:* Pérez implies that Chicanos have been offended when he has reminded them of their Mexican heritage; they insist on being seen as American citizens. What does this say about assimilation and identity? Does the Chicano officer's comment about Mexicans reveal contempt for immigrants? Have other ethnic groups—Jews, Italians, the Irish—resented the presence of unassimilated and poorer arrivals from their homelands?

EVALUATING STRATEGY

1. Why is a minor incident like a fender-bender a better device to explain the plight of the undocumented immigrant than a dramatic one?

2. How does Pérez use dialogue to advance the narrative? Is it better to let people speak for themselves?

APPRECIATING LANGUAGE

1. What words does Pérez use to trivialize the damage caused by the accident?
2. What word choices and images highlight the importance of documents in the lives of illegal immigrants?

WRITING SUGGESTIONS

1. Write a short narrative detailing a minor event that taught you something. A brief encounter with a homeless person may have led you to change your opinions of the poor. Perhaps you discovered your dependence on energy one afternoon when your apartment building lost power and you were unable to use your computer to finish an assignment, watch the evening news, prepare dinner, or even open the garage door to get your car.
2. *Collaborative writing:* Working with a group of students, discuss your views on immigration. Take notes and write a brief statement outlining your group's opinion. If major differences emerge during your discussion, split into subgroups and draft pro and con statements.

Martin Gansberg

Martin Gansberg (1920–1995) grew up in Brooklyn and worked as a reporter, editor, and book reviewer for the *New York Times* for over forty years. His 1964 article about a woman who was fatally stabbed while her neighbors watched but failed to call the police stunned readers and caused a national outrage. Psychologists blamed the impact of television for causing what they called "the bystander effect." Editorials cited the incident as sign of urban alienation and social apathy. Critics later claimed that Gansberg's article exaggerated events and that his dramatic opening line created the false impression that the neighbors passively watched the entire incident from beginning to end. In fact, most witnesses only heard what they thought was a late-night argument, and the most vicious part of the attack occurred out of sight of many neighbors. The man convicted of the 1964 murder of Kitty Genovese, Winston Moseley, remains in prison. He was denied parole for the thirteenth time in 2008.

Thirty-Eight Who Saw Murder and Didn't Call the Police

Source: From *The New York Times,* March 27, 1964, © 1964 The New York Times. All rights reserved. Used by permission.

This article appeared four months after the assassination of President Kennedy, when many commentators and most of the public were troubled by social unrest, crime, violence, and a growing sense that America was, as some put it, a "sick society." Consider how today's cable news commentators and bloggers would react to a similar event.

1 For more than half an hour 38 respectable, law-abiding citizens in Queens watched a killer stalk and stab a woman in three separate attacks in Kew Gardens.

2 Twice their chatter and the sudden glow of their bedroom lights interrupted him and frightened him off. Each time he returned, sought her out, and stabbed her again. Not one person telephoned the police during the assault; one witness called after the woman was dead.

3 That was two weeks ago today.

4 Still shocked is Assistant Chief Inspector Frederick M. Lussen, in charge of the borough's detectives and a veteran of 25 years of homicide investigations. He can give a matter-of-fact recitation on many murders: But the Kew Gardens slaying baffles him—not because it is a murder, but because the "good people" failed to call the police.

5 "As we have reconstructed the crime," he said, "the assailant had three chances to kill this woman during a 35-minute period. He returned twice to complete the job. If we had been called when he first attacked, the woman might not be dead now."

6 This is what the police say happened beginning at 3:20 A.M. in the staid, middle-class, tree-lined Austin Street area:

7 Twenty-eight-year-old Catherine Genovese, who was called Kitty by almost everyone in the neighborhood, was returning home from her job as manager of a bar in Hollis. She parked her red Fiat in a lot adjacent to the Kew Gardens Long Island Rail Road Station, facing Mowbray Place. Like many residents of the neighborhood,

she had parked there day after day since her arrival from Connecticut a year ago, although the railroad frowns on the practice.

8   She turned off the lights of her car, locked the door, and started to walk the 100 feet to the entrance of her apartment at 82-70 Austin Street, which is in a Tudor building with stores in the first floor and apartments on the second.

9   The entrance to the apartment is in the rear of the building because the front is rented to retail stores. At night the quiet neighborhood is shrouded in the slumbering darkness that marks most residential areas.

10   Miss Genovese noticed a man at the far end of the lot, near a seven-story apartment house at 82-40 Austin Street. She halted. Then, nervously, she headed up Austin Street toward Lefferts Boulevard, where there is a call box to the 102nd Police Precinct in nearby Richmond Hill.

11   She got as far as a streetlight in front of a bookstore before the man grabbed her. She screamed. Lights went on in the 10-story apartment house at 82-67 Austin Street, which faces the bookstore. Windows slid open and voices punctuated the early-morning stillness.

12   Miss Genovese screamed: "Oh, my God, he stabbed me! Please help me! Please help me!"

13   From one of the upper windows in the apartment house, a man called down: "Let that girl alone!"

14   The assailant looked up at him, shrugged, and walked down Austin Street toward a white sedan parked a short distance away. Miss Genovese struggled to her feet.

15   Lights went out. The killer returned to Miss Genovese, now trying to make her way around the side of the building by the parking lot to get to her apartment. The assailant stabbed her again.

16   "I'm dying!" she shrieked. "I'm dying!"

17   Windows were opened again, and lights went on in many apartments. The assailant got into his car and drove away. Miss Genovese staggered to her feet. A city bus, 0–10, the Lefferts Boulevard line to Kennedy International Airport, passed. It was 3:35 A.M.

18   The assailant returned. By then, Miss Genovese had crawled to the back of the building, where the freshly painted brown doors to the apartment house held out hope for safety. The killer tried the first door; she wasn't there. At the second door, 82-62 Austin Street, he saw her slumped on the floor at the foot of the stairs. He stabbed her a third time—fatally.

19   It was 3:50 by the time the police received their first call, from a man who was a neighbor of Miss Genovese. In two minutes they were at the scene. The neighbor, a 70-year-old woman, and another woman were the only persons on the street. Nobody else came forward.

20   The man explained that he had called the police after much deliberation. He had phoned a friend in Nassau County for advice, and then he had crossed the roof of the building to the apartment of the elderly woman to get her to make the call.

21   "I didn't want to get involved," he sheepishly told police.

22   Six days later, the police arrested Winston Moseley, a 29-year-old business machine operator, and charged him with homicide. Moseley had no previous record. He is married, has two children and owns a home at 133-19 Sutter Avenue, South Ozone Park, Queens. On Wednesday, a court committed him to Kings County Hospital for psychiatric observation.

23   When questioned by the police, Moseley also said that he had slain Mrs. Annie May Johnson, 24, of 146-12 133d Avenue, Jamaica, on Feb. 29 and Barbara Kralik, 15, of 174-17 140th Avenue, Springfield Gardens, last July. In the Kralik case, the police are holding Alvin L. Mitchell, who is said to have confessed to that slaying.

24   The police stressed how simple it would have been to have gotten in touch with them. "A phone call," said one of the detectives, "would have done it." The police may be reached by dialing "0" for operator or SPring 7-3100.

25   Today witnesses from the neighborhood, which is made up of one-family homes in the $35,000 to $60,000 range with the exception of the two apartment houses near the railroad station, find it difficult to explain why they didn't call the police.

26   A housewife, knowingly if quite casually, said, "We thought it was a lovers' quarrel." A husband and wife both said, "Frankly, we were afraid." They seemed aware of the fact that events might have been different. A distraught woman, wiping her hands in her apron, said, "I didn't want my husband to get involved."

27   One couple, now willing to talk about that night, said they heard the first screams. The husband looked thoughtfully at the bookstore where the killer first grabbed Miss Genovese.

28   "We went to the window to see what was happening," he said, "but the light from our bedroom made it difficult to see the street." The wife, still apprehensive, added: "I put out the light and we were able to see better."

29   Asked why they hadn't called the police, she shrugged and replied: "I don't know."

30   A man peeked out from a slight opening in the doorway to his apartment and rattled off an account of the killer's second attack. Why hadn't he called the police at the time? "I was tired," he said without emotion. "I went back to bed."

31   It was 4:25 A.M. when the ambulance arrived to take the body of Miss Genovese. It drove off. "Then," a solemn police detective said, "the people came out."

UNDERSTANDING CONTEXT

1. What details of this murder transformed it from a local crime story into an event that captured national attention?

2. How did the duration of the attack add to the significance of the neighbors' failure to call the police?

3. What reasons did the residents of Kew Gardens give for not taking action?

4. Gansberg mentions that William Moseley is a married homeowner with two children. Would these details surprise readers? Do most people have stereotyped notions about violent criminals?

5. Gansberg describes the neighborhood as being middle class. Is this significant? Why or why not?

6. *Critical thinking:* Do you think this article describes an isolated event or captures common-place attitudes and behaviors? Would most people call 911 today? Have you or anyone you know reported a crime in progress? Do you believe that urban life and television violence have desensitized people to crime and led them to passively watch rather than help? Do you think the same situation could occur in a small town? Is it a fact of modern life or human nature that leads people to avoid getting involved?

EVALUATING STRATEGY

1. What impact does the first line have? Although it states facts and not a point of view, can you consider it a thesis statement? Why or why not?

2. Gansberg includes details such as times and addresses. Why is this expected in a newspaper article? Does the author's inclusion of objective facts give the article greater authority?

3. Gansberg includes several direct quotations by neighbors explaining their actions that night. Are direct quotes more effective than paraphrases? Why?

4. *Critical thinking:* Does the opening line imply to you that all the witnesses passively watched the attack from beginning to end? Do writers, especially reporters, have an ethical responsibility to be accurate? Do you believe some journalists distort or exaggerate events to make their stories more dramatic?

APPRECIATING LANGUAGE

1. Gansberg uses passive voice to describe the actions of neighbors that night, stating "lights went out" and "windows opened." What impact does this have?

2. What verbs does Gansberg use to describe the victim's calls for help? What effect do they have?

3. What words does Gansberg use to describe the witnesses after the attack?

4. Gansberg uses the word "shrugged" to describe both the killer and a witness. Do you think this was deliberate? Why or why not?

WRITING SUGGESTIONS

1. Write a brief narrative about a recent incident and try objectively to reconstruct an accurate timeline of events. Include details about times, dates, locations, and participants, as for a newspaper report.

2. *Collaborative writing:* Discuss Gansberg's article with a group of students. Are they aware of similar incidents? Have they observed people's reaction to the plight of a person in distress? Do they believe most people are apathetic to victims of violence? Why or why not? Use division to organize your group's responses. If the group comes up with opposing viewpoints, consider using comparison to prepare contrasting statements.

James Dillard is a physician who specializes in rehabilitation medicine. In this narrative, first published in the "My Turn" column in *Newsweek,* he relates an incident that nearly ended his medical career.

A Doctor's Dilemma

As you read this narrative, keep in mind how most people expect physicians to respond in an emergency.

1 It was a bright, clear February afternoon in Gettysburg. A strong sun and layers of down did little to ease the biting cold. Our climb to the crest of Little Roundtop wound past somber monuments, barren trees and polished cannon. From the top, we peered down on the wheat field where men had fallen so close together that one could not see the ground. Rifle balls had whined as thick as bee swarms through the trees, and cannon shots had torn limbs from the young men fighting there. A frozen wind whipped tears from our eyes. My friend Amy huddled close, using me as a wind breaker. Despite the cold, it was hard to leave this place.

2 Driving east out of Gettysburg on a country blacktop, the gray Bronco ahead of us passed through a rural crossroad just as a small pickup truck tried to take a left turn. The Bronco swerved, but slammed into the pickup on the passenger side. We immediately slowed to a crawl as we passed the scene. The Bronco's driver looked fine, but we couldn't see the driver of the pickup. I pulled over on the shoulder and got out to investigate.

3 The right side of the truck was smashed in, and the side window was shattered. The driver was partly out of the truck. His head hung forward over the edge of the passenger-side window, the front of his neck crushed on the shattered windowsill. He was unconscious and starting to turn a dusky blue. His chest slowly heaved against a blocked windpipe.

4 A young man ran out of a house at the crossroad. "Get an ambulance out here," I shouted against the wind. "Tell them a man is dying."

5 I looked down again at the driver hanging from the windowsill. There were six empty beer bottles on the floor of the truck. I could smell the beer through the window. I knew I had to move him, to open his airway. I had no idea what neck injuries he had sustained. He could easily end up a quadriplegic. But I thought: he'll be dead by the time the ambulance gets here if I don't move him and try to do something to help him.

6 An image flashed before my mind. I could see the courtroom and the driver of the truck sitting in a wheelchair. I could see his attorney pointing at me and thundering at the jury: "This young doctor, with still a year left in his residency training, took it upon himself to play God. He took it upon himself to move this gravely injured man, condemning him forever to this wheelchair . . ." I imagined the millions of dollars in award money. And all the years of hard work lost. I'd be paying him off for the rest of my life. Amy touched my shoulder. "What are you going to do?"

7 The automatic response from long hours in the emergency room kicked in. I pulled off my overcoat and rolled up my sleeves. The trick would be to keep enough

traction straight up on his head while I moved his torso, so that his probable broken neck and spinal-cord injury wouldn't be made worse. Amy came around the driver's side, climbed half in and grabbed his belt and shirt collar. Together we lifted him off the windowsill.

8   He was still out cold, limp as a rag doll. His throat was crushed and blood from the jugular vein was running down my arms. He still couldn't breathe. He was deep blue-magenta now, his pulse was rapid and thready. The stench of alcohol turned my stomach, but I positioned his jaw and tried to blow air down into his lungs. It wouldn't go.

9   Amy had brought some supplies from my car. I opened an oversize intravenous needle and groped on the man's neck. My hands were numb, covered with freezing blood and bits of broken glass. Hyoid bone—God, I can't even feel the thyroid cartilage, it's gone . . . OK, the thyroid gland is about there, cricoid rings are here . . . we'll go in right here . . .

10   It was a lucky first shot. Pink air sprayed through the IV needle. I placed a second needle next to the first. The air began whistling through it. Almost immediately, the driver's face turned bright red. After a minute, his pulse slowed down and his eyes moved slightly. I stood up, took a step back and looked down. He was going to make it. He was going to live. A siren wailed in the distance. I turned and saw Amy holding my overcoat. I was shivering and my arms were turning white with cold.

11   The ambulance captain looked around and bellowed, "What the hell . . . who did this?" as his team scurried over to the man lying in the truck.

12   "I did," I replied. He took down my name and address for his reports. I had just destroyed my career. I would never be able to finish my residency with a massive lawsuit pending. My life was over.

13   The truck driver was strapped onto a backboard, his neck in a stiff collar. The ambulance crew had controlled the bleeding and started intravenous fluid. He was slowly waking up. As they loaded him into the ambulance, I saw him move his feet. Maybe my future wasn't lost.

14   A police sergeant called me from Pennsylvania three weeks later. Six days after successful throat-reconstruction surgery, the driver had signed out, against medical advice, from the hospital because he couldn't get a drink on the ward. He was being arraigned on drunk-driving charges.

15   A few days later, I went into the office of one of my senior professors, to tell the story. He peered over his half glasses and his eyes narrowed. "Well, you did the right thing medically of course. But, James, do you know what you put at risk by doing that?" he said sternly. "What was I supposed to do?" I asked.

16   "Drive on," he replied. "There is an army of lawyers out there who would stand in line to get a case like that. If that driver had turned out to be a quadriplegic, you might never have practiced medicine again. You were a very lucky young man."

17   The day I graduated from medical school, I took an oath to serve the sick and the injured. I remember truly believing I would be able to do just that. But I have found out it isn't so simple. I understand now what a foolish thing I did that day. Despite my oath, I know what I would do on that cold roadside near Gettysburg today. I would drive on.

UNDERSTANDING CONTEXT

1. What was Dillard's goal in publishing this narrative in a national newsmagazine?

2. Does this narrative serve to contrast idealism and reality? How does Dillard's oath conflict with his final decision?

3. Does the fact that the victim was drinking have an impact on your reactions to the doctor's actions? Does Dillard seem to show contempt for his patient?

4. *Critical thinking:* Does this essay suggest that there is an undeclared war between doctors and lawyers? Do medical malpractice suits improve or diminish the quality of medicine? Are lawyers to blame for the writer's decision to "drive on"?

EVALUATING STRATEGY

1. *Other modes:* Does this narrative also serve as a persuasive argument? Is the story a better vehicle than a standard argumentative essay that states a thesis and presents factual support?

2. Does this first-person story help place the reader in the doctor's position? Is this a more effective strategy than writing an objective third-person essay about the impact of malpractice suits?

3. Why does Dillard mention that the patient later disobeyed his doctors' orders and left the hospital so he could get a drink?

4. How do you think Dillard wanted his readers to respond to the essay's last line?

APPRECIATING LANGUAGE

1. What words does Dillard use to dramatize his attempts to save the driver's life? How do they reflect the tension he was feeling?

2. What language does Dillard use to demonstrate what he was risking by trying to save a life?

3. What kind of people read *Newsweek?* Do you find this essay's language suitable?

WRITING SUGGESTIONS

1. Relate an emergency situation you experienced or encountered. Using Dillard's essay as a model, write an account capturing what you thought and felt as you acted.

2. Write a letter to the editor of *Newsweek* in response to Dillard's essay. Do you find his position tenable? Are you angry at a doctor who vows not to help accident victims? Or do you blame the legal community for putting a physician in this position?

3. *Collaborative writing:* Discuss Dillard's essay with a small group of students and compose a short letter to the editor as a response. If members of your group have conflicting points of view, consider developing opposing letters.

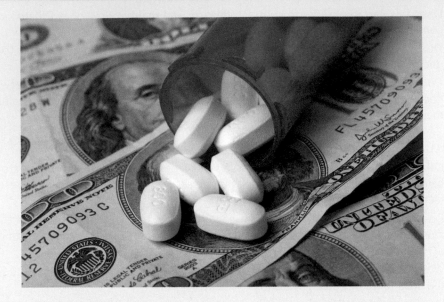

© D. Hurst/Alamy

The Health Care Crisis

All health systems have pluses and minuses; all ration health care in some way. We ration it, harshly, by income and price. People with money and access command top-notch care. Those without scramble for what they can get. Big businesses negotiate good group-health insurance. Small businesses are pushed against the wall. The healthy find private policies, the sick get kicked out. That's the American way.

Jane Bryant Quinn

A century ago most physicians in the United States had only a fragmentary knowledge of medicine. Only 10 percent had a college degree. Some medical schools did not require applicants to have a high school diploma and granted a license with just six months' training. Apprenticed to older doctors, medical students learned by observation. Little connection was made between research and practice. Equipped with dubious medicines and crude surgical techniques, doctors were frequently able to provide their patients with little more than emotional support.

The twentieth century saw a revolution in medical science, education, and technology. Extensive operations that required weeks of hospital care were replaced with minimally invasive procedures performed in outpatient clinics. New generations of drugs improved the quality of life for millions. Doctors became heroic figures, portrayed as selfless role models of skill, wisdom, and compassion. Americans came to expect immediate access to high-tech medical care.

Yet each year patients die or suffer injuries from medical malpractice. Surgeons make mistakes. Hospitals fail to follow postoperative procedures. Patients develop infections and drug interactions. According to an Institute of Medicine report, 98,000 hospital patients died from preventable medical errors in 1998. To protect themselves from lawsuits, doctors and hospitals carry malpractice insurance. In recent years many doctors who have never been sued have seen their premiums rise from $30,000 to over $100,000 a year. In response, doctors have refused to treat high-risk patients, moved from states with high jury awards, or switched specialties to lower their rates. Leo Boyle argues that "the problem of medical malpractice is that it occurs far too often . . . killing more people than AIDS, breast cancer, or automobile crashes." Philip K. Howard insists the legal system has failed to address the problem, noting, "Most victims of error get nothing, while others win lottery-like jury awards even when the doctor did nothing wrong."

As medical technology has increased so has its cost. The Centers for Medicare and Medicaid Services estimated that $2.34 trillion was spent on health care in the United States in 2008—$7,681 per person. Health care costs now represent 16 percent of the nation's economy. Combined, Medicare and Medicaid spent over $800 billion in 2008. The rising costs of health care are affecting American corporations. In 2005 General Motors reported that health care costs added $1,600 to the price of every vehicle sold. Providing health insurance for employees and retirees has made it harder for American corporations to compete with cheaper imports, further encouraging companies to send jobs overseas, where both labor and benefits are cheaper.

Advances in medical technology have also continued to raise ethical questions about providing health care for the poor, using technology to extend the lives of the terminally ill, pricing new drugs, and using fetal stem cells in research.

Before reading the articles listed below, consider these questions:

1. *Examine the ads for doctors, hospitals, and malpractice attorneys in your local Yellow Pages. How do doctors and lawyers represent themselves to the public?*
2. *Is litigation the best way to remedy medical malpractice?* Does suing a few doctors on behalf of individual patients lead to reform or simply encourage doctors to practice "defensive medicine" and order unnecessary tests?
3. *Do hospital dramas and drug commercials give the public unrealistic expectations of medical technology?*
4. *What kind of health care coverage, if any, do you or members of your family have?*
5. *Who should pay for those who can afford health insurance?*

E-READINGS ONLINE

Use InfoTrac College Edition, available through **CourseMate for** *The Sundance Writer*, to find the full text of each article online.

Leo Boyle. "The Truth about Medical Malpractice."
The Association of American Trial Lawyers argues the malpractice crisis is not caused by litigation but by preventable medical error. Malpractice, Boyle asserts, kills more Americans each year than AIDS or breast cancer.

Andis Robeznieks. "The Fear Factor: Malpractice Reforms Haven't Done Much to End Defensive Medicine."
The fear of being sued leads doctors to order needless tests and procedures, which costs the health care system over $45 billion a year.

Dan Frosch. "Your Money or Your Life: When Getting Sick Means Going Broke."
The middle class now accounts for nearly 90 percent of those declaring bankruptcy because of medical expenses.

Jane Bryant Quinn. "Our 'Kindness Deficit' of Care: We Ration Health Care, Harshly, by Income and Price."
Those with generous medical benefits or money can afford top-notch care; the poor scramble for what they can get.

Don Peck. "Putting a Value on Health."
The way to arrest spiraling costs is to admit that we already do what we say we never will—ration health care—and then figure how to do that better.

Jane M. Orient. "Embattled Doctors and Patients."
The health care reform legislation passed by Congress will only increase insurance premiums, making health care less affordable.

Maren C. Stewart. "Control Obesity, Control Costs."
Two-thirds of Americans are overweight, a condition that is responsible for one-fourth of the nation's health care costs.

K. J. Lee. "A Solution for America's Healthcare Crisis."
Health care costs could be lowered by eliminating waste and inefficiency and providing physicians and hospitals with "accurate, real-time, transparent data."

Christian Kryder. "The 'F' Word in Healthcare."
Eliminating fraud could cut $250 billion in current health care costs.

Michael Marschke. "To Die Well."
The elderly and dying should be given palliative care to provide comfort in their last days rather than aggressive and expensive procedures designed to cure them.

Jill Lepore. "The Politics of Death."
Medical technology has increased life expectancy and extended terminal illnesses so that "the longer we live, the longer we die. Over one-quarter of Medicare money now pays for medical services provided in the final year of life.

CRITICAL READING AND THINKING

1. Do you detect a "war" between doctors and lawyers?
2. Is there a better way of identifying and punishing incompetent or irresponsible physicians than costly litigation?
3. Does litigation force medical professionals to raise standards, or does it only raise costs?

4. How has the cost of health care affected individuals, corporations, and the national economy?
5. Will upper-income professionals resist change in health care policy because they fear losing some of their benefits in order to create a system that provides care for the uninsured?
6. Should health care coverage be linked to employment?
7. How important are statistics in these articles? Do they provide compelling evidence of a crisis? What role do case histories—stories about specific people—play in these articles? Is one kind of support more effective? Should writers rely on more than one type of evidence to develop persuasive argument?

WRITING SUGGESTIONS

1. If you or someone you know has been involved in a medical malpractice case, write a short essay describing what you learned from the experience.
2. Craft a brief letter responding to one or more of the writers, agreeing or disagreeing with the views expressed.
3. *Collaborative writing:* Review these articles with a group of students and discuss a single issue, such as medical malpractice, insurance benefits, or medical costs. Develop an essay dividing the group's observations into categories or contrasting opposing viewpoints.
4. *Other modes:*
   - Write a short *process* paper suggesting a fair method of handling malpractice cases.
   - Write a brief *definition* of "medical malpractice." What distinguishes malpractice from an honest error in judgment?
   - Develop a *cause-and-effect* essay detailing the causes and effects of rising health care costs. What are the causes—incompetent medical professionals, aggressive trial lawyers, patient expectations, or new technology? What are the effects on patients, the medical profession, public health, employers, the federal budget, and the American economy? You may limit your paper by discussing a single cause or effect.
   - Write a *persuasive* essay suggesting one or more solutions to one aspect of the crisis in health care.

RESEARCH PAPER

You can develop a research paper about the health care crisis by conducting further research, guided by one of the following questions:

- How much of the health care crisis is related to lifestyle issues such as smoking, obesity, diet, and alcohol and drug use? Can personal choices decrease the incidence of disease and lower family medical expenses?
- Would Americans accept a national health care system that would provide basic coverage for all citizens but limit treatment options?

■ Will corporations pressure employees to accept fewer health care benefits to compete in the global economy?

■ Can advances in medical technology lower health care costs by diagnosing diseases at an earlier stage or identifying conditions that can be prevented with drugs or changes in lifestyle?

FOR FURTHER READING

To locate additional sources on health care, enter *health care industry* as a search term in InfoTrac College Edition (available through your English CourseMate at **www.cengagebrain.com**) or one of your college library's databases, and examine readings under the following key subdivisions:

analysis	economic aspects
beliefs, opinions, attitudes	ethical aspects
case studies	political aspects

ADDITIONAL SOURCES

Using a search engine, enter one or more of the following terms to locate additional sources:

health care costs	medical malpractice
Medicare	medical malpractice insurance
health care crisis	national health insurance
right to die	euthanasia
living wills	HMOs

See the Evaluating Internet Source Checklist on pages 553–554. See Chapter 24 for documenting sources.

George Orwell was the pen name of Eric Blair (1903–1950), who was born in India, the son of a British official. Blair attended the prestigious Eton school but joined the Indian Imperial Police instead of attending university. After four years of service in Burma, he left to pursue a writing career. His first book, *Down and Out in Paris and London,* explored the plight of the poor and homeless during the depression. His later books included *Animal Farm* and *1984.*

Shooting an Elephant

Source: "Shooting an Elephant" from *Shooting an Elephant and Other Essays* by George Orwell. Copyright © 1950 by Sonia Brownell Orwell and renewed 1978 by Sonia Pitt-Rivers. By permission.

As you read the narrative, published in 1936, consider what message about imperialism Orwell was trying to communicate to his British audience. What is his implied thesis? How does he use comparison, description, and persuasion in developing this narrative?

1   In Moulmein, in Lower Burma, I was hated by large numbers of people—the only time in my life that I have been important enough for this to happen to me. I was subdivisional police officer of the town, and in an aimless, petty kind of way anti-European feeling was very bitter. No one had the guts to raise a riot, but if a European woman went through the bazaars alone somebody would probably spit betel juice over her dress. As a police officer I was an obvious target and was baited whenever it seemed safe to do so. When a nimble Burman tripped me up on the football field and the referee (another Burman) looked the other way, the crowd yelled with hideous laughter. This happened more than once. In the end the sneering yellow faces of young men that met me everywhere, the insults hooted after me when I was at a safe distance, got badly on my nerves. The young Buddhist priests were the worst of all. There were several thousands of them in the town and none of them seemed to have anything to do except stand on street corners and jeer at Europeans.

2   All this was perplexing and upsetting. For at that time I had already made up my mind that imperialism was an evil thing and the sooner I chucked up my job and got out of it the better. Theoretically—and secretly, of course—I was all for the Burmese and all against their oppressors, the British. As for the job I was doing, I hated it more bitterly than I can perhaps make clear. In a job like that you see the dirty work of Empire at close quarters. The wretched prisoners huddling in the stinking cages of the lock-ups, the grey, cowed faces of the long-term convicts, the scarred buttocks of the men who had been flogged with bamboos—all these oppressed me with an intolerable sense of guilt. But I could get nothing into perspective. I was young and ill-educated and I had had to think out my problems in the utter silence that is imposed on every Englishman in the East. I did not even know that the British Empire is dying, still less did I know that it is a great deal better than the younger empires that are going to supplant it. All I knew was that I was stuck between my hatred of the empire I served and my rage against the evil-spirited little beasts who tried to make my job impossible. With one part of my mind I thought of the British Raj as an unbreakable tyranny, as something clamped down, *in saecula saeculorum,* upon the will of prostrate peoples; with another part I thought that the greatest joy in the world would be to drive a bayonet into a Buddhist priest's guts. Feelings like these

are the normal byproducts of imperialism; ask any Anglo-Indian official, if you can catch him off duty.

3   One day something happened which in a roundabout way was enlightening. It was a tiny incident in itself, but it gave me a better glimpse than I had had before of the real nature of imperialism—the real motives for which despotic governments act. Early one morning the sub-inspector at a police station the other end of the town rang me up on the phone and said that an elephant was ravaging the bazaar. Would I please come and do something about it? I did not know what I could do, but I wanted to see what was happening and I got on to a pony and started out. I took my rifle, an old .44 Winchester and much too small to kill an elephant, but I thought the noise might be useful *in terrorem*. Various Burmans stopped me on the way and told me about the elephant's doings. It was not, of course, a wild elephant, but a tame one which had gone "must." It had been chained up as tame elephants always are when their attack of "must" is due, but on the previous night it had broken its chain and escaped. Its mahout, the only person who could manage it when it was in that state, had set out in pursuit, but he had taken the wrong direction and was now twelve hours' journey away, and in the morning the elephant had suddenly reappeared in the town. The Burmese population had no weapons and were quite helpless against it. It had already destroyed somebody's bamboo hut, killed a cow and raided some fruit-stalls and devoured the stock; also it had met the municipal rubbish van, and, when the driver jumped out and took to his heels, had turned the van over and inflicted violence upon it.

4   The Burmese sub-inspector and some Indian constables were waiting for me in the quarter where the elephant had been seen. It was a very poor quarter, a labyrinth of squalid bamboo huts, thatched with palm-leaf, winding all over a steep hillside. I remember that it was a cloudy stuffy morning at the beginning of the rains. We began questioning the people as to where the elephant had gone, and, as usual, failed to get any definite information. That is invariably the case in the East; a story always sounds clear enough at a distance, but the nearer you get to the scene of events the vaguer it becomes. Some of the people said that the elephant had gone in one direction, some said that he had gone in another, some professed not even to have heard of any elephant. I had almost made up my mind that the whole story was a pack of lies, when we heard yells a little distance away. There was a loud, scandalised cry of "Go away, child! Go away this instant!" and an old woman with a switch in her hand came round the corner of a hut, violently shooing away a crowd of naked children. Some more women followed, clicking their tongues and exclaiming; evidently there was something there that the children ought not to have seen. I rounded the hut and saw a man's dead body sprawling in the mud. He was an Indian, a black Dravidian coolie, almost naked, and he could not have been dead many minutes. The people said that the elephant had come suddenly upon him round the corner of the hut, caught him with its trunk, put its foot on his back and ground him into the earth. This was the rainy season and the ground was soft, and his face had scored a trench a foot deep and a couple of yards long. He was lying on his belly with arms crucified and head sharply twisted to one side. His face was coated with mud, the eyes wide open, the teeth bared and grinning with an expression of unendurable agony. (Never tell me, by the way, that the dead look peaceful. Most of the corpses I have

seen looked devilish.) The friction of the great beast's foot had stripped the skin from his back as neatly as one skins a rabbit. As soon as I saw the dead man I sent an orderly to a friend's house nearby to borrow an elephant rifle. I had already sent back the pony, not wanting it to go mad with fright and throw me if it smelled the elephant.

5 The orderly came back in a few minutes with a rifle and five cartridges, and meanwhile some Burmans had arrived and told us that the elephant was in the paddy fields below, only a few hundred yards away. As I started forward practically the whole population of the quarter flocked out of their houses and followed me. They had seen the rifle and were all shouting excitedly that I was going to shoot the elephant. They had not shown much interest in the elephant when he was merely ravaging their homes, but it was different now that he was going to be shot. It was a bit of fun to them, as it would be to an English crowd; besides, they wanted the meat. It made me vaguely uneasy. I had no intention of shooting the elephant—I had merely sent for the rifle to defend myself if necessary—and it is always unnerving to have a crowd following you. I marched down the hill, looking and feeling a fool, with the rifle over my shoulder and an ever-growing army of people jostling at my heels. At the bottom, when you got away from the huts, there was a metalled road and beyond that a miry waste of paddy fields a thousand yards across, not yet ploughed but soggy from the first rains and dotted with coarse grass. The elephant was standing eighty yards from the road, his left side towards us. He took not the slightest notice of the crowd's approach. He was tearing up bunches of grass, beating them against his knees to clean them and stuffing them into his mouth.

6 I had halted on the road. As soon as I saw the elephant I knew with perfect certainty that I ought not to shoot him. It is a serious matter to shoot a working elephant—it is comparable to destroying a huge and costly piece of machinery—and obviously one ought not to do it if it can possibly be avoided. And at that distance, peacefully eating, the elephant looked no more dangerous than a cow. I thought then and I think now that his attack of "must" was already passing off; in which case he would merely wander harmlessly about until the mahout came back and caught him. Moreover, I did not in the least want to shoot him. I decided that I would watch him for a little while to make sure that he did not turn savage again, and then go home.

7 But at that moment I glanced round at the crowd that had followed me. It was an immense crowd, two thousand at the least and growing every minute. It blocked the road for a long distance on either side. I looked at the sea of yellow faces above the garish clothes—faces all happy and excited over this bit of fun, all certain that the elephant was going to be shot. They were watching me as they would watch a conjuror about to perform a trick. They did not like me, but with the magical rifle in my hands I was momentarily worth watching. And suddenly I realised that I should have to shoot the elephant after all. The people expected it of me and I had got to do it; I could feel their two thousand wills pressing me forward, irresistibly. And it was at this moment, as I stood there with the rifle in my hands, that I first grasped the hollowness, the futility of the white man's dominion in the East. Here was I, the white man with his gun, standing in front of the unarmed native crowd—seemingly the leading actor of the piece; but in reality I was only an absurd puppet pushed to and fro by the will of those yellow faces behind. I perceived in this moment that when the white man

turns tyrant it is his own freedom that he destroys. He becomes a sort of hollow, posing dummy, the conventionalised figure of a sahib. For it is the condition of his rule that he shall spend his life in trying to impress the "natives" and so in every crisis he has got to do what the "natives" expect of him. He wears a mask, and his face grows to fit it. I had got to shoot the elephant. I had committed myself to doing it when I sent for the rifle. A sahib has got to act like a sahib; he has got to appear resolute, to know his own mind and do definite things. To come all that way, rifle in hand, with two thousand people marching at my heels, and then to trail feebly away, having done nothing—no, that was impossible. The crowd would laugh at me. And my whole life, every white man's life in the East, was one long struggle not to be laughed at.

8   But I did not want to shoot the elephant. I watched him beating his bunch of grass against his knees, with that preoccupied grandmotherly air that elephants have. It seemed to me that it would be murder to shoot him. At that age I was not squeamish about killing animals, but I had never shot an elephant and never wanted to. (Somehow it always seems worse to kill a *large* animal.) Besides, there was the beast's owner to be considered. Alive, the elephant was worth at least a hundred pounds; dead, he would only be worth the value of his tusks—five pounds, possibly. But I had got to act quickly. I turned to some experienced-looking Burmans who had been there when we arrived, and asked them how the elephant had been behaving. They all said the same thing: he took no notice of you if you left him alone, but he might charge if you went too close to him.

9   It was perfectly clear to me what I ought to do. I ought to walk up to within, say, twenty-five yards of the elephant and test his behaviour. If he charged I could shoot, if he took no notice of me it would be safe to leave him until the mahout came back. But also I knew that I was going to do no such thing. I was a poor shot with a rifle and the ground was soft mud into which one would sink at every step. If the elephant charged and I missed him, I should have about as much chance as a toad under a steam-roller. But even then I was not thinking particularly of my own skin, only the watchful yellow faces behind. For at that moment, with the crowd watching me, I was not afraid in the ordinary sense, as I would have been if I had been alone. A white man mustn't be frightened in front of "natives"; and so, in general, he isn't frightened. The sole thought in my mind was that if anything went wrong those two thousand Burmans would see me pursued, caught, trampled on and reduced to a grinning corpse like that Indian up the hill. And if that happened it was quite probable that some of them would laugh. That would never do. There was only one alternative. I shoved the cartridges into the magazine and lay down on the road to get a better aim.

10   The crowd grew very still, and a deep, low, happy sigh, as of people who see the theatre curtain go up at last, breathed from innumerable throats. They were going to have their bit of fun after all. The rifle was a beautiful German thing with cross-hair sights. I did not then know that in shooting an elephant one should shoot to cut an imaginary bar running from ear-hole to ear-hole. I ought therefore, as the elephant was sideways on, to have aimed straight at his ear-hole; actually I aimed several inches in front of this, thinking the brain would be further forward.

11   When I pulled the trigger I did not hear the bang or feel the kick—one never does when a shot goes home—but heard the devilish roar of glee that went up from the

crowd. In that instant, in too short a time, one would have thought, even for the bullet to get there, a mysterious, terrible change had come over the elephant. He neither stirred nor fell, but every line of his body had altered. He looked suddenly stricken, shrunken, immensely old, as though the frightful impact of the bullet had paralysed him without knocking him down. At last, after what seemed a long time—it might have been five seconds, I dare say—he sagged flabbily to his knees. His mouth slobbered. An enormous senility seemed to have settled upon him. One could have imagined him thousands of years old. I fired again into the same spot. At the second shot he did not collapse but climbed with desperate slowness to his feet and stood weakly upright, with legs sagging and head drooping. I fired a third time. That was the shot that did for him. You could see the agony of it jolt his whole body and knock the last remnant of strength from his legs. But in falling he seemed for a moment to rise, for as his hind legs collapsed beneath him he seemed to tower upwards like a huge rock toppling, his trunk reaching skyward like a tree. He trumpeted, for the first and only time. And then down he came, his belly towards me, with a crash that seemed to shake the ground even where I lay.

12　　I got up. The Burmans were already racing past me across the mud. It was obvious that the elephant would never rise again, but he was not dead. He was breathing very rhythmically with long rattling gasps, his great mound of a side painfully rising and falling. His mouth was wide open—I could see far down into caverns of pale pink throat. I waited a long time for him to die, but his breathing did not weaken. Finally I fired my two remaining shots into the spot where I thought his heart must be. The thick blood welled out of him like red velvet, but still he did not die. His body did not even jerk when the shots hit him, the tortured breathing continued without a pause. He was dying, very slowly and in great agony, but in some world remote from me where not even a bullet could damage him further. I felt that I had got to put an end to that dreadful noise. It seemed dreadful to see the great beast lying there, powerless to move and yet powerless to die, and not even to be able to finish him. I went back for my small rifle and poured shot after shot into his heart and down his throat. They seemed to make no impression. The tortured gasps continued as steadily as the ticking of a clock.

13　　In the end I could not stand it any longer and went away. I heard later that it took him half an hour to die. Burmans were arriving with dahs and baskets even before I left, and I was told they had stripped his body almost to the bones by the afternoon.

14　　Afterwards, of course, there were endless discussions about the shooting of the elephant. The owner was furious, but he was only an Indian and could do nothing. Besides, legally I had done the right thing, for a mad elephant has to be killed, like a mad dog, if its owner fails to control it. Among the Europeans opinion was divided. The older men said I was right, the younger men said it was a damn shame to shoot an elephant for killing a coolie, because an elephant was worth more than any damn Coringhee coolie. And afterwards I was very glad that the coolie had been killed; it put me legally in the right and it gave me a sufficient pretext for shooting the elephant. I often wondered whether any of the others grasped that I had done it solely to avoid looking a fool.

UNDERSTANDING CONTEXT

1. What is Orwell's goal in relating this incident? What does this event symbolize?
2. What roles does Orwell play in the narrative? How does his behavior as a police officer conflict with his personal views?
3. What are Orwell's attitudes toward the Burmese?
4. Orwell's readers were primarily British. What was he trying to impress upon them?
5. *Critical thinking:* Consider Orwell's statement, "With one part of my mind I thought of the British Raj [rule over India] as an unbreakable tyranny . . . with another part I thought that the greatest joy in the world would be to drive a bayonet into a Buddhist priest's guts." What does this admission reveal?

EVALUATING STRATEGY

1. Orwell opens the essay with the statement, "I was hated by large numbers of people." What impact does that have on readers? Does it do more than simply attract attention?
2. How does Orwell balance his role between narrator and participant?
3. *Other modes:* Can this essay also serve as an example? Is the killing of the elephant representative of a larger issue?

APPRECIATING LANGUAGE

1. What metaphors does Orwell use in telling the story?
2. Underline the figurative language Orwell uses on page 223 to describe the labored death of the elephant. What images does he use to create a sense of horror?
3. Orwell calls the Burmese "natives," "coolies," and "Burmans." He describes their huts as "squalid" and the rice paddies as a "miry waste." What does this suggest about his view of Asia?

WRITING SUGGESTIONS

1. *Critical thinking:* Orwell relates an incident in which he played a role that conflicted with his personal beliefs. Write a brief narrative about an event that placed you in a similar situation. Have your roles as employee, manager, spouse, parent, student, or friend caused you to act against your values? Select a single event and write a short narrative, clearly outlining how the actions you were compelled to take contrasted with what you really felt at the time. Have you ever been compelled to lie on behalf of others?
2. *Collaborative writing:* Work with other students to create a short statement analyzing Orwell's message about political power and the nature of abusive governments. Have each group member write a draft and then work to combine ideas into a single statement. If there are major differences in ideas, develop a comparison or division paper to contrast or list these different views.

WRITING BEYOND THE CLASSROOM

Metro Hotel
New York

INCIDENT REPORT
July 23, 2011
Sandra Berman
Legal Department

RE: Disturbance at Central Assurance Annual Meeting, Continental
Ballroom 7/22/11 7:30–7:45 P.M.

At approximately 7:30 last evening I left my office and encountered a
disturbance outside the Continental Ballroom, where Central Assurance
was holding its annual meeting. A woman was shouting at a female
security guard, insisting she be allowed into the ballroom. I approached
this woman and asked her to identify herself. She refused and demanded
entry into the meeting. I politely asked her to show a pass or a room key.
Central Assurance required that security only allow invited guests with
passes into the meeting. This woman, who finally identified herself as
Sharon Engleman, never produced any credentials.

   I politely asked that she lower her voice and leave the premises
unless she could produce either a pass to the meeting or a hotel key.
At this point George Muir of Central Assurance came from the ballroom,
identified himself, and explained to me that Ms. Engleman had been part
of a class action lawsuit and was demanding to address the shareholders.
He stated that their attorneys had told both her and her attorneys that
she had no legal right to appear at a shareholders' meeting because she
was neither an employee of Central Assurance nor a stockholder.

   At this point Ms. Engleman began screaming obscenities and
demanded to distribute flyers to the shareholders. I told her she could
leave her flyers on the table outside the ballroom. She then pushed both
Mr. Muir and myself. The security guard called for assistance. Ted Wilson
of hotel security arrived and immediately asked Ms. Engleman to leave
the hotel. When she refused, he called the police. At approximately
7:45 P.M. two NYPD officers arrived and escorted Ms. Engleman from the
building. On her way out she shouted obscenities at me and threatened
to sue the hotel.

   I reported this incident to Frank Canon, Vice President of Central
Assurance when the meeting ended at 10:35 P.M.

   Please contact me for further information on this matter.

Roisin Reardon
Special Events Coordinator

UNDERSTANDING CONTEXT

1. What is the purpose of this narrative?
2. Who is the immediate and potential extended audience for this document?
3. Why would this report be useful for an attorney representing the hotel?
4. *Critical thinking:* How might the threat of a lawsuit compel a professional to document his or her actions?

EVALUATING STRATEGY

1. How can a writer deal with events that do not have a clearly established time reference?
2. Are there missing details that you feel should be included?

APPRECIATING LANGUAGE

1. Why is word choice important in reports like this?
2. Why do you think the author repeats the word "politely"?

WRITING SUGGESTIONS

1. Create an objective report of a situation you witnessed, such as a car accident, demonstration, rally, athletic game, or live concert.
2. *Collaborative writing:* Working with a group of students, read the report and discuss your impressions. Did the hotel employee appear to behave professionally and responsibly? What image does she project in her report? Do you see anything in the tone or style of the report that seems inappropriate? Why or why not?

RESPONDING TO IMAGES

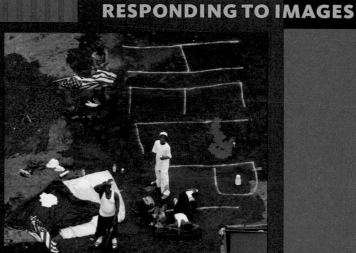

Victims of Hurricane Katrina seeking help, New Orleans, 2005
© Smiley N. Pool/Dallas Morning News/CORBIS

1. Describe your first response to this photograph. What led the people to write a message when their plight would have been obvious? Do you recall your reactions to television coverage of Katrina victims trapped on roof-tops, on highway overpasses, and in the Superdome? Do you believe the criticisms of the government's response were fair or unfair?

2. The victims in New Orleans lived in a world-famous city familiar to many tourists and media personalities. Would victims of a disaster in a remote part of Kansas or Idaho receive as much attention? Does familiarity with a location affect how people perceive images? Millions of people who never visited New York City, for example, had seen the World Trade Center in pictures, movies, and television programs. Did that make its destruction on September 11 more palpable and dramatic? Had terrorists killed the same number of people by flying planes into five-story apartment buildings in a smaller city, would the images be as striking? Why or why not?

RESPONDING TO IMAGES

3. *Visual analysis:* What role do the flags play in this image? What statement do they make? Why would victims use flags to attract attention? Consider the impact of the messages painted on the roofs. Few photographs include text. Do these words create a natural caption?

4. *Collaborative writing:* Work with a group of students and develop a caption for this photograph to be used in a high school history book. Create a caption that is accurate and objective. Pay attention to the use of words and the impact of connotations. If members of your group disagree, develop opposing captions.

5. *Other modes:*
   - Write a *description* essay that analyzes the images present in this photograph, such as the flag, the messages, and the people's gestures.
   - Write a *cause-and-effect* essay that outlines the impact this image has on the public. Does an image like this lead many Americans to view the response to Katrina along racial lines?
   - Write a *classification* paper that establishes how you think emergency workers should respond in a disaster. Which victims should be rescued first? Which victims should be rescued last?
   - Write a *persuasive* essay that suggests how local, state, and federal agencies can better coordinate their responses to avoid duplication and indecision.

NARRATION CHECKLIST

Before submitting your paper, review these points:

✔ Does your narrative have a clear focus?

✔ Can your readers clearly follow the chronology of events?

✔ Do you write in a consistent tense? Does your narrative contain illogical shifts from past to present?

✔ Does the narrative flow evenly, or is it cluttered with unnecessary detail?

✔ Does your narrative maintain a consistent point of view? Do you switch from first to third person without reason?

✔ Does your narrative suit your purpose, reader, and discourse community?

Access the English CourseMate for this text at **www.cengagebrain.com** for additional information on writing narration.

Example
Presenting Illustrations

What Is Example?

Examples illustrate an idea, issue, problem, situation, or personality type. Examples are used to establish a definition or support a thesis. After defining an *adjective* as "a word modifying a noun or pronoun," a textbook may provide readers with examples: *red, new, tall, rich*. The achievements of movie directors can be demonstrated with scenes from their films. The case history of a single patient can illustrate the symptoms of a mental disorder. Writers also use examples to support an argument. An attorney filing a claim of sexual harassment may present specific violations to substantiate a client's case. Students demanding greater campus security might list recent thefts in a letter to the dean to substantiate the need for increased protection.

An example differs from a narration or a description in that the details do not characterize a single person, place, or event, but supply information about a type. A narrative essay might tell the story of a man or woman winning the Boston Marathon after recovering from a serious accident. An example essay would relate the athlete's story to illustrate how people can overcome challenges. A description essay provides details about an entrepreneur turning an abandoned church into a bookstore. An example essay would use these details as an illustration of recycling abandoned buildings.

Purpose: To Inform or Persuade

Writers clarify abstract ideas and prevent confusion by giving readers specific examples:

> Dorm residents may use small electrical devices—*hair dryers, laptops, or electric shavers*—but are prohibited from operating major appliances—*microwaves, toaster ovens, or refrigerators.*
>
> —*Student Manual*

■ Informative examples should be accurate and specific—ones readers will readily recognize and understand.

■ The language used in developing informative examples should suit the audience. Writers must choose words carefully and be conscious of how connotations will influence readers.

Writers also use examples to support a thesis.

Thesis	*Fraternities do not promote binge drinking. For example,* last month's Greek Week
Examples	sponsored fifteen separate events that drew 7,500 participants. Alcohol was
	served only to those of legal drinking age, and IDs were checked by licensed
	security guards. The campus police reported no drinking-related violations.
	On the contrary, the English Department's Poetry in the Park festival resulted
	in thirteen citations for illegal drinking and a drunk-driving arrest.

—Letter to the editor

- Persuasive examples should be ones readers will identify and accept. Democrats are not likely to be impressed by a writer who uses only endorsements by Republicans to support a political argument. High school students may lack the sense of history needed to appreciate examples drawn from the Depression or World War II.

- Because examples are often isolated incidents, they should also be supported by evidence demonstrating a general trend—statistics, surveys, and expert testimony.

Extended Examples

Writers may use a single extended example—often in the form of a narrative—to explain an idea or support an argument. Extended examples allow writers to tell a story, create human interest, and provide a context for evidence such as quotations and statistics. Media entrepreneur Tony Brown used the failing of a single black business to illustrate the African American community's failure to patronize black entrepreneurs:

> It was a day of celebration when Rick Singletary opened the largest Black-owned super-market in the country in Columbus, Ohio—a spectacular $4.4 million operation. He had worked for a major grocery chain for fourteen years and started his own store with his life savings, those of his mother, and a government-insured loan from the Reagan administration. He located Singletary Plaza Mart in the Black community because he knew there was a need for a grocery store there, and because he wanted to create jobs for Blacks.
>
> The entrepreneur needed only a $200,000-a-week volume to keep 130 Black people working. And yet, in a tragedy that exemplifies the real reason why Black America has never been able to compete with White America, Singletary's store failed. Although his research has shown that Blacks in Columbus spent $2.5 million per week on groceries, he could not get them to spend even $200,000 of it in the store he had built in their own neighborhood.

Tony Brown, "Death of a Dream"

Advantages

- Extended examples clarify concepts by telling a story that can arouse interest, build suspense, and dramatize factual detail.

- Extended examples allow writers to explore an issue in depth by creating a microcosm. By understanding a specific item in detail, readers can appreciate the complexity of the larger issue it represents.

Disadvantages

■ Readers may dismiss a single example as a random event or exception that has no wider significance. The use of other evidence, such as facts and statistics, can bolster the importance of the example.

■ Extended examples may not be representative. Because no two people, objects, or events are exactly alike, no individual example is likely to fully illustrate a subject. An extended example of a child learning to read, an alcoholic seeking sobriety, or a prosecutor preparing a case may be misleading. Readers may assume that a strictly personal trait is shared by the general population. Extended examples require accurate commentary to prevent confusion.

Lists of Examples

To overcome problems that can occur with a single example, writers often present more than one illustration. By listing a number of examples, they hope that readers will find it easier to identify their subject. Larry Orenstein uses a series of short examples of people who die in unusual circumstances to define his term "odd enders":

> Some people become Odd Enders by accident. In 1947, an eccentric U.S. recluse, while carrying food to his equally reclusive brother, tripped a burglar trap in his house and was crushed to death under bundles of old newspapers, three breadboxes, a sewing machine and a suitcase filled with metal. His brother starved to death.
>
> In 1982, a 27-year-old man fired two shotgun blasts at a giant saguaro cactus in the desert near Phoenix. The shots caused a 23-foot section of the cactus to fall and crush him to death. That same year, an elderly Louisiana man with ailing kidneys was waving a gun at quarreling relatives when it went off. The bullet severed a tube from his dialysis machine, and he bled to death.
>
> —*Larry Orenstein, "Odd Enders"*

Advantages

■ Using a number of examples demonstrates a range of possibilities.

■ Readers who might misinterpret a single example are more likely to gain a fuller understanding of the subject if more than one illustration is given.

Disadvantages

■ A list of examples can be too brief to fully explain or represent an issue and may offer only superficial illustrations. To counteract this problem, writers often vary the length of examples, briefly listing some while describing others in depth.

■ A list of isolated examples can appear to be simply a collection of random events that provides weak support for an argument. Including facts, testimony, and statistics can provide additional evidence.

■ Although a series of brief examples can create a fast-paced essay, they can lack focus. Lists of examples should be carefully organized in a logical pattern.

WRITING ACTIVITY

List examples that would support the following general statements.

1. People will try almost anything to lose weight.

2. Parents must develop methods to spend more time with their children.

3. Consumer decisions affect the environment.

4. The American economy has overcome many challenges.

5. Technology is robbing people of personal privacy.

6. Movies and television present stereotyped images of women.

7. Today's job market demands computer literacy.

8. Automobiles require special attention.

9. Marriage demands compromise.

10. The Internet has influenced journalism.

Hypothetical Examples

Examples can be fictional, usually narratives of possible situations. Writers often use hypothetical examples to explain or dramatize a point.

Thesis	Make sure you report all injuries—even superficial wounds—to your supervisor before leaving the plant. For
Hypothetical example	*example,* if you fall and hurt your knee but fail to inform your supervisor, you may be unable to prove the injury was work related and be unable to receive full benefits if you later discover surgery is required.

Advantages

- Hypothetical examples are useful when no factual example exists or if actual situations are too complicated to serve as explanations.
- Hypothetical examples allow writers to speculate about possible events.
- Fictional examples are useful when writers wish to avoid bias and subjective judgments. Factual examples may create controversy or lead to personal interpretations.

Disadvantages

- Hypothetical examples are not based in fact. They offer only possible events and actions and provide weak evidence for arguments. Hypothetical examples require support from other forms of evidence to support a thesis.
- Hypothetical examples can seem distant and unrealistic. They can be made effective if they include facts and provide realistic scenarios readers will recognize.

Factual Examples

Factual examples use actual events and people to explain an idea or illustrate a point:

Thesis	Make sure you report all injuries—even superficial wounds—to your supervisor before leaving the plant. Last spring a shipping
Factual example	clerk injured her knee on the loading dock. Thinking she had suffered only a minor bruise, she completed her shift and went home without informing her supervisor. During the night she awoke in great pain and went to the emergency room where doctors discovered a fracture requiring surgery. Because she could not prove the injury occurred at work, she had to pay over $2,500 in insurance co-payments.

Advantages

- Factual examples command attention because they are based in actual events, involving people readers may know or at least identify with.
- Factual illustrations can be documented, dramatizing the reality of the issue or problem.

Disadvantages

- Factual examples may contain specific details that are not generally representative.
- Because factual examples usually describe past events, some readers may infer that they are irrelevant to current circumstances.

WRITING ACTIVITY

Provide a hypothetical or factual example to support or illustrate the following thesis statements:

1. Peer pressure drives adolescents to engage in self-destructive behavior.

2. Motion pictures influence fashion trends.

3. Many people purchase pets without considering how they will care for them.

4. Credit cards lead some consumers to spend recklessly.

5. Operating a small business can entail great risk.

6. Public schools are failing to prepare students for college.

7. Attitudes toward child abuse have changed in the last two decades.

8. Many undergraduates find it almost impossible to complete a bachelor's degree in four years.

9. Television gives children unrealistic expectations.

10. A false allegation, even if proved untrue, can ruin a person's reputation.

Strategies for Writing Example: Prewriting and Planning

Critical Thinking and Prewriting

1. **You can begin writing an example essay in two ways.** Select a person, place, situation, event, or object that illustrates a trend or general condition:
   - A power failure prevents you from printing an assignment, illustrating our dependence on energy.
   - A fraudulent charge appears on your credit card statement, providing an example of identity theft.

   Or select a general concept, idea, or subject and explain it to readers by using one or more examples:
   - Describe your interpretation of a "no-win situation" and support it with examples.
   - Explain the qualities of a role model by providing examples of men and women who demonstrate these traits.

2. **Consider your readers' perceptual world.** The attitudes, education, values, and experiences of your readers determine how they will respond to examples you use to inform or persuade your audience. Midwesterners may not understand examples requiring familiarity with New York City politics. Young people may not recognize famous individuals known to their parents.

3. **Engage critical thinking.** Examples, like statistics, can be both persuasive and misleading. No matter how interesting or compelling, examples are individual events, persons, or situations and may not be representative of the whole. The fact that a healthy eighty-five-year-old man has smoked heavily since adolescence does not disprove the overwhelming evidence that tobacco causes disease. Examples are anecdotal accounts and rarely provide convincing support for an argument unless supplemented with other forms of evidence. Ask yourself the following:
   - Are your examples truly representative, or are they exceptions to a general rule or condition?
   - Can your examples be supported by facts, testimony, surveys, or statistics?

4. **Begin listing examples.** Use brainstorming, listing, and asking questions to generate as many examples as you can. Freewrite to explore longer or extended examples.

Planning

1. **Clearly define the general principle, rule, situation, or fact the example is going to illustrate.** Examples can become simple narratives unless they support a clearly defined subject.

2. **Determine whether your essay would benefit from a single extended example or a series of examples.**

3. **Organize examples using a chronological, spatial, or emphatic pattern.** Create a timeline for longer or extended examples to focus the narrative.

4. **Determine the best placement for the thesis and definitions.** Beginning with an example can arouse interest and present facts before the thesis

is stated. This is useful when you are confronting a biased or hostile audience.

5. **Review your thesis before writing.**
   - Is it clearly stated?
   - Does it express a general idea or principle that can be illustrated or proven by examples?

6. **Review your examples.**
   - Do the examples clearly support the thesis?
   - Are the examples ones readers will understand and appreciate?
   - Are the examples arranged in a logical pattern?

Strategies for Writing Example: Writing the First Draft

Writing the First Draft

1. **Use the plan as a guide but be open to additional examples.** As you write, you may expand examples, discover new ones, or discard some on your list as irrelevant or unworkable.

2. **Distinguish between relevant and incidental events.** Because your examples are supposed to illustrate a general situation, it is important that your text indicate which elements are wholly personal or accidental. Stress items that support the thesis:

   Ted Smith, *like all AIDS patients in the study,* had been HIV positive for at least five years but had not developed outward symptoms beyond slight fatigue. He took the new drug and within six weeks reported increased energy and stamina. *Unlike the other patients,* Smith continued to take AZT. He reported mild to severe headaches lasting ten to fifteen minutes after taking the new drug. This side effect occurred in 20 percent of patients in the study.

3. **Use introductory and transitional statements to link examples and the thesis:**

   Crime is increasing on this campus. Bicycle theft, *for example,* . . .
   Kai Long lost ten pounds in two weeks on this diet, *illustrating* . . .

Strategies for Writing Example: Revising and Editing

Revising

1. **Review the plan and thesis.**
   - Is the thesis stated in terms readers can understand?
   - Can the thesis be refined to more sharply delineate what the examples illustrate?

2. **Do the examples support your thesis?** Remember an example is more than a narrative or a description. It should explain an idea or support a point of view.

(Continued)

3. **Is other evidence needed to make a stronger argument?**
   - Can facts, quotations, or statistics be blended into the essay to offer additional proof?
4. **Decide whether your point is better supported by hypothetical or factual examples.**
   - You may wish to mix factual and hypothetical examples to provide actual details and unbiased illustrations.
5. **Measure the number and value of examples.**
   - Are enough examples presented to illustrate all phases of the subject?
   - Do examples provide separate illustrations or are they merely repetitive?
6. **Are examples clearly organized or do they form a random pattern?**
   - You may want to experiment with a different kind of organization (such as chronological, spatial, or emphatic) to be sure you choose the most effective style.

Editing and Proofreading

1. **Examine examples for consistency in voice, tone, style, and tense.** A list of examples can appear chaotic if there are awkward shifts.
   - Keep examples in the same tense and voice. Avoid shifting from first to third person or from past to present unless there are logical transitions.
2. **Review diction for unintended connotations.** Because examples are supposed to illustrate and explain an idea, careful word choice is essential to avoid misleading readers.
3. **Examine paragraph breaks and transitions for clarity.** Readers will rely on structure to follow examples and relate them to a general principle.
4. **Make the opening and final examples memorable.** First and last impressions are most likely to influence readers and give them illustrations they can recall and repeat to others.

STUDENT PAPER

This paper was written in response to the following assignment in a freshman composition course:

> Write a 500-word essay that illustrates a current social phenomenon with an example of someone you know or have met. Your paper might illustrate the struggles of single mothers, the perils of dating online, the dilemma of telling a falsehood. Make sure your paper clearly defines the subject you are illustrating. Document the use of any outside sources.

FIRST DRAFT WITH INSTRUCTOR'S COMMENTS

Title?

My former tennis partner Terrell Williams stopped coming to the courts in late September.

adverb

When I ran into him in the library he tells me he can't play anymore. I thought maybe his

badly

shoulder was acting up again, because last season he tore it very bad. It took weeks for him

Avoid tense shift/run-on tense shift

to recover and it almost seemed he would have to quit the track team as well.

Instead Terrell tells me he had started a business to pay for books and tuition fees. Terry

father's

had discovered, almost by accident, that a company near his fathers repair shop purchased

wooden forklift pallets. This firm pays five dollars for intact pallets and three dollars for

broken ones. Driving to school the next day, Terry noticed abandoned pallets tossed beside

not parallel

dumpsters, stacked in alleys, and many were leaning against convenience stores. On his way

home that afternoon he stopped to ask some store managers, landlords, delivery drivers if he

wordy

could have the pallets they were discarding ~~or leaving behind~~. A convenience store owner not

only let him have the pallets but offered to pay him twenty dollars a week to get rid of them.

Terry borrowed his father's 1999 Ford van and began picking up pallets on his way home

from school. After a week he was earning fifty to a hundred dollars a day. As the semester

passed, he developed contacts with local merchants who informed him of major deliveries.

Now he could sometimes load up his van and get a hundred dollars' worth of pallets in one

stop. Factory managers began stacking spare pallets in alleys for him.

Terry gave his father fifty dollars a week for use of the van and paid for gas and new

tires. The van was put to hard use and soon needed a brake job and a tune up. Terry still

managed to generate enough profit to pay for school, his books, and rent.

expand, what kind?

Terry is really an example of a new kind of entrepreneur.

(Continued)

REVISION NOTES

This is an interesting topic to write about, but this is really a description or a narrative—not an example. Only the last sentence points out that your friend represents something larger. Remember, an example is not the story or a description of a single person, place, object, or situation—it represents a larger trend, problem, or issue. What does Terry represent? What "new kind of entrepreneur"?

REVISED DRAFT

Jack Chu   **Communication Skills 151**

Guerrilla Entrepreneur

Last semester Pauline Feldman spoke at the business school to promote her new book, *Guerrilla Entrepreneurs,* about a new breed of small business owners, particularly those in the inner city who often operate in an expanding underground economy. Instead of getting traditional jobs, guerilla entrepreneurs discover an overlooked opportunity and launch a business venture. "In a tough job market," she noted, "it is hard for young people to find work when downsized professionals with years of experience, connections, and proven skills are willing to take entry level jobs." She suggested that more young people will have to become guerrilla entrepreneurs and create their own careers.

No one better illustrates this phenomenon than Terrell Williams, my former tennis partner. I say former because Terry stopped coming to the courts in late September. When I ran into him in the library, he explained that in order to pay for tuition and save for a new car, he had started a business.

Terry discovered, almost by accident, that a company near his father's repair shop purchased wooden forklift pallets. This firm pays five dollars for intact pallets and three dollars for broken ones. Driving to school the next day, Terry noticed abandoned pallets tossed beside dumpsters, stacked in alleys, and propped against convenience stores. On his way home that afternoon, he stopped to ask store managers, landlords, and delivery drivers if he could have their discarded pallets. A convenience store owner not only allowed him to take the pallets but agreed to pay Terry twenty dollars a week to get rid of them.

Terry borrowed his father's 1999 Ford van and began picking up pallets on his way home from school. After a week he was earning fifty to a hundred dollars a day. As the semester passed, he developed contacts with local merchants who informed him of major deliveries. Now he could sometimes load up his van and get a hundred dollars worth of pallets in one stop. Factory managers began stacking spare pallets in alleys for him.

Terry gave his father fifty dollars a week for use of the van and paid for gas and new tires. The van was put to hard use and soon needed a brake job and a tune up. Terry still managed to generate enough profit not only to pay for school, his books, and rent but save an extra thousand dollars to buy a car.

Terry represents any number of guerrilla entrepreneurs who seize an opportunity and create a new business. Like the other people chronicled in Pauline Feldman's book, Terry feels a great sense of pride in his accomplishment but also experiences great stress. He knows that the battered van may have to be replaced. He has thought of purchasing a second van and hiring another driver, but insurance costs, liability issues, and the paperwork have led him to decide to stay a one-man enterprise. And like many of the guerilla entrepreneurs Pauline Feldman describes, Terry has no plans to continue his business after he graduates. "It's a means to an end," he says. "After I go to law school, I hope I never see another pallet."

Works Cited

Feldman, Pauline. "Become a Guerilla Entrepreneur." The New School of Business, Chicago. 15 Oct. 2011. Keynote Speech.

Williams, Terrell. Personal interview. 22 Mar. 2012.

QUESTIONS FOR REVIEW AND REVISION

1. What is a *guerrilla entrepreneur*?

2. Does the student's example clearly illustrate the definition provided? Why or why not?

3. Do you know people who could serve as examples of guerrilla entrepreneurs?

4. This essay uses a single narrative example. Is this an effective device? Would it be better to provide short sketches of three or four entrepreneurs?

5. Are there details that could be eliminated from the essay?

6. The student refers to a talk by Pauline Feldman. Does the student rely too much on this source? How important it is to accurately summarize the ideas of others before expanding on them with your own?

7. Read the paper aloud. Are there sentences that could be rewritten for clarity?

WRITING SUGGESTIONS

1. Using this essay as a model, write an example essay about a person you know who represents a social trend—a downsized executive, a homeowner facing foreclosure, a single parent, or a workaholic. Make sure you clearly define the trend you are illustrating.

2. *Collaborative writing:* Working with others, write an essay illustrating how working students balance job and academic responsibilities. Use a number of examples to reveal common problems and solutions.

Suggested Topics for Writing Example

General Assignments

Write an example paper on any of the following topics. Your example may inform or persuade. You may use both factual and hypothetical examples.

1. Begin with a point of view. State your opinion on one of the following issues and use examples as illustrations:

   American materialism

   Television violence

The prevailing attitude on your campus about mandatory drug testing, capital punishment, smoking, abortion, date rape, affirmative action, or any other controversial topic

Courage

Illegal immigration

2. Alternatively, begin with a specific person, place, item, or event and explain its greater significance, demonstrating how it illustrates or symbolizes a general trend or concept:

- Describe a common behavior you have observed. What does this action represent? You might see road rage as an example of growing selfishness or littering as a sign of disrespect for public property.
- Write about an incident that taught you a lesson. What does this episode reveal about society, human nature, your family, or friends?
- Select a location, such as a shopping mall, high school, coffee shop, or summer camp, and explain what it represents about American society.
- Describe a television program, concert, website, or movie that represents what you consider to be good or bad in popular culture.
- Relate a dilemma you have faced in your own life. How does it illustrate a situation faced by others?

Writing in Context

1. Imagine that you have been asked to explain to foreign students the American attitude toward a specific issue or value, such as marriage, money, crime, or education. Illustrate your response with examples. You may demonstrate a range of opinions by listing differing attitudes and supplying each with at least one example.

2. Write a letter to the editor of a magazine that you read to praise or criticize its coverage. Support your views with examples.

3. Write a response to an essay question that asks for historical examples of movements that changed American society.

4. Write a hypothetical example illustrating the proper course of action in an emergency.

Strategies for Reading Example

When reading the example essays in this chapter, keep the following questions in mind.

Context

1. What is the author's purpose—to inform or persuade? What does the example illustrate?

2. What is the thesis or general point? Is it clearly defined? Can you restate it in your own words?

3. What can you tell about the intended audience? Are the examples targeted to a specific group of readers? Are the illustrations ones that general readers can recognize and appreciate?

Strategy

1. Does the writer use a single extended example or a list?

2. Does the author use other forms of support—facts, testimony, statistics?

3. Are the examples convincing? Do they truly represent a general condition, or are they drawn out of context?

4. How is the essay organized?

5. Where is the thesis or general principle placed in the essay? Would it be more effective if located elsewhere?

6. What transitional devices are used to organize the examples?

Language

1. Do the tone, style, and diction used to relate the example suit the writer's purpose?

2. What role do connotations play in relating examples? How do they shape the reader's perception?

READING TO LEARN

As you read the example essays in this chapter, note techniques you can use in your own writing:

- **"Homeless" by Anna Quindlen** uses a single, extended example of a homeless woman to explore an urban problem of poverty and dislocation.

- **"Mexicans Deserve More Than *La Mordida*" by Joe Rodriguez** relates an incident of police corruption as an example of a national problem in Mexico.

- **"What's in a Word?" by Sharon Begley** uses a series of specific examples to demonstrate how words not only express meaning but also influence how we perceive the world around us.

- **"Attacking Student Loan Debt" by Carolyn M. Brown** uses an extended example to dramatize the problem of student loan debt and then presents a "five-step blueprint" to show a student how to "annihilate his debt."

- **"Covenant House Needs Your Help"** presents three short biographies of troubled young people to motivate donors to contribute to a social agency.

Anna Quindlen

Anna Quindlen (1952–) graduated from Barnard College in 1974 and began working as a reporter in New York. After writing articles for the *New York Post,* she took over the "About New York" column for the *New York Times.* In 1986 she started her own column, "Life in the Thirties." Her collected articles were published in *Living Out Loud* in 1988. She has written numerous op-ed pieces for the *Times* on social and political issues. In 1992 she received the Pulitzer Prize. The following year she published another collection of essays, *Thinking Out Loud: On the Personal, the Political, the Public, and the Private.* Quindlen has also written six novels: *Rise and Shine, Object Lessons, One True Thing, Black and Blue, Every Last One,* and *Blessings.*

Homeless

Source: "Homeless" from *Living Out Loud* by Anna Quindlen. Copyright © 1987 by Anna Quindlen. By permission.

In this essay Quindlen illustrates the plight of the homeless by presenting a single example, a woman named Ann whom she discovered living in the Port Authority Terminal. As you read the essay, determine which attributes of this woman's situation are wholly personal and which represent the general homeless population.

introduction of example

1 Her name was Ann, and we met in the Port Authority Bus Terminal several Januarys ago. I was doing a story on homeless people. She said I was wasting my time talking to her; she was just passing through, although she'd been passing through for more than two weeks. To prove to me that this was true, she rummaged through a tote bag and a manila envelope and finally unfolded a sheet of typing paper and brought out her photographs.

pictures

2 They were not pictures of family, or friends, or even a dog or cat, its eyes brown-red in the flashbulb's light. They were pictures of a house. It was like a thousand houses in a hundred towns, not suburb, not city, but somewhere in between, with aluminum siding and a chain-link fence, a narrow driveway running up to a one-car garage and a patch of backyard. The house was yellow. I looked on the back for a date or a name, but neither was there. There was no need for discussion. I knew what she was trying to tell me, for it was something I had often felt. She was not adrift, alone, anonymous, although her bags and her raincoat with the grime shadowing its creases had made me believe she was. She had a house, or at least once upon a time had had one. Inside were curtains, a couch, a stove, potholders. You are where you live. She was somebody.

home and identity

3 I've never been very good at looking at the big picture, taking the global view, and I've always been a person with an overactive sense of place, the legacy of an Irish grandfather. So it is natural that the thing that seems most wrong with the world to me right now is that there are so many people with no homes. I'm not simply talking about shelter from the elements, or three square meals a day or a mailing address to which the welfare people can send the check—although I know that all these are important for survival. I'm talking about a home, about precisely those kinds of feelings that have wound up in cross-stitch and French knots on samplers over the years.

importance of a home

4 Home is where the heart is. There's no place like it. I love my home with a ferocity totally out of proportion to its appearance or location. I love dumb things about it: the hot-water heater, the plastic rack you drain dishes in, the roof over my head, which occasionally leaks. And yet it is precisely those dumb things that make

Sam Diephuis/Jupiterimages

it what it is—a place of certainty, stability, predictability, privacy, for me and for my family. It is where I live. What more can you say about a place than that? That is everything.

5   Yet it is something that we have been edging away from gradually during my lifetime and the lifetimes of my parents and grandparents. There was a time when where you lived often was where you worked and where you grew the food you ate and even where you were buried. When that era passed, where you lived at least was where your parents had lived and where you would live with your children when you became enfeebled. Then, suddenly where you lived was where you lived for three years, until you could move on to something else and something else again. And so we have come to something else again, to children who do not understand what it means to go to their rooms because they have never had a room, to men and women whose fantasy is a wall they can paint a color of their own choosing, to old people reduced to sitting on molded plastic chairs, their skin blue-white in the lights of a bus station, who pull pictures of houses out of their bags. Homes have stopped being homes. Now they are real estate.

home vs. real estate

6   People find it curious that those without homes would rather sleep sitting up on benches or huddled in doorways than go to shelters. Certainly some prefer to do so because they are emotionally ill, because they have been locked in before and they are damned if they will be locked in again. Others are afraid of the violence and trouble they may find there. But some seem to want something that is not available in shelters, and they will not compromise, not for a cot, or oatmeal, or a shower with special soap that kills the bugs. "One room," a woman with a baby who was sleeping on her sister's floor, once told me, "painted blue." That was the crux of it; not size or location, but pride of ownership. Painted blue.

importance of ownership

7   This is a difficult problem, and some wise and compassionate people are working hard at it. But in the main I think we work around it, just as we walk around it when it is lying on the sidewalk or sitting in the bus terminal—the problem, that is. It has been customary to take people's pain and lessen our own participation in it by turning it into an issue, not a collection of human beings. We turn an adjective into a noun: the poor, not poor people; the homeless, not Ann or the man who lives in the box or the woman who sleeps on the subway grate. Sometimes I think we would be better off if we forgot about the broad strokes and concentrated on the details. Here is a woman without a bureau. There is a man with no mirror, no wall to hang it on. They are not the homeless. They are people who have no homes. No drawer that holds the spoons. No window to look out upon the world. My God. That is everything.

homeless vs. people without homes

UNDERSTANDING CONTEXT

1. What is Quindlen's thesis? Can you state it in your own words?

2. What attitude does Quindlen have about homeless people? What is the worst aspect of their situation?

3. *Critical thinking:* Quindlen states that people use language to lessen their involvement with others by turning "an adjective into a noun: the poor, not poor people." What does she mean? Can you think of other examples?

EVALUATING STRATEGY

1. What role does Ann play in the article? Would an essay about homeless people be as effective without a personal example?

2. Quindlen focuses on the snapshot of Ann's home. What is significant about this detail? What does the picture represent to Ann?

3. What concrete details does Quindlen use to record the condition of homeless people?

4. *Critical thinking:* Quindlen at one point states, "I've never been very good at looking at the big picture, taking the global view." Is it effective for a writer to admit shortcomings or explain his or her approach to the subject? Does this explain why the article does not include statistics or surveys providing a "global view" of the issue?

APPRECIATING LANGUAGE

1. What connotation does the word *home* have? What does it bring to mind when you hear or see the word? How does Quindlen use readers' perceptions to highlight what homeless people lack?

2. What words does Quindlen use to describe Ann? What attitude does her word choice reflect?

3. Discuss the different meanings of *home* and *real estate*.

WRITING SUGGESTIONS

1. Write an essay about a social problem, using a single person to illustrate the issue. Focus on how this one person represents challenges faced by others with the same problem.

2. Select a friend, historical figure, or current celebrity you admire and write an essay using him or her to illustrate a personality trait or quality. A famous athlete might represent determination. A close friend might illustrate selflessness.

3. *Collaborative writing:* Work with a group of students and discuss a social problem, personality trait, political issue, or academic subject. Then select a person, real or hypothetical, to explain it. A local politician arrested on drug charges might illustrate the problem of addiction. A fictional student could portray the problems students face in determining a major.

Joe Rodriguez served as an editorial writer for the *San Jose Mercury News* before becoming one of the newspaper's staff columnists. He has written extensively about life in northern California, commenting on Mexican American identity, bilingual education, gun control, drugs, and city planning. He has published several articles about the price of urban renewal, stating, "There's more humanity in one block of real neighborhood than in a square mile of a subdivision."

Mexicans Deserve More Than *La Mordida*

Source: "Mexicans Deserve More than La Mordida" by Joe Rodriquez. From Knight-Ridder/Tribune Services, April 1, 1997. Copyright © 1997, KRT. Distributed by McClatchy-Tribune Information Services.

As you read Rodriguez's essay, notice how he uses a minor incident to represent a complex social problem. Consider whether this bribery incident illustrates a problem greater than the corruption found in other countries.

1 "I wouldn't give you a dime for Mexico!"

2 My father used to tell us that every time Mexico broke his heart. He was *muy indio,* with dark reddish brown skin, huge calloused hands and a handsomely hooked nose. On our occasional trips to Tijuana to visit relatives, he'd see Indian women begging on the streets, Indian kids selling Chiclets chewing gum, and white-skinned Mexicans owning and running everything.

3 "Not a dime for Mexico!"

4 He was more Mexican than I'll ever be, more Mexican than any Harvard-educated technocrat, any Spanish-looking *gachupin,* any middle-class Zapatista guerrilla-intellectual, or any bald-headed ex-president crook from Mexico City's ritzy Polanco district. My father wasn't referring to the nation's people, but to a political and social system that still fosters extreme poverty, discrimination and injustice, and to the privileged and the ruthless who benefit by it.

5 I should have remembered my Dad's dime recently when two Mexico City policemen pulled me over for making an illegal left-hand turn at the Monument of Cuauhtemoc on the famous Paseo de la Reforma boulevard.

6 I was driving back into the giant city after three days in the countryside. I had escaped a traffic accident only minutes earlier. I was hot, tired, grumpy and jumpy. I was driving a rental car. These conditions made me the perfect *pollo* for these two uniformed coyotes.

7 Both cops got out. The older one checked out the rental plates. The younger one wanted to see my driver's license.

8 "Where's your hotel?" he asked.

9 Right over there, I said, the Maria Cristina Hotel on Rio Lerma Street.

10 "I don't know any hotel by that name," he said. "Prove it. Show me something from the hotel."

11 I fumbled through my wallet, finally producing a card-key from the hotel. The dance between the cops and me had begun.

12 "I see," the young policeman said. "What are you doing in Mexico?"

Sam Diephuis/Jupiterimages

13   I'm a journalist, I said. I'd been reporting in Queretaro state.

14   "You know," he said, "for making that illegal turn, we're going to have to take away your driver's license and the plates from the car."

15   I said, What? Why can't you just give me a ticket?

16   He then walked away and asked the other, older, policeman, "How do you want to take care of this?"

17   The veteran officer then took over.

18   "The violation brings a fine of 471 pesos," he told me. "But we still have to take your plates and license. You can pick them up at police headquarters when you pay the fine. Or, I can deliver them to you tomorrow at your hotel, but only after you pay."

19   By now, I figured this was all B.S., but I wasn't absolutely sure. Who ever heard of license plate confiscation for minor traffic violations? Still, I didn't know what my rights were as a motorist. Why didn't I prepare myself for something like this?

20   "So, since you say you need the car," the cop said, "*¿Nos podemos arreglar esto de otra manera?* (Can we take care of this another way?)."

21   I would prefer a ticket, I said.

22   The veteran cop stretched his arms upward, relaxed a bit, and then rested his forearms on my door. He leaned in and stuck his face inches from mine, and smiled.

23   "*Lo que tenemos aqui, se llama la corrupción,*" he said. "What we have here is called corruption."

24   So there it was—*la mordida*—the bite, the bribe, a complex government system based not on civil service, but on bribery, political patronage, personal favoritism and individual gain.

25   Everybody in Mexico knows that corruption is rampant among the local, state and federal police forces and the military. A national agency has even taken out full-page newspaper ads asking people not to pay off corrupt cops, saying "*la mordida* spreads as easily as rabies."

26   Just last month, Mexico's national drug czar, a well-respected general, was arrested for protecting a northern drug lord. Corruption at the top only emboldens the small-fries like these two brown-shirted Mexico City cops.

27   Mexico's people deserve so much better. It is their personal integrity and family strength that carry the nation, despite the incompetence and dishonesty of the ruling party and corrupt officials big and small. And it's well within the United States' ability to step up the few binational efforts that exist to train Mexican police officers—the honest and sharp ones—in modern methods and ethics.

28   I wish I had thought about that and my father's dime and refused to play the game as I sat parked on Mexico City's most prominent boulevard, but I didn't.

29   "What do you say you help us out with 500 pesos?" the veteran cop said.

30   What do you mean, I said. The violation is worth less than that.

31   "400 pesos."

32   I don't have that much, I said, lying through my teeth.

33   "300 pesos."

34   We got stuck on 300 pesos for a while until he came down to 250 pesos, or about $31.25 in American dollars. I thumbed through my wallet for the bills, trying to keep him from seeing that I had much more money.

35   "Listen," he said. "You're a journalist from the United States. *Tu ganas pura lana.* You make lots of money. You can give me 300 pesos easy."

36   I don't make a lot of money, I said. My newspaper does, not me. I'm not rich. I'm just another Mexican like you trying to get by.

37   He wasn't moved.

38   Once I had the 250 pesos out of my wallet, he handed me a notebook through the window.

39   "Put the money in this so people don't see it pass hands."

40   I put the money in the notebook and gave it to him. He asked me once again for more.

41   "*Andale, hombre,*" he said. "You can give me another 50 pesos. Consider it my tip."

UNDERSTANDING CONTEXT

1. How would you describe *la mordida* in your own words?

2. What attitude toward *la mordida* does the statement "Not a dime for Mexico" reflect?

3. Does this minor request for a bribe—which could occur in any country— illustrate something unique to Mexico?

4. *Critical thinking:* Why is bribery wrong? How does corruption, even in trivial matters, affect people's faith in their government and institutions?

EVALUATING STRATEGY

1. Rodriguez selects a minor incident to reveal the nature of *la mordida*. Would a major bribery scandal involving national elections be a better example?

2. Would a series of shorter examples better represent the extent of *la mordida* in Mexican society?

3. Why is dialogue important in relating this example?

4. What role does the writer play in this example? Why are his reactions important?

APPRECIATING LANGUAGE

1. What does the writer's choice of words reveal about his attitude toward *la mordida?*

2. *La mordida* literally means "the bite" in Spanish. What connotations does "the bite" have?

WRITING SUGGESTIONS

1. Illustrate a common social problem or incident with a personal experience. You might provide an example of online dating, road rage, littering, sexual harassment, sports gambling, or binge drinking.

2. *Collaborative writing:* Work with a group of students and develop a list of social problems—discrimination, corruption, alcoholism, and so forth—and then select one and provide one or more examples revealing the nature and extent of the problem.

Sharon Begley

Sharon Begley graduated from Yale University and joined *Newsweek* magazine in 1977 as an editorial assistant. After serving as an assistant editor in the late 1970s, she became a general editor in 1983. During her career at *Newsweek,* Begley wrote numerous articles on science and health issues. She left the magazine to write the "Science Journal" column for the *Wall Street Journal*. Five years later, Begley returned to *Newsweek* as a senior editor.

What's in a Word?

In this Newsweek *article, Begley uses a number of examples to illustrate the way words may shape our thoughts and perceptions. Differences in cultural perceptions and attitudes can be explained, in part, by differences in language.*

1   Language may shape our thoughts.

2   When the Viaduct de Millau opened in the south of France in 2004, this tallest bridge in the world won worldwide accolades. German newspapers described how it "floated above the clouds" with "elegance and lightness" and "breathtaking" beauty. In France, papers praised the "immense" "concrete giant." Was it mere coincidence that the Germans saw beauty where the French saw heft and power? Lera Boroditsky thinks not.

3   A psychologist at Stanford University, she has long been intrigued by an age-old question whose modern form dates to 1956, when linguist Benjamin Lee Whorf asked whether the language we speak shapes the way we think and see the world. If so, then language is not merely a means of expressing thought, but a constraint on it, too. Although philosophers, anthropologists, and others have weighed in, with most concluding that language does not shape thought in any significant way, the field has been notable for a distressing lack of empiricism—as in testable hypotheses and actual data.

4   That's where Boroditsky comes in. In a series of clever experiments guided by pointed questions, she is amassing evidence that, yes, language shapes thought. The effect is powerful enough, she says, that "the private mental lives of speakers of different languages may differ dramatically," not only when they are thinking in order to speak, "but in all manner of cognitive tasks," including basic sensory perception. "Even a small fluke of grammar"—the gender of nouns—"can have an effect on how people think about things in the world," she says.

5   As in that bridge. In German, the noun for bridge, *Brucke,* is feminine. In French, *pont* is masculine. German speakers saw prototypically female features; French speakers, masculine ones. Similarly, Germans describe keys (*Schlüssel*) with words such as hard, heavy, jagged, and metal, while to Spaniards keys (*llaves*) are golden, intricate, little, and lovely. Guess which language construes key as masculine and which as feminine? Grammatical gender also shapes how we construe abstractions. In 85 percent of artistic depictions of death and victory, for instance, the idea is represented by a man if the noun is masculine and a woman if it is feminine, says Boroditsky. Germans tend to paint death as male, and Russians tend to paint it as female.

6   Language even shapes what we see. People have a better memory for colors if different shades have distinct names—not English's light blue and dark blue, for instance, but Russian's *goluboy* and *sinly*. Skeptics of the language-shapes-thought claim have argued that that's a trivial finding, showing only that people remember what they saw in both a visual form and a verbal one, but not proving that they actually see the hues differently. In an ingenious experiment, however, Boroditsky and colleagues showed volunteers three color swatches and asked them which of the bottom two was the same as the top one. Native Russian speakers were faster than English speakers when the colors had distinct names, suggesting that having a name for something allows you to perceive it more sharply. Similarly, Korean uses one word for "in" when one object is in another snugly (a letter in an envelope), and a different one when an object is in something loosely (an apple in a bowl). Sure enough, Korean adults are better than English speakers at distinguishing tight fit from loose fit.

7   In Australia, the Aboriginal Kuuk Thaayorre use compass directions for every spatial cue rather than right or left, leading to locutions such as "there is an ant on your southeast leg." The Kuuk Thaayorre are also much more skillful than English speakers at dead reckoning, even in unfamiliar surroundings or strange buildings. Their language "equips them to perform navigational feats once thought beyond human capabilities," Boroditsky wrote on Edge.org.

8   Science has only scratched the surface of how language affects thought. In Russian, verb forms indicate whether the action was completed or not—as in "she ate [and finished] the pizza." In Turkish, verbs indicate whether the action was observed or merely rumored. Boroditsky would love to run an experiment testing whether native Russian speakers are better than others at noticing if an action is completed, and if Turks have a heightened sensitivity to fact versus hearsay. Similarly, while English says "she broke the bowl" even if it smashed accidentally (she dropped something on it, say), Spanish and Japanese describe the same event more like "the bowl broke itself." "When we show people video of the same event," says Boroditsky, "English speakers remember who was to blame even in an accident, but Spanish and Japanese speakers remember it less well than they do intentional actions. It raises questions about whether language affects even something as basic as how we construct our ideas of causality."

UNDERSTANDING CONTEXT

1. Can you state Begley's thesis in your own words?
2. How, in Begley's view, do differences in language explain why the French and Germans described the same bridge in such different terms?
3. How does the gender of a word affect the way people see an idea, object, or concept?
4. Why does Lera Boroditsky believe the Kuuk Thaayorre of Australia have such a good sense of direction?
5. *Critical thinking:* Does Begley's article indicate why precise and sensitive translations are necessary in order to conduct diplomatic negotiation? Might one language view a word in a positive light, while another sees it negatively?

EVALUATING STRATEGY

1. What evidence does Begley use to support her thesis?

2. Are the examples Begley presents, such as words for keys or an action like a broken bowl, easy to understand?

3. Begley asks rhetorical questions. Is this an effective device? Why or why not? Could a writer pose too many questions?

4. *Critical thinking:* Begley notes that "the field has been notable for a distressing lack of empiricism—as in testable hypotheses and actual data." Is this a significant admission? It is important for someone analyzing an issue to comment on the status of research or the quality of available evidence? Why or why not?

APPRECIATING LANGUAGE

1. English does not have gender—everything is simply "the." Some languages, such as French, German, and Spanish, have masculine and feminine designations such as *der Mann* and *die Frau*. Should Begley have explained this more fully for English speakers who have never studied a foreign language? Why or why not?

2. *Critical thinking:* Do you think there may be significant differences within the same language? Do men and women, blacks and whites, New Yorkers and Texans have different responses to the same words? Might, for example, the word "gun" lead people in Manhattan to think of crime and violence and remind people in Montana of hunting trips and family outings?

WRITING SUGGESTIONS

1. Analyze the language used to describe a recent event, issue, or controversy. What words were used in the press, on television, or by your friends to describe the firing of a football coach, a student protest, a new law, a change in policy, or the closing of a local company? Do you detect any bias in these examples? What words or phrases were the most significant, in your view, and what did they reveal about people's attitudes?

2. *Collaborative writing:* Work with a group of students and analyze some common slang expressions. What do they suggest about the way members of your generation view themselves and the world around them? Write a short essay that uses specific examples. Do you perceive a common theme in the slang you hear on campus?

Carolyn M. Brown is editor at large for *Black Enterprise* and has published articles on a range of issues, including domestic violence, racial profiling, retirement, unemployment trends, investment opportunities, small business development, and personal finance.

Attacking Student Loan Debt

Source: "Attacking Student Loan Debt" by Carolyn M. Brown. *Black Enterprise,* October 2010, pp. 73(2). By permission.

In this essay Carolyn M. Brown uses an extended example to illustrate the problem of student debt and then outlines a five-step process to eliminate it.

1 Bryan Mitchell has always taken pride in getting a good education. "College was the next step after high school. There was no question about it, no breaks in between," says Mitchell, who holds a bachelor's degree in business administration from The University of New Haven (UNH). But the cost of attending the private institution has left the 25-year-old saddled with $120,000 in student loan debt after four years.

2 Mitchell's debt is a combination of money he used for UNH's tuition and fees, estimated at $15,000 per semester. All together he has two subsidized federal loans (through Sallie Mae) at 6.5% and eight unsubsidized bank loans with interest rates ranging from 2.5% to 9.75%. Each month he pays $700 toward the interest. The debts are nearly one-third of his $2,600 monthly net income.

3 With his large education debt, Mitchell isn't terribly unique. As of June 2010, for the first time ever, Americans collectively owed more in student loans than in credit card debt, according to Mark Kantrowitz, publisher of FinAid.org and FastWeb.com. In August, Americans owed $826.5 billion in revolving credit accounts and about $830 billion in federal and private student loans.

4 Financial experts consider education loans to be "good debt" because students use the borrowed money to increase their earning potential. But student loans can be burdensome and can take 10 to 20 years to pay off. Today, the average college undergraduate leaves school with roughly $20,000 of loan debt while the typical under [sic] graduate student amasses debt ranging from $30,000 to $120,000.

5 A do-it-yourself attitude led to Mitchell's whopping education debt. "I didn't seek help from anyone, not my parents, no family or friends. I wanted to do things all on my own," he says. "I have been really independent ever since I was a little kid."

6 Mitchell began his path to college financing on the right foot: He filled out the Free Application for Federal Student Aid, the form financial aid offices use for awarding funds. His mistake, he now realizes, was that he didn't actively seek assistance from his university's financial aid department. A counselor there could have helped him investigate any loans, grants, and special programs for which he might have been eligible. Instead, he opted to borrow directly from various banks whose interest rates on student loans were relatively high.

7   Loans from private banks are attractive to many students because the application process may be easier, but in the long run, private loans are typically more expensive. Banks charge a higher rate of interest because the student doesn't put forth collateral for the loan.

8   Mitchell isn't making the same mistakes with his graduate education, which he hopes to complete by 2012. His employer is paying for his master's degree in management from Saint Joseph College in West Hartford. He works full time as an admissions officer at Goodwin College in East Hartford, and he earns $40,000 a year after a recent promotion.

9   Aside from his student loans, Mitchell has no other debt. His 2004 Nissan Maxima, a gift from his parents, is paid for. Mitchell who says he has maintained good credit habits since being approved for his first credit card at age 16, has steered clear of high credit card balances. "I am really against using credit cards unless it is a big purchase," he explains. "Usually, I try to pay it off quickly."

The Advice

Mitchell is committed to making lifestyle changes in order to take on his financial challenge. This means squeezing dollars wherever he can, including taking on a part-time job, cutting back on living expenses, and applying for tax credits on student loan interest payments. He will also consult a tax adviser to see if he qualifies for any public service forgiveness programs or income-based repayment programs.

Black Enterprise has drafted a seven-year, five-step blueprint to help Mitchell annihilate his debt.

- **Trim living expenses.** Mitchell is currently renting a one-bedroom apartment at $600 a month. He has the potential to save $200 by getting a two-bedroom apartment at $800 a month and splitting that expense with a roommate. This would allow him to apply an additional $2,400 annually toward his student loan debt recommends Vicki R. Brackens, ChFC (chartered financial consultant), senior financial planner at Brackens Financial Solutions Network, an office of MetLife in Syracuse, New York.

- **Boost discretionary income.** Mitchell plans to earn an extra $200 every week working part time at his local gym as a personal trainer. Also, the recent promotion, which increased his annual salary by $5,000, gives him a chance to put roughly an additional $400 per month toward tackling his debt. He should use this money to pay down the loan principal, so that he is not only paying his required interest payments, advises Brackens. Mitchell should continue making the monthly $700 interest payment. To make extra principal payments, he should use the $1,400 he expects to have each month ($800 from part-time work, $400 from salary increase, $200 from rent reduction). Once he completes his master's studies and receives another salary increase, he will likely receive an automatic raise in status and income—around $60,000 to $70,000 a year, according to his employer. Based on his original loan terms, his total payments would be $232,800 over

20 years. With the seven-year plan, his total would be $169,680, saving $63,120 in total loan payments, says Brackens.

■ **Pay down loan principals.** While consolidation may bring more convenience and possibly lower the monthly payments, the long-range impact is an increase in the time period to repay the loan and an increase in total interest paid, explains Brackens. He should start applying extra payments to the principal of the loan that has the highest interest rate until it's paid off. For example, he would pay $1,400 extra on his Sallie Mae (or SLM) private student loan for $6323 at 9.75%. Then apply the extra $1,400 to his SLM private student loan for $4,652 at 9.75% and then the SLM private student loan for $26,781 at 8.75%, continuing to do this for the loan with the next highest interest rate until all 10 loans are paid off. But Brackens cautions that he must attach a separate check for the extra payment to a letter detailing he wants the money applied to the principal and which loan to apply it to; otherwise it will go to the interest, which is the typical policy of most lending institutions.

■ **Build a cash reserve.** Mitchell should set aside $100 a month in savings. While his main goal is debt reduction, preparing for emergencies should never be forgotten, says Brackens. She suggests he add his $2,000 contest winnings to his $2,000 cash reserve. Also, he should move his savings into an interest-bearing money market account or high-yield savings account. In six years, (if the interest yield were 1.25%), Mitchell could amass more than $13,000.

■ **Stay put with 401(k) contribution.** Mitchell should stay at the 5% contribution level for his 401(k) account and not worry about any other investments. Right now, if he dilutes his resources trying to achieve too many financial objectives, he will end up carrying debt for a longer period (and at a higher cost) than he needs to, says Brackens. At 25 years of age, Mitchell has a long time horizon that allows him to plow all available cash toward his debts. If he can get his debt to zero in seven years, he should have money to apply toward building an investment portfolio.

■ **Advice to others.** Attending a state college or university may drastically reduce your cost. State schools provide residents with lower tuition rates and also offer state-based college grants. Also, after selecting the college of your choice be sure to visit or call your school's financial aid office to get assistance with your financing options.

UNDERSTANDING CONTEXT

1. What does Bryan Mitchell represent? Is his situation unusual, in Brown's view?
2. How did Mitchell amass so much student debt? Could any of it been avoided?
3. What must Mitchell do to reduce his debt? Do these steps seem realistic?
4. *Critical thinking:* In the past people were willing to borrow money for education, confident that a college degree would lead to a good job that provided enough income to pay off student loans and support a comfortable lifestyle. Do you think many individuals and families are as confident about their futures today? Are people seeking alternative ways to finance college or even questioning whether it pays to go to college?

EVALUATING STRATEGY

1. Brown uses a single extended example. Is this an effective device? Would her essay be more effective if she profiled more than a single student? Why or why not?

2. Would a hypothetical example be less effective than a real one? Why or why not?

3. Brown introduces facts and numbers about national trends. Why are these important? Does an extended example need additional support to explain its significance?

4. *Other modes:* How does Brown transition from example to *persuasion* and *process*?

APPRECIATING LANGUAGE

1. Why do financial experts consider education loans to be "good debt"? What other examples would constitute "good debt" in your view? How would you define "bad debt"?

2. What words does Brown use to describe Mitchell's debt? What connotations do they have?

3. *Critical thinking:* Consider the word *debt*. What connotations does it have? Do some people equate *debt* with "shame" or "guilt." Do people prefer to use other words with fewer negative connotations, such as *principal* or *balance,* to describe what they owe?

WRITING SUGGESTIONS

1. Use one or more real or hypothetical examples to demonstrate a problem; then provide steps to remedy it. You might describe someone who smokes, overeats, or fails to exercise and then outline steps to overcome this behavior.

2. *Collaborative writing:* Working with a group of students, discuss the problem of financing a college education. Then develop an essay using several examples that illustrate different methods of paying for college.

CRITICAL ISSUES

Image by © Robert Harding World Imagery/Corbis

Debtor Nation

America's financial situation is unsustainable. In 2009 the federal government spent $3.5 trillion but collected only $2.1 trillion in revenue. The result was a $1.4 trillion deficit, up from $458 billion in 2008. That's 10 percent of gross domestic product, a level unseen since World War II.

Veronique De Rugy

The national debt is a big number, but it is not excessive. On a relative basis, the federal debt burden has hardly changed over the past twenty years. . . . the overall percentage the U. S. spends to service its debt (currently less than 3 percent of GDP) is lower than it was in the late 1980s and most of the 1990s.

Zachary Karabell

The United States of America has a national debt exceeding $14 trillion. According to the Federal Reserve, Americans themselves owe another $14 trillion in mortgages, car loans, and credit card balances. States across the country owe trillions of dollars, much of it in future pension obligations to their public employees. In addition, interest payments on the debt may cost the US government as much as $900 billion a year by 2020. Medicare, Medicaid, and Social Security costs are expected to soar as the Baby Boom generation begins to retire. Medicare alone is facing a shortfall of $38 trillion in future years.

The growing debts, both federal and state, will have profound effects on the United States at home and abroad. Before leaving office in 2011, California Governor Arnold Schwarzenegger called for cutting the state's prison staff by 6,000, releasing 22,000 inmates, closing nearly fifty state parks, and reducing funding for state agencies by 10 percent. Incoming governor Jerry Brown called for more budget cuts and higher taxes. Diplomats and defense analysts have reasoned that the United States can no longer maintain its status as a military superpower. Richard Sinnreich, a retired army officer and defense consultant, sees parallels between America today and the British Empire a century ago. "As a debtor nation with an exploding deficit and little hope in the near term of correcting either condition," he notes, "we have a special need to reconcile our ambitions with our resources." Ben Rhodes, a national security consultant, argues that many of America's adversaries have adopted the strategy "to sit back and let America burn its resources until we are overextended." America's allies are taking note of how its global position may be weakened by its fiscal crisis. British historian Niall Ferguson alerted Australians that "The US faces the nasty arithmetic of Imperial decline." The rising influence of China and the "sudden waning of American power" will bring "a dramatic change in the global balance of power," forcing Australia to rethink its strategic relationship with the United States.

Politicians and economists are currently debating how to rescue the United States from decades of economic stagnation at home and a loss of prestige and influence abroad. For many, debt is a problem that should be addressed through austerity—cutting government spending. Veronique De Rugy argues that the debt is unsustainable. "The more we borrow," she states, "the higher the cost of borrowing." Soon the United States will spend more on interest payments than it does on defense, education, and Homeland Security. Massive debts inhibit the economic growth needed to create jobs and fund investments in new technologies. De Rugy believes massive cuts in government spending will restore the nation's economic health:

> If these growing deficits aren't addressed by immediately and dramatically slashing spending. . . . We are about to embark on the most massive transfer of wealth from younger taxpayers to older ones in American history. It will not just be unprecedented but unfair. Our children will have to pay for the decisions we make today. . . . We need to reform entitlement spending, put both military and domestic spending on the chopping block, and start selling off federal assets. Better to do it now than during a fire sale later.

Other economists maintain that such measures will only hinder growth. Cutting investments for the future to pay down debt, they argue, is self-defeating. Commenting in *Time* in 2010, Zachary Karabell recalled that during the Great Depression of the 1930s "the orthodoxy of austerity and budget cutting hobbled the world and led to a decade of deflation and depression." To stimulate the economy in a recession and invest in the future, debt may be necessary:

> Debt can be foolish, as the housing crisis demonstrated. But it can be a powerful tool when properly used. . . . Any business leader will tell you that you can't cut your way to prosperity. . . . If the philosophy of austerity dictates policy from now on, our children and grandchildren will not praise us for the reduced deficits we leave them; they will reproach us for refusing to mobilize our vast resources to reinvent ourselves. But we were being prudent, we will say. No, they will reply, you were being cheap. You were running scared.

The quality of life for Americans in the next two decades will be largely determined by how the nation, states, cities, and consumers determine how to manage debt.

Before reading the articles in the list below, consider the following questions:

1. *How big is the national debt?* Is it sustainable? How do economists forecast future debts?
2. *Are all debts the same?* Is debt ever "good" or "necessary"?
3. *How do writers describe government expenditures?* How does "spending" differ from "investing"?
4. *How much of the national debt is caused by the country's demographics—a growing population of older people who are living longer and requiring more and more expensive health care?*
5. *What is an "entitlement"?* Should all citizens receive the same benefits? Should benefits like Medicare and Social Security be means-tested so wealthy retirees receive less than those with lower incomes?

E-READINGS ONLINE

Use InfoTrac College Edition, available through your English CourseMate at **www .cengagebrain.com,** to find the full text of each article online.

Shawn Tully. "We Owe What? The Next Crisis: America's Debt."
The government's need for revenue will probably lead to a VAT, a national sales tax to be paid mostly by the middle class.

Kevin D. Williamson. "The Other National Debt."
In addition to the $14 trillion national debt, state and local governments owe $2.5 trillion, much of it pensions and health care promised to public employees.

Thomas I. Palley. "America's Exhausted Growth Paradigm."
The massive consumer borrowing that drove the American economy for the past generation can no longer continue, forcing major policy changes to spark future growth.

Veronique De Rugy. "Our Unsustainable Debt: America is on the Verge of Financial Disaster."
Massive cuts in government spending are required to avert a fiscal crisis that will penalize future generations.

Zachary Karabell. "Debt Doesn't Matter."
Arguing that "you can't cut your way to prosperity," Karabell insists the populist concern about the debt ignores the fact that the economy and future generations would benefit from more government stimulus, not less.

Fareed Zakaria. "Defusing the Debt Bomb."
A 25 percent national sales tax and a 25 percent income tax for those making over $100,000 a year, an end to mortgage interest deductions, and raising the retirement age by a few years are needed to address the national debt.

Paul Ryan. "Red Alert."
A Republican Congressman offers a "Roadmap to America's Future" which calls for changes in entitlements, health care, and taxation to solve the nation's fiscal crisis.

Paul Krugman. "The Flimflam Man."
A Nobel-Prize-winning economist attacks Paul Ryan's "Roadmap" because it would only "cut benefits for the middle class while slashing taxes on the rich" and increase future deficits.

James K. Galbraith. "On The Economics of Deficits."
The national debt is caused, Galbraith argues, not by government overspending but by the recession itself, especially high unemployment.

Christine Hauser. "Written Off, Not Paid Off."
The reported drop in credit card debt is caused not by consumers being frugal but by financial institutions writing off billions of dollars of credit card debt as losses.

Charles K. Wilber. "Awakening the Giant: Strategies for Restarting the U.S. Economy."
The 2009 stimulus was too weak "to kick-start the economy into a growth path" and more government spending is needed to create jobs and reduce future deficits.

CRITICAL READING AND THINKING

1. How do the various authors define America's fiscal crisis?
2. Which authors believe that spending cuts are needed to avert a financial meltdown? Which authors argue the government should continue spending to stimulate the economy to lower future deficits? What evidence do authors use to justify their views?
3. How important are statistics in discussing the economy? Do authors explain the sources of the data they cite?
4. How difficult is it to forecast future economic trends? Can a war, new technologies, a global crisis, or changes in consumer behavior create unforeseen challenges or opportunities?

5. Do arguments about deficits lead to debates about the role of government? Do some writers appear to use the issue of debt to attack government spending on social and health care programs? Do other writers appear to favor government spending rather than tax reduction to stimulate economic growth?

WRITING SUGGESTIONS

1. Write an essay describing the impact the nation's debt will have on your generation. Do you think most college students understand how the country's financial situation will determine their future? How aware are they of their own debts?

2. *Collaborative writing:* Working with other students, develop a list of suggestions consumers can take to reduce their personal debt. Do most people understand what interest they are paying on their student loans, car loans, and credit cards? Can students finance their education without taking on massive debt?

3. *Other modes:*
   - *Define* "austerity." Does the term have positive or negative connotations? Would voters respond differently to a politician using terms like "responsible" or "affordable" to describe spending cuts?
   - Write a *division* paper that describes different causes or effects of the nation's fiscal crisis.
   - *Classify* solutions to the national debt from the least to most radical or most to least realistic.
   - Write a *cause-and-effect* essay that provides reasons why or why not the retirement age should be raised to reduce Social Security spending. Should future retirees have to reach the age of 68 or 70 before receiving benefits?
   - Write a *comparison* essay contrasting arguments for and against cutting government spending to address the deficit.

RESEARCH PAPER

You can develop a research paper about debt by conducting further research to explore a range of issues:

- Examine the fiscal health of a government program such as Social Security or Medicare. How much revenue does the program collect currently? How much does it pay out? How fiscally sound is the program? What changes are needed to guarantee it can meet its future obligations?
- How will the retirement of the baby boom generation affect the American economy? Will the doubling of retirees drain the federal budget of resources, leaving less money to benefit the young?
- Review public opinion polls and analyze your findings. How many of those polled view the national debt as a serious problem? How many favor cutting government spending?

■ How will the nation's fiscal problems affect a particular industry or field? Will high-tech companies offering less expensive medical technology boom because governments and insurance companies are seeking to save money? Will NASA and other federal programs suffer because of reduced budgets? Will real estate remain depressed because fewer people will be able to qualify for mortgages? How might the nation's financial situation affect the field you are planning to enter?

FOR FURTHER READING

To locate additional sources on debt, enter *national debt* as a search term in InfoTrac College Edition, available through your English CourseMate at **www.cengagebrain .com,** or one of your college library's databases, and examine readings under key subdivisions:

analysis	economic aspects
cases	forecasts and trends
causes of	political aspects

ADDITIONAL SOURCES

Using a search engine, enter one or more of the following terms to locate additional sources:

national debt	Social Security
Medicare	unemployment
Federal Reserve	credit cards
student loans	public employee pensions

See the Evaluating Internet Source Checklist on pages 533–534. See Chapter 24 for documenting sources.

Covenant House

Covenant House is the nation's largest shelter program for homeless youth. Begun in 1969 by a priest who took in six runaways during a blizzard, the program has grown to serve thousands each year. The agency is supported by almost entirely by donations from individuals.

Covenant House Needs Your Help

As you read this web page soliciting support, notice how examples are used to dramatize the plight of homeless youth and illustrate the program's services.

© 2005 Covenant House

UNDERSTANDING CONTEXT

1. What services does Covenant House provide?
2. Why does Covenant House need financial support?

3. Why do homeless youths face greater challenges today?

4. What is the mission of Covenant House?

EVALUATING STRATEGY

1. What purpose do examples serve? Is it important to provide names of those served? Why or why not?

2. What role do statistics play? Is it important to balance examples with factual detail?

3. How effective is the visual impact of this web page? Do you find it easy to read? Does it communicate at a glance? Does the photograph grab attention and demonstrate the severity of the problem of homeless young people?

APPRECIATING LANGUAGE

1. Does this level of diction seem appropriate for a mass audience?

2. Do you think using the word *kid* is effective? Why or why not? Might some readers object to this term?

WRITING SUGGESTIONS

1. Develop the text for a fund-raising brochure or web page using examples for support. Determine the best examples that would both dramatize a social problem and demonstrate how the organization works to solve it.

2. *Collaborative writing:* Discuss this web page with a group of students and then develop a process essay that explains step by step how you would conduct a national fund-raising campaign to draw attention to the problem of homeless youth and encourage donations.

RESPONDING TO IMAGES

Image by © Virgo Productions/Corbis

1. Describe your immediate reaction to this picture. Do you see it as an example of innocent childhood or a growing social problem?

2. Compare this photograph to the one on page 183. Do you see a connection between them? Would placing these images side by side change people's opinions of two boys playing with toy guns?

3. *Visual analysis:* This picture depicts two white middle-class boys in cowboy hats playing with guns. Would reactions differ if the boys were African American or Latino and wore gang caps? Why or why not?

4. *Collaborative writing:* Discuss this image with a group of students and develop a series of captions that use word choice to create positive and negative connotations.

5. *Other modes:*
   - Write a *cause-and-effect* essay that explains the effect that toy guns have on children. Do they lead children to glamorize or trivialize the use of deadly force?
   - *Compare* the effect of children playing cowboy, cops and robbers, or army with other children versus playing violent video games alone. Is one activity more harmful? Why or why not?
   - Write a *process* paper advising parents how to monitor their children's play activity to identify potential problems, such as a fascination with guns or violence.
   - Write a *persuasive* essay that argues for or against banning the sale of toy guns to children.

EXAMPLE CHECKLIST

Before submitting your paper, review these points:

✔ Does your paper have a clearly stated thesis or main point?

✔ Do the examples directly illustrate the thesis? Are there any irrelevant details that may mislead or confuse readers?

✔ If you use a single extended example to persuade, can it be supported with facts, statistics, or quotations?

✔ Are the examples clearly organized? Do they follow a logical pattern?

✔ Should the thesis appear at the opening, middle, or conclusion of the essay?

✔ Read your paper aloud. How does it sound? Do the examples support the thesis? Are there clear transitions between examples?

 Access the English CourseMate for this text at **www.cengagebrain.com** for additional information on writing example essays.

Definition
Establishing Meaning

What Is Definition?

Effective communication requires that writers and readers have a shared language. Words and ideas must be *defined* to eliminate confusion and misinterpretation. Definitions limit or explain the meaning of a word or concept. As a college student you have probably devoted much of your time to mastering new terms and their definitions.

Clearly stated definitions play a critical role in academic, professional, government, and business writing. To prevent confusion, conflict, and litigation, many union contracts, insurance policies, and leases include definitions so all parties will share a common interpretation of important terms. Government documents and business reports frequently include glossaries to familiarize readers with new or abstract terms. Failing to understand a definition can be costly. A tenant who does not understand a landlord's definition of *excessive noise* may face eviction. The car buyer who misinterprets the manufacturer's definition of *normal use* may void his or her warranty.

The word *definition* leads most students to think of a dictionary. But defining involves more than simply looking up the meaning of a word. Definitions are not always precise or universally accepted. Distinctly different definitions exist. To be an effective writer in college and in your future profession, it is important to appreciate the range of definitions, from standard to personal:

- **Standard definitions** are universally accepted and rarely subject to change. Words such as *tibia, dolphin, uranium, felony,* and *turbine* have exact meanings that are understood and shared by scholars, professionals, and the general public.

- **Regulatory definitions** are officially designated terms that are subject to change. The NFL, IRS, FAA, school boards, insurance companies, and the Catholic Church issue definitions to guide policy, control operations, inform the public, and make decisions. The IRS definition of *deductible meal allowance* can change yearly. Congress may pass a bill that changes the Veterans Administration's definition of *service-connected disability*. One health insurance company may pay for a liver transplant while another carrier refuses, defining the procedure as *experimental*. Regulatory definitions can change or be limited to a specific region, organization, or discipline. The building codes of New York and San Francisco may have varying definitions of what buildings are *structurally sound*.

Maria Toutoudaki/jupiterimages

Sam Diephuis/jupiterimages

- **Evolving definitions** reflect changes in community attitudes, social values, government policies, and scientific research. In the nineteenth century, hitting children was a widely accepted method of discipline called *corporal punishment*. Today, the same behavior would be defined as *child abuse*. Decades ago medical and psychological texts defined *homosexuality* as a mental disease. In 1973 the American Psychological Association voted to remove homosexuality from its list of psychological disorders. Evolving definitions track social change but rarely shift as abruptly as regulatory definitions.

- **Qualifying definitions** limit meanings of words or concepts that are abstract or subject to interpretation. How does one define *alcoholic*? At what point do doctors label a patient *obese* or *senile*? When does a young person become a *juvenile delinquent*? Some definitions are hotly debated within a discourse community. Researchers, politicians, and social commentators continually argue over whether drug addiction, for example, should be defined as a *disability* that entitles people to receive benefits.

- **Cultural definitions** are shaped by the history, values, and attitudes of a national, ethnic, or religious group. In some countries it is customary to offer cash or gifts to government officials as a *tribute* in return for their services. In the United States the same action would be considered an illegal *bribe*.

- **Personal definitions** are used by writers to express individual interpretations of words or ideas. A writer can frame an entire essay such as Ellen Goodman's "The Company Man" (see page 281), to establish a personal definition. Your concept of a good parent or a desirable career would be a personal definition.

WRITING ACTIVITY

Determine what type of definition would best suit each of the following topics. In some instances, there may be more than one possible definition.

1. Internal combustion engine

2. Second-degree murder

3. Addiction

4. Inflation

5. Cyberspace

6. Stalking

7. Existentialism

8. Road rage

9. Pornography

10. Altimeter

The Purpose of Definition

Definitions generally provide a common or shared understanding of a word, but they can also be used to persuade readers to accept a point of view. A prosecutor may define a young defendant's actions as *vandalism,* while the defense attorney tells jurors to consider his or her client's actions a *teenage prank.* A proposal to ban handguns could be praised as a *protection of public safety* or criticized as *a denial of individual rights.* How writers define terms and ideas greatly influences readers' perceptions.

Connotations play a large role in shaping persuasive definitions. To transform public attitudes and change their perceptions, writers frequently urge readers to redefine something—for example, to change their perceptions to see striking a child as *abuse* instead of *spanking* or to accept *graffiti* as *street art.* Because business owners sensed that *shoplifting* was generally dismissed as a petty offense, many began using the term *retail theft* to emphasize its criminality.

WRITING ACTIVITY

Provide persuasive definitions for the following terms. Your definition can reflect your personal opinions and values.

1. Family values
2. Domestic violence
3. Treason
4. Racism
5. Social justice
6. Capitalism
7. Welfare reform
8. Poverty
9. Role models
10. Patriotism

Methods of Definition

Writers create definitions using a number of strategies:

1. **Defining through synonyms** is the simplest method of providing meaning for a word or concept. Glossaries and dictionaries customarily define technical terms or foreign words with synonyms. *Costal* refers to *rib.* *Messer* can be translated as *knife.* A *casement* can be explained as a *window.*

- Because no two words are exact equivalents, be cautious about using a single word in a definition. Be aware of connotations that may distort meanings.

2. **Defining by description** provides details about a subject and gives readers a sense of what it might look, feel, taste, smell, or sound like. Defining *costrel* as "a small flask with a loop or loops that is suspended from a belt" provides readers with a clear picture of the object. Descriptive definitions also can demonstrate how something operates. An *airbag* can be defined as "a rapidly inflated cushion designed to protect automobile passengers in a collision."
   - Describing objects in action creates a clear picture. Because some items may have many functions, a writer must indicate exceptions or alternative actions to prevent oversimplification.

3. **Defining by example** provides specific illustrations to establish meaning. A *felony* can be defined as "a serious crime such as murder, sexual assault, or burglary." Examples establish meaning through identification. Telling a fourth-grade class that "a verb is a word that expresses action" is not as effective as providing examples children can easily recognize: *run, buy, talk, sell, build, think.*
   - Complex or abstract concepts are easier to comprehend if defined by example.

4. **Defining by comparison** uses analogies; this strategy is particularly useful for less familiar terms and concepts. A television reporter covering a space mission might define NASA terminology using comparison. To explain the term *power down*, she remarks that the astronauts are "conserving power by turning off nonessential electrical devices, much like switching off the radio and windshield wipers on a car."
   - Because they can oversimplify complex ideas, comparative definitions must be used carefully.

5. **Extended definitions** qualify or limit the meaning of abstract, disputed, or highly complex words or concepts. Such words as *sin, love,* and *racism* cannot be adequately defined through synonyms, brief descriptions, or a few examples. A complete definition might require several paragraphs or pages.

Strategies for Writing Definition: Prewriting and Planning

Critical Thinking and Prewriting

1. **Determine the goal of your definition—to inform or persuade.** Decide whether your purpose is to explain the meaning of a subject to readers or influence their perceptions about it.

2. **Write a list of ideas, people, items, concepts, theories, and places.** One way of starting is simply to begin isolating possible topics. At first, list as many ideas as possible. Refer to the list on pages 751–752 for possible ideas.

3. **Review the list and note the best ways of defining selective topics.** Some topics may be challenging to define because they are complex, controversial, or elusive. If you find a particular subject difficult, explore another idea.
   - Use synonyms for words or concepts that have direct equivalents. Be sure to remind readers of subtle distinctions.

- Use examples to illustrate your subject.
- Compare the subject with others that readers may find easier to recognize and comprehend.

Planning

1. **Write a clearly stated one-sentence definition of your subject if possible.** Try to focus your thoughts by stating a working thesis to target your planning.

2. **Define your role.** Your definition can be based on personal observation and opinion or standard principles and methods followed in a specific discipline or profession.

3. **Consider your audience.** What knowledge do your readers have? Your definition should offer recognizable examples in language they will understand. Determine what uses your audience has for the definition. Will readers have to base future decisions based on your definition? Will this definition dictate or guide their actions?

4. **Use a balance of defining methods.** Each method of defining has advantages and disadvantages. It is usually effective to blend descriptions, synonyms, examples, and comparisons.

5. **Determine the best place to locate your thesis—at the beginning, middle, or conclusion.** A controversial issue may alienate or confuse readers. Before stating your thesis, you may wish to present a narrative, a fact, or a statistic.

6. **Organize your essay.** Arrange your material in a logical pattern—spatial, chronological, or emphatic.
   - Address common misconceptions about your topic at the opening.
   - Provide clear transitions between points.
   - Conclude the essay with a memorable statement or shorthand version summarizing the key points of your definition.

Strategies for Writing Definition: Writing the First Draft

Writing the First Draft

1. **Keep extended definitions on target.** Refer to your plan and thesis as you write. Extended examples are designed to illustrate a point. You can easily become enveloped in the narrative and include details that may be interesting but do not advance the purpose of the essay.
   - Remember that your goal is to *define* the topic, not tell a story.

2. **Use or refer to existing definitions.** Instead of creating your own definition, you can often adopt or make use of an existing one. If you accept the American Psychological Association's definition of *compulsion,* you can simply restate the definition for readers. When you use existing definitions,

(Continued)

acknowledge their sources. If you disagree with an existing official definition, restate it and then demonstrate how your interpretation differs.

3. **Clearly summarize the definition in a sentence or two.** Readers are not likely to recall ideas scattered throughout an essay. If possible, distill your main points into one or two clearly stated sentences that readers can underline for easy reference.

4. **Define abstract or elusive topics by setting boundaries.** John Ciardi suggested that in trying to define an elusive concept like *happiness,* "the best one can do is to try to set some extremes to the idea and then work in toward the middle."
   - Openly state what your subject is *not,* in order to set firm boundaries and reduce reader confusion.
   - Provide examples in a pro and con fashion, illustrating what does and does not fall within the boundaries of your definition. If you are trying to define *racial profiling,* for instance, you might list those actions that constitute unfair profiling and those that do not.

Strategies for Writing Definition: Revising and Editing

Revising

1. **Review your plan; then examine the content of your draft.**
   - Does your paper *define* the topic or merely *describe* it? A description of an SUV provides details about its appearance, whereas a definition of an SUV allows readers to distinguish this type of vehicle from vans, station wagons, and pickup trucks.

2. **Review your thesis or summary.**
   - Do you provide a clearly stated definition that readers can remember or highlight for future reference?

3. **Analyze extended definitions for irrelevant or missing details.**
   - Does the narrative simply tell a story or does it *define* the subject by supplying facts, observations, and details needed to inform or persuade readers?

4. **Review informative definitions for clarity.**
   - Are the limits of the definition clearly stated and supported by facts and details?
   - Are readers given measurements, distinguishing features, visual illustrations, or rules so that they can identify the subject when they encounter it?

5. **Review persuasive definitions for critical thinking.**
   - In shaping opinion, do you take your readers' existing knowledge and attitudes into account? Do you address their existing conceptions?

- Do you show how your definition differs from others?
- Have you avoided logical fallacies (see pages 39–41)?

6. **Review the introduction and conclusion.**
   - Does the opening introduce the subject and arouse interest? Should the thesis appear in the beginning or follow an initial narrative or fact?
   - Does the conclusion create a strong impression readers will remember?

7. **Review the overall structure of the body.**
   - Is the supporting material clearly organized and joined by transitional statements? Do the separate paragraphs serve to advance the definition?

Editing and Proofreading

1. **Review your choice of words.**
   - Does your paper contain words that require further definition to prevent confusion?
   - Are there any connotations that may alienate or mislead readers?

2. **Read your paper aloud.**
   - Are there awkward, wordy, or repetitive phrases you can delete or revise?

3. **Review the thesis statement.**
   - Is your definition clearly stated and easy to remember?

4. **Use peer editing.**
   - Ask readers whether they can restate your definition in their own words. If they cannot, revise your thesis or add more details and examples.

STUDENT PAPER

This paper was written in response to the following assignment:

> Invent a definition for a social issue or problem you have experienced. You may support your definition with factual research or personal observation. Make sure your paper clearly defines the subject and does not simply describe it.

FIRST DRAFT WITH INSTRUCTOR'S COMMENTS

Composition 112   Leni Mandel

Delete, too general   *maybe*
Fathers are probably the most important people in our lives except may be for our

mothers. They are supposed to teach us a lot. But my father was kind of a *Vague*

disappointment. *Needs stronger opening*

(Continued)

Like half the members of my generation, I am the product of what used to be called a "broken home." My parents divorced when I was eight. I lived with my mother all the time and would see my father every other weekend. And every summer my dad took me on a vacation lasting two weeks. *Wordy, condense*

My father, like many of his generation, was a Disneyland dad. He always arrived on time, brought me stuff, and took me to places I wanted to go. He bought me a lot of clothes and toys and gave me things my mothers would not get for me. He was always kind and generous. But I found it disappointing that though he gave me things and took me places he never

redundant

really acted like a real Dad. I think divorced dads can be generous and responsible when it comes to paying bills. I know my dad always came through when my mom told him she needed money for us. When we needed school clothes or had to see to the dentist he sent my mom extra money without any problems.

comma   *redundant*

But even so, my Dad never really acted like a real Dad.

have

He could of done so much more. Looking back, I really feel cheated. My dad was there

Add comma, run-on

for me but he never acted like a real father just a Disneyland Dad.

REVISION NOTES

This paper is a description, not a definition. A description provides details about an individual person, place, or thing. Definition presents details about a type of person, place, or thing. You call your father a "Disneyland Dad." What exactly is a "Disneyland Dad"? You need to define that term. You can use your father as an illustrative example. Make sure your essay contains a clear definition of a "Disneyland Dad" that readers will be able to understand.

REVISED DRAFT

Composition 112   Leni Mandel

Disneyland Dads

Like half the members of my generation, I am the product of what used to be called a "broken home." My parents divorced when I was eight. I lived with my mother and saw my father on alternate weekends and two weeks during the summer.

My father, like many of his generation, was a classic Disneyland Dad. The Disneyland Dad is usually found at malls, little league fields, upscale pizza restaurants, and ice cream parlors. He is usually accompanied by a child busily eating food forbidden by Mom, wearing new clothes, or playing with expensive toys. The Disneyland Dad dispenses cash like an ATM and provides an endless supply of quarters for arcade games. Whether they are motivated by guilt, frustration, or an inability to parent, Disneyland Dads substitute material items for fatherly advice, guidance, and discipline.

While my mother furnished the hands-on, day-to-day parenting, my father remained silent. My mother monitored my eating habits, my friends, my grades, even the programs I watched on television. But without daily contact with my mother, my father found it difficult to make decisions about my upbringing. He was afraid of contradicting Mom. So he showered me with gifts and trips. He expanded my wardrobe, gave me my first pieces of real jewelry, introduced me to Broadway shows, and took me to Disneyland—but he did not help me with school, teach me about the job market, give me insight into boys, or allow me to be anything more than a spoiled consumer.

As I grew older, my relationship with my father became strained. Weekends with him were spent shopping, going to movies, playing tennis, and horseback riding—activities I loved, but activities that limited opportunities for anything but casual conversation.

Like most of my friends, I came to view my father as more of an uncle than a parent. He was a beloved family figure, someone who could be counted on for some extra cash, new clothes, a pizza. And like most of my friends, I was troubled by the gulf that widened between my father and myself. I talked, argued, and made up with my mother as I went through my teens. Both of us changed over the years. But my father remained the same—the generous but distant Disneyland Dad.

The Disneyland Dad is a neglected figure. While books and daytime talk shows focus on the plight of single moms, few people offer advice for the fathers. Men in our society are judged by success and conditioned to dispense tokens of their achievement to their children. We kids of divorce want all the things the Disneyland Dad can offer, but we really need his attention, his guidance, his experience, his mentoring. Someone has to help Disneyland Dads become fathers.

QUESTIONS FOR REVIEW AND REVISION

1. What tone does the term "Disneyland Dad" have? Is it suitable for a serious essay? What connotations does it suggest?

2. Does this student really *define* or merely *describe* Disneyland Dads?

3. Does the paper include enough details to outline the qualities of a Disneyland Dad?

4. The student uses quotation marks to highlight certain words. Do you find this an effective technique?

5. *Blending the modes:* Where does the student use *narration* and *comparison* to develop the essay? Does the final paragraph state a *persuasive argument?*

6. Did the student follow the instructor's suggestions? Do you sense she appreciates the difference between description and definition?

7. Read the paper aloud. Can you detect awkward or vague passages that would benefit from revision?

WRITING SUGGESTIONS

1. Invent a term that defines a personality type, and illustrate it using a parent, friend, or coworker as an example.

2. *Collaborative writing:* Discuss this paper with several students, and collect ideas for a process paper that offers tips to teenage children on how to communicate with a Disneyland Dad.

Suggested Topics for Writing Definition

General Assignments

Write a definition on any of the following topics. Your definition will probably use other modes: narration, description, example, comparison, or persuasion. Choose your terminology carefully and avoid words with misleading connotations. Remember, your main goal is to *define,* not describe or tell a story. Give your readers ways of recognizing your subject on their own.

- A successful professional in your field, such as a good defense attorney, contractor, nurse, or teacher
- A good relationship
- Domestic violence
- Stalking
- An educated person
- A healthy lifestyle
- Self-respect
- Racism
- The level of insanity a defendant must exhibit to be deemed not liable for his or her actions
- Terrorism

Writing in Context

1. Imagine you have been asked to write a brief brochure about college life, to be distributed to disadvantaged high school students. The principal stresses that she fears many of her students lack independent study skills and the discipline needed to succeed in college. Define the characteristics of a good college student, stressing hard work and study habits.

2. You have been asked to participate in a panel on sexual harassment. In preparation, provide two definitions of sexual harassment—one expressing attitudes, feelings, and statements you have encountered from males on campus, the other from females. Try to be objective and state differences fairly.

Strategies for Reading Definition

As you read the definition essays in this chapter, keep the following questions in mind.

Context

1. Which type of definition is the author developing—standard, regulatory, evolving, qualifying, cultural, or personal?
2. What is the author's purpose—to inform or persuade?
3. What is the nature of the context, audience, discipline, or writing situation? Is the writer addressing a general or specific reader?

Strategy

1. What methods of definition does the writer use—synonyms, examples, comparisons, or descriptions?
2. Is the definition limited to a specific incident or context, or can it be applied generally? Is the writer defining a particular person or personality trait that could be shared by millions?
3. Does the writer provide personal examples, or does he or she rely on official sources to establish the definition?

Language

1. What role do word choice and connotation play in establishing the definition?
2. What do the tone and level of language reveal about the writer's purpose and intended audience?

READING TO LEARN

As you read the definition essays in this chapter, note techniques you can use in your own writing.

- **"Dyslexia" by Eileen Simpson** presents a standard definition of a common learning disability.

- **"The Company Man" by Ellen Goodman** uses a single extended example to define the qualities of a workaholic.

- **"Listening to Madness" by Alissa Quart** explains "Mad Pride," a movement of the mentally ill to reject the definition of "disease" and embrace their "differences."

- **"What is an Act of Terror?" by Jo Ellen Green Kaiser** questions how we define "terrorism" by comparing "acts of terror" with "acts of war."

Eileen Simpson

Eileen Simpson was a psychotherapist who struggled for years to overcome dyslexia, a reading disorder that affects more than 20 million Americans. She wrote several books, including *Poets in Their Youth,* a memoir of her marriage to the poet John Berryman. Other books based on her personal experiences explored problems of children growing up without parents. This section comes from her 1979 book *Reversals: A Personal Account of Victory over Dyslexia.*

Dyslexia

Source: "Dyslexia from Reversals" by Eileen Simpson. Copyright © 1979, 1991 by Eileen Simpson. By permission.

Simpson provides a standard definition of an existing term by examining its Greek and Latin roots and then demonstrates the effects dyslexia has on its victims. Notice that she supplies examples to help readers fully appreciate the implications of a widely misunderstood disorder.

1 Dyslexia (from the Greek, *dys*, faulty + *lexis*, speech, cognate with the Latin *legere*, to read), developmental or specific dyslexia as it's technically called, the disorder I suffered from, is the inability of otherwise normal children to read. Children whose intelligence is below average, whose vision or hearing is defective, who have not had proper schooling, or who are too emotionally disturbed or brain-damaged to profit from it belong in other diagnostic categories. They, too, may be unable to learn to read, but they cannot properly be called dyslexics. [definition of dyslexia] [defining what dyslexia is not]

2 For more than seventy years the essential nature of the affliction has been hotly disputed by psychologists, neurologists, and educators. It is generally agreed, however, that it is the result of a neurophysiological flaw in the brain's ability to process language. It is probably inherited, although some experts are reluctant to say this because they fear people will equate "inherited" with untreatable. Treatable it certainly is: not a disease to be cured, but a malfunction that requires retraining. [dyslexia not a "disease" but a "malfunction"]

3 Reading is the most complex skill a child entering school is asked to develop. What makes it complex, in part, is that letters are less constant than objects. A car seen from a distance, close to, from above, or below, or in a mirror still looks like a car even though the optical image changes. The letters of the alphabet are more whimsical. Take the letter *b*. Turned upside down it becomes a *p*. Looked at in a mirror, it becomes a *d*. Capitalized, it becomes something quite different, a *B*. The *M* upside down is a *W*. The *E* flipped over becomes Ǝ. This reversed *E* is familiar to mothers of normal children who have just begun to go to school. The earliest examples of art work they bring home often have I LOVƎ YOU written on them.

4 Dyslexics differ from other children in that they read, spell, and write letters upside down and turned around far more frequently and for a much longer time. In what seems like a capricious manner, they also add letters, syllables, and words, or, just as capriciously, delete them. With palindromic words (was-saw, on-no), it is the order of the letters rather than the orientation they change. The new word makes sense, but not the sense intended. Then there are other words where the changed order—"sorty" for story—does not make sense at all. [gives examples]

Sam Diephuis/jupiterimages

277

5 The inability to recognize that g, *g*, and *G* are the same letter, the inability to maintain the orientation of the letters, to retain the order in which they appear, and to follow a line of text without jumping above or below it—all the results of the flaw—can make of an orderly page of words a dish of alphabet soup.

effects of dyslexia on reading

6 Also essential for reading is the ability to store words in memory and to retrieve them. This very particular kind of memory dyslexics lack. So, too, do they lack the ability to hear what the eye sees, and to see what they hear. If the eye sees "off," the ear must hear "off" and not "of," or "for." If the ear hears "saw," the eye must see that it looks like "saw" on the page and not "was." Lacking these skills, a sentence or paragraph becomes a coded message to which the dyslexic can't find the key.

7 It is only a slight exaggeration to say that those who learned to read without difficulty can best understand the labor reading is for a dyslexic by turning a page of text upside down and trying to decipher it.

8 While the literature is replete with illustrations of the way these children write and spell, there are surprisingly few examples of how they read. One, used for propaganda purposes to alert the public to the vulnerability of dyslexics in a literate society, is a sign warning that behind it are guard dogs trained to kill. The dyslexic reads:

specific example

a Wurring
Guard God
Patoly

for

Warning
Guard Dog
Patrol

and, of course, remains ignorant of the danger.

9 Looking for a more commonplace example, and hoping to recapture the way I must have read in fourth grade, I recently observed dyslexic children at the Educational Therapy Clinic in Princeton, through the courtesy of Elizabeth Travers, the director. The first child I saw, eight-year-old Anna (whose red hair and brown eyes reminded me of myself at that age), had just come to the Clinic and was learning the alphabet. Given the story of "Little Red Riding Hood," which is at the second grade level, she began confidently enough, repeating the title from memory, then came to a dead stop. With much coaxing throughout, she read as follows:

specific example

Grandma you a top. Grandma [looks over at picture of Red Riding Hood]. Red Riding Hood [long pause, presses index finger into the paper. Looks at me for help. I urge: Go ahead] the a [puts head close to the page, nose almost touching] on Grandma

for

Once upon a time there was a little girl who had a red coat with a red hood. Etc.

10 "Grandma" was obviously a memory from having heard the story read aloud. Had I needed a reminder of how maddening my silences must have been to Miss Henderson, and how much patience is required to teach these children, Anna, who took almost ten minutes to read these few lines, furnished it. The main difference

between Anna and me at that age is that Anna clearly felt no need to invent. She was perplexed, but not anxious, and seemed to have infinite tolerance for her long silences.

11   Toby, a nine-year-old boy with superior intelligence, had a year of tutoring behind him and could have managed "Little Red Riding Hood" with ease. His text was taken from the *Reader's Digest's Reading Skill Builder,* Grade IV. He read:

specific example

> A kangaroo likes as if he had but truck together warm. His saw neck and head do not . . . [Here Toby sighed with fatigue] seem to feel happy back. They and tried and so every a tiger Moses and shoots from lonesome day and shouts and long shore animals. And each farm play with five friends . . .

12   He broke off with the complaint, "This is too hard. Do I have to read any more?" His text was:

> A kangaroo looks as if he had been put together wrong. His small neck and head do not seem to fit with his heavy back legs and thick tail. Soft eyes, a twinkly little nose and short front legs seem strange on such a large strong animal. And each front paw has five fingers, like a man's hand.

13   An English expert gives the following bizarre example of an adult dyslexic's performance:

specific example

> An the bee-what in the tel mother of the biothodoodoo to the majoram or that emidrate eni eni Krastrei, mestriet to Ketra lotombreidi to ra from treido as that.

14   His text, taken from a college catalogue the examiner happened to have close at hand, was:

> It shall be in the power of the college to examine or not every licentiate, previous to his admission to the fellowship, as they shall think fit.

specific example

15   That evening when I read aloud to Auntie for the first time, I probably began as Toby did, my memory of the classroom lesson keeping me close to the text. When memory ran out, and Auntie did not correct my errors, I began to invent. When she still didn't stop me, I may well have begun to improvise in the manner of this patient—anything to keep going and keep up the myth that I was reading—until Auntie brought the "gibberish" to a halt.

UNDERSTANDING CONTEXT

1. What basic definition does Simpson provide? What misinterpretation does she note can occur if a condition is considered "inherited"?

2. How does Simpson summarize controversies in the field of research? What do scientists from different disciplines agree on?

3. What is the implication to dyslexics and their parents that dyslexia is "not a disease to be cured, but a malfunction that requires retraining"?

4. *Critical thinking:* How can this disorder affect a child's development if it is not detected?

EVALUATING STRATEGY

1. Why is it effective to provide an etymology of the word *dyslexia* at the opening? Does this help satisfy reader curiosity about a term many people have heard but do not fully understand?

2. How does Simpson's introduction of personal experience affect the definition? Does this add a human dimension to her definition, or does it detract from its objectivity? Would the inclusion of personal experience be appropriate in a textbook?

3. Do the examples of dyslexic reading dramatize the effects of this disorder? Would an explanation alone suffice to impress readers with the crippling effects of a reading disorder?

4. *Other modes:* How does Simpson use *description* and *narration* to develop her definition? What role can stories or case studies provide readers seeking to understand a complex subject?

APPRECIATING LANGUAGE

1. Simpson is defining a complex disorder. How does her language indicate that she is seeking to address a general audience? Would the vocabulary differ in a definition written for psychology students?

2. Simpson cites an example of a dyslexic reading a warning sign as "propaganda." Does the use of this word weaken her argument that dyslexia is a serious condition? Why or why not?

3. How does Simpson define the term *palindromic*?

WRITING SUGGESTIONS

1. Write a concisely worded definition of *dyslexia* in your own words.

2. *Critical writing:* Write an essay expressing your view on how dyslexics should be graded in college. Should students with dyslexia be allowed more time on essay tests, be offered special tutorial services, or be given alternative assignments and examinations? Can students with disabilities be accommodated while maintaining academic standards?

3. *Collaborative writing:* Working with several other students, craft a brief explanation of dyslexia to be incorporated into a brochure for parents of children with learning impairments. Keep your audience in mind, and avoid making negative comments that might upset parents.

Ellen Goodman (1941–) was born in Massachusetts and graduated from Radcliffe College. She worked for *Newsweek* and the *Detroit Free Press* before joining the *Boston Globe* in 1967. Until her retirement in 2010, Goodman's column "At Large" was widely syndicated throughout the United States. As an essayist and television commentator, Goodman has discussed feminism, changes in family life, sexual harassment, and male and female relationships. Her essays have been collected in several books, including *Close to Home, At Large,* and *Turning Points.*

The Company Man

Source: "The Company Man" from *Close to Home* by Ellen Goodman. Copyright © 1979 by The Washington Post Group. By permission.

Instead of using a number of illustrations to develop a definition, Goodman presents a single, extended example of a person who fits her personal view of a workaholic.

1 He worked himself to death, finally and precisely, at 3:00 A.M. Sunday morning.

2 The obituary didn't say that, of course. It said that he died of a coronary thrombosis—I think that was it—but everyone among his friends and acquaintances knew it instantly. He was a perfect Type A, a workaholic, a classic, they said to each other and shook their heads—and thought for five or ten minutes about the way they lived.

3 This man who worked himself to death finally and precisely at 3:00 A.M. Sunday morning—on his day off—was fifty-one years old and a vice-president. He was, however, one of six vice-presidents, and one of three who might conceivably—if the president died or retired soon enough—have moved to the top spot. Phil knew that.

4 He worked six days a week, five of them until eight or nine at night, during a time when his own company had begun the four-day week for everyone but the executives. He worked like the Important People. He had no outside "extracurricular interests," unless, of course, you think about a monthly golf game that way. To Phil, it was work. He always ate egg salad sandwiches at his desk. He was, of course, overweight, by 20 or 25 pounds. He thought it was okay, though, because he didn't smoke.

5 On Saturdays, Phil wore a sports jacket to the office instead of a suit, because it was the weekend.

6 He had a lot of people working for him, maybe sixty, and most of them liked him most of the time. Three of them will be seriously considered for his job. The obituary didn't mention that.

7 But it did list his "survivors" quite accurately. He is survived by his wife, Helen, forty-eight years old, a good woman of no particular marketable skills, who worked in an office before marrying and mothering. She had, according to her daughter, given up trying to compete with his work years ago, when the children were small. A company friend said, "I know how much you will miss him." And she answered, "I already have."

8 "Missing him all these years," she must have given up part of herself which had cared too much for the man. She would be "well taken care of."

9 His "dearly beloved" eldest of the "dearly beloved" children is a hardworking executive in a manufacturing firm down South. In the day and a half before the

funeral, he went around the neighborhood researching his father, asking the neighbors what he was like. They were embarrassed.

10   His second child is a girl, who is twenty-four and newly married. She lives near her mother and they are close, but whenever she was alone with her father, in a car driving somewhere, they had nothing to say to each other.

11   The youngest is twenty, a boy, a high-school graduate who has spent the last couple of years, like a lot of his friends, doing enough odd jobs to stay in grass and food. He was the one who tried to grab at his father, and tried to mean enough to him to keep the man at home. He was his father's favorite. Over the last two years, Phil stayed up nights worrying about the boy.

12   The boy once said, "My father and I only board here."

13 At the funeral, the sixty-year-old company president told the forty-eight-year-old widow that the fifty-one-year-old deceased had meant much to the company and would be missed and would be hard to replace. The widow didn't look him in the eye. She was afraid he would read her bitterness and, after all, she would need him to straighten out the finances—the stock options and all that.

14   Phil was overweight and nervous and worked too hard. If he wasn't at the office, he was worried about it. Phil was a Type A, a heart-attack natural. You could have picked him out in a minute from a lineup.

15   So when he finally worked himself to death, at precisely 3:00 A.M. Sunday morning, no one was really surprised.

16   By 5:00 P.M. the afternoon of the funeral, the company president had begun, discreetly of course, with care and taste, to make inquiries about his replacement. One of the three men. He asked around: "Who's been working the hardest?"

UNDERSTANDING MEANING

1. How does Goodman define a workaholic? Why does she assert that Phil's heart attack was directly related to his career?

2. What does Goodman's definition imply about the quality of Phil's life? What does she suggest that it was lacking?

3. What, if anything, seems to have driven Phil?

4. Goodman mentions that Phil provided well for his widow. Is Phil, a hardworking vice president who cares about his family, an ideal man in the eyes of many women? If Phil were African American or Hispanic, would he be viewed as a "role model"? Would a "company woman" be seen as a feminist?

5. *Critical thinking:* Americans have long admired hard workers. Franklin, Edison, Henry Ford, and Martin Luther King Jr. became legendary for their accomplishments. On the other hand, Americans long for more leisure time. Is there a double standard? Do we want to spend more time with our friends and family but expect our doctors, lawyers, contractors, and stockbrokers to work overtime for us, meet our deadlines, and always be a phone call away?

EVALUATING STRATEGY

1. Would Goodman's definition be stronger if she included more than one example?

2. What impact does the final paragraph have? How does this reinforce her point?

APPRECIATING LANGUAGE

1. Goodman places certain phrases in quotation marks—"well taken care of " and "dearly beloved." What is the effect of highlighting these terms?

2. What does the term "company man" suggest? Would "church man" or "advocacy man" provoke different responses?

WRITING SUGGESTIONS

1. Develop your own definition of *workaholic*. Can it be defined in hours worked or by the degree of stress a job creates? Does an actor or writer working eighty hours a week to rehearse a play or write a novel fit the category of *workaholic?* Is a mother with young children by definition a workaholic?

2. *Collaborative writing:* Speak with fellow students, and write a short statement in response to the question, "What do we owe our employers?"

Alissa Quart

Alissa Quart is a contributing editor for *Columbia Journalism Review,* where she writes a column. She has also written articles for *Newsweek, Mother Jones,* and the *New York Times Magazine.* Her books include *Branded: The Buying and Selling of Teenagers* (2003) and *Hothouse Kids* (2006). Quart was a Nieman Fellow at Harvard University in 2009–10.

Listening to Madness

This article, first published in Newsweek *in 2009, explains why some mental patients reject the traditional definition of mental illness as a "disease," often embracing their condition as "unusual ways of processing information and emotion" and calling for an acceptance of what they call "mental diversity."*

1   "We don't want to be normal," Will Hall tells me. The 43-year-old has been diagnosed as schizophrenic, and doctors have prescribed antipsychotic medication for him. But Hall would rather value his mentally extreme states than try to suppress them, so he doesn't take his meds. Instead, he practices yoga and avoids coffee and sugar. He is delicate and thin, with dark plum polish on his fingernails and black fashion sneakers on his feet, his half Native American ancestry evident in his dark hair and dark eyes. Cultivated and charismatic, he is also unusually energetic, so much so that he seems to be vibrating even when sitting still.

2   I met Hall one night at the offices of the Icarus Project in Manhattan. He became a leader of the group—a "mad pride" collective—in 2005 as a way to promote the idea that mental-health diagnoses like bipolar disorder are "dangerous gifts" rather than illnesses. While we talked, members of the group—Icaristas, as they call themselves—scurried around in the purple-painted office, collating mad-pride fliers. Hall explained how the medical establishment has for too long relied heavily on medication and repression of behavior of those deemed "not normal." Icarus and groups like it are challenging the science that psychiatry says is on its side. Hall believes that psychiatrists are prone to making arbitrary distinctions between "crazy" and "healthy," and to using medication as tranquilizers.

3   "For most people, it used to be, 'Mental illness is a disease—here is a pill you take for it,'" says Hall. "Now that's breaking down." Indeed, Hall came of age in the era of the book *Listening to Prozac.* He initially took Prozac after it was prescribed to him for depression in 1990. But he was not simply depressed, and he soon had a manic reaction to Prozac, a not uncommon side effect. In his frenetic state, Hall went on to lose a job at an environmental organization. He soon descended into poverty and started to hear furious voices in his head; he walked the streets of San Francisco night after night, but the voices never quieted. Eventually, he went to a mental-health clinic and was swiftly locked up. Soon after, he was diagnosed with schizophrenia. He was put in restraints and hospitalized against his will, he says. For the next year, he bounced in

and out of a public psychiatric hospital that he likens to a prison. The humiliation and what he experienced as the failure of the medication were what turned him against traditional treatment. Since then, Hall has been asking whether his treatment was really necessary. He felt sloshily medicated, as if he couldn't really live his life.

4 Hall and Icarus are not alone in asking these questions. They are part of a new generation of activists trying to change the treatment and stigma attached to mental illness. Welcome to Mad Pride, a budding grassroots movement, where people who have been defined as mentally ill reframe their conditions and celebrate unusual (some call them "spectacular") ways of processing information and emotion.

5 Just as some deaf activists prefer to embrace their inability to hear rather than "cure" it with cochlear implants, members of Icarus reject the notion that the things that are called mental illness are simply something to be rid of. Icarus members cast themselves as a dam in the cascade of new diagnoses like bipolar and ADHD. The group, which now has a membership of 8,000 people across the U.S., argues that mental-health conditions can be made into "something beautiful." They mean that one can transform what are often considered simply horrible diseases into an ecstatic, creative, productive or broadly "spiritual" condition. As Hall puts it, he hopes Icarus will "push the emergence of mental diversity."

6 Embracing "mental diversity" is one thing, but questioning the need for medication in today's pill-popping world is controversial—and there have been instances in which those who experience mental extremes harm themselves or others. Icaristas argue that some of the severely mentally ill may avoid taking medication, because for some the drugs don't seem to help, yet produce difficult side effects. And while some side effects like cognitive impairment are surely debilitating, others are more subtle, such as the vague feeling that people are not themselves. Icaristas call themselves "pro-choice" about meds—some do take their drugs, but others refuse.

7 Mad pride has its roots in the mad-liberation movement of the 1960s and '70s, when maverick psychiatrists started questioning the boundaries between sane and insane, and patients began to resist psychiatric care that they considered coercive. But today the emphasis is on support groups, alternative health and reconsidering diagnostic labeling that can still doom patients to a lifetime of battling stigma. Icarus also frames its mission as a somewhat literary one—helping "to navigate the space between brilliance and madness." Even the name Icarus, with its origin in the Greek myth of a boy who flew to great heights (brilliance) but then came too close to the sun (madness) and hurtled to his death, has a literary cast.

8 Although Icarus and Hall focus on those diagnosed as mentally ill, their work has much broader implications. Talking to Hall, I was acutely aware just how much their stance reflects on the rest of us—the "normal" minds that can't read through a book undistracted, the lightly depressed people, the everyday drunks who tend toward volatility, the people who "just" have trouble making eye contact, those ordinary Americans who memorize every possible detail about Angelina Jolie.

9 After all, aren't we all more odd than we are normal? And aren't so many of us one bad experience away from a mental-health diagnosis that could potentially

limit us? Aren't "normal" minds now struggling with questions of competence, consistency or sincerity? Icarus is likewise asking why we are so keen to correct every little deficit—it argues that we instead need to embrace the range of human existence.

10   While some critics might view Icaristas as irresponsible, their skepticism about drugs isn't entirely unfounded. Lately, a number of antipsychotic drugs have been found to cause some troubling side effects.

11   There are, of course, questions as to whether mad pride and Icarus have gone too far. While to his knowledge no members have gravely harmed themselves (or others), Hall acknowledges that not everyone can handle the Icarus approach. "People can go too fast and get too excited about not using medication, and we warn people against throwing their meds away, being too ambitious and doing it alone," he says.

12   But is this stance the answer? Jonathan Stanley, a director of the Treatment Advocacy Center, a nonprofit working to provide treatment for the mentally ill, is somewhat critical. Stanley, who suffers from bipolar illness with psychotic features, argues that medication is indispensable for people with bipolar disease or with schizophrenia. Stanley's group also supports mandatory hospitalization for some people suffering severe mental illness—a practice that Icarus calls "forced treatment."

13   Scholars like Peter Kramer, author of *Listening to Prozac* and *Against Depression*, also take a darker view of mental extremes. "Psychotic depression is a disease," Kramer says. As the intellectual who helped to popularize the widespread use of antidepressants, Kramer is nonetheless enthusiastic about Icarus as a community for mad pride. Yet he still argues that mental health diagnoses are very significant. "In an ideal world, you'd want good peer support like Icarus—for people to speak up for what's right for them and have access to resources—and also medication and deep-brain stimulation," he says.

14   For his part, Hall remains articulate, impassioned and unmedicated. He lives independently, in an apartment with a roommate in Oregon, where he is getting a master's in psychology at a psychoanalytic institute. He maintains a large number of friendships, although his relationships, he says, are rather tumultuous.

15   Nevertheless, it's not so easy. Hall periodically descends into dreadful mental states. He considers harming himself or develops paranoid fantasies about his colleagues and neighbors. Occasionally, he thinks that plants are communicating with him. (Though in his mother's Native American culture, he points out, this would be valued as an ability to communicate with the spirit world.)

16   On another night, I had dinner with eight Icarus members at a Thai restaurant in midtown Manhattan. Over Singha beer, they joked about an imaginary psycho-active medication called Sustain, meant to cure "activist burnout." It was hard to imagine at the dinner what Hall had suffered. While he and his "mad" allies were still clearly outsiders, they had taken their suffering and created from it an all-too-rare thing: a community.

UNDERSTANDING CONTEXT

1. How would you define the "Mad Pride" movement?

2. Why do some mental patients reject the definition of their condition as a "disease" and refuse to take prescribed medications?

3. Does the fact that drugs often have serious side effects indicate that the condition they are designed to treat is not serious? Why or why not?

4. *Critical thinking:* How difficult is it for parents, educators, employers, and medical professionals to determine who is mentally ill and needs intervention and treatment? When is someone "sick" and when is someone simply "different"?

EVALUATING STRATEGY

1. Does the opening quotation make an effective introduction? Why or why not? Is a claim of not wanting to be "normal" bound to grab attention?

2. *Blending the modes:* How does Quart use *comparison* to develop her article?

3. Quart uses numerous quotations in her essay. Is this an effective device? Why or why not?

APPRECIATING LANGUAGE

1. What words do people in the Mad Pride movement use to describe their mental condition? What connotations do these words have?

2. Look up the word *Icarus* in a dictionary or encyclopedia. Why might people in the Mad Pride movement decide to use this name? What does Icarus represent? Would others associate Icarus with self-destructive recklessness?

3. *Critical thinking:* People with physical disabilities have rejected words like *invalid* or *cripple*, which they believe belittle or degrade them. Is it natural that people with mental issues are sensitive about terms used by society to describe them or their condition?

WRITING SUGGESTIONS

1. Write a short essay examining how groups of people have changed widely held attitudes by changing the words used to define them. Why, for instance, did African Americans reject the word *Negro* during the Civil Rights movement of the 1960s? Why did feminists reject language that defined jobs using male and female terms, arguing that *mailmen*, *policemen*, and *stewardesses* should be called *letter carriers*, *police officers*, and *flight attendants*?

2. *Collaborative writing:* Work with a group of students and develop your own definition of mental illness. When would your group define someone as being sick enough to require professional help? When, for instance, would you contact college administrators, family members, or mental health professionals about a classmate's or a roommate's behavior?

Jo Ellen Green Kaiser graduated from Yale University and received a PhD in American Literature and Critical Theory from the University of California–Berkeley. Formerly managing editor and associate publisher at *Tikkun*, she is now the chief editor of *Zeek* and executive director of Zeek Media Inc. She is also co-editor of *Righteous Indignation: A Jewish Call for Justice* (2008).

What Is an Act of Terror?

Source: Jo Ellen Green Kaiser, "What Is An Act of Terror?" *Tikkun* Magazine, Sept-Oct 2006, 14(1). Copyright © 2006 Tikkun: A Quarterly Interfaith Critique of Politics, Culture & Society. By permission.

In this editorial, published in Tikkun *magazine in 2006, Jo Ellen Green Kaiser first distinguishes between "acts of terror" and "acts of war," then argues why the United States should resist labeling political adversaries "terrorists."*

1 When Hezbollah began bombing Israel this summer, U.S. politicians and pundits were quick to call the action an "act of terror." It was not. It was an "act of war." The difference is not semantic.

2   What makes a bombing an "act of terror"? Terror is violent and unexpected, but so is war itself. We don't call either the bombing of Hiroshima or the bombing of Pearl Harbor acts of terror, though both were terrifyingly destructive.

3   War itself is terrifying. Horror, panic, an intense fear of danger to come—that defines the experience of war. What makes "acts of terror" different from "acts of war" is that the danger we fear is unknown. We don't know who has attacked us, or why, or how to find them. They operate outside our known political universe.

4   Since 9/11, however, the terms "terror" and "war" have been collapsed. The Bush administration pursues a "war on terror," as if the unknown could be brought permanently to bay. Yet even as he suggests terror can be tamed, Bush increasingly populates the realm of terror, casting ordinary enemies of the state as terrorists. We saw this in the lead-up to the current Gulf War, in which Iraq itself was almost never named. Instead, the enemy was the evil, cartoon-like Saddam whose motives were unclear and whose weapons unknown—as if the state of Iraq and its long history did not exist.

5   It's not an exaggeration to say that the Bush administration was able to persuade Americans to make preemptive war against a sovereign nation-state through the power of the rhetoric of "terror." In the Bush worldview, the "American way of life" is not only the best possible way to live but the only possible way. It is an extraordinarily myopic worldview that suggests those who espouse any other ideological position must simply not know any better. Those who are introduced to the "American way" and yet still reject it are seen as beyond reason. Like Saddam, they operate on the "outside," in an unfathomable and unknowable ideological space. One cannot understand them, cannot negotiate with them, can only attack and hope to destroy them. They are terrorists.

6   The rhetoric of terrorism supplies the logic for unending war. While we hope for a messianic age "when the world will be one," for the forseeable future, humanity will continue to be divided by radically different understandings of how we must live in the world. There will always be those who oppose the values we share with their

own. If we insist on characterizing our ideology as the only one possible, we will have created the necessity for the terrorists—the outsiders—we so fear.

7   The alternative is to understand the human world as a complex web of competing ideological positions, some of which are deeply oppositional. We need not accept the validity of these positions. There are even times when our ethical duty is to go to war over ideology, as in the U.S. Civil War or World War II. Yet acknowledging that there are acceptable ideologies other than our own invites mutual recognition and negotiation over differences.

8   Such a stance will also help us recognize those who desire to be seen as terrorists—those who not only refuse to recognize the validity of any position other than their own, but who do not wish to be known themselves—in short, those who desire to be on the "outside." Osama Bin Laden stands there; Saddam Hussein did not.

9   As the United States formulates a strategy for Lebanon and for Iran, we must be wary of references to "terrorist" states and "terrorist" leaders. Iran is not an unknown quantity, nor for that matter is Hezbollah. Radical as it is, Hezbollah operates within a field of differences, its political arm participating in the multiethnic parliament of Lebanon. Arguing that Hezbollah is not a terrorist organization does not imply support—Hezbollah's launch of rockets into Israel was an act of war, to which Israel had the right to respond. It only implies that Hezbollah is not "outside" the world in which we operate.

10   Terrorism is a strategy of fear. Calling enemies terrorists only plays into those fears, implying that we can only protect ourselves by clinging more tightly to what is ours and rejecting more clearly that which is outside. We will be stronger, and better able to confront the threats that we face, when we can characterize our enemies as people like us, with their own beliefs and fears.

UNDERSTANDING CONTEXT

1.   What is Jo Ellen Green Kaiser's thesis? Can you restate it in your own words?

2.   How does Kaiser define *terrorism?* How does it differ from *war* in her view?

3.   Do you think victims see a difference in being bombed by terrorists or by soldiers? Why or why not?

4.   Why does Kaiser believe that instead of dismissing enemies as "terrorists" we should view them "as people like us, with their own beliefs and fears"?

5.   *Critical thinking:* Do you see a difference between a group dedicated to committing terrorism and an organization with a political ideology that uses terrorism as a strategy to achieve its goals? Have revolutionaries engaged in acts of terrorism to overthrow authoritarian regimes or resist foreign occupation?

EVALUATING STRATEGY

1.   How effective is Kaiser's introduction?

2.   How does Kaiser organize her essay? What role do paragraphs play?

3.   *Other modes:* Where does Kaiser use *examples, comparison,* and *persuasion* to develop her essay?

APPRECIATING LANGUAGE

1. What connotation does *terrorism* have? How does it differ from *war*?

2. What is a "preemptive war"?

3. How would you define what Kaiser calls "the strategy of fear"?

WRITING SUGGESTIONS

1. Using Kaiser's essay as a model, use a definition to develop a persuasive argument. Do you consider drug addicts "criminal" or "sick"? Should the definition of "unsportsmanlike conduct" be expanded? Who would you define as "rich"? What is "underemployment" and how should it be addressed?

2. *Collaborative writing:* Working with a group of students, discuss Kaiser's article and then develop a definition of terrorism. Your group might develop its essay by listing events you would define as acts of terrorism and acts you would not. If members have conflicting views, consider developing opposing statements.

CRITICAL ISSUES

© Eyebyte/Alamy

The War on Terrorism

How can you defeat an enemy who thinks he's on a mission from God? A hundred days and one war later, we know the answer: B-52's, for starters.

Charles Krauthammer

The instinct to retaliate with bombing is an anachronism. Fewer than twenty men had brought us to our national knees. . . . The government's answer was that we were good and love freedom and these people are bad and hate it. That vapid answer came from a national culture that has lost its talent for healthy guilt.

Daniel C. Maguire

Shortly after the attacks of September 11, 2001, President Bush announced a war against terrorism. Speaking to reporters two weeks later, Paul Wolfowitz, Deputy Secretary of Defense, outlined the direction of the war:

> It's not going to be solved by some limited military action. It's going to take, as the President has said and Secretary Rumsfeld has said, a broad and sustained campaign against the terrorist networks and the states that support those terrorist networks.

Within weeks the United States began military operations that would topple the Taliban regime in Afghanistan, a move that cost few American casualties and was widely supported by the public at home and its Allies abroad.

The passage of the Patriot Act and the invasion of Iraq, however, led critics to question if these actions would defeat terrorists or simply erode civil liberties at home, hurt America's image abroad, and create more anger in the Muslim world, encouraging more terrorism. Among those who supported President Bush were columnist Thomas Friedman, who argued that the United States had to project its power in the Middle East:

> The "right reason" for this war was the need to partner with Iraqis . . . to build a progressive Arab regime. Because the real weapons of mass destruction that threaten us were never Saddam's missiles. The real weapons that threaten us are the growing number of angry, humiliated young Arabs and Muslims, who are produced by failed or failing Arab states—young people who hate America more than they love life.

Arab and Muslim commentators viewed the invasion differently, seeing it as a dangerous misstep in attempting to curb terrorism. Husain Haqqani, a Pakistani journalist, suggested an alternative strategy to counter extremism in the Muslim world:

> The United States must avoid any impulse to act as an imperial power, dictating its superior ways to "less civilized" peoples. It should be prepared to accept Islamic pride and Arab nationalism as factors in the region's politics, instead of backing narrowly based elites to do its bidding. Patient engagement, rather than the flaunting of military and financial power, should characterize this new phase of U.S. intervention in the heart of the Islamic world.

For some Americans, the concept of a never-ending "war on terrorism" raised concerns. Susan Sontag believed the term *war* itself was inappropriate to describe the actions America must take:

> There are no endless wars. But there are declarations of the extension of power by a state that believes it cannot be challenged.
>
> America has every right to hunt down the perpetrators of these crimes and their accomplices. But this determination is not necessarily a war. Limited, focused military engagements abroad do not translate into "wartime" at home. There are better ways to check America's enemies, less destructive of constitutional rights and international agreements that serve the public interest of all, than continuing to invoke the dangerous, lobotomizing notion of endless war.

Before reading the articles listed below, consider these questions:

1. *Was the proper response to the attack on September 11th a "war"?* What action should the president take to confront international terrorism?
2. *Did toppling regimes in Afghanistan and Iraq make America more or less secure?* Did the demonstration of military power shatter the ambitions of extremists or only fuel the humiliation and resentment that breed terrorism?
3. *Why did terrorists target the United States?* Do most Americans understand why their nation is viewed with so much hatred throughout Africa and Asia?
4. *When will a war on terror end, if ever?* Can we expect the United States to be a nation under threat for next ten, twenty, or fifty years?
5. *Do you think America will suffer another major attack in the future?* How likely do think it is that terrorists will cause mass casualties? Is a major attack with biological, chemical, or nuclear weapons probable?
6. *Are expensive military campaigns overseas making the United States stronger or weaker?*

E-READINGS ONLINE

Search for each article by author or title in InfoTrac College Edition, available through your English CourseMate at **www.cengagebrain.com**.

Fareed Zakaria. "We're Safer Than We Think."
Al Qaeda has been "whittled down to about 400 fighters" and "militant Islam's appeal has plunged" throughout the Muslim world.

Chuck Freilich. "Armageddon and the Threat of Nuclear Terrorism."
The United States "must take into account that a nuclear terrorist threat could emerge in the foreseeable future, and act accordingly to minimize that threat using prevention and deterrence."

John Mueller. "Nuclear Bunkum: Don't Panic: bin Laden's WMD are Mythical, Too."
Concerns about Al Qaeda acquiring weapons of mass destruction are overblown, with much of the "intelligence" coming from "a loveable rogue" eager to sell fictional accounts.

Michiko Kakutani. "The Attack Coming From Bytes, Not Bombs."
Rival powers and terrorist groups could launch a devastating cyber attack on the United States that could shut down power plants, cause chemical plant and pipeline explosions, erase critical data, and paralyze the nation's economy.

Ronald Brownstein. "Dangerous Trends in the War on Terror."
Intensified efforts by terrorists to recruit Muslim Americans and growing suspicion about Islam in the United States "can reinforce and accelerate each other if leaders in both communities don't act."

Philip Mudd. "Containing Terror."
Terrorism, like communism during the cold war is "a social movement that must be held in check."

Jacob Sullum. "The Wide Net of 'Material Support': The War on Terrorism Becomes a War on Free Speech."
Those who advise radical groups how to seek peaceful resolutions to their grievances risk being prosecuted for "providing material support" to terrorists.

Paul Pillar and John Nagl. "Is Afghanistan the Right War?"
With terrorists coming from Nigeria and Yemen and the chances that the Taliban would not harbor Al Qaeda again, Paul Pillar, a former intelligence officer, believes the war in Afghanistan is unnecessary. In contrast, John Nagl, a security advisor and military veteran, argues that "counterinsurgency in Afghanistan is the least bad of the options available."

Caryle Murphy. "The War on Terrorism: Why It Will Be a Long One."
Arab Muslims, a Middle East correspondent notes, do not hate us, only our foreign policy. To win the war on terrorism, America "must help moderate Muslims find their voices."

A. Tariq Karim. "Terrorism: Addressing Its Root Causes."
Terrorists are bred in unjust and undemocratic societies in which fanatics preaching hatred and bigotry offer the only alternative to oppression.

Howard Zinn. "Operation Enduring War."
The war against terrorism is a war without end that turns attention away from the most deadly enemies who "are not in caves and compounds abroad but in the corporate boardrooms and governmental offices where decisions are made that consign millions to death and misery."

CRITICAL READING AND THINKING

1. How do the various authors define *terrorism*?
2. Why was America attacked, according to these authors?
3. What do the authors see as the cause of terrorism?
4. What do these authors see as the proper response to terrorism?
5. Why do some authors believe that the United States must improve its relations with the Muslim world to defeat terrorism?

WRITING SUGGESTIONS

1. Write an essay about how the war on terrorism has affected your life. Have you witnessed more security at airports? Do you have family or friends serving in the military? What attitudes have you observed among family, friends, coworkers, and other students? Is terrorism something they talk about?

2. *Collaborative writing:* Working with other students, develop an essay outlining what your group believes are the best strategies for opposing terrorism. If students disagree, consider drafting opposing essays.

3. *Other modes:*
   - Write a *cause-and-effect* essay that explains the causes of terrorism and/or the effects it has on society.
   - Develop a *classification* essay that explains what you consider the most to least likely future terrorist attacks or the least to most successful ways of improving national security.
   - Write an essay that uses an *example* of what you consider the best or worst decision the administration has made on the war on terrorism.
   - Write a *process* essay that explains what steps the United States should take to defeat terrorism.

RESEARCH PAPER

You can develop a research paper about the war on terrorism by conducting further research to explore a range of issues:

- How do different experts, commentators, and governments define *terrorism*?
- How have Europeans responded to America's war on terrorism, especially the invasion of Iraq?
- How has the Muslim world responded to extremism and terrorism?
- What motivates terrorists to attack civilian populations?
- Do historians and political commentators see terrorism as evidence of a "clash of civilizations" between Islam and the West or a conflict between a small group of extremists and the rest of the world, including mainstream Muslims?

FOR FURTHER READING

To locate additional sources, enter *terrorism* as a search term in InfoTrac College Edition, available through your English CourseMate at **www.cengagebrain.com,** or one of your college library's databases, and examine readings under key subdivisions:

analysis	history
cases	military aspects
ethical aspects	public opinion

ADDITIONAL SOURCES

Using a search engine, enter one or more of the following terms to locate additional sources:

terrorism	Homeland Security
nuclear terrorism	al Qaeda
Osama bin Laden	causes of terrorism
effects of terrorism	war on terrorism
terrorist organizations	suicide bombers

See the Evaluating Internet Source Checklist on page 533–534. See Chapter 24 for documenting sources.

Don Rosenberg

Don Rosenberg is a psychologist and therapist in Milwaukee. He wrote the following definition of depression for a brochure to be distributed in a mental health clinic.

What Is Depression?

Source: "What is Depression?" by Don Rosenberg. Reprinted by permission of the author.

As you read this definition, notice that it is directed to people who may suffer from depression. How does it differ from a definition of depression you might find in a psychology textbook?

WHAT IS DEPRESSION?

Depression is an internal state—a feeling of sadness, loss, "the blues," deep disappointment. *When it is more severe, you may have feelings of irritability, touchiness, guilt, self-reproach, loss of self-esteem, worthlessness, hopelessness, helplessness, and even thoughts of death and suicide.* It may include such other feelings as tearfulness, being sensitive and easily hurt, loss of interests, loss of sexual drive, loss of control in life, feeling drained and depleted, anger at yourself, and loss of the ability to feel pleasure.

It may be accompanied by *physical symptoms* similar to the sense of profound loss, including:

- *loss of appetite,* often with weight loss, but sometimes we find increased eating
- *insomnia or early morning waking,* often 2–4 times per night, nearly every day, but sometimes we see a need to sleep excessively
- moving and speaking slows down, but sometimes we see *agitation*
- *fatigue or loss of energy* nearly every day
- *loss of concentration,* foggy and indecisive
- sometimes includes anxious and headachy feelings and also *frequent crying*

Besides the physical sensations and emotions of depression, depressed people may *withdraw, may brood or ruminate about problems,* have trouble remembering things, wonder if they would be better off dead, and become very concerned about bodily symptoms and pains. They may be grouchy, sulking, restless, and unwilling to interact with family and friends.

UNDERSTANDING CONTEXT

1. What role does definition play in the treatment of any disorder? Do people need to find a name or a label for what troubles them? Is that the first step to coping with or resolving a problem?
2. Can you define *depression* in your own words?
3. What are the physical symptoms of depression?

Sam Diephuis/jupiterimages

EVALUATING STRATEGY

1. How effective are the techniques used for emphasis—underlining, italics, bulleted points?

2. How is the message directed to its readers? Do you sense that only those experiencing these symptoms are likely to read this document?

APPRECIATING LANGUAGE

1. How does Rosenberg describe depression? Do the words create impressions people are likely to recognize?

2. There are few technical or professional terms in this definition. Does this sacrifice accuracy? Why or why not?

WRITING SUGGESTIONS

1. Take a definition from the glossary section of a textbook and write a general version for an audience of clients, consumers, or students.

2. *Collaborative writing:* Discuss a common problem or issue with fellow students: job insecurity, lack of sleep, stressful family relationships, stalking, or child care. Select a term you often overhear and provide a clear definition for it. Have each member of the group list features of this term. Try to incorporate objective elements. Have the group prepare two versions—one designed for an "official" publication, such as the college catalog or textbook, the other for an informal handout.

RESPONDING TO IMAGES

JIM BOURG/Reuters/Landov

Anti-gay marriage protest in Boston, 2004

1. What is your first reaction to this photograph? Do you find this an effective form of protest? Does the use of the "1 + 1 = ____" argument make a strong point or does it seem simplistic? Can you think of other "1 + 1 = ____" arguments?

2. How important are definitions in law and public policy? How should we define *marriage, stalking, terrorism, obscenity,* and *sexual harassment?*

3. *Visual analysis:* Note the wording of the sign. What connotations does the word "preserve" have? Does it imply that traditional marriage is under attack? Would signs using negative terms to denounce gay marriage be less effective? Would they appear hateful? Why or why not? What signs might supporters of gay marriage use? How could they communicate a positive message?

4. *Critical thinking:* The man is clearly holding the sign aloft to be seen by a photographer. In a visual society do people feel compelled to condense their message to a slogan? Does it reduce complex issues to simplistic phrases or sound bites?

5. *Collaborative writing:* Working with a group of students, select a current political or social issue and discuss the role definition plays. Identify opposing viewpoints and write a definition statement that expresses each position. How, for instance, do people who argue over free speech define obscenity, or how do those who debate gun control define "the right to bear arms"?

DEFINITION CHECKLIST

Before submitting your paper, review these points:

✔ Is your purpose clear—to inform or persuade?

✔ Do you avoid defining a word with the same word, such as "a diffusion pump diffuses"?

✔ Is your level of technical or professional language suited to your audience?

✔ Does your definition provide enough information and examples so that readers can restate your thesis in their own words?

✔ Are there existing definitions you can use for reference or contrast?

✔ Do extended definitions contain illustrations, narratives, or comparisons readers may misinterpret or not recognize?

✔ Do you state the essence of your definition in a short summary statement readers can remember or highlight for future reference?

 Access the English CourseMate for this text at **www.cengagebrain.com** for additional information on writing definitions.

Comparison and Contrast
Indicating Similarities and Differences

What Is Comparison and Contrast?

Comparison and contrast answers the questions: How are things alike or different? What distinguishes a gasoline engine from a diesel engine? Is it cheaper to buy or lease a new car? What separates a misdemeanor from a felony? How is a viral infection different from a bacterial one? All of these questions can be addressed by examining similarities and differences.

You have probably encountered questions on essay examinations that require comparison-and-contrast responses:

Compare the industrial output of the North and South at the outbreak of the Civil War.

How do the rules of evidence differ in criminal and civil proceedings?

Which arrangement offers business owners greater protection of personal assets—full or limited partnerships?

At the end of *The Great Gatsby* Nick Carraway decides to return to the West because he is too "squeamish" for the East. What differences did Fitzgerald see between the East and West?

Comparison-and-contrast writing is commonly used to organize research papers. You might compare two short stories by Edgar Allan Poe in an English course, explain the differences between methods of depreciation in accounting, or contrast conflicting theories of childhood development in psychology. Comparison-and-contrast writing is also used by engineers to explain the fuel efficiency of different engines, by architects to discuss alternative plans to modernize a building, and by social workers to determine the better program to assist the homeless.

The Purposes of Comparison and Contrast

Writers use comparison and contrast for five purposes:

1. **To draw distinctions between related subjects.** In many instances, comparison is used to eliminate confusion. Many people, for instance, mistake an *optician*, who makes and sells eyeglasses, for an *optometrist*, who performs eye examinations and prescribes lenses. Comparison can pair extended definitions to show readers the difference, for example, between air-cooled and water-cooled engines or

cross-country and downhill skiing. *When drawing distinctions, writers explain differences between similar subjects but do not choose one over the other.*

2. **To recommend a choice between two things.** Television commercials compare competing products. Political campaign brochures urge voters to support a candidate over his or her rival. Articles in medical journals argue that one drug is more effective than another. Government studies assert that one air-quality standard is preferable to another. The basic purpose of stating recommendations is to *persuade readers to make a choice.*

3. **To examine advantages and disadvantages.** Instead of comparing and contrasting two separate plans, people, objects, or ideas, a paper can contrast the good and bad points of a single subject. A report might examine a proposed shopping mall, detailing its positive effects on employment while describing its negative impact on nearby property values.

4. **To show how one subject has changed.** A television critic might argue that a TV series lacks the quality shown in its first season. A sportswriter might compare a team's performance this season with last season's. An employee might explain how a company has changed since it was purchased by a multinational corporation. A student could use a "before and after" comparison to illustrate how a friend changed following the loss of a job or the death of a family member.

5. **To propose an idea, criticize a change, or make a prediction.** Writers can state an argument by comparing a problem with a proposed solution. A city engineer could describe current traffic jams and parking problems, then explain how widened streets and new parking garages could resolve congestion. A doctor could describe a patient's existing lifestyle as a cause of obesity, and then propose a diet and exercise program as solution. A congressman might criticize a policy intended to stimulate small businesses and create jobs by pointing out that in reality it has hurt entrepreneurs and caused layoffs. To show that a curriculum change has improved education, a principal could contrast students' previous test scores with their current performance. An environmentalist might predict how climate change will affect the planet by comparing current conditions with those expected in the future.

Selecting Topics for Comparison-and-Contrast Papers

When developing a paper using comparison and contrast, you must be sure your subjects share enough common points for meaningful discussion. You can compare two sports cars, two action adventure films, two diets, or two political theories. But comparing a sports car to a pickup truck or an adventure film to a romantic comedy is not likely to generate more than superficial observations. In addition, comparisons have to be carefully limited, especially for comparisons of broad or complex subjects. To examine the differences between American and Chinese cultures, Yi-Fu Tuan (p. 317) limits his focus to the different ways Americans and Chinese view space and place. By exploring this limited topic in depth, he reveals more about Chinese culture in a page or two than might be shown in a twenty-page essay attempting to address religion, politics, economics, history, and social customs. To compare two presidents, for instance, you might focus on their relations with the press, their foreign policies, or their ability to respond in a crisis.

WRITING ACTIVITY

Use prewriting techniques to develop ideas on the following pairs. If you are unfamiliar with one topic, select another one that stimulates your thoughts. List similarities and note differences. Consider how you might limit the scope of your comparison. Your goal may be to inform or recommend.

1. Buying versus leasing a car

2. Two people you know well: your parents, two bosses, or two close friends

3. American versus Asian attitudes toward family, career, marriage, or government

4. Your generation's attitudes or values versus those of your parents' generation

5. Liberal versus conservative views of government, justice, poverty, or national defense

6. Two opposing views of the war in Afghanistan

7. Two popular bands, filmmakers, fashion designers, or political candidates

8. Best and worst airlines, hotels, landlords, bosses, restaurants, or doctors you have encountered

9. Two cities or regions of the country

10. Print versus online journalism

Organizing Comparison-and-Contrast Papers

Perhaps the most frustrating problem writers face in writing comparison and contrast is organizing ideas. Without careful planning, you may find yourself shifting awkwardly back and forth between subjects. Your readers may have difficulty following your train of thought and may confuse one subject with another. Whether drawing distinctions or making recommendations, writers use two basic methods of organizing comparison-and-contrast writing.

Subject by Subject

The *subject-by-subject* method divides the paper into two sections. Writers state all the information about topic A and then discuss topic B. Usually, the actual comparisons are drawn in the second part of the paper, where B is discussed in relation to A. In a short paper about two types of life insurance, the student first explains "whole life" insurance and then describes "term" insurance. Because the purpose is to explain, the conclusion of the following paper does not offer a recommendation.

Vicki Shimi   Econ 101

Whole Life and Term Insurance

Most life insurance companies offer a variety of life insurance products, investments, and financial services. Two of the most common policies provided are whole life and term insurance.

Whole life insurance is the oldest and most traditional form of life insurance. Life insurance became popular in the nineteenth century as a way of protecting the buyer's dependents in the event of premature death. A purchaser would select a policy amount to be paid to his or her beneficiaries after his or her death. Payments called premiums were made on a yearly, quarterly, or monthly basis. As the policyholder paid premiums, the policy gained cash value. Part of the payment earned interest like money in a bank account. Insurance served as an investment tool, allowing people to save for retirement and giving them access to guaranteed loans. For a low interest fee, insurance holders could borrow against the cash value of their policies.

Term insurance, introduced in the twentieth century, serves the same basic purpose as whole life insurance, protecting the buyer's dependents. Unlike whole life, however, no cash value accrues. In a sense, the policyholder is "renting" insurance, purchasing only a death benefit. The advantage of term insurance is its low cost. Because there is no money set aside for investment, the premiums are lower. This allows a person to afford a larger policy. A term policy for $100,000 could be cheaper than a whole life policy for $50,000.

The type of insurance a person needs depends on his or her income, family situation, investment goals, savings, and obligations. Most investment counselors agree, however, that anyone with a spouse or children should have some form of life insurance protection.

Advantages

- The subject-by-subject method is a simple, straightforward method of organizing your essay and thus is useful if you have limited time.
- The subject-by-subject method is suited for short, highly readable papers.
- Abstract topics, such as economic theories, religious beliefs, and scientific principles, are often easier to organize in a subject-by-subject method because few individual features are shared by both subjects.

Disadvantages

- Long papers organized subject by subject are difficult to follow. A twenty-page report, for instance, would read like two ten-page papers fastened together. It would be difficult for readers to recall enough details from the first subject to appreciate how it differs from the second.

■ Because subjects are discussed separately, it is difficult to present specific facts side by side. Readers are forced to page back and forth to compare details, such as prices and statistics.

Point by Point

The *point-by-point* method organizes the comparison of A and B on a series of specific subtopics. Following an introduction, A and B are discussed in a number of comparisons. Hotels, for example, have common features: location, appearance, atmosphere, number of rooms, banquet facilities, and rates. In the following paper, the writer organizes information about two hotels in each paragraph. In this instance, the writer makes a recommendation, stating her clear preference for one of the hotels in both the introduction and conclusion.

English 100   Jack Phelan

St. Gregory and Fitzpatrick Hotels

Campus organizations and academic conventions visiting the city hold special events at either the St. Gregory or the Fitzpatrick. Both are large convention hotels, but for many reasons the St. Gregory is more desirable.

Opened in 1892, the St. Gregory is the oldest surviving hotel in the city. The Fitzpatrick is the newest, having opened just last spring. The St. Gregory has a commanding view of State Street. The Fitzpatrick is part of the $200 million Riverfront Centre.

The chief attraction of the St. Gregory is its famed domed lobby, ornamented with carved mahogany and elaborate brass and marble fittings. Admiral Dewey was presented with the key to the city here following his victory in Manila Bay in 1898. In contrast, the sleek Fitzpatrick is noted for its sweeping thirty-story atrium. The open lobby is banked with massive video screens broadcasting subtitled stock market reports, news, and sports.

The main lounge of the St. Gregory is the Pump Room, a plush, turn-of-the-century Irish bar decorated with gilt-framed paintings of the Emerald Isle. The Fitzpatrick features two bars. Homerun, a sports bar, is popular with local students and young professionals. The Exchange is a smaller, quieter bar that is a favorite of visiting executives. Copiers, fax machines, and computers are available in the nearby Executive Centre.

Both hotels offer a range of room rates. The cheapest rooms at the St. Gregory are $95 a night. Though small, they are comfortable. The Fitzpatrick has only a dozen single traveler rooms for $125. Double rooms at the St. Gregory range from $175 to $259, depending on size and decor. All Fitzpatrick double rooms are identical and cost $195. In addition to convention rates, the St. Gregory offers 20 percent student discounts. The Fitzpatrick offers only corporate discounts.

(Continued)

> Both hotels provide excellent convention services. Since most professors and academic delegates have access to university computers and fax machines, they prefer the historic elegance of the St. Gregory. Students especially appreciate discount rates and the availability of public transport to the university.

Advantages

- The point-by-point method is useful in organizing long papers that can be broken into units. Instead of splitting a twenty-page report into two ten-page sections, you can create a series of related comparisons.
- This method allows writers to place specific details side by side so that readers can easily compare prices, dimensions, and figures without having to search through the entire document.
- A point-by-point approach is useful in preparing a document for multiple readers. Because it is organized in sections, a reader can easily identify the information most relevant to his or her purpose.

Disadvantages

- The point-by-point method can be difficult to use if the subjects are abstract and lack detail. Comparing two philosophies or two films may be easier to organize by discussing each separately.
- The point-by-point method can distort a topic if the specific points of comparison are poorly chosen. Major issues can be overlooked or minimized and minor details overemphasized unless the categories are carefully planned.

Blending the Methods

Writers often blend elements of both methods in a single essay. As you read the comparison-and-contrast entries in this chapter you will notice that few exactly fit either method. But as with all writing, clear organization is essential to avoid confusion, especially when your essay addresses more than one topic.

WRITING ACTIVITY

Select ideas from the previous exercise or develop ones from the following topics and create an outline using the subject-by-subject method, point-by-point method, or a blend of methods.

1. The sense of privacy in a small town versus a large city

2. America before and after a major event, such as the civil rights movement, World War II, the women's movement, or 9/11

(Continued)

3. The way husbands and wives are depicted on television

4. Media images of New York and California

5. The quality of a football team's offense and defense

6. Reality TV shows

7. Male and female attitudes about sex, dating, or relationships

8. Growing up in a single-parent versus two-parent family

9. Two common views of death, abortion, poverty, or a recent campus controversy

10. Working for a salary versus working for an hourly wage

Strategies for Writing Comparison: Prewriting and Planning

Critical Thinking and Prewriting

1. **List possible topics in a tandem fashion:**

    U.S. & Canadian health care　　　　Two NFL or NBA teams

    Public schools & choice schools　　　Owning versus renting a home

    ■ Leave space beneath each possible topic so that you can list details side by side.

2. **Choose related topics.** The subjects you select must have enough in common to establish meaningful similarities and enough in contrast to establish more than trivial differences.

    ■ Once you have a list of topics, scan down the pairs to find topics that are suitable for your task.

    ■ Avoid general comparisons that only state obvious and well-known observations.

3. **Select a single topic that has changed.** Instead of comparing two people, two jobs, or two neighborhoods, you might write a before-and-after essay that shows how a subject has changed over time. Has your old neighborhood changed? Has a new boss altered the way you work? Is a favorite TV show better or worse this season than last?

4. **Determine your purpose.** Is your goal to explain differences between two topics or to recommend one subject over another?

- Critical thinking is particularly important in persuading readers to accept your opinions. Consider the common errors you should avoid (see pages 39–41 in Chapter 4).

5. **Examine categories for balance.** Because comparisons often measure advantages and disadvantages, it is easy to make lapses in critical thinking by ignoring points of comparison. You can easily demonstrate that nuclear power is superior to solar energy—as long as you overlook the critical problem of safety and radioactive waste.

   - Make sure that you avoid weighting your essay to favor one subject over another by stressing the advantages of one while emphasizing the disadvantages of another.

6. **Consider using graphs and charts to demonstrate differences in facts, number, or statistics.**

7. **Test ideas through peer review.** Ask fellow students whether you have failed to consider important points of comparison.

Planning

1. **Consider your audience.** Before you can compare two items, you may have to explain background information. Before comparing two treatments for arthritis, it may be necessary to explain the nature of the disease and define basic medical terms.

2. **Review the scope of the assignment and your thesis.** Because you are discussing more than a single topic, it is important to focus your subject.

3. **Determine which method suits your purpose.** A short, nontechnical paper might be best organized using the subject-by-subject method. Longer works with details that should be placed side by side are better developed using the point-by-point method.

4. **Clearly state your thesis.** Whether your goal is to inform or persuade, your comparison needs a well-stated thesis.

5. **Prioritize points.** Determine the most important points of comparison. You may come up with many ideas but not have the space or time to fully develop them.

6. **Develop an outline.** Because you are handling two topics, you may find that you need a more detailed outline to write a comparison than to write a narrative or description.

   - If you find it difficult to develop a point-by-point outline, consider developing a subject-by-subject outline for a rough draft.

Strategies for Writing Comparison: Writing the First Draft

Writing the First Draft

1. **Focus on the goal of your comparison to guide the draft.** Use your thesis to direct your writing. When you discover new ideas, determine whether they will help support the point of your comparison.

2. **Get your ideas on paper by writing separate descriptions.** If you find it difficult to get started or follow a detailed outline, it may be easier to describe each subject separately.

3. **Most comparisons consist of paired descriptions.** Make your descriptions effective by creating dominant impressions, describing people and objects in action, and including dialogue to give voice to people.

4. **Use parallel structures to organize comparisons.** Readers will find your ideas easier to follow and easier to evaluate if you place ideas in a consistent pattern:

   > Shelly Longwood is a federal prosecutor with no political experience who is an outspoken supporter for victims' rights. Her opponent, Sandy Berman, is a judge and former county supervisor who is a strong advocate of community policing.

   Both candidates are described in a matching pattern—current job, political experience, policy.

5. **Be aware of the impact of connotations.** The words you select in describing your topics will influence your readers' interpretations.
   - If you are seeking to distinguish differences between related subjects, avoid using words that may suggest unintended preferences.
   - In making a recommendation, positive and negative connotations and associations will be important tools in pointing out advantages and disadvantages.

6. **Keep the length of your paper in mind as you write.** It is always difficult to measure how many ideas and details you will develop as you write. When you discuss two topics, you may find your essay lengthening.
   - If you realize that to cover all the points on your outline, your paper will be far longer than desired, review your plans. You may wish to tighten your thesis, restrict your topic, discard minor points, or possibly abandon your topic for a more workable one.

Strategies for Writing Comparison: Revising and Editing

Revising

1. **Review your plan and read your draft for its overall impact.**
   - Is the thesis clear? Does your paper accurately establish differences or effectively state a recommendation?

- Is each subject fully developed and described with enough detail?
- Is the draft focused? Or is it too long, too confused?
- Does the draft fulfill the needs of the assignment?

2. **Evaluate the way you describe or define each subject.**
   - Do you accurately and precisely define what you are comparing?
   - Have you limited the topics?
   - Are there misconceptions or vague statements that require greater clarity?

3. **Review the organization.** Is the paper logically organized? Should you consider rewriting the paper using a different method?

4. **Examine the information you have included.** Does the essay present enough facts, observations, and details about *both* subjects?

5. **Evaluate transitions between ideas.**
   - Can readers follow your train of thought? Are there clear shifts from one topic to another?
   - Can paragraph breaks and other devices help readers follow your ideas?

6. **Review the emphasis of main points.** Are the main points of the comparison clearly highlighted and easy to remember?

7. **Study the impact of the introduction and conclusion.**
   - Does the introduction set up the comparison and introduce your purpose and thesis?
   - Does the conclusion make a final impression, restate the significant differences, or reinforce your recommendations?

8. **Evaluate the use of any visuals.**
   - Do they clearly illustrate similarities and differences in your subjects?
   - Do the images add value to your writing, or are they unrelated or distracting?
   - Are graphs or charts based on accurate data? Are the visual aids easy to understand?

Editing and Proofreading

1. **Read the paper aloud. Listen to your sentences.**
   - Are there awkward or repetitive phrases?
   - Do any passages require streamlining or greater detail?

2. **Review your choice of words.**
   - Do you accurately define each subject and main points?
   - Do the connotations of your words reflect your meaning?

3. **Use peer editing to identify problems you may have overlooked.**

STUDENT PAPER

This is a draft of a comparison paper a student wrote after reading a book and some articles on education.

FIRST DRAFT WITH INSTRUCTOR'S COMMENTS

Alfred Leone   English 112

Comparison Essay

School Reforms

needs more focused introduction   *cut, vague, obvious*

Today in America schools are important. They train students to perform in college

and compete in the world today. They play a vital role in shaping the future. But our

schools are not doing their job. They need reform. Two types of alternative schools

explain

have been tried. They could be the future. But they may need to be

reformed, too.

Magnet schools started in 1970s mostly to overcome segregation without the use

avoid repetition

of unpopular forced busing. The government provided extra money for these <u>special</u>

explain the "same principles"

schools that usually had some kind of <u>special</u> focus like the arts or high tech. Many

charter schools today use many of the same principles although charter schools are not

always public.

Both charter and magnet schools sought to remedy long-standing problems in public school

performance by offering students and parents an alternative to standard public schools. These

schools, however, have not been without their critics. "I sometimes think we are simply seeing a

placebo effect in some of these schools. The books, the tests, the teachers may be the same, but

a new sign on the door and the fact that it takes some effort to apply, not only attracts motivated

(Continued)

students but energizes them to try harder because they are told and tell themselves they are special" (Smith 10–11). *explain this source, link to your text.*

Both magnet schools and charter schools have given students, often very poor ones, more options for their education. Not all students think alike or learn alike. Not all have the same interests. Public schools have to meet the most common needs and cannot always *SP* accomodate gifted or challenged students. Charter schools are often more focused because of their charter, which makes them accountable. Charters have a time limit. Unlike a public *fragment* high school that will stay in operation for as long as students walk through the door. A char- *run-on* ter school must achieve specific goals with a certain time frame (usually three to five years), or they will be shut down. *This belongs in first paragraph*

Our public schools are substandard. A recent *Newsweek* survey revealed that American students are now scoring below fifteen other countries in math and seventeen other countries in science. Even more troubling to experts is that in some major cities less than 40% of minority students will graduate high school. Major US corporations report that it is easier to hire skilled workers in Asia than the United States, where as many as two-third of the job applicants fail a simple math test (Rankin 12).

Magnet and charter schools have had some success in the past. They need to redesigned for the twenty-first century and made more widely available.

Works Cited

Rankin, Gwen. "Schools Flunk." *Newsweek* 10 Oct. 2012: 12–14. Print.
Smith, Sara. *School Reform: Hopes, Dreams, and Scams.* New York: Putnam, 2011. Print.

(Continued)

REVISION NOTES

This is a good topic. You have located good sources. But the paper could be improved with careful revision and editing:

1. *The paper needs clearer organization. Introduce the subject of schools, explaining problems with public schools. Discuss magnet schools, then charter schools.*

2. *Provide a clearer definition of both magnet and charter schools.*

3. *When you introduce outside sources, link them to your text and explain their importance. Who is Sara Smith? Why is her opinion significant? What is her book based on?*

4. *Edit for spelling, fragments, and run-ons.*

REVISED DRAFT

Alfred Leone   English 112

Comparison Essay

Experiments in Education Reform:
Magnet and Charter Schools

Our public schools are substandard. A recent *Newsweek* survey revealed that American students are now scoring below fifteen other countries in math and seventeen other countries in science. Even more troubling to experts is that in some major cities less than 40% of minority students will graduate high school. Major US corporations report that it is easier to hire skilled workers in Asia than the United States, where as many as two-thirds of the job applicants fail a simple math test (Rankin 12). Two alternatives to standard public schools—magnet schools and charter schools—could improve student performance, if they are redesigned for the twenty-first century.

Magnet schools were developed in the 1970s as a way of integrating schools without forced busing. Magnet schools are public schools that offer a special curriculum focusing on college preparation, high technology, the performing arts, or business. Because they draw students district-wide, the hope is that they will attract diverse populations. Cities established magnet schools to obtain federal funding and meet court-ordered desegregation requirements. Academically, magnet schools have a mixed record. Sara Smith, former White House advisor on education, conducted a review of two hundred magnet schools and noted, "Because their primary goal was creating diversity, academic excellence became a secondary concern" (11). Smith believes, however, that magnet schools, if properly redesigned, could increase student achievement, especially in "stressed, under-funded school districts losing their best and brightest to private academies" (12).

Charter schools, like magnet schools, offer students a special curriculum. Unlike magnet schools, however, not all charter schools are public. In some districts private

(Continued)

and religious institutions can be designated charter schools and receive public funding. Unlike magnet schools, charter schools are often exempted from the school district's ordinary rules and regulations. Instead, they operate under a charter, a contract that stipulates specific objectives the schools must achieve within a certain time, usually three to five years. If they fail to achieve their goals, they lose their charter and close. Freed from standard requirements, charter schools can experiment with new approaches to teaching and testing.

The record on magnet and charter schools has been mixed. It is difficult to measure their success in many cases because of high transfer rates and the lack of uniform testing data. Some private charter schools have been so mismanaged that they have run out of money and closed mid-semester, leaving students scrambling to find openings in other institutions. Even when alternative schools prove to be successful, it is hard to prove whether it is the school or the student. Smith wonders if student motivation rather than innovative teaching techniques is responsible for improved performance. "I sometimes think," she argues, "we are simply seeing a placebo effect in some of these schools. The books, the tests, the teachers may be the same, but a new sign on the door and the fact that it takes some effort to apply not only attracts serious students but energizes them to try harder, because they are told and they tell themselves they are special" (Smith, 10–11).

With education needing reform, it is time magnet and charter schools receive a full review to identify their successes and replicate those in regular schools most students attend.

Works Cited

Rankin, Gwen. "Schools Flunk." *Newsweek* 10 Oct. 2012: 12–14. Print.
Smith, Sara. *School Reform: Hopes, Dreams, and Scams.* New York: Putnam, 2011. Print.

QUESTIONS FOR REVIEW AND REVISION

1. Is the thesis of this essay clear? Can you restate it in your own words? Does the paper try to cover too much material in a short paper? Would it be better to focus on one aspect of magnet and charter schools, such as their faculty, testing, or graduation requirements?

2. Would a revised introduction and conclusion provide greater focus?

3. What audience does the student seem to address?

4. *Critical thinking:* Why is it important to provide information about the person quoted in the essay?

5. How effectively does the student organize the comparison? What role does paragraph structure play?

6. Does the student follow the instructor's suggestions? Is this version a great improvement over the first draft?

7. Read the paper aloud. Do you detect any passages that could be revised to reduce wordiness and repetition?

WRITING SUGGESTIONS

1. Write a 500-word essay comparing two nations, cities, or neighborhoods. Stress similarities most readers would be unaware of.

2. *Collaborative writing:* Discuss this paper with a group of students. Ask each member to suggest possible changes. Do they find common areas needing improvement?

Suggested Topics for Writing Comparison and Contrast

General Assignments

Write a comparison paper on one of the following topics. You may use either the subject-by-subject or point-by-point method of organization. Your paper will likely blend both of these approaches. *Clearly determine your purpose—to inform or persuade.*

- High school and college
- Your best and worst jobs
- Renting versus owning a home
- The two most influential teachers/coaches/supervisors you have known
- Two popular sitcoms/newsmagazines/soap operas/talk shows/reality shows
- How a television series, football team, band, or neighborhood has changed over time
- Your best and worst college courses
- A then and now comparison that describes a current problem and proposes a solution
- Advantages and disadvantages of owning your own business
- A current problem and a proposed solution

Writing in Context

1. Imagine you have been asked by a British newsmagazine to write an article explaining the pro and con attitudes that Americans have about a controversial topic, such as immigration, gun control, capital punishment, abortion, or welfare reform. Your article should be balanced and objective and should provide background information rather than just express your personal opinion.

2. Write the text for a brief pamphlet directed to high school seniors comparing high school and college. You may wish to use a chart format to compare specific points.

3. Write an e-mail to a friend comparing the best and worst aspects of your college, dorm, neighborhood, or job.

4. Examine a website about cars, computers, or entertainment. Post a comment describing its best and worst features.

5. Compare two popular student clubs or restaurants for a review in the campus newspaper. Direct your comments to students who are interested in inexpensive but interesting entertainment.

Strategies for Reading Comparison and Contrast

In reading the comparison-and-contrast essays in this chapter, keep these questions in mind.

Context

1. What is the writer's goal—to draw distinctions or to recommend a choice?
2. What details does the writer present about each subject?
3. Who is the intended audience? Is the essay directed to a general or a specific reader?
4. Is the comparison valid? Is the writer comparing two subjects in a fair manner? Have any points been overlooked?
5. Does the author have an apparent bias?
6. If the comparison makes a recommendation, does the selection seem valid? What makes the chosen subject superior to others? What evidence is presented?

Strategy

1. What is the basic pattern of the comparison—subject by subject, point by point, or a blend?
2. Does the author use a device to narrow the topic or to advance the comparison?
3. Does the writer use visual aids, such as graphs, charts, or highlighted text?
4. Is the essay easy to follow? Are transitions between subjects clearly established by paragraph breaks and other devices?

Language

1. Does the writer use words with connotations that ascribe positive or negative qualities to one or both of the subjects? How does the author characterize the topics?
2. What do the diction, level of language, and use of technical terms reveal about the intended audience?
3. If the writer is suggesting a choice, how does the language demonstrate his or her preference?

READING TO LEARN

As you read the comparison essays in this chapter, note techniques you can use in your own writing.

- **"Chinese Place, American Space" by Yi-Fu Tuan** uses the subject-by-subject method to organize his comparison between Americans and the Chinese. Note that Tuan devotes more space to the less-familiar topic of China than the United States.

- **"Grant and Lee" by Bruce Catton** compares the two great Civil War generals, not as military leaders but as symbols of two visions of America.

- **"A Fable for Tomorrow" by Rachel Carlson** uses a "before and after" description of a mythical town to dramatize the impact pesticides have on the environment.

- **"Reinventing the American Dream" by Christopher Jencks** compares the Republican definition of the American Dream—a land of freedom and limited government—with the Democratic vision of a country of shared prosperity and security.

Yi-Fu Tuan

Yi-Fu Tuan (1930–) was born in China and later moved to the United States. Now a geography professor in Madison, Wisconsin, he has studied the cultural differences between America and his native country. He states that he writes "from a single perspective—namely that of experience." In this article published in *Harper's,* he compares the way people in two cultures view their environments.

Chinese Place, American Space

Source: "Chinese Place, American Space" by Yi-Fu Tuan. Reprinted with permission from Yi-Fu Tuan.

Cultures as diverse as America's and China's have many points of difference. In attempting to provide insight into their differences in a brief essay, Yi-Fu Tuan focuses on the concept of space and location. Americans, he asserts, are less rooted to place and are future oriented. The Chinese, savoring tradition, are deeply tied to specific locations. Note that Yi-Fu Tuan devotes most of his essay to describing the less-familiar Chinese houses and values.

1 Americans have a sense of space, not of place. Go to an American home in exurbia, and almost the first thing you do is drift toward the picture window. How curious that the first compliment you pay your host inside his house is to say how lovely it is outside his house! He is pleased that you should admire his vistas. The distant horizon is not merely a line separating earth from sky, it is a symbol of the future. The American is not rooted in his place, however lovely: his eyes are drawn by the expanding space to a point on the horizon, which is his future.

thesis
American space
American home

2 By contrast, consider the traditional Chinese home. Blank walls enclose it. Step behind the spirit wall and you are in a courtyard with perhaps a miniature garden around a corner. Once inside his private compound you are wrapped in an ambiance of calm beauty, an ordered world of buildings, pavement, rock, and decorative vegetation. But you have no distant view: nowhere does space open out before you. Raw nature in such a home is experienced only as weather, and the only open space is the sky above. The Chinese is rooted in his place. When he has to leave, it is not for the promised land on the terrestrial horizon, but for another world altogether along the vertical, religious axis of his imagination.

transition
Chinese home
Chinese place

3 The Chinese tie to place is deeply felt. Wanderlust is an alien sentiment. The Taoist classic *Tao Te Ching* captures the ideal of rootedness in place with these words: "Though there may be another country in the neighborhood so close that they are within sight of each other and the crowing of cocks and barking of dogs in one place can be heard in the other, yet there is no traffic between them; and throughout their lives the two peoples have nothing to do with each other." In theory if not in practice, farmers have ranked high in Chinese society. The reason is not only that they are engaged in a "root" industry of producing food but that, unlike pecuniary merchants, they are tied to the land and do not abandon their country when it is in danger.

4 Nostalgia is a recurrent theme in Chinese poetry. An American reader of translated Chinese poems may well be taken aback—even put off—by the frequency, as well as the sentimentality, of the lament for home. To understand the strength of this sentiment, we need to know that the Chinese desire for stability and rootedness in place is prompted by the constant threat of war, exile, and the natural disasters of

flood and drought. Forcible removal makes the Chinese keenly aware of their loss. By contrast, Americans move, for the most part, voluntarily. Their nostalgia for home town is really longing for a childhood to which they cannot return: in the meantime the future beckons and the future is "out there," in open space. When we criticize American rootlessness, we tend to forget that it is a result of ideals we admire, namely, social mobility and optimism about the future. When we admire Chinese rootedness, we forget that the word "place" means both a location in space and position in society: to be tied to place is also to be bound to one's station in life, with little hope of betterment. Space symbolizes hope; place, achievement and stability.

final comments on American and Chinese values

UNDERSTANDING CONTEXT

1. How does the author see a difference between "space" and "place"?
2. What do the traditional designs of American and Chinese homes reveal about cultural differences?
3. Why do the Chinese honor farmers?
4. What historical forces have shaped the Chinese desire for "rootedness"? How is American history different?
5. What negative aspects does Yi-Fu Tuan see in the Chinese sense of place?

EVALUATING STRATEGY

1. The writer really devotes only a single paragraph to describing American concepts of space. Why? Is the essay out of balance? Discuss whether a comparison paper should devote half its space to each topic.
2. Is the author objective? Is it possible for a writer to discuss cultures without inserting a measure of bias?

APPRECIATING LANGUAGE

1. What words does Yi-Fu Tuan use in describing the two cultures? Do they seem to differ in connotation?
2. Does the word *rootlessness* suggest something negative to most people? How does Yi-Fu Tuan define it?
3. Look up the word *wanderlust*. How does a German term suit an essay comparing American and Chinese cultures?

WRITING SUGGESTIONS

1. If you have lived in or visited another country or region within the United States, write a brief essay outlining how it differs from your home. Just as Yi-Fu Tuan used the concept of space to focus a short article, you may wish to limit your comparison to discussing eating habits, dress, attitudes toward work, music, or dating practices.
2. *Collaborative writing:* Ask a group of students about their attitudes toward rootlessness and place. Determine how often students have moved in their lives. How many have spent their entire lives in a single house or apartment? Write a few paragraphs outlining the attitudes expressed by the group.

Bruce Catton (1899–1978) grew up listening to stories of Civil War veterans. His own college career was interrupted by service in the First World War. Catton went to work as a reporter for the *Cleveland Plain Dealer* and later served as information director for several government agencies. In 1953 his book *A Stillness at Appomattox* became a best seller, and Catton received a Pulitzer Prize. He wrote several other books about the Civil War and edited *American Heritage* magazine for two decades.

Grant and Lee

Source: "Grant and Lee" by Bruce Catton. From *The American Story* by Earll Schenk Miers. Reprinted by permission of the U.S. Capitol Historical Society.

Perhaps no other essay is as widely anthologized as a sample of comparison writing than Catton's "Grant and Lee," which first appeared in a collection, The American Story. *Directed to a general audience, the essay seeks to contrast the two most famous generals of the Civil War.*

1   When Ulysses S. Grant and Robert E. Lee met in the parlor of a modest house at Appomattox Court House, Virginia, on April 9, 1865, to work out the terms for the surrender of Lee's Army of Northern Virginia, a great chapter in American life came to a close, and a great new chapter began.

2   These men were bringing the Civil War to its virtual finish. To be sure, other armies had yet to surrender, and for a few days the fugitive Confederate government would struggle desperately and vainly, trying to find some way to go on living now that its chief support was gone. But in effect it was all over when Grant and Lee signed the papers. And the little room where they wrote out the terms was the scene of one of the poignant, dramatic contrasts in American history.

3   They were two strong men, these oddly different generals, and they represented the strengths of two conflicting currents that, through them, had come into final collision.

4   Back of Robert E. Lee was the notion that the old aristocratic concept might somehow survive and be dominant in American life.

5   Lee was tidewater Virginia, and in his background were family, culture, and tradition . . . the age of chivalry transplanted to a New World which was making its own legends and its own myths. He embodied a way of life that had come down through the age of knighthood and the English country squire. America was a land that was beginning all over again, dedicated to nothing much more complicated than the rather hazy belief that all men had equal rights and should have an equal chance in the world. In such a land Lee stood for the feeling that it was somehow of advantage to human society to have a pronounced inequality in the social structure. There should be a leisure class, backed by ownership of land; in turn, society itself should be keyed to the land as the chief source of wealth and influence. It would bring forth (according to this ideal) a class of men with a strong sense of obligation to the community; men who lived not to gain advantage for themselves, but to meet the solemn obligations which had been laid on them by the very fact that they were privileged. From them the country would get its leadership; to them it could look for the higher values—of thought, of conduct, of personal deportment—to give it strength and virtue.

6   Lee embodied the noblest elements of this aristocratic ideal. Through him, the landed nobility justified itself. For four years, the Southern states had fought a desperate war to uphold the ideals for which Lee stood. In the end, it almost seemed as if the Confederacy fought for Lee; as if he himself was the Confederacy . . . the best thing that the way of life for which the Confederacy stood could ever have to offer. He had passed into legend before Appomattox. Thousands of tired, underfed, poorly clothed Confederate soldiers, long since past the simple enthusiasm of the early days of the struggle, somehow considered Lee the symbol of everything for which they had been willing to die. But they could not quite put this feeling into words. If the Lost Cause, sanctified by so much heroism and so many deaths, had a living justification, its justification was General Lee.

7   Grant, the son of a tanner on the Western frontier, was everything Lee was not. He had come up the hard way and embodied nothing in particular except the eternal toughness and sinewy fiber of the men who grew up beyond the mountains. He was one of a body of men who owed reverence and obeisance to no one, who were self-reliant to a fault, who cared hardly anything for the past but who had a sharp eye for the future.

8   These frontier men were the precise opposite of the tidewater aristocrats. Back of them, in the great surge that had taken people over the Alleghenies and into the opening Western country, there was a deep, implicit dissatisfaction with a past that had settled into grooves. They stood for democracy, not from any reasoned conclusion about the proper ordering of human society, but simply because they had grown up in the middle of democracy and knew how it worked. Their society might have privileges, but they would be privileges each man had won for himself. Forms and patterns meant nothing. No man was born to anything, except perhaps to a chance to show how far he could rise. Life was competition.

9   Yet along with this feeling had come a deep sense of belonging to a national community. The Westerner who developed a farm, opened a shop, or set up in business as a trader, could hope to prosper only as his own community prospered— and his community ran from the Atlantic to the Pacific and from Canada down to Mexico. If the land was settled, with towns and highways and accessible markets, he could better himself. He saw his fate in terms of the nation's own destiny. As its horizons expanded, so did his. He had, in other words, an acute dollars-and-cents stake in the continued growth and development of his country.

10   And that, perhaps, is where the contrast between Grant and Lee becomes most striking. The Virginia aristocrat, inevitably, saw himself in relation to his own region. He lived in a static society which could endure almost anything except change. Instinctively, his first loyalty would go to the locality in which that society existed. He would fight to the limit of endurance to defend it, because in defending it he was defending everything that gave his own life its deepest meaning.

11   The Westerner, on the other hand, would fight with an equal tenacity for the broader concept of society. He fought so because everything he lived by was tied to growth, expansion, and a constantly widening horizon. What he lived by would survive or fall with the nation itself. He could not possibly stand by unmoved in the

face of an attempt to destroy the Union. He would combat it with everything he had, because he could only see it as an effort to cut the ground out from under his feet.

12   So Grant and Lee were in complete contrast, representing two diametrically opposed elements in American life. Grant was the modern man emerging; beyond him, ready to come on the stage, was the great age of steel and machinery, of crowded cities and a restless burgeoning vitality. Lee might have ridden down from the old age of chivalry, lance in hand, silken banner fluttering over his head. Each man was the perfect champion of his cause, drawing both his strengths and his weaknesses from the people he led. Yet it was not all contrast, after all. Different as they were—in background, in personality, in underlying aspiration—these two great soldiers had much in common. Under everything else, they were marvelous fighters. Furthermore, their fighting qualities were really very much alike.

13   Each man had, to begin with, the great virtue of utter tenacity and fidelity. Grant fought his way down the Mississippi Valley in spite of acute personal discouragement and profound military handicaps. Lee hung on in the trenches at Petersburg after hope itself had died. In each man there was an indomitable quality . . . the born fighter's refusal to give up as long as he can still remain on his feet and lift his two fists.

14   Daring and resourcefulness they had, too; the ability to think faster and move faster than the enemy. These were the qualities which gave Lee the dazzling campaigns of Second Manassas and Chancellorsville and won Vicksburg for Grant.

15   Lastly, and perhaps greatest of all, there was the ability, at the end, to turn quickly from war to peace once the fighting was over. Out of the way these two men behaved at Appomattox came the possibility of a peace of reconciliation. It was a possibility not wholly realized, in the years to come, but which did, in the end, help the two sections to become one nation again . . . after a war whose bitterness might have seemed to make such a reunion wholly impossible. No part of either man's life became him more than the part he played in their brief meeting in the McLean house at Appomattox. Their behavior there put all succeeding generations of Americans in their debt. Two great Americans, Grant and Lee—very different, yet under everything very much alike. Their encounter at Appomattox was one of the great moments of American history.

UNDERSTANDING CONTEXT

1. What does Catton see as the most striking difference between the generals?
2. How did Grant and Lee differ in background and sense of allegiance?
3. What were the historical forces that shaped the two men?
4. *Critical thinking:* Essentially, Catton is telling the story of a confrontation between victor and vanquished, yet his account does not seem to depict the men as winner and loser. Catton does not dwell on what made Grant victorious or on the causes for Lee's defeat. What does this reveal about his purpose?

EVALUATING STRATEGY

1. How does Catton organize the essay?

2. *Critical thinking:* The Civil War was, in part, a battle over slavery. Catton does not mention this issue. Does his account appear to be ethically neutral, suggesting that neither side was morally superior in its war aims?

APPRECIATING LANGUAGE

1. Does Catton appear to be neutral or biased in his description of the two men?

2. What does the tone, level of language, and word choice suggest about Catton's intended audience?

WRITING SUGGESTIONS

1. Write an essay comparing two people in the same profession. Compare two teachers, coaches, landlords, attorneys, ministers, or coworkers. Try to focus on their personalities and philosophies rather than on their appearance. You may wish to limit your paper to a specific attitude, situation, or behavior.

2. *Collaborative writing:* Work with a group of students to write a short dramatic scene based on Catton's essay. Use set descriptions to establish the locale, and invent dialogue. Discuss with members of the group how Lee and Grant might have sounded. What words might they have chosen? How would their vocabulary indicate their different backgrounds?

Rachel Carson (1907–1964) was a marine biologist known for the literary quality of her writing. She won critical acclaim with her first two books, *The Sea Around Us* (1951) and *The Edge of the Sea* (1955). Then, in 1962, she hit the best-seller list with *Silent Spring,* a frightening exposé of the hazards that insecticides and weed killers were posing to both wildlife and human beings. As much as anything else, this one book can be said to have launched the modern environmental movement.

A Fable for Tomorrow

Source: "A Fable for Tomorrow" from *Silent Spring* by Rachel Carson. Copyright © 1962 by Rachel L. Carson. Copyright © renewed 1990 by Roger Christie. By permission.

Rapid industrialization both in manufacturing and agriculture brought unprecedented material advantages to the developed world throughout the first half of the twentieth century. At the same time, insufficient notice was being taken of the damages such industrialization was inflicting on the natural environment. Although Silent Spring *is a well-researched book by a reputable scientist, it is intended for a general audience. The following preface to that book is an imaginative rendering of the eventual consequences of continued indifference to the environment.*

1 There was once a town in the heart of America where all life seemed to live in harmony with its surroundings. The town lay in the midst of a checkerboard of prosperous farms, with fields of grain and hillsides of orchards where, in spring, white clouds of bloom drifted above the green fields. In autumn, oak and maple and birch set up a blaze of color that flamed and flickered across a backdrop of pines. Then foxes barked in the hills and deer silently crossed the fields, half hidden in the mists of the fall mornings.

2   Along the roads, laurel, viburnum and alder, great ferns and wildflowers delighted the traveler's eye through much of the year. Even in winter the roadsides were places of beauty, where countless birds came to feed on the berries and on the seed heads of the dried weeds rising above the snow. The countryside was, in fact, famous for the abundance and variety of its bird life, and when the flood of migrants was pouring through in spring and fall people traveled from great distances to observe them. Others came to fish the streams, which flowed clear and cold out of the hills and contained shady pools where trout lay. So it had been from the days many years ago when the first settlers raised their houses, sank their wells, and built their barns.

3   Then a strange blight crept over the area and everything began to change. Some evil spell had settled on the community: mysterious maladies swept the flocks of chickens; the cattle and sheep sickened and died. Everywhere was a shadow of death. The farmers spoke of much illness among their families. In the town the doctors had become more and more puzzled by new kinds of sickness appearing among their patients. There had been several sudden and unexplained deaths, not only among adults but even among children, who would be stricken suddenly while at play and die within a few hours.

4   There was a strange stillness. The birds, for example—where had they gone? Many people spoke of them, puzzled and disturbed. The feeding stations in the backyards were deserted. The few birds seen anywhere were moribund; they trembled violently and could not fly. It was a spring without voices. On the mornings that had once throbbed with the dawn chorus of robins, catbirds, doves, jays, wrens, and scores of other bird voices there was now no sound; only silence lay over the fields and woods and marsh.

5   On the farms the hens brooded, but no chicks hatched. The farmers complained that they were unable to raise any pigs—the litters were small and the young survived only a few days. The apple trees were coming into bloom but no bees droned among the blossoms, so there was no pollination and there would be no fruit.

6   The roadsides, once so attractive, were now lined with browned and withered vegetation as though swept by fire. These, too, were silent, deserted by all living things. Even the streams were now lifeless. Anglers no longer visited them, for all the fish had died.

7   In the gutters under the eaves and between the shingles of the roofs, a white granular powder still showed a few patches; some weeks before it had fallen like snow upon the roofs and the lawns, the fields and streams.

8   No witchcraft, no enemy action had silenced the rebirth of new life in this stricken world. The people had done it themselves.

9   This town does not actually exist, but it might easily have a thousand counterparts in America or elsewhere in the world. I know of no community that has experienced all the misfortunes I describe. Yet every one of these disasters has actually happened somewhere, and many real communities have already suffered a substantial number of them. A grim specter has crept upon us almost unnoticed, and this imagined tragedy may easily become a stark reality we all shall know.

10 What has already silenced the voices of spring in countless towns in America? This book is an attempt to explain.

UNDERSTANDING CONTEXT

1. What sort of a world does Carson describe in the first two paragraphs of the essay?
2. Can you tell exactly what it is that causes the change between the world of the first two paragraphs and the world described next? What do you know about what caused the devastation?
3. What does Carson mean when she says the people had done it themselves?
4. What is Carson's purpose in providing this fictional account of destruction?

EVALUATING STRATEGY

1. Note each reference to silence. How do all of those references relate to the title of the book Carson is introducing, *Silent Spring?*
2. How does Carson use a "before and after" comparison to make her point?

APPRECIATING LANGUAGE

1. The first two paragraphs describe the town in almost fairytale language. In the remainder of the essay, which specific words help capture the negative atmosphere that Carson is trying to create?

2. Although Carson is a scientist, she chose to use in this introduction language that would be easily understood by the layperson. Why do you think she might have made that choice?

WRITING SUGGESTIONS

1. You may have seen specific places go through a transformation on a smaller scale of the sort Carson describes. Write two paragraphs in which you first describe a place as you once knew it and then as it exists now.

2. People also go through transformations. Write two paragraphs in which you first describe a person as he or she once was, then describe that person as he or she is now.

CRITICAL ISSUES

Image by © Ashley Cooper/Picimpact/CORBIS

Sign showing the former edge of retreating glacier in Alaska

The Environment

The sooner we start doing something about global warming the better, because by the time that everyone agrees that global warming has started, it could be too late to do much about it.

S. George Philander

One day, our models will make sense of all the existing data, and scientists will tease new data from yet unknown sources. When that happens, global warming may turn out to be real; it may even turn out to be man-made. In that case, then maybe we will have to shoulder the enormous burden the warming lobby wants us to take on now.

Dolly Setton

In 1850 there were one hundred fifty glaciers in Glacier National Park. Today there are fifty. Grinnell Glacier, which once spread over 576 acres, now covers less than 200 acres. Scientists estimate that the last glacier may melt by 2030.

Melting glaciers are just one indicator of long-term climate change. In the summer of 1990 oystermen in Delaware Bay discovered more and more empty shells in their nets. The oysters had been killed by a parasite that thrives in warmer waters. Rising ocean temperatures have destroyed coral reefs in the South Pacific. In Antarctica ice shelves thousands of years old have crumbled, causing sections the size of Rhode Island to break off and drift out to sea and melt.

For two hundred years humans have poured hundreds of billions of tons of carbon into the atmosphere from factories, power plants, automobiles, trains, and aircraft. The natural "sinks" that absorb carbon dioxide—ocean, soil, and plants—do not have the capacity to offset these added emissions. As early as 1896 the Swedish chemist Svante Arrhenius, noting the growth of industrialization and use of fossil fuels, predicted that carbon dioxide emissions would increase and raise the Earth's temperature. Some scientists, however, question assumptions about the cause of global warming, a few doubting whether it is occurring at all.

In addition to concerns about climate change, the reliance on expensive imported oil has led to calls for new, cleaner sources of energy. Scientists and economists debate the efficiency and costs of a variety of ways to generate power. Wind and solar are perhaps the cleanest, but they are erratic and currently only produce a fraction of the nation's energy needs. Biofuels use domestically grown plants that free the United States from imported oil, but they take large amounts of land away from agricultural use, drive up food costs, and require massive amounts of fertilizer that can be toxic. The United States possesses large reserves of natural gas, which burns cleaner than oil and could lessen American dependence on foreign sources of energy. But extracting natural gas from the earth can contaminate drinking water and cause serious health problems. Nuclear power has proved to be an efficient source of energy, but concerns about radiation and the safe disposal of dangerous waste lead many to resist building new reactors.

Environmentalists, who traditionally were concerned about pollution coming from smokestacks and car exhaust pipes, have detected new health hazards. Throughout the developed world billions of people dispose of old electronic products. Millions of computers, television sets, laptops, calculators, and cell phones are discarded each year. Many of these devices contain dangerous chemicals that are released when these products are compacted into landfills or broken up by recyclers.

More recently, scientists have discovered another source of pollution—chemicals from discarded cosmetics and pharmaceuticals that have appeared in the soil, drinking water, and fish consumed by humans. Sewage treatment plants designed to remove organic wastes are not always able to filter out pharmaceutical pollutants.

China and India are rapidly industrializing, producing hundreds of millions of new middle-class consumers who want homes, cars, computers, air conditioning—all of which will further strain the Earth's resources.

Before reading the articles, consider the following questions:

1. *Do most people understand enough about science to evaluate claims about climate change and other environmental threats?*
2. *Can the need to generate new industries and create new jobs be reconciled with concerns about the environment? Do businesses move factories overseas where environmental regulations are less strict?*
3. *Why has global warming become a political issue?*
4. *Do you think consumers who are accustomed to inexpensive energy and the the convenience of disposal products are willing to change their lifestyles to protect the environment?*
5. *Do concerns about the environment wane during recessions? Does the immediate need for jobs surpass concerns about long-term environmental change?*

E-READINGS ONLINE

Search for each article by author or title on InfoTrac College Edition, available through your English CourseMate at **www.cengagebrain.com.**

Al Gore. "We Can't Wish Away Climate Change."
As a global leader, the United States must take steps to reduce carbon emissions to induce China to enact similar policies.

S. Fred Singer. "Global Warming: Man-Made or Natural?"
Mistaken concerns about global warming will "distort energy policies in a way that severely will damage national economies, decrease standards of living, and increase poverty."

Erika Engelhaupt. "Engineering a Cooler Earth."
Researchers are exploring ideas to lower the Earth's temperature by reflecting sunlight by making clouds whiter and spraying sulfur into the stratosphere.

Iain Murray. "Nuclear Power? Yes, Please."
To end our reliance on oil, "we will need nuclear facilities to power our plug-in hybrid electric cars or to make the hydrogen for our fuel cells."

Harvey Wasserman. "Nukes Are Not Green."
Because "the price of a melt-down or terror attack at an American nuke is beyond calculation," atomic energy is not the solution to climate change.

Thomas Friedman. "Dreaming the Possible Dream."
Entrepreneurs have demonstrated revolutionary technology that turns carbon dioxide emissions from coal and natural gas powered plants into building materials instead of entering the atmosphere.

Michael Grunwald. "The Clean Energy Scam."
Instead of being "eco-friendly," ethanol "increases global warming, destroys forests and inflates food prices."

George Johnson. "Plugging into the Sun."
Two hundred fifty acres of curved mirrors in the Nevada desert generate enough electricity to power 14,000 households.

Chris Carroll. "High-Tech Trash."
Each year the world discards 50 million tons of cell phones, VCRs, TVs, and computers, much of which ends up in landfills, releasing lead, mercury, and other toxic elements into the soil and water.

Jeffrey Kluger. "Flushed Away."
The pharmaceuticals that "keep us healthy" can "make the water supply sick."

CRITICAL READING AND THINKING

1. What do authors see as the cause of climate change?
2. What solutions do environmentalists outline to combat global warming? Do they seem practical?
3. Does it seem that each alternative to fossil fuels—bio-fuels, nuclear energy, and solar power—has serious disadvantages? Is there such a thing as truly green and practical sources of energy?
4. Can a consumer-driven society take steps to protect the environment without limiting economic growth?
5. Will people be willing to pay more for electric or hybrid vehicles? Why or why not?
6. Could a commitment to new, high-tech energy production create new industries and millions of new jobs? Why or why not?

WRITING SUGGESTIONS

1. Write an essay about your own environmental habits. Does concern about the environment influence your buying decisions, driving habits, and waste disposal? Do you recycle? How do you dispose of used motor oil, old prescription medicine, and plastics?
2. *Collaborative writing:* Discuss climate change with other students and write a paper outlining your group's views on its seriousness. If members have differing opinions, write a pro and con paper to contrast opposing views or a classification paper ranking their responses.
3. *Other modes:*
   - Write a brief *narrative* of an environmental crisis—Three Mile Island, Love Canal, the BP oil spill—and explain its significance in changing public opinion and shaping environmental policy.
   - *Compare* two alternative energy sources—clean coal and natural gas or wind and solar. Which is more environmentally friendly? Which is more practical?
   - *Classify* alternative energy sources from the cleanest to the least clean or from the most to least practical.
   - Use *process* to inform consumers about steps they can take in their daily lives to reduce their negative impact on the environment.
   - Respond to one of the readings by writing a *persuasive* essay agreeing or disagreeing with the author's views.

RESEARCH PAPER

You can develop a research paper about the environment by conducting further research to explore a range of issues:

■ How will the growth of China and India impact climate change? Can nations dedicated to rapidly expanding their economies be expected to consider halting growth to stem pollution? Will their demand for energy drive up the price of oil, forcing nations to explore alternatives?

■ How should pollution be measured? Natural gas burns cleaner than oil, but its extraction from the earth can pollute ground water. Nuclear energy is "clean," but the mining and processing of uranium and the construction of reactors releases large amounts of carbon. What is clean energy?

■ Examine a single alternative energy source. How efficient is it? How much carbon and other pollutants are released during its entire process? Is it cost-effective? What unique technical challenges, if any, need to be overcome?

■ How have other nations dealt with environmental issues? Do other countries recycle more than the United States, devote more funds to research, or have higher environmental standards?

■ What role has the Internet played in reducing carbon emissions? For a small amount of electricity, messages once sent by truck or airplane are delivered instantly around the world. Websites have replaced the needs for printing and shipping and recycling paper documents. Could other technologies further reduce pollution?

FOR FURTHER READING

To locate additional sources, enter *global warming* and *pollution* as search terms in InfoTrac College Edition, available through your English CourseMate at **www. cengagebrain.com** or one of your college library's databases, and examine readings under key subdivisions:

analysis	economic aspects
case studies	forecasts and trends
causes of	political aspects
control	public opinion

ADDITIONAL SOURCES

Using a search engine, enter one or more of the following terms to locate additional sources:

climate change	global warming
pollution	clean energy
nuclear power	hybrid cars
recycling	solar power

See the Evaluating Internet Source Checklist on pages 533–534. See Chapter 24 for documenting sources.

Christopher Jencks is the Malcolm Wiener Professor of Social Policy at Harvard University's Kennedy School of Government. He has taught at the University of Chicago, Northwestern University, and the University of California at Santa Barbara. His books include *The Academic Revolution* (with David Reisman), *The Homeless, Inequality, Who Gets Ahead?* and *Rethinking Social Policy.*

Reinventing the American Dream

Source: "Reinventing the American Dream" by Christopher Jencks. *The Chronicle of Higher Education,* Oct 17, 2008. Reprinted with permission from Christopher Jencks.

In this article, Jencks compares the Republican and Democratic views of the American Dream and explains why both will have to be reinvented.

1 The American Dream sounds like apple pie and motherhood. Everyone is for it.

2 But when everyone endorses an ideal, whether it's the American Dream, equal opportunity, or justice, you can be pretty sure that they disagree about what the ideal means, and that the appearance of agreement is being achieved by talking past one another.

3 There are at least two competing versions of the American Dream, and they are not only different but mutually incompatible. Perhaps even more alarming is the fact that they will both need to be reinvented if our children and grandchildren are to inhabit a livable planet.

4 In one version, this country is the place where anyone who builds a better mousetrap can get rich. To do that, the mousetrap builder will need a lot of help: workers to make the mousetraps, salespeople to put them in the hands of consumers, and security guards to prevent the world from beating a path to the inventor's door and helping themselves. In order to get rich, mousetrap developers will also have to pay their workers far less than they make themselves. Otherwise there won't be enough money left over from mousetrap sales to make the inventor rich.

5 This version of the American Dream emphasizes individual talent and effort. It favors freedom and opposes government regulation. And it belongs to the Republican Party.

6 Democrats have another version of the American Dream: Everyone who works hard and behaves responsibly can achieve a decent standard of living. But the definition of a decent standard of living is a moving target. For those who came of age before 1950, it usually meant a steady job, owning a house in a safe neighborhood with decent schools, and believing that your children would have a chance to go to college even if you did not.

7 True, lots of people who worked hard and behaved responsibly didn't realize this dream. Blue-collar workers were laid off during recessions through no fault of their own, and their jobs often disappeared when technological progress allowed employers to produce more stuff with fewer workers. Still, more and more people achieved this dream between 1945 and 1970, so the Democratic version of the American Dream had broader appeal than the Republican version, in which a smaller number of people could get much richer.

Sam Diephuis/jupiterimages

8   Since the early 1970s, however, all that has changed.

9   The American economy has been under siege. Real per capita disposable income has continued to grow, but the average annual increase has fallen, from 2.7 percent between 1947 and 1973 to 1.8 percent between 1973 and 2005. Of course, even a 1.8 percent annual increase in purchasing power is far more than the human species achieved during most of its history, and it is also far more than we are likely to achieve in the future unless we do a lot of creative accounting.

10   What transformed the political landscape was not the slowdown in growth but the distributional change that accompanied it. From 1947 to 1973, the purchasing power of those in the bottom 95 percent of the income distribution rose at the same rate as per capita disposable income, about 2.7 percent a year. Among families in the top 5 percent, the growth rate was 2.2 percent. From 1973 to 2006, however, the average annual increase in the purchasing power of the bottom 95 percent was only .6 percent. The top 5 percent, in contrast, managed to maintain annual growth of 2.0 percent, which was almost the same as what they enjoyed before 1973.

11   That's a lot of numbers, but what my students at the Kennedy School call the "take-away" is pretty simple: After 1973, when economic growth slowed, America had a choice. We would have tried to share the pain equally by maintaining the social contract under which living standards had risen at roughly the same rate among families at all levels. Or we could have treated the slowdown in growth as evidence that the Democratic version of the American Dream didn't work, and that we should try the Republican version, in which we all look out for ourselves, some people get rich, and most get left behind.

12   We chose the Republican option.

13   That formulation is deceptive, of course, because voters did not have a clear choice. Many Democratic politicians accepted the Republican argument that the cure for slower growth was to make markets more competitive and government regulation less onerous. Very few Democrats argued that an adverse shift in the distribution of private-sector earnings was something the government should insure Americans against, like a Mississippi flood or a terrorist attack on the World Trade Center. In that respect the Democrats were very different from the parties of the left in Western Europe, but quite similar to the parties of the left in most other English-speaking countries.

14   One reason for Anglophone caution about protecting the citizenry from an adverse shift in the distribution of income is that English-speaking economists (which is to say almost all economists, even in non-English-speaking countries) were mostly blaming the rise in economic inequality on what they called "skill-biased technological change." That argument was correct as far as it went, but it didn't go very far and was therefore deeply misleading.

15   In their new book, *The Race Between Education and Technology* (Belknap Press/ Harvard University Press, 2008), Claudia Goldin and Lawrence F. Katz argue— convincingly, in my view—that demand for skilled workers has indeed risen since 1973. But they also argue that demand for skilled workers rose no faster after 1973 than it had between 1910 and 1973.

16   What changed was that before 1973, the supply of skilled workers grew at about the same rate as demand, so relative wages were fairly stable. After 1973 the supply of

skilled workers grew far more slowly, even though demand kept rising. That imbalance played a significant role in raising inequality, at least between 1975 and 2000.

17   Between 1940 and 1980, the number of years of school completed by the average worker rose almost one year every decade (actually, .86 years). Between 1980 and 2005, the increase was only half that (.43 years per decade). If you exclude GEDs, administrative data indicate that high-school graduation rates have hardly changed since the early 1970s. At the same time, immigration has increased the supply of unskilled workers.

18   Those changes might not have led to a deterioration of wages and working conditions among unskilled workers if we had tried to protect their livelihoods, but we didn't. Congress and presidents let the minimum wage lag farther and farther behind inflation from 1981 to 2006. Large employers and the National Labor Relations Board made it harder to organize unions. Weaker unions found it harder to protect their members, and that, in turn, reduced the number of workers who wanted to join.

19   Again, this is a complicated story, but the take-away is pretty straightforward. Since 1973 both the federal government and the states have made less effort to raise the educational attainment of the young. They have also made less effort to protect the incomes of the less educated.

20   Why should that be? I'm not sure, but I have a hypothesis. Forty-some years ago, I was attending a White House conference on higher education and ran into Edmund G. (Pat) Brown, who was then governor of California, as we waited for an elevator. I had been studying at the University of California, and I asked him about the university's budget problems.

21   Brown, a Democrat, said the university always had budget problems when the Democrats controlled the state. Having always thought of Democrats as big spenders and friends of education, I was startled and asked why, just as we reached his floor. His parting answer was (roughly): "Democrats want to spend money on everything; Republicans only want to spend money on highways and the university, where they went and expect to send their children."

22   I don't know if that hypothesis holds up empirically, but I do think one big reason we have done so little to raise educational attainment since 1973 is that both federal and state budgets are much tighter. We cut the share of the gross domestic product going to national defense from 10 percent in 1959 to 5.5 percent in 1973 to 4.0 percent in 2006. But since 1973, that reduction has been more than offset by the government's increased spending on health care and Social Security. Even expenditures per student on K-through-12 education have risen faster than expenditures per student on higher education. According to the National Center for Education Statistics, expenditures per student in public elementary and secondary schools doubled between 1970–71 and 2000–1, even adjusted for inflation. Real expenditures per student in public colleges and universities rose only 35 percent during that period.

23   One alternative to keeping young people in school longer might have been to regulate the economy in ways analogous to what Germany, France, the Low Countries,

and Scandinavia did to keep wages relatively equal. In truth, though, we would have had to both expand education and regulate the labor market to keep alive the Democratic version of the American Dream. Regulation arouses even more resistance from employers than does taxation. And unlike their European counterparts, American employers usually have something close to a veto over policy changes that don't involve national security.

24   Employers argue that regulating the market drives up costs and slows job growth. Growth statistics for the past 50 years offer some support for that claim. But since 1970, annual growth has been only about a tenth of a percentage point higher in inegalitarian countries than in egalitarian countries. To be sure, income is not all that matters, and dumb regulations can certainly slow job growth and generate high unemployment. But there is no reason why egalitarian regulations have to be dumb.

25   In any case, few Democratic politicians think voters would accept that approach to solving the economic problems of the bottom 95 percent, and I think they are right, at least in the short run. In the long run, a concerted effort to revive a Democratic version of the American Dream might change the rhetorical environment, but meanwhile, the Democrats would have to resign themselves to a long period in the wilderness, with no assurance that their strategy would ever appeal to most voters. Few politicians want to take such a risk.

26   In the long run, moreover, both the Democratic and Republican versions of the American Dream will have to be rethought. They both focus heavily on income and material consumption. The idea that we can keep raising our material standard of living without making most of the planet too hot for human habitation is, I think, mistaken. Even the idea that we have 20 or 30 years to make the necessary adjustments appears wrongheaded.

27   So I'm afraid reinventing the American Dream really means trying to wean ourselves from the illusion that we all need and deserve more stuff. If we are to survive, we need a different definition of progress. That definition will need to focus on human needs like physical health, material security, individual freedom, and time to play with our children and smell the roses.

28   I'm not saying that material goods are unimportant. People need food to sustain them, a home in which they can afford to live until they die, and medical advice when they are sick. But I'm not sure people my age (71) need a million-dollar machine to keep us alive another year or two. And I am quite sure that most of us could live without 85 percent of the stuff we buy in places other than grocery stores and gas stations.

29   An American Dream that doesn't destroy the planet will have to involve a more-equal distribution of basic material goods. It will also have to involve more emphasis on the quality of the services we consume than on the quality of our possessions. Perhaps most important, it will have to involve more emphasis on what we can do for others and less emphasis on what we can get for ourselves.

30   There is just one small problem. I have no idea how to get from here to there. That makes me a pessimist.

UNDERSTANDING CONTEXT

1. How does Jencks describe the conflicting visions of the American Dream embraced by the Republican and Democratic parties? Do you detect any bias in his comparison? Which vision better represents your own definition of the American Dream?

2. How did the American economy change after 1973?

3. Why have workers' wages failed to rise?

4. *Critical thinking:* Why does Jencks believe that both perceptions of the American Dream must be reinvented? Do both versions of American success require a level of consumption that is unsustainable?

EVALUATING STRATEGY

1. How does Jencks use comparison to explain conflicting visions of the American Dream?

2. *Critical thinking:* In two places Jencks states a number of statistics, then summarizes the main points in a simple explanation he calls the "takeaway." Do you think this is an effective way of connecting with readers who may not understand or remember complex data? Have professors used a similar technique giving lectures? Might some readers find this approach patronizing?

3. *Blending the modes:* Where does Jencks use *narration, definition,* and *persuasion* to develop his essay?

4. Jencks ends his essay stating that he has no idea how to achieve the solutions he advocates. Does this weaken his argument? Might some readers be impressed by his honesty?

APPRECIATING LANGUAGE

1. Does Jencks describe the opposing views of the American Dream in neutral terms? Do you detect any bias in his choice of words?

2. Jencks uses the term *egalitarian.* How would you define this term?

3. How does Jencks want to redefine the term *progress*?

WRITING SUGGESTIONS

1. Write a short essay defining your vision of the American Dream. Do you follow Jencks's depiction of the Republican or the Democratic version or a blend?

2. *Collaborative writing:* Discuss Jencks's essay with a group of students and ask them to respond to his argument that "reinventing the American Dream really means trying to wean ourselves from the illusion that we all need and deserve more stuff." Record students' responses and write an essay summarizing their views. If they have conflicting opinions, consider developing a comparison or classification essay.

Peggy Kenna and Sondra Lacy

Peggy Kenna and Sondra Lacy are communications specialists based in Arizona who work with foreign-born employees. In addition, they provide cross-cultural training to executives conducting international business. Kenna is a speech and language pathologist who specializes in accent modification. Kenna and Lacy have collaborated on a series of fifty-page booklets that compare American and foreign business organizations, habits, behaviors, and negotiating styles. Widely sold in airports, these booklets give Americans tips on doing business overseas.

Communication Styles: United States and Taiwan

Source: "Communication Styles: United States and Taiwan" from *Business Taiwan* by Peggy Kenna and Sondra Lacy. Copyright © 1994 by The McGraw-Hill Companies, Inc. By permission.

This section from Business Taiwan *contrasts American and Taiwanese styles of communicating. Designing their booklets for quick skimming, Kenna and Lacy use charts to highlight cultural differences.*

UNITED STATES	TAIWAN
■ *Frank*	■ *Subtle*
1 Americans tend to be very straightforward and unreserved. The people of Taiwan often find them abrupt and not interested enough in human relationships.	Frankness is not appreciated by the people of Taiwan. They particularly dislike unqualified negative statements.
■ *Face-saving less important*	■ *Face-saving important*
2 To Americans accuracy is important but errors are tolerated. Admitting mistakes is seen as a sign of maturity. They believe you learn from failure and therefore encourage some risk taking.	The Chinese do not like to be put in the position of having to admit a mistake or failure. They also do not like to tell you when they don't understand your point.
3 Americans believe criticism can be objective and not personal; however, all criticism should be done with tact.	You also should not admit too readily when you don't know something as it can cause you to lose face.
■ *Direct eye contact*	■ *Avoid direct eye contact*
4 Direct eye contact is very important to Americans since they need to see the nonverbal cues the speaker is giving. Nonverbal cues are a very important part of the American English language. Americans use intermittent eye contact when they are speaking but fairly steady eye contact when they are listening.	Holding the gaze of another person is considered rude.

(Continued)

Sam Diephuis/jupiterimages

UNITED STATES	TAIWAN
■ *Direct and to the point*	■ *Indirect and ambiguous*
5 Americans prefer people to say what they mean. Because of this they tend to sometimes miss subtle nonverbal cues. Americans are uncomfortable with ambiguousness and don't like to have to "fill in the blanks." They also tend to discuss problems directly.	People in Taiwan dislike saying "no." They may not tell you when they don't understand. They often hedge their answers if they know you won't like the answer. If they say something like, "We'll think about it," they may mean they aren't interested.
	They dislike discussing problems directly and will often go around the issue, which can be frustrating for Americans. 6
	The Chinese language (Mandarin) is so concise that the listener needs to use much imagination to "fill in the gaps." 7
■ *"Yes" means agreement*	■ *"Yes" means "I hear"*
Americans look for clues such as nodding of the head, a verbal "yes" or "uh huh" in order to determine if their arguments are succeeding.	People in Taiwan do not judge information given to them so they do not indicate agreement or disagreement; they only nod or say "yes" to indicate they are listening to you. 8
	The people of Taiwan believe politeness is more important than frankness so they will not directly tell you "no." The closest they will come to "no" is "maybe." 9

UNDERSTANDING CONTEXT

1. What appear to be the major differences between American and Taiwanese methods of communicating?
2. Why is it important for Americans to be sensitive about making direct eye contact with Taiwanese?
3. How do Americans and Taiwanese accept failure?
4. *Critical thinking:* Why would this booklet be valuable to Americans visiting Taiwan on business? Does such a brief, to-the-point guide risk relying on stereotypes?

EVALUATING STRATEGY

1. How easy is this document to read and review? How accessible would the information be if it were written in standard paragraphs?

2. What does the directness of the document reveal about the intended audience? Would it be suitable for a college classroom?

APPRECIATING LANGUAGE

1. What language do the writers use in describing the Taiwanese? Do they attempt to be neutral, or does their word choice favor one nationality over another?

2. Kenna and Lacy suggest that many Taiwanese find Americans to be "abrupt." Is this a good word choice? Does the guide express common prejudices?

WRITING SUGGESTIONS

1. Using Kenna and Lacy's entry as a source, write a short *process* paper instructing how an American should present an idea or product in Taiwan. Assume you are writing to sales representatives traveling to Taiwan for the first time. Provide step-by-step suggestions for how they should conduct themselves from the moment they enter a seminar room to make a presentation.

2. *Collaborative writing:* Working with a group of students, discuss the differences between high school teachers and college instructors, then develop a chart contrasting their attitudes toward absenteeism, late homework, tests, and research papers.

RESPONDING TO IMAGES

Henry Ford II Introduces the 1949 Ford

Image by © Bettmann/CORBIS

CONTEXT: *The Ford Motor Company faced bankruptcy following World War II. In 1949 it introduced a streamlined car with many new features that became so popular it was called "the car that saved Ford." Over a million were produced.*

1. What is your first reaction to this photograph? What does this image represent to you? Is it a quaint image of an old-fashioned car or a reminder of a time when America dominated cutting-edge technology?

2. How could this image be used to illustrate a comparison between past and present?

3. *Visual analysis:* Could Ford use this image today to remind car buyers, investors, and Congress that it has overcome adversity in the past? Would this image paired next to a modern Ford make an effective ad? Why or why not?

4. How have car ads changed in recent years? Once status symbols, cars are now associated with pollution, energy waste, government bailouts, and

RESPONDING TO IMAGES

safety problems. How can a troubled auto company use images to overcome negative assumptions and win consumer confidence?

5. *Critical thinking:* What kind of car do American automakers need to produce today to win back the market share they have lost to foreign companies?

6. *Collaborative writing:* Discuss this image with other students. Work together and develop a new caption or a brief description to use this photo in an ad. What product or service would you promote with this picture—a TV show set in the fifties, life insurance, a modern car, or a political organization lobbying for or against American corporations?

7. *Other modes:*
   - Write a *description* of this photograph for a high school history book.
   - Write a *cause and effect* essay explaining the effects of globalization on American companies or what must be done to create manufacturing jobs in the United States.
   - Develop a *division or classification* essay discussing consumer reactions to foreign-made products.
   - Write a *persuasive* essay stating your position on globalization.

COMPARISON AND CONTRAST CHECKLIST

✔ Are your subjects closely enough related to make a valid comparison?

✔ Have you identified the key points of both subjects?

✔ Have you selected the best method of organizing your paper?

✔ Is the comparison easy to follow? Are transitions clear?

✔ Does the comparison meet reader needs and expectations?

✔ Have you defined terms or provided background information needed by readers to fully appreciate the comparison?

✔ Is your thesis clearly stated and located where it will have the greatest impact?

 Access the English CourseMate for this text at **www.cengagebrain.com** for additional information on writing comparison and contrast essays.

Process

Explaining How Things Work and Giving Directions

What Is Process?

Process writing shows how things work or how specific tasks are accomplished. The first type of process writing is a *directed form of narration* that explains how something occurs or operates. Biology textbooks describe how the heart functions by separating its actions into a series of steps. A chain-of-events explanation also can show how an engine works, how inflation affects the economy, how the IRS audits an account, or how police respond to a 911 call.

The second type of process writing gives *directions for completing a specific task*. Recipes, owners' manuals, textbooks, and home repair articles provide readers with step-by-step directions to bake a cake, rotate tires, create a website, write a research paper, detect a computer virus, or fix a leaking roof.

Explaining How Things Work

Just as division writing seeks to explain an abstract or complex subject by separating it into smaller categories, process writing separates the workings of complicated operations into steps or stages. In the essay "How Our Skins Got Their Color" (page 363) Marvin Harris explains the role sunlight and Vitamin D played in giving human beings different complexions:

> Vitamin D can be obtained from a few foods, primarily the oils and livers of marine fish. But inland populations must rely on the sun's rays and their own skins for the supply of this crucial substance. The particular color of a human population's skin, therefore, represents in large degree a trade-off between the hazards of too much versus too little solar radiation: acute sunburn and skin cancer on the one hand, and rickets and osteomalacia on the other. It is this trade-off that largely accounts for the preponderance of brown people in the world and for the general tendency for skin color to be darkest among equatorial populations and lightest among populations dwelling at higher latitudes.

When you write explanations, it is important to consider your readers' existing knowledge. You may need to define technical terms, use illustrative analogies such as comparing the heart to a pump or a computer virus to a human infection, and relate brief narratives so that readers will understand the process. Some writers will use an extended analogy, comparing a nuclear power plant to a teakettle or terrorism to a brush fire.

WRITING ACTIVITY

Develop an outline listing ideas for a paper explaining one of the following topics:

1. The admissions procedure at your college
2. The functions of the heart, lungs, or liver
3. The way you perform a task at home, at school, or in your job
4. The formation of a hurricane or tornado
5. The process determining which teams will play in the World Series or the Super Bowl
6. The way couples resolve conflicts
7. The process of how a bill becomes a law
8. The procedure of a civil or criminal trial
9. The way children learn to walk, talk, or read
10. The process of getting married, filing for divorce, or adopting a child

Strategies for Writing Explanations

Critical Thinking and Prewriting

1. **List possible topics that can be explained in a short paper.**
2. **Prewrite to explore the most promising topics.** Use freewriting and brainstorming to identify topics best suited to the assignment. Avoid overly complex subjects that require extensive background explanation or are subject to numerous interpretations.
3. **Study your topic carefully.** Note the principal features that need emphasis. Highlight features that are commonly confused or might be difficult for readers to understand.

Planning

1. **Determine how much background information is needed.** Your readers may require, for example, a basic knowledge of how normal cells divide before being able to comprehend the way cancer cells develop. In some instances, you have to address widely believed misconceptions. In explaining criminal investigation methods, you might have to point out how actual police operations differ from those depicted on television.
2. **Define clear starting and ending points.** In some cases the process may have an obvious beginning and end. Flowers emerge from buds, grow, turn color, and
(Continued)

fall off. But the process of a recession may have no clear-cut beginning and no defined end. If you were to write a paper about the process of getting a divorce, would you stop when final papers are signed or continue to discuss alimony and child visitation rights? When does a divorce end?

3. **Separate the process into logical stages.** Readers will naturally assume all the stages are equally significant unless you indicate their value or importance. Minor points should not be overemphasized by being divided into distinct steps.

4. **Develop an outline listing steps and major points to guide the first draft.**

5. **Determine whether visual aids such as photographs, diagrams, or charts can illustrate the process.**

Writing the First Draft

1. **Keep your audience in mind as you write.**
   - Realize that someone reading your process paper likely knows less than you do.
   - Consider your readers' perceptual world as you explain ideas. What analogies or references will they understand?

2. **Use transitional phrases and paragraph breaks to separate stages.** Statements such as "at the same time" or "two days later" can help readers follow the chronology and direction of events.

3. **Stress the importance of time relationships.** Process writing creates a slow-motion explanation that can be misleading if the chain of events naturally occurs in a short period. You can avoid this confusion by opening with a real-time description of the process:

> The test car collided with the barrier at thirty-five miles an hour. In less than a tenth of a second the bumper crumpled, sending shock waves through the length of the vehicle as the fenders folded back like a crushed beer can. At the same instant sensors triggered the air bag to deploy with a rapid explosion so that it inflated before the test dummy struck the steering wheel.

The rest of the paper might repeat this process in several pages, slowly relating each stage in great detail.

4. **Use images, details, narratives, and examples to enrich the description of each stage.**

5. **Alert readers to possible variations.** If the process is subject to change or alternative forms, present readers with the most common type. Indicate, either in the introduction or in each stage, that exceptions or variations can occur.

Revising

1. **Review your plan and goals; then read your paper aloud with your reader in mind.**

- Determine whether your paper provides enough information to explain the process.
- Examine your paper for terms or concepts that need definition or further explanation.

2. **Review transitions and paragraph breaks for clarity.**
   - Do not cluster too many important ideas into a single step.
   - Avoid exaggerating the significance of a minor point by isolating it as a single step.

3. **Review the use of visual aids for accuracy.**

4. **Use peer review to test your paper.**
   - Ask others how easy it is for them to understand the process. What improvements could be made?

Editing and Proofreading

1. **Read the paper aloud to test for clarity.**
   - Make sure that you define technical or widely misunderstood terms.
   - Examine the level of diction to determine whether it is suited to your readers' existing knowledge.

2. **Use peer editing to locate errors you may have missed.**

Giving Directions

Directions are step-by-step instructions guiding readers through a specific goal or task. Recipes and repair manuals show readers how to prepare a meal or change a tire. Process writing can also include advice on buying a house or negotiating a loan. In "Fender Benders: Legal Dos and Don'ts" (page 359), Armond D. Budish provides this tip for drivers involved in a minor collision:

> **1. Stop! It's the Law.**
> No matter how serious or minor the accident, stop immediately. If possible, don't move your car—especially if someone has been injured. Leaving cars as they were when the accident occurred helps the police determine what happened. Of course, if your car is blocking traffic or will cause another accident where it is, then move it to the nearest safe location.

Budish, like many other writers, finds it effective to tell people what *not* to do. Negative instructions work best when you are trying to get readers to change their habits or avoid common errors. Budish's last tip warns drivers not to make a frequent mistake:

> **10. Don't Be Too Quick to Accept a Settlement.**
> If the other driver is at fault and there's any chance you've been injured, don't rush to accept a settlement from that person's insurance company. You may not know the extent of your injuries for some time, and once you accept a settlement, it's difficult to get an "upgrade." Before settling, consult with a lawyer who handles personal injury cases.

WRITING ACTIVITY

Select one of the topics below and use prewriting techniques to develop a plan for a short set of directions. Remember to consider each target audience.

1. Provide directions to the campus stadium for out-of-town visitors arriving at the local airport. Give readers visual references, such as landmarks, to identify key intersections.

2. Inform people how to sell items on eBay.

3. Tell people how *not* to plan a family vacation.

4. Instruct students how to balance work and school.

5. Direct consumers on using credit wisely; warn them about accumulating debt.

6. Provide safety tips for vacationers renting a sailboat, motorbike, or snowmobile.

7. Warn senior citizens about a common telemarketing scam; provide tips to identify fraudulent offers.

8. Advise new homeowners on the most important actions they can take to protect the environment.

9. Use your own experience to create a list of suggestions to help students study for exams, save money on books, lose weight, read faster, save time, or exercise.

10. Offer tips to parents concerned about their children's use of the Internet. Alert them to potential hazards and suggest remedies.

For giving instructions, you may find it useful to number steps and provide visual aids, such as diagrams, charts, photographs, or maps. Highlighting, bold type, and underlining can dramatize text and make the document easy to read in an emergency.

Strategies for Writing Directions

Critical Thinking and Prewriting

1. **List possible topics under the phrase "How to . . ."**
   - Select subjects you are familiar with and can fully explain in a page or two of directions:

     How to change the oil in your car

     How to write a will without a lawyer

     How to cook in a wok

     How to save money on clothes

     How to choose the right day care center

2. **Prewrite to explore the most promising topics.**
   - Limit the subject to a single task or problem—how to change a tire instead of how to maintain your car.
3. **Consider your audience carefully.** Unlike other types of writing, giving directions requires you to ask people to not only *read* but also *act on* your ideas.
   - Determine how much knowledge your readers have.
   - Consider any misconceptions or confusion that must be addressed before proceeding.

Planning

1. **Define the scope of your directions.** Directions must be focused, especially if you are providing step-by-step instructions rather than advice.
   - Clearly define the task or goal; you should be directing readers to accomplish something specific. Directions must be goal-centered.
2. **Define clear starting and ending points.** Give readers clear instructions about when to start the process and when to end it. In providing first-aid instructions, for example, you must first teach readers to identify situations in which actions must be taken and end with telling them when to stop.
3. **Make sure directions are self-contained.** A recipe, for example, should list *all* the ingredients, appliances, and instructions required to accomplish the task.
   - Readers should not be directed to another source for information to complete the process.
4. **Break the process into even steps.** Avoid placing too much information or too many actions in a single step.
5. **Consider using numbered steps.** Readers find it easier to follow numbered steps and can mark their places if interrupted.
6. **Consider using visual aids such as charts, graphs, diagrams, maps, or photographs to illustrate the process.** Make sure visuals are clearly labeled and directly connected to specific steps in the written directions.
7. **Prepare a clearly organized outline.**

Writing the First Draft

1. **Using your outline as a guide, write a draft, keeping your goal and your readers in mind.**
2. **Provide complete instructions.** Do not tell readers to "remove the flat tire" without explaining the process or to "put the cake in the oven for thirty minutes until it's done" without describing what it is supposed to look like when it is "done."
   - Remember, readers are doing this process for the first time and must rely on your directions; give full details about each step.

(Continued)

3. **Give negative instructions.** Tell people what *not* to do, especially if you know that people are prone to make errors, skip steps, substitute cheaper materials, or ignore potential problems.

4. **Warn readers of possible events that they may misinterpret as mistakes.** If, at some point in the process, the mixture readers are working with suddenly changes color or the machine they are operating makes excess noise, they may assume they have made a mistake and stop. If someone assembling a desk discovers that the legs are wobbly, he or she may think the product is defective. If this is normal—if the legs tighten up when the drawers are installed—let readers know.

5. **Consider using visual aids.** Large print, capital letters, bold or italic type, and underlining can highlight text for easy reading.
   - Remember, readers may have to refer to your document while working, so make it easy to skim.

6. **Warn readers of any potential hazards to their safety, health, property, or the environment.**
   - Warn readers about dangerous chemicals, fire hazards, and electrical shocks that could threaten their safety or health.
   - Alert readers to potential property damage that can result from improper use of materials.
   - Inform readers of any legal sanctions they may encounter. Warn car owners about the proper disposal of used motor oil or old tires.
   - Remind homeowners to check local building codes before starting major projects that may require permits.

Revising

1. **Review your outline and then read your draft for completeness, organization, and readability.**
   - Directions should be stated in short, precise sentences. Delete wordy or unnecessary phrases. Instead of writing "The next thing you should do is . . . ," use numbered steps.
   - Directions should provide clear descriptions of each step. Telling readers to "sand the tabletop" may leave them wondering whether they should simply remove rough edges or work on the surface until it is as smooth as glass.
   - Let readers know when each step ends—each step should have a defined goal.

2. **Review the overall organization and transitions.** Have you broken the process into workable steps? Is too much information placed in a single step?

3. **Examine any visual aids for accuracy.** Make sure any diagrams, maps, or charts are clearly labeled and directly support the text of the document.

4. **Test your writing through peer review.** Writing directions is challenging because it is hard to put yourself in the place of someone lacking information or a skill that might be second nature to you.
   - Ask people to read your paper; then quiz them on important points.
   - Readers unfamiliar with the process may spot missing critical information that you have overlooked.

Editing and Proofreading

1. **Read the paper aloud to test for clarity.** In explaining a process it is important to use language readers can understand.
   - Make sure you define technical or commonly misunderstood terms.
   - Examine the level of diction to determine whether it is suited to your readers' existing knowledge.
2. **Use peer editing to locate errors that you may have missed.**

STUDENT PAPER

This paper was written in response to the following assignment:

> Write a 500-word process paper providing directions to accomplish a specific task. You may include graphs, charts, diagrams, or numbered steps.

FIRST DRAFT WITH INSTRUCTOR'S COMMENTS

Eric Masson   Composition 101

Use more specific title **Home Safety**

wordy opening, trim

Homeowners are generally only concerned about security when they plan to take a vaca-

tion. When they take off for a week or two to the mountains or down the shore, they install

explain

additional locks, set <u>timers</u>, purchase sophisticated monitoring systems, talk to neighbors,

and hope their homes will not be robbed while they are enjoying themselves. But the real-

good point

ity is different. Most homes are not burglarized while their owners are thousands of miles

(Continued)

away. Most houses are robbed before 9 P.M., often while their owners are near or inside the

residence. Your house is more likely to be robbed while you are grilling in the backyard or

watching a football game than when you are on a cruise or camping trip.

qualify

There are things you can do to make your home <u>burglar proof.</u>

The most important thing you can do is to take steps in case a burglary does happen.

Good advice

You will have to prove any loss. So it makes sense to make a list of your valuables. Photo-

graph or videotape each room in your house. Keep receipts of major purchases. Store these

in a safe deposit box. Review your insurance to see if special items like furs, artwork, or coin

collections are covered. It is also important to identify valuables. Engrave computers, televi-

sions, cameras, stereos, and DVD players with your name or an identifying number. Police

often discover stolen property but have no way of contacting the owner.

A really important thing to remember is to always lock your doors. Nothing is more

tempting to a criminal than an open garage door or unlatched screen door. <u>Lock up even</u>

Wordy, revise sentences

<u>when you plan to visit a neighbor for "just a minute" because that "minute" can easily turn</u>

<u>into a half an hour, giving a burglar plenty of time for a burglary.</u>

Many people buy very expensive and high-tech security systems but leave them off

slang

most of the time because they are so hard to use. A cheap alarm system used <u>24-7</u> is better

¶ new paragraph, different topic

than one used just now and then. It can also be important to trim shrubbery around doors

and windows to keep burglars from having a hiding place.

vague

It is very important to network with neighbors and <u>let them know what is going on.</u> Let

neighbors know if you expect deliveries or contractors. Thieves have posed as moving crews,

casually looting a house and loading a truck while neighbors looked on.

Thieves are usually reluctant to leave the first floor, which usually has a number of exits.

They don't like going into attics or basements where they might get trapped, so that is

where to hide valuables.

And finally, call the police the moment you discover a break-in. If you return home and find

evidence of a break–in, do not go inside the home. The thieves, who could be armed ~~with weapons,~~

might still be inside. Use your cell phone or go to a neighbor's to call the police. Never attempt to

confront a burglar yourself. No personal possession is worth risking death or a disabling injury.

REVISION NOTES

This is a good topic, but your instructions could be made clearer and easier to follow.

* Qualify your opening remark. No one can promise to make a home "burglar proof" but you can suggest ways to reduce the risk of break-ins.

* Number steps and use titles to highlight each of your suggestions. Stress verbs to highlight actions readers should take. Numbered steps can reduce wordy and repetitive transitional statements like "another important thing is."

REVISED DRAFT

Eric Masson   Composition 101

Securing Your Home

Homeowners frequently think of security only when planning a vacation. Leaving home for a week or two, they install additional locks, set timers to trigger lights, purchase sophisticated monitoring systems, alert neighbors, and hope their homes will not be robbed in their absence. But most homes are robbed before 9 P.M., often while their owners are near or inside the residence. Your house is more likely to be robbed while you are grilling in the backyard or watching a football game in a basement rec room than when you are on a cruise or camping trip.

Although it is impossible to make any home "burglar proof," there are some actions you can take to protect your home and property:

1. **Document your assets.** Make a list of your valuables. Photograph or videotape each room in your home. Keep receipts of major purchases. Store these and other important

(Continued)

records in a safe deposit box so you can prove any losses. Review your insurance policies to see if special items like furs, artwork, or coin collections are covered.

2. **Identify valuables.** Engrave computers, televisions, cameras, stereos, and DVD players with your name or an identifying number. Police often discover stolen property but have no way of contacting the owners.

3. **Always lock your doors.** Nothing attracts a thief more than an open garage or unlatched screen door. Lock up even when you plan to visit a neighbor for "just a minute." That "minute" can easily become half an hour, plenty of time for a burglary to occur. Don't leave doors open if you are going to be upstairs or in the basement.

4. **Install only security systems you will use.** Many homeowners invest in expensive, high-tech security systems that are so cumbersome they leave them off most of the time. A cheap alarm system used twenty-four hours a day provides more protection than a state-of-the-art system used randomly.

5. **Trim shrubbery around entrances and windows.** Don't provide camouflage for burglars. Thieves can easily conceal themselves behind foliage while jimmying doors and windows.

Trim hedges below window level.   ©Corbis

6. **Network with neighbors.** Let neighbors know if you expect deliveries, house guests, or contractors. Thieves have posed as moving crews, casually looting a house and loading a truck while neighbors look on.

7. **Store valuables in attics and basements.** Thieves are reluctant to venture beyond the ground floor, which usually offers numerous exits in case of detection. Attics and basements, therefore, provide more security for valuable or hard to replace items.

Finally, call the police the moment you discover a burglary has occurred. If you return home and find evidence of a break-in, ***do not go inside!*** The thieves, who could be armed, might still be on the premises. Use a cell phone or ask a neighbor to call the police. Never attempt to confront a burglar yourself. No personal possession is worth risking death or a disabling injury.

QUESTIONS FOR REVIEW AND REVISION

1. The student offers seven directions. Would these be easier to recall if emphasized by the subtitle "Seven Tips to Keep Your Home Secure"? Would it be better to introduce the steps stating "there are seven actions you can take" instead of "some actions"? Why or why not?

2. What misconceptions does the student address?

3. How important is the final warning?

4. The student writes in the second person, directly addressing the readers. Would the paper be less effective if written in third person? Why or why not?

5. Do the level of language, diction, and tone suit the intended audience?

6. Did the student follow the instructor's suggestions?

7. Read the paper aloud. Is this document easy to read and easy to remember? Could revisions increase its clarity?

8. The student included a photograph in the final draft. Is it effective? Why or why not?

WRITING SUGGESTIONS

1. Using this paper as a model, write a set of instructions directed to a general audience about improving the performance of a car, installing a new computer program, planning a trip or a wedding, losing weight, choosing a pet, preparing for a job interview, or another topic of your choice.

2. *Collaborative writing:* Discuss this paper with other students. Using some of its ideas, work together to write a brief set of instructions on securing a dorm room or an apartment.

Suggested Topics for Writing Process

General Assignments

Explaining How Things Work

Write a process paper on any of the following topics. Assume you are writing to a general, college-educated audience. You may develop your explanation using narratives, comparisons, and definitions. Explain the process as a clearly stated chain of events. Draw from your own experiences.

- How students register for courses
- The operation of an appliance, such as a microwave, washing machine, or refrigerator
- The process of a disease or disability
- The training of new employees
- How a computer virus works
- The way the body loses fat through diet or exercise
- A method of introducing a new product in the marketplace

- How restaurants prevent food poisoning
- A legal process, such as an arrest, eviction, or bankruptcy
- How real-estate agents sell a house

Giving Directions

Write a process paper giving specific directions to complete a specific task. You may wish to place your instructions in numbered steps rather than standard paragraphs. Remember to highlight potential hazards.

- How to protect your computer against viruses
- How to purchase a new or used car
- How to deter a mugger or attacker
- How to quit smoking
- How to find a job
- How to avoid identity theft
- How to create a website
- How to treat a second-degree burn
- How to teach children to save money, eat properly, read books, or avoid dangerous situations

Writing in Context

1. Write step-by-step directions telling freshmen how to register for classes online. Make sure your instructions are complete. You might, for instance, have to explain to new students how to read a class schedule and define abbreviations or terms like "prerequisite" or "honors class." When you complete a draft of your paper, review it carefully to see whether you have left out any essential information.

2. Select a process that you have learned on a job and write instructions suitable for training a new employee. Consider how your job may have changed. Give trainees the benefit of your experience and add tips that might not be included in the standard job descriptions. Warn readers, for instance, of common problems that arise.

3. Select a process from one of your textbooks and rewrite it for a sixth-grade class. Simplify the language and use analogies that sixth graders will understand.

Strategies for Reading Process

As you read the process entries in this chapter, keep these questions in mind.

Context

1. What is the writer's goal—to explain or instruct?
2. Is the goal clearly stated?

3. What are the critical stages or steps in the process?

4. What errors should readers avoid?

Strategy

1. What is the nature of the intended audience? How much existing knowledge does the writer assume that readers have?

2. How are steps or stages separated? Are transitions clearly established?

3. Are the instructions easy to follow?

4. Are any special effects, such as highlighting, numbered steps, and visual aids, skillfully used?

Language

1. Are technical terms clearly defined and illustrated?

2. Does the writer use concrete words to create clear images of what is being explained?

READING TO LEARN

As you read the process essays in this chapter, note techniques you can use in your own writing.

- **"How to Mark a Book" by Mortimer Adler** uses numbered steps to explain the most effective way to read a book.

- **"Fender Benders: Legal Dos and Don'ts" by Armond D. Budish** uses numbered steps to inform drivers what to do if they are involved in a minor car accident. He also gives negative directions, telling readers what not to do.

- **"How Our Skins Got Their Color" by Marvin Harris** explains the natural process that led humans to develop different complexions.

- **"How to Land the Job You Want" by Davidyne Mayleas** uses numbered steps to show readers how to find jobs.

- **"My First Conk" by Malcolm X** explains how blacks processed their hair to develop an argument about race and identity.

Mortimer Adler

Mortimer Adler (1902–2001) was born in New York City. He taught psychology at Columbia University, then moved to Chicago, where he taught the philosophy of law for more than twenty years. He resigned from the University of Chicago in 1952 to head the Institute for Philosophical Research in San Francisco. His books include *How to Read a Book* and *Philosopher at Large: An Intellectual Autobiography*. Adler became famous as an editor of the *Encyclopedia Britannica* and a leader of the Great Books Program of the University of Chicago. This program encouraged adults from all careers to read and discuss classic works. This essay first appeared in the *Saturday Review of Literature* in 1940.

How to Mark a Book

Source: "How to Mark a Book" from *How to Read a Book* by Mortimer J. Adler and Charles Van Doren. Copyright © 1940 by Mortimer J. Adler. Copyright renewed © 1967 by Mortimer J. Adler. Copyright © 1972 by Mortimer J. Adler and Charles Van Doren. By permission.

Before reading Adler's essay, consider your own reading habits. Do you read with a pen in your hand? Do you scan a work first or simply begin with the first line? Do you take notes? Do you have problems remembering what you read?

introduction

1   You know you have to read "between the lines" to get the most out of anything. I want to persuade you to do something equally important in the course of your reading. I want to persuade you to "write between the lines." Unless you do, you are not likely to do the most efficient kind of reading. I contend, quite bluntly, that marking up a

thesis

book is not an act of mutilation but of love.

2   You shouldn't mark up a book which isn't yours. Librarians (or your friends) who lend you books expect you to keep them clean, and you should. If you decide that I

disclaimer

am right about the usefulness of marking books, you will have to buy them. Most of the world's great books are available today, in reprint editions, at less than a dollar.

3   There are two ways in which one can own a book. The first is the property right you establish by paying for it, just as you pay for clothes and furniture. But this act of purchase is only the prelude to possession. Full ownership comes only when you

defines "full ownership"

have made it a part of yourself, and the best way to make yourself a part of it is by writing in it. An illustration may make the point clear. You buy a beefsteak and transfer it from the butcher's icebox to your own. But you do not own the beefsteak in the most important sense until you consume it and get it into your bloodstream. I am arguing that books, too, must be absorbed in your bloodstream to do you any good.

4   Confusion about what it means to *own* a book leads people to a false reverence

"false reverence for paper"

for paper, binding, and type—a respect for the physical thing—the craft of the printer rather than the genius of the author. They forget that it is possible for a man to acquire the idea, to possess the beauty, which a great book contains, without staking his claim by pasting his bookplate inside the cover. Having a fine library doesn't prove that its owner has a mind enriched by books; it proves nothing more than that he, his father, or his wife, was rich enough to buy them.

classifies three types of book owners

5   There are three kinds of book owners. The first has all the standard sets and best-sellers—unread, untouched. (This deluded individual owns woodpulp and ink,

Sam Diephuis/jupiterimages

not books.) The second has a great many books—a few of them read through, most of them dipped into, but all of them as clean and shiny as the day they were bought. (This person would probably like to make books his own, but is restrained by a false respect for their physical appearance.) The third has a few books or many— every one of them dogeared and dilapidated, shaken and loosened by continual use, marked and scribbled in from front to back. (This man owns books.)

6   Is it false respect, you may ask, to preserve intact and unblemished a beautifully printed book, an elegantly bound edition? Of course not. I'd no more scribble all over a first edition of *Paradise Lost* than I'd give my baby a set of crayons and an original Rembrandt! I wouldn't mark up a painting or a statue. Its soul, so to speak, is inseparable from its body. And the beauty of a rare edition or of a richly manufactured volume is like that of a painting or a statue.

7   But the soul of a book *can* be separated from its body. A book is more like the score of a piece of music than it is like a painting. No great musician confuses a symphony with the printed sheets of music. Arturo Toscanini reveres Brahms, but Toscanini's score of the C-minor Symphony is so thoroughly marked up that no one but the maestro himself can read it. The reason why a great conductor makes notations on his musical scores—marks them up again and again each time he returns to study them—is the reason why you should mark your books. If your respect for magnificent binding or typography gets in the way, buy yourself a cheap edition and pay your respects to the author.

8   Why is marking up a book indispensable to reading? First, it keeps you awake. (And I don't mean merely conscious; I mean wide awake.) In the second place, reading, if it is active, is thinking, and thinking tends to express itself in words, spoken or written. The marked book is usually the thought-through book. Finally, writing helps you remember the thoughts you had, or the thoughts the author expressed. Let me develop these three points. *[explains need to write as you read]*

9   If reading is to accomplish anything more than passing time, it must be active. You can't let your eyes glide across the lines of a book and come up with an understanding of what you have read. Now an ordinary piece of light fiction, like say, *Gone with the Wind,* doesn't require the most active kind of reading. The books you read for pleasure can be read in a state of relaxation, and nothing is lost. But a great book, rich in ideas and beauty, a book that raises and tries to answer great fundamental questions, demands the most active reading of which you are capable. You don't absorb the ideas of John Dewey the way you absorb the crooning of Mr. Vallee. You have to reach for them. That you cannot do while you're asleep. *[defines "active reading"]*

10   If, when you've finished reading a book, the pages are filled with your notes, you know that you read actively. The most famous active reader of great books I know is President Hutchins, of the University of Chicago. He also has the hardest schedule of business activities of any man I know. He invariably reads with a pencil, and sometimes, when he picks up a book and pencil in the evening, he finds himself, instead of making intelligent notes, drawing what he calls "caviar factories" on the margins. When that happens, he puts the book down. He knows he's too tired to read, and he's just wasting time.

why write? 11   But, you may ask, why is writing necessary? Well, the physical act of writing, with your own hand, brings words and sentences more sharply before your mind and preserves them better in your memory. To set down your reaction to important words and sentences you have read, and the questions they have raised in your mind, is to preserve those reactions and sharpen those questions. Even if you wrote on a scratch pad, and threw the paper away when you had finished writing, your grasp of the book would be surer. But you don't have to throw the paper away. The margins (top and bottom, as well as side), the end-papers, the very space between the lines, are all available. They aren't sacred.

12   And, best of all, your marks and notes become an integral part of the book and stay there forever. You can pick up the book the following week or year, and there are all your points of agreement, disagreement, doubt, and inquiry. It's like resuming an interrupted conversation with the advantage of being able to pick up where you left

reading as
conversation
off. And that is exactly what reading a book should be: a conversation between you and the author. Presumably he knows more about the subject than you do; naturally, you'll have the proper humility as you approach him. But don't let anybody tell you that a reader is supposed to be solely on the receiving end. Understanding is a two-way operation; learning doesn't consist in being an empty receptacle. The learner has to question himself and question the teacher. He even has to argue with the teacher, once he understands what the teacher is saying. And marking a book is literally an expression of your differences, or agreements of opinion, with the author.

13   There are all kinds of devices for marking a book intelligently and fruitfully. Here's the way I do it:

uses numbered
steps and italics
for emphasis
1. *Underlining:* of major points, of important or forceful statements.
2. *Vertical lines at the margin:* to emphasize a statement already underlined.
3. *Star, asterisk, or other doo-dad at the margin:* to be used sparingly, to emphasize the ten or twenty most important statements in the book. (You may want to fold the bottom corner of each page on which you use such marks. It won't hurt the sturdy paper on which most modern books are printed, and you will be able to take the book off the shelf at any time and, by opening it at the folded-corner page, refresh your recollection of the book.)
4. *Numbers in the margin:* to indicate the sequence of points the author makes in developing a single argument.
5. *Numbers of other pages in the margin:* to indicate where else in the book the author made points relevant to the point marked; to tie up the ideas in a book, which, though they may be separated by many pages, belong together.
6. *Circling of key words or phrases.*
7. *Writing in the margin, or at the top or bottom of the page, for the sake of:* recording questions (and perhaps answers) which a passage raised in your mind; reducing a complicated discussion to a simple statement; recording the sequence of major points right through the book. I use the endpapers at the back of the book to make a personal index of the author's points in the order of their appearance.

14   The front end-papers are, to me, the most important. Some people reserve them for a fancy bookplate. I reserve them for fancy thinking. After I have finished reading the book and making my personal index on the back endpapers, I turn to the front and try to outline the book, not page by page, or point by point (I've already done that at the back), but as an integrated structure, with a basic unity and an order of parts. This outline is, to me, the measure of my understanding of the work.

15   If you're a die-hard anti-book-marker, you may object that the margins, the space between the lines, and the end-papers don't give you room enough. All right. How about using a scratch pad slightly smaller than the page-size of the book—so that the edges of the sheets won't protrude? Make your index, outlines, and even your notes on the pad, and then insert these sheets permanently inside the front and back covers of the book.

16   Or, you may say that this business of marking books is going to slow up your reading. It probably will. That's one of the reasons for doing it. Most of us have been taken in by the notion that speed of reading is a measure of our intelligence. There is no such thing as the right speed for intelligent reading. Some things should be read quickly and effortlessly, and some should be read slowly and even laboriously. The sign of intelligence in reading is the ability to read different things according to their worth. <u>In the case of good books, the point is not to see how many of them you can get through, but rather how many can get through you—how many you can make your own.</u> A few friends are better than a thousand acquaintances. If this be your aim, as it should be, you will not be impatient if it takes more time and effort to read a great book than it does a newspaper. *(goal of reading good books)*

17   You may have one final objection to marking books. You can't lend them to your friends because nobody else can read them without being distracted by your notes. Furthermore, you won't want to lend them because a marked copy is a kind of intellectual diary, and lending it is almost like giving your mind away.

18   If your friend wishes to read your *Plutarch's Lives, Shakespeare,* or *The Federalist Papers,* tell him gently but firmly to buy a copy. You will lend him your car or your coat—but your books are as much a part of you as your head or your heart. *(conclusion)*

UNDERSTANDING CONTEXT

1. In Adler's view, when do you really *own* a book? What makes a book truly yours? What makes a book like a steak?

2. What does Adler mean by the "soul" of a book? How does respecting it differ from respecting its "body"?

3. Why is it important, in Adler's view, to write as you read?

4. *Critical thinking:* This essay was first published more than seventy years ago. Are Adler's suggestions any different from the study skills you may have learned in high school or college?

EVALUATING STRATEGY

1. What audience is Adler addressing?
2. *Other modes:* Where does Adler use *comparison, description,* and *classification* in developing this essay?
3. Adler provides seven suggestions that are stated in italics and numbered. If this advice were written in a standard paragraph, would it be as effective? Why or why not?

APPRECIATING LANGUAGE

1. The *Saturday Review of Literature* had a general but highly literate readership, much like that of today's *New Yorker* or *Vanity Fair.* Does the tone and style of the article seem suited to this audience?
2. Are there any words, phrases, references, or expressions in this seventy-year-old article that need updating?

WRITING SUGGESTIONS

1. Using Adler's seven suggestions, write a brief one-page guide on active reading directed to high school students.
2. *Collaborative writing:* Adler presents tips for active reading. Work with a group of students and discuss their experiences in studying for examinations. Record your ideas and suggestions, and then write a well-organized list of tips to help new students develop successful study skills.

Armond D. Budish is an attorney and consumer-law reporter. He practices law in Ohio, where he writes columns on consumer issues for the *Cleveland Plain Dealer*. He has also published articles for *Family Circle* magazine. His book *How to Beat the Catastrophic Costs of Nursing Home Care* was published in 1989.

Fender Benders: Legal Dos and Don'ts

Source: "Fender Benders: Do's and Don't's" by Armond D. Budish. From *Family Circle* Magazine, July 19, 1994 issue. Copyright © 1994 by Armond D. Budish. By permission.

As you read this article, notice how Budish makes use of numbered steps and bold type to make this Family Circle *article easy to skim.*

1   The car ahead of you stops suddenly. You hit the brakes, but you just can't stop in time. Your front bumper meets the rear end of the other car. *Ouch!*

2   There doesn't seem to be any damage, and it must be your lucky day because the driver you hit agrees that it's not worth hassling with insurance claims and risking a premium increase. So after exchanging addresses, you go your separate ways.

3   Imagine your surprise when you open the mail a few weeks later only to discover a letter from your "victim's" lawyer demanding $10,000 to cover car repairs, pain and suffering. Apparently the agreeable gentleman decided to disagree, then went ahead and filed a police report blaming you for the incident and for his damages.

4   When automobiles meet by accident, do you know how to respond?

5   Here are 10 practical tips that can help you avoid costly legal and insurance hassles.

1. Stop! It's the Law.

6   No matter how serious or minor the accident, stop immediately. If possible, don't move your car—especially if someone has been injured. Leaving the cars as they were when the accident occurred helps the police determine what happened. Of course, if your car is blocking traffic or will cause another accident where it is, then move it to the nearest safe location.

7   For every rule there are exceptions, though. If, for example, you are rear-ended at night in an unsafe area, it's wisest to keep on going and notify the police later. There have been cases in which people were robbed or assaulted when they got out of their cars.

2. Zip Loose Lips.

8   Watch what you say after an accident. Although this may sound harsh, even an innocent "I'm sorry" could later be construed as an admission of fault. Also be sure not to accuse the other driver of causing the accident. Since you don't know how a stranger will react to your remarks, you run the risk of making a bad situation worse.

9   Remember, you are not the judge or jury; it's not up to you to decide who is or is not at fault. Even if you think you caused the accident, you might be wrong. For example: Assume you were driving 15 miles over the speed limit. What you probably were not aware of is that the other driver's blood-alcohol level exceeded the legal limits, so he was at least equally at fault.

3. Provide Required Information.

10 If you are involved in an accident, you are required in most states to give your name, address and car registration number to: any person injured in the accident; the owner, driver or passenger in any car that was damaged in the accident; a police officer on the scene. If you don't own the car (say it belongs to a friend or your parents), you should provide the name and address of the owner.

11 You must produce this information even if there are no apparent injuries or damages and even if you didn't cause the accident. Most states don't require you to provide the name of your insurance company, although it's usually a good idea to do so. However, *don't* discuss the amount of your coverage—that might inspire the other person to "realize" his injuries are more serious than he originally thought.

12 What should you do if you hit a parked car and the owner is not around? The law requires you to leave a note with your name, and the other identifying information previously mentioned, in a secure place on the car (such as under the windshield wiper).

4. Get Required Information.

13 You should obtain from the others involved in the accident the same information that you provide them with. However, if the other driver refuses to cooperate, at least get the license number and the make and model of the car to help police track down the owner.

5. Call the Police.

14 It's obvious that if it's a serious accident in which someone is injured, the police should be called immediately. That's both the law and common sense. But what if the accident seems minor? Say you're stopped, another car taps you in the rear. If it's absolutely clear to both drivers that there is no damage or injury, you each can go your merry way. But that's the exception.

15 Normally, you should call the police to substantiate what occurred. In most cities police officers will come to the scene, even for minor accidents, but if they won't, you and the other driver should go to the station (of the city where the accident occurred) to file a report. Ask to have an officer check out both cars.

16 If you are not at fault, be wary of accepting the other driver's suggestion that you leave the police out of it and arrange a private settlement. When you submit your $500 car-repair estimate several weeks later, you could discover that the other driver has developed "amnesia" and denies being anywhere near the accident. If the police weren't present on the scene, you may not have a legal leg to stand on.

17 Even if you *are* at fault, it's a good idea to involve the police. Why? Because a police officer will note the extent of the other driver's damages in his or her report, limiting your liability. Without police presence the other driver can easily inflate the amount of the damages.

6. Identify Witnesses.

18   Get the names and addresses of any witnesses, in case there's a legal battle some time in the future. Ask bystanders or other motorists who stop whether they saw the accident; if they answer "yes," get their identifying information. It is also helpful to note the names and badge numbers of all police officers on the scene.

7. Go to the Hospital.

19   If there's a chance that you've been injured, go directly to a hospital emergency room or to your doctor. The longer you wait, the more you may jeopardize your health and the more difficult it may be to get reimbursed for your injuries if they turn out to be serious.

8. File a Report.

20   Every driver who is involved in an automobile incident in which injuries occur must fill out an accident report. Even if the property damage is only in the range of $200 to $1,000, most states require that an accident report be filed. You must do this fairly quickly, usually in 1 to 30 days. Forms may be obtained and filed with the local motor vehicle department or police station in the city where the accident occurred.

9. Consider Filing an Insurance Claim.

21   Talk with your insurance agent as soon as possible after an accident. He or she can help you decide if you should file an insurance claim or pay out of your own pocket.

22   For example, let's say you caused an accident and the damages totaled $800. You carry a $250 deductible, leaving you with a possible $550 insurance claim. If you do submit a claim, your insurance rates are likely to go up, an increase that will probably continue for about three years. You should compare that figure to the $550 claim to determine whether to file a claim or to pay the cost yourself. (Also keep in mind that multiple claims sometimes make it harder to renew your coverage.)

10. Don't Be Too Quick to Accept a Settlement.

23   If the other driver is at fault and there's any chance you've been injured, don't rush to accept a settlement from that person's insurance company. You may not know the extent of your injuries for some time, and once you accept a settlement, it's difficult to get an "upgrade." Before settling, consult with a lawyer who handles personal injury cases.

24   When you *haven't* been injured and you receive a fair offer to cover the damage to your car, you can go ahead and accept it.

UNDERSTANDING CONTEXT

1. What problems can motorists have if they are careless about handling even minor accidents?

2. What are some of the most important things you should do if involved in a fender bender?

3. Why should you go to the hospital even if you have what appears to be a minor injury?

4. *Critical thinking:* Should this article be printed as a pamphlet and distributed to drivers' education classes? Have you known anyone who has gotten into difficulties that could have been avoided if he or she had followed the writer's advice?

EVALUATING STRATEGY

1. How does Budish arouse reader attention in the opening?

2. How effective are the numbered steps? Would the article lose impact if printed in standard paragraphs?

3. How easy is this article to remember? Can you put it down and recall the main points?

APPRECIATING LANGUAGE

1. This article was written for *Family Circle*. Does the language appear to be targeted to a female audience?

2. Why does Budish, who is an attorney, avoid legal terminology?

3. Does Budish's language create concrete images that make strong impressions to dramatize his subject?

WRITING SUGGESTIONS

1. Using this article as a model, provide the general public with a similar list of tips to prevent heart disease, deter muggers, prepare their children for school, or save money for retirement.

2. *Collaborative writing:* Work with a group of students to provide tips for new students on campus. Use peer review to make sure you do not overlook details in guiding students to accomplish a specific goal.

Marvin Harris (1927–2001) was born in Brooklyn and received degrees from Columbia University. After teaching at Columbia for many years, Harris moved to the University of Florida, where he served as a graduate research professor in anthropology. Harris conducted research in Harlem, Africa, South America, and Asia. He published several scholarly works but is best known for books written for general readers such as *Cows, Pigs, Wars, and Witches: The Riddles of Culture* and *Cannibals and Kings: The Origins of Cultures*. Much of Harris's work focused on how people's basic needs for food and shelter influence their culture.

How Our Skins Got Their Color

Source: "How Our Skins Got Their Color" from *Our Kind: Who We Are, Where We Came From, Where We Are Going* by Marvin Harris, pp. 111–114. Copyright © 1969 by Marvin Harris. By permission.

In this essay from Our Kind: Who We Are, Where We Came From, Where We Are Going *(1988), Harris explains how human beings developed different skin colors. In reading this account, determine how he addresses a topic laden with controversy.*

1 Most human beings are neither very fair nor very dark, but brown. The extremely fair skin of northern Europeans and their descendants, and the very black skins of central Africans and their descendants, are probably special adaptations. Brown-skinned ancestors may have been shared by modern-day blacks and whites as recently as ten thousand years ago.

2 Human skin owes its color to the presence of particles known as melanin. The primary function of melanin is to protect the upper levels of the skin from being damaged by the sun's ultraviolet rays. This radiation poses a critical problem for our kind because we lack the dense coat of hair that acts as a sunscreen for most mammals. Hairlessness exposes us to two kinds of radiation hazards: ordinary sunburn, with its blisters, rashes, and risk of infection; and skin cancers, including malignant melanoma, one of the deadliest diseases known. Melanin is the body's first line of defense against these afflictions. The more melanin particles, the darker the skin, and the lower the risk of sunburn and all forms of skin cancer. This explains why the highest rates for skin cancer are found in sun-drenched lands such as Australia, where light-skinned people of European descent spend a good part of their lives outdoors wearing scanty attire. Very dark-skinned people such as heavily pigmented Africans of Zaire seldom get skin cancer, but when they do, they get it on depigmented parts of their bodies—palms and lips.

3 If exposure to solar radiation had nothing but harmful effects, natural selection would have favored inky black as the color for all human populations. But the sun's rays do not present an unmitigated threat. As it falls on the skin, sunshine converts a fatty substance in the epidermis into vitamin D. The blood carries vitamin D from the skin to the intestines (technically making it a hormone rather than a vitamin), where it plays a vital role in the absorption of calcium. In turn, calcium is vital for strong bones. Without it, people fall victim to the crippling diseases rickets and osteomalacia. In women, calcium deficiencies can result in a deformed birth canal, which makes childbirth lethal for both mother and fetus.

4 Vitamin D can be obtained from a few foods, primarily the oils and livers of marine fish. But inland populations must rely on the sun's rays and their own skins

for the supply of this crucial substance. The particular color of a human population's skin, therefore, represents in large degree a trade-off between the hazards of too much versus too little solar radiation: acute sunburn and skin cancer on the one hand, and rickets and osteomalacia on the other. It is this trade-off that largely accounts for the preponderance of brown people in the world and for the general tendency for skin color to be darkest among equatorial populations and lightest among populations dwelling at higher latitudes.

5   At middle latitudes, the skin follows a strategy of changing colors with the seasons. Around the Mediterranean basin, for example, exposure to the summer sun brings high risk of cancer but low risk for rickets; the body produces more melanin and people grow darker (i.e., they get suntans). Winter reduces the risk of sunburn and cancer; the body produces less melanin, and the tan wears off.

6   The correlation between skin color and latitude is not perfect because other factors—such as the availability of foods containing vitamin D and calcium, regional cloud cover during the winter, amount of clothing worn, and cultural preferences—may work for or against the predicted relationship. Arctic-dwelling Eskimos, for example, are not as light-skinned as expected, but their habitat and economy afford them a diet that is exceptionally rich in both vitamin D and calcium.

7   Northern Europeans, obliged to wear heavy garments for protection against the long, cold, cloudy winters, were always at risk for rickets and osteomalacia from too little vitamin D and calcium. This risk increased sometime after 6000 B.C., when pioneer cattle herders who did not exploit marine resources began to appear in northern Europe. The risk would have been especially great for the brown-skinned Mediterranean peoples who migrated northward along with the crops and farm animals. Samples of Caucasian skin (infant penile foreskin obtained at the time of circumcision) exposed to sunlight on cloudless days in Boston (42°N) from November through February produced no vitamin D. In Edmonton (52°N) this period extended from October to March. But further south (34°N) sunlight was effective in producing vitamin D in the middle of the winter. Almost all of Europe lies north of 42°N. Fair-skinned, nontanning individuals who could utilize the weakest and briefest doses of sunlight to synthesize vitamin D were strongly favored by natural selection. During the frigid winters, only a small circle of a child's face could be left to peek out at the sun through the heavy clothing, thereby favoring the survival of individuals with translucent patches of pink on their cheeks characteristic of many northern Europeans. . . .

8   If light-skinned individuals on the average had only 2 percent more children survive per generation, the changeover in their skin color could have begun five thousand years ago and reached present levels well before the beginning of the Christian era. But natural selection need not have acted alone. Cultural selection may also have played a role. It seems likely that whenever people consciously or unconsciously had to decide which infants to nourish and which to neglect, the advantage would go to those with lighter skin, experience having shown that such individuals tended to grow up to be taller, stronger, and healthier than their darker siblings. White was beautiful because white was healthy.

9   To account for the evolution of black skin in equatorial latitudes, one has merely to reverse the combined effects of natural and cultural selection. With the sun directly overhead most of the year, and clothing a hindrance to work and survival,

vitamin D was never in short supply (and calcium was easily obtained from vegetables). Rickets and osteomalacia were rare. Skin cancer was the main problem, and what nature started, culture amplified. Darker infants were favored by parents because experience showed that they grew up to be freer of disfiguring and lethal malignancies. Black was beautiful because black was healthy.

UNDERSTANDING CONTEXT

1. What is Harris's thesis?
2. What is the "natural" color for human skin?
3. What caused people to develop different complexions?
4. What role did sunlight play in human evolution?
5. *Critical thinking:* What impact could this scientific explanation of skin color have on debates about race and discrimination? Can biological aspects of humanity be separated from social, cultural, political, or psychological attitudes?

EVALUATING STRATEGY

1. How does Harris organize his essay?
2. What research does Harris use to support his views?
3. *Blending the modes:* Where does Harris use *narration, comparison,* and *definition* in his explanation?

APPRECIATING LANGUAGE

1. How does Harris define *melanin*?
2. Does Harris's selection of words describing color contain connotations that suggest a bias? Is his essay wholly objective? How often does he use words such as *white* and *black*?
3. Would the average newspaper reader be able to understand this essay? What does the level of language suggest about the intended audience?

WRITING SUGGESTIONS

1. Using this essay for background information, draft a brief explanation about skin color for an elementary school brochure on race relations. Use easily understood language, and employ comparisons and short narratives to explain scientific principles. Avoid words that may have negative connotations.
2. *Critical writing:* Write an essay analyzing the effect reading this essay had on you. Did it affect your attitudes toward people of different races? Does the knowledge that all humans probably once shared the same complexion change the way you view yourself?
3. *Collaborative writing:* Discuss Harris's essay with a group of students. What value does a scientific explanation of skin color have in addressing racial problems? Would it be beneficial to share this information with children? Record members' reactions, and create a short statement about the importance of understanding the origins of skin color. If members disagree, consider developing pro and con responses.

Davidyne Mayleas

Davidyne Mayleas attended the University of Chicago and New York University, where she majored in banking and finance. After college she became a freelance journalist and social critic. She has written articles for popular magazines, such as *Reader's Digest* and *Esquire*. She is most noted for her investment and career advice. She has published several books, including *The Hidden Job Market for the 8os* and *By Appointment Only*.

How to Land the Job You Want

Source: "How to Land the Job You Want" by Davidyne Mayleas. Originally appeared in *Empire* Magazine. Copyright © 1976 by Davidyne Mayleas. By permission.

After graduation, you will no doubt enter the job market. As you read this essay, consider how you can make use of Mayleas's instructions.

1 Louis Albert, 39, lost his job as an electrical engineer when his firm made extensive cutbacks. He spent two months answering classified ads and visiting employment agencies—with zero results. Albert might still be hunting if a friend, a specialist in the employment field, had not shown him how to be his own job counselor. Albert learned how to research unlisted openings, write a forceful résumé, perform smoothly in an interview, even transform a turndown into a job.

2   Although there seemed to be a shortage of engineering jobs, Albert realized that he still persuaded potential employers to see him. This taught him something—that his naturally outgoing personality might be as great an asset as his engineering degree. When the production head of a small electronics company told him that they did not have an immediate opening, Albert told his interviewer, "You people make a fine product. I think you could use additional sales representation—someone like me who understands and talks electrical engineer's language, and who enjoys selling." The interviewer decided to send Albert to a senior vice president. Albert got a job in sales.

3   You too can be your own counselor if you put the same vigorous effort into *getting* a job as you would into *keeping* one. Follow these three basic rules, developed by placement experts:

4 **1. Find the hidden job market.** Classified ads and agency listings reveal only a small percentage of available jobs. Some of the openings that occur through promotions, retirements and reorganization never reach the personnel department. There are three ways to get in touch with this hidden market:

5   *Write a strong résumé with a well-directed cover letter and mail it to the appropriate department manager in the company where you'd like to work.* Don't worry whether there's a current opening. Many managers fill vacancies by reviewing the résumés already in their files. Dennis Mollura, press-relations manager in the public-relations department of American Telephone and Telegraph, says, "In my own case, the company called me months after I sent in my résumé."

6   *Get in touch with people who work in or know the companies that interest you.* Jobs are so often filled through personal referral that Charles R. Lops, executive employment manager of the J. C. Penney Co., says, "Probably our best source for outside people comes from recommendations made by Penney associates themselves."

7 *"Drop in" on the company.* Lillian Reveille, employment manager of Equitable Life Assurance Society of the United States, reports: "A large percentage of the applicants we see are 'walk-ins'—and we do employ many of these people."

8 **2. Locate hidden openings.** This step requires energy and determination to make telephone calls, see people, do research, and to keep moving despite turndowns.

9 *Contact anyone who may know of openings,* including relatives, friends, teachers, bank officers, insurance agents—anyone you know in your own or an adjacent field. When the teachers' union and employment agencies produced no teaching openings, Eric Olson, an unemployed high-school math instructor, reviewed his talent and decided that where an analytical math mind was useful, there he'd find a job. He called his insurance agent, who set up an interview with the actuarial department of one of the companies he represented. They hired Olson.

10 It's a good idea to contact not only professional or trade associations in your field, but also your local chamber of commerce and people involved in community activities. After Laura Bailey lost her job as retirement counselor in a bank's personnel department, she found a position in customer relations in another bank. Her contact: a member of the senior-citizens club that Mrs. Bailey ran on a volunteer basis.

11 *Use local or business-school libraries.* Almost every field has its own directory of companies, which provides names, addresses, products and/or services, and lists officers and other executives. Write to the company president or to the executive to whom you'd report. The vice president of personnel at Warner-Lambert Co. says, "When a résumé of someone we could use—now or in the near future—shows up 'cold' in my in-basket, that's luck for both of us."

12 *Consult telephone directories.* Sometimes the telephone company will send you free the telephone directories of various cities. Also, good-sized public libraries often have many city directories. Fred Lewis, a cabinetmaker, checked the telephone directories of nine different cities where he knew furniture was manufactured. At the end of five weeks he had a sizable telephone bill, some travel expenses—and ten interviews which resulted in three job offers.

13 **3. After you find the opening, get the job.** The applicants who actually get hired are those who polish these six job-getting skills to perfection:

14 *Compose a better résumé.* A résumé is a self-advertisement, designed to get you an interview. Start by putting yourself in an employer's place. Take stock of your job history and personal achievements. Make an inventory of your skills and accomplishments that might be useful from the employer's standpoint. Choose the most important and describe them in words that stress accomplishments. Avoid such phrases as "my duties included. . . ." Use action words like planned, sold, trained, managed.

15 Ask a knowledgeable business friend to review your résumé. Does it stress accomplishment rather than duties? Does it tell an employer what you can do for him? Can it be shortened? (One or two pages should suffice.) Generally, it's not wise to mention salary requirements.

16 *Write a convincing cover letter.* While the résumé may be a copy, the cover letter must be personal. Sy Mann, director of research for Aceto Chemical Co., says: "When

I see a mimeographed letter that states, 'Dear Sir, I'm sincerely interested in working for your company,' I wonder, 'How many other companies got this valentine?'" Use the name and title of the person who can give you the interview, and be absolutely certain of accuracy here. Using a wrong title or misspelling a prospective employer's name may route your correspondence directly to an automatic turndown.

17   *Prepare specifically for each interview.* Research the company thoroughly; know its history and competition. Try to grasp the problems of the job you're applying for. For example, a line in an industry journal that a food company was "developing a new geriatric food" convinced one man that he should emphasize his marketing experience with vitamins rather than with frozen foods.

18   You'll increase your edge by anticipating questions the interviewer might raise. Why do you want to work for us? What can you offer us that someone else cannot? Why did you leave your last position? What are your salary requirements?

19   An employer holds an interview to get a clearer picture of your work history and accomplishments, and to look for characteristics he considers valuable. These vary with jobs. Does the position require emphasis on attention to detail or on creativity? Perseverance or aggressiveness? Prior to the interview decide what traits are most in demand. And always send a thank-you note immediately after the interview.

20   *Follow-up.* They said you would hear in a week; now it's two. Call them. Don't wait and hope. Hope and act.

21   *Supply additional information.* That's the way Karen Halloway got her job as fashion director with a department store. "After my interview I sensed that the merchandise manager felt I was short on retail experience. So I wrote to him describing the 25 fashion shows I'd staged yearly for the pattern company I'd worked for."

22   *Don't take no for an answer.* Hank Newell called to find out why he had been turned down. The credit manager felt he had insufficient collection experience. Hank thanked him for his time and frankness. The next day, Hank called back saying, "My collection experience is limited, but I don't think I fully emphasized my training in credit checking." They explored this area and found Hank still not qualified. But the credit manager was so impressed with how well Hank took criticism that when Hank asked him if he could suggest other employers, he did, even going so far as to call one. Probing for leads when an interview or follow-up turns negative is a prime technique for getting personal referrals.

23   The challenge of finding a job, approached in an active, organized, realistic way, can be a valuable personal adventure. You can meet new people, develop new ideas about yourself and your career goals, and improve your skills in dealing with individuals. These in turn can contribute to your long-term job security.

UNDERSTANDING CONTEXT

1. What is the "hidden job market"? How can people discover opportunities that are not advertised?

2. What are the best sources of locating openings other than the want ads?

3. How should job seekers prepare résumés and cover letters?

4. *Critical thinking:* Students attend college to prepare for careers, but do colleges effectively train their graduates to enter the job market? Could schools do a better job of giving their students the skills needed to locate and secure employment?

EVALUATING STRATEGY

1. How effective is the opening narrative? Does it dramatize the need for Mayleas's instructions? Does it grab attention?

2. Review Mayleas's use of paragraphing, numbering, and italics. Could the article be made any easier to skim and remember?

3. *Critical thinking:* Process writers often number points and develop short, easy-to-remember instructions so readers can recall advice and apply it later. Is there a risk, however, that a complex concept can be reduced to a superficial slogan?

APPRECIATING LANGUAGE

1. Mayleas uses verbs to begin each instruction—"Find the hidden job market" and "Write a convincing cover letter." Why is it important to emphasize verbs in giving directions?

2. Seeking a job can be stressful and depressing. Underline words the writer uses to build reader confidence and create a positive tone.

WRITING SUGGESTIONS

1. Based on your own experiences, write a short set of instructions for students seeking jobs in a business you have worked in. Make your directions as specific as possible.

2. *Collaborative writing:* Discuss these tips with a group of students. Brainstorm and add suggestions; then write a short list of directions to help new students find part-time jobs on or off campus.

Job search want ads   © Peter Griffin/Alamy

The Job Market

As much as you may appreciate the love and guidance your parents give you, you must figure out who you are and what you want to do. And your doing so is an absolute requirement if you want to have a fulfilling career.

Pamela M. McBride

College students typically begin looking for jobs during spring break in their senior year, often with little direction or preparation. Many will waste valuable time, miss opportunities, or find themselves "taking jobs" rather than "launching careers." Employment experts note that most job seekers, especially recent graduates, make common mistakes in searching for jobs, preparing résumés, and interviewing.

Eighty percent of job openings are never advertised. They are not listed in want ads, bulletin boards, or websites. To locate the best of these opportunities, job seekers have to look for them by networking—locating people who have the job they want or know someone who does.

Students can begin networking long before graduation. Before deciding on a major, they should determine whether their courses and degree will prepare them for the work they want to do and whether they will be prepared to find a job when they graduate. Talking to or e-mailing people who have the job you want can provide valuable advice. Professional organizations, volunteer work, and internships can generate contacts with potential employers.

Developing networking and interviewing skills can help students find jobs and prepare them to make future career shifts. Outsourcing, changing government policies, shifts in the global economy, and constantly advancing technologies will force most of today's graduates to change careers, not jobs, four or five times in their lives.

With experts predicting unemployment to remain high for several years, it is important to understand how to explore the hidden job market, network to establish contacts, and interview effectively.

Before reading the articles listed below, consider the following questions:

1. *How did you determine your major?* Do you know what you want to do with your life? Do you know what people really do in the careers you want to pursue? Do you know whether jobs in this field are growing or declining and what they pay?
2. *If you were looking for a job today, what method would you use to locate openings?*
3. *Do you know what you would include on your résumé?* Have you seen copies of successful résumés? Do you know not only what information to include but also how to present it?
4. *What questions do you expect to be asked at an interview?*
5. *Are you aware of the economic trends that will affect your future career?* Are you entering a job market that is expanding or shrinking?
6. *Do you know ways of improving your prospects of getting a job when you graduate?* Are there professional organizations you can join? Are there part-time or summer jobs that can give you relevant experience? If you cannot locate a job, are there opportunities for volunteer work that can provide experience or valuable contacts?

E-READINGS ONLINE

Search for each article by author or title on InfoTrac College Edition, available through your English CourseMate at **www.cengagebrain.com**.

Alexei Bayer. "Broken Jobs Machine: Why Unemployment Remains High."
The sectors that created the most jobs before the recession—financial services, real estate, and hospitality—depend on consumers having large amounts of discretionary cash and are unlikely to rebound in an era of austerity.

Stephen S. Roach. "More Jobs, Worse Work."
More than 80 percent of jobs created in recent years have been in low-end professions, making it harder for applicants to find desirable employment.

Jyoti Thottam. "Where the Good Jobs Are Going."
Software developers, engineers, and accountants who earned $70,000 or $80,000 a year are increasingly losing jobs to professionals in India who are willing to do the same job for less than $10,000.

Sean Gregory. "Five Jobs for Our Shores: Afraid of Outsourcing? Here Are Some Growing Fields That Won't Be Farmed Out to Overseas Workers."

Oil prospecting, physical training, transportation, health care, and money management offer well-paying jobs that cannot be sent overseas.

InfoWorld. "Off the Record: The Myth of Job Security."
In one decade the US economy "created 318 million new jobs and destroyed 300 million of them," forcing workers to always "keep one eye on the job market."

Ariel Kaminer. "The Job of Finding a New Job."
Job counselors help the unemployed discover what they are good at, what they like doing, and what jobs are available.

Careers and Colleges. "10 Job-Hunting Mistakes and How Not to Make Them."
Job seekers must make determined efforts to locate jobs among the 80 percent that are never advertised.

Pamela M. McBride. "You're a Graduate and No Job—Now What?"
To obtain jobs new graduates must dedicate their time, evaluate their search techniques, and cultivate their networks.

Walter C. Vertreace. "How to Find Your Dream Job in a Nightmare Economy."
A challenging job market does not mean that graduates should abandon their dreams and take the first job offer that comes their way.

Linda D. Wilson. "How to Create a Career Networking System."
Networking, the most effective method of finding a job, consists of three basic steps—find, meet, and apply.

PR Newswire. "5 Tips on How to Find a Job by Marketing Yourself Online."
Online exchanges give job seekers marketing tools that help them rise above the competition.

Kathy Williams. "Can You Ace 10 Tough Job Interview Questions?"
Learning how to answer difficult questions can help applicants stand out and project a positive image.

CRITICAL READING AND THINKING

1. How can students prepare themselves for entering the job market?
2. What common mistakes should applicants avoid in looking for jobs and writing résumés?
3. What questions are commonly asked at interviews?
4. What changes are occurring in the American economy, and how do they affect the job market?
5. Why do workers with good jobs have to keep an eye on the job market?

WRITING SUGGESTIONS

1. Write a self-assessment essay that analyzes your personal strengths and weaknesses, likes and dislikes, skills and abilities and that analyzes the career you

intend to pursue. Have you talked with anyone who has the kind of job you want? Do you really know what people do in this profession, or have your impressions been shaped by what you have heard or seen on television?

2. *Collaborative writing:* Working with other students, discuss what you have learned about the job market, interviewing, and writing résumés. Take notes and work together to present your group's advice in a process paper listing suggestions in numbered steps.

3. *Other modes:*
   - Write a *cause-and-effect* essay that explains why many companies are outsourcing jobs overseas.
   - Write a *description* of your ideal first job.
   - Develop a *classification* essay that ranks jobs from the most to least desirable.
   - Create a *comparison* essay that shows how technology or economic trends have changed an industry, a specific business, or the nature of a job.
   - Write a personal *definition* of what you consider an ideal career.

RESEARCH PAPER

You can develop a research paper about the job market by conducting further research to explore a range of issues:

- What economic, political, and technological forces are shaping today's job market?
- How is outsourcing affecting the job market?
- Why have labor unions lost power?
- Do women still face barriers to advancement?
- Do fewer jobs offer health care benefits and pensions? Will more workers be forced to become personally responsible for providing their own health insurance and retirement savings?

FOR FURTHER READING

To locate additional sources about the job market, enter these search terms into InfoTrac College Edition, available through your English CourseMate at **www.cengagebrain.com** or one of your college library's databases:

Employment
Subdivisions: analysis
                cases
                forecasts and trends
                surveys

Employment Interviewing
Subdivisions: analysis
                ethical aspects
                methods

Résumés

Subdivisions: analysis
design and construction
ethical aspects
evaluation
planning
surveys

ADDITIONAL SOURCES

Using a search engine, enter one or more of the following terms to locate additional sources:

employment résumés	job interviews
career trends	outsourcing
labor unions	worker benefits
glass ceiling	employment trends
job forecasts	hidden job market

See the Evaluating Internet Sources Checklist on pages 533–534. See Chapter 24 for documenting sources.

Malcolm X (1925–1965) was born Malcolm Little in Omaha, Nebraska, where his father worked as a preacher. While in prison for robbery, Malcolm converted to the Black Muslim faith. He changed his last name to X to reject his "slave name" and dramatize African Americans' loss of heritage. He became a rising force in the Nation of Islam and in 1963 was named its first "national minister." After a trip to Mecca, he converted to orthodox Islam and rejected the racial views advocated by Black Muslims. He founded the Muslim Mosque, Inc., in 1964. A year later, he was shot and killed at a Harlem rally.

My First Conk

In this section from his autobiography, Malcolm X explains the process of "conking," or straightening hair, popular with some African Americans in the 1940s and 1950s. As you read this essay, note how Malcolm X explains the process, then uses it as an example in an argument about black identity.

1 Shorty soon decided that my hair was finally long enough to be conked. He had promised to school me in how to beat the barbershops' three- and four-dollar price by making up congolene, and then conking ourselves.

2 I took the little list of ingredients he had printed out for me, and went to a grocery store, where I got a can of Red Devil lye, two eggs, and two medium-sized white potatoes. Then at a drugstore near the poolroom, I asked for a large jar of Vaseline, a large bar of soap, a large-toothed comb and a fine-toothed comb, one of those rubber hoses with a metal spray-head, a rubber apron and a pair of gloves.

3 "Going to lay on that first conk?" the drugstore man asked me. I proudly told him, grinning, "Right!"

4 Shorty paid six dollars a week for a room in his cousin's shabby apartment. His cousin wasn't at home. "It's like the pad's mine, he spends so much time with his woman," Shorty said. "Now, you watch me—"

5 He peeled the potatoes and thin-sliced them into a quart-sized Mason fruit jar, then started stirring them with a wooden spoon as he gradually poured in a little over half the can of lye. "Never use a metal spoon; the lye will turn it black," he told me.

6 A jelly-like, starchy-looking glop resulted from the lye and potatoes, and Shorty broke in the two eggs, stirring real fast—his own conk and dark face bent down close. The congolene turned pale-yellowish. "Feel the jar," Shorty said. I cupped my hand against the outside, and snatched it away. "Damn right, it's hot, that's the lye," he said. "So you know it's going to burn when I comb it in—it burns bad. But the longer you can stand it, the straighter the hair."

7 He made me sit down, and he tied the string of the new rubber apron tightly around my neck, and combed up my bush of hair. Then, from the big Vaseline jar, he took a handful and massaged it hard all through my hair and into the scalp. He also thickly Vaselined my neck, ears and forehead. "When I get to washing out your head, be sure to tell me anywhere you feel any little stinging," Shorty warned me, washing

his hands, then pulling on the rubber gloves, and tying on his own rubber apron. "You always got to remember that any congolene left in burns a sore into your head."

8   The congolene just felt warm when Shorty started combing it in. But then my head caught fire.

9   I gritted my teeth and tried to pull the sides of the kitchen table together. The comb felt as if it was raking my skin off.

10   My eyes watered, my nose was running. I couldn't stand it any longer; I bolted to the washbasin. I was cursing Shorty with every name I could think of when he got the spray going and started soap-lathering my head.

11   He lathered and spray-rinsed, lathered and spray-rinsed, maybe ten or twelve times, each time gradually closing the hot-water faucet, until the rinse was cold, and that helped some.

12   "You feel any stinging spots?"

13   "No," I managed to say. My knees were trembling.

14   "Sit back down, then. I think we got it all out okay."

15   The flame came back as Shorty, with a thick towel, started drying my head, rubbing hard. *"Easy, man, easy!"* I kept shouting.

16   "The first time's always worst. You get used to it better before long. You took it real good, homeboy. You got a good conk."

17   When Shorty let me stand up and see in the mirror, my hair hung down in limp, damp strings. My scalp still flamed, but not as badly; I could bear it. He draped the towel around my shoulders, over my rubber apron, and began again Vaselining my hair.

18   I could feel him combing, straight back, first the big comb, then the fine-tooth one.

19   Then, he was using a razor, very delicately, on the back of my neck. Then finally, shaping the sideburns.

20   My first view in the mirror blotted out the hurting. I'd seen some pretty conks, but when it's the first time, on your own head, the transformation, after the lifetime of kinks, is staggering.

21   The mirror reflected Shorty behind me. We both were grinning and on top of my head was this thick, smooth sheen of shining red hair—real red—as straight as any white man's.

22   How ridiculous I was! Stupid enough to stand there simply lost in admiration of my hair now looking "white," reflected in the mirror in Shorty's room. I vowed that I'd never again be without a conk, and I never was for many years.

23   This was my first really big step toward self-degradation: when I endured all of that pain, literally burning my flesh to have it look like a white man's hair. I had joined that multitude of Negro men and women in America who are brainwashed into believing that the black people are "inferior"—and white people "superior"—that they will even violate and mutilate their God-created bodies to try to look "pretty" by white standards.

24   Look around today, in every small town and big city, from two-bit catfish and soda-pop joints into the "integrated" lobby of the Waldorf-Astoria, and you'll see conks on black men. And you'll see black women wearing these green and pink and purple and red and platinum-blonde wigs. They're all more ridiculous than a

slapstick comedy. It makes you wonder if the Negro has completely lost his sense of identity, lost touch with himself.

25   You'll see the conk worn by many, many so-called "upper class" Negroes, and, as much as I hate to say it about them, on all too many Negro entertainers. One of the reasons that I've especially admired some of them, like Lionel Hampton and Sidney Poitier, among others, is that they have kept their natural hair and fought to the top. I admire any Negro man who has never had himself conked, or who has had the sense to get rid of it—as I finally did.

26   I don't know which kind of self-defacing conk is the greater shame—the one you'll see on the heads of the black so-called "middle class" and "upper class," who ought to know better, or the one you'll see on the heads of the poorest, most down-trodden, ignorant black men. I mean the legal-minimum-wage ghetto-dwelling kind of Negro, as I was when I got my first one. It's generally among these poor fools that you'll see a black kerchief over the man's head, like Aunt Jemima; he's trying to make his conk last longer, between trips to the barbershop. Only for special occasions is this kerchief-protected conk exposed—to show off how "sharp" and "hip" its owner is. The ironic thing is that I have never heard any woman, white or black, express any admiration for a conk. Of course, any white woman with a black man isn't thinking about his hair. But I don't see how on earth a black woman with any race pride could walk down the street with any black man wearing a conk—the emblem of his shame that he is black.

27   To my own shame, when I say all of this I'm talking first of all about myself—because you can't show me any Negro who ever conked more faithfully than I did. I'm speaking from personal experience when I say of any black man who conks today, or any white-wigged black woman, that if they gave the brains in their heads just half as much attention as they do their hair, they would be a thousand times better off.

UNDERSTANDING CONTEXT

1. What motivated black people to endure the painful "conking" process?
2. Why does Malcolm X see the conk as an "emblem of shame"?
3. Why is Malcolm X especially disturbed by the sight of conks worn by middle-class and professional African Americans?
4. *Critical thinking:* A century ago, Jewish immigrants were urged, often by American Jews, to shave their beards and discard traditional garments in order to succeed in the New World. Are these changes harmless adaptations to a new culture or do they represent a form of self-loathing? Do you see current examples of men and women altering their identity?

EVALUATING STRATEGY

1. Malcolm X begins the essay with a story, told without any commentary. Do you find it effective to explain the process, then discuss its social significance?
2. How does Malcolm X use dialogue to bring the narrative to life?

3. *Other modes:* Can you consider this essay a blend of process, example, and argument? What parts do these elements play in the essay?

4. *Critical thinking:* Social critics generally comment on social behavior from a distance. How does the story of his own conking give Malcolm X greater insight into black self-degradation? Without introducing his own experiences, what effect would the last four paragraphs have?

APPRECIATING LANGUAGE

1. What language does Malcolm X use to dramatize the pain of being conked?

2. At one point, Malcolm X states he was "brainwashed." Why is this a key term? How did popular culture "brainwash" generations of African Americans to admire "whiteness" and despise black identity?

3. Malcolm X uses the word *shame* repeatedly. How do you define *shame*?

WRITING SUGGESTIONS

1. Write a short essay about a process you have experienced—getting your ears pierced, applying for a loan, trying out for a team, auditioning for a part. First describe the process; then comment on what you learned about yourself and society.

2. *Collaborative writing:* Discuss the last sentence of the essay with a number of students. Do many people—of all races—devote more attention to their hair than their brains? Write a list of examples showing how people seek to alter their appearance to achieve a new identity.

WRITING BEYOND THE CLASSROOM

As you read these instructions about conducting a self-assessment, determine whether you would find them easy to follow. Are they clearly organized and do they provide enough detail?

STEIN AND GIOTTA ASSOCIATES

Conducting a self-assessment

Transitioning to a new career after losing a job can be stressful. You may feel bitter, confused, and anxious. Stein and Giotta specializes in helping displaced professionals find new and rewarding employment opportunities. Before meeting with your assigned consultant, follow these guidelines to identify your strengths and weaknesses. The more you know about yourself, the better prepared you will be to benefit from our services.

1. **Examine your work history and ask yourself these two questions:**
   What three things did I like about my past jobs?
   What three things did I hate?

2. **Identify your strengths and weaknesses:**
   List three of your greatest strengths or abilities.
   List three of your greatest problems or weaknesses.

3. **Create a priority list of the following items you want in a new career. Think carefully and add comments about each one.**
   a. income
   b. job security
   c. the ability to work independently
   d. chance for advancement
   e. personal satisfaction
   f. opportunity to learn new skills
   g. pension and benefits
   h. status

4. **Write a paragraph describing your ideal job.**

5. **List five things you will have to accomplish to get this job.**

UNDERSTANDING CONTEXT

1. What questions should applicants ask themselves about their past jobs?
2. What items should applicants prioritize in considering their future careers?
3. *Critical thinking:* The last question asks applicants to list things they will have to do to get their ideal job. Is it useful to ask people to identify these tasks themselves rather than tell them what to do? Do people have to take charge of their own job search even when they seek professional assistance? Why or why not?

EVALUATING STRATEGY

1. Why are numbered points useful in giving these directions?
2. How does asking questions engage readers? Does it force them to take responsibility for their success?

APPRECIATING LANGUAGE

1. What does the level of diction and word choice reveal about the intended audience?
2. Do the authors successfully avoid overly technical language that some readers would find difficult?

WRITING SUGGESTIONS

1. Write your own self-assessment, identifying your strengths and weaknesses, what is important to you in a job, and what you will have to accomplish to get your ideal job.
2. *Collaborative writing:* Using this document as a model, work with a group of students and create an academic self-assessment to help students identify their strengths and weaknesses and what it will take to succeed in college.

RESPONDING TO IMAGES

Image by © Joseph Sohm; Visions of America/CORBIS

1. What is your immediate reaction to this photograph? Are you registered to vote? How many times have you voted? If not, why not?

2. In recent elections as many as half the eligible voters did not cast ballots. Why do people fail to vote?

3. Do you think negative campaign tactics and the emphasis on fund-raising alienates voters? If elections were based on reasonable debates instead of attack ads would more people take an interest in politics?

4. *Critical thinking:* Do you think the voting process could be streamlined? Should citizens be able to vote online? Do people mistrust the accuracy and security of voting machines? Should the nation have a uniform method of voting that is reliable and verifiable? Why or why not?

5. *Visual analysis:* What impression does the informal style of the banner create? Does it look amateurish or inviting? Why the exclamation point?

6. *Collaborative writing:* Discuss this photograph with a group of students. Ask each student if they know people who do not or refuse to vote. Write a list of suggestions that would encourage more people, especially young people, to vote.

(Continued)

RESPONDING TO IMAGES

7. *Other modes:*
- Write a brief *narrative* essay describing the first time you voted or decided not to vote. What led you to act the way you did?
- *Contrast* the way you think political campaigns and voting should be carried out and the way they occur in reality. Organize your views subject by subject or point by point to prevent confusion.
- Write a short essay that uses an *example* of a recent incident or scandal that has led people to question the political process.
- Write a *persuasive* essay calling for a change in the way the political parties select presidential nominees.

PROCESS CHECKLIST

Before submitting your paper, review these points:

✔ Is the process clearly defined?

✔ Do you supply background information that readers need?

✔ Is the information easy to follow? Is the chain of events or the sequence of steps logically arranged?

✔ Could the text be enhanced by large print, bold or italic type, diagrams, or charts?

✔ Are your instructions complete? Do readers know when one step is over and another begins?

✔ Do your instructions alert readers to normal changes that they might mistake for errors?

✔ Are hazards clearly stated?

✔ Did you use peer review to test your document?

 Access the English CourseMate for this text at **www.cengagebrain.com** for additional information about process writing.

Division and Classification
Separating into Parts and Rating Categories

What Are Division and Classification?

Division separates a subject into parts; **classification** rates subjects on a scale. Both are used to make complex subjects easier to understand and help in decision making. Poorly written division and classification, however, can misinform and mislead readers. Division and classification can be based on official and objective designations established by researchers, government agencies, corporations, organizations, or experts. They can also be created by individuals to express personal observations and opinions.

Division

If you enter a hospital, you will probably see signs directing you to different departments, for example, cardiology, radiology, psychiatry, and pediatrics. Universities consist of separate colleges, such as business and liberal arts. American literature can be divided into courses by historical era (nineteenth- and twentieth-century writers), by genre (poetry, fiction, and drama), or by special interest (women's literature, black literature, and science fiction). Discount stores organize products into housewares, clothing, linens, and other departments. Corporations place personnel into different divisions, such as design, production, maintenance, marketing, sales, and accounting. If you call your cable company's 800 number, a recorded voice may direct you to press one number for billing and another for technical support.

Division makes complicated subjects easier to comprehend and work with. The human body is overwhelmingly intricate. In order to understand how it functions, medical disciplines divide it into systems: digestive, respiratory, nervous, musculoskeletal, reproductive, and others. By studying individual systems, medical students come to a fuller understanding of how the whole body operates. Crime is such a vast social problem that writers discuss it in terms of traditional divisions—robbery, car theft, homicide, fraud, and so on—or invent their own categories, dividing crime by causes: power, greed, identity, and revenge.

The website Depression-help-resource.com, for instance, uses division to explain widely accepted types of depression:

Maria Toutoudaki/jupiterimages

Sam Diephuis/jupiterimages

Post Partum Depression—Major depressive episode that occurs after having a baby. Depressive symptoms usually begin within four weeks of giving birth and can vary in intensity and duration.

Seasonal Affective Disorder (SAD)—A type of depressive disorder which is characterized by episodes of major depression which reoccur at a specific time of year (e.g., fall, winter). In the past two years, depressive periods occur at least two times without any episodes that occur at a different time.

Anxiety Depression—Not an official depression type (as defined by the DSM). However, anxiety often also occurs with depression. In this case, a depressed individual may also experience anxiety symptoms (e.g. panic attacks) or an anxiety disorder (e.g., PTSD, panic disorder, social phobia, generalized anxiety disorder).

In this case division presents readers with a series of definitions. Division can be used to organize a set of narratives, descriptions, processes, or persuasive arguments.

WRITING ACTIVITY

Select one of the following topics and divide it into subtopics. You can use an existing division or invent one of your own.

1. Customers you encountered in a recent job

2. Tests students face in college

3. Student housing on or off campus

4. Blind dates

5. Jobs in a particular career

6. Diets

7. Television programs

8. Current movies

9. Cars

10. Popular night spots

Strategies for Writing Division

Critical Thinking and Prewriting

1. **Clearly define your subject.** If you do not initially limit the overall topic, you will find it difficult to break it down into parts.

2. **Determine whether your division is official or personal.** Are you using a method established by others or creating one of your own?

3. **Avoid oversimplifying your subject.** You have no doubt seen magazine articles announcing three kinds of bosses, four types of marriages, or five methods of child rearing. Writers often invent descriptive or humorous labels, warning you to avoid the "toxic controller" or advising you how to negotiate with the "whiny wimp." Although these divisions can be amusing and insightful, they can trivialize or oversimplify a subject. Not all people or situations can neatly fit into three or four types.

Planning

1. **Write a clear thesis statement or definition at the top of the page to guide planning.**

2. **Select a division method that includes all parts of the whole.** If you divide college students into three types, for example, make sure everyone on campus can be included in one group. Eliminate potential gaps. You cannot simply divide students into Protestants, Catholics, and Jews if some are Muslims or agnostics. Acknowledge exceptions.

3. **Make sure individual parts fit only one category.** If you were to divide businesses by location—north, south, east, and west—how would you address a company with operations on both coasts? If items can fit in more than a single category, your method of division may not suit your subject. It might be better to discuss businesses in terms of products, gross sales, or size rather than location.

4. **Indicate the size of each group.** If you state that students pay for college in three ways—by scholarships, loans, and personal savings—many readers will assume that a third of students pay their own way, when, in fact, they may constitute less than 1 percent of the whole. If you cannot supply precise percentages, indicate the group's general size: "The vast majority of students rely on loans, while only a very small minority are able to finance their education with personal savings."

5. **Explain possible exceptions and changes.** You may have to explain that it is possible for an item to belong to more than one category at a time or change categories:

   > Some students use more than one method to pay for college. They may have enough scholarship money to cover their first year or two, rely on personal savings to finance a few semesters, then borrow to pay for the rest.

(Continued)

6. **Avoid creating categories that include too many differences.** Not all items within a category are going to be identical, but to make sense a division should have a focus. If you were examining people in different age groups, it would be logical to write about people in their twenties, thirties, forties, and fifties. But a category of those in their sixties would include both working and retired people, those still paying into Social Security and those receiving benefits. It might be more accurate to subdivide this group into those from sixty to sixty-five, and those sixty-six to seventy.

7. **Determine what other modes you will use.** A division essay is usually a collection of related narratives, definitions, arguments, examples, processes, or descriptions. Study your subject and select the best method of addressing each subtopic.

8. **Develop an outline that clearly divides your topic to guide the first draft.**

Writing the First Draft

1. **Focus your writing by clearly envisioning your purpose.** Divisions should help explain a subject and make it easier to work with.

2. **Follow guidelines for writing other modes—definition, narrative, example, process, and so forth—in developing each category.**

3. **Use parallel structures to develop categories.** Readers will find your categories easier to follow if you provide a common pattern of development. In discussing three types of cities, you might discuss size, population, major industry, climate, and social life, in that order.
   - Readers must be able to compare common points of each subject to understand their similarities and differences.

4. **Monitor the length of your draft.** Because of their complexity, division papers can become lengthy. If you realize that your subject is too ambitious and would take ten pages to fully address a topic selected for a 500-word essay, you may wish to return to prewriting to narrow your topic or select a different subject.

5. **Be open to new ideas but remain focused.** As you write, new ideas may occur to you. You may add new categories, expand discussion, or restrict your thesis—but avoid going off topic.

Revising

1. **Examine your thesis and overall draft.**
   - Is the thesis clearly stated? Is your purpose clear? Does the essay help readers understand a complex subject or only confuse the issue?
   - Does your method of division make sense? Does it draw meaningful or only arbitrary distinctions between items?

2. **Review the essay for balance and thoroughness.**
   - Do some sections need expansion and others trimming?

3. **Analyze the essay for parallel development.**
   - Do you follow a general pattern to discuss each item so that readers can easily compare them, or are the subtopics presented in a jumbled manner that mixes narratives, definitions, and examples without a common thread?
4. **Are the divisions clearly defined?**
   - Can some items be placed in more than one division?
5. **Do the divisions account for every part of the whole?**
   - Are there any items left over that do not fit any of your categories?
6. **Do you explain possible exceptions?**
7. **Use peer review.**
   - Ask others to review your essay for clarity and completeness.

Editing and Proofreading

1. **Review word choice for accuracy and connotations.**
   - Are your subheadings meaningful and easy to remember?
   - Do some words have connotations that may mislead readers?
   - Do technical terms require definition or qualification?
2. **Read your paper aloud to identify errors.**
3. **Use peer editing to locate errors you may have missed.**

Classification

Like division, classification breaks a complex subject into parts. But for classification, the categories are ranked or rated according to a single standard. Teachers grade tests A, B, C, D, or F according to the number of correct answers. Car insurance companies set prices based on drivers' ages, past accidents, and the value of their vehicles. Fire departments rank fires as one, two, three, four, or five alarms to determine how much equipment to send. Prisons are classified minimum, medium, and maximum security. During the football season, teams are ranked by their wins and losses.

Classification helps people to make decisions and to direct actions. Classifications can set prices, establish salaries, and in some cases save lives. The importance of classification is demonstrated by the use of triage in emergency medicine. When a hospital is flooded with accident victims, doctors place patients into three categories: those who will die with or without immediate medical attention, those who will survive without emergency care, and those who will survive only if treated without delay. The last group is given priority to ensure that doctors do not waste time on the dying or those with minor injuries.

Like division, classification can be objective and official or personal. The movie listings in a newspaper may display a number of stars next to an R-rated film. The R rating, officially established by the MPAA (see page 421), is an official classification that will appear in every newspaper listing, television commercial, theater trailer, poster, and website. The number of stars, however, will vary with each newspaper, reflecting the personal opinion of a local critic.

The National Weather Service, for example, uses the Saffir-Simpson Hurricane Wind Scale measuring sustained wind speeds of one minute to officially rank hurricanes in five clearly defined categories:

Category 1 (74–95 mph) *Very dangerous winds will produce some damage.* Large branches of trees will snap and shallow-rooted trees can be toppled.

Category 2 (96–110 mph) *Extremely dangerous winds will cause extensive damage.* Many shallowly rooted trees will be snapped or uprooted and block numerous roads.

Category 3 (111–130 mph) *Devastating damage will occur.* Many trees will be snapped or uprooted, blocking numerous roads.

Category 4 (131–155 mph) *Catastrophic damage will occur.* Most trees will be snapped or uprooted and power poles downed. Fallen trees and power poles will isolate residential areas.

Category 5 (over 155 mph) *Catastrophic damage will occur.* Nearly all trees will be snapped or uprooted and power poles downed. Fallen trees and power poles will isolate residential areas.

In contrast, James Austin (page 403) uses classification to explain his personal view that there are four levels of chance or luck, ranging from "pure blind luck" that benefits anyone to "luck that is peculiar to one person."

WRITING ACTIVITY

Select one of the following topics and develop at least three classifications. Remember to use a single standard to rate the topic, such as price, quality, size, performance, or severity.

1. Home security systems
2. Professional athletes or teams
3. Local restaurants
4. College professors
5. Investments
6. Job security
7. Drug use
8. Friendships
9. Facebook pages
10. Courses in your major

Strategies for Writing Classification

Critical Thinking and Prewriting

1. **Avoid confusing classification with division.** Remember classification does not just separate a subject into types or parts, but rates them on a scale.

2. **Determine whether your classification is official or personal.** Are you using a scale established by others or creating one of your own?

3. **To focus prewriting, start with a scale.** Because classification rates subjects on a standard, you can easily identify workable subjects and discard unusable ones if you work with a scale. You might develop a generic chart to explore topics, using one to five stars, an A–F grading system, or a 1–10 scale to rate your topics.

Planning

1. **Establish a clearly defined standard of measurement.** If you plan to classify cars by price, determine whether you are going to use wholesale or dealer prices. If you rate cars by resale value, establish the methods used to obtain your figures.

2. **Do not mix standards.** The most common mistake writers make in classification is mixing standards. You can classify cars by price, engine performance, reliability, or safety—but you can't write a paper about cars that discusses one as being safe, another as being expensive, and another as being easy to maintain.

3. **Define each category clearly.** To successfully teach writing, for example, an English professor must provide students with a clear understanding of what distinguishes an A paper from a B paper. Even if you are making up your own categories, each one should be clearly defined so readers can understand what separates each classification.

4. **Arrange categories in order.** Organize the categories so they follow a ladder-like progression, such as judging items from the best to the worst, the cheapest to most expensive, or the newest to the oldest.

5. **Provide enough categories or classes to include all parts of the whole.** If you classify cars as being either American or foreign-made, how would you account for Toyotas produced in the United States or Chryslers assembled in Mexico?

6. **Make sure all topics fit only one class.** Every unit should fit only a single category. Make sure you have no leftover items that either can fit in more than one class or cannot be accounted for.

7. **Note any exceptions or variations to the classification.**

Writing the First Draft

1. **As you write, keep your goal in mind—to rate items on a scale.**

2. **Use concrete language and details to distinguish each class and describe each item.** Avoid vague or general descriptions. Be as accurate as you can in defining standards.

(Continued)

3. **Illustrate each class with examples readers can identify.** Consider your audience carefully to select items they will understand. If you rate films, refer to movies your readers will recognize.

4. **Use parallel structures to develop categories.** Develop common reference points so that readers can distinguish between categories and compare examples.

5. **Monitor the length of your draft.** As with division, a classification paper can easily balloon into a much longer essay. If you realize that to fully classify your subject, your essay will expand beyond the scope of the assignment, consider narrowing your topic or selecting a new subject.

6. **Note new ideas, but remember your goal—to rate items on a common scale.**

Revising

1. **Analyze your thesis.**
   - Is your overall subject clearly defined?

2. **Review your method of classification.**
   - Does your classification make meaningful or only arbitrary distinctions between items? Will your scale help people understand the subject and make decisions?
   - Are your categories clearly defined?
   - Are there any gaps between categories? Do categories overlap?
   - Are the categories arranged in a progressive order, moving from small to large, cheap to costly, worst to best, or strongest to weakest?

3. **Examine the categories for balance and completeness.**
   - Are some categories sharply defined and others vaguely worded?
   - Are some categories illustrated with several examples and others with just one?

4. **Can all items or parts be placed on your scale? Do you account for variations or exceptions?**

5. **Use peer review to identify areas needing improvement.**

Editing and Proofreading

1. **Read your paper aloud.**
   - Is your paper stated in concrete, accurate language?
   - Do any terms require further clarification or definition?
   - Do some words have connotations that may confuse readers?

2. **Consider using visual aids.**
   - Would your classification be easier to understand and recall if the text were supported by a chart, graph, or grid?

3. **Use peer editing to locate errors you may have missed.**

Using Division and Classification

Writers often use both division and classification to make decisions and explain ideas or actions. A travel guide might divide local restaurants by type—seafood, steak, Italian, or Mexican—and then classify them by quality or price range. A financial planner could present clients with different types of investments—stocks, bonds, and mutual funds–and then classify each by risk or rate of return. A first aid manual might use division to explain the different causes of burns—contact with heat, radiation, chemicals, or electricity—and then use classification to rank them first, second, or third degree based on their severity. In answering a 911 call, a dispatcher uses division to determine whether the emergency requires a police, fire department, or ambulance response. With further information, he or she uses classification to measure the size or severity of the emergency, to determine how many police officers or paramedics to send.

STUDENT PAPER

This paper was written in response to the following assignment:

> Write a 500-word paper using division or classification to discuss a current social or political issue. Remember, to create clearly defined categories and explain possible exceptions.

FIRST DRAFT WITH INSTRUCTOR'S COMMENTS

Sandra Loman   English 200

Entitlements

weak intro
Entitlements are going to be a major issue for years. They are going to dominate politics for
                                        affect
years. How we deal with them is going to <u>effect</u> the economy, taxes, and jobs for years to

come. We are going hear about them for a long time, but how many Americans even know
                        pronoun?
what an "entitlement" is and why <u>they</u> are important?
        wordy
      The oldest entitlement we have is Social Security. It got started in the Depression of the

1930s. Everyone knows this program because we all have a Social Security number. It is a
wordy
<u>program not in that much bad shape like the others.</u> People pay a lot into the program, but

(Continued)

it is paying out more than it collects. By 2037 it is expected to run out. Next is Medicare that

provides medical care for the old. This program is rapidly expanding for two major reasons.

and

More people are getting old,^ they are living longer. Also, all the innovations in drugs and

run-on

surgery that keep old people going are costing more and more each year. *informal*

wordy

Medicaid is another entitlement that is costing more and more for a whole number of

reasons. It provides health care for low-income people.

Health care is getting more expensive. Plus, in the recent deep recession, more peo-

ple were eligible because they lost their jobs.

Put together these three programs consume a large part of the federal budget. As the

population of old people grows, these programs take on a life of their own, getting big-

ger and bigger. As a result the government has to tax more, borrow more, or spend less on

everything else. The government made promises with these entitlements, and they seem

sacred. But they are getting so expensive a lot of people, even liberals who fought hard to

create these programs, are wondering how to pay for them. *run-on*

Entitlements are hard for politicians to debate without controversy. The moment any-

pronoun?

one talks about changes, it sounds like they want to punish the poor and the old, the most

vulnerable people in our country, people who really need help. People expect these pro-

weak

grams to be there. Members of their families probably get benefits every month.

But at the same time, they get upset when they see how much the government takes out of

their paycheck*S* every week.

It is going to take strong leadership to address this growing problem and come up with a fair solution. We are going to hear the word "entitlement" for a very long time.

REVISION NOTES

* Significant topic.

* Before discussing entitlements, you need to provide a clear definition of them.

* This is the type of topic that requires outside sources. Provide specific numbers to demonstrate to readers the importance of your topic. Remember to document sources.

* Edit sentences for clarity. Revise vague and awkward phrases.

REVISED DRAFT

Sandra Loman   English 200

Entitlements: The Big Three

Political debates, talk shows, and blogs are increasingly dominated by a single word— "entitlements." Many Americans, however, are confused about what entitlements are and why they are so important.

In his *Handbook of American Government,* Erick Rosen defines entitlements as "federal programs that distribute payments based on fixed formulas to citizens who meet certain criteria, such as the disabled, the poor, or the elderly" (271). Unlike programs like defense or NASA, entitlements do not require annual congressional appropriations. As more people meet the criteria, by turning 65, for example, the more money the government automatically pays out.

Three large entitlement programs consume 41% of the 2010 federal budget and are expected to grow dramatically:

Social Security ($708 billion)

Founded in 1935 as a pension program for seniors, Social Security was expanded in 1956 to provide benefits for the disabled. Social Security is funded by a payroll tax of 6.2%, which is matched by employers, so that someone making $100,000 a year is contributing $12,400

(Continued)

to the program. Today 52 million people—one in six Americans—receive monthly Social Security payments. In the next generation, the population of retirees will almost double. Under the current formulas, Social Security will begin paying out more than it collects in payroll taxes by 2015 (Mandel 46).

Medicare ($468 billion)

Created in 1965, Medicare provides health care coverage for Americans over 65, people with certain disabilities, and everyone with "end stage renal disease" (Lech 17). Like Social Security, Medicare is funded by a payroll tax of 1.45%, which is matched by employers, so the person making $100,000 a year is contributing $2,900 to the program. The number of Americans entitled to receive Medicare will grow from 47 million in 2010 to 80 million in 2030 (Lech 19).

Medicaid ($285 billion)

Medicaid was established in 1965 to provide health care coverage for low-income individuals and families. Unlike Medicare, it is funded by both the federal and state governments, with the federal government paying about 57% of the expenses. Currently two-thirds of nursing home residents and one-third of childbirths qualify for Medicaid payments. In 2008 nearly 50 million people were eligible to receive Medicaid benefits. With the nursing home population expected to rise with the aging Baby Boom generation, expenses are predicted to increase significantly over the next twenty years ("Medicaid").

In 2010 these entitlements totaled $1.4 trillion. Under the current formulas, expenses are expected to grow rapidly in the future. Nancy Kwan, a budget specialist for a Congressional study group, predicts that health care entitlements alone will "increase from 4% of our GDP in 2007 to 12% in 2050." Her analysis shows that "expenses are increasing not just because the number of people becoming eligible for Medicare and Medicaid is growing but because of rising costs per patient."

The burden for taxpayers will also grow. In 1955, Kwan noted, there were nine workers paying into Social Security for every retiree collecting benefits. Now the ratio is 3.9 workers for every retiree. By 2030 that number will drop to 2.4.

Candidates running for office are reluctant to discuss either raising taxes or cutting benefits, but the numbers are getting harder to ignore. It is going to take strong leadership to address this growing problem and come up with fair solutions. We are going to hear the word "entitlement" for a very long time.

Works Cited

Kwan, Nancy. Interview by Joe Scarborough. *Morning Joe*. MSNBC. 9 Feb. 2011. Television.

Lech, Albert. "Budget Realities." *Federal Forum*. Sep. 2011: 15–29. Print.

Mandel, Rachel. "Social Security." *American Dimensions*. Oct. 2011: 35–53. Print.

"Medicaid." *CNN.com*. Cable News Network, 21 Oct. 2011. Web. 25 Oct. 2011.

Rosen, Erik. *Handbook of American Government*. New York: Scribners, 2011. Print.

QUESTIONS FOR REVIEW AND REVISION

1. What's the student's thesis?
2. How does the student define her standard of measurement?
3. What value does this division have in explaining her subject?
4. Is each entitlement clearly defined?
5. How effectively does the student use outside sources? Are they clearly and smoothly integrated into her text?
6. Is the paper properly documented using MLA guidelines (see pages xxx–xxx)?
7. Read the essay aloud. Can you detect weak or awkward passages that need revision?
8. How effectively did the student follow the instructor's suggestions?

WRITING SUGGESTIONS

1. Using this paper as a model, write a similar division paper that breaks down a topic into parts or types. You might divide a football team into offense, defense, and special teams or explain different products or services provided by a local business.
2. *Collaborative writing:* Discuss this essay with other students. Do they think that their peers appreciate the impact entitlement programs will have on their future? Write a classification paper ranking levels of awareness of the issue.

Suggested Topics for Writing Division and Classification

General Assignments

Separating into Parts

Write a division essay on any of the following topics. Your division may make use of standard categories or ones you invent. Remember to clearly state the way you are dividing your subject. Each subject or example should be supported with definitions, brief narratives, or descriptions.

- Dates you have had
- Basketball, football, or baseball teams
- Career opportunities in your field
- Popular music
- Student housing
- Computer systems you have worked with
- Charitable organizations
- Women's groups
- Local restaurants

Rating Categories

Write a classification essay on any of the following topics. Make sure to use a single method rating the subtopics from best to worst, easiest to hardest, least desirable to most desirable, or least expensive to most expensive.

- Jobs you have had
- Diets
- Talk shows
- Current movies
- Professors, coaches, or bosses you have known
- Football teams
- Cars
- Websites
- Hotels

Writing in Context

1. Assume you have been asked by a national magazine to write about students' political attitudes. You may develop your essay by division or classification. You can discuss politics in general terms of liberal and conservative attitudes or concentrate on a single issue, such as capital punishment or legalizing marijuana.
2. Write a humorous paper about campus fashion by dividing students into types. Invent titles or labels for each group and supply enough details so that readers can readily fit the people they meet into one of your categories.

Strategies for Reading Division and Classification

As you read the division and classification entries in this chapter, keep these questions in mind.

Context

1. What is the writer trying to explain by dividing or classifying the subject? Does the writer have another goal—to inform, entertain, or persuade?
2. Do the divisions risk oversimplifying the subject?
3. Do the classification essays have a clearly defined scale or standard?
4. Do the standards seem fair or adequate? Do they accurately measure what they claim to evaluate?

Strategy

1. How does the writer introduce or establish the divisions or classes?
2. How does the author illustrate each type with other modes such as *example, definition,* or *narrative*?

3. Does the writer use an existing, long-established standard or one he or she invented?
4. Is the goal of the paper to explain items or recommend one over others?

Language

1. What does the level of language reveal about the intended audience?
2. What words does the author use to describe or define categories? Do the connotations of any of these words reveal positive or negative attitudes toward specific items? Do you detect a bias?

READING TO LEARN

As you read the division and classification essays in this chapter, note techniques you can use in your own writing.

■ **"Friends, Good Friends—and Such Good Friends" by Judith Viorst** uses division to describe seven types of friends.

■ **"Four Kinds of Chance" by James Austin** classifies levels of chance or luck from the most obvious to the most obscure.

■ **"Ways of Meeting Oppression" by Martin Luther King** uses division to explain different ways people respond to oppression.

■ **"Death and Justice: How Capital Punishment Affirms Life" by Edward Koch** uses division to organize an argument for capital punishment by refuting seven common objections to the death penalty.

Judith Viorst

Judith Viorst (1936–) is best known for the columns she writes for *Redbook*. She has published several children's books, including *Alexander and the Terrible, Horrible, No Good, Very Bad Day* (1982) and *Sad Underwear and Other Complications* (1995). She has also written a number of collections of light verse, including *It's Hard to Be Hip Over Thirty and Other Tragedies of Modern Life* (1970), *How Did I Get to Be Forty and Other Atrocities* (1984), and *Suddenly Sixty and Other Shocks of Later Life* (2000). She has also published a novel, *Murdering Mr. Monti: A Merry Little Tale of Sex and Violence* (1994).

Friends, Good Friends—and Such Good Friends

Source: "Friends, Good Friends–and Such Good Friends" by Judith Viorst. Originally appeared in *Redbook* Magazine. Copyright © 1977 by Judith Viorst. By permission.

Before reading this essay, consider the friends you have had in your life. Do they belong to different types? Were school friends different from neighborhood friends or friends you have met through relatives?

<table>
<tr><td>Introduction
Definition of
"friend"</td><td>1</td><td>Women are friends, I once would have said, when they totally love and support and trust each other, and bare to each other the secrets of their souls, and run—no questions asked—to help each other, and tell harsh truths to each other (no, you can't wear that dress unless you lose ten pounds first) when harsh truths must be told.</td></tr>
<tr><td></td><td>2</td><td>Women are friends, I once would have said, when they share the same affection for Ingmar Bergman, plus train rides, cats, warm rain, charades, Camus, and hate with equal ardor Newark and Brussels sprouts and Lawrence Welk and camping.</td></tr>
<tr><td>division into
types</td><td>3</td><td>In other words, I once would have said that a friend is a friend all the way, but now I believe that's a narrow point of view. For the friendships I have and the friendships I see are conducted at many levels of intensity, serve many different functions, meet different needs, and range from those as all-the-way as the friendship of the soul sisters mentioned above to that of the most nonchalant and casual playmates.</td></tr>
<tr><td></td><td>4</td><td>Consider these varieties of friendship:</td></tr>
<tr><td>type #1
examples</td><td>5</td><td>1. Convenience friends. These are women with whom, if our paths weren't crossing all the time, we'd have no particular reason to be friends: a next-door neighbor, a woman in our car pool, the mother of one of our children's closest friends, or maybe some mommy with whom we serve juice and cookies each week at the Glenwood Co-op Nursery.</td></tr>
<tr><td></td><td>6</td><td>Convenience friends are convenient indeed. They'll lend us their cups and silverware for a party. They'll drive our kids to soccer when we're sick. They'll take us to pick up our car when we need a lift to the garage. They'll even take our cats when we go on vacation. As we will for them.</td></tr>
<tr><td></td><td>7</td><td>But we don't, with convenience friends, ever come too close or tell too much; we maintain our public face and emotional distance. "Which means," says Elaine, "that I'll talk about being overweight but not about being depressed. Which means I'll admit being mad but not blind with rage. Which means that I might say that we're pinched this month but never that I'm worried sick over money."</td></tr>
</table>

Sam Diephuis/jupiterimages

8   But which doesn't mean that there isn't sufficient value to be found in these friendships of mutual aid, in convenience friends.

9   2. <u>Special-interest friends.</u> These friendships aren't intimate, and they needn't involve kids or silverware or cats. Their value lies in some interest jointly shared. And so we may have an office friend or a yoga friend or a tennis friend or a friend from the Women's Democratic Club. *(type #2 examples)*

10   "I've got one woman friend," says Joyce, "who likes, as I do, to take psychology courses. Which makes it nice for me—and nice for her. It's fun to go with someone you know and it's fun to discuss what you've learned, driving back from the classes." And for the most part, she says, that's all they discuss.

11   "I'd say that what we're doing is *doing* together, not being together," Suzanne says of her Tuesday-doubles friends. "It's mainly a tennis relationship, but we play together well. And I guess we all need to have a couple of playmates."

12   I agree.

13   My playmate is a shopping friend, a woman of marvelous taste, a woman who knows exactly *where* to buy *what*, and furthermore is a woman who always knows beyond a doubt what one ought to be buying, I don't have the time to keep up with what's new in eyeshadow, hemlines and shoes, and whether the smock look is in or finished already. But since (oh, shame!) I care a lot about eyeshadow, hemlines, and shoes, and since I don't *want* to wear smocks if the smock look is finished, I'm very glad to have a shopping friend.

14   3. <u>Historical friends.</u> We all have a friend who knew us when . . . maybe way back in Miss Meltzer's second grade, when our family lived in that three-room flat in Brooklyn, when our dad was out of work for seven months, when our brother Allie got in that fight where they had to call the police, when our sister married the endodontist from Yonkers and when, the morning after we lost our virginity, she was the first, the only, friend we told. *(type #3 examples)*

15   The years have gone by and we've gone separate ways and we've little in common now, but we're still an intimate part of each other's past. And so whenever we go to Detroit we always go to visit this friend of our girlhood. Who knows how we looked before our teeth were straightened. Who knows how we talked before our voice got un-Brooklyned. Who knows what we ate before we learned about artichokes. And who, by her presence, puts us in touch with an earlier part of ourself, a part of ourself it's important never to lose.

16   "What this friend means to me and what I mean to her," says Grace, "is having a sister without sibling rivalry. We know the texture of each other's lives. She remembers my grandmother's cabbage soup. I remember the way her uncle played the piano. There's simply no other friend who remembers those things."

17   4. <u>Crossroads friends.</u> Like historical friends, our crossroads friends are important for *what was*—for the friendship we shared at a crucial, now past, time of life. A time, perhaps, when we roomed in college together; or worked as eager young singles in the Big City together; or went together, as my friend Elizabeth and I did, through pregnancy, birth, and that scary first year of new motherhood. *(type #4 examples)*

18   Crossroads friends forge powerful links, links strong enough to endure with not much more contact than once-a-year letters at Christmas. And out of respect for those crossroads years, for those dramas and dreams we once shared, we will always be friends.

type #5 examples

19   5. <u>Cross-generational friends.</u> Historical friends and crossroads friends seem to maintain a special kind of intimacy—dormant but always ready to be revived—and though we may rarely meet, whenever we do connect, it's personal and intense. Another kind of intimacy exists in the friendships that form across generations in what one woman calls her daughter-mother and her mother-daughter relationships.

20   Evelyn's friend is her mother's age—"but I share so much more than I ever could with my mother"—a woman she talks to of music, of books and of life. "What I get from her is the benefit of her experience. What she gets—and enjoys—from me is a youthful perspective. It's a pleasure for both of us."

21   I have in my own life a precious friend, a woman of 65 who has lived very hard, who is wise, who listens well; who has been where I am and can help me understand it; and who represents not only an ultimate ideal mother to me but also the person I'd like to be when I grow up.

22   In our daughter role we tend to do more than our share of self-revelation; in our mother role we tend to receive what's revealed. It's another kind of pleasure—playing wise mother to a questing younger person. It's another very lovely kind of friendship.

type #6 examples

23   6. <u>Part-of-a-couple friends.</u> Some of the women we call our friends we never see alone—we see them as part of a couple at couples' parties. And though we share interests in many things and respect each other's views, we aren't moved to deepen the relationship. Whatever the reason, a lack of time or—and this is more likely—a lack of chemistry, our friendship remains in the context of a group. But the fact that our feeling on seeing each other is always, "I'm so glad she's here" and the fact that we spend half the evening talking together says that this too, in its own way, counts as a friendship.

24   (Other part-of-a-couple friends are the friends that came with the marriage, and some of these are friends we could live without. But sometimes, alas, she married our husband's best friend; and sometimes, alas, she is our husband's best friend. And so we find ourself dealing with her, somewhat against our will, in a spirit of what I'll call *reluctant* friendship.)

type #7 examples

25   7. <u>Men who are friends.</u> I wanted to write just of women friends, but the women I've talked to won't let me—they say I must mention man-woman friendships too. For these friendships can be just as close and as dear as those that we form with women. Listen to Lucy's description of one such friendship:

26   "We've found we have things to talk about that are different from what he talks about with my husband and different from what I talk about with his wife. So sometimes we call on the phone or meet for lunch. There are similar intellectual interests—we always pass on to each other the books that we love—but there's also something tender and caring too."

27   In a couple of crises, Lucy says, "he offered himself for talking and for helping. And when someone died in his family he wanted me there. The sexual, flirty part of our friendship is very small, but *some*—just enough to make it fun and different."

She thinks—and I agree—that the sexual part, though small, is always *some*, is always there when a man and a woman are friends.

28   It's only in the past few years that I've made friends with men, in the sense of a friendship that's *mine*, not just part of two couples. And achieving with them the ease and the trust I've found with women friends has value indeed. Under the dryer at home last week, putting on mascara and rouge, I comfortably sat and talked with a fellow named Peter. Peter, I finally decided, could handle the shock of me minus mascara under the dryer. Because we care for each other. Because we're friends.

29   8. <u>There are medium friends, and pretty good friends, and very good friends indeed, and these friendships are defined by their level of intimacy.</u> And what we'll reveal at each of these levels of intimacy is calibrated with care. We might tell a medium friend, for example, that yesterday we had a fight with our husband. And we might tell a pretty good friend that this fight with our husband made us so mad that we slept on the couch. And we might tell a very good friend that the reason we got so mad in that fight that we slept on the couch had something to do with that girl who works in his office. But it's only to our very best friends that we're willing to tell all, to tell what's going on with that girl in his office.

[margin note: levels of friendship classified by intimacy]

30   The best of friends, I still believe, totally love and support and trust each other, and bare to each other the secrets of their souls, and run—no questions asked—to help each other, and tell harsh truths to each other when they must be told.

31   But we needn't agree about everything (only 12-year-old girl friends agree about *everything*) to tolerate each other's point of view. To accept without judgment. To give and to take without ever keeping score. And to *be* there, as I am for them and as they are for me, to comfort our sorrows, to celebrate our joys.

UNDERSTANDING CONTEXT

1. What was Viorst's original view of women friends? How did she define them?

2. How do convenience friends differ from special-interest friends? Are they both superficial relationships in many ways? Why or why not?

3. Viorst states that she did not want to include men in her article, but her female friends insisted that man–woman friendships should be included. Does this reflect a social change? Do you think women today have more friendships with men, especially in the workplace, than their mothers or grandmothers did?

4. *Critical thinking:* Viorst writes almost exclusively about female friendship. Do you think that men, too, have the same type of friends—convenience friends, special-interest friends, historical friends, and so on? Are male friendships different?

EVALUATING STRATEGY

1. Viorst divides friends into types rather than classifying them from best friends to acquaintances. Does her approach make more sense? Can friendships change? Can a convenience friend become over time your best friend?

2. Viorst mentions other women in her essay. Does this make her observations more effective? If she limited her commentary to only her friends, would the essay be as influential?

3. *Blending the modes:* Where does Viorst use *description* and *comparison* to develop her essay?

4. *Critical thinking:* Viorst wrote this essay in 1977. Since then has technology created new communities and new friendships? Should online friends be included?

APPRECIATING LANGUAGE

1. This essay first appeared in *Redbook*. Is there anything in her word choices or tone that indicate she was writing to a female audience?

2. Consider the words we use to describe people we include in our lives: *friend, acquaintance, colleague, partner, pal.* Do men and women define these words differently?

WRITING SUGGESTIONS

1. Write a short essay about the types of friendships you have developed. Have you maintained many friendships that began in childhood? Why or why not?

2. Write a classification essay categorizing people who only take from friends, those who share with friends, and those who only seem to give in relationships. Provide examples of each type.

3. *Collaborative writing:* Discuss Viorst's essay with a group of students. Do her comments seem to apply exclusively to women's friendships? Why or why not? Write a brief comparison paper contrasting the different ways men and women develop friendships. Is one gender more competitive? Do men or women seem to have or need more friends?

Dr. James Austin (1925–) graduated from Harvard Medical School and is a specialist in neurology. He devoted more than twenty years to research on the brain. While serving as professor and chairman of the Department of Neurology at the University of Colorado Medical School, he received the American Association of Neuropathologists Prize. Austin has also earned a reputation as a writer with an ability to make complicated scientific issues understandable to general readers.

Four Kinds of Chance

Source: "Four Kinds of Chance" from *Chase, Chance and Creativity: The Lucky Art of Novelty* by James Austin, pp. 70–77. Copyright © 2003 by Massachusetts Institute of Technology. By permission.

James Austin has written widely on the role of chance or luck in scientific discovery. In this article, written for the Saturday Review *(1974), he classifies the four kinds of chance that occur in scientific research. Luck, he explains, is not as simple as drawing a winning hand in poker. As you read the article, consider how many of the varieties of chance you have experienced.*

1 What is chance? Dictionaries define it as something fortuitous that happens unpredictably without discernable human intention. Chance is unintentional and capricious, but we needn't conclude that chance is immune from human intervention. Indeed, chance plays several distinct roles when humans react creatively with one another and with their environment.

2   We can readily distinguish four varieties of chance if we consider that they each involve a different kind of motor activity and a special kind of sensory receptivity. The varieties of chance also involve distinctive personality traits and differ in the way one particular individual influences them.

3   Chance I is the pure blind luck that comes with no effort on our part. If, for example, you are sitting at a bridge table of four, it's "in the cards" for you to receive a hand of all 13 spades, but it will come up only once in every 6.3 trillion deals. You will ultimately draw this lucky hand—with no intervention on your part—but it does involve a longer wait than most of us have time for.

4   Chance II evokes the kind of luck Charles Kettering had in mind when he said: "Keep on going and the chances are you will stumble on something, perhaps when you are least expecting it. I have never heard of anyone stumbling on something sitting down."

5   In the sense referred to here, Chance II is not passive, but springs from an energetic, generalized motor activity. A certain basal level of action "stirs up the pot," brings in random ideas that will collide and stick together in fresh combinations, lets chance operate. When someone, *anyone*, does swing into motion and keeps on going, he will increase the number of collisions between events. When a few events are linked together, they can then be exploited to have a fortuitous outcome, but many others, of course, cannot. Kettering was right. Press on. Something will turn up. We may term this the Kettering Principle.

6   In the two previous examples, a unique role of the individual person was either lacking or minimal. Accordingly, as we move on to Chance III, we see blind luck, but in camouflage. Chance presents the clue, the opportunity exists, but it would

be missed except by that one person uniquely equipped to observe it, visualize it conceptually, and fully grasp its significance. Chance III involves a special receptivity and discernment unique to the recipient. Louis Pasteur characterized it for all time when he said: "Chance favors only the prepared mind."

7   Pasteur himself had it in full measure. But the classic example of his principle occurred in 1928, when Alexander Fleming's mind instantly fused at least five elements into a conceptually unified nexus. His mental sequences went something like this: (1) I see that a mold has fallen by accident into my culture dish; (2) the staphylococcal colonies residing near it failed to grow; (3) the mold must have secreted something that killed the bacteria; (4) I recall a similar experience once before; (5) if I could separate this new "something" from the mold, it could be used to kill staphylococci that cause human infections.

8   Actually, Fleming's mind was exceptionally well prepared for the penicillin mold. Six years earlier, while he was suffering from a cold, his own nasal drippings had found their way into a culture dish, for reasons not made entirely clear. He noted that nearby bacteria were killed, and astutely followed up the lead. His observations led him to discover a bactericidal enzyme present in nasal mucus and tears, called lysozyme. Lysozyme proved too weak to be of medical use, but imagine how receptive Fleming's mind was to the penicillin mold when it later happened on the scene!

9   One word evokes the quality of the operations involved in the first three kinds of chance. It is *serendipity*. The term describes the facility for encountering unexpected good luck, as the result of: accident (Chance I), general exploratory behavior (Chance II), or sagacity (Chance III). The word itself was coined by the Englishman-of-letters Horace Walpole, in 1754. He used it with reference to the legendary tales of the Three Princes of Seren-dip (Ceylon), who quite unexpectedly encountered many instances of good fortune on their travels. In today's parlance, we have usually watered down *serendipity* to mean the good luck that comes solely by accident. We think of it as a result, not an ability. We have tended to lose sight of the element of sagacity, by which term Walpole wished to emphasize that some distinctive personal receptivity is involved.

10   There remains a fourth element in good luck, an unintentional but subtle personal prompting of it. The English Prime Minister Benjamin Disraeli summed up the principle underlying Chance IV when he noted that "we make our fortunes and we call them fate." Disraeli, a politician of considerable practical experience, appreciated that we each shape our own destiny, at least to some degree. One might restate the principle as follows: *Chance favors the individualized action.*

11   In Chance IV the kind of luck is peculiar to one person, and like a personal hobby, it takes on a distinctive individual flavor. This form of chance is oneman-made, and it is as personal as a signature. . . . Chance IV has an elusive, almost miragelike, quality. Like a mirage, it is difficult to get a firm grip on, for it tends to recede as we pursue it and advance as we step back. But we still accept a mirage when we see it, because we vaguely understand the basis for the phenomenon. A strongly heated layer of air, less dense than usual, lies next to the earth, and it bends the light rays as they pass through. The resulting image may be magnified as if by a telescopic lens in the atmosphere, and real objects, ordinarily hidden far out of sight over the horizon, are brought forward and revealed to the eye. What happens in a mirage then, and in this form of chance, not only appears farfetched but indeed is farfetched.

12   About a century ago, a striking example of Chance IV took place in the Spanish cave of Altamira.* There, one day in 1879, Don Marcelino de Sautuola was engaged in his hobby of archaeology, searching Altamira for bones and stones. With him was his daughter, Maria, who had asked him whether she could come along to the cave that day. The indulgent father had said she could. Naturally enough, he first looked where he had always found heavy objects before, on the *floor* of the cave. But Maria, unhampered by any such preconceptions, looked not only at the floor but also all around the cave with the open-eyed wonder of a child! She looked up, exclaimed, and then he looked up, to see incredible works of art on the cave ceiling! The magnificent colored bison and other animals they saw at Altamira, painted more than 15,000 years ago, might lead one to call it "the Sistine Chapel of Prehistory." Passionately pursuing his interest in archaeology, de Sautuola, to his surprise, discovered man's first paintings. In quest of science, he happened upon Art.

13   Yes, a dog did "discover" the cave, and the initial receptivity was his daughter's, but the pivotal reason for the cave paintings' discovery hinged on a long sequence of prior events originating in de Sautuola himself. For when we dig into the background of this amateur excavator, we find he was an exceptional person. Few Spaniards were out probing into caves 100 years ago. The fact that he—not someone else—decided to dig that day in the cave of Altamira was the culmination of his passionate interest in his hobby. Here was a rare man whose avocation had been to educate himself from scratch, as it were, in the science of archaeology and cave exploration. This was no simple passive recognizer of blind luck when it came his way, but a man whose unique interests served as an active creative thrust—someone whose own actions and personality would focus the events that led circuitously but inexorably to the discovery of man's first paintings.

14   Then, too, there is a more subtle manner. How do you give full weight to the personal interests that imbue your child with your own curiosity, that inspire her to ask to join you in your own musty hobby, and that then lead you to agree to her request at the critical moment? For many reasons, at Altamira, more than the special receptivity of Chance III was required—this was a different domain, that of the personality and its actions.

15   A century ago no one had the remotest idea that our caveman ancestors were highly creative artists. Weren't their talents rather minor and limited to crude flint chippings? But the paintings at Altamira, like a mirage, would quickly magnify this diminutive view, bring up into full focus a distant, hidden era of man's prehistory, reveal sentient minds and well-developed aesthetic sensibilities to which men of any age might aspire. And like a mirage, the events at Altamira grew out of de Sautuola's heated personal quest and out of the invisible forces of chance we know exist yet cannot touch. Accordingly, one may introduce the term *altamirage* to identify the quality underlying Chance IV. Let us define it as the facility for encountering unexpected good luck as the result of highly individualized action. Altamirage goes well beyond the boundaries of serendipity in its emphasis on the role of personal action in chance.

---

*The cave had first been discovered some years before by an enterprising hunting dog in search of game. Curiously, in 1932 the French cave of Lascaux was discovered by still another dog.

16   Chance IV is favored by distinctive, if not eccentric, hobbies, personal lifestyles, and modes of behavior peculiar to one individual, usually invested with some passion. The farther apart these personal activities are from the area under investigation, the more novel and unexpected will be the creative product of the encounter.

UNDERSTANDING CONTEXT

1.   What are the four categories of chance?
2.   What is meant by "blind" or "dumb" luck? Give some examples from your own life.
3.   What is the Kettering Principle? Would Edison's famous trial-and-error experiments to discover a filament for the incandescent light bulb fit this kind of chance?
4.   How does the Pasteur principle differ from the Kettering Principle?
5.   How did the dog's discovery of a cave differ from "blind luck" or Chance I?
6.   *Critical thinking:* How often have you discovered things by chance? What role has chance played in your career and education? Does understanding Austin's four kinds of chance enhance your ability to be "lucky" in the future? Can you "make your own kind of luck"?

EVALUATING STRATEGY

1.   What principle does Austin use to divide chance into four categories?
2.   What examples does Austin use to illustrate each type? Are they accessible by a general audience?
3.   Would a chart aid in explaining the four types of chance?
4.   *Blending the modes:* How does Austin make use of *definition* and *narration* in developing his classification essay?

APPRECIATING LANGUAGE

1.   How much technical language does Austin include?
2.   *Critical thinking:* Is part of Austin's task in this article to invent new terms to create categories of chance? Do most of our words for chance—*luck*, *fortune*, *lot*—all suggest the same meaning?

WRITING SUGGESTIONS

1.   List a number of instances in your life you considered lucky. Using Austin's four categories, write a paper categorizing your experiences. Have you ever gotten past Chance I?
2.   *Collaborative writing:* Discuss the role of chance with a group of students. Do many people use the idea of chance to dismiss the accomplishments of others? Do people use luck as an excuse for not trying? Talk about these issues, and then collaborate on a short paper suggesting how Austin's concept of chance should be taught to children.

Martin Luther King Jr. (1929–1968) was a leading figure in the civil rights movement in the 1950s and 1960s. A noted minister, King blended his deeply felt religious values and his sense of social justice. He created the Southern Christian Leadership Conference, organized many demonstrations, and lobbied for voting rights. In 1964 he received the Nobel Peace Prize. He was assassinated in 1968.

Ways of Meeting Oppression

In this section from his 1958 book Stride Toward Freedom, *King classifies three ways that oppressed people have responded to their condition. King uses classification as a method to make a persuasive argument urging readers to accept his recommended choice of action.*

1 Oppressed people deal with their oppression in three characteristic ways. One way is acquiescence: The oppressed resign themselves to their doom. They tacitly adjust themselves to oppression, and thereby become conditioned to it. In every movement toward freedom some of the oppressed prefer to remain oppressed. Almost 2,800 years ago Moses set out to lead the children of Israel from the slavery of Egypt to the freedom of the promised land. He soon discovered that slaves do not always welcome their deliverers. They become accustomed to being slaves. They would rather bear those ills they have, as Shakespeare pointed out, than flee to others that they know not of. They prefer the "fleshpots of Egypt" to the ordeals of emancipation.

2 There is such a thing as the freedom of exhaustion. Some people are so worn down by the yoke of oppression that they give up. A few years ago in the slum areas of Atlanta, a Negro guitarist used to sing almost daily: "Been down so long that down don't bother me." This is the type of negative freedom and resignation that often engulfs the life of the oppressed.

3 But this is not the way out. To accept passively an unjust system is to cooperate with that system; thereby the oppressed become as evil as the oppressor. Nonco-operation with evil is as much a moral obligation as is cooperation with good. The oppressed must never allow the conscience of the oppressor to slumber. Religion reminds every man that he is his brother's keeper. To accept injustice or segregation passively is to say to the oppressor that his actions are morally right. It is a way of allowing his conscience to fall asleep. At this moment the oppressed fails to be his brother's keeper. So acquiescence—while often the easier way—is not the moral way. It is the way of the coward. The Negro cannot win the respect of his oppressor by acquiescing; he merely increases the oppressor's arrogance and contempt. Acquiescence is interpreted as proof of the Negro's inferiority. The Negro cannot win the respect of the white people of the South or the peoples of the world if he is willing to sell the future of his children for his personal and immediate comfort and safety.

4 A second way that oppressed people sometimes deal with oppression is to resort to physical violence and corroding hatred. Violence often brings about momentary

results. Nations have frequently won their independence in battle. But in spite of temporary victories, violence never brings permanent peace. It solves no social problem; it merely creates new and more complicated ones.

5   Violence as a way of achieving racial injustice is both impractical and immoral. It is impractical because it is a descending spiral ending in destruction for all. The old law of an eye for an eye leaves everybody blind. It is immoral because it seeks to humiliate the opponent rather than win his understanding; it seeks to annihilate rather than to convert. Violence is immoral because it thrives on hatred rather than love. It destroys community and makes brotherhood impossible. It leaves society in monologue rather than dialogue. Violence ends by defeating itself. It creates bitterness in the survivors and brutality in the destroyers. A voice echoes through time saying to every potential Peter, "Put up your sword."* History is cluttered with the wreckage of nations that failed to follow this command.

6   If the American Negro and other victims of oppression succumb to the temptation of using violence in the struggle for freedom, future generations will be the recipients of a desolate night of bitterness, and our chief legacy to them will be an endless reign of meaningless chaos. Violence is not the way.

7   The third way open to oppressed people in their quest for freedom is the way of nonviolent resistance. Like the synthesis in Hegelian philosophy, the principle of nonviolent resistance seeks to reconcile the truths of two opposites—the acquiescence and violence—while avoiding the extremes and immoralities of both. The nonviolent resister agrees with the person who acquiesces that one should not be physically aggressive toward his opponent; but he balances the equation by agreeing with the person of violence that evil must be resisted. He avoids the nonresistance of the former and the violent resistance of the latter. With nonviolent resistance, no individual or group need submit to any wrong, nor need anyone resort to violence in order to right a wrong.

8   It seems to me that this is the method that must guide the actions of the Negro in the present crisis in race relations. Through nonviolent resistance the Negro will be able to rise to the noble height of opposing the unjust system while loving the perpetrators of the system. The Negro must work passionately and unrelentingly for full stature as a citizen, but he must not use inferior methods to gain it. He must never come to terms with falsehood, malice, hate, or destruction.

9   Nonviolent resistance makes it possible for the Negro to remain in the South and struggle for his rights. The Negro's problem will not be solved by running away. He cannot listen to the glib suggestion of those who would urge him to migrate en masse to other sections of the country. By grasping his great opportunity in the South he can make a lasting contribution to the moral strength of the nation and set a sublime example of courage for generations yet unborn.

---

*The apostle Peter had drawn his sword to defend Christ from arrest. The voice was Christ's, who surrendered himself for trial and crucifixion (John 18:11).

10   By nonviolent resistance, the Negro can also enlist all men of good will in his struggle for equality. The problem is not a purely racial one, with Negroes set against whites. In the end, it is not a struggle between people at all, but a tension between justice and injustice. Nonviolent resistance is not aimed against oppressors but against oppression. Under its banner consciences, not racial groups, are enlisted.

UNDERSTANDING CONTEXT

1. Briefly describe the three ways people respond to oppression, according to King. Do you know of other ways? Do some people respond to oppression by blaming each other?

2. Humility is a Christian value. How does King, a minister, argue that humble acceptance of injustice is immoral?

3. King admits that nations have achieved freedom through violence, but why does he reject violence for African Americans?

EVALUATING STRATEGY

1. Why does King use classification to suggest a solution instead of writing a simple persuasive argument?

2. What transitional statements does King use to direct his readers?

3. How does King use religious values to advance his argument?

APPRECIATING LANGUAGE

1. How does King define the difference between "acquiescence" and "nonviolent resistance"?

2. What do King's use of biblical analogies and reference to Hegelian philosophy reveal about his intended audience?

WRITING SUGGESTIONS

1. Use this essay as a model to write your own classification paper persuading people to accept one method over others to respond to a common problem, such as the end of a relationship, the loss of a loved one, being victimized, or discovering a partner's infidelity. Discuss why other responses are less desirable than the one you recommend.

2. *Collaborative writing:* Discuss King's classifications with a group of students. How many people suffering oppression in the world today appear to be following the "third way"? Have a member take notes; then work together to draft a short paper dividing or classifying, if possible, your group's observations.

Edward Irving Koch

Blending the Modes

Edward Irving Koch (1924–) was born in the Bronx, New York. After attending City College of New York from 1941 to 1943, he was drafted into the army and subsequently received two battle stars. In 1948 he received his LLB degree from the New York University School of Law. After serving for two years in the New York City Council and nine years in Congress, he was elected mayor of New York City in 1977 and served three terms. He has written twelve books, including four novels.

Death and Justice: How Capital Punishment Affirms Life

Source: "Death and Justice: How Capital Punishment Affirms Life" by Edward I. Koch. From The New Republic, April 15, 1985 issue. Reprinted with permission from Edward Koch.

In this article Edward Koch uses division and persuasion to argue for the death penalty by listing and refuting seven common objections to capital punishment.

1 Last December a man named Robert Lee Willie, who had been convicted of raping and murdering an 18-year-old woman, was executed in the Louisiana state prison. In a statement issued several minutes before his death, Mr. Willie said: "Killing people is wrong. . . . It makes no difference whether it's citizens, countries, or governments. Killing is wrong." Two weeks later in South Carolina, an admitted killer named Joseph Carl Shaw was put to death for murdering two teenagers. In an appeal to the governor for clemency, Mr. Shaw wrote: "Killing is wrong when I did it. Killing is wrong when you do it. I hope you have the courage and moral strength to stop the killing."

2 It is a curiosity of modern life that we find ourselves being lectured on morality by cold-blooded killers. Mr. Willie previously had been convicted of aggravated rape, aggravated kidnapping, and the murders of a Louisiana deputy and a man from Missouri. Mr. Shaw committed another murder a week before the two for which he was executed, and admitted mutilating the body of the 14-year-old girl he killed. I can't help wondering what prompted these murderers to speak out against killing as they entered the death-house door. Did their newfound reverence for life stem from the realization that they were about to lose their own?

3 Life is indeed precious, and I believe the death penalty helps to affirm this fact. Had the death penalty been a real possibility in the minds of these murderers, they might well have stayed their hand. They might have shown moral awareness before their victims died, and not after. Consider the tragic death of Rosa Velez, who happened to be home when a man named Luis Vera burglarized her apartment in Brooklyn. "Yeah, I shot her," Vera admitted. "She knew me, and I knew I wouldn't go to the chair."

4 During my 22 years in public service, I have heard the pros and cons of capital punishment expressed with special intensity. As a district leader, councilman, congressman, and mayor, I have represented constituencies generally thought of as liberal. Because I support the death penalty for heinous crimes of murder, I have sometimes been the subject of emotional and outraged attacks by voters who find my position reprehensible or worse. I have listened to their ideas. I have weighed

Sam Diephuis/jupiterimages

their objections carefully. I still support the death penalty. The reasons I maintain my position can be best understood by examining the arguments most frequently heard in opposition.

5   1. The death penalty is "barbaric." Sometimes opponents of capital punishment horrify with tales of lingering death on the gallows, of faulty electric chairs, or of agony in the gas chamber. Partly in response to such protests, several states such as North Carolina and Texas switched to execution by lethal injection. The condemned person is put to death painlessly, without ropes, voltage, bullets, or gas. Did this answer the objections of death penalty opponents? Of course not. On June 22, 1984, the New York Times published an editorial that sarcastically attacked the new "hygienic" method of death by injection, and stated that "execution can never be made humane through science." So it's not the method that really troubles opponents. It's the death itself they consider barbaric.

6   Admittedly, capital punishment is not a pleasant topic. However, one does not have to like the death penalty in order to support it any more than one must like radical surgery, radiation, or chemotherapy in order to find necessary these attempts at curing cancer. Ultimately we may learn how to cure cancer with a simple pill. Unfortunately, that day has not yet arrived. Today we are faced with the choice of letting the cancer spread or trying to cure it with the methods available, methods that one day will almost certainly be considered barbaric. But to give up and do nothing would be far more barbaric and would certainly delay the discovery of an eventual cure. The analogy between cancer and murder is imperfect, because murder is not the "disease" we are trying to cure. The disease is injustice. We may not like the death penalty, but it must be available to punish crimes of cold-blooded murder, cases in which any other form of punishment would be inadequate and, therefore, unjust. If we create a society in which injustice is not tolerated, incidents of murder—the most flagrant form of injustice—will diminish.

7   2. No other major democracy uses the death penalty. No other major democracy—in fact, few other countries of any description—are plagued by a murder rate such as that in the United States. Fewer and fewer Americans can remember the days when unlocked doors were the norm and murder was a rare and terrible offense. In America the murder rate climbed 122 percent between 1963 and 1980. During that same period, the murder rate in New York City increased by almost 400 percent, and the statistics are even worse in many other cities. A study at M.I.T. showed that based on 1970 homicide rates a person who lived in a large American city ran a greater risk of being murdered than an American soldier in World War II ran of being killed in combat. It is not surprising that the laws of each country differ according to differing conditions and traditions. If other countries had our murder problem, the cry for capital punishment would be just as loud as it is here. And I daresay that any other major democracy where 75 percent of the people supported the death penalty would soon enact it into law.

8   3. An innocent person might be executed by mistake. Consider the work of Adam Bedau, one of the most implacable foes of capital punishment in this country. According to Mr. Bedau, it is "false sentimentality to argue that the death penalty should be abolished because of the abstract possibility that an innocent person

might be executed." He cites a study of the 7,000 executions in this country from 1893 to 1971, and concludes that the record fails to show that such cases occur. The main point, however, is this. If government functioned only when the possibility of error didn't exist, government wouldn't function at all. Human life deserves special protection, and one of the best ways to guarantee that protection is to assure that convicted murderers do not kill again. Only the death penalty can accomplish this end. In a recent case in New Jersey, a man named Richard Biegenwald was freed from prison after serving 18 years for murder; since his release he has been convicted of committing four murders. A prisoner named Lemuel Smith, who, while serving four life sentences for murder (plus two life sentences for kidnapping and robbery) in New York's Green Haven Prison, lured a woman corrections officer into the chaplain's office and strangled her. He then mutilated and dismembered her body. An additional life sentence for Smith is meaningless. Because New York has no death penalty statute, Smith has effectively been given a license to kill.

9   But the problem of multiple murder is not confined to the nation's penitentiaries. In 1981, 91 police officers were killed in the line of duty in this country. Seven percent of those arrested in the cases that have been solved had a previous arrest for murder. In New York City in 1976 and 1977, 85 persons arrested for homicide had a previous arrest for murder. Six of these individuals had two previous arrests for murder, and one had four previous murder arrests. During those two years the New York police were arresting for murder persons with a previous arrest for murder on the average of one every 8.5 days. This is not surprising when we learn that in 1975, for example, the median time served in Massachusetts for homicide was less than two-and-a-half years. In 1976 a study sponsored by the Twentieth Century Fund found that the average time served in the United States for first-degree murder is ten years. The median time served may be considerably lower.

10   4. Capital punishment cheapens the value of human life. On the contrary, it can be easily demonstrated that the death penalty strengthens the value of human life. If the penalty for rape were lowered, clearly it would signal a lessened regard for the victims' suffering, humiliation, and personal integrity. It would cheapen their horrible experience, and expose them to an increased danger of recurrence. When we lower the penalty for murder, it signals a lessened regard for the value of the victim's life. Some critics of capital punishment, such as columnist Jimmy Breslin, have suggested that a life sentence is actually a harsher penalty for murder than death. This is sophistic nonsense. A few killers may decide not to appeal a death sentence, but the overwhelming majority make every effort to stay alive. It is by exacting the highest penalty for the taking of human life that we affirm the highest value of human life.

11   5. The death penalty is applied in a discriminatory manner. This factor no longer seems to be the problem it once was. The appeals process for a condemned prisoner is lengthy and painstaking. Every effort is made to see that the verdict and sentence were fairly arrived at. However, assertions of discrimination are not an argument for ending the death penalty but for extending it. It is not justice to exclude everyone from the penalty of the law if a few are found to be so favored. Justice requires that the law be applied equally to all.

12   6. Thou Shalt Not Kill. The Bible is our greatest source of moral inspiration. Opponents of the death penalty frequently cite the sixth of the Ten Commandments in an attempt to prove that capital punishment is divinely proscribed. In the original Hebrew, however, the Sixth Commandment reads, "Thou Shalt Not Commit Murder," and the Torah specifies capital punishment for a variety of offenses. The biblical viewpoint has been upheld by philosophers throughout history. The greatest thinkers of the 19th century—Kant, Locke, Hobbes, Rousseau, Montesquieu, and Mill—agreed that natural law properly authorizes the sovereign to take life in order to vindicate justice. Only Jeremy Bentham was ambivalent. Washington, Jefferson, and Franklin endorsed it. Abraham Lincoln authorized executions for deserters in wartime. Alexis de Tocqueville, who expressed profound respect for American institutions, believed that the death penalty was indispensable to the support of social order. The United States Constitution, widely admired as one of the seminal achievements in the history of humanity, condemns cruel and inhuman punishment, but does not condemn capital punishment.

13   7. The death penalty is state-sanctioned murder. This is the defense with which Messrs. Willie and Shaw hoped to soften the resolve of those who sentenced them to death. By saying in effect, "You're no better than I am," the murderer seeks to bring his accusers down to his own level. It is also a popular argument among opponents of capital punishment, but a transparently false one. Simply put, the state has rights that the private individual does not. In a democracy, those rights are given to the state by the electorate. The execution of a lawfully condemned killer is no more an act of murder than is legal imprisonment an act of kidnaping. If an individual forces a neighbor to pay him money under threat of punishment, it's called extortion. If the state does it, it's called taxation. Rights and responsibilities surrendered by the individual are what give the state its power to govern. This contract is the foundation of civilization itself.

14   Everyone wants his or her rights, and will defend them jealously. Not everyone, however, wants responsibilities, especially the painful responsibilities that come with law enforcement. Twenty-one years ago a woman named Kitty Genovese was assaulted and murdered on a street in New York. Dozens of neighbors heard her cries for help but did nothing to assist her. They didn't even call the police. In such a climate the criminal understandably grows bolder. In the presence of moral cowardice, he lectures us on our supposed failings and tries to equate his crimes with our quest for justice.

15   The death of anyone—even a convicted killer—diminishes us all. But we are diminished even more by a justice system that fails to function. It is an illusion to let ourselves believe that doing away with capital punishment removes the murderer's deed from our conscience. The rights of society are paramount. When we protect guilty lives, we give up innocent lives in exchange. When opponents of capital punishment say to the state: "I will not let you kill in my name," they are also saying to murderers: "You can kill in your own name as long as I have an excuse for not getting involved."

16   It is hard to imagine anything worse than being murdered while neighbors do nothing. But something worse exists. When those same neighbors shrink back from justly punishing the murderer, the victim dies twice.

UNDERSTANDING CONTEXT

1. Many people oppose the death penalty because of the value they place on human life. How does Koch argue that he favors capital punishment for the same reason?
2. Explain how Koch can dislike the death penalty but insist that it is necessary.
3. Why is the death penalty, in Koch's view, perhaps more necessary in this country than elsewhere?
4. How does Koch respond to the common argument that the death penalty violates the Ten Commandments?
5. Why does Koch believe that an execution by the state is different than an execution by an individual?
6. *Critical thinking:* You have probably heard various arguments both for and against capital punishment. Did Koch present any new points or make a more compelling case than others? Did his essay influence your views on the death penalty? Why or why not?

EVALUATING STRATEGY

1. Koch announces his plan for organizing his essay in paragraph 4. Is this an effective strategy? Why or why not?
2. *Other modes:* What analogy does Koch use to explain the need for executing those who commit heinous crimes? Why does he say this comparison is not perfect?
3. What support does Koch use? What types of evidence are most effective and least effective in your view?

APPRECIATING LANGUAGE

1. How would you describe Koch's tone and style? Is it suited to his topic? Why or why not?
2. Do you detect any emotional language in this essay? When writing about an issue like capital punishment, should writers use emotionally charged words? Why or why not?

WRITING SUGGESTIONS

1. Koch addresses seven arguments against capital punishment. Select one reason and write a persuasive essay supporting or rejecting this argument.
2. *Collaborative writing:* Discuss the issue of capital punishment with a group of students and have each one write a statement explaining when, if ever, they believe a convicted criminal should receive the death penalty. Write an essay using classification to organize the responses from the strongest advocate to the strongest opponent of the death penalty.

CRITICAL ISSUES

Jupiter Images

The Criminal Justice System

What Winston Churchill once said about democracy can probably also be said about the adversary system of criminal justice: It may well be the worst system of justice, "except [for] all the other [systems] that have been tried from time to time."

Alan M. Dershowitz

The system is seriously flawed. It disproportionately affects the poor and the African-American community. It makes too many mistakes. Too many prisoners are unjustly placed on death row because of poor representation at trial. Too many others spend irretrievable chunks of their lives behind bars because of false identifications or shoddy police work or inadequate legal representation.

National Catholic Reporter

During the last decade violent crime has steadily dropped, particularly in major cities. Safer streets have, in part, help revitalize urban America, which has experienced a rapid growth in upscale housing and commercial redevelopment. At the same time, the nation's prison population has risen dramatically. Over six million citizens—one in every 32 Americans—are in jail, on probation or parole, or in prison. While many Americans cite falling crime statistics as signs of progress, others, like Paul Butler, a former prosecutor, examine the social cost on those communities in which one in three males are under the supervision of the criminal justice system and more young men are in prison than in college:

> These costs are both social and economic, and they include the large percentage of black children who live in female-headed, single-parent households; a perceived dearth of men "eligible" for marriage; the lack of male role models for black children, especially boys; the absence of wealth in the black community; and the large unemployment rate among black men.

Elizabeth Palmberg argues that the war on drugs has increased racial disparities in the criminal justice system, so that "four out of five state drug prisoners are African American or Latino, although these groups comprise only 22 percent of drug users. . . . and these disparities permeate every level of the criminal justice system, from policing to parole."

Popular television programs have highlighted the use of DNA to identify the guilty and exonerate the innocent. By proving the innocence of convicts, DNA has demonstrated the unreliability of other forms of evidence such as eyewitness testimony. But even when DNA evidence conclusively proves that someone has been wrongly convicted, it does not always lead to immediate release. Bob Herbert noted in *The New York Times* that "once an innocent person is trapped in the system, it's extremely difficult to get him—or her—extricated." Complicating the use of DNA evidence is the fact that many of the current experts who testify in court have as little as two weeks' training.

The introduction of cameras in courtrooms in the 1990s allowed Americans who had only seen fictionalized courtroom dramas to witness real trials. Anna Quindlen argues that cameras should be allowed in courtrooms to let people see how the legal process "takes this messy stew of evidence and egos and transmutes it finally through order, instruction and deliberation into a system that gets it right a good bit of the time." In contrast, Jack Litman, a defense attorney, believes that cameras can intimidate witnesses and harm victims because "there is an enormous difference between . . . testifying before 12 people and 12 million people."

Before reading the articles listed below, consider the following questions:

1. *Do you think the criminal justice system is basically fair to victims, witnesses, and defendants?*
2. *Do you think trials should be televised?* Have you ever watched televised trials? What did you learn by watching actual courtroom proceedings? How do they differ from courtroom dramas?
3. *Do you think GPS devices and other monitoring technology can make probation and parole more effective? Could technology punish people and prevent crime without putting offenders in jail?*
4. *Do celebrity and high-profile trials give the public a distorted view of the criminal justice system?*
5. *Have you ever served on a jury or appeared in court?* How did your experiences shape your view of the criminal justice system?

E-READINGS ONLINE

Search InfoTrac College Edition, available through your English CourseMate at **www. cengagebrain.com,** by author or title to find the full text of the following articles online.

Anna Quindlen. "Lights, Camera, Justice for All."
Because the point of public trials was to let people in, Quindlen argues "in the 21st century, letting the people in means letting the cameras in."

Felicity Barringer. "Lawyers Are Divided on Cameras in the Courtroom."
Jack Litman, a defense attorney, questions the impact televised trials can have on witnesses and victims.

Leonard Post. "Citing Low Pay, Lawyers Refuse Indigent Cases."
Because of low pay, many lawyers refuse to represent poor defendants, denying them adequate counsel and leading judges to dismiss charges against criminals when lawyers cannot be found to defend them.

Elizabeth Palmberg. "Seeing Green: Why the Penal System Isn't Colorblind."
The war on drugs has increased racial disparities in the justice system so that black teenagers convicted of drug crimes are 48 times more likely to be sent to prison than white teenagers.

Graeme Wood. "Prison Without Walls."
Of all the Americans "serving time" only one-third are behind bars. The rest circulate in society with their movements, restricted by conditions of parole or probation, increasingly monitored by GPS.

Adam Liptak. "Locked Away Forever."
Almost ten thousand Americans are serving life sentences for crimes they committed before they turned eighteen.

National Catholic Reporter. "Flawed Prison System Hurts Us All."
Noting that over six million Americans are currently in jail, on parole, or probation, the *National Catholic Reporter* argues that "we can't keep locking people away and trying to forget they exist. Humans, even those who have broken the law, deserve better, and even tough sentences eventually end."

Bob Herbert. "Trapped in the System."
Despite conclusive DNA evidence that he did not commit the crime, Ryan Matthews remains on death row because "freeing someone who has been wrongfully convicted is a torturously slow and difficult process, with no guarantee at any time that it will end positively."

Adam Liptak. "You Think DNA Evidence Is Foolproof? Try Again."
DNA evidence has proven the unreliability of other forms of evidence, but it cannot create a "foolproof" system of justice because DNA tests are conducted by fallible technicians and presented in court by poorly trained "experts."

Thomas N. Faust. "Shift the Responsibility of Untreated Mental Illness Out of the Criminal Justice System."
Noting that 16 percent of inmates are severely mentally ill, the executive director of the National Sheriffs' Association argues that prisons "have started to become psychiatric hospitals."

David Rose. "Locked Up to Make Us Feel Better."
Petty criminals are increasingly given life sentences not for crimes they committed but to protect the public from their future behavior, so prisons may soon house more inmates for "preventative detention" than murder.

CRITICAL READING AND THINKING

1. What do the various authors see as strengths and weaknesses in the criminal justice system?
2. How has DNA evidence changed perceptions of the fairness of the criminal justice system?
3. What do some authors view as causes for racial disparities in the justice system?
4. What are the benefits and risks of televising trials?
5. Why do few Americans appear to be concerned about the large numbers of people in prison? Do people feel safer? Do they see imprisoning large numbers of mostly young and poor males as an acceptable trade-off for lowered crime rates?

WRITING SUGGESTIONS

1. Write an essay about one aspect of the criminal justice system that you have observed. Have you ever been a victim of crime, appeared in court, or served on a jury? Describe your most surprising finding or observation. Was the system better or worse than you expected?
2. *Collaborative writing:* Working with other students, develop an essay outlining what your group believes would be the best ways to improve the criminal justice system to make sure victims are fairly treated and defendants adequately represented.
3. *Other modes:*
   ■ Write a *comparison* paper that contrasts the ways different people view the police, courts, or prison system.
   ■ Use a single trial, crime, defendant, or victim as an *example* of a problem in the criminal justice system.
   ■ Write an essay that explores the *causes* or *effects* of racial disparities in sentencing offenders.
   ■ Develop a *division* paper that discusses three or four of the most pressing challenges to the criminal justice system.
   ■ Write a *classification* essay that outlines the most to least effective ways of dealing with people who break the law.

RESEARCH PAPER

You can develop a research paper about the criminal justice system by conducting further research to explore a range of issues:

■ Why has crime dropped?
■ Why has the prison population expanded?
■ What flaws in the justice system have been revealed by the use of DNA evidence? Has it, for example, led more people to oppose capital punishment?

- What representation do poor defendants receive in your area? Are state or local public defenders adequately funded and supported? Do the poor get fair trials?
- Examine media coverage of a sensational criminal trial. Are the stories balanced? Do you detect bias for or against the defendant, witnesses, the attorneys, or the victim?

FOR FURTHER READING

To locate additional sources on the criminal justice system, enter these search terms into InfoTrac College Edition, available through your English CourseMate at **www .cengagebrain.com,** or another one of your college library's databases:

Administration of Criminal Justice
Subdivisions: analysis
                  beliefs, opinions, and attitudes
                  economic aspects
                  evaluation
                  forecasts and trends
                  political aspects
                  public opinion
                  social aspects

DNA Identification
Subdivisions: analysis
                  cases
                  laws, regulations, and rules
                  methods

Prisons
Subdivisions: analysis
                  demographic aspects
                  history
                  personal narratives
                  psychological aspects
                  social aspects

ADDITIONAL SOURCES

Using a search engine, enter one or more of the following terms to locate additional sources:

DNA testing	prisons	insanity defense
public defenders	televised trials	criminal justice system
capital punishment	parole	community service
Innocence Project	juvenile justice	mandatory sentencing

See the Evaluating Internet Sources Checklist on pages 533–534. See Chapter 24 for documenting sources.

The Motion Picture Association of America was founded in 1922 as the trade association of the American film industry. The organization's initial goal was to curb widespread criticism of motion pictures by improving the public image of the movie industry. It established production codes to counter state and local censorship boards that threatened to disrupt film distribution. In 1968 the MPAA, in partnership with theater owners, developed a rating system for motion pictures alerting the public, especially parents, of objectionable content.

CONTEXT: *The Red Carpet Ratings Service e-mails parents the ratings of newly released films. This announcement on page 421, designed to resemble a movie poster, appeared on the MPAA website.*

UNDERSTANDING CONTEXT

1. Who is the target audience for this announcement?
2. What method of classification does the MPAA use to rate films?
3. *Critical thinking:* Why does a trade organization representing motion pictures feel the need to rate its own products? Does this strike you as being self-defensive or socially responsible? Do you think many parents would like to see a rating system for music? Why or why not?

EVALUATING STRATEGY

1. How effective is the design of this announcement?
2. What does the title "Parents: Stay Ahead of the Curve!" suggest to you? What parental concerns does it address?
3. *Critical thinking:* How might a movie studio executive use this announcement to answer critics of the film industry?

APPRECIATING LANGUAGE

1. What do the words *red carpet* suggest? Do you think it makes an effective name for this service? Why or why not?
2. Do you think the wording of the classifications is clear? What is the difference between "not suitable" and "inappropriate" or "suggesting guidance" and "strongly cautioning"? Do you think these labels provide accurate information for parents making decisions about what movies their children should and should not see?
3. The MPAA originally used X as its most restrictive designation. It changed the listing to NC-17 in the 1980s. What connotation does X-rated have? Why would the MPAA want to eliminate this term?

Sam Diephuis/jupiterimages

Motion Picture Association of America/Motion Picture
Association of America

WRITING SUGGESTIONS

1. Write an essay about your experiences with movie ratings. Did your parents restrict the movies you were allowed to see as a child based on the ratings? If you have children, do you use ratings to select movies? Why or why not?

2. *Collaborative writing:* Work with a group of students to establish a similar rating system for music. Which artists and groups would your group rate PG or R? If members disagree, develop opposing statements.

RESPONDING TO IMAGES

Symbols of three monotheistic religions   © SÈbastien DÈsarmaux/Godong/Corbis

1. What is your first impression of this photograph?

2. Could you use this image as a book cover, billboard, or poster? Would it grab attention? What message does it convey in your eyes? Are there places in the world where a poster like this would stir controversy, even violent protests?

3. What does this photograph reveal about the power of symbols? What visual connotations do these images represent?

4. *Visual analysis:* Does representing three religions this way imply equality? Might some people be offended by the suggestion that their faith is equal or similar to others and not recognized as the one true faith?

5. Write an essay classifying the ways people might respond to this photograph.

6. *Collaborative writing:* Share this image with a group of students and ask each to write a caption before you discuss the photograph. What do the captions suggest? Can you divide them into groups or classify them by most positive to most negative?

RESPONDING TO IMAGES

7. *Other modes:*

- Write a short *narrative* about a situation in which you encountered someone of another faith. What did you learn from this experience?
- *Compare* how people regard those of another faith. Are some people respectful and tolerant? Are others suspicious and hostile? How can a diverse society accommodate people with different religious values?
- Write a *process* essay detailing how public schools should explain religion in courses like history or social studies. Give step-by-step directions to ensure a fair presentation of different faiths. Include negative instructions, indicating what should be avoided.

DIVISION AND CLASSIFICATION CHECKLIST

Before submitting your paper, review these points:

✔ Have you clearly defined your goal—to write a division or classification paper?

✔ Do you make meaningful divisions or classifications? Does your paper oversimplify a complex subject?

✔ Are your categories clearly defined?

✔ Do you avoid overlapping categories?

✔ Do you use parallel patterns to develop categories and items?

✔ Do all the parts of your subject clearly fit into a single category? Are there any items left over?

 Access the English CourseMate for this text at **www.cengagebrain.com** for additional information on division and classification essays.

Cause and Effect

Determining Reasons and Measuring and Predicting Results

What Is Cause and Effect?

What causes terrorism? How will Hurricane Katrina affect the future of New Orleans? Why are more children being diagnosed with autism? What causes global warming? How did Microsoft dominate the software market? How will budget cuts affect education? Would a handgun ban reduce street crime? What causes addiction? How will a new appointment change the Supreme Court? Why did you choose this college? How did being fired, surviving an accident, or breaking up with someone affect you? The answers to all these questions call for the use of **cause and effect,** writing that seeks to determine reasons why something occurred or measure and predict results.

Historians devote much of their work to analyzing the causes of events. Did Lenin cause the Russian Revolution or did the revolution create Lenin? Why did Hitler rise to power? What led to the women's movement of the 1970s? Historians also consider the ramifications of current events and speculate about the future. Will another oil crisis occur? What role will China play in the twenty-first century? Will a global economy diminish national sovereignty? How will the growing number of Hispanics influence presidential campaigns?

Nearly all professions and disciplines engage in cause-and-effect reasoning. Marketers try to determine why a product succeeded or failed. Engineers work to discover why a test motor exploded. Medical researchers investigate what causes normal cells to become cancerous and examine the results of experimental treatments. City planners predict the effect a major earthquake would have on emergency services. Social workers study the results of welfare reform. Educators consider if curriculum changes will cause students to achieve higher SAT scores. Crash investigators examine the wreckage of an airliner to determine the cause of an accident.

Many of the papers you will be assigned in college and much of the writing you will do in your career will be developed using cause and effect. Identifying the reasons that something occurred can be challenging. Measuring results and determining future outcomes, no matter how much evidence you analyze, can remain largely guesswork. Critical thinking skills are essential to successfully produce cause-and-effect writing.

Determining Causes

During the 1920s physicians and surgeons noticed that many of their lung cancer patients were heavy smokers. An observable association was discovered, but no clear proof of a cause-and-effect relationship. Not all lung cancer patients smoked, and millions of smokers were free of the disease. Though many scientists were concerned, they had no clear evidence that tobacco caused cancer. In fact, for the next twenty years cigarette advertisements featured endorsements by doctors who claimed the calming effect of nicotine reduced stress and prevented stomach ulcers. It was not until 1964 that researchers had assembled enough data to convince the surgeon general of the United States that smoking caused cancer, leading him to proclaim cigarettes a health hazard.

In some instances causes can be established through investigation and research. Doctors can diagnose an infection as the cause of a fever. Accountants can study financial records to discover why a company lost money. But many controversial issues remain subject to debate. Why are American schools failing to educate children? John Taylor Gatto (page 449) studied the problem and determined that television and schools have detrimental effects on children's lives:

> Two institutions at present control our children's lives—television and schooling, in that order. Both of these reduce the real world of wisdom, fortitude, temperance, and justice to a never-ending, nonstop abstraction. In centuries past, the time of a child and adolescent would be occupied in real work, real charity, real adventures, and the real search for mentors who might teach what one really wanted to learn.

When evaluating a writer attempting to establish a cause, consider the amount of evidence, the degree of objective analysis, and the willingness to qualify assertions. If General Motors saw an increase in car sales after a major promotional campaign,

WRITING ACTIVITY

Select one of the following topics and develop ideas using a variety of prewriting strategies.

1. The reasons you or your parents selected this college or university

2. Causes of domestic violence, poverty, racism, or other social problem

3. Reasons why many Americans do not vote

4. The major causes of conflict between parents and children

5. Why a team won or lost a recent game

6. The reason you hold a certain belief about abortion, capital punishment, or any other highly debated issue

7. Why teenagers start smoking

8. Reasons explaining a current fad, fashion trend, popularity of a television show, or a celebrity's success

9. Why people gamble

10. The reason for America's high homicide rate

does it prove the commercials were successful? Could additional sales be attributed to a change in interest rates, easier credit, a price increase in imported cars, or a surge in consumer confidence? It would take careful research to determine if the advertising directly contributed to the sales results.

Measuring and Predicting Effects

Writers use cause and effect to measure and predict effects. By gathering evidence, evaluating data, and considering alternative interpretations, experts attempt to determine the effect of a new drug, a change in social policy, or a technological innovation. John Brooks (page 438), for instance, studied the effects of the telephone:

> What has the telephone done to us, or for us, in the hundred years of its existence? A few effects suggest themselves at once. It has saved lives by getting rapid word of illness, injury, or famine from remote places. By joining with the elevator to make possible the multistory residence or office building, it has made possible—for better or worse—the modern city.

As with determining causes, measuring effects can be challenging. How can the government measure the effects of a tax cut designed to stimulate the economy? If businesses report higher profits and unemployment drops, can these results be attributed to the tax cut? Could a rising demand for American products from overseas, a change in interest rates, or a drop in the price of oil also be credited for the surge in the economy?

Predicting future outcomes can be challenging because evidence may be difficult to collect or may be subject to various interpretations. In addition, numerous unforeseen factors can take place to alter expected events. A school board that determines to close schools because of a declining birthrate may fail to account for an influx of immigrants or the closure of private schools that would place more students into the public system.

Peter Moskos (page 452) argues that because addictive drugs are dangerous, they should be legalized to regulate and reduce their use. Legalization of drugs, he predicts, would reduce both crime and consumption:

> Illegal drug dealers sell to anyone. Legal ones are licensed and help keep drugs such as beer, cigarettes, and pharmaceuticals away from minors. Illegal dealers settle disputes with guns. Legal ones solve theirs in court. Illegal dealers fear police. Legal ones fear the IRS.
>
> Less use. Regulation can reduce drug use. In two generations, we've halved the number of cigarette smokers not through prohibition but through education, regulated selling, and taxes. And we don't jail nicotine addicts. Drug addiction won't go away, but tax revenue can help pay for treatment. . . . It's unlikely that repealing federal drug laws would result in a massive increase in drug use. . . .

In contrast, Lee P. Brown (page 455) argues that legalization would not reduce demand:

> Some argue that drug enforcement should be replaced by a policy of "harm reduction," which emphasizes decriminalization and medical treatment over law enforcement and interdiction. But people do not use drugs simply because they are illegal. Equally significant, effective enforcement reduces drug supply, increases price, lowers the numbers of users, and

decreases hard-core drug use. There is an inverse relationship between the price of cocaine and the number of people seeking emergency room treatment. . . . Legalization does not get to the problem's core . . . it fails to answer why more drug availability would not lead to more drug use and more devastating consequences.

When examining writing that predicts future effects, consider the amount of evidence presented, the recognition of other factors that may affect results, and the use of critical thinking.

WRITING ACTIVITY

Select one of the following topics and develop ideas using a variety of prewriting strategies.

1. The effect of cable television on popular culture

2. The result of a recent policy change at your college or job

3. Effects you have experienced from exercising or changing your diet

4. The ways a Supreme Court ruling changed law, society, or people's attitudes

5. The long-term effects of a past scandal, confrontation, strike, or demonstration in your community

6. The effects losing a job can have on a person's self-esteem

7. Side effects you or someone else experienced from medication

8. How an affair affects a marriage or long-term relationship

9. The impact of graffiti on a neighborhood

10. The effects of television advertising on children

Strategies for Planning Cause and Effect

Critical Thinking and Prewriting

1. **Review critical thinking.** Before beginning to write, review Strategies for Increasing Critical Thinking (pages 38–39) and Avoiding Errors in Critical Thinking (pages 39–41).
   - Read about deduction and induction (see pages 466–468).
   - Appreciate the importance of close observation and objective evaluation.
   - Remind yourself to distinguish between fact and opinion in developing topics.

(Continued)

2. **Develop potential topics using the following devices.**
List events, situations, actions, and decisions; then explore their causes.

Examples: *Causes:*

Homelessness

Illiteracy

Addiction

Teen obesity

Your decision to quit a job

List events, situations, actions, and decisions; then explore their effects.

Examples: *Effects:*

Recent changes in financial aid policy

Rising or decreasing crime rate

Your parents' divorce

Being downsized

Moving into your own apartment

3. **Determine the goal of your paper—to establish causes, measure results, or predict future outcomes.**

4. **Select topics suitable to your purpose.** Consider the scope of the assignment and the amount of time you can devote to research and writing.
   - Keep the length of your paper and the due date in mind as you develop your topic.

5. **List as many causes or effects as you can.**
   - Use prewriting techniques—clustering or freewriting—to develop a list of causes or effects.
   - Do not edit this list; jot down any ideas, though they may seem irrelevant. Because your topic may change, don't discard ideas that might stimulate further thought.

6. **Search for supporting material.** Conduct an online search using key words in your topic to discover additional insights and supporting material for your paper.
   - Evaluate sources carefully. Look for signs of bias, unproven assumptions, or mistakes in logic.

7. **Determine whether visuals can enhance your paper.** Photographs, charts, and graphs can illustrate or document causes and effects.

Planning

1. **Write a clear thesis statement listing the main causes or effects at the top of the page to guide planning.**

2. **Qualify your approach.** It can be difficult to discuss all the causes or effects of a complex subject. Limit your discussion, stating in the introduction how you intend to establish causes or measure results.
   - If you are writing about a controversial or complex issue, admit that other interpretations exist and justify your thesis.

3. **Evaluate your reader's needs.** What evidence does your reader require to accept your conclusions? Are government statistics more impressive than expert testimony? Does any background information have to be presented? Are there misconceptions that must be addressed or terms that need to be defined?

4. **Offer logical, acceptable evidence.**

5. **Revise your list of causes and effects.**
   - Delete minor, repetitive, or marginal ideas.
   - Highlight those points needing further development; use prewriting techniques to explore these issues further.
   - Examine each item on your list. Can some be separated into two causes or three separate effects? Can closely related points be combined?

6. **Write a new list, ranking points by order of importance.** Examine the number of points you have developed, considering the goal of the document. Would it be better to discuss one or two causes in depth or provide a list of eight reasons with only brief support and explanation?

7. **Use division or classification to organize causes or effects.**
   - Order ideas from the least to most important or most to least important. Place your most significant ideas in the opening or closing, where reader attention is highest.

Strategies for Writing Cause and Effect

Writing the First Draft

1. **Focus on the thesis to keep your writing on track.**
2. **Keep the scope of the paper in mind as you write; consider limiting the topic if the draft becomes too lengthy.**
3. **Qualify remarks, noting possible exceptions or alternative interpretations.** Avoid making absolute statements that can be easily refuted by readers who recognize a single exception.
4. **Use other modes to organize your discussion of causes and effects.** You can use *comparison* to discuss alternative interpretations, *classification* to present a spectrum of causes or effects, and *example* to illustrate ideas.

(Continued)

5. **Use transitional statements and paragraph breaks to signal shifts between separate causes or effects.**

6. **Make notes as you write.** Jot down new ideas or questions that come up to guide revisions and further drafts.

Strategies for Revising and Editing Cause and Effect

Revising

1. **Review the entire essay.**
   - Does your paper meet the needs of the writing assignment?
   - Did your topic prove suitable for the scope of the assignment?

2. **Examine your thesis and list of causes or effects.**
   - Is the thesis clearly stated? Can it be further refined?
   - Have you supplied enough supporting evidence?

3. **Review your discussion of causes and effects.**
   - Does your paper devote too much space to minor points? Do more causes and effects need to be presented?
   - Does your paper offer only a superficial list of ideas? Should you narrow the thesis and discuss fewer causes or effects in greater detail?

4. **Examine your paper for critical thinking.**
   - Review your use of induction and deduction. Do you jump to conclusions or ignore alternative interpretations? Do you base your reasoning on untested assumptions?
   - Have you avoided making errors in logic (see pages 39–41)?

5. **Review the introduction and conclusion.**
   - Does the first paragraph clearly announce your purpose, limit the topic, and qualify your approach?
   - Does the conclusion end the paper on a strong point by emphasizing the significance of your causes and effects?

6. **Review the use of visual aids.**
   - Are they appropriate for this paper?
   - Do they accurately and effectively illustrate or document the causes or effects you discuss?

7. **Use peer review to identify areas needing improvement.**

Editing and Proofreading

1. **Read your paper aloud.**
   - Are ideas stated in concrete language readers can understand?

- Do some terms require further clarification or definition?
- Do the tone and style of your words reflect your purpose?

2. **Review the structure of your paper.**
   - Are transitions clear? Could changes in paragraphing or revised transitional statements make the essay easier to follow?

3. **Use peer editing to locate errors you may have missed.**

STUDENT PAPER

This paper was written in response to the following assignment:

> Write an essay explaining the causes or analyzing the effects of a social phenomenon, technological change, economic problem, or political issue. You might discuss causes for the popularity of a fad, the effect of the Internet on political campaigns, or reasons behind recent protests over immigration policies.

FIRST DRAFT WITH INSTRUCTOR'S COMMENTS

Tony Lobanco   Comp. 112

title?   *needs stronger intro*

Why do so many people throughout the world who once used to dream of coming to

vague

America now hate it.*?* It seems like all we hear about these days is how much people all over

the world now hate the US. Anti-American feelings seem to have swept the whole globe in

vague

the last decade. Sure, "Yankee, Go Home!" was a cliché protest sign, but now it's all over.

vague

Many people say that the reasons people in the world hate us vary a lot. Take for exam-

ple US military presence throughout Europe, Asia, Africa, and South America, ~~for instance~~.

People hostile to the United States see US Navy ships dock in their ports. Sixty years after

WWII America still has bases in England and Germany.

Another reason is American popular culture. Maybe all the sex and violence Hollywood,

hip-hop, and TV put out troubles ministers, rabbis, and priests in this country, but it assaults the

(Continued)

vague
mindsets of Muslims throughout the world. We know that all the stuff Hollywood puts out is

fantasy. We see normal Americans working, going to school, raising kids, and paying bills. But

in other countries the only Americans they see are Tony Soprano and the *Sex in the City* girls. All

they know about us are sex, greed, and violence. So when their kids begin to sing along with Brit-

slang, too informal
ney or wear their hair like Paris, these people go nuts and see it like the end of their culture.

vague
All of this has been said before. I think maybe one reason the hatred of the US has gone

up in the last twenty years has to do with the Cold War ending. Like Gwen Patterson said,

"the deep and enduring rage against the winner of the Cold War is something we did not

expect or understand" (359). *Expand this last point/ Who is Gwen Patterson?*

Works Cited

Patterson, Gwen. *Why The Towers Fell*. Chicago: U of Chicago P, 2009. Print.

REVISION NOTES

Your essay lists common reasons why people in other countries resent the United States. It does not say much that is new. It restates the obvious. Your last paragraph, however, introduces an idea that might give you something original and interesting to write about. Focus on this reason. How did the end of the Cold War cause a rise in anti-American sentiment around the globe? You mention Gwen Patterson—who is she? Why is her quote significant?

REVISED DRAFT
Why They Hate Us

In the days following the attacks of September 11, 2001, many shocked Americans wondered why people hated the United States. The horror of watching planes flying into buildings was matched by the disbelief and anger many felt watching people in the Middle East dancing in the streets, honking car horns, and passing out candy to children like it was a holiday. Polls taken in the Middle East revealed that large numbers of people approved of

Image by © Reuters/CORBIS

Osama bin Laden and viewed the hijackers not as terrorists but heroes and martyrs. As President Bush prepared for the war in Iraq, many Europeans began criticizing the United States. Polls in Germany and France showed that many Europeans believed the CIA was responsible for the 9/11 attacks. Seeing former allies view the United States with suspicion and hostility troubled many Americans.

Why do they all hate us? Scholars, reporters, and diplomats have given us a lot of reasons. They suggest that anti-Americanism is caused by jealousy, fears of modernity, our support for Israel, and the sense that Western culture is eroding traditional customs and values.

But none of these reasons is new. America has been making movies that offend foreign tastes for eighty years. The United States has supported Israel since 1948. The main cause for rising anti-Americanism, I think, is the end of the Cold War. For almost fifty years the world was dominated by two superpowers—the United States and Soviet Union. The state of conflict made America look less threatening and violent in contrast to a Communist dictatorship that killed and jailed millions.

(Continued)

People in West Germany may have grumbled about being under America's shadow, but they only had to look over the Berlin Wall to realize it was a lot better than being in East Germany under Soviet domination. There was no comparison between living in North or South Korea, either. Arabs and other Muslims may have resented America's support for Israel, but they knew the United States believed in the freedom of religion. The Soviets were officially atheists and denounced all religion. The spread of American influence may have weakened Islamic values, but the growth of Soviet-sponsored Communist movements in Pakistan, Iran, Indonesia, and Algeria threatened to abolish Islam.

The Cold War made America look like the lesser of two evils. We were the good cop in a good cop–bad cop scenario. People resented American power and influence, but had reasons to fear the Communists.

Now that the Cold War is over, the world has only one superpower. We no longer look like the good cop or the lesser evil. To many people in the world the United States is a global bully, an economic giant, and a cultural titan—all of which make other nations feel weak, intimidated, and second-rate. And no people like feeling second-rate. Gwen Patterson, a Brookings Middle East scholar, ended her extensive review of Arab media with the observation that "the deep and enduring rage against the winner of the Cold War is something we did not expect or understand" (359).

Works Cited

Patterson, Gwen. *Why The Towers Fell*. Chicago: U of Chicago P, 2009. Print.

QUESTIONS FOR REVIEW AND REVISION

1. What is the student's thesis? Can you state it in your own words?
2. Does the student present enough evidence to support the thesis? What, if anything, could strengthen this essay?
3. How effective is the opening? Does it grab attention and dramatize the student's subject? What changes, if any, would you make?
4. *Blending the modes:* How does the student use *narrative, comparison,* and *persuasion* to develop the essay?
5. Did the student follow the instructor's suggestions? Did the student develop an original topic?
6. Read the essay aloud. Do you detect any informal or unclear sentences that could be more clearly stated?
7. In the final draft the student added a photograph. Is this an effective addition to the essay or a distraction? What should guide the inclusion of visuals in a written document?
8. *Critical thinking:* Why is it important to explain the source of quotations used as support?

WRITING SUGGESTIONS

1. Using the student's essay as a model, describe the causes for another phenomenon—the popularity of reality television shows, a campus fad, rising consumer debt, the prices of homes in your area, the local job market, or differences between male and female attitudes on a certain subject.

2. *Collaborative writing:* Discuss the student essay with a group of students and suggest ways for the United States to counter anti-Americanism around the world. What can the government, institutions, corporations, nonprofit organizations, and individuals do to improve America's image?

Suggested Topics for Writing Cause and Effect

General Assignments

Write a cause-and-effect paper on any of the following topics. Your paper can focus on determining causes, measuring effects, or explaining both causes and effects. Cause-and-effect papers often require research to present evidence. It is possible to use cause and effect in less formal papers, in which you offer personal experience and observations as support. Review Strategies for Increasing Critical Thinking (pages 38–39).

Write a paper *explaining the causes* of the following topics:

- Teenage pregnancy
- Domestic violence
- Your choice of major or career goal
- A recent campus or local scandal, incident, or controversy
- The success or failure of a local business, organization, or event
- The victory or defeat of a political candidate
- Your decision to take a course of action—to quit smoking, to begin exercising, to join or leave an organization, to pursue a job, to end a relationship
- Apathy toward the poor
- Current attitudes about an ethnic, political, religious, or social group
- Divorce

Write a paper *measuring the effects* of the following topics:

- The Internet
- Immigration
- Harsher drunk-driving laws
- Camera cell phones
- Welfare reform
- Living in a dorm
- Airport security

■ A recent policy change at the federal, state, local, or college level
■ Single-parent families
■ Terrorism

Writing in Context

1. Analyze in a short essay a recent event on your campus, in your community, or at your place of work. Examine what caused this event to take place. If several causes exist, you may use division to explain them or classification to rank them from the most to least important.

2. Write a letter to the editor of the college newspaper predicting the effects of a current policy change, incident, or trend in student behavior.

3. Imagine that a job application asks you to write a 250-word essay presenting your reasons for choosing your career. Write a one-page essay that lists your most important reasons. As you write, consider how an employer would evaluate your response.

Strategies for Reading Cause and Effect

As you read the cause-and-effect entries in this chapter, keep the following questions in mind.

Context

1. What is the writer's purpose—to establish causes, measure results, or predict outcomes? Does the writer use cause and effect to simply report a change or to support a persuasive argument?

2. Subject the essay to critical reading. Does the writer avoid logical fallacies (see Chapter 4)? Are causes and effects clearly linked—or can they simply be time relationships or the results of coincidence?

3. Does the writer qualify his or her conclusions? Does he or she acknowledge alternative interpretations?

Strategy

1. Where does the author place the thesis—at the outset or after presenting evidence? Could it be located elsewhere in the essay?

2. What evidence does the author present—personal observations, statistics, scientific studies, the testimony of experts? Is the evidence sufficient? Is it fairly and accurately presented?

3. How does the author organize the essay? Could the entry be easier to follow if causes or effects were presented in numbered lists?

4. Does the writer practice critical thinking? Does the writer mistake symptoms for causes, assume past trends will continue, or base conclusions on unproven assumptions?

5. What other modes does the writer use—narration, comparison, definition?

Language

1. Does the author's choice of words indicate bias?

2. What roles do diction and connotation play in stating causes and results?

3. What do the tone and style suggest about the writer's intended audience? Are technical terms defined?

READING TO LEARN

As you read the cause and effect essays in this chapter, note techniques you can use in your own writing.

■ **"The Effects of the Telephone" by John Brooks** analyzes how the telephone revolutionized human experience.

■ **"Why Schools Don't Educate" by John Taylor Gatto** lists reasons why schools are failing to educate and children are failing to learn.

■ **"Who's Listening to Your Cell Phone Calls?" by Louis Mizell Jr.** uses a series of examples to dramatize the effects of intercepted cell phone calls.

■ **"Too Dangerous Not to Regulate" by Peter Moskos** argues that the legalization of drugs will cause a lessening of violence.

■ **"End the Demand, End the Supply" by Lee P. Brown** predicts that legalizing drugs will only increase their use.

John Brooks

John Brooks (1920–1993) published his first novel, *The Big Wheel,* in 1949. His second novel, *The Man Who Broke Things,* appeared in 1958. Brooks's nonfiction book about corporations in the 1980s, *The Takeover Game,* became a best seller. Brooks, who served as a trustee of the New York Public Library for fifteen years, contributed articles to the *New Yorker* for four decades.

The Effects of the Telephone

Source: "The Effects of the Telephone" from *Telephone: The First Hundred Years* by John Brooks, pp. 8–9. Copyright © 1975, 1976 by John Brooks. By permission.

In this brief essay, Brooks outlines how the telephone has shaped human lives and perceptions. Before reading this article, consider what your life would be like without a telephone. How much do you depend on the phone?

opening
question
obvious
effect

1 What has the telephone done to us, or for us, in the hundred years of its existence? A few effects suggest themselves at once. It has saved lives by getting rapid word of illness, injury, or famine from remote places. By joining with the elevator to make possible the multistory residence or office building, it has made possible—for better or worse—the modern city. By bringing about a quantum leap in the speed and ease with which information moves from place to place, it has greatly accelerated the rate of scientific and technological change and growth in industry. Beyond doubt it has crippled if not killed the ancient art of letter writing. It has made living alone possible for persons with normal social impulses; by so doing, it has played a role in one of the greatest social changes of this century, the breakup of the multigenerational

possible effects

household. It has made the waging of war chillingly more efficient than formerly. Perhaps (though not probably) it has prevented wars that might have arisen out of international misunderstanding caused by written communication. Or perhaps—again not probably—by magnifying and extending irrational personal conflicts based on voice contact, it has caused wars. Certainly it has extended the scope of human conflicts, since it impartially disseminates the useful knowledge of scientists and the babble of bores, the affection of the affectionate and the malice of the malicious.

2   But the question remains unanswered. The obvious effects just cited seem inadequate, mechanistic; they only scratch the surface. Perhaps the crucial effects are evanescent and unmeasurable. Use of the telephone involves personal risk because it involves exposure; for some, to be "hung up on" is among the worst of fears; others dream of a ringing telephone and wake up with a pounding heart. The tele-

psychological
effects

phone's actual ring—more, perhaps, than any other sound in our daily lives—evokes hope, relief, fear, anxiety, joy, according to our expectations. The telephone is our nerve-end to society.

3   In some ways it is in itself a thing of paradox. In one sense a metaphor for the times it helped create, in another sense the telephone is their polar opposite. It is small and gentle—relying on low voltages and miniature parts—in times of hugeness and violence. It is basically simple in times of complexity. It is so nearly human, recreating voices so faithfully that friends or lovers need not identify themselves by

438

name even when talking across oceans, that to ask its effects on human life may seem hardly more fruitful than to ask the effect of the hand or the foot. The Canadian philosopher Marshall McLuhan—one of the few who have addressed themselves to these questions—was perhaps not far from the mark when he spoke of the telephone as creating "a kind of extra-sensory perception."

closing
quotation

UNDERSTANDING CONTEXT

1. What does Brooks see as the principal effects of the telephone? Has it had any negative consequences?

2. Why does he see the telephone as "a thing of paradox"?

3. *Critical thinking:* What lessons about the telephone can be applied to cyberspace? Does the Internet connect people in more ways than the typical one-on-one connection of a telephone conversation?

EVALUATING STRATEGY

1. Most people have grown up with telephones. Many carry cell phones in pockets and purses. How does Brooks prompt readers to question something they take for granted? Could you imagine writing a similar essay about cars, ballpoint pens, or supermarkets?

2. *Critical thinking:* Brooks states that the telephone and elevator made the high-rise and the modern city possible. Does this suggest that it can be difficult to isolate a single cause? Do technological and social changes intertwine and interact to create unintended results?

APPRECIATING LANGUAGE

1. Brooks states that the telephone is "nearly human." How does he personalize the telephone, linking it to human emotions?

2. Brooks avoids technical language in his essay. Would the introduction of scientific terminology weaken his essay?

3. Consider Brooks's observation that the "telephone is our nerve-end to society." Does the telephone link you to others, to the world? When you need to reach someone, do you instinctively think of calling instead of writing or visiting them?

WRITING SUGGESTIONS

1. Using Brooks's article as a model, write your own essay explaining the effects of another common invention—blogs, camera cell phones, online shopping, or credit cards.

2. *Collaborative writing:* Work with a group of students to discuss the effects of computers on children and society. Develop a list of positive and negative effects and write a brief essay comparing the benefits and dangers.

Louis R. Mizell, Jr.

Louis R. Mizell Jr. was a special agent and intelligence officer for the US State Department. He is now president of Mizell and Company, an international firm specializing in crime prevention. Mizell frequently appears on television commenting on home and personal security issues. He has published a series of books on personal safety. In 1998 he published *Invasion of Privacy*, analyzing how modern technology has compromised personal privacy and security.

Who's Listening to Your Cell Phone Calls?

Source: "Who's Listening to Your Cellular and Cordless Phone Calls" from *Invasion of Privacy* by Louis R. Mizell. Copyright © 1998 Louis R. Mizell, Jr. By permission.

Before reading this passage from Invasion of Privacy, *consider how often you have used or have seen friends use cell phones. Do people assume their conversations are private?*

1 More than forty million cellular phones are currently in use in the United States, and the numbers are dramatically increasing each year.

2 On any given day, thousands of eavesdroppers intercept, record, and listen to conversations made from cellular and so-called cordless phones. These eavesdroppers include curious neighbors, business competitors, stalkers, journalists, private investigators, and even espionage agents.

3 In California, spies for hire cruise the highways of Hollywood and the Silicon Valley, hoping to steal valuable trade secrets from executives talking on their car phones. Armed with radio scanners, tabloid reporters in New York monitor conversations of the rich, famous, and infamous, hoping to get a front-page scoop. In Florida, a ham operator monitoring the poolside conversations of a prominent lawyer got incredible inside information on three divorce cases.

4 Cellular telephone conversations can be easily monitored by anyone with a radio scanner, but it is a violation of state and federal law to do so intentionally. A 1993 law made it illegal to make or sell radio scanners that pick up cellular calls, but the law didn't make it illegal to own the old scanners. Furthermore, it is rather easy, although illegal, to modify a legal police scanner so that it will pick up cellular conversations.

5 The problem is that there are hundreds of thousands of the old radio scanners in circulation and an equal number of people who don't care about the law. "How are they going to catch me and how are they going to prove it?" said one ham operator who listens to his neighbors' cellular conversations "just for the fun of it."

6 In truth, only a very small percentage of the people who have been monitored ever learn that their calls were intercepted. An even smaller percentage of the perpetrators are ever caught. Curious kooks, corporate snoops, and spies for hire who use intercepted information are usually smart enough not to publicize where they got it.

7 "I really couldn't care less if someone listens to my conversations," said a schoolteacher from Indiana. "I'm not discussing my love life or national security." One of the biggest problems concerning privacy and portable phones is that most people do not realize how even innocent information can be used by criminals and other

opportunists. Another problem is that just because you don't care if someone is listening to your conversation, the person you are talking to might care very much.

8   Burglars are known to monitor the calls of people discussing evening or weekend plans. Knowing that the occupants are going to be away, the burglars enter their homes.

9   Doctors and lawyers frequently discuss everyday business on cellular phones. In one case, a doctor was notified that a VIP patient had tested positive for AIDS. The information was intercepted, and before long, the VIP's medical status was common knowledge. In another case, a lawyer from Ohio reviewed a client's prenuptial agreement with a second lawyer who was using a cellular telephone. A teenage neighbor of the second lawyer intercepted the conversation. "Before long, the whole damn neighborhood knew about our secret wedding and my financial situation," said the angry groom-to-be.

10   Stalking, or inappropriate pursuit, has become a dangerous epidemic in the United States and is evolving into one of the most insidious threats to personal privacy. Many researchers estimate that more than 200,000 women, men, and children are currently being harassed, threatened, and endangered by stalkers.

11   Stalking may begin with an innocuous contact and then, through misinterpretation or delusion, the pursuer escalates to harassment, surveillance, threats, and sometimes murder.

12   I have been involved in seven cases and am aware of many more in which stalkers intercepted cellular phone conversations and used the intelligence to harass their targets.

13   A jobless and toothless forty-one-year-old man, hooked on amphetamines, became infatuated with a fifteen-year-old girl whom he first noticed at a state swimming competition. "He's really scary and keeps showing up wherever I go," explained the frightened swimmer. "It's like he always knows where I'm going to be."

14   The young lady had good reason to be scared; the man had a long history of bizarre and criminal behavior. On one occasion, he burglarized a home and fell asleep in a teenage girl's bed. The horrified family called the police who arrested the man and confiscated handcuffs and a number of stolen house keys.

15   Released on good behavior, the "nonviolent" criminal was once again free to victimize others. We can't prove what his ultimate plans were concerning our fifteen-year-old client, but we did prove that he had a scanner in his car and had recorded the swimmer's mother as she talked on various cell phones, including a car phone. Two of the taped conversations informed the stalker where his target would be. "I've got to pick my daughter up at McDonald's at 4:30," she mentioned to one friend. "The swim team is celebrating at the Hyatt tonight," she told her neighbor. Needless to say, the stalker showed up at both locations.

16   Eavesdropping on cellular phones is only one of the issues that worry privacy advocates. There is also concern that cellular phones will be used by police and sophisticated criminals to locate the caller.

17   Unbeknownst to most consumers, cellular phones are portable homing devices that allow police and others to pinpoint the caller's position. Police have used this tool to locate a wide range of criminals and kidnap victims. Privacy advocates worry that police will abuse this tool to spy on innocent citizens.

18   When a cellular phone is switched to the On position, it emits a low-power signal to the network to announce which cell site it is in. A cell site is a zone served by a single relay station and is generally several square miles in size. When a caller moves out of one cell site, the call is automatically switched to a different cell site.

19   By using a technique called triangulation, police are able to get a directional fix on the cellular signal and pinpoint the phone's cell site or location. This is the technique police used to locate the car owned by the slain father of basketball great Michael Jordan. Triangulation techniques have also been used by intelligence agencies to locate enemy radio sites and by ocean search-and-rescue teams to pinpoint the location of vessels.

20   There are dozens of cases in which triangulation techniques have assisted law enforcement worldwide.

21   When the Los Angeles police needed to locate O. J. Simpson during the now-famous highway chase, they received court-ordered help from a mobile phone company and were able to locate the Ford Bronco by tracing its cellular phone radio signal. In Colombia, ruthless drug boss Pablo Escobar was finally located and shot dead by police after they traced his mobile telephone's radio signal. Police in the United States located fugitive lawyer Nicholas Bissell, Jr., in Nevada on November 26, 1996, after tracing calls he made on his cellular telephone. Bissell was running from the law after being convicted of fraud, embezzlement, and abuse of power.

22   Another advantage of cellular tracing from a law enforcement perspective is that cellular phones can tell police not only where a suspect is going but also where he has been.

23   A federal drug informant is accused of booby-trapping a briefcase in an unsuccessful attempt to kill a U.S. prosecutor. Using the informant's cellular phone records, prosecutors showed that he was in the same town on the same day where the would-be assassination kit was purchased.

24   Unlike hard-line telephones that most people have in their homes, customers pay for each local cellular call. The billing record for each cellular call shows the cell site from which it was made.

25   Privacy advocates recognize that cellular call tracing can be a great tool for law enforcement, but they argue that the bad will outweigh the good if police abuse their powers.

26   "Police have no right to know my location just because they reason that I might be relevant to some investigation," explained a law-abiding political science professor. "I want to make sure police cannot track and follow a person using a mobile phone unless they obtain a full wiretap warrant." At present, police only need a simple subpoena, which is easier to obtain than a wiretap warrant, to legally intercept cell phone signals.

27   "I bet the good professor would change his mind real quickly if his daughter were kidnapped," countered a police captain. "We don't have the time, the resources, or the inclination to snoop on law-abiding citizens. . . . We only use cellular tools to catch criminals," he protested. "Shouldn't we be more worried about the way rapists and burglars invade our privacy and less worried about taking crime-fighting weapons from the police?"

UNDERSTANDING CONTEXT

1. Why are cell phones easy to monitor? What makes them different from traditional telephones?
2. Why have laws banning police scanners that can pick up cell calls failed to curb illegal monitoring?
3. How can even innocent calls expose people to risk?
4. How do cell phones work as homing devices? How can police use them to track people's movements?
5. *Critical thinking:* Can anyone be sure that his or her legal, medical, or financial records are secure? Even if you never use a cell phone, can you be sure that conversations by your lawyer, doctor, or broker are not being monitored?

EVALUATING STRATEGY

1. How effective is the evidence Mizell presents? Do you find it convincing? Do you think it will change people's use of cell phones?
2. *Blending the modes:* How does Mizell use *narration* and *cause and effect* in developing his analysis?

APPRECIATING LANGUAGE

1. Mizell uses words such as "kook" in his essay. Does the use of slang make the essay easy to read, or does it detract from the seriousness of the subject?
2. Mizell's book is targeted to a wide audience. Do you find his style readable? Can you easily remember facts and details? Would the use of technical or legal terminology lend the article greater authority?

WRITING SUGGESTIONS

1. Write an essay analyzing how technology—cell phones, e-mail, computers, the Internet, security video cameras—have robbed citizens of their privacy. Is there any way to protect people from stalkers and hackers who might monitor phone calls or illegally access computer files and post the information on a web page?
2. *Collaborative writing:* Working with a group of students, review Mizell's article, and write a short process paper instructing consumers about cell phone use. Remind people to avoid discussing sensitive issues or providing information that could be used by burglars or stalkers.

Privacy in the Electronic Age

The Internet's greatest impact has been its ability to provide a voice for the many people who have no formal opportunity to speak in the real world.

Thomas A. Workman

Two years ago I warned that we were in danger of sleepwalking into a surveillance society. Today I fear that we are in fact waking up to a surveillance society that is already all around us.

Richard Thomas

The Internet, cell phones, YouTube, MySpace, Facebook, and Twitter have changed the fabric of modern life. Individuals can now operate corporations from a laptop, conducting business worldwide without the need for an expensive office or support staff. Parents can keep track of children without having to play phone tag. Corporations can keep in touch with employees and customers in real time. Accident victims can summon immediate help by cell phone and be instantly located by GPS. Stolen automobiles and lost pets can be tracked by satellite.

But these conveniences have eroded personal privacy. Cell-phone records can be used to track a person's location. The average New Yorker is photographed twenty-three times a day by surveillance cameras in apartment lobbies, stores, elevators, and street corners. An embarrassing photograph taken at a party that once might have circulated in a single office or high school can be posted online. Erin Andrews, a sportscaster, was secretly videotaped undressing in her hotel room by a predator. Posted online where it could be viewed, shared, and downloaded by anyone, the video turned a single violation of privacy into a never-ending global personal assault.

Today 70 percent of teenagers have online profiles, which often contain personal information or potentially compromising postings. Few realize that an innocent family snapshot posted on a personal page may reveal a house number or a license plate that could be used by predators to stalk victims.

A survey of 500 adolescents revealed that over half had received e-mails containing inappropriate sexual content. Ilene Berson, a professor of child and family studies, finds that teenagers are especially vulnerable online because for them "the Net is a kind of make-believe world where the regular expectations and rules don't seem to apply. They don't consider that once you turn off the computer, it might spill over into their life."

Employers frequently examine job applicants' online profiles, as do attorneys who screen potential clients and witnesses for damaging or compromising postings. Alarmed that a simple Google search produces unflattering images or comments, many professionals hire companies specializing in cleaning up online reputations by deleting or burying negative information.

The Internet has raised First Amendment issues. Should high school teachers who post racist comments online or whose Facebook page depicts them drinking or behaving inappropriately be terminated or suspended? Should schools discipline students who slander principals with online parodies they produce at home?

The near-universal use of cell-phone cameras and sites like YouTube have created a new global medium that can make anyone a journalist capable of recording a historical event for a worldwide audience. In 2009, cell phones could broadcast images of street demonstrations in Iran that the government tried to block and did not cover on its official media. Sites like YouTube and blogs allowed dissidents to disseminate information and inform the outside world. Later, Iranian security police tracked cell-phone accounts and examined online postings to locate and detain dissidents. Ironically, the demonstrator who uses a cell-phone camera to publicize a protest against a repressive regime also provides that regime with the evidence it needs to identify dissidents.

Before reading these articles, consider these questions:

1. *Have you posted photographs or personal information on a MySpace or Facebook page?* Have you considered whether you have revealed too much of your identity?
2. *Have you observed people taking pictures or videos of others at parties or public events without their knowledge?* Would you feel violated if you discovered that someone had posted your picture online without your permission?
3. *Should an employer evaluate applicants based on pictures they may have posted in high school or college?*
4. *Would you conduct an online search to locate information about a person before responding to a request for a date or hiring a babysitter?*
5. *Do cell phones and the Internet create citizen journalists who can bypass censorship or do they provide tools to distort events and manipulate perceptions of events?*
6. *Does the presence of surveillance cameras make you feel spied upon or protected?*

E-READINGS ONLINE

Search for each article by author or title using InfoTrac College Edition, available through your English CourseMate at **www.cengagebrain.com.**

Michael Isikoff. "The Snitch in Your Pocket."
Most of the owners of the nation's 277 million cell phones do not realize their devices can allow authorities to track their movements in real time.

David Hatch. "Tracking Your Every Move."
ICanStalkU.com, an educational tool, reveals how easily personal data can be compromised online. A teenager's simple Tweet instantly revealed her name, photograph, and current location.

Jamie Malanowski. "Big Brother: How a Million Surveillance Cameras in London Are Proving George Orwell Wrong."
Not far from the flat where Orwell wrote his prophetic novel, thirty-two CCTV cameras run 24 hours a day, creating a "surveillance society" that has eroded privacy but given the public a greater sense of personal security.

John Caher. "No Warrant Needed for GPS Car-Tracking."
Because drivers have no expectation of privacy on the open road, a federal judge has ruled that the police do not need a warrant to use GPS devices to track a suspect.

Chloe Albanesius and Erik Rhey. "Are You on the Map?"
Online map services like Google Maps, which include street-view images of public buildings and private homes, concern citizens and security experts who fear these images can be used by predators and terrorists to target victims.

Thomas A. Workman. "The Real Impact of Virtual Worlds."
Students who post videos of themselves participating in risky or outrageous activities should be viewed as engaging in "misdirected recreation rather than purposeful misconduct."

Maria Giffen. "Online Privacy: When Your Life Goes Public."
Seventy percent of high school students have online profiles, and over half have posted their own photos, with little realization how their actions in cyberspace may affect their futures.

Shannon P. Duffy. "The MySpace Suspensions."
Schools that have suspended students for posting lewd parodies of their principals on home computers have raised First Amendment issues.

Andrew Tanick. "Can Facebook Cost You a Job?"
Increasingly, employers are examining social networking sites to screen job applicants and monitor employees.

Healthcare Risk Management. "Cell Phone Cameras Are Creating Liability Risk for Health Care Facilities."
Because employees have used cell-phone cameras to violate the privacy of vulnerable patients, supervisors must monitor their presence in health care facilities that would never allow employees to carry traditional cameras.

Michael Fertik. "10 Ways to Protect Your Privacy Online."
Consumers can take simple steps—from blocking cookies to closing old accounts—to protect their privacy online.

CRITICAL READING AND THINKING

1. What do the various authors see as the advantages and disadvantages of electronic devices?
2. How has the cell-phone camera changed our notions of privacy?
3. What dangers do young people expose themselves to online?
4. Should teachers be suspended or terminated because their Facebook or MySpace pages show them partying and drinking away from school?
5. Should attorneys be allowed to introduce online profiles as evidence to discredit witnesses in court?

WRITING SUGGESTIONS

1. Write an essay about one aspect of the electronic age you have observed. Have you noticed anyone posting personal information or photographs on MySpace or Facebook that you think could have negative consequences? Do young people think before they post?

2. *Collaborative writing:* Work with a group of students and write a set of guidelines people should follow before posting on social networking sites.

3. *Other modes:*
   - Write a *narrative* essay about a personal experience involving a cell phone or the Internet that illustrates the advantages or disadvantages of the electronic age.
   - Write a paper that outlines the *effects* of social networking.
   - Use *comparison* to identify the advantages and disadvantages of cell-phone cameras, social networking sites, or GPS systems.
   - Write a *persuasive* paper supporting or criticizing schools that suspend students for posting online parodies accusing principals or teachers of criminal conduct.
   - Use *analysis* to study how the concept of privacy has changed in the electronic age.

RESEARCH PAPER

You can develop a research paper about privacy in the electronic age by conducting further research to explore a range of issues:

- What cases about online postings have tested First Amendment rights?
- Do employers have the right to monitor employee use of company computers, cell phones, and other electronic devices?
- Have surveillance cameras lowered crime?
- Have terrorists used the Internet to recruit followers, disseminate propaganda, and plan attacks?
- Can police and courts effectively deter online stalking?

FOR FURTHER READING

To locate additional sources on privacy in the electronic age, enter these search terms into InfoTrac College Edition, available through your English CourseMate at **www.cengagebrain.com** or another one of your college library's databases:

Privacy
Subdivisions: analysis
                    beliefs, opinions, and attitudes
                    ethical aspects
                    forecasts and trends
                    political aspects
                    public opinion
                    social aspects

Wireless Telephones

Subdivisions: analysis

laws, regulations, and rules

public opinion

E-mail

Subdivision: analysis

ethical aspects

laws, regulations, and rules

political aspects

public opinion

Online Social Networks

Subdivisions: analysis

ethical aspects

laws, regulations, and rules

political aspects

ADDITIONAL SOURCES

Using a search engine, enter one or more of the following terms to locate additional sources:

surveillance cameras	GPS systems	Facebook
online predators	privacy	Twitter etiquette
e-mail privacy	identity theft	data mining
YouTube	bloggers	Google

See the Evaluating Internet Sources Checklist on pages 533–534.

John Taylor Gatto

John Taylor Gatto (1935–) taught in New York City public schools for twenty-five years and was named the city's Teacher of the Year three times. He has published several books about public education, including *Dumbing Us Down, The Exhausted School,* and *The Empty Child.* Since leaving teaching, Gatto has become a public speaker, addressing audiences at the White House and NASA's Goddard Space Flight Center.

Why Schools Don't Educate

Source: "Why Schools Don't Educate" by John Taylor Gatto. From the acceptance speech for the *New York State Teacher of the Year Award,* January 31, 1990. By permission.

In this section from a speech Gatto presented after receiving an award, he outlines the effects schools and television have had on children. As you read his list, consider if there could be other causes for the symptoms he observes.

1 Two institutions at present control our children's lives—television and schooling, in that order. Both of these reduce the real world of wisdom, fortitude, temperance, and justice to a never-ending, nonstop abstraction. In centuries past, the time of a child and adolescent would be occupied in real work, real charity, real adventures, and the real search for mentors who might teach what one really wanted to learn. A great deal of time was spent in community pursuits, practicing affection, meeting and studying every level of the community, learning how to make a home, and dozens of other tasks necessary to becoming a whole man or woman.

2 But here is the calculus of time the children I teach must deal with:

3 Out of the 168 hours in each week, my children must sleep fifty-six. That leaves them 112 hours a week out of which to fashion a self.

4 My children watch fifty-five hours of television a week, according to recent reports. That leaves them fifty-seven hours a week in which to grow up.

5 My children attend school thirty hours a week; use about eight hours getting ready, going, and coming home; and spend an average of seven hours a week in homework—a total of forty-five hours. During that time they are under constant surveillance, have no private time or private space, and are disciplined if they try to assert individuality in the use of time or space. That leaves twelve hours a week out of which to create a unique consciousness. Of course my kids eat, too, and that takes some time—not much, because we've lost the tradition of family dining. If we allot three hours a week to evening meals we arrive at a net amount of private time for each child of nine hours.

6 It's not enough. It's not enough, is it? The richer the kid, of course, the less television he watches, but the rich kid's time is just as narrowly proscribed by a broader catalogue of commercial entertainments and his inevitable assignment to a series of private lessons in areas seldom of his choice.

7 And these things are, oddly enough, just a more cosmetic way to create dependent human beings, unable to fill their own hours, unable to initiate lines of meaning to give substance and pleasure to their existence. It's a national disease, this

dependency and aimlessness, and I think schooling and television and lessons—the entire Chatauqua idea—have a lot to do with it.

8   Think of the things that are killing us as a nation: drugs, brainless competition, recreational sex, the pornography of violence, gambling, alcohol, and the worst pornography of all—lives devoted to buying things—accumulation as a philosophy. All are addictions of dependent personalities and that is what our brand of schooling must inevitably produce.

9   I want to tell you what the effect is on children of taking all their time—time they need to grow up—and forcing them to spend it on abstractions. No reform that doesn't attack these specific pathologies will be anything more than a facade.

10   1. The children I teach are indifferent to the adult world. This defies the experience of thousands of years. A close study of what big people were up to was always the most exciting occupation of youth, but nobody wants to grow up these days, and who can blame them. Toys are us.

11   2. The children I teach have almost no curiosity, and what little they do have is transitory; they cannot concentrate for very long, even on things they choose to do. Can you see a connection between the bells ringing again and again to change classes, and this phenomenon of evanescent attention?

12   3. The children I teach have a poor sense of the future, of how tomorrow is inextricably linked to today. They live in a continuous present; the exact moment they are in is the boundary of their consciousness.

13   4. The children I teach are ahistorical; they have no sense of how the past has predestined their own present, limiting their choices, shaping their values and lives.

14   5. The children I teach are cruel to each other; they lack compassion for misfortune, they laugh at weakness, they have contempt for people whose need for help shows too plainly.

15   6. The children I teach are uneasy with intimacy or candor. They cannot deal with genuine intimacy because of a lifelong habit of preserving a secret self inside an outer personality made up of artificial bits and pieces, of behavior borrowed from television or acquired to manipulate teachers. Because they are not who they represent themselves to be, the disguise wears thin in the presence of intimacy, so intimate relationships have to be avoided.

16   7. The children I teach are materialistic, following the lead of schoolteachers who materialistically "grade" everything—and television mentors who offer everything in the world for sale.

17   8. The children I teach are dependent, passive, and timid in the presence of new challenges. This timidity is frequently masked by surface bravado or by anger or aggressiveness, but underneath is a vacuum without fortitude.

18   I could name a few other conditions that school reform will have to tackle if our national decline is to be arrested, but by now you will have grasped my thesis, whether you agree with it or not. Either schools, television, or both have caused these pathologies. It's a simple matter of arithmetic. Between schooling and television, all the time children have is eaten up. That's what has destroyed the American family; it no longer is a factor in the education of its own children.

UNDERSTANDING CONTEXT

1. How, in Gatto's opinion, are education and television linked in children's lives?
2. How has television affected children's views of the world and their attitudes toward others?
3. Gatto states that schoolchildren are "cruel" and "passive." Can one be both cruel and passive?
4. *Critical thinking:* Gatto states that "children live in a continuous present" without a sense of past and future. Is this a natural attribute of childhood or something induced by television? Doesn't television at least portray popular history?

EVALUATING STRATEGY

1. How effective is Gatto's use of numbered steps?
2. All of Gatto's eight points open with the statement, "The children I teach . . ." Does this repetition become redundant or build emphasis?
3. What risk does a writer run in criticizing children? How might parents respond?
4. *Blending the modes:* Where does Gatto use *example*, *comparison*, and *persuasion* to develop his essay?

APPRECIATING LANGUAGE

1. Gatto uses the word *ahistorical.* How would you define this word?
2. Gatto calls "being devoted to buying things" the "worst pornography of all." Is *pornography* an effective word choice?

WRITING SUGGESTIONS

1. Write your own essay detailing the effects television has had on your generation or children you observe. Do your observations parallel those of Gatto?
2. *Collaborative writing:* Discuss Gatto's article with a group of students. Record their observations on school reform. Select the major ideas and use them to draft a letter to a local school board suggesting ways of improving education.

Peter Moskos is a former Baltimore police officer and Harvard graduate who is now an assistant professor at the John Jay College of Criminal Justice and the CUNY Graduate Center in the Department of Sociology. In his book *Cop in the Hood* (2008), which describes his experiences as a police officer in East Baltimore, Moskos called for reforming the legal system and legalizing drugs.

Too Dangerous Not to Regulate

Source: "Drugs Are Too Dangerous Not To Regulate–We Should Legalize Them: The nation's drug problem should be controlled through regulation and taxation" by Peter Moskos. *U.S. News & World Report*, July 25, 2008. By permission.

In this U.S. News & World Report *article, published in 2008, Moskos argues that the war on drugs has resulted in increased addiction, gang violence, and human suffering. Legalizing and regulating drugs, he predicts, would lessen drug use.*

1 Drugs are bad. So let's legalize them.

2 It's not as crazy as it sounds. Legalization does not mean giving up. It means regulation and control. By contrast, criminalization means prohibition. But we can't regulate what we prohibit, and drugs are too dangerous to remain unregulated.

3 Let's not debate which drugs are good and which are bad. While it's heartless to keep marijuana from terminally ill cancer patients, some drugs—crack, heroin, crystal meth—are undoubtedly bad. But prohibition is the issue, and, as with alcohol, it doesn't work. Between 1920 and 1933, we banned drinking. Despite, or more likely because of, the increased risk, drinking became cool. That's what happens when you delegate drug education to moralists. And crime increased, most notoriously with gangland killings. That's what happens when you delegate drug distribution to crooks. Prohibition of alcohol ended in failure, but for other drugs it continues.

4 Law enforcement can't reduce supply or demand. As a Baltimore police officer, I arrested drug dealers. Others took their place. I locked them up, too. Thanks to the drug war, we imprison more people than any other country. And America still leads the world in illegal drug use. We can't arrest and jail our way to a drug-free America. People want to get high. We could lock up everybody and still have a drug problem. Prisons have drug problems.

5 Illegal production remains high. Since 1981, the price of cocaine has dropped nearly 80 percent. Despite the ongoing presence of U.S. and other troops, Afghanistan has been exporting record levels of opium, from which heroin is made. Poor farmers may not want to sell to criminals, but they need to feed their families, and there is no legal market for illegal drugs. Al Qaeda in Afghanistan, the FARC in Colombia, and drug gangs in Mexico all rely on drug prohibition. A legal drug trade would do more to undermine these terrorists than military action would. If we taxed drugs, profits would go to governments, which fight terrorists.

6 Illegal drug dealers sell to anyone. Legal ones are licensed and help keep drugs such as beer, cigarettes, and pharmaceuticals away from minors. Illegal dealers settle disputes with guns. Legal ones solve theirs in court. Illegal dealers fear police. Legal ones fear the IRS.

7   Less use. Regulation can reduce drug use. In two generations, we've halved the number of cigarette smokers not through prohibition but through education, regulated selling, and taxes. And we don't jail nicotine addicts. Drug addiction won't go away, but tax revenue can help pay for treatment.

8   The Netherlands provides a helpful example. Drug addiction there is considered a health problem. Dutch policy aims to save lives and reduce use. It succeeds: Three times as many heroin addicts overdose in Baltimore as in all of the Netherlands. Sixteen percent of Americans try cocaine in their lifetime. In the Netherlands, the figure is less than 2 percent. The Dutch have lower rates of addiction, overdose deaths, homicides, and incarceration. Clearly, they're doing something right. Why not learn from success? The Netherlands decriminalized marijuana in 1976. Any adult can walk into a legally licensed, heavily regulated "coffee shop" and buy or consume top-quality weed without fear of arrest. Under this system, people in the Netherlands are half as likely as Americans to have ever smoked marijuana.

9   It's unlikely that repealing federal drug laws would result in a massive increase in drug use. People take or don't take drugs for many reasons, but apparently legality isn't high on the list. In America, drug legalization could happen slowly and, unlike federal prohibition, not be forced on any state or city. City and state governments could decide policy based on their needs.

10   The war on drugs is not about saving lives or stopping crime. It's about yesteryear's ideologues and future profits from prison jobs, asset forfeiture, court overtime pay, and federal largess.

11   We have a choice: Legalize drugs, or embark on a second century of failed prohibition. Government regulation may not sound as sexy or as macho as a "war on drugs," but it works better.

UNDERSTANDING CONTEXT

1. What is Moskos's thesis? Can you state it in your own words?
2. Why does Moskos believe that legalizing drugs should not be seen as a surrender in the fight against drugs?
3. What effect would legalizing drugs have on terrorists?
4. Why does Moskos believe that legalizing drugs would not increase their use?
5. *Critical thinking:* Why does Moskos see the war on drugs as a failure? Why can law enforcement not stop illegal drug use?

EVALUATING STRATEGY

1. How effective is Moskos's introduction?
2. How does Moskos use comparisons to support his thesis? Are they effective? Can a writer rely too much on analogies?
3. How does Moskos address opposing arguments?
4. *Critical thinking:* How does Moskos use his experience as a police officer to establish his credibility as an authority on drugs?

APPRECIATING LANGUAGE

1. Does the word *legalization* suggest acceptance or approval? How does Moskos try to define the word?

2. Moskos refers to beer and cigarettes as "drugs." Do you think many readers will equate beer with heroin? Why or why not?

WRITING SUGGESTIONS

1. Using Moskos's article as a model, write a cause-and-effect essay that analyzes the success or failure of a social or government policy. Has school choice improved education? Have drunk-driving laws changed people's behavior?

2. *Collaborative writing:* Working with a group of students, discuss Moskos's article and determine if you agree or disagree with his view. Write an essay stating your group's views. If members have conflicting opinions, consider developing a comparison paper stating opposing viewpoints.

Lee P. Brown (1937–) earned a degree in criminology from Fresno State University in 1960. He earned a master's degree in criminology from the University of California–Berkeley, from which he also received his doctorate in 1970. He headed police departments in Atlanta, Houston, and New York City before becoming the first African American mayor of Houston, Texas, in 1997. In 1993 he served as the Director of the Office of National Drug Control Policy (the nation's "drug czar") under President Clinton.

End the Demand, End the Supply

Source: "Drugs Are a Major Social Problem, We Cannot Legalize Them" by Lee P. Brown. *U.S. News & World Report,* July 25, 2008. Reprinted with permission from Wright's Media

In this article, which appeared with Peter Moskos's article in U.S. News & World Report *in 2008, Brown rejects Moskos's call for the legalization of drugs.*

1 Illegal drugs continue to be a major problem in America. They will never be legalized, and they should not be.

2 Advocates of legalization argue that drug prohibition only makes things worse. They argue that crime, the spread of HIV, and violence are major consequences of drug prohibition. But these represent only part of the damage caused by drug use. Consider drug-exposed infants, drug-induced accidents, and loss of productivity and employment, not to mention the breakdown of families and the degeneration of drug-inflicted neighborhoods. These too are consequences of drugs.

3 Others argue that drugs affect only the user. This is wrong. No one familiar with alcohol abuse would suggest that alcoholism affects the user solely. And no one who works with drug addicts will tell you that their use of drugs has not affected others— usually family and friends.

4 Some argue that drug enforcement should be replaced by a policy of "harm reduction," which emphasizes decriminalization and medical treatment over law enforcement and interdiction. But people do not use drugs simply because they are illegal. Equally significant, effective enforcement reduces drug supply, increases price, lowers the number of users, and decreases hard-core drug use. There is an inverse relationship between the price of cocaine and the number of people seeking emergency room treatment.

5 Legalization advocates claim widespread support. But the fact is that there is no broad public or political outcry for the decriminalization of drugs.

6 Contrary to what the advocates of legalization say about the European models, decriminalization has not worked there. The Dutch policy of "responsible" drug use has resulted in thousands of foreigners going to the Netherlands to buy drugs. These users then commit crimes to support their habits and drain Dutch taxpayers to provide treatment for their addictions. The number of marijuana and heroin users has increased significantly.

7 The British experience of controlled distribution of heroin resulted in the doubling of the number of recorded new addicts every 16 months between 1960 and 1967. That experiment was ended.

8   A 1994 resolution opposing drug legalization in Europe that was signed by representatives of several European cities stated in part that "the answer does not lie in making harmful drugs more accessible, cheaper and socially acceptable. Attempts to do this have not proven successful."

9   Supply and demand. An effective drug policy must focus on reducing the demand for drugs through prevention, education, and treatment without overlooking enforcement and working with source countries. That was the policy that I developed while serving as the nation's "drug czar" under President Clinton. The formula is simple: no demand, no supply.

10   In 1988, the House Select Committee on Narcotics Abuse and Control, chaired by Rep. Charles Rangel, a New York Democrat, held hearings on the possible legalization of drugs. The questions asked by Rangel then are equally relevant today: Which drugs would we legalize—heroin, cocaine, methamphetamines, and PCP, as well as marijuana? What would we do with addicts? Would we support their habit for life or pay for their treatment? What would we do about those who are only experimenting? Would legalization contribute to their addiction? What would prevent a black market from emerging?

11   Because these and other questions cannot be answered to the satisfaction of the U.S. public and our lawmakers, America will never legalize drugs.

12   Legalization does not get to the problem's core. In seeking to satisfy the few, it subverts the best interests of all. In purporting to provide a quick, simple, costless cure for crime and violence, it fails to answer why more drug availability would not lead to more drug use and more devastating consequences.

13   We must, however, change our drug policy and view drug use as a public health problem, not just a problem for the criminal justice system.

UNDERSTANDING CONTEXT

1. What is Brown's thesis? Can you state it in your own words?
2. How does Brown counter Moskos's argument that decriminalization has lowered drug use in Europe?
3. How, in Brown's view, does effective law enforcement decrease drug use?
4. Why does Brown believe that legalization would have negative consequences?
5. *Critical thinking:* Are there any points on which Moskos and Brown agree?

EVALUATING STRATEGY

1. How does Brown introduce his personal experience to establish credibility?
2. *Blending the modes:* How does Brown use *comparison* to develop his cause-and-effect essay?
3. Brown argues that law enforcement reduces supply. Would his argument be stronger if he included facts or statistics to support this assertion? Why or why not?

APPRECIATING LANGUAGE

1. Brown places words like "harm reduction" and "responsible" in quotation marks. What impact does this have? What is he trying to suggest about these terms?

2. *Critical thinking:* Brown uses the term "supply and demand" as being critical to combating drug use. Do you think many programs simply focus on one aspect of the issue, such as cutting demand through education or limiting supply by arrests and seizures? Would society have to stress both supply and demand for such programs to be effective? Why or why not?

WRITING SUGGESTIONS

1. Using Moskos's and Brown's articles as models, write a short essay stating your prediction about the legalization of drugs. If drugs were legalized but regulated like alcohol or cigarettes, would more people use drugs? Would it reduce crime by eliminating gangs? Would it make the drug problem better or worse?

2. *Collaborative writing:* Discuss Moskos's and Brown's articles with a group of students and ask which author they find more convincing and why. Write a short essay reflecting the ideas of your group. If members disagree, consider writing a comparison essay presenting pro and con views.

WRITING BEYOND THE CLASSROOM

CAMPUS HEALTH OFFICE
Health alert
Sharing of prescription medication

Background

Recent studies have shown that one in four Americans share prescription drugs with others. A campus survey revealed that 18% of students reported giving prescription medication to friends. The most commonly shared drugs included painkillers and antidepressants.

Causes

- Peer pressure
- Desire to help friends in distress, provide immediate relief, spare friends cost of physician or hospital visits
- Lack of understanding of potential risks
- General belief that prescription medications are safer than illegal or "street drugs"

Effects

- Accidental overdoses
- Allergic reactions and interactions with other medications
- Masking of symptoms, delaying needed medical evaluation and treatment
- Fraudulent requests for additional medication

Recommendations

The college must educate students about the dangers of sharing prescription medication.

- Include a unit on sharing prescription medications in freshman orientation.
- Add banner message on Student Life website with link to Campus Health.
- Remind coaches, health instructors, biology instructors, therapists, and counselors who have contact with students to instruct them about the dangers of sharing prescription medication.
- Post warnings in dorms, classroom buildings, locker rooms, student union.

UNDERSTANDING CONTEXT

1. Why do people share prescription drugs?
2. What are the harmful effects of sharing medication?
3. Why do people fail to recognize the hazards of providing medication to friends?
4. How can a college make students appreciate the dangers of sharing prescription drugs?

EVALUATING STRATEGY

1. How effective is the use of bulleted points and short sentences? Would the same message stated in standard paragraphs be as effective? Why or why not?
2. This alert labels sections "Causes," "Effects," and "Recommendations." Is this effective? Why or why not?
3. *Blending the modes:* How does the alert move from causes and effects to making a *persuasive* argument?

APPRECIATING LANGUAGE

1. What audience does the alert seem to address? Can you detect any technical terms that would be unfamiliar to general readers?
2. What language is used to characterize the people who give their medication to friends?

WRITING SUGGESTIONS

1. Using this health alert as a model, write a similar alert to warn students about identity theft, smoking, binge drinking, cheating, or any other harmful activity. Use bulleted lists to make your message easy to skim and remember.
2. *Collaborative writing:* Working with a group of students, review this health alert and "translate" its bulleted points into standard sentences and paragraphs for a short article suited for the college newspaper or campus website.

RESPONDING TO IMAGES

A real estate agent holding a FORECLOSURE sign

Antenna/Jupiter Images

1. What is your first reaction to this picture? What words come to mind?

2. Does this photograph illustrate a national crisis or a family crisis or both?

3. Could you imagine using this photograph as a political campaign poster? What caption could accompany it? How could a caption shape the picture's message?

4. *Critical thinking:* Who do you think is most responsible for the mortgage crisis—officials who deregulated the financial industry, irresponsible lenders, or people who bought houses they knew they could not afford?

5. *Visual analysis:* How does the sign contrast with the house? Does it appear to attack or call into question homeownership? What does the house represent? What indications reveal that this is a posed rather than a candid photograph?

6. *Collaborative writing:* Discuss this photograph with a group of students and have each one write a caption. What does each person's caption represent? Can a photograph like this serve as a kind of Rorschach test that reveals an individual's perceptual world?

7. *Other modes:*
   - Develop a *comparison* essay that uses a before-and-after approach to examine how the 2008 recession changed the real estate market, availability of credit, and perceptions about houses as investment tools.
   - Write a *narrative* essay about someone you know who has lost his or her home or is struggling to pay a mortgage.

CAUSE-AND-EFFECT CHECKLIST

Before submitting your paper, review these points:

✔ Is your thesis clearly stated?

✔ Are causes clearly stated, logically organized, and supported by details?

✔ Are conflicting interpretations disproven or acknowledged?

✔ Are effects supported by observation and evidence? Do you avoid sweeping generalizations and unsupported conclusions?

✔ Do you anticipate future changes that might alter predictions?

✔ Do you avoid making errors in critical thinking, especially hasty generalization and mistaking an effect for a cause?

✔ Have you tested your ideas through peer review?

 Access the English CourseMate for this text at **www.cengagebrain.com** for additional information on writing cause and effect

Argument and Persuasion
Influencing Readers

What Are Argument and Persuasion?

We are bombarded by argument and persuasion every day. TV commentators encourage us to change our opinions about capital punishment or immigration. Sales brochures convince us to invest in stocks or purchase life insurance. Billboards, e-mail, magazine ads, and television commercials urge us to buy computers, automobiles, perfumes, and soft drinks. Political candidates solicit our votes. Public service announcements warn us against smoking and drunk driving.

As a student you have to develop persuasive arguments in essays and research papers to demonstrate your skills and knowledge. After graduation you will need a persuasive résumé and cover letter to enter the job market. In your career you will have to impress clients, motivate employees, justify decisions, defend actions, and propose new ideas with well-stated arguments and persuasive appeals.

Arguments are assertions designed to convince readers to accept an idea, adopt a solution, or change their opinions. Writers use reason and facts to support their arguments, often disproving or disputing conflicting theories or alternative proposals in the process. Attorneys prepare written arguments stating why a client has a valid claim or deserves a new trial. Scientists present the results of experiments to argue for new medical treatments or to disprove current assumptions. Economists assemble data to support arguments to raise or lower interest rates.

Persuasive Appeals

In ancient times Aristotle and other philosophers established three classic persuasive appeals to convince people to accept ideas or take action: **logos, pathos,** and **ethos.** Today these appeals appear in television commercials, political campaign speeches, business proposals, and ordinary e-mail. Because each appeal has advantages and disadvantages, writers often use more than one.

Logos

Logos (**Logic**) supports a point of view or proposed action with critical thinking (see Chapter 4), reasoned arguments, and evidence such as the following:

    Test results—Findings established by experiments or research
    Statistics—Data represented as numbers and percentages
    Documents—Materials such as diaries, letters, reports, photographs, and videos generated by participants or witnesses of specific events or situations

Sam Diephuis/jupiterimages

Maria Toutoudaki/jupiterimages

Expert testimony—Opinions by respected authorities

Eyewitness testimony—Statements by those who observed or experienced an event or situation

Interpretation—Critical reading and analysis of accepted laws, principles, contracts, and other documents, such as the Constitution

Examples—Specific instances, events, or cases

Hypothetical examples—Fictional examples used to illustrate ideas

Surveys—Polls of public opinion or interviews with sample audiences

Logic is widely used in academic, business, and government writing. Attorneys use expert testimony, forensic evidence, and interpretations of legal principles to persuade judges and juries. You probably used logic in preparing high school research papers.

Advantages

- Provides evidence for major decisions, especially group decisions
- Presents facts readers can independently verify
- Offers support readers can use to persuade others or defend decisions

Disadvantages

- Demands high degree of reader attention and concentration
- May require specialized knowledge
- Takes time to present and absorb

Pathos

Pathos **(Emotion)** uses images, sensations, or shock techniques to lead people to react in a desired manner. Emotional appeals call on people's deeply felt needs and desires for the following:

Creativity—The desire for recognition and self-expression

Achievement—The desire to attain money, fame, or professional accomplishments

Independence—The drive to be unique, to stand out, to be an individual

Conformity—The need to be part of a group, to have friends, to be one of the "in" group

Endurance—The desire to be recognized for bearing burdens others have avoided or could not bear; feeling successful by simply surviving

Fear—The need to resist, avoid, or defeat threats to self, family, or the community, to fight crime, cancer, or terrorism

Popularity—The desire to be accepted, respected, admired by friends, coworkers, or the opposite sex

Emotional appeals are widely used in public relations, marketing, advertising, and political campaigns. Sex appeal is used to sell products ranging from cars to shampoo. Images of starving children will provoke pity and empathy, encouraging people to donate money or lobby politicians for government action. Fear of crime, terrorism, disease, or job loss can be used to motivate audiences to vote for a candidate or support a change in policy.

Advantages

- Produces immediate responses
- Requires little special knowledge or preparation

Disadvantages

- Can be short-lived
- Provides little support that can be shared with others

Ethos

Ethos **(Ethics)** uses shared values to influence readers. Appeals based on ethics may call upon reasoning but do not rest wholly on the logical analysis of evidence. Like emotional appeals, those based on ethics reflect deeply held convictions rather than personal motivations.

Religion—The desire to follow the rules and behavior espoused by one's faith—to be a good Jew, Christian, or Muslim

Patriotism—The drive to place one's country above personal needs, to sacrifice for community ("Ask not what your country can do for you; ask what you can do for your country.")

Standards—The desire to be a good citizen, a good lawyer, or a good parent, to express the higher ideals of a community, profession, or social role

Humanitarianism—A secular appeal to help others, save the environment, protect the weak, or be "a citizen of the world"

Ethical appeals form the basis of many sermons, editorials, and political speeches that emphasize shared values and beliefs.

Advantages

- Calls upon readers' core values
- Can inspire others to make sacrifices

Disadvantages

- Appeals to a limited audience with shared values
- Assumes readers share writer's definition of values such as patriotism, Christianity, or loyalty

Blending Appeals

To create effective persuasive messages, writers frequently blend factual details with emotionally charged human interest stories. A fund-raising letter for a children's shelter might use the emotional story of a single child to arouse sympathy, provide facts and statistics to demonstrate the severity of the problem, and then conclude with an ethical appeal for financial support:

MAKE A DIFFERENCE

Pathos:
emotional example
demonstrating a
problem

Thirteen-year-old Sandy Lopez will not have to sleep in a doorway tonight. Abandoned by abusive parents, she spent six weeks living in subway stations and alleys before she came to Safe Haven. Today she has a warm bed, clean clothes, and regular meals. She is back in school, making friends, and studying music.

Logos:
factual support
presenting a
solution

Since 1986 Safe Haven has helped thousands of homeless children find shelter, counseling, and support. Eighty percent of our clients complete high school and almost a third graduate from college.

But Safe Haven has only 90 beds and every day has to turn away dozens of the 2,000 homeless children who live in the streets, where they often succumb to drugs, prostitution, and alcohol abuse. To meet the growing need, Safe Haven needs your help to build a new dorm, hire more counselors, and expand its job training center.

Ethos:
ethical call
to action

Living in one of the richest cities in the world, can we ignore the children who sleep in our streets? Make a difference. Contribute to Safe Haven today.

WRITING ACTIVITY

Select one or more of the following writing situations and give examples of the best appeal or appeals. Note advantages and disadvantages of each appeal.

1. A fund-raising brochure for a day care center, to be distributed in churches

2. An announcement encouraging students to avoid binge drinking

3. A congressional candidate's letter to voters advocating privatizing Social Security

4. A school board's letter urging parents to attend parent–teacher meetings

5. The text of a public service announcement reminding people to vote

6. A minister's appeal to his or her congregation to donate money to victims of a natural disaster

7. A scientist's statement to Congress urging further funds for genetic research

8. A homeowner's appeal to an alderman for street repairs in his or her neighborhood

9. An automobile manufacturer's letter to car owners explaining the need for a recall to repair an engine defect

10. An environmental group's letter requesting that the city cease using lawn chemicals in public parks

Understanding Logic: Deduction and Induction

Logic is the most important appeal used in college and professional writing. Two of the basic terms in logic—**deduction** and **induction**—are commonly misunderstood and are worth reviewing. Many of the problems we encounter as students, consumers, employees, family members, and citizens involve deductive and inductive thinking. Whether you are constructing an argument using deduction or induction, it is important to avoid *logical fallacies*—errors in critical thinking (see pages 39–41).

Deduction

Deduction is a logical argument stated in a formula or syllogism with the following components:

Major Premise—a general statement of what is true or assumed to be true.

Minor Premise—a specific example, case, or situation

Conclusion—the result

Example:

MAJOR PREMISE: All full-time students are eligible for financial aid.

MINOR PREMISE: Jane Kwan is a full-time student.

CONCLUSION: *Jane Kwan is eligible for financial aid.*

Sample Major Premises

warranties	union contracts	lease agreements
insurance policies	employee manuals	building codes
IRS regulation	the Constitution	traffic laws

Sample Minor Premises

an employee applying for early retirement
a renter considering subletting her apartment
a restaurateur thinking of turning an old duplex into a steak house.

All these situations require the use of deduction. A 57-year-old employee would have to check his or her employee or union contract to see if he or she is old enough for early retirement. A lease determines whether renters are allowed to sublet. Zoning ordinances stipulate whether a residential building can be converted into commercial property.

If the major premise in deductive reasoning is incorrect or vaguely worded, problems can emerge. Many lawsuits concern disputed interpretations of a major premise, such as

Tenants can be evicted for excessive noise.

What constitutes "excessive noise"—continually disturbing neighbors with a loud stereo or hosting a single wild party? Who decides what is "excessive noise"? Do the standards differ between an apartment building housing the elderly and one filled with college students? Can you argue against eviction if the police were never called and no neighbor filed a complaint? Is the landlord the sole judge of a tenant's behavior? If landlords and tenants have different interpretations of the terms of a lease, conflicts can occur.

Before signing a contract or making a verbal agreement with an employer or contractor, review it carefully. Any clause two parties accept will become a major premise. In writing rules, policies, or regulations for employees, make sure you define ideas clearly and illustrate them with examples:

> Employees may use a sick day to attend the funeral of an immediate family member—
> a parent, sibling, child, or the parent, sibling, child of your spouse.

QUESTIONS

1. Can you think of instances where you have encountered problems in deduction? Have you had disputes based on conflicting interpretations of a lease, warranty, tax regulation, or school policy?

2. Do you see any potential problems with the following rules or major premises? Could different interpretations create confusion or conflicts?
   - Disadvantaged students have priority for on-campus jobs.
   - Students must have completed a substantial amount of work to be eligible for a course extension.
   - Employees can be terminated for excessive tardiness.

Induction

Unlike deduction, induction does not begin with a premise or assertion of what is true. Instead, an inductive argument starts with evidence, bits of information. From these specifics, a general conclusion is drawn. Induction can be illustrated by a simple diagram:

```
       XXX    XXX        XX    X      evidence
         XXXXXX        XXX
       XXX   XX      X    XX
         XXXXXX        XXX   X
```
_____*inductive leap*_____

CONCLUSION

Examples of evidence:

surveys and polls	interviews	test results
historical documents	eyewitness testimony	photographs
financial records	crime-scene evidence	statistics

Induction is used by physicians to make a diagnosis. Based on observations, test results, and the patient's history, doctors establish the reason for a medical complaint. Detectives investigating a crime scene collect evidence that is examined to identify suspects. Pollsters conduct voter surveys to determine the likely outcome of an election. Stockbrokers review a company's current sales, debts, market share, and competition to advise potential investors. In all these cases, professionals assemble data, analyze it, and then make an "inductive leap" to draw a conclusion. No one can be 100 percent sure that he or she has properly assembled and interpreted the information; there is always a degree of doubt.

A criminal trial best illustrates the inductive process. In a murder case, the prosecutor presents evidence of the defendant's guilt—eyewitness testimony, fingerprints, expert witnesses, and so forth—and tells the jury that all the evidence adds up to a clear guilty verdict. The defense attorney may introduce contradictory evidence or question the interpretation of the prosecution's evidence to argue that there is not enough proof to conclude that the defendant is guilty. Lawyers don't use the term *inductive leap*—but the legal concept of *reasonable doubt* is very close.

We use inductive logic in making decisions. In choosing a new apartment, we weigh a number of factors—rent, location, appearance, appliances, and the like—and then make a decision based on our observations. To determine if a used car is worth $5,000, we take a test drive, check the tires for wear, determine the mileage, ask the previous owner about problems, and check the car's blue-book value. From this information we conclude whether the car merits its price.

As with deduction, problems occur with inductive logic. Evidence may be improperly collected, overlooked, or misinterpreted. Public opinion polls can contain leading questions that encourage people to respond in a certain way. Surveys may not include all the subjects they are supposed to measure. Eyewitnesses may have faulty memories or misinterpret what they have seen. Even when statistics are accurately collected, it can be difficult to determine what they mean. If reports of identity theft increase, does it prove that identity theft is on the rise or only that more cases are being reported? Minor pieces of evidence may be given too much importance, while significant results are ignored or minimized. People with preconceived opinions may select only that evidence that supports their point of view.

QUESTIONS

1. How often have you used induction in solving problems or making decisions? What problems have you encountered?

2. Have you observed the use of inductive reasoning during televised trials? How effective have cross-examinations been in raising reasonable doubt?

3. Do your textbooks in other courses offer methods of collecting and evaluating evidence? Do disciplines value different types of evidence? Do some courses stress statistics, whereas others rely on expert opinion?

Persuasion and Audience

Whenever you write, you should consider your audience—the people who will read your papers, e-mail, reports, and letters. A narrative or description will only be effective if readers understand the definitions, examples, and details you present to support your thesis. In writing persuasion, however, you have to consider your readers more carefully. Unlike a narrative or a description, an argument seeks not to simply tell a story or share information but to influence people to change their minds or take action. Readers of persuasive writing are more likely to be critical, even hostile to your viewpoints. To win support, you may have to refute alternative arguments, dismiss competing interpretations of evidence, or admit the value of opposing ideas. The psychologist Carl R. Rogers studied problems in communications and emphasized the importance of building trust by addressing audience concerns and objections. *Rogerian* arguments work to build consensus by showing respect to people holding opposing viewpoints.

Appealing to Hostile Readers

Perhaps the most challenging problem writers face is attempting to persuade a hostile audience—readers you know or expect will have negative attitudes about you, the organization you represent, or the ideas you advocate. Although no technique will magically convert opponents into supporters, you can overcome a measure of hostility and influence those who may be undecided with a few strategies:

1. **Openly admit differences.** Instead of attempting to pretend that no conflict exists, frankly state that your view may differ from that of your readers. This honest admission can achieve a measure of objectivity and respect.

2. **Responsibly summarize opposing viewpoints.** By fairly restating your opponents' views, you convince readers to agree with you and you demonstrate objectivity.

3. **Avoid making judgmental statements.** Don't label people with differing views with hostile or negative language. Use neutral terms to make distinctions. If you call your views "right" and your readers' "wrong," you will have difficulty getting people to accept your thesis, because in the process they will have to accept your insults as valid. Demeaning language will only alienate readers.

4. **Stress shared values, experiences, and problems.** Build bridges with your readers by emphasizing past cooperation and common concerns.

5. **Ask readers to maintain an open mind.** Don't demand or expect to convert readers, but keep in mind that almost everyone will agree to try to be open-minded and receptive to new ideas.

6. **Overcome negative stereotypes.** Play the devil's advocate to determine what negative stereotypes your readers might have about you, the organization you represent, or your thesis. Include examples, references, evidence, and stories in your paper to counter these negative impressions.

WRITING ACTIVITY

Select one of the following writing contexts and list some strategies to overcome hostile reactions. What facts, narratives, appeals, or approaches would help advance the writer's thesis? What issues does the writer have to address? How can he or she counter objections? What information would the writer have to include?

1. An African American writing a letter to the editor of a conservative business magazine arguing for stronger affirmative action policies

2. A feminist writing an article about sexual harassment directed to business owners and managers

3. A real estate developer writing to a community group opposing the construction of a new shopping mall

4. A student group writing to alumni to suggest that funds being raised for a new athletic facility be spent on computer labs

5. A district attorney explaining to a crime victim why her attacker has been allowed to plead to a lesser charge and receive probation rather than a prison sentence

6. A defense attorney drafting opening remarks to a jury in a highly publicized child abuse case

7. A tenant writing to a landlord urging him to add security features, such as deadbolts, to apartments

8. A college administrator developing an open letter to students defending a campus organization's decision to invite a controversial public speaker

9. A person acquitted but believed by many to be guilty of a violent sexual assault addressing a school board about why he or she should keep a teaching position

10. A director of the Food and Drug Administration explaining to AIDS patients why a new drug requires further testing before being approved for human use, even for the terminally ill

Strategies for Planning Argument and Persuasion

Critical Thinking and Prewriting

1. **List as many topics, problems, issues, controversies, debates, and decisions you can think of.** Brainstorm, freewrite briefly, and list questions to isolate promising topics.

2. **Review the scope of the assignment.** Effective argument-and-persuasion papers require substantial evidence and reasoning.
   - Topics like capital punishment, gun control, abortion, and sexual harassment are difficult to address in a short paper unless you take a unique approach or develop a new angle. Avoid writing papers that simply repeat commonly stated positions.
   - Discard topics that require extensive research or are simply too complex be fully addressed given the limits of your paper.

3. **Determine the goal of your essay—to persuade readers to accept your opinion or to motivate readers to take action or alter their behavior.**

4. **Consider your audience.** Define your readers and their perceptual world. List the past experiences, social roles, values, norms, attitudes, and reference groups that may influence their thinking.
   - Determine their immediate attitude toward your topic. Are your readers likely to be open-minded and neutral or bring strongly held opinions to the issue?
   - List questions and concerns your readers may have.
   - List appeals readers will relate to and respond to.

5. **Develop a thesis statement and a list of principal appeals with your readers in mind.**

6. **List evidence needed to support your thesis.** Conduct a computer search using keywords to locate current sources about your topic.
   - Evaluate sources carefully for accuracy and bias.

Planning

1. **Review critical thinking.** Before writing a plan, review Strategies for Increasing Critical Thinking (pages 38–39) and Common Errors in Critical Thinking (pages 39–41).

2. **Write your thesis statement at the top of the page to guide planning.** Qualify your thesis, avoiding generalizations, absolute statements, and unsupported assumptions.

3. **Develop an introduction that arouses attention, establishes your approach, and uses persuasive appeals to create a favorable relationship with readers.**
   - You may wish to open your essay with a question, a narrative, a quote, or a statistic that illustrates or dramatizes the issue.
   - Consider carefully whether you wish to announce your thesis immediately or present supporting details or answer potential objections before presenting an opinion that may alienate readers.

4. **Do not mistake propaganda for persuasion.** Do not assume that hurling accusations, using inflated statistics, employing shock tactics, or demonizing

(Continued)

your opponents will make your argument successful. People resent manipulation, and potential supporters may be alienated by exaggerated arguments and appeals they find objectionable or false.

5. **Organize ideas in order of importance.** Place the most convincing appeal or argument at the beginning or end of your paper, where reader attention is strongest.

6. **Consider using visuals.** Photographs, charts, and diagrams can add effective support to a persuasive message—provided they are carefully selected and properly presented.

   ■ Select images that suit the appeals you are using. The image of a starving child may offer moving support for a fund-raising poster using emotional appeal but would be inappropriate in an academic paper. Charts, diagrams, and graphs can help readers appreciate data in a business report but add little to an essay based on ethical appeals.

   ■ Avoid using images that may alienate readers. (See Strategies for Using Visuals in College Writing in Chapter 28).

7. **Conclude the paper with a thought-provoking impression or a clear call to action.** End the paper with a final fact, example, or quotation that will influence readers to consider your thesis, perhaps even read more to fully understand your point of view. If your goal is to direct people to alter their behavior, present explicit instructions so that motivated readers can take immediate action.

Strategies for Writing Argument and Persuasion

Writing the First Draft

1. **Keep your thesis and audience in mind as you write.** Select appeals, ideas, and facts your readers will understand and respond to.

2. **Qualify remarks, noting possible alternative views.** Avoid making absolute statements that can be easily refuted by citing a single exception.

3. **Recognize the strength and weakness of each appeal.** Balance emotional appeals with facts. Dramatize statistics with human interest. Adapt ethical appeals to your readers' perceptual world.

4. **Present factual detail in ways readers can understand.** Use examples, analogies, and narratives to illustrate and dramatize evidence.

5. **Use transitional phrases and paragraph breaks to signal shifts between main points of your argument.**

6. **Keep the scope of the assignment in mind as you write, and consider limiting the topic if the draft becomes too lengthy.**

7. **Anticipate reader objections.** Play the devil's advocate as you write. Consider how you can overcome or counter readers' negative assumptions about your thesis.

Strategies for Revising and Editing Argument and Persuasion

Revising

1. **Review the needs of the writing assignment; then examine your entire essay.**
   - On first reading, does your essay meet the needs of the assignment?
   - Is the topic suitable?
   - Is the thesis clearly stated?
   - If you are motivating readers to do something, are they given a clearly defined course of action to follow?

2. **Examine your use of appeals.**
   - Are logical appeals clear, accurate, and suitable to your task?
   - Do you present clear, convincing evidence your readers will accept?
   - Do emotional appeals avoid bias or propaganda that may offend readers or cause a backlash?
   - Are ethical appeals suited to your audience? Do your readers share the values you call upon?

3. **Review critical thinking.** Do you avoid common errors in critical thinking (see pages 39–41)?

4. **Examine the placement of your thesis.** Should the thesis be placed at the opening or end of the essay? Would it be more effective to present background information, address reader objections, and clear up misconceptions before announcing your point of view?

5. **Review your introduction and conclusion.**
   - Does the first paragraph clearly announce your purpose, limit the topic, and qualify your approach? Does it grab attention and prepare readers to accept your message?
   - Does the conclusion urge readers to consider your thesis or direct them to take action?

6. **Examine the paper's structure.**
   - Are there clear transitions between main points?
   - Could paragraph breaks be altered to demonstrate shifts and emphasize ideas?

(Continued)

7. **Review your use of visuals.** Do they support your message? Are they appropriate, effective, and clearly presented?
8. **Use peer review to identify areas needing improvement.**

Editing and Proofreading

1. **Read your paper aloud.**
   - Are ideas stated in specific language readers can understand?
   - Do any words have connotations unsuited to your purpose or audience?
   - Do the tone and style suit your topic, audience, and message?
2. **Use peer editing to locate errors you may have missed.**

STUDENT PAPER

This paper was written in response to the following assignment:

> Write a 500–750 word persuasive essay about a current social or political issue. Avoid writing about subjects such as abortion or capital punishment unless you can provide a new or unique angle. Document use of any outside sources.

FIRST DRAFT WITH INSTRUCTOR'S COMMENTS

This college, like many others, has and needs a Black Student Union. It has nothing to do

Weak, vague *What does everyone "seem to think"?* *What claims?*

with what everyone seems to think it has. A lot of people who make these claims have never

even bothered to visit the Black Student Union or bothered to check the facts they saw in

the paper. *What did they see in the paper?*

   People say black students are getting paid to run their organization, which is so totally

wordy, revise

not the case. In fact, the Black Student Union only receives money to operate a study center

SP *Words missing?*

that, in fact, serves lots of non-blacks because the Acamdemic Support Center. The union

received money last year, but most of it went to fix the building, which does belong to the

university.

(Continued)

"fostering"?

Many people criticize the Black Student Center for ~~foresting~~ racial discrimination.

This is not the case. We live in integrated dorms, attend integrated classes, and play

well stated

on integrated teams. The few hours a week a student might spend at the BSU hardly

threatens to create racial isolation. Other students have specialized centers, and no

one seems bothered about that. In addition, people have accused the BSU of being a

hotbed of radical politics. I see no evidence of this. *explain, expand*

Black students need the BSU. Black students are a minority on this campus.

It is easy for them to feel alienated and isolated. And they are at high risk for

failure. "Since only one of eight black males entering a university will graduate, it

is imperative that we seek remedies to support their academic achievement and

Link quote to your text, explain who Smith is.

professional advancement"(Smith). And the BSU does just that. Black students

have problems finding friends and building positive reinforcement networks that

provide needed personal support. Because few of their friends in high school

were college-bound, they had to isolate themselves and study on their own. This

habit, however, is not always the best strategy in college. Many students benefited

from "social promotion" and when they get to college, they discover that their

A's and B's were really more equal to C's and D's in better suburban schools. The

Black Student Union offers African American students a place to relax, to interact

with older students, and work to make the university a more hospitable place for

minorities.

Works Cited

Smith, Dean. *Black Males in Crisis.* New York: Scribners, 2011. Print.

(Continued)

REVISION NOTES

You have an interesting topic for a persuasive essay, but you need to make several improvements to produce a truly effective paper.

* You mention that the Black Student Union has critics and refer to the recent newspaper article. Expand this point. Explain the claims and criticisms of those who oppose the Black Student Union, then disprove or discount them point by point.

* You need to provide additional factual support to counter charges that the Union is getting too much money.

* Document sources fully. You list the Smith book in Works Cited but do not show the page reference for the quote you use.

* Finally, read your draft out loud. Missing words, awkward sentences, and wordy phrases are easier to hear than see.

REVISED DRAFT

Why a Black Student Union?

Before any controversial issue can be discussed, there is usually a certain amount of misinformation to deal with. This is clearly the case with the Black Student Union. Many students have voiced concern and written letters to the editor since the college paper revealed that $540,000 was being allocated to the Union (Kane 1). The article stated that $52,000 was going to salaries, making the Black Student Union the only student organization with a paid staff.

First of all, the bulk of the money allocated to the Union is dedicated to renovating the building, which is university property. Constructed in 1962, the building has not had major repairs since 1974. Roof leaks, first reported to the administration three years ago, have led to substantial and costly damage. In addition, it is the only building that was not retrofitted with new heating and air conditioning systems in 1996 (CSU 22). Also, the building still does not comply with the Americans with Disabilities Act. Wheelchair ramps must be installed by court order (CSU 23).

Second, no one at the Union receives a salary for student activities. Five graduate students are paid to tutor remedial classes. Given the lack of space in the cramped Academic Support Center, use of the Black Student Union makes sense and creates more openings in the Center. Many non-black students attend classes and remedial seminars at the Union. Less than half the graduates of the Internet course last semester were African American (Kane 2).

(Continued)

But there are other objections to the Union. Why should blacks have their own facility? Many on campus see the presence of a black student union as a kind of self-imposed apartheid. The Union has also been criticized for being the center of racially hostile militancy.

The Black Student Union hardly threatens to impose a new kind of segregation. We live in integrated dorms, attend integrated classes, participate in integrated sports, and serve on mostly white and Asian academic committees. The few hours a week a student might spend at the BSU hardly threatens racial isolation—any more than the women's center risks ending coeducation or the Newman Center pits Catholics against Protestants. From my own observations, I see little evidence of the radical and extremist politics union opponents mention. The most popular event the Black Student Union holds is Career Week, when black students line up to meet representatives from AT&T, IBM, Bank One, and 3M. Most students are concerned about academic performance and career options rather than radical politics. True, the Union has sponsored some controversial speakers, but so has the university itself. Much of the "extremist literature" cited in a campus editorial is not distributed by the Union. The Union receives a lot of free literature in the mail, which has been traditionally displayed in the lobby. When it was brought to the attention of the board that some of the pamphlets were anti-Semitic, members took quick steps to screen incoming publications and discard "hate literature."

The real purpose of the Union is to assist African Americans to succeed on campus. Comprising less than 5% of the student body, blacks easily feel alienated, particularly those who graduated from predominately black high schools. After studying the experiences of black students in fifteen major colleges, Dean Smith concluded, "Since only one of eight black males entering a university will graduate, it is imperative that we seek remedies to support their academic achievement and professional advancement" (12). Many black students have difficulty forming friendships and joining organizations. Often there were only a handful of college-bound students in their schools. To survive, they had to isolate themselves, studying alone to avoid associating with peers resentful of their dedication to academics. Outcasts in high school, these students find college bewildering. They are not accustomed to participating in class or working in groups. They often discover that they are woefully unprepared for college. Coming from schools with 50–75% dropout rates, many suffered from "social promotion." They discover that their A's and B's are only equal to C's and D's in better suburban schools. The Black Student Union offers African American students a place to relax, interact with older students, and work to make the university a more hospitable place for minorities.

Given the history of discrimination and disadvantage faced by African Americans, the Union can be a positive asset. Is it a crutch, an undeserved luxury? No one can deny that black students feel handicapped on campus. No one complains about the cost of wheelchair ramps and elevators which benefit a handful of physically disabled students. Why should we ignore the crippling legacy of racism?

Works Cited

California State University Budget Office. CSU Facilities Report. Sacramento, 2011. Web. 5 May 2011.

Kane, Kelly. "BSU Funding Furor." *Campus Times* 1 May 2011: 1–2. Print.

Smith, Dean. *Black Males in Crisis.* New York: Scribners, 2011. Print.

QUESTIONS FOR REVIEW AND REVISION

1. What is the student's thesis?
2. What negative assumptions does the student seek to address? How does he counter them?
3. What audience does the writer appear to address? What appeals does the student use?
4. How much of the paper is driven by responding to opponents' criticisms? Is this a useful device?
5. How effective is the conclusion? Does comparing disabled students to African Americans make a valid point? Would you suggest an alternative ending?
6. Read the paper aloud. Are there passages that should be deleted or expanded?
7. Did the student follow the instructor's suggestions?

WRITING SUGGESTIONS

1. Using this paper as a model, write a similar essay taking a position on a current campus controversy. Assume you are addressing a hostile audience. Respond to their objections without criticizing or demeaning those who disagree with your thesis.
2. *Collaborative writing:* Discuss this paper with a group of students. Have a member record comments by the group. Work together to write a short statement approving or disapproving of the concept of establishing separate student unions. If members disagree, consider writing pro and con versions.

Suggested Topics for Writing Argument and Persuasion

General Assignments

Write a persuasive argument to a general audience on one of the following topics. You may use one or more appeals. You can frame your paper in the form of an essay, letter, flyer, advertisement, or other document.

- Community and police relations
- The drinking age
- The way colleges prepare or fail to prepare graduates for the job market
- Censorship of the Internet
- Affirmative action
- Minimum wage
- Unemployment
- Medical malpractice
- Family values
- The insanity defense

Select one of the following issues and craft a persuasive essay targeted to one of the audiences listed.

Issues	Audiences
Medicare reform	Suburban residents
Distribution of condoms in public schools	Minority police officers
	Senior citizens
Gun control	Public health workers
Recycling	Retired schoolteachers
Legalization of marijuana for medical purposes	Small-business owners
	Inner-city teenagers
Prayer in public schools	Young parents
Bilingual education	
Internet consumer fraud	

Writing in Context

1. Imagine you have become close to a highly respected member of your community. This person is well regarded by your family and may have a key role in your future. He or she invites you to join an organization that actively supports a view on abortion that is opposite to yours. Write a letter persuading this person to understand your reasons for declining the offer. State your disagreement in neutral terms without creating animosity or angering someone you wish to remain on friendly terms with.

2. Write a letter to the editor of the campus newspaper about a problem or situation you have observed but that no one seems willing to address. Urge the college community to take notice and possibly take action.

Strategies for Reading Argument and Persuasion

As you read the argument and persuasion entries in this chapter, keep these questions in mind.

Context

1. What is the author's thesis? What does he or she want readers to accept? Is the writer persuading readers to accept an opinion or motivate them to take action?
2. How credible is the thesis? Does it make sense? Are alternative views discussed?
3. How does the author characterize those who advocate differing views?
4. Does the writer appear to have an unfair bias?

Strategy

1. Which appeals does the writer use? Does he or she blend logic and emotion, evidence with ethics?
2. Do the appeals seem effective, given the intended audience?

(Continued)

3. Where does the author place the thesis?
4. Are emotional appeals suitable or do they reflect bias?
5. Does the writer avoid errors in critical thinking?
6. Does the reader appear to anticipate a sympathetic, neutral, or hostile audience?

Language

1. What role does connotation play in shaping arguments using logical, emotional, or ethical appeals?
2. What does the author's choice of words reveal about the intended audience?
3. Does word choice indicate bias?

READING TO LEARN

As you read the argument and persuasion essays in this chapter, note techniques you can use in your own writing:

- **"In Praise of the 'F' Word" by Mary Sherry** uses an extended example to support her argument that the threat of failure is a powerful teaching tool.

- **"Hyphenated Americans" by Armstrong Williams** argues that retaining ethnic identities erodes the commitment to a common civil society.

- **"Still Hyphenated Americans" by Julianne Malveaux** insists that in celebrating Black History Month, African Americans are only celebrating the hyphenated status history gave them.

- **"The Case for Walking Away" by Jane Bryant Quinn** uses expert testimony to support her argument that in some cases declaring bankruptcy is a sensible strategy that allows consumers to start afresh.

- **"Filing for Bankruptcy is Not a Smart Financial Move" by Tamara E. Holmes** opens with a personal extended example supported by expert testimony to argue that the negative consequences of declaring bankruptcy outweigh its benefits.

- **"Nuclear Power is a Clean Energy Source" by Patrick Moore** opens with an explanation by an environmentalist why he changed his opinion on the benefits of nuclear energy.

- **"Nuclear Energy Pollutes" by Sherwood Ross** relies on evidence taken from a book by an anti-nuclear advocate to build an argument against nuclear power.

Mary Sherry

Mary Sherry (1940–) writes from her experience as a parent, a writer, and a teacher. She writes articles and advertising copy, owns a small publishing firm in Minnesota, and for many years has taught remedial and creative writing to adults.

In Praise of the "F" Word

Source: "In Praise of the 'F' Word" by Mary Sherry. From *Newsweek,* May 6, 1991. By permission.

For years teachers passed students who should have failed because of the social stigma associated with being left behind one's peers. In this 1991 article from Newsweek, *Sherry argues that simply failing students who do not try would provide the motivation they might need to take school seriously.*

1   Tens of thousands of 18-year-olds will graduate this year and be handed meaningless diplomas. These diplomas won't look any different from those awarded their luckier classmates. Their validity will be questioned only when their employers discover that these graduates are semiliterate.

— Introduction

2   Eventually a fortunate few will find their way into educational repair shops—adult-literacy programs, such as the one where I teach basic grammar and writing. There, high-school graduates and high-school dropouts pursuing graduate-equivalency certificates will learn the skills they should have learned in school. They will also discover they have been cheated by our educational system.

3   As I teach, I learn a lot about our schools. Early in each session I ask my students to write about an unpleasant experience they had in school. No writers' block here! "I wish someone would have made me stop doing drugs and made me study." "I liked to party and no one seemed to care." "I was a good kid and didn't cause any trouble, so they just passed me along even though I didn't read well and couldn't write." And so on.

— examples

4   I am your basic do-gooder, and prior to teaching this class I blamed the poor academic skills our kids have today on drugs, divorce and other impediments to concentration necessary for doing well in school. But, as I rediscover each time I walk into the classroom, before a teacher can expect students to concentrate, he has to get their attention, no matter what distractions may be at hand. There are many ways to do this, and they have much to do with teaching style. However, if style alone won't do it, there is another way to show who holds the winning hand in the classroom. That is to reveal the trump card of failure.

5   I will never forget a teacher who played that card to get the attention of one of my children. Our youngest, a world-class charmer, did little to develop his intellectual talents but always got by. Until Mrs. Stifter.

6   Our son was a high-school senior when he had her for English. "He sits in the back of the room talking to his friends," she told me. "Why don't you move him to the front row?" I urged, believing the embarrassment would get him to settle down. Mrs. Stifter looked at me steely-eyed over her glasses. "I don't move seniors," she said. "I flunk them." I was flustered. Our son's academic life flashed before my eyes. No teacher had ever threatened him with that before. I regained my composure and

— extended example

managed to say that I thought she was right. By the time I got home I was feeling pretty good about this. It was a radical approach for these times, but, well, why not? "She's going to flunk you," I told my son. I did not discuss it any further. Suddenly English became a priority in his life. He finished out the semester with an A.

Recognition of the limits of using a single example as support, provides additional details

7   I know one example doesn't make a case, but at night I see a parade of students who are angry and resentful for having been passed along until they could no longer even pretend to keep up. Of average intelligence or better, they eventually quit school, concluding they were too dumb to finish. "I should have been held back" is a comment I hear frequently. Even sadder are those students who are high-school graduates who say to me after a few weeks of class, "I don't know how I ever got a high-school diploma."

Direct quotations as support

Statement of problem

8   Passing students who have not mastered the work cheats them and the employers who expect graduates to have basic skills. We excuse this dishonest behavior by saying kids can't learn if they come from terrible environments. No one seems to stop to think that—no matter what environments they come from—most kids don't put school first on their list unless they perceive something is at stake. They'd rather be sailing.

9   Many students I see at night could give expert testimony on unemployment, chemical dependency, abusive relationships. In spite of these difficulties, they have decided to make education a priority. They are motivated by the desire for a better job or the need to hang on to the one they've got. They have a healthy fear of failure.

Proposed solution

10   People of all ages can rise above their problems, but they need to have a reason to do so. Young people generally don't have the maturity to value education in the same way my adult students value it. But fear of failure, whether economic or academic, can motivate both.

Thesis

Explanation of what is needed for solution to work

11   Flunking as a regular policy has just as much merit today as it did two generations ago. We must review the threat of flunking and see it as it really is—a positive teaching tool. It is an expression of confidence by both teachers and parents that the students have the ability to learn the material presented to them. However, making it work again would take a dedicated, caring conspiracy between teachers and parents. It would mean facing the tough reality that passing kids who haven't learned the material—while it might save them grief for the short term—dooms them to long-term illiteracy. It would mean that teachers would have to follow through on their threats, and parents would have to stand behind them, knowing their children's best interests are indeed at stake. This means no more doing Scott's assignments for him because he might fail. No more passing Jodi because she's such a nice kid.

Conclusion: Call to action

12   This is a policy that worked in the past and can work today. A wise teacher, with the support of his parents, gave our son the opportunity to succeed—or fail. It's time we return this choice to all students.

UNDERSTANDING CONTEXT

1. What was Sherry's purpose in writing the essay? Does she have in mind certain types of students? Are there students who should be excluded from her plan?

2. When Sherry discusses the students she works with in night school, what reasons does she say they had for not doing well in school? How do they feel about their education?

3. Why are the students Sherry teaches motivated to learn what they failed to learn when they were younger?

4. Why does Sherry call the threat of failure a positive teaching tool?

5. Why would it take a concerted effort of parents and teachers for her suggestion to work?

6. *Critical thinking:* Do you feel that the threat of failure would motivate students to do better in school than they would without that threat? Is Sherry right in thinking that students do not perceive failure to be a real threat? Have things changed since Sherry published this essay in 1991?

EVALUATING STRATEGY

1. Is the title effective in grabbing attention? Why or why not?

2. *Blending the modes:* Where does Sherry use *comparison, example,* and *cause and effect*?

3. How does Sherry establish herself as someone who has a right to express an opinion on this subject? In other words, how does she present a trustworthy ethos?

4. Would students in Grades K–12 be able to get past their emotional response to failing and understand the logic? If you failed a course and were told it would be good for you in the long run, would you agree?

APPRECIATING LANGUAGE

1. What does Sherry mean when she refers to failure as the "trump card" of education?

2. What does Sherry suggest with her term "educational repair shops" in the second paragraph?

3. Is Sherry's tone and style suited to a newsmagazine like *Newsweek?* Why or why not?

WRITING SUGGESTIONS

1. Write a short essay that agrees or disagrees with Sherry's argument about failing students.

2. *Collaborative writing:* Discuss Sherry's essay with a group of students and ask them about the grading policies in their high schools. Were failing grades given routinely or rarely? Were students passed based on attendance? Write a short essay organizing the group's observations using division or classification.

© Garry Gay/Alamy Limited

Public Schools

If an unfriendly foreign power had attempted to impose on America the mediocre educational performance that exists today, we might well have viewed it as an act of war. . . . We have, in effect, been committing an act of unthinking, unilateral educational disarmament.

A Nation at Risk

In 1983 the Reagan administration released *A Nation at Risk,* a study that charged, "Our society and its educational institutions seem to have lost sight of the basic purposes of schooling, and of the high expectations and disciplined effort needed to attain them." The report claimed that a "rising tide of mediocrity" in public schools threatened America's position in a world of "determined, well-educated, and strongly motivated competitors."

A Nation at Risk has fueled three decades of debate about education. Jonathan Kozol, author of *Savage Inequalities,* argues that urban schools fail because of unfair distribution of resources. While suburban districts allocate up to $15,000 a year on each student, urban schools provide less than $8,000. Critics of public schools argue that funding alone does not explain poor performance. Blake Hurst, a former school district president, notes that although Missouri spent nearly $2 billion to reduce class sizes and build new schools in Kansas City, there was little change in test scores. At one point the state devoted 44 percent of its education budget to 9 percent of the student population. Despite this infusion of added resources, the Kansas City School District failed to improve and lost its accreditation in 2000.

Teachers are at the center of the education debate. Damon Moore, a public school teacher, states that legislators, administrators, and parents cannot improve education. "Reform's last chance," he argues, "rests in the hearts and minds of those who are fighting the battle up front—in the classroom." Others claim that teachers and teachers unions are responsible for failing schools. "Some teachers," Sheila Cherry states, "would sacrifice students' futures to save their jobs." Such critics as Lisa Snell charge that teachers and schools disguise their failures by labeling children learning disabled. Special education classes, originally designed to serve the mentally retarded, now teach 12 percent of all students, 90 percent of whom have been diagnosed with learning disabilities.

Frustrated by bureaucracy, lowered standards, and unsafe schools, educators have called for a range of alternatives to traditional public schools. Charter schools, special schools set up independently within a public school system, now serve half a million students. They promised to be more rigorous and accountable, but *American School and University* found that "like traditional public schools, charter schools run the gamut from inspiring successes to disappointing failures." Some cities have experimented with choice or voucher systems, which provide low-income families with vouchers they can apply to public or private schools. Like charter schools, choice schools have produced mixed results. A growing number of parents now educate their children at home, arguing that Internet resources, educational videos, and museum trips can provide a richer and more challenging educational experience than overcrowded public schools plagued with shortages and violence.

Although advocating different strategies to improve schools, educators and education critics still see America as a nation at risk.

Before reading the articles listed below, consider the following questions:

1. *Do Americans value education?* Do you know parents who never attend a parent-teacher conference or PTA meeting but never miss their children's football or soccer games?
2. *How should schools be funded?* Is it fair that suburban schools receive more funds than urban schools? Should school funding be based on something other than property taxes?
3. *Do teachers have enough or too much influence?*
4. *Do standardized tests improve education?* Tests, proponents assert, identify a school's strengths and weaknesses. Critics argue tests are unfair and lead schools to simply suspend marginal students so they won't be tested and lower the school average.

E-READINGS ONLINE

Search for each article by author or title using InfoTrac College Edition, available through your English CourseMate at **www.cengagebrain.com.**

Evan Thomas and Pat Wingert. "Schoolyard Brawl."
Michelle Rhee, former chancellor of the District of Columbia school system, believes in paying teachers based on merit and firing bad ones. In contrast, Randi Weingarten, head of the nation's second-largest teachers' union, defends tenure and promotions based on seniority.

Gregory Shafer. "What's Literacy Got to Do with It?"
In practice, the schools designed to assist the poor "actually constitute the engine that stultifies change and hinders revolt."

Mike Kennedy. "Charter Schools: Threat or Boon to Public Schools?"
Charter schools, which now enroll 575,000 students, "run the gamut from inspiring successes to disappointing failures."

Jonathan Kozol. "Malign Neglect."
A specialist in basic education uses statistics to demonstrate dramatic funding disparities between urban and suburban schools.

Blake Hurst. "End of an Illusion."
A former school district president concludes from a study of the Kansas City School District that more money is not the answer to ailing schools.

Gregory Kent. "Celebrating Mediocrity? How Schools Shortchange Gifted Students."
In attempting to provide all children with equal educational opportunities, public schools fail to help gifted students reach their full potential.

Lisa Snell. "Special Education Confidential: How Schools Use the 'Learning Disability' Label to Cover Up Their Failures."
Two million students would not have been labeled learning disabled "if the public schools they attended had provided proper, rigorous, and early reading instruction."

Joe Klein. "How the Teachers Killed a Dream."
A journalist explains how a multimillionaire in Michigan tried to endow several charter schools in Detroit—and how the teachers stopped him.

Jodie Morse. "Learning While Black."
A staff writer for *Time* magazine points to evidence that black students are more likely to be disciplined than white students for the same behavior.

Steven Brill. "The Teachers' Unions' Last Stand."
Teachers unions, which have long advocated lifetime tenure, are facing a growing demand to evaluate teachers based on performance.

Gregory Rome and Walter Block. "Schoolhouse Socialism."
School vouchers will not improve educational opportunities and will "end up destroying private schools, turning them instead into relabeled state schools."

George W. Liebman. "Will the U.S. Get Left Behind?: We Must Improve Our High Schools." Liebman poses seven essential questions to consider in evaluating public schools.

CRITICAL READING AND THINKING

1. What do these authors see as the major problems in our schools?
2. Do these authors believe that the solution to failing schools is providing more money or creating new systems?
3. What role do teachers play in school reform? Should they have more or less influence on educational policies?
4. How can schools be held more accountable? Do standardized tests work?
5. How effective are educational alternatives, such as charter and choice schools?

WRITING SUGGESTIONS

1. Write an essay evaluating your own high school experience. Did you attend a public, private, or charter school? Do you feel your school adequately prepared you to enter college or obtain a job? What would have made your high school better?
2. *Collaborative writing:* Work with a group of other students and discuss the causes for the poor performance of many of the nation's schools. Why do so many students drop out? Why are so many high school graduates unprepared for college? Why do American students score lower on standardized tests than students from many Third World countries? List the major causes. Your group may use division to organize them in categories or classification to rank them by importance.
3. *Other modes:*
   - Write a *description* essay about your best learning experience.
   - Develop a *comparison* essay contrasting two schools or two teachers.
   - Create a *definition* of an ideal school or teacher.
   - Write a *process* essay giving parents suggestions on how to make sure their children get a good education.

RESEARCH PAPER

You can develop a research paper about public schools by conducting further research to explore a range of issues:

- How effective has the No Child Left Behind initiative been in reforming education?
- Have schools made effective use of new technology?
- What role have teachers' unions played in recent educational debates?
- What role have special interest groups had in shaping educational policy?
- What are the current problems, concerns, or controversies in your local schools?

FOR FURTHER READING

To locate additional sources on public schools, enter these search terms into InfoTrac College Edition, available through your English CourseMate at **www.cengagebrain .com** or another one of your college library's databases:

Public Schools
Subdivisions: analysis
                evaluation
                finance
                forecasts and trends
                political aspects
                public opinion

Education
Subdivisions: beliefs, opinions, and attitudes
                comparative analysis
                evaluation
                government finance
                research surveys

Charter Schools
Subdivisions: analysis
                evaluation
                finance
                standards

ADDITIONAL SOURCES

Using a search engine, enter one or more of the following terms to locate additional sources:

public schools	teachers unions	school choice
charter schools	school standards	No Child Left Behind
home schooling	PTA	public school funding
dropout rates	standardized testing	SAT scores

See the Evaluating Internet Source Checklist on pages 533–534. See Chapter 24 for documenting sources.

Armstrong Williams (1959–) is a talk show host and columnist who has written on a range of issues concerning African Americans. His books include *Beyond Blame: How We Can Succeed by Breaking the Dependency Barrier* (1995) and *Letters to a Young Victim: Hope and Healing in America's Inner Cities* (1996). Williams is a frequent commentator on cable news programs.

Hyphenated Americans

Source: "Hyphenated Americans" by Armstrong Williams. From www.armstrong-williams.com, Nov. 7, 2000. By permission.

In this column, Williams argues against Americans retaining an ethnic identity that emphasizes separateness and erodes allegiance to a common civil society.

1 Over the past year, small, trite hyphens have been appearing on the campaign trail: Bush courts the African-American vote; the Muslim-American vote will make the difference in Michigan; Gore simultaneously appeals to California's Asian-American population and New York's Jewish-American community; Nader attempts to tap into the Native-American segment of our voting populace. Like deadly spore, these hyphens are replicating everywhere, supplanting our identities as Americans with a tribal ID card.

2 Hopefully now, our elected president will make a renewed effort to regard the citizens of this country not as rival clans, but as humans. To understand the importance of this issue, follow me for a moment, from the political to the personal. With little cultural debate, much of the country now chooses to define themselves not as Americans, but as the proud embodiments of various tribes. We no longer share this vast country. Instead, there is a nation for blacks and a nation for Asians and a nation for gays and Hispanics, one for Jews and whites, with each tribe pledging allegiance not to a unified nation-state, but to their own subjective cultural identity.

3 So what exactly is a hyphenated American? No one really asks. They understand only that Americans must not be called "Americans" in this day and age. To do so would be to violate the tenets of political correctness, and to invite disaster—at least at suburban dinner parties. Those who dare find strength in their authentic experiences, rather than always trying to go about things as an American might, are deemed traitors to their tribe and soon find themselves joined to no one. This is the new cultural narrative in America: what matters is not your unique experience as a human-American, but rather your ability to identify with some vague tribal concept.

4 Of course, there are those who swell with pride at being hyphenated Americans. They would argue that those small hyphens keep intact their unique struggles and heritage. Such people might even point to the important symbolic function that such a hyphen serves: it pushes the hyphenated-American experience into the mainstream, therefore reducing any cultural hangover from America's less tolerant past.

5 In reality though, the argument for rooting oneself in a tribal identity seems terribly destabilizing to the concept of multicultural unity. To insist that we are all hyphenated Americans is pretty much the same thing as asserting that no one is an American. The major implication: your America is not my America. The idea of civic unity becomes clouded as hyphenated Americans increasingly identify with their

Sam Diephuis/jupiterimages

489

cultural "I," rather than the civic "we." The great hope that our civil rights leaders had about getting beyond the concept of warring tribes and integrating to form a more perfect union falls by the wayside of these small hyphens.

6   I fear that we are reverting from a highly centralized country to a set of clans separated by hyphens. Herein lies the danger: when you modify your identity to distinguish it from other clans, you tend to modify your personal attitudes as well. You make the "others" what you need them to be, in order to feel good about your own little tribe. The best in the other "tribes" therefore becomes obscured, as does any unity of understanding. Instead, we distill the cultural "others" into the most easily identifiable symbols: Blacks as criminals; Asians as isolationists; Italians as gangsters; Muslims as fanatics; Jews as stingy; Latin Americans as illegal immigrants; whites as racists. We perpetuate these stereotypes when we willingly segregate ourselves into cultural tribes, even when we know that in our individual lives, we are so much more than this.

7   Our cultural prophets once dreamt of achieving a nation not of warring tribes, but of humans. Presently, we fail this vision, and we fail ourselves.

UNDERSTANDING CONTEXT

1. What observations did Williams make during the 2000 presidential campaign? What troubled him the most?

2. Why does Williams view ethnic identities as damaging to the nation and civic society?

3. Do you observe that many people on your campus or neighborhood prefer to see themselves as African-Americans, Hispanics, Jews, or Irish-Americans rather than "Americans"?

4. Does identity with an ethnic heritage always imply a political point of view? Why or why not?

5. *Critical thinking:* Is an ethnic identity undercut by other associations and influences? Do the poor and unemployed of all ethnic groups have more in common with each other than with middle-class professionals with whom they share a common ancestry? Why or why not? Do New Yorkers have a geographical identity that distinguishes them from people of the same ethnicity who live in Texas or Oregon? Do entrepreneurs, doctors, teachers, police officers, and landlords have shared interests that overcome ethnic identities? Can a highly technological and complex society like the United States really break up along ethnic lines?

EVALUATING STRATEGY

1. Williams opens his essay by observing political campaigns. Is this an effective device? Does it reveal how politicians view the voting public?

2. Can you easily summarize Williams's thesis in a single sentence? Why or why not? Is his point clearly stated?

APPRECIATING LANGUAGE

1. How does Williams define "hyphenated Americans"? How does he define "multicultural society"?

2. Williams uses the terms *tribe* and *clans* to describe ethnic groups and ethnic loyalty. What connotations do these words have? Do some people find terms like *tribal* and *clan* demeaning or offensive?

3. Williams places the word *other* in quotation marks. Today many commentators use the term *other* to describe people who are seen as outsiders, enemies, or threats. Look up this word in a dictionary. What does the word *other* mean to you? What connotations does it have?

WRITING SUGGESTIONS

1. Write a short essay explaining the way you vote for political candidates. Does your ethnic identity influence the way you vote? Are you more likely to support candidates who share your background? Why or why not?

2. *Collaborative writing:* Working with a group of students, discuss Williams's essay and ask each member if they agree or disagree with his position on ethnic identity. Write an essay that summarizes your group's views using classification to organize their views from those who strongly agree to those who strongly disagree with Williams's argument.

Julianne Malveaux

Julianne Malveaux (1953–) was born in San Francisco. She studied economics at Boston College and later attended the Massachusetts Institute of Technology, where she received a PhD in economics in 1980. She has published articles on economics and social policy in *Ms.*, *Essence*, *Emerge*, and the *Progressive*. Her recent books include *Sex, Lies, and Stereotypes: Perspectives of a Mad Economist* (1994) and *Wall Street, Main Street, and the Side Street: A Mad Economist Takes a Stroll* (1999).

Still Hyphenated Americans

Source: "Still Hyphenated Americans" by Julianne Malveaux. Reprinted with permission from Julianne Malveaux.

Malveaux wrote this column in response to the question, "Why celebrate Black History Month?" Malveaux argues that African Americans are only celebrating the hyphenated status history gave them.

1 "Why are we still celebrating Black History Month," the young white woman asks me. Until then, our airplane conversation had been casual, companionable. We'd spoken of trivia for nearly an hour, of changed travel conditions, the flight delay, of the plastic knives we'd been handed. My seatmate, a California college student, was traveling to Washington, D.C. to visit friends, and brimmed over with questions about sightseeing in Washington. Then she lowered her voice just a bit, asked if I minded an "awkward" question, and asked about Black History Month.

2 I didn't know whether to chuckle or to scream. Seventy-five years after Dr. Carter G. Woodson established Negro History week in 1926, folks are still wondering why we should commemorate black history. We need look no further than the words of one of our nation's most-quoted African Americans, Dr. Martin Luther King, Jr., who wrote, "The mistreatment of the Negro is as old as the most ancient history book, and as recent as today's newspaper." As long as African American life and history are not fully represented on newspaper pages, in the broadcast media, or in the history books, it makes sense to commemorate African American History Month.

3 The Association for the Study of Afro-American Life and History annually selects a black history month theme. Their website, www.asalh.org, lists themes for the next several years. This year, the theme is The Color Line Revisited: Is Racism Dead? I shared the theme with my young seatmate who assured me that class, not race, is what separates Americans. Rubbing shoulders in the first class cabin of the plane, she wondered, "You can't honestly say you've been discriminated against in your life, have you?"

4 Discrimination is an institutional, not an individual phenomenon. How else but discrimination do we explain the differentials between African American and white income, unemployment rates, and homeownership levels. Those simple statistics make it clear that African Americans and whites have very different realities. If the overall unemployment rate were 9.8 percent, as the black rate was in January, we'd be talking about a depression and designing programs to put people back to work. Instead, President Bush's new budget cuts employment and training programs from $225 million to $45 million, a cut of nearly 80 percent. These programs, targeted

Sam Diephuis/jupiterimages

492

to some of our nation's largest cities, provide important training to high-risk young people, many of whom are African American. To cut such programs at this time is tantamount to cutting the defense budget in wartime, but we know that President Bush has done no such thing. Indeed, while job-training funds are being slashed by millions of dollars, the President proposes increasing defense spending by $48 billion more this year.

5   The nation's indifference to high black unemployment rates speaks to the difference in our realities. Many whites see themselves as Americans, while African Americans are hyphenated only because our realities are hyphenated. We'll feel like "regular" Americans when we have "regular" experiences (meaning, no racial profiling, among other things), when our "regular" history is reflected in our nation's statuary (how many cities literally have no public monuments to African American people) and libraries.

6   The unemployment rate difference isn't the only place the color line is drawn. Seventy-one percent of all whites own their homes, compared to 48 percent of African Americans. The gap is a function of redlining and discrimination in lending, both of which have been convincingly demonstrated by contemporary research. But when a home is the largest asset in most people's portfolio, too many African Americans are denied the opportunity to accumulate wealth when they can't buy homes. Restrictive covenants no longer prevent people from owning, but implicitly restrictive lending policies are as effective today as racist covenants were two generations ago.

7   To be sure, the color line is fuzzier than it has ever been. Our airwaves frequently broadcast the lifestyles of the black and beautiful—the Oprah Winfreys, Michael Jordans, Condoleeza Rices and Colin Powells of the world. As proud as we are of African American icons, it would be foolhardy to suggest that all black people share experiences with these icons. At the other end, one in four African Americans and forty percent of African American children live in poverty. Is racism real? No question. We commemorate Black History Month because it is an important way to recognize the many contributions African American people have made to our nation, because our nation, despite the progress it has made, still fails to systematically acknowledge black history. Until our textbooks spill over with stories of the slaves who built our nation's capital, the African American patriots who fought and died for our country, and the African American scientists whose inventions have shaped our lives, I will gleefully commemorate African American History Month. I shouldn't be the only one celebrating, African American history is American history! We hyphenated Americans are merely celebrating the hyphen that history handed us.

UNDERSTANDING CONTEXT

1. Why does Malveaux argue that Black History Month should be celebrated?
2. What does Malveaux mean by "institutional" discrimination? Why does she reject the idea that social problems are "about class, not race"?

3. When, in her view, will African Americans be able to feel like "regular Americans"?

4. *Critical thinking:* Malveaux comments on the "black and beautiful" celebrities like Oprah Winfrey, Michael Jordan, and Colin Powell. Do you think the presence of successful African Americans leads people to believe that racism no longer exists?

EVALUATING STRATEGY

1. How does Malveaux use the comments of the white passenger to open her essay? Is this a valuable device to introduce a controversial issue?

2. What facts and statistics does Malveaux use to support her thesis? Why is factual support important in this essay?

APPRECIATING LANGUAGE

1. How does Malveaux define "hyphenated Americans"?

2. Is Malveaux's diction, tone, and style suited for a newspaper column, which many people will skim rather than read? What challenges do columnists face in writing about complex and difficult issues?

WRITING SUGGESTIONS

1. Write a letter agreeing or disagreeing with Malveaux's column. Could you argue that other groups, such as Hispanics and Asians, are far less represented in the nation's history books, media, and public institutions?

2. *Collaborative writing:* Discuss Malveaux's column with a group of students and ask if public schools should teach American history by highlighting ethnic differences or weaving them into a single unified version of our past. Should black history be taught separately? Why or why not? Write an essay summarizing your group's view. If students have differing opinions, use comparison or division and classification to organize their opinions.

Jane Bryant Quinn (1939–) was born in Niagara Falls, New York, and graduated from Middlebury College in Vermont. She is a contributing editor for *Newsweek*, where she wrote a column about personal finance for thirty years. She has published columns in *Woman's Day* and *Good Housekeeping* and appeared as a commentator for ABC and CBS. Her books include *Everyone's Money Book* (1978), *Smart and Simple: Financial Strategies for Busy People* (1996), and *Making the Most of Your Money—Completely Revised* (2009).

The Case for Walking Away

Source: "The Case for Walking Away" by Jane Bryant Quinn. *Newsweek*, January 12, 2009, p. 62. By permission.

In this Newsweek *article published in 2009, Jane Bryant Quinn argues why, in some cases, bankruptcy is a sensible strategy consumers should use to save assets and preserve resources needed to start over.*

1 Normally I'd say suck it up, cut spending and repay your debt. But not if you're going broke.

2 In January, we're supposed to sit down and organize our personal finances. This year I'll risk my good-girl reputation with a subversive idea: go bankrupt in 2009. If you're reaching the end of your rope, don't try to hold on. Save what you can.

3 It's painful and humiliating even to consider bankruptcy, let alone join that crowd in the courthouse corridor, waiting for your name to be called. Normally I'd say suck it up, cut spending and repay your consumer debt. But that's not always possible, especially with an economic tsunami rolling over your home, job and health insurance.

4 Most families, honorable to the end, struggle longer than they should, says Katie Porter, a law professor at the University of Iowa. By the time they give in, they've lost assets they could have used to start over again. That defeats the point of bankruptcy—to stop the self-blame and hopelessness that goes with bad luck and bad bills, and give yourself a second chance.

5 The right time to go bankrupt is when you're financially stuck but still have assets to protect. You can use Chapter 7, the most popular type, only once in eight years, so draw up a "no kidding" plan for living on your income when you're finally clear. "If you're out of work, try not to go bankrupt until you have a new job and can see what's ahead of you," says Harvard Law School professor Elizabeth Warren.

6 It's a mistake to tap your retirement accounts to make minimum payments on monstrous bills. IRAs and 401(k)s are largely protected in bankruptcy, as is most of your child's 529 college-savings account. This money is your future. Leave it alone and use credit cards for your necessities. Card issuers know that some of their customers will fail. That's why they charge elephant fees.

7 Your health is your future, too. You're doing your family no favors by forgoing medical treatment because you can't pay. Bankruptcy eliminates medical as well as consumer debt.

8 Bankruptcy can even help you save your home, especially with home values down and so many mortgages underwater. You're allowed to keep a limited amount

Sam Diephuis/jupiterimages

495

of home equity in most states. If the house is worth less than the mortgage plus your home-equity exemption, you can file for Chapter 7 bankruptcy, wipe out your consumer debts and still keep your home, provided that your mortgage payments are up to date, says Stephen Elias, a California bankruptcy attorney and coauthor of Nolo Press's do-it-yourself bankruptcy books. If your house is worth more, however, or you're behind on your payments, it will likely be sold.

9   When you're behind on the mortgage but have a new job with money coming in, choose a Chapter 13 workout. Your lawyer will negotiate a three- to five-year plan for paying your debts, including the mortgage arrears. Some people stay in the plan just long enough to get current on their mortgage and then resume their normal lives, Porter says. The next Congress may sweeten Chapter 13 by allowing a judge to reduce (or "cram down") your mortgage principal if the debt amounts to more than the house is worth. That would save a lot of homes.

10   Don't try to preserve your house if you're going broke. Stop making payments, stay there while foreclosure is underway, then move out and rent. If the mortgage is underwater, "you're already functionally renting because you have no equity," says Adam Levitin, a professor at Georgetown University Law Center. In theory, many states allow lenders to chase you for the sum still owed after the house is sold. But that's rare, Warren says. Lenders know that you probably can't pay.

11   Foreclosures stay on your record for seven years and bankruptcies for 10. If you re-establish good bill-paying habits, you may get decent credit even sooner. And you'll start fresh, which is what a new year ought to bring.

UNDERSTANDING CONTEXT

1. What is Quinn's thesis? Can you state it in your own words?
2. What are the benefits of declaring bankruptcy? How can it help people make a fresh start?
3. What are the differences between Chapter 7 and Chapter 13 forms of bankruptcy?
4. In what situations can people declare bankruptcy and still keep their homes?
5. *Critical thinking:* Do you think many consumers are ill informed about what bankruptcy means? Should bankruptcy be viewed as a failure or a strategy? Does declaring bankruptcy carry a stigma? Does this stigma lessen during a deep recession marked by high unemployment? Why or why not?

EVALUATING STRATEGY

1. How does Quinn address readers who might be biased against those who declare bankruptcy?
2. What evidence does Quinn use to support her argument?
3. *Blending the modes:* Where does Quinn use *comparison*, *example*, and *process* to develop her argument?

4. *Critical thinking:* How much of Quinn's article is about changing popular perceptions of bankruptcy? Do many people equate bankruptcy with irresponsibility? How can a writer advocate declaring bankruptcy without appearing to encourage negligent behavior?

APPRECIATING LANGUAGE

1. Quinn calls her advice "subversive." What does this term imply? How does it address her readers' likely attitudes toward bankruptcy?

2. What does the use of words like "painful and humiliating" suggest about perceptions of bankruptcy?

3. Quinn states that credit card companies charge "elephant fees." Does this term suggest they are unfairly high? Why or why not? Does her use of the term imply that declaring bankruptcy to erase credit card debt is an acceptable strategy?

WRITING SUGGESTIONS

1. Write a short article agreeing or disagreeing with Quinn's thesis. Do you believe that bankruptcy is ever justified?

2. *Collaborative writing:* Working with a group of students, take information from Quinn's article to create a bulleted list about declaring bankruptcy for a website about personal finance.

Tamara E. Holmes

Tamara E. Holmes graduated from Howard University with a BA in journalism in 1994. She has published articles about personal finance, careers, business, and technology for *Black Enterprise*, *Working Mother*, *Essence*, and *USA Today*. She has edited publications for Howard University and the Baltimore City Public School System.

Filing for Bankruptcy is Not a Smart Financial Move

Source: "Filing for Bankruptcy Is Not a Smart Financial Move" by Tamara E. Holmes. *Black Enterprise*, February 2005, p. 159(1). By permission.

Holmes opens with the story of a single consumer, then provides expert testimony as support to argue against using bankruptcy as a strategy for resolving financial problems.

1　In 1994, Mia Conyer of Baltimore had dug herself into a financial hole. "I had a car that I had purchased at a very high interest rate of 24%," says the 36-year-old professional, who was 19 when she purchased the car. By the time she realized she couldn't afford it, it was too late. "I returned the car with a voluntary repossession and they hit me with the balance and started garnishing my wages." At the advice of a relative, Conyer filed for bankruptcy under Chapter 7 of the U.S. Bankruptcy Code, a move that she regrets. "It may seem like a quick fix, but [the bankruptcy] just fell off my credit report a couple of months ago," she says. Bankruptcy prevented Conyer from getting credit for 10 years.

2　Each year, millions of people file for bankruptcy hoping to create a clean financial slate. For some, it is a last-ditch effort to wipe out debts, but for others like Conyer, it can do more harm than good.

3　"It's a horrendous mistake for people to have maybe $5,000 or $8,000 worth of credit card debt or a car note to file bankruptcy," says Brooke Stephens, author of *Talking Dollars and Making Sense: A Wealth-Building Guide for African-Americans* (McGraw-Hill; $14.95). She says bankruptcy should be a last resort used "when you absolutely have no assets, no income, nothing on the horizon to resolve the problem."

4　But before you determine whether your particular situation warrants filing bankruptcy, you should familiarize yourself with the different kinds.

5　There are two common types of bankruptcy. Under Chapter 7, a consumer's assets are liquidated and the proceeds are given to a trustee who pays off as many debts as possible. Those debts that cannot be paid off are discharged. A Chapter 13 filing is more of a reorganization plan under which a consumer keeps assets such as property. Some assets are exempt, such as a 401(k) or a car, but it varies from state to state. A plan is drawn up for debts to be paid over a period of three to five years or less. Certain debts such as back taxes, student loans, alimony, and child support cannot be discharged.

6　Rod Griffin, public affairs manager for Experian credit agency, says many consumers don't realize that a Chapter 7 bankruptcy will remain on a credit report for 10 years, while a Chapter 13 bankruptcy will stay for seven years. Even if your claim is rejected by the court, it will still appear on your credit report. Griffin says if a lender extends credit to someone who has filed for bankruptcy, his or her interest rates are generally much higher.

7   Ted Travis, vice president and operations manager with Residential Home Loan Centers in Laurel, Maryland, works with borrowers who have filed for bankruptcy under Chapter 13 to refinance their homes and use the equity to pay off debts. Such an action, called a bankruptcy buyout, must be approved by the Bankruptcy Court. While it enables consumers to pay off the debt sooner, it does nothing to take the bankruptcy mark off of a credit report until seven years has passed, and customers are still likely to get a less favorable rate.

8   Legislation that would make it more difficult for consumers to file for bankruptcy under Chapter 7 is making its way through Congress, which some analysts say is enticing people to file now before such laws come to pass, while others simply want a chance to start over and prove they can now manage their finances responsibly.

9   For Conyer, good money management skills are now a must. "I'm trying to rebuild from scratch because everything that I had already built up got taken away," she says. "Once you file—whether you're doing good, bad, or indifferent—it's there [on your credit report]. That's the first thing lenders see."

UNDERSTANDING CONTEXT

1.   What is Holmes's thesis? Can you restate it in your own words?

2.   What are the negative consequences of declaring bankruptcy?

3.   What debts cannot be discharged by a Chapter 13 bankruptcy?

4.   Are there negative consequences for even filing a claim for bankruptcy?

5.   *Critical thinking:* Based on Holmes's and Quinn's articles, when do you think a person should declare bankruptcy? At what points do the benefits outweigh the negative consequences?

EVALUATING STRATEGY

1.   Holmes opens and closes her article with a personal example. Is this an effective device? Why or why not?

2.   How does Holmes introduce expert testimony into her article? Are direct quotes more effective than paraphrases? Why or why not?

3.   How does Holmes explain the difference between Chapter 7 and Chapter 13 bankruptcy?

4.   *Other modes:* Where does Holmes use *narration, example, comparison,* and *cause and effect* to develop her essay?

APPRECIATING LANGUAGE

1.   What key words in the statements Holmes quotes dramatize her point? What does this suggest about the way writers should use direct quotations as support?

2.   How does the tone and style of Holmes's description of bankruptcy differ from Quinn's?

3. *Critical thinking:* What connotations does the word *bankruptcy* have? Does it explain the use of euphemisms such as "restructured debt"? How can language shape the way readers view bankruptcy?

WRITING SUGGESTIONS

1. Write a short essay persuading readers to accept your own view of bankruptcy. When, if ever, should people declare bankruptcy? Do you see a moral distinction between responsible consumers who declare bankruptcy because of job loss or massive medical bills and those who bought houses they could not afford and maxed out credit cards buying luxury items?

2. *Collaborative writing:* Discuss Quinn's and Holmes's views on bankruptcy with a group of students and poll their attitudes on bankruptcy. If you can agree, work together to create a definition essay that clearly states under what circumstances people should consider filing for bankruptcy. If members of the group have conflicting opinions, consider using comparison to develop opposing viewpoints or classification to place opinions on a scale.

Patrick Moore

Patrick Moore (1947–) was born in British Columbia and received his PhD in ecology from the Institute of Animal Resource Ecology, University of British Columbia. An early member of Greenpeace, he was originally an outspoken opponent of nuclear energy. Moore became president of the Greenpeace Foundation in 1977 and served for nine years. After leaving Greenpeace, Moore changed many of his views on energy and land use. He is the cofounder of Greenspirit Strategies, a consulting firm that works with governments and corporations on environmental and energy issues. Unlike many other environmentalists, Moore now believes that nuclear energy should play a role in meeting future energy demands.

Nuclear & Green

Source: "Nuclear & Green" by Patrick Moore. *The New York Post*, February 23, 2007. By permission.

In this article, Moore explains why he changed his position on nuclear energy and argues that nuclear energy should be utilized because it does not emit carbon or other pollutants.

1 As cofounder and former leader of Greenpeace, I once opposed nuclear energy. But times have changed, and new facts of compelling importance have emerged—and so my views have changed as well, as have those of a growing number of respected, independent environmentalists around the world.

2 There are few places where nuclear power makes as much sense or is as im-portant as in New York. Indeed, the state is a microcosm of the challenges America and the world face to have ample, clean and reasonably priced electricity. As such, I strongly support renewal of the license for the Indian Point nuclear plants in Westchester, which provides 30 percent or so of the electricity used in the New York metro area.

3 Let me explain.

4 Climate change is now high on the global agenda, and I believe nuclear energy holds the greatest potential to arrest the dangers we face from global warming. It is the only non-greenhouse-gas-emitting power source capable of effectively replacing fossil fuels and satisfying growing demand.

5 Hydroelectric is largely built to capacity. And while other key renewable energy sources will play a growing role, wind and solar power are unreliable and intermit-tent. They simply can't provide "baseload" electricity—especially in densely popu-lated areas like downstate New York.

6 And with Mayor Bloomberg's 2030 Commission projecting the growth of the city's population by 1 million over the next few decades, New York's power needs can't be expected to shrink.

7 Worldwide, nuclear energy is one of the safest industrial sectors. Here in North America, no one has been harmed in the entire history of civilian nuclear-power generation. Indeed, it's proven safer to work at a nuclear power plant than in the finance or real-estate sectors.

8 Nuclear energy is already the No. 2 source of electricity in the United States; it accounts for nearly 30 percent of New York state's electricity.

9   Another environmental benefit: Nuclear power plants improve air quality by reducing smog.

10   Downstate New York arguably has the worst air quality of any region in the country, thanks to high levels of ozone and particulate pollution.

11   The five boroughs and four other New York counties—Nassau, Orange, Rockland and Suffolk—are in violation of both the U.S. Environmental Protection Agency's ozone standards and its regulations on fine particulate matter.

12   It is well established that this pollution has harmful health effects, especially for children and the elderly. This needs to be addressed now.

13   Because of the many environmental and economic benefits, dozens of business associations, labor unions, community groups and others support Indian Point license renewal.

14   Nuclear energy also makes economic sense. The cost of producing nuclear energy in the United States is on par with coal and hydroelectric. That's a very important consideration in New York, which has the country's second-highest electricity costs. This impacts the poor and elderly, in particular, and makes it difficult for the business sector to operate efficiently as well.

15   What about nuclear waste? The notion is misleading. This used fuel is not waste. After its first cycle, spent fuel still contains 95 percent of its energy. Future generations will be able to put this valuable resource to work, powering the country.

16   Nuclear energy is not a silver bullet—it alone can't meet all of our energy needs. But the path toward cleaner air lies in the reduction of fossil fuels in favor of a mix of nuclear and renewable energy.

17   A growing consensus among environmentalists, politicians, industry and labor groups, academics and community leaders strongly supports a move in that direction.

18   Nearly 70 percent of Americans think more needs to be done to reduce greenhouse-gas emissions. I believe nuclear energy is well positioned to help achieve this goal and bring New York in line with the federal Clean Air Act.

19   The time for fresh thinking and renewed leadership on New York's energy needs is now.

UNDERSTANDING CONTEXT

1. How does Moore explain why he changed his views on nuclear energy?

2. What are the benefits of nuclear energy, in Moore's view?

3. Why does Moore believe that other alternative energy sources do not supplant the need for nuclear power?

4. *Critical thinking:* Two of the major objections to nuclear energy are safety and the disposal of radioactive waste. How effectively does Moore answer these objections?

EVALUATING STRATEGY

1. How effective is Moore's introduction? Does a writer who openly admits changing his or her position suggest thoughtfulness? Why or why not?

2. Moore mentions that nuclear power is the second source of electricity in the United States. Is this an important fact to include? Why or why not?

3. *Critical thinking:* Moore argues that "it is safer to work at a nuclear power plant than in the finance or real-estate sectors." Does this statement adequately address concerns about radioactive waste and the threat of accidents?

APPRECIATING LANGUAGE

1. What words and phrases does Moore use to persuade readers that nuclear energy is needed?

2. Moore insists that the notion of "nuclear waste" is misleading. What does the word *waste* imply? Should Moore have supplied an alternative term?

WRITING SUGGESTIONS

1. Write a short essay stating your own views on nuclear energy. You might comment on your initial impressions of atomic power. Have past nuclear accidents, such as Chernobyl in the Ukraine or Fukushima in Japan, shaped your perceptions? Are you aware if your city or state relies on a nuclear power plant for electricity?

2. *Collaborative writing:* Discuss Moore's article with a group of students and then work together to create a comparison paper that outlines the advantages and disadvantages of nuclear power. If your group can reach a consensus, write a thesis statement outlining your group's view. If members disagree, consider drafting opposing viewpoints.

Sherwood Ross

Sherwood Ross was born in Chicago and received a BA from the University of Miami in Coral Gables. He worked as a speechwriter and press aide to Mayor Richard J. Daley before becoming a reporter for the *Chicago Daily News*. He is now a media consultant to colleges, labor unions, and magazine editors. A civil rights activist, he was News Director for the National Urban League. He has published hundreds of articles on issues such as terrorism, civil rights, and the environment.

Nuclear Power Not Clean, Green or Safe

Source: "Nuclear Power Not Clean, Green or Safe" by Sherwood Ross. Reprinted with permission from Sherwood Ross.

Sherwood Ross argues that nuclear energy is "not clean, green, or safe" because reactors produce dangerous waste, could be targeted by terrorists, and require vast amounts of fossil fuels to process uranium.

1 In all the annals of spin, few statements are as misleading as [former] Vice President [Dick] Cheney's that the nuclear industry operates "efficiently, safely, and with no discharge of greenhouse gases or emissions," or [former] President [George W.] Bush's claim America's 103 nuclear plants operate "without producing a single pound of air pollution or greenhouse gases."

Nuclear Power Is Not the Answer

2 Even as the White House refuses to concede global warming is really happening, it touts nuclear power as the answer to it as if it were an arm of the Nuclear Energy Institute (NEI), the industry's trade group. NEI's advertisements declare, "Kids today are part of the most energy-intensive generation in history. They demand lots of electricity. And they deserve clean air."

3 In reality, not only are vast amounts of fossil fuels burned to mine and refine the uranium for nuclear power reactors, polluting the atmosphere, but those plants are allowed "to emit hundreds of curies of radioactive gases and other radioactive elements into the environment every year," Dr. Helen Caldicott, the antinuclear authority, points out in her book *Nuclear Power Is Not the Answer*.

4 What's more, the thousands of tons of solid radioactive waste accumulating in the cooling pools next to those plants contain "extremely toxic elements that will inevitably pollute the environment and human food chains, a legacy that will lead to epidemics of cancer, leukemia, and genetic disease in populations living near nuclear power plants or radioactive waste facilities for many generations to come," she writes. Countless Americans are already dead or dying as a result of those nuclear plants and that story is not being effectively told.

Nuclear Energy Produces Dangerous By-Products

5 To begin with, over half of the nation's dwindling uranium deposits lie under Navajo and Pueblo tribal land, and at least one in five tribal members recruited to mine the ore were exposed to radioactive gas radon 220 and "have died and are continuing to die of lung cancer," Caldicott writes. "Thousands of Navajos are still affected by uranium-induced cancers," she adds.

6   As for uranium tailings [radioactive sand] discarded in the extraction process, 265-million tons of it have been left to pile up in, and pollute, the Southwest, even though they contain radioactive thorium. At the same time, uranium 238, also known as "depleted uranium," (DU) a discarded nuclear plant byproduct, "is lying around in thousands of leaking, disintegrating barrels" at the enrichment facilities in Oak Ridge, Tenn.; Portsmouth, Ohio; and Paducah, Ky.; where ground water is now too polluted to drink, Caldicott writes.

7   Fuel rods at every nuclear plant leak radioactive gases or are routinely vented into the atmosphere by plant operators. "Although the nuclear industry claims it is 'emission' free, in fact it is collectively releasing millions of curies annually," the author reports.

Safety Standards Are Lacking

8 Speaking of safety, since the Three Mile Island (TMI) plant meltdown on March 28, 1979, some 2,000 Harrisburg [Pennsylvania] area residents settled sickness claims with operators' General Public Utilities Corp. and Metropolitan Edison Co., the owners of TMI.

9   Area residents' symptoms included nausea, vomiting, diarrhea, bleeding from the nose, a metallic taste in the mouth, hair loss, and red skin rash, typical of acute radiation sickness when people are exposed to whole-body doses of radiation around 100 rads, said Caldicott, who arrived on the scene a week after the meltdown.

10   David Lochbaum, of the Union of Concerned Scientists, believes nuclear plant safety standards are lacking and predicted another nuclear catastrophe in the near future, stating, "It's not if but when." Not only are such plants unsafe but the spent fuel is often hauled long distances through cities to waste storage facilities where it will have to be guarded for an estimated 240,000 years.

11   "The magnitude of the radiation generated in a nuclear power plant is almost beyond belief," Caldicott writes. "The original uranium fuel that is subject to the fission process becomes 1 billion times more radioactive in the reactor core. A thousand megawatt nuclear power plant contains as much long-lived radiation as that produced by the explosion of 1,000 Hiroshima-sized bombs."

Nuclear Plants Produce Too Much Waste

12 Each year, operators must remove a third of the radioactive fuel rods from their reactors as they have become contaminated with fission products. The rods are so hot they must be stored for 30 to 60 years in a heavily shielded building continuously cooled by air or water lest they burst into flame, and afterwards packed into a container.

13   "Construction of these highly specialized containers uses as much energy as construction of the original rector itself, which is 80 gigajoules per metric ton," Caldicott points out.

14   What's a big construction project, though, when you don't have to pay for it? In the 2005 Energy Bill, Congress allocated $13-billion in subsidies to the nuclear power industry. Between 1948 and 1998, the U.S. government subsidized the industry with $70-billion of taxpayer monies for research and development, corporate Socialism pure and simple.

15   As for safety, an accident or terrorist strike at a nuclear facility could kill people by the thousands. About 17-million people live within a 50 mile radius of the two Indian Point reactors in Buchanan, New York, just 35 miles from Manhattan. Suicidal

terrorists, Caldicott noted, could disrupt the plant's electricity supply by ramming a speedboat packed with explosives into their Hudson River intake pipes, where water is sucked in to cool the reactors. Over time, the subsequent meltdown could claim an estimated 518,000 lives.

Nuclear Power Is Not Clean, Green, or Safe

16 Caldicott points out there are truly green and clean alternative energy sources to nuclear power. She refers to the American plains as "the Saudi Arabia of wind," where readily available rural land in just several Dakota counties "could produce twice the amount of electricity that the United States currently consumes." Now that sounds clean, green, and safe. And I betcha it could be done through free enterprise, too. Somebody, quick, call in the entrepreneurs!

UNDERSTANDING CONTEXT

1. Why does Ross believe that nuclear energy is not "clean, green, or safe"?
2. How dangerous is radioactive waste?
3. What threat would a terrorist attack on a nuclear reactor pose?
4. *Critical thinking:* Patrick Moore states that it is safer to work in a nuclear power plant than in real estate. Ross mentions the uranium ore miners dying of lung cancer. To measure the safety of any energy source, does the entire process have to be examined, from initial collection to waste disposal? Why or why not?

EVALUATING STRATEGY

1. Ross heavily relies on a single source, Helen Caldicott's book *Nuclear Power Is Not the Answer.* Does this weaken his argument? Why or why not? Would including other types of evidence or additional testimony strengthen his essay? Why or why not?
2. The nuclear accident at Three Mile Island Ross mentions occurred in 1979. Should he have provided more background detail to people who are unfamiliar with the incident?
3. Ross ends his essay offering an alternative energy source—wind. After devoting pages to an anti-nuclear argument, should he have supplied more details about the energy source he suggests as a replacement? Why or why not?

APPRECIATING LANGUAGE

1. What words does Ross use to characterize the safety of nuclear energy?
2. Ross quotes Helen Caldicott's claim that the American plains are "the Saudi Arabia of wind." What does this phrase mean?

WRITING SUGGESTIONS

1. Write an essay that agrees or disagrees with Sherwood Ross's view of nuclear energy.
2. *Collaborative writing:* Nuclear reactors emit no carbon, but fossil fuels are consumed to mine and process uranium ore and construct the reactors. Biofuels burn cleaner than oil but require fossil-fueled vehicles to plant, fertilize, and harvest crops used to make fuel. Work with a group of students to establish a standard that should be used to fully measure the carbon output and environmental impact of energy sources.

Feeding America is a nonprofit organization founded to "create a hunger-free America." It distributes food, increases public awareness, and advocates policies to benefit the hungry. Each year Feeding America provides 2 billion pounds of food and supports fifty thousand local charitable agencies that operate shelters, food pantries, after-school programs, and soup kitchens.

Child Hunger Facts

This web page is part of a group presenting facts about hunger in various American communities. Note that unlike many appeals to help people needing relief, this web page relies on logical rather than emotional appeals.

Child Hunger Facts

CHILD HUNGER FACTS

The problem of childhood hunger is not simply a moral issue. Child hunger hampers a young person's ability to learn and becomes more likely to suffer from poverty as an adult. Scientific evidence suggests that hungry children are less likely to become productive citizens.

We address child hunger through two national programs:

Kids Cafe

BackPack Program

Facts of Child Hunger in America

- Nearly 14 million children are estimated to be served by Feeding America, over 3 million of which are ages 5 and under. i
- According to the USDA, over 17 million children lived in food insecure (low food security and very low food security) households in 2009. ii
- 20% or more of the child population in 16 states and D.C. are living in food insecure households. The states of Arkansas (24.4 percent) and Texas (24.3 percent) have the highest rates of children in households without consistent access to food.(Cook, John, *Child Food Insecurity in the United States: 2006-2008.* iii
- The top five states with the highest rate of food insecure children under 18 are Arkansas, Texas, Arizona, Missouri, Mississippi, as well as the District of Columbia
- Proper nutrition is vital to the growth and development of children, particularly for low-income children. 62 percent of all client households with children under the age of 18 participated in a school lunch program, but only 14 percent participated in a summer feeding program that provides free food when school is out. i
- 54 percent of client households with children under the age of 3 participated in the Special Supplemental Nutrition Program for Women, Infants, and Children (WIC). i
- 32 percent of pantries, 42 percent of kitchens, and 18 percent of shelters in the Feeding America network reported "many more children in the summer" being served by their programs. i
- Emergency food assistance plays a vital role in the lives of low-income families. In 2002, more than half of the nonelderly families that accessed a food pantry at least once during the year had children under the age of 18. iv
- 15.5 million or approximately 20.7 percent of children in the U.S. live in poverty.
- Research indicates that even mild undernutrition experienced by young children during critical periods of growth impacts the behavior of children, their school performance, and their overall cognitive development. vi
- In fiscal year 2009, 48 percent of all SNAP participants were children. vii
- During the 2009 federal fiscal year, 19.5 million low-income children received free or reduced-price meals through the National School Lunch Program.Unfortunately, just 2.2 million of these same income-eligible children participated in the Summer Food Service Program that same year. viii

i Rhoda Cohen, J. Mabli, F., Potter, Z., Zhao. *Hunger in America 2010.* Feeding America. February 2010.

ii Nord, Mark, M. Andrews. S. Carlson. United States Department of Agriculture/Economic Research Service *Household Food Security in the United States, 2008.*

iii Cook, John. Feeding America. *Child Food Insecurity in the United States: 2006-2008.*

v DeNavas-Walt, Carmen, B.D. Proctor, C.H. Lee. U.S. Census Bureau, Income, Poverty, and Health Insurance Coverage in the United States: 2008. September 2009.

vi Leftin, Joshua, Gothro, A., Eslami, E.. USDA, Office of Analysis, Nutrition and Evaluation. Characteristics of Supplemental Nutrition Assistance Program Households: Fiscal Year 2009, October 2010.

vii Wolkwitz, Kari. USDA, Office of Analysis, Nutrition and Evaluation. Characteristics of Food Stamp Households: Fiscal Year 2008, September 2009.

viii USDA, FNS. National School Lunch Program: Participation and Lunches Served. Data preliminary as of June 2010.

UNDERSTANDING CONTEXT

1. What does Feeding America want people to know about childhood hunger?
2. How can malnutrition affect a child's future?
3. What facts does the web page present?

EVALUATING STRATEGY

1. How does Feeding America persuade readers to appreciate that childhood hunger "is not simply a moral issue"?
2. What appeals are used in this web page?
3. What evidence is presented as support?
4. *Critical thinking:* This web page includes documentation, citing the US Department of Agriculture and US Census Bureau as sources for its statistics. Is this important? Does it add credibility to the message? Do most websites provide documentation for the evidence they present? Does the use of government statistics make a website appear more credible and the organization more reliable?

APPRECIATING LANGUAGE

1. This web page avoids emotional language, such as "crisis" or "desperate need." What does this suggest about the intended audience? Would including emotional language make the web page more effective or detract from its credibility?
2. How is the term "food insecure" defined?

WRITING SUGGESTIONS

1. Create a similar web page that educates the public about another social problem by presenting factual details.
2. *Collaborative writing:* Working with a group of students, create a fund-raising ad or e-mail that uses emotional appeals to raise funds to fight child hunger. Your group may search stock photo websites for appropriate photographs to accompany your text. Make sure your ad not only dramatizes the problem but also demonstrates how readers' contributions can make a difference.

RESPONDING TO IMAGES

Cairo demonstration, 2011   Image by © Ron Havio/VII/Corbis

1. What is your first reaction to this photograph? Does it require a caption?

2. *Visual analysis:* Does this image dramatize the impact of social networking and globalization? Why would a demonstrator in an Arab country use English in a protest sign?

3. The man is clearly posing for a camera. Can even the most objective reporting distort events? Does one demonstration in one city fairly represent the mood of an entire country? Would a photograph of people conducting routine business a few blocks away alter your perceptions? Why or why not?

4. *Critical thinking:* How have social networking, cell phones, and websites altered the world's politics? Does a revolution require a party apparatus anymore to overturn a government? Does social networking create a new form of journalism that can counter state-controlled media?

5. *Collaborative writing:* Discuss this image with a group of students. Have each student develop a caption. Review the captions and study the use of connotations. Are some captions objective? Do some seem alarmist? Which caption would best suit a high school textbook? What does this photograph say about the global nature of the English language?

RESPONDING TO IMAGES

6. *Other modes:*
   - Write an essay that describes the *effects* of social networking in politics.
   - Use *division* to outline different ways social networking is changing society.
   - Write a *persuasive* essay outlining your views on the way social networking can unite consumers, protesters, and others who may not have a party or lobbying organization to represent their views.
   - Use *example* to illustrate the effect of globalization.

ARGUMENT AND PERSUASION CHECKLIST

Before submitting your paper, review these points:

- ✔ Is your message clearly defined?
- ✔ Does your paper meet readers' needs? Do you provide the support they need to accept your thesis?
- ✔ Do you support your views with adequate evidence?
- ✔ Do you anticipate reader objections and alternative points of view?
- ✔ Do you balance the strengths and weaknesses of logical, ethical, and emotional appeals?
- ✔ Do you avoid overstated, sentimental, or propagandist appeals?
- ✔ Do you avoid preaching to the converted? Will only those who already agree with you accept your arguments?
- ✔ Do you make it easy for undecided readers to accept your position without feeling manipulated or patronized?
- ✔ Have you tested your argument with peer review?

 Access the English CourseMate for this text at **www.cengagebrain.com** for additional information about argument and persuasion.

The Research Paper

3

Conducting Research

*The research paper is, in the fullest sense, a discovery and
an education that leads you beyond texts, beyond a library,
and encourages you to investigate on your own.*

—Audrey J. Roth

What Is Research?

Your ability to write effective research papers greatly determines your success in
college. Instructors assign research papers because, unlike objective tests, they
measure your ability to solve problems, apply knowledge, gather evidence, and
interpret data.

Learning how to write a good research paper not only improves your academic
performance but sharpens the critical thinking skills needed in most careers. Although few people write traditional research papers after they leave college, almost
every professional uses the same methods to produce annual reports, market studies, product evaluations, proposals, and e-mail. Executives, administrators, attorneys,
entrepreneurs, and scientists must base their decisions and recommendations on
information. The ability to locate accurate sources, evaluate evidence, and interpret
findings is essential for success in any field.

Common Misconceptions

Before undertaking a research paper, it is important to understand what a research
paper is *not*.

A research paper is *not* a summary of everything you can find about your topic. The
goal in writing a research paper is not to present a collection of facts and quotations
"about" a topic. Although it is important to survey information, using twenty sources
instead of ten will not necessarily improve the quality of your paper. *The goal of a research paper is to present carefully selected evidence that supports your thesis.*

A research paper does *not* simply repeat what others have written. A research paper is
more than a string of quotations and summaries. Research writers not only collect evidence but also evaluate and interpret it. *The focus of a research paper is your thesis and
commentary—not pages of text you have cut and pasted from the Internet.*

(Continued)

Maria Toutoudaki/jupiterimages

Sam Diephuis/jupiterimages

> **A research paper does *not* merely support a preconceived point of view.** Honest research starts with a topic or question. You should only reach a conclusion and develop a thesis after carefully examining a body of evidence. *Selecting facts and quotes to support what you already believe is not research.*
>
> **A research paper does *not* include the ideas of others without documentation.** Including the ideas and words of others in your text without attribution is plagiarism. *Whenever you add facts, quotations, and summaries of outside sources, you must identify them (see Chapter 24 on using and documenting sources).*

Conducting Research: An Overview

Writing a research paper can be made less intimidating and less arduous if you break the process into key steps:

1. **Understand the scope of the assignment.**

2. **Select an appropriate topic.**

3. **Conduct preliminary research.**

4. **Limit the topic and develop a working thesis.**

5. **Create a timeline.**

6. **Collect and evaluate relevant evidence.**

1. Understand the scope of the assignment.

Even when instructors allow students to select topics themselves, most provide directions that outline the scope of the assignment. Students may be required to use a certain number of sources, present evidence in a specific manner, or address a particular issue, as in the following two examples:

> Analyze a contemporary social problem and propose a solution. State a clear thesis and support it with outside sources that include at least one personal interview. Your paper should be five to eight pages long and documented in MLA style.

> Select a noted trial, Supreme Court decision, or scandal and examine its lasting impact on the law, American institutions, or perceptions of justice. Your paper should be six to eight pages long and documented in APA style.

■ **Make sure you fully understand all the requirements of an assignment and refer to them throughout the process.** Perhaps the most common mistake students make is failing to address the needs of the assignment. Once you begin looking up sources and examining data, you can be easily led astray and write a paper that is interesting but fails to meet the instructor's requirements. *Every time you start to work on your paper, review the assignment to keep your research on track.*

- **Ask your instructor for clarification of any points you find confusing.** Once you have a topic in mind, ask your instructor if he or she thinks it is suitable. Your instructor may provide valuable tips on what subjects to avoid or how to look for sources.

- **Make copies of any instructor handouts, web pages, or notes, and keep them next to your computer or in your backpack or briefcase for quick reference.** Refer to these guidelines when visiting the library or searching the Internet. Make sure your research remains focused on sources that address the needs of the assignment.

2. Select an appropriate topic.

The first step in writing a research paper is selecting a topic or topics. Until you begin collecting evidence, you may not be sure if the subjects you start with are workable. Often, subjects that you might find interesting at first become unmanageable because sources are lacking or too numerous to handle.

Strategies for Selecting a Topic

1. **Select a topic that matches the assignment.** If your instructor requires you to include personal interviews, you may find it difficult to locate people with specialized knowledge. For example, you may find local mental health professionals who can tell you about depression or addiction. But it may be very difficult to locate anyone who has treated multiple-personality disorder.

2. **Select a topic that interests you.** Brainstorm to discover whether your existing knowledge and experiences apply to the assignment. Discuss possible topics with your instructor or friends and ask for suggestions.

3. **Consider your long-term goals.** In addition to fulfilling a course requirement, a research paper may help you explore your career goals or locate information you can use in your job or business. Make sure that your personal interests do not conflict with the goals of the assignment—refer to the instructor's guidelines to keep your project on track.

4. **Select a topic that is flexible.** Until you begin researching, you cannot tell how much information is readily available. Think of your topic as an accordion, something that may have to be compressed or expanded based on what you discover.

5. **Be willing to alter or reject topics.** Your first topic is only a starting point. If you find it difficult to work with, drop it and select another. Do not feel obligated to stick with something unless required to by your instructor. Use prewriting techniques such as clustering, brainstorming, and asking questions to develop new approaches to your topic.

(Continued)

6. **Select more than one topic to start.** At this point no decision is final. Until you begin investigating ideas, you may not know whether a topic will be suitable. If you are unsure which topic to pursue, sketch out two or three for preliminary research.

Topics to Avoid

Difficulties commonly arise from the following kinds of topics, which are often best avoided altogether.

- **Topics that rely on a single source.** Research papers coordinate information from several sources. If you select an event covered in one news story or a process explained by a single set of instructions, you will not be able to achieve one of the major goals of a research paper. Check with your instructor if you are interested in a topic with only a single source.

- **Highly controversial topics—unless you can develop a new approach.** It is unlikely you can write anything about capital punishment or abortion that has not already been stated—unless you look at the issue from a unique perspective. Controversial subjects may be difficult to research because many of the sources are biased. Discuss your topic with your instructor and ask for recommended approaches or alternative subjects.

- **New topics.** Issues raised by events that have just happened may be difficult to research because little has been published except news reports and fragmentary comments. A quick Internet search might locate all the reliable material currently available.

- **Topics lacking credible sources.** Conducting research about UFOs, psychic phenomena, and alternative medicine can be difficult because sources may be anecdotal and unscientific. Avoid conspiracy-related issues. By their nature, these topics resist objective investigation. A reference librarian can suggest sources or a new topic.

- **Popular topics.** Like writing about a controversial topic, it may be difficult to find something new to say about an issue many students have written about. Popular issues may be hard to research because many of the books may already be checked out of the library.

- **Topics difficult to narrow or expand.** Until you begin discovering sources, you will not know how complex your task will be. If you select a topic that resists alterations, you may be forced to reject it in favor of a more manageable subject.

3. Conduct preliminary research.

Once you have selected a topic or topics, you are ready to explore your subject. Your goal at this point is not to locate specific sources for your research paper but to survey the field of knowledge, get a sense of the discipline, identify schools of thought, and research trends, areas of conflict, and new discoveries.

Strategies for Conducting Preliminary Research

1. **Review textbooks and lecture notes.** Textbooks often include endnotes, bibliographies, and footnotes that can direct you to books, articles, and websites about specific issues. In addition, textbooks and your notes can help you create a list of people, events, ideas, and places to use as online search terms.

2. **Search online encyclopedias and reference works.** Online reference sources, such as Answers.com (**www.answers.com**) and Bartleby.com (**www.bartleby.com**), offer online dictionaries, cross-referenced encyclopedias, and lists of websites that can provide a broad overview of your subject and links to specific sources.

(Continued)

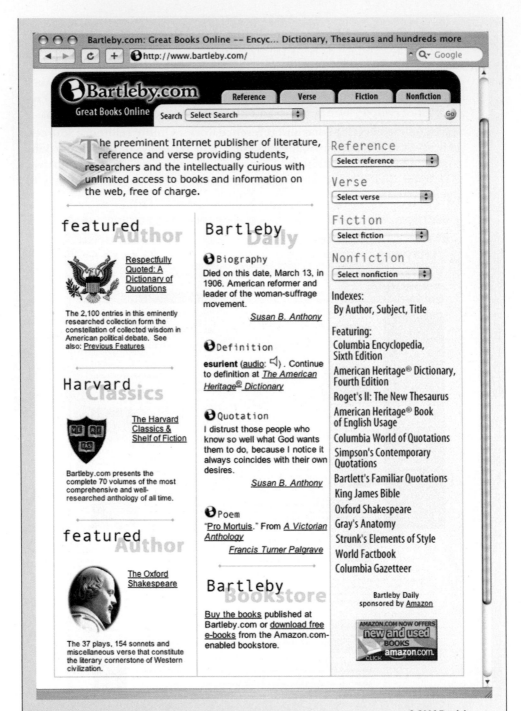

3. **Search the Internet.** There are a variety of popular search engines you can use to survey information available on your subject:

Bing	**www.bing.com**
Excite	**www.excite.com**
Google	**www.google.com**
Lycos	**www.lycos.com**
Yahoo!	**www.yahoo.com**

Each of these search engines accesses millions of sites on the Internet. Students unfamiliar with searching the Internet are often frustrated by the overwhelming list of unrelated hits they receive. Entering *Martin Luther King* may generate a list of thousands of websites about Billy *Martin*, *Martin Luther*, and *King* George III.

Search engines provide tools to narrow your search. To use these tools efficiently, keep the following suggestions in mind:

- Check the spelling of search terms, especially names.
- Make search terms as specific as possible.
- Put quotation marks around search words or phrases. Entering "*Leopold and Loeb*" will locate only documents containing this phrase, eliminating documents about King *Leopold* or *Loeb* Realty. See page 520 for a sample Internet search on "leopold and loeb."
- Use the Boolean search operators AND, OR, NOT. Entering *Orwell AND Nature* locates sites containing both terms. Entering *Orwell NOT Nature* excludes sites containing the second term. Entering *Orwell OR Nature* locates sites containing either term.
- Check to be sure information is up-to-date by examining websites for dates they were created or last updated.
- Take advantage of subject directories, offered by many search engines, such as Yahoo! and Google. Surveying the subject categories related to your preliminary topic may help you search more efficiently.

4. **Review specialized encyclopedias, dictionaries, and directories.** A general encyclopedia, such as the *Encyclopedia Britannica,* may offer only brief commentaries on subjects and will not include minor people, events, or subjects. The reference room of your library is likely to have specialized encyclopedias that may offer substantial entries, such as the following:

Biography
Who's Who in the World
Contemporary Authors

(Continued)

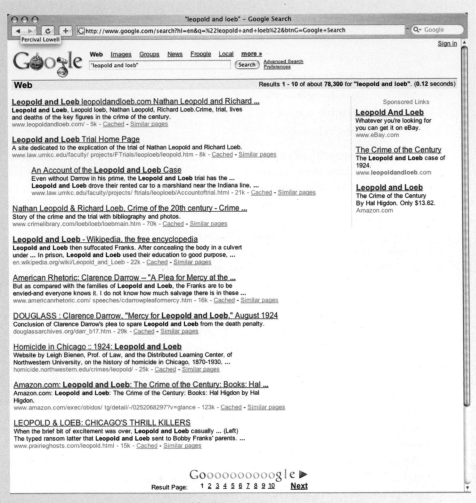

Google search using "leopold and loeb"   Google, Inc.

Business/Economics
Dictionary of Banking and Finance
Encyclopedia of Economics

Education
Encyclopedia of Education
The International Encyclopedia of Education

Sample website result from Leopold and Loeb search

Engineering
The Engineering Index
Information Sources in Engineering

History
Dictionary of American History
An Encyclopedia of World History

Literature
Cassell's Encyclopedia of World Literature
The Oxford Companion to American Literature

Political Science
The Blackwell Encyclopedia of Political Thought
Encyclopedia of American Political History

Psychology
Dictionary of Psychology
Encyclopedia of Human Behavior

Science/Technology
Dictionary of Mathematics
Encyclopedia of Medical History

(Continued)

Social Sciences
Dictionary of Anthropology
Encyclopedia of Crime and Justice

5. **Review indexes, databases, and abstracts.** Available in print and online, these references are valuable tools in conducting research. Databases list articles. Many provide abstracts that briefly summarize articles, usually in a single paragraph. If the complete text is available, you may download and save the file for later reading and note taking. Skimming abstracts allows you to quickly review a dozen articles in the time it would take to locate a magazine and find a single article. Abstracts not only list the source of the full article but also indicate its length and special features, such as photographs or tables. Such sources as *Psychological Abstracts* and *Criminal Justice Abstracts* provide summaries in specific disciplines.

Sample Abstract from *Expanded Academic Index*

	Database: Expanded Academic Index
	Subject: aids (disease) in motion pictures
Title	TV Movies of the first decade of AIDS (American Values and Images)
Magazine	Journal of Popular Film and Television, Spring 1993 v 21 n 1 p19 (8)*
Authors	Author: Frank Pilipp and Charles Shull
Summary	Abstract: The decade of 1983–1993 has produced several full-length feature films which respond to the AIDS epidemic. Three of them, 'As Is,' 'Andre's Mother,' and 'An Early Frost' undoubtedly portray the virus as non-partisan when it comes to gender, color, or sexual orientation, although they fail to destroy the image of AIDS as being a purely homosexual disease. The disease instead is viewed as punishment inflicted on the main characters and their families for their violation of middle-class norms and values.
Listings for related articles	Subjects: Gays—portrayals, depictions, etc. Motion pictures—criticism, interpretation, etc.
	AIDS (disease) in motion pictures—criticism, interpretation, etc.
	Features: illustration; photograph
	AN: 14558418

* indicates eight page article

■ Common online indexes and databases include
ABC Political Science
ABI/Inform
Academic Search
Biography & Genealogy Master Index
Business Abstracts
Business Newsbank
CARL UnCover
Contemporary Authors
Dissertation Abstracts
Education Index
ERIC
General Science Index
Historical Abstracts
Humanities Index
Masterplots
Medline
MLA Bibliography
National Criminal Justice Reference Service
Newspaper Abstracts
Psychological Literature
Reader's Guide Abstracts
Sociological Abstracts
Women's Resources International

E-Research Activity

Exploring Preliminary Research Online

Explore the sources available online or at your library.

1. Search Answers.com (www.answers.com) for articles on the following topics. Scroll through the entire article to locate cross-references and links.

Chicago	Leopold and Loeb	plagiarism
immigration	General Motors	global warming

2. Search the Internet for websites on the same topics using one or more of the following search engines:

www.google.com	**www.altavista.com**	**ww.yahoo.com**
www.bing.com	**ww.excite.com**	

Follow the search engine's advanced search directions to focus your search and reduce the number of unrelated sites.

3. Examine the list of online databases available in your library.

4. Search a business database for a company you have worked for or done business with (such as Taco Bell, Coca-Cola, The Home Depot, Bath & Body Works, or Proctor and Gamble).

5. Use Medline to generate a list of articles about a medical problem you or a family member has experienced (for example, carpal tunnel syndrome, diabetes, or autism).

6. Use a general database, such as Readers' Guide or InfoTrac College Edition (available through your English CourseMate at **www.cengagebrain.com**) to obtain a list of recent articles on one or more of the following topics:

caffeine	federal witness protection program
Alzheimer's disease	high-definition television
Russell Crowe	Hubble Space Telescope

7. Using one of the articles you identified in E-Research Activity 1, save the file to a drive and then print a hard copy of the first page of the text.

8. Send the file of links you created in E-Research Activity 2 as an e-mail attachment to your own e-mail address for later retrieval. This method might be necessary if you locate an article on a database but have no way to save the file.

A Note on Conducting Preliminary Research

Remember, your goal at this point is to simply survey the field, to get an overall feel for your subject. Don't get bogged down with details or allow yourself to become overwhelmed by the complexity or number of sources.

- Determine whether there is sufficient material on your subject to work with.
- Look for ways to limit your topic.
- Identify patterns in the data: conflicting points of view, clusters of related articles, key figures or authors, current theories, or research trends.
- Allow sources to direct you to new topics or new approaches to your subject.

Continually refer to your instructor's guidelines to keep your search on track.

4. Limit the topic and develop a working thesis.

After surveying the field of knowledge, consider whether your topic is worth pursuing. If you cannot find enough material or if the sources are too diverse or scattered, you may wish to consider a new subject. In most instances, the preliminary material you have located may help you further limit your topic. Notice how the sequences of titles below result in a more targeted topic.

Credit Crisis
Credit Cards
Consumers and Credit Cards
College Students and Credit Cards

Famous Trials
Role of the Media in High-Profile Trials
Leopold and Loeb Case
Role of the Press in the Leopold and Loeb Case

Asking questions can help target your paper and prevent you from simply summarizing the work or the ideas of others:

Why do so many college students face substantial credit card debt?
Did media coverage affect the outcome of the Leopold and Loeb case?

At this point you may be able to develop a working thesis, a starting point for your research paper. Although it may be general and subject to change, the working thesis moves beyond a narrowed topic or question to make a tentative statement:

Colleges should regulate credit card promotions on their campuses.
Excessive media coverage influenced the outcome of the Leopold and Loeb case.

A working thesis is a tentative statement subject to change. A working thesis is a tool to guide your research; keep an open mind and be willing to alter your opinion.

5. Create a timeline.

In developing a long paper, make sure you devote enough time for each stage in the writing process. Don't spend six weeks gathering materials and try to write, revise, edit, and proofread a ten-page paper over a weekend.

- **Note the due date and work backward to create a schedule that allows sufficient time for each stage in the writing process.**

May 10	Paper due
May 5	Target date for completion
May 1	Final draft prepared for final editing and proofreading
April 25	Second draft completed
April 15	First draft completed for revision and rewriting
April 10	Final outline completed, final thesis
April 5	Research completed and sources selected
March 15	Topic narrowed, working thesis, and research initiated
March 10	Topic selected and preliminary research started
March 5	Research project assigned

- **Chart your progress on a calendar to keep on track.**
- **Establish cutoff dates for major stages in the process.** If you cannot find enough material by a fixed date, talk with your instructor and consider changing topics. If you find too much material, narrow your topic.
- **Don't allow the research stage to expand past a specific date.** Keep the scope of the assignment and the length of the paper in mind to guide the quantity of material you collect.

6. Collect and evaluate relevant evidence.

The type of evidence you will need to support your thesis will depend on the discipline, the topic, and the scope of the assignment. There are two kinds of sources: primary and secondary.

Primary sources—original documents and observations; works of art, such as novels, poems, and plays; historical documents; letters; diaries; autobiographies; speeches; interviews; raw data, such as polls or observations of experiments; eyewitness testimony; photographs of events

Secondary sources—interpretations and analysis of primary sources; literary criticism, commentaries, biographies, analytical studies, reviews, editorials

You may use only primary or secondary sources or a combination. A literary paper might focus on a novel (primary source) and include biographical material about the author and critical interpretations (secondary sources). An economics paper on a recent market trend may examine stock market statistics (primary sources) and comments by experts (secondary sources).

Types of Evidence

Primary documents—regulations, minutes, speeches, contracts, laws, reports, letters, diaries, e-mail, policies, manuals, or press releases created by governments, corporations, individuals, and organizations.

Advantages: provide objective data and serve as a basis to examine the validity of secondary sources, such as criticism and interpretation

Disadvantages: may require specialized training to access or understand. Documents, such as speeches and e-mail, can be misleading if taken out of context.

Criticism—Analysis of events, works of art, ideas, problems, or proposals by historians, political commentators, literary critics, or scientists.

Advantages: provides useful quotations from experienced experts

Disadvantages: although written by experts, all criticism is largely opinion and can be biased. Avoid relying on a single critic. Balance personal opinions with alternative viewpoints or other forms of evidence.

Testimony—statements, narratives, comments, or interviews by individuals. *Primary evidence* would be statements by eyewitnesses and participants in events. *Secondary evidence* would be commentary by experts.

Advantages: provides dramatic human interest and thought-provoking insights

Disadvantages: may be anecdotal, fragmentary, or biased; should be balanced with other forms of evidence

Facts and statistics—Objective details and information presented in numbers such as census data or stock prices.

Advantages: provide objective evidence readers expect in research documents

Disadvantages: can be poorly collected or presented in a biased manner to distort events. Facts and statistics can lack impact and may be balanced with testimony to create human interest.

(Continued)

Research and experiments—Data collected through academic studies or laboratory experimentation.

> **Advantages:** can provide objective evidence that can be verified by other sources
>
> **Disadvantages:** can require specialized training to understand. Studies may be biased in their design or results misinterpreted.

Polls and surveys—measure opinions and attitudes of the general public or specialized populations.

> **Advantages:** offer insight into past or current attitudes about a person, issue, or event
>
> **Disadvantages:** can be highly biased and subject to manipulation

Media reports—newspaper, website, television, and magazine reports.

> **Advantages:** provide short, factual stories that are easily read; offer insight into current events
>
> **Disadvantages:** written to be meet deadlines, based on immediate impressions; can be fragmentary and inaccurate

Because each type of evidence has advantages and disadvantages, most writers use a variety of sources to achieve balance and a fuller picture of their subject.

How to Locate Library Sources

Large university libraries may have their collections separated by discipline or department. Look for maps or guides to locate materials. Though the books may be arranged on different floors or even in different buildings on your campus, all libraries will use either the Library of Congress or Dewey Decimal system. Libraries organize books, magazines, videos, and other sources by *call numbers*. Call numbers are standard. *The Grapes of Wrath*, for example, will have the same Library of Congress call number in the Boston College library as it does at the University of New Mexico.

Library of Congress System

A	General Works
B	Philosophy/Religion
C	History/Auxiliary Sciences
D	History/Topography (except America)
E–F	America
G	Geography
H	Social Sciences (Psychology, Sociology, etc.)
J	Political Science
K	Law
L	Education
M	Music
N	Fine Arts
P	Language and Literature

Q	Science
R	Medicine
S	Agriculture
T	Technology
U	Military Science
V	Naval Science
Z	Bibliography and Library Science

Dewey Decimal System

000–099	General Works
100–199	Philosophy and Psychology
200–299	Religion
300–399	Social Science
400–499	Language
500–599	Pure Science
600–699	Technology/Applied Sciences
700–799	The Arts
800–899	Literature
900–999	History

Computerized Catalogs

Online catalogs list a library's holdings of books, magazines, videos, and other sources. The exact instructions for searching a catalog will vary slightly. Most systems provide on-screen directions to locate specific works by subject, author, or title.

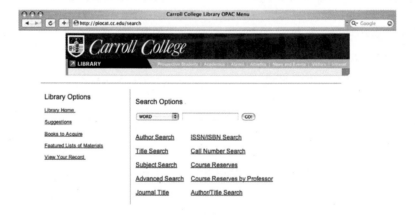

If you do not have a particular source in mind, you can enter a subject or topic:

Leopold and Loeb

LIST OF ITEMS   12 ITEMS MATCH YOUR SEARCH

ITEM	AUTHOR	TITLE	
1	Bellak, Leopold, 1916	The schizophrenic syndrome, Leo	1967
2	Busch, Francis X	Prisoners at the bar: an accou	1952
3	Compulsion	[video recording]	1995
4	Darrow, Clarence, 1857	Clarence Darrow pleas in defen	1926
5	Darrow, Clarence, 1857–	The plea of Clarence Darrow in	1924
6	DeFord, Miriam Allen	Murderers sane and mad	1965
7	Geis, Gilbert	Crimes of the century: from Leo	1998
8	Higdon, Hal	The crime of the century	1975
9	Levin, Meyer, 1905–	Compulsion–New York, Simon	1956
10	Loeb, Leo, 1869–	The venom of Heloderma	1913
11	McKernan, Maureen	The amazing crime and trial	1924
12	Vaughn, Betty Ann Erick	The forensic speaking in the	1948

By highlighting or entering the number of the source, you can access specific information about it:

AUTHOR	Higdon, Hal
TITLE	The crime of the century : the Leopold and Loeb case by Hal Higdon.
	New York : Putnam, [c1975]
LOCATION	College Library Main Book Collection
	3rd Floor West, Room 3191
CALL NO.	HV6245 H46
STATUS	Not checked out
DESCRIPTION	380 p., [8] leaves of plates: ill; 24 cm.
NOTES	Includes index. Bibliography: p. 368
	ISBN: 0399114912
	OCLC NUMBER: 01801383

Once you have located the call number for a source, you can search for it in the library.

■ When you locate the book, look at the books next to it. Libraries organize books by subject, so you may find other useful titles on the same shelf.

Computerized catalogs are often linked to other libraries so you can search for sources located at other campuses or in local public libraries. They also list databases of abstracts and articles. Ask a librarian if you can access the library's databases from a remote site (for example, at home, in your dorm room, or from a laptop with Internet connection).

■ If this option is available, you may need a current user name and password to gain access.

Locating Periodicals

Libraries refer to magazines and journals as *periodicals* or *serials*. You can locate a magazine or a newspaper in the catalog or *serials holding list*. But this will simply explain where *Newsweek* or the *New York Times* is located in the building—in bound volumes, microfilm, or online. To find which articles and issues to search for, you have to consult specific databases (see page 523). Databases list articles under keywords. The *MLA Bibliography*, for instance, lists articles about literature and authors:

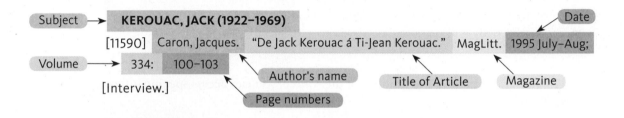

Subject → **KEROUAC, JACK (1922–1969)**

[11590]   Caron, Jacques.   "De Jack Kerouac á Ti-Jean Kerouac."   MagLitt.   1995 July–Aug;

Volume → 334:   100–103
[Interview.]

Author's name   Title of Article   Magazine   **Date**
Page numbers

Fiction
[11591] Oates, Joyce Carol; Dauzat, Pierre-Emmanuel, translator. "Au bout de la route."
MagLitt. 1995 July–Aug; 334: 96–99.

Letters
[11592] "Letters from Jack Kerouac to Ed White, 1947–68." MissR. 1994; 17(3): 107–60
[Includes letters (1947–1968) to White, Ed.]

Prose/Some of the Dharma
[11593] Sampas, John, foreword; Stanford, David, ed. and introd. Some of the Dharma. New
York, NY: Viking; 1997. 420pp. ISBN 0-670-84877-8 [And poetry.Edition.]

Other Sources

In addition to books and periodicals, libraries contain government documents, statistics, microfilms, audio and video recordings, photographs, and film. Your library may have special collections of artifacts not included in most databases. Depending on your topic, you may be able to obtain valuable information from corporations, organizations, federal agencies, state and local governments, or historical and professional societies.

Selecting and Evaluating Sources

Database and Internet searches may provide you with hundreds, even thousands, of sources. Before you begin printing or photocopying, consider the type and number of sources needed. Without planning a list, you may waste a great deal of time collecting sources that may be interesting but unsuited to your paper.

Strategies for Selecting and Evaluating Sources

1. **List the types of sources needed to support your working thesis.** Review the assignment, instructor's directions, your preliminary research, and your working thesis to develop a list of needed sources, as with the following two examples:

   Working Thesis:
   Colleges should regulate credit card promotions on their campuses.

   Sources needed:

   > Data, examples of student credit problems
   > Examples of colleges with vested interests in credit card issuers
   > Evidence this is serious problem
   > Interviews, analysis of experts

   Working Thesis:
   Excessive media coverage influenced the outcome of the Leopold and Loeb case.

   Sources needed:

   > Background/summary of Leopold & Loeb case
   > Biographical information of principal figures in Leopold and Loeb case
   > Description of press in Chicago in 1920s
   > Actual 1924 newspaper accounts
   > Assessment of effects of press on judge's decision

   For a ten-page paper, you may need only one or two biographical sources—not five or six. Make sure you select enough sources for each item on your list.

2. **Collect a variety of evidence.** If you are writing a paper about the homeless, you may wish to balance personal accounts with statistics and expert opinions. A paper about *Native Son* might benefit from sources from black history or accounts of contemporary race relations in addition to critical studies of the book and biographies of the author Richard Wright.

3. **Avoid collecting needless or repetitive data.** Although it is important to grasp the sweep and range of material about your subject, avoid collecting more items than you need.

(Continued)

- Select the most useful sources, briefly noting similar articles for confirmation.
- Refer to the assignment and your working thesis to keep your research focused.
- Skim books and long documents by examining tables of contents and indexes to measure their usefulness before checking them out.

4. **Select reliable sources.** Recognized publishers, magazines, and established databases such as MLA, Westlaw, and Psychological Abstracts are edited by professionals who follow established standards. Articles appearing in *The New England Journal of Medicine, The Harvard Law Review*, or *Nursing* have been reviewed by physicians, attorneys, and nurses. Small press publications and individual websites, however, may produce material based solely on rumor, anecdotal observation, and facts taken out of context. **Do not assume that all the books in the library or sites on the Internet are of equal value.**

- **Evaluate books** by checking online reviews. Examine the author's use of sources. Does the book include a bibliography? Does the author provide endnotes and support his or her conclusions with facts, quotations, or statistics? Is the author's biography available in *Who's Who* or other databases? Use the author's name or book title as a search term and examine any comments or reviews it generates. Does the author seem biased?
- **Evaluate magazines** by reviewing other issues and examining the editorial staff. Determine the audience for the magazine. Publications designed for general readers, such as *Reader's Digest* or *People*, are less rigorous about checking specific facts than professional journals in law or medicine.
- **Evaluate websites** by seeking confirming articles on established databases. Examine the server or producer of the website. Is it a professional organization, university, or government agency? Or is it a small, amateur, or personal site? Does the information seem biased or objective?

5. **Distinguish between fact and opinion.** In evaluating sources it is important to separate factual data from interpretation and analysis. The author of a book, magazine article, or website might accurately report a change in oil prices but present a highly personal and subjective interpretation or prediction.

6. **Examine sources for lapses in critical thinking.** Remember that all the books, articles, and websites you discover were created by human beings who, despite their degrees or expertise, may be biased or mistaken.

- Do not assume that everything you read is accurate or true.
- Facts may be misrepresented, conclusions misguided, and alternative interpretations ignored. Review Strategies for Increasing Critical Thinking on pages 38–39.

EVALUATING INTERNET SOURCES CHECKLIST

As you search for sources online, determine their value and reliability.

✔ **Source:** What is the domain name of the source? The URL—the site's Internet address—can help you evaluate an online source.

Domain	Source
.com	company or for-profit organization
.edu	college or university
.gov	government
.mil	military
.net	Internet provider
.ny.us	New York state government
.org	nonprofit organization or individual

Does a reputable organization sponsor the site? Is this organization likely to be impartial in its examination of the information? Does the organization benefit from persuading you to accept its position? Do you detect inflammatory language that reveals bias or prejudice?

✔ **Authorship:** Does the site mention the author or webmaster? This information is often noted at the bottom of the site's home page, but does not always appear on internal pages. Does the author or webmaster include an e-mail address? An e-mail to the author or webmaster can yield valuable insights.

✔ **Credibility:** If you are able to identify the site's author, can you also determine whether he or she has significant knowledge about the topic? Does the site present objective information or express personal opinions? Does the author include his or her résumé or biography?

- To check if the author has also published books, check your library's online catalog or Amazon.com (www.amazon.com), which lists books and often includes reader reviews.

- Place the author's full name in quotation marks and enter it as a search term using a search engine like Yahoo! or Google to locate biographical information.

✔ **Purpose:** Can you determine the site's intended purposes? Is the site designed to present all available evidence? Does it seem to take a side? Is the site intended to inform readers or to sell a product or service?

✔ **Audience:** Does the site expect its readers to have an opinion? Does the site encourage its readers to form an opinion based solely on the information presented? Or does the site invite further investigation by providing links to related sites?

✔ **Language:** Is the information presented in a manner that allows any reader to understand it? Is specialized terminology included? Does its presence have a negative effect on the general reader's comprehension?

(Continued)

✔ **Presentation:** Has the site been planned and designed well? Is it easy to navigate? Are the links active, current, and relevant? Does the text reflect that careful planning has been devoted to it, including thorough proofreading? Don't allow impressive graphics, sound, and video to substitute for accuracy in the information.

✔ **Timeliness:** Many sites are not dated, making it difficult to determine the currency of the information. If dates do not appear, test links to see if they are still active. Place key terms and phrases in quotations and use them as search terms to determine dates and perhaps locate more recent sources.

✔ **Critical Thinking:** Do you detect errors in critical thinking, such as hasty generalizations, dependence on anecdotal evidence, faulty comparisons, false authorities, or attacking personalities? See pages 39–41.

Strategies for Overcoming Problems with Research

Students frequently encounter common problems in conducting library research.

1. **There are no sources on the topic.** If your library and Internet search fails to yield sufficient results, review the subject and search terms you are using.
   ■ Check the spelling of your keywords.
   ■ Check a thesaurus for synonyms.
   ■ Review the Library of Congress subject headings for alternative search terms.
   ■ Review textbooks, encyclopedias, and other reference sources for search terms.
   ■ Ask a reference librarian or your instructor for suggestions.

2. **There are sources about the subject but none are related to the specific topic or working thesis.** If you are analyzing the role of the mother in *Death of a Salesman,* you may find numerous articles on the play or Willy Loman but nothing on his wife. You do not have to find articles that exactly match your topic or thesis. Because one of the goals of a research paper is originality, your thesis may address unexplored territory. You can still use related or background sources. Biographies of Arthur Miller might yield insights into the attitudes represented by Linda Loman. Critical commentaries may provide views about the Loman family that relate to Linda's role in the play.
   ■ Pointing out the lack of sources can be crucial in demonstrating the value of your paper and the uniqueness of your approach.

3. **Sources present conflicting findings or opinions.** Experts often disagree. As a student you are not expected to resolve conflicts among experts, but you should report what you find.
   ■ On the basis of your evaluation of the evidence, you may side with one group or alter your thesis to conclude that at present it is impossible to make a definitive statement.

4. **There are several books and articles, but they present the same information or refer to a common original source.** If you discover that the five books you have selected present the same material, select the most representative, relevant, or best-written source.

   ■ Although you may select only a single source, it is important to comment on the consensus of expert opinion. Acknowledge that other writers share the same views.

5. **The only available sources are fragmentary, biased, outdated, inaccurate, or unprofessional.** In some instances the only available sources will lack substance or quality. A controversial historical incident may have produced a rash of inflammatory editorials, biased newspaper accounts, or subjective memoirs by adversaries.

   ■ Ask your instructor whether you should consider changing your topic.
   ■ Consult a reference librarian for alternative sources.
   ■ As a researcher you are not responsible for the lack of evidence or the quality of sources you can locate—but you should comment on the limited value of existing evidence.

Taking Notes

Traditional textbooks suggest students record notes on index cards. Placing single facts or quotations on separate cards makes it easy to shuffle and reorder them after developing an outline. Today most students photocopy or print pages and highlight selected passages. Others copy online text directly onto a computer disk or download and save full articles.

Whatever method you use, it is essential to accomplish three tasks when recording information from outside sources:

1. **Accurately record information you will need to cite the source.**

   Books: author's full name, full title (including any subtitle), publisher, place of publication, and year.

   ■ If a publisher lists several cities, choose the first location listed.
   ■ Note editions, translators, editors, or forewords.

   Articles: author's full name, full title (including any subtitle), full title of the magazine or newspaper, edition, volume, pages, and date.

   ■ If you photocopy pages from a book or magazine, write the information directly on the copies for future reference.

   Film: title, director, studio, city, year of release.

   (Continued)

Video: title, director, production company, city, date of production or original broadcast.

Online sources: author's (or editor's) full name, title of website or document, sponsoring organization, date (if provided), date you accessed the source, and full URL or Internet address. (Bookmark or print online resources for future reference.)

2. **Double-check your notes for accuracy.** If you take notes rather than photocopy a source, make sure that you have properly copied facts, numbers, and names. Understand the difference between quoting and paraphrasing sources, as the following example shows:

Original text:

When Robert Moses began building playgrounds in New York City, there were 119. When he stopped, there were 777. Under his direction, an army of men that at times during the Depression included 84,000 laborers reshaped every park in the city and then filled the parks with zoos and skating rinks, boathouses and tennis houses, bridle paths and golf courses, 288 tennis courts and 673 baseball diamonds.

The Power Broker by Robert A. Caro

Student note card, full direct quotation:

Robert A. Caro, *The Power Broker.* New York: Vintage, 1975. Print.

"When Robert Moses began building playgrounds in New York City, there were 119. When he stopped, there were 777. Under his direction, an army of men that at times during the Depression included 84,000 laborers reshaped every park in the city and then filled the parks with zoos and skating rinks, boathouses and tennis houses, bridle paths and golf courses, 288 tennis courts and 673 baseball diamonds." p. 7

Student note card, partial direct quotation using ellipsis (. . .) to show omitted text:

Robert A. Caro, *The Power Broker.* New York: Vintage, 1975. Print.

"When Robert Moses began building playgrounds in New York City, there were 119. When he stopped, there were 777. Under his direction, an army of men . . . reshaped every park in the city. . . ." p. 7

■ In deleting details, make sure that your notes accurately reflect the meaning of the original text. Do not take quotations out of context that alter the author's point of view.

Student note card, paraphrase, putting text into his or her own words:

Robert A. Caro, *The Power Broker.* New York: Vintage, 1975. Print.

Robert Moses increased the number of New York City playgrounds from 119 to 777. During the Depression as many as 84,000 workers restored every city park, embellishing them with zoos, playgrounds, and hundreds of tennis courts and baseball diamonds. p. 7

Even though the student is not copying Robert Caro word for word, he or she will have to cite Caro in the research paper to acknowledge the source of the statistics.

3. **Label research materials.**
   - Make sure that you print or photocopy all the material needed. To save paper, some library printers do not automatically print the last page of an article. Make sure your copies are complete.
   - Clip or staple articles to prevent pages from becoming mixed up.
   - Label, number, or letter your sources for easy reference. You may find it useful to write note cards for some or all of your sources so that they can be easily arranged on your desk.

4. **Organize database files.**
   - For files you've downloaded from databases, consolidate them and make a backup disk.
   - As a quick and easy reference, consolidate abstracts of the articles to form a single file that provides an overview of the items that you've identified as potentially useful.

Primary Research

Conducting Interviews

Interviews allow you to collect information from professionals, eyewitnesses, and others with direct experience about your topic. Interviews, however, can be challenging to conduct and analyze.

1. **Determine whether interviews will provide useful information.** Not all subjects are conducive to interviews. You may be unable to identify a local expert on your topic. Print and electronic sources may be more useful.
   - Many print articles serve as interviews because they are written by experts and eyewitnesses. In addition, in writing an article a person has the opportunity to check facts, verify recollections, and evaluate responses more carefully than in an interview.

2. **Locate backup sources if possible.** Because interviews can be difficult to arrange and subjects may have to cancel a meeting at the last moment, avoid basing your whole paper on interviews.
   - Search for print or electronic sources that can provide information needed to support your working thesis.

3. **Identify possible subjects.** Ask your instructor or network with local organizations, corporations, and government agencies to locate people who may be willing to provide interviews.
   - Because scheduling meetings may be difficult, locate several prospects.

4. **Determine the information or insights you wish to obtain from an interview.** There is no reason to use an interview to gather background information that you can easily obtain from other sources. However, conducting an interview gives you an opportunity to ask questions, to interact with a source, to ask an expert or witness to comment on other sources, or to help you locate resources you may have overlooked.

5. **Schedule interviews in advance.** Because it may be difficult to find a time and place to meet people and last-minute changes can occur, schedule interviews well in advance. If you can, offer the subject additional dates and times in case the first appointment you arrange must be postponed.

6. **Provide subjects with questions in advance.** Reporters and television interviewers usually prefer not to give people questions in advance because they seek spontaneous reactions. As a researcher, however, you are seeking information. Giving subjects a few days or a week to consider the topic of your interview may help them focus their thoughts or locate information.

7. **Ask specific questions.** An interview is not a conversation or an endless monologue. You should ask specific questions to produce comments that you can use in your paper:

   > As a director of a program for the homeless, could you say how many of the homeless suffer from mental illness?
   >
   > What is the biggest obstacle preventing the homeless from gaining independence?

8. **Ask consistent questions.** If you are interviewing more than one subject, don't ask one person, "How many of the homeless are mentally ill?" and then ask another, "How many of the homeless are schizophrenic?" If you use conflicting terms, you will not be able to compare results.

9. **Do not record the interview without permission.** For professional or legal reasons, many subjects will not allow you to record an interview. Ask in advance whether they will permit sound recording.

10. **Ask how the subject wishes to be credited.** An attorney working for the US Department of Labor may not wish to be viewed as speaking for the federal government. A physician may prefer not to have his or her hospital mentioned in your paper.

11. **Review the interview material with your subject to ensure accuracy.** Make sure you have accurately recorded names, facts, and statistics. Take careful notes during the interview and verify that you have accurately represented the subject's thoughts.

12. **Use the interview to verify evidence or seek new sources.** If you have the opportunity to interview a practicing psychiatrist, you can ask him or her whether he or she is familiar with a book you have read or a new study found on the Internet. You might also ask the physician for suggested readings or other interview subjects.

■ Although you do not want a single source to heavily influence how you shape your final paper, you may wish to ask an expert to review your sources and thesis.

13. **Recognize the limits of interviews.** Interviews can be compelling because they bring you face to face with your topic. But remember, an interview presents a single person's experiences or point of view. The observations of one person may be highly individualistic and not representative of others. His or her views should be given no more weight than a book or a website.

Conducting Surveys

Surveys can be used to gather specific information about a particular population or to measure that population's knowledge, beliefs, or attitudes about a particular person, issue, or problem. A sociology student researching the homeless could, for example, survey the residents of a local shelter to determine their level of education. A business student studying consumer attitudes toward online shopping might distribute a questionnaire to new car buyers, asking if they would consider buying a car from an online dealer.

Like interviews, surveys can be time-consuming and very challenging.

1. **Measure your ability to conduct a survey.** Surveys require time and effort to conduct as well as collect and analyze their results.
   ■ Will you have enough time to conduct a survey?
   ■ Will conducting a survey detract from your ability to search for library and online sources?
   ■ Will the survey reveal valuable information? Is it necessary? Ask your instructor for guidance.

2. **Develop backup sources.** Determine if you can support your working thesis with other forms of evidence in case you have to terminate the survey.
   ■ Much of the statistical data available in the library or online is the result of surveys.

3. **Determine clearly what you are seeking to measure.** A survey should have a clear goal—for example, to assess the education level of the residents of a homeless shelter or measure the attitudes of car buyers toward online car dealers.

4. **Craft the measuring instrument carefully.** Whether surveys are conducted online, on paper, over the phone, or in personal interviews, they must use a standard instrument. Your results will only be valid if all the subjects respond to the same questions.
   ■ Questions or categories should be as specific as possible. If you simply ask residents of a homeless shelter if they completed high school, negative responses will include people who left school in sixth grade and those only a few credits short of a high school diploma. It would be more effective to ask respondents to record the last year of school completed or check a box referring to a specific level of education. Asking car buyers, "Would you consider buying a car

from an online dealer?" will only produce simplistic responses. More detailed questions would more adequately reflect consumer attitudes:

1. Would you consider buying a car from an online dealer?

___ Definitely   ___ Possibly   ___ Probably not   ___ Definitely not

2. If you answered "Probably not" or "Definitely not," check the reasons for this response. Check all items that apply:

   ___ Fear of revealing personal or financial information online
   ___ Reluctance to deal with new or unknown businesses
   ___ Loyalty to local car dealers
   ___ Desire to develop personal relationship with sales staff
   ___ Concern for service and warranty repair
   ___ Desire to test-drive several cars
   ___ Unfamiliarity with the Internet

- Review your instrument carefully for unconscious bias. Examine your use of diction; avoid words with unintended subjective connotations.
- Do not ask loaded questions that prompt a desired response, such as "Should we stop wasting money on welfare?" or "Do you support the mayor's urban renewal program that will destroy the city's low-income housing?"
- Use peer review to test your instrument for lapses in critical thinking, missing questions, or misleading statements.

5. **Clearly identify your subjects.** Surveys will be useful only if the population being evaluated is clearly defined. Who will you consider homeless—long-term residents of a shelter or those seeking refuge for a single night? How will you determine who is a "car buyer"?

6. **Determine how to conduct the survey.** You can conduct a series of personal interviews, distribute questionnaires in person, or contact subjects by telephone, mail, or e-mail.
   - If you talk with people directly or by phone, make sure you ask the same questions in the same order. Use a standard form to record responses.
   - Distribute questionnaires in person, if possible, to standardize the time and manner in which respondents answer.
   - Realize that in many instances only 5 percent of people will respond to a survey. Be prepared to mail or e-mail hundreds of questionnaires to develop a useful number of responses.

7. **Develop a workable method of collecting and interpreting responses.** Consider using forms that can be visually or electronically scanned.

8. **Document your research methods.** Surveys have value only if you carefully record how you selected subjects, the rationale used to construct the measuring instrument, and the number of responses collected.

9. **Maintain a timeline.** Keep an eye on the calendar. You must allow sufficient time not only to conduct surveys but also to analyze results and edit and present your findings. Don't devote too much time to a single step in the process.

10. **Review Common Errors in Critical Thinking (pages 39–41) to test your methods of research and analysis.**

Locating and Evaluating Visuals

For some assignments graphs, charts, tables, and photographs are essential sources that should be included in your paper. In other instances, you may develop your own graphics to highlight data or include your own photographs. However, in some courses assignments focus primarily on text and visuals can be of limited value.

Strategies for Locating and Evaluating Visuals

1. **Determine the importance of visuals.** If visuals provide essential information, scan, download, or photocopy tables, photographs, graphs, and charts you find in print or online documents for future use.
   - Make sure you note the source of the visual.
   If visuals will only dramatize a point in your text or supply added interest to your paper, scan, download, and photocopy visuals as you come across documents but do not devote time to locating additional visuals at this point.
   - Do not spend time looking for visuals that is better spent locating text sources.
2. **Search online library galleries, educational websites, and stock photo services for images.** Libraries, educational websites, and stock photo services such as the following offer millions of commercial, historical, and news photographs; illustrations; and graphics:
   New York Public Library Digital Gallery
   > **http://digitalgallery.nypl.org/nypldigital/index.cfm**
   Libraryspot.com
   > **http://libraryspot.com/images.htm**
   Teacher Tap Visual Resources: Photos and Clip Art
   > **http://www.eduscapes.com/tap/topic20.htm**
   - Study the site's search engine to narrow your search. Most sites list links and allow you to search for images in specific categories, such as historical, commercial, art, news, people, or graphics.
3. **Before selecting visuals, examine them for relevance, distortion, or bias.**
   - See Strategies for Analyzing Visual Images (pages 630–631)
   - See Strategies for Analyzing Graphics (page 636)
4. **If you take your own photographs, document the subject, location, and date for each image.**

RESEARCH ACTIVITY

1. **Use library or online sources to answer the following questions:**
   a. Where is the headquarters for B. F. Goodrich?
   b. When and where was Jack Nicholson born?
   c. Who is the current mayor of San Diego?
   d. When did Ford produce the Edsel?
   e. Who developed methadone?

2. **Create a list of sources for one of the following topics:**
   a. The construction of the Lincoln Tunnel
   b. The role of the green monkey in AIDS
   c. The 1919 World Series scandal
   d. Protecting elephant herds from ivory poachers
   e. Reviews of a current Broadway play or new motion picture

3. **Review selections in the Reader section of this book to develop topics and identify sources.**
   a. Use databases or the Internet to search for information about an author.
   b. Use one of the questions following an article to develop a topic.
   c. Examine an article you have read for keywords to guide a database or online search.

RESEARCH CHECKLIST

As you conduct your research, consider these questions:

✔ Do you fully understand the needs of the assignment? Do you know what your instructor expects in terms of topic, content, sources, and documentation?

✔ Have you narrowed your topic sufficiently to target a search for sources?

✔ Has your preliminary research given you a global view of the field? Can you detect trends or patterns in the research, prevailing theories, or conflicts?

✔ Have you developed a flexible working thesis to guide your research?

✔ Have you explored database and online sources as well as books and articles?

✔ Are you keeping the final paper in mind as you conduct research? If you sense your paper is expanding beyond its target length, narrow your topic.

✔ Does the material you select accurately and fairly represent the wider spectrum of research material, or are you taking material out of context to support a preconceived thesis?

✔ Are you recording the data needed to document your sources in the final paper?

If you have difficulties locating material, ask your instructor or reference librarian for assistance.

For Further Reading

Badke, William. *The Survivor's Guide to Library Research.*

Berdie, Douglas R., et al. *Questionnaires: Design and Use.*

Converse, Jean M. *Survey Questions: Handcrafting the Standardized Questionnaire.*

Dillman, Don A. *Mail and Telephone Surveys: The Total Design Method.*

Harmon, Charles. *Using the Internet, Online Services, and CD-ROMs for Writing Research and Term Papers.*

Harnack, Andrew, and Eugene Kleppinger. *Online! A Reference Guide to Using Internet Resources.*

Roth, Audrey J. *The Research Paper: Process, Form, and Content.*

Rubin, Herbert J., and Irene S. Rubin. *Qualitative Interviewing: The Art of Hearing Data.*

Shepherd, Robert D. *Writing Research Papers: Your Complete Guide to the Process of Writing a Research Paper, from Finding a Topic to Preparing the Final Draft.*

Woodward, Jeannette A. *Writing Research Papers: Investigating Resources in Cyberspace.*

E-Sources

The Library of Congress
> **http://www.loc.gov**

Cornell University Library: The Seven Steps of the Research Process
> **http://olinuris.library.cornell.edu/ref/research/skill1.htm**

Cornell University Library: Critically Analyzing Information Sources
> **http://olinuris.library.cornell.edu/ref/research/skill26.htm**

 Access the English CourseMate for this text at **www.cengagebrain.com** for additional information on conducting research.

Writing the Research Paper

A good research paper is actually the result or culmination of many rough drafts.

—Jeanette A. Woodward

What Is a Research Paper?

The research paper is the standard method of demonstrating your skills in college. Collecting data, assembling quotations, finding evidence, evaluating sources, and developing a thesis are essential to laying the groundwork for your paper. But before you plunge into working with sources and making citations, it is important to take three preliminary steps:

1. **Review the needs of the assignment.** If you have not examined the instructor's requirements recently, refresh your memory. Study handouts, course websites, and your notes.
   - Do you fully understand what is expected in terms of topic, content, sources, and format? If you are unsure, talk with your instructor.
   - Do your working thesis, sources, and notes fit the scope of the assignment? Should some sources be discarded? Should other avenues of research be pursued?

2. **Take a global look at your sources and notes.** Review the full scope of what your research has revealed. Consider the whole body of evidence you have discovered, including those items you examined but did not select.
   - What have you learned about the subject? Have you uncovered information that leads you to narrow your topic or refine the thesis?
   - Do sources contradict or disprove your assumptions? Should you rethink your point of view?
   - What do the sources reveal about the state of knowledge about your topic? Is there consensus or conflict? Are there patterns in the evidence?
   - How reliable are the sources? Are they based on objective analysis, thorough research, and controlled experiments, or are they biased or rely on anecdotal data?
   - Are there sources that can be grouped together, such as articles by experts who share the same opinion or similar statistics? Can some sources be considered duplicates?

Sam Diephuis/Jupiterimages

Maria Toutoudak/Jupiterimages

- Can you prioritize sources? Which are the most important?
- Can critical thinking help you analyze the value of what you have located?

3. **Reshape your paper by reviewing your topic, examining the evidence, and refining the working thesis.**

Refine Your Thesis and Develop an Outline

After examining your sources, refine the thesis. If you have limited the original topic, you may need to develop a thesis that addresses the new focus of your paper. In writing shorter papers, you may have needed only a brief plan or list of ideas to guide the first draft. But in writing a research paper, it is useful to develop a full outline to organize ideas and sources.

Working Thesis

Colleges should regulate credit card promotions on their campuses.

Revised Thesis

Colleges, many of which allow credit card companies to operate on their campuses and sometimes share in the substantial profits, must regulate the way corporations promote their products and educate their students in money management.

Working Outline

A working outline is a rough guide to direct your first draft. Because it is not likely to be read by anyone other than yourself, it does not have to follow any particular format. Use it as a blueprint to organize your main points and sources. (See pages 569–570 for a sample formal outline.)

I. INTRO—Students and debt
    A. Student credit card debt
    B. Thesis statement

II. Campus credit card promotions
    A. Jessica Jackson (Hsu)
    B. Promotion offers (Hughes, p. 176)

III. Credit card company collaboration with colleges
    A. Revenue from alumni cards
    B. Plans to market cards to students
    C. College promotion of card use (Hsu)

IV. Expanded credit use
    A. University of Wisconsin report ("University")
    B. Northwestern students (Hughes, p. 176)
    C. Ferris & Fingerhut quotes (Terrell)
    D. Hughes quote (p. 176)

(Continued)

V. Credit crisis
   A. Derrick Jackson quote (Hsu)
   B. Campus counseling
VI. Solutions to crisis
   A. University of Wisconsin report ("University")
   B. Valdez interview
VII. Conclusion and Valdez quote

Along with an outline, develop a timeline to chart your progress. Make sure you budget enough time for each stage of the writing process, including revising and editing.

Strategies for Developing an Outline

1. **Write a clear thesis statement.** The thesis is the mission statement of your paper. It should provide a clear focus for the paper and direct the first draft.
   - Use the thesis statement as a guide for selecting outside sources.
2. **Develop an outline that meets the needs of the assignment.** Make sure that your outline addresses the goals of the paper and the instructor's requirements.
3. **Don't expect that your sources will neatly fall into place like pieces of a puzzle.** In many instances, the evidence you find may be fragmentary and lead in different directions. Outline your ideas and observations, weaving into the text those sources that confirm your point of view.
4. **Use sources to support your views; don't simply summarize them.** An outline forms a framework for the first draft. Indicate where you will place supporting quotations, facts, or statistics.
   - Do not feel obligated to include all the sources you have located.
5. **Leave ample space for changes.**
6. **Label your sources A, B, C, or a short title for easy reference.**
7. **Separate longer sources for use in multiple places.** If you have located a long quotation, do not feel obligated to place it in a single block of text. Instead, you may select two or three sections and distribute them throughout the paper.
   - In separating longer passages, make sure you do not distort the source's meaning by taking ideas out of context.

8. **Design an introduction that announces the topic, sets up the thesis, and prepares readers for the direction of the paper.** Because research papers can be long and complex, it is important to give readers a road map, an explanation of what will follow.

   ■ An introduction can present the thesis, provide a rationale for the methods of research, or comment on the nature of sources.

   ■ Introductions can be used to address research problems, commenting on the lack of reliable data or conflicting opinions. Introductions can also include a justification of your approach that anticipates reader objections.

   ■ As in writing any paper, you will probably come up with new ideas while writing the draft. After revising the body, you may wish to rewrite the opening and closing.

9. **Organize the body by using the modes of organization.** Clear structure plays an important role in making your paper readable and convincing. Without a clear pattern of organization, your paper may become a confusing list of quotations and statistics.

   ■ Use modes such as *comparison* and *division* to organize evidence.

   ■ Use transitional statements and paragraph breaks to signal changes in direction.

10. **Craft a conclusion that ends the paper on a strong point rather than a simple summary of points.** Although it may be useful to review critical points at the end of a long paper, the conclusion should leave the reader with a memorable fact, quotation, or restatement of the thesis.

Writing the Research Paper

Your goal in writing the first draft, as in any paper, is to get your ideas on paper. Using outside sources, however, complicates the writing process. Students often make common errors in approaching the evidence they have collected.

Strategies for Using Sources

1. **Avoid simply reporting on what you found.** The quotations, facts, and statistics you have selected should support your point of view. Avoid what some writers call the "string of pearls" effect of simply patching together outside sources with little original commentary or analysis:

   > When it first opened on Broadway, *Death of a Salesman* had a great impact on audiences (Stein 19). According to Sally Lyman, "The play captured the hidden anxiety coursing through postwar America" (17). Another critic, Timothy Baldwin, stated, "This play made

   (Continued)

the audience face its greatest fear—growing old" (98). Fred Carlson said that he walked out of the theater shaken and deeply moved (23).

■ Although outside sources may be interesting and worth quoting or paraphrasing, *your* ideas, interpretations, and arguments should form the basis of the paper.

2. **Explain any lack of sources.** If you select a new, unknown, or uncommon subject, there may be few sources directly supporting your thesis. Although readers might be impressed by your argument, they may question why you have not supported your ideas with evidence. An instructor may question whether you thoroughly researched your topic. Commenting on the lack of sources can both demonstrate the uniqueness of your approach and justify the absence of outside sources:

> Critics of *Death of a Salesman* have concentrated on the male characters, examining Willy Loman's dreams, his relationship to Biff, his sons' conflicts. Of 125 articles published in the last four years about this play, none focus on the essential role of Linda Loman, who serves as the axis for the male conflicts in the play.

3. **Summarize conflicting opinions.** One of the responsibilities of a researcher is to fairly represent the available body of evidence. If respected authorities disagree, you should explain the nature of the controversy:

> Scientists debate whether this disorder is hereditary. Yale researchers Brown and Smith cite the British twin study as evidence of a genetic link (35–41). However, both the American Medical Association and the National Institute of Health insist the small numbers of subjects in the twin study do not provide sufficient evidence to support any conclusions (Kendrick 19–24).

4. **Indicate whether sources represent widely held views.** If multiple sources present the same information, select the most thorough, most recent, or best-written one, but indicate its ideas are shared by others:

> Nearly all experts on teenage suicide support Jane Diaz's observation that low self-esteem, stress, and substance abuse are the principal contributing factors to the current rise in adolescent suicide (Smith 28; Johnson 10–15; King 89–92).

5. **Comment on the quality as well as quantity of your sources.** Indicate if sources are fragmentary, dated, or biased:

> Although the 1908 railroad strike received national attention, few major newspapers offered more than superficial reports. Sensational accounts of lynching, rape, and murder appeared in New York and Chicago tabloids. The radical *Torch of Labor* blamed the deaths of two strikers on a plot engineered by Wall Street bankers. The conservative *Daily World* insisted union organizers were bent on overthrowing the government. Most sources, however, do agree that Red Williams played a critical role in organizing a labor protest that ultimately weakened the emerging Transport Workers Union.

Guidelines for Using Direct Quotations

Direct quotations give power and authority to your research paper by introducing the words of others just as they were written or stated. But to be effective, direct quotations must be carefully chosen, accurately presented, and skillfully woven into the text of your paper.

1. **Limit use of direct quotations.** Avoid reproducing long blocks of text, unless direct evidence is essential for accuracy or emphasis. In many instances, you can summarize and paraphrase information.

   ■ Use direct quotations when they are brief, memorable, and so well stated that a paraphrase would reduce their impact. Avoid using direct quotations when you can accurately restate the information in a documented paraphrase.

   ■ Remember, the focus of a research paper is *your* ideas, observations, and conclusions, not a collection of direct quotations.

2. **Link direct quotations into your commentary.** Avoid isolating quotations.

   Faulty:

   Television advertising exploded in the Fifties. **"Advertising agencies increased spending on television commercials from $10 million in 1948 to $2 billion in 1952" (Smith 16).** These revenues financed the rapid development of a new industry.

   Revised:

   Television advertising exploded in the Fifties. **According to Kai Smith, "Advertising agencies increased spending on television commercials from $10 million in 1948 to $2 billion in 1952" (16).** These revenues financed the rapid development of a new industry.

   Or

   Television advertising exploded in the Fifties, with advertising agencies increasing spending **"from $10 million in 1948 to $2 billion in 1952" (Smith 16).** These revenues financed the rapid development of a new industry.

3. **Introduce block quotes with a complete sentence followed by a colon:**

   The Quiz Show Scandal of the 1950s shook public confidence in the new medium. The idea that the highly popular shows were rigged to ensure ratings infuriated and disillusioned the public:

   > NBC received thousands of letters and telephone calls from irate viewers who felt cheated. Although the public readily accepted that Westerns and soap operas were fictional, they believed that the teachers and housewives who appeared on shows like "Twenty-One" were "real people" like themselves. Having followed their favorite contestants week after week, loyal viewers strongly identified with people they considered genuine. Learning that all the furrowed brows and lip biting were choreographed, they felt duped. (Brown 23)

4. **Provide background information to establish the value of direct quotations.** Bibliographical entries at the end of your paper may explain a source but do not help readers understand its significance.

Faulty:
> President Roosevelt showed signs of declining health as early as 1942. Sheridan noted, "His hands trembled when writing, he complained of headaches, and he often seemed unable to follow the flow of conversation around him" (34–35).

Revised:
> President Roosevelt showed signs of declining health as early as 1942. George Sheridan, a young naval aide who briefed the White House during the Battle of Midway, was shocked by the President's condition. Sheridan noted, "His hands trembled when writing, he complained of headaches, and he often seemed unable to follow the flow of conversation around him" (34–35).

5. **Indicate quotations within quotations.** Although most writers try to avoid using direct quotations that appear in another source, sometimes it cannot be avoided. You can easily indicate a quote within a quote with "quoted in" (abbreviated in MLA style to "qtd. in").

Original Source:
From Sandra Bert's *The Plague* (page 23)

> The medical community of San Francisco was overwhelmed by the sudden increase in AIDS cases in the early 1980s. Tim Watson, a resident at the time, said, "It was like being hit by a tidal wave. We went home every night absolutely stunned by the influx of dying young men."

Research Paper quoting Tim Watson:
> Within a few years the number of AIDS cases, especially in the Bay Area, exploded. Physicians were shocked by the rising numbers of patients with untreatable infections. "It was like being hit by a tidal wave," Watson remembered (qtd. in Bert 23).

6. **Accurately delete unneeded material from quotations.** You can abbreviate long quotations, deleting irrelevant or unimportant details by using ellipsis points (. . .). Three evenly spaced periods indicate words have been deleted from a direct quotation.

Original:
> The governor vetoed the education bill, which had been backed by a coalition of taxpayers and unions, because it cut aid to inner city schools.
>
> *—James Kirkland*

Shortened quotation using ellipsis points:
> Kirkland reported that "the governor vetoed the education bill . . . because it cut aid to inner city schools."

- Use a period and three ellipsis points (four dots. . . .) to indicate deletion of one or more full sentences.
- Avoid making deletions that distort the original meaning. Do not eliminate qualifying statements.

Original:
> Given the gang wars, the failure of treatment programs, the rising number of addicts, I regretfully think we should legalize drugs until we can find better solutions to the problem.
>
> *—Mayor Wells*

Improper use of ellipsis points:
> At a recent press conference, Mayor Wells stated, "I . . . think we should legalize drugs . . ."

7. **Use brackets to insert words or indicate alterations.** In some instances, you may have to insert a word to prevent confusion or a grammatical error.

Original:
> George Roosevelt [no relation to the President] left the Democratic Party in 1935, troubled by the deepening Depression. Roosevelt considered the New Deal a total failure.
>
> —*Nancy Stewart*

Brackets enclose inserted word to prevent confusion:
> As the Depression deepened, many deserted the Democratic Party, seeking more radical solutions to the worsening economy. According to Stewart, "[George] Roosevelt considered the New Deal a total failure."

Original:
> Poe, Whitman, and Ginsburg are among some of America's greatest poets.
>
> —*John Demmer*

Brackets enclose altered verb:
> Demmer states that "Poe . . . [is] among some of America's greatest poets."

Strategies for Citing Sources

Citing where you obtained information for your paper serves three key purposes:

1. **Citations prevent allegations of plagiarism.** Plagiarism—presenting the facts, words, or ideas of someone else as your own—has serious consequences. In many colleges students who submit a plagiarized paper will automatically fail the course. In some schools, students will be expelled. Outside of academics, plagiarism (often called "copyright infringement") has ruined the careers of politicians, artists, and executives. Prominent columnists and reporters have been fired from newspapers and magazines for using the ideas of others without acknowledging their original source. Hollywood studios have been sued by artists who claim ideas from their rejected screenplays were used in other films.

   ■ Accurate documentation protects you from plagiarism by clearly labeling borrowed facts and ideas.

2. **Citations support your thesis.** Attorneys arguing a case before a judge or jury present labeled exhibits to prove their theory of a case. As a researcher, you support your thesis by introducing expert testimony, facts,

(Continued)

case histories, and eyewitness accounts. Like an attorney, you have to clearly identify the source for evidence for it to be credible. A paper about crime that draws upon statistics from the FBI and studies from the Justice Department will be more credible than one relying on personal websites, blogs, and opinions.

- The more controversial your thesis, the more readers will demand supporting evidence.

3. **Citations refer readers to other sources.** Citations not only illustrate which ideas originated with the writer and which were drawn from other sources, but they also tell readers where they can find more information. Through your citations, readers may learn of a biography or a website offering additional evidence.

Exceptions to Citing Sources

You do not need to use citations for every fact, quotation, or idea you present in your paper.

1. **Common expressions or famous quotations.** Famous sayings by such people as Shakespeare, Jesus, or Benjamin Franklin (for example, "To err is human" or "I am the resurrection") do not have to be cited, even when presented as direct quotations. If you are unsure, ask your instructor.

2. **Facts considered in the "realm of common knowledge."** You do not have to provide a citation if you referred to a source to check a fact that is readily available in numerous sources:

> Shakespeare's birthplace
> The number of counties in Illinois
> The date *Death of a Salesman* opened on Broadway.
> Babe Ruth's 1927 batting average

Sources Requiring Documentation

In almost every other instance, however, you have to acknowledge the use of outside material.

1. **Direct quotations.** Whenever you quote a source word for word, you must place it in quotation marks and cite its source.

2. **Indirect quotations or paraphrases.** Even if you do not copy a source but state the author's ideas in your own words, you must cite the source. Changing a few words or condensing a page of text into a few sentences does not alter the fact that you are using someone else's ideas.

3. **Specific facts, statistics, and numbers subject to change.** Data will be credible and acceptable only if you present the source. If you state, "Last year 54,450 drunk drivers were arrested in California," readers will naturally wonder where you obtained that number. Statistics make credible evidence only if readers trust their source.

4. **Graphs, charts, and other visual aids.** Indicate the source of any graphic you reproduce.

   ■ You must also cite the source for information you use to create your own visual.

Strategies for Revising and Editing Research Papers

1. **Review the assignment, thesis, and working outline.**
2. **Examine your draft for use of sources.**
   ■ Does the draft fulfill the needs of the assignment?
   ■ Does the text support the thesis?
   ■ Is the thesis properly placed? Should it appear in the opening or the conclusion?
   ■ Are enough sources presented?
   ■ Is there any evidence that should be included or deleted?
   ■ Do you provide enough original commentary or is your paper merely a collection of facts and quotations?
3. **Read the draft aloud.**
   ■ Does the paper have an even style and tone? Are there awkward transitions between sources and your commentary?
4. **Revise the introduction and conclusion.**
5. **Edit for mechanical and spelling errors. Make sure your paper follows the appropriate style for documenting sources (see pages 555–563 and 573–582 for guidelines).**

Documentation Styles

The two most common documentation styles used in the humanities and social sciences are MLA and APA. Both methods provide guidelines for placing parenthetical notes after quoting or paraphrasing outside sources and for listing them at the end of the paper. Many textbooks suggest recording each source on a note card so they can be easily shuffled and placed in alphabetical order. If you are writing on a computer, you may find it easier to scroll down and enter each source as you refer to it.

MLA Style

Created by the Modern Language Association, the MLA style is used in language and literature courses. Parenthetical notes citing the author or title and page numbers are inserted after quotations and paraphrases. At the end of the paper all the sources are alphabetized on a "Works Cited" page. For full details about using MLA style, consult the *MLA Handbook for Writers of Research Papers,* seventh edition (recommended for college students); or the MLA website at **http://www.mla.org/style/handbook_faq.** Another excellent source is the *MLA Style Manual and Guide to Scholarly Publishing,* third edition. This "MLA Style" section is based on current guidelines from the seventh edition of the *Handbook.*

Strategies for Writing Parenthetical Notes

Parenthetical notes, also called citations, usually include an author's last name and a page number for print sources. If no author is listed, titles—sometimes abbreviated—are used. To keep the notes as brief as possible, the MLA format does not precede page numbers with p., pp., or commas. The parenthetical note is considered part of the sentence and comes before the final mark of punctuation. Notes should be placed as close to the source as possible without interrupting the flow of the text.

1. **Parenthetical notes include author and page number.** A direct quotation from Ralph Ellison's novel *Invisible Man* is indicated with a parenthetical note placed after it:

   > The novel's unnamed character calls himself invisible because society does not recognize him as a human being. He defends his retreat from society, realizing that many would view his decision as a sign of irresponsibility. "Responsibility," he argues, "rests on recognition, and recognition is a form of agreement" (Ellison 14).

2. **Parenthetical notes include only page numbers if the author is clearly identified in the text:**

   > Sheila Smitherin praised Ellison's novel, stating that modern black literature "was born on the pages of *Invisible Man*" (32).

3. **If two or more sources are cited within a sentence, notes are inserted after the material that is quoted or paraphrased:**

   > Smith stated that the novel "exposed the deep-rooted racism society was unwilling to confront" (34), leading one columnist to argue that the book should be taught in every high school (Wilson 12–13).

4. **Long quotations are indented one inch from the left margin without quotation marks:**

> The Group Theater revolutionized American drama. According to Frank Kozol, the members tried to create something then unseen on the New York stage:
>> Clurman and his followers wanted to develop a new kind of theater. They not only wanted to produce new, socially relevant plays, but create a new relationship between playwright and cast. It would be a collective effort. Designed to be a theater without stars, actors lived together and shared living expenses. They were infused with the revolutionary spirit of the times. The Group Theater soon launched the career of Clifford Odets, whose plays were among the most poignant depictions of life during the Great Depression. (Taylor 34–35)

Notice that the parenthetical note appears outside the final punctuation of the last sentence of a block quotation.

5. **Avoid long parenthetical notes for nonprint and electronic sources without authors by mentioning the source in the text:**

> According to the *National Mortgage Bankers Association's 2012 Annual Report,* "The nation faces a crisis, but it is a crisis that is both manageable and containable" (58).

Strategies for Writing a Works Cited Page

List all sources you have cited on a separate sheet at the end of your paper, titled "Works Cited." If you include a list of works you have read for background but have not actually cited, title the page "Works Consulted."

NOTE: MLA revised its format in 2009. Older books and websites may contain outdated guidelines. Make sure to follow the current requirements:

- **Italicize books and magazines rather than underline them (*Time* not <u>Time</u>).**
- **Delete URLs for most electronic sources. Use "Web." to indicate online material.**
- **Place angle brackets around website URLs, <www.cnn.com>, when web addresses are needed or your instructor requires them.**

- Arrange the list of works alphabetically by the author's last name or first significant word of the title if no author is listed:

  Jones, Wilson. *Chicago Today*. New York: Putnam, 2012. Print.
  "A New Look for Toronto." *Toronto Magazine* Fall 2011: 21. Print.

- For sources with more than one author, alphabetize by the first author's last name:

  Zinter, Mary, and Jan Ames. *First Aid*. New York: Dial, 2012. Print.

(Continued)

- Begin each entry even with the left margin, and indent subsequent lines five spaces. Double-space the entire page. Do not separate entries with additional spaces.

    Abrams, Jane. "Rebuilding America's Cities." *Plain Dealer* [Cleveland] 21 Jan. 2002: 12. Print.

    Brown, Gerald. *The Death of the Central City: The Malling of America.* New York: Macmillan, 2003. Print.

- If listing more than one source for an author, alphabetize the works but list the author's last name only once, substituting three hyphens for the name in subsequent citations:

    Keller, Joseph. *Assessing Blame.* New York: Columbia UP, 2003. Print.

    ---. *Quality Control.* New York: Miller, 2000. Print.

NOTE: Include the medium for each source: Print, Web, Film, Television, DVD, Radio, Telephone Interview, CD-ROM, LP, or Performance.

Guidelines for Listing Sources in Works Cited and Parenthetical Notes

Books

1. Write the author's last name, first name, then any initial. Copy the name as written on the title page. "C. W. Brown" would appear as:

    Brown, C. W.

    Omit any degrees or titles such as Ph.D. or Dr.

2. State the full title of the book. Place a colon between the main heading and any subtitle. Italicize all the words and punctuation in the title, except for the final period.

    Brown, C. W. *Sharks and Lambs: Wall Street in the Nineties.*

3. Record the city of publication, publisher, date of publication, and medium of publication. If the book lists several cities, use only the first. If the city is outside the United States, add an abbreviation for the country. If an American city may be unfamiliar, you can include an abbreviation for the state. Record the main words of the publisher, deleting words like "publishing" or "press" (Monroe for Monroe Publishing Company). Use the initials "UP" for "University Press." End the citation with the last year of publication and the medium consulted.

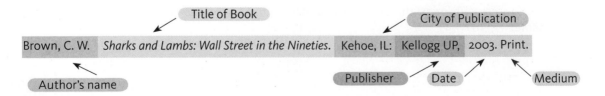

Brown, C. W. *Sharks and Lambs: Wall Street in the Nineties.* Kehoe, IL: Kellogg UP, 2003. Print.

Title of Book · City of Publication · Author's name · Publisher · Date · Medium

Book with Two or Three Authors

WORKS CITED ENTRY: Smith, David, John Adams, and Chris Cook. *Writing Online*. New York: Macmillan, 2012. Print.

PARENTHETICAL NOTE: (Smith, Adams, and Cook 23–24)

Books with Four or More Authors

WORKS CITED ENTRY: Chavez, Nancy, et al. *Mexico Today*. New York: Putnam, 2011. Print.

PARENTHETICAL NOTE: (Chavez et al. 87)

Book with Corporate Author

WORKS CITED ENTRY: National Broadcasting Company. *Programming Standards*. New York: National Broadcasting Company, 2012. Print.

PARENTHETICAL NOTE: (National Broadcasting Company 112)

To avoid a cumbersome parenthetical note, you can mention the author or title in the text:

> According to the National Broadcasting Company's *Programming Standards,* "No single executive should be able to cancel a program" (112).

Book with Unnamed Authors

WORKS CITED ENTRY: *New Yale Atlas*. New York: Random House, 2009. Print.

PARENTHETICAL NOTE: (*New Yale Atlas* 106)

Book with Multiple Volumes

WORKS CITED ENTRY: Eisenhower, Dwight. *Presidential Correspondence*. Vol. 2. New York: Dutton, 1960. Print.

PARENTHETICAL NOTE: (Eisenhower 77)

If you cite more than one volume in your paper, indicate the number:

> (Eisenhower 2: 77)

Book in Second or Later Edition

WORKS CITED ENTRY: Franklin, Marcia. *Modern France*. 3rd ed. Philadelphia: Comstock, 1987. Print.

PARENTHETICAL NOTE: (Franklin 12)

Work in an Anthology

WORKS CITED ENTRY: Ford, John M. "Preflash." *The Year's Best Fantasy*. Ed. Ellen Datlow and Terri Windling. New York: St. Martin's, 2009. 65–82. Print.

PARENTHETICAL NOTE: (Ford 65–66)

Note: If you include more than one work from the same anthology, list the anthology in the Works Cited section separately under the editors' names and list individual entries in a shortened form:

Ford, John M. "Preflash." Datlow and Windling 65–82.

Book in Translation

WORKS CITED ENTRY: Verne, Jules. *Twenty Thousand Leagues under the Sea*. Trans. Michel Michot. Boston: Pitman, 1992. Print.

PARENTHETICAL NOTE: (Verne 65)

Book with Editor or Editors

WORKS CITED ENTRY: Benson, Nancy, ed. *Ten Great American Plays*. New York: Columbia UP, 2002. Print.

PARENTHETICAL NOTE: (Benson 23)

Book in a Series

WORKS CITED ENTRY: Swessel, Karyn, ed. *Northern Ireland Today*. New York: Wilson, 2003. Print. Modern Europe Ser. 3.

PARENTHETICAL NOTE: (Swessel 34)

Periodicals

Newspaper Article

WORKS CITED ENTRY:

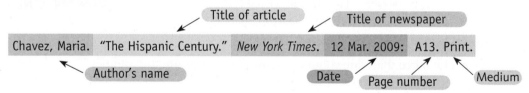

PARENTHETICAL NOTE: (Chavez)

Note: If an article has only one page, page numbers are not included in parenthetical notes.

Magazine Article

WORKS CITED ENTRY: Janssen, Mary. "Iran Today." *Time* 25 Mar. 2009: 34+. Print.

Note: If an article appears on nonconsecutive pages, list the first page followed by a "+" sign.

PARENTHETICAL NOTE: (Janssen 38)

Scholarly Article

WORKS CITED ENTRY: Grant, Edward. "The Hollywood Ten: Fighting the Blacklist."
California Film Quarterly 92.2 (2002): 14–32. Print.

PARENTHETICAL NOTE: (Grant 21–23)

Newspaper or Magazine Article with Unnamed Author

WORKS CITED ENTRY: "The Legacy of the Gulf War." *American History* 12 Mar. 2003:
23–41. Print.

PARENTHETICAL NOTE: ("Legacy" 25)

Note: Long titles can be abbreviated to a key word or phrase.

Other Print Sources

Encyclopedia Article with Author

WORKS CITED ENTRY:

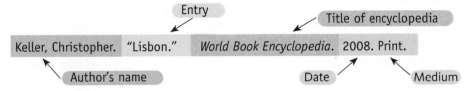

Note: Provide edition number if given.

PARENTHETICAL NOTE: (Keller)

Note: Page numbers are not used with works in which articles are arranged alphabetically.

Encyclopedia Article with Unnamed Author

WORKS CITED ENTRY: "Lisbon." *Columbia Illustrated Encyclopedia*. 2009. Print.

PARENTHETICAL NOTE: ("Lisbon")

Pamphlet with Author

WORKS CITED ENTRY: Tindall, Gordon, ed. *Guide to New York Churches*. New York:
Chamber of Commerce, 2012. Print.

PARENTHETICAL NOTE: (Tindall 76–78)

Pamphlet with Unnamed Author

WORKS CITED ENTRY: *Guide to New York Museums*. New York: Columbia University,
2008. Print.

PARENTHETICAL NOTE: (*Guide* 176–82)

The Bible

WORKS CITED ENTRY: *Holy Bible.* Grand Rapids, MI: Zondervan, 1988. Print. New Intl. Vers.

Note: Titles of sacred texts are not italicized, unless they are specific editions.

PARENTHETICAL NOTE: (Mark 2: 4–9)

Note: In the first parenthetical note, give the title of this specific bible in italics, with a comma, before the book and chapter.

Nonprint Sources

Parenthetical Notes for Nonprint Sources

Because nonprint sources often have long titles, parenthetical notes can be cumbersome and interrupt the flow of your sentences:

> Cases of depression rise during periods of high unemployment (*National Mental Health Association's Annual Address 2008*). Drug and alcohol abuse, divorce, and suicide also increase (*Losing the American Dream*).

You can avoid long parenthetical notes by mentioning the source in your sentence. This also allows you to introduce or explain who or what you are quoting or paraphrasing:

> The *National Mental Health Association's Annual Address 2008* observes that cases of depression rise during periods of unemployment. The documentary film *Losing the American Dream* notes that drug and alcohol abuse, divorce, and suicide also increase.

Film

WORKS CITED ENTRY:

Note: You may wish to include names of performers, directors, or screenwriters if they are of special interest to readers. These names should be inserted between the title and the distributor.

PARENTHETICAL NOTE: (*Casino*)

Television Program

WORKS CITED ENTRY: "The Long Goodbye." *Law and Order.* Dir. Jane Hong. Writ. Peter Wren. Perf. Rita Colletti, Diane Nezgod, and Vicki Shimi. NBC. WTMJ, Milwaukee. 12 May 2009. Television.

PARENTHETICAL NOTE: ("Long Goodbye")

Video Recording

A videocassette, DVD, slide program, laser disc, and so on, can be cited as you would a film. If the original release date is relevant, include it.

WORKS CITED ENTRY: *Colonial Williamsburg*. Compiled by Janet Freud. American Home Video, 2010. DVD.

PARENTHETICAL NOTE: (*Colonial Williamsburg*)

Live Performance of a Play

WORKS CITED ENTRY: *All My Sons*. By Arthur Miller. Dir. Anita Dayin. Lyric Theater, New York. 10 May 2009. Performance.

PARENTHETICAL NOTE: (*All My Sons*)

Speech

WORKS CITED ENTRY: Goode, Wilmont. "America in the Next Century." Chicago Press Club. 12 Oct. 2009. Speech.

PARENTHETICAL NOTE: (Goode)

Personal or Telephone Interview

WORKS CITED ENTRY: Weston, Thomas. Personal interview. 21 May 2011.

In the preceding citation, you would substitute "Telephone" for "Personal" if the interview was conducted by telephone.

PARENTHETICAL NOTE: (Weston)

Electronic Sources

Web Pages

Web pages vary greatly but most contain standard data to be included in a citation:

1. The name of the author or editor.
2. The title of the work (use italics for independent works and quotations marks for those that are parts of larger works).
3. Title of the website in italics (if different from the title of the work).
4. The version or edition if listed.
5. The publisher or sponsor of the website or "n. p." if unavailable.
6. The day, month, year of publication or "n.d." if unavailable.
7. The medium: "Web."
8. The day, month, and year of access (the date you looked at, downloaded, or printed the material.)

WORKS CITED ENTRY: Irish American Heritage Center (Chicago). Home page. 5 Apr. 2006. Web. 10 May 2006.

PARENTHETICAL NOTE: (Irish American Center)

Work from Library or Personal Subscription Service such as **InfoTrac, EBSCO,** or **Lexis-Nexis**

WORKS CITED ENTRY: Hsu, Lisa. "In Bad Faith: Academics, Ethics, and Credit Card Promotions." *The New Collegian* 27.3 (2011): 72. *InfoTrac College Edition.* Web. 5 May 2012.

PARENTHETICAL NOTE: (Hsu)

Electronic Journal Article

WORKS CITED ENTRY: Smith, Perry. "Truman Capote and Kansas." *Phoenix* 2.7 (2011). Web. 15 Mar. 2011.

PARENTHETICAL NOTE: (Smith)

Online Newspaper Article

WORKS CITED ENTRY: "*Long Day's Journey into Night* Production Disappointing." *New York Times* 17 Mar. 2011. Web. 22 Apr. 2012.

PARENTHETICAL NOTE: ("*Long Day's Journey*")

Reference Database

WORKS CITED ENTRY: *The Emerald Project: Irish Literature from 1500–2000.* 2000. Boston University. Web. 21 Oct. 2012.

PARENTHETICAL NOTE: (*The Emerald Project*)

Electronic Texts

Many books are available online. Because they lack page numbers, mention the title within the text to avoid long parenthetical notes.

WORKS CITED ENTRY: Gissing, George. *Demos.* London, 1892. *The Online Books Page.* Ed. Charles Aldarondo. Jan. 2002. Project Gutenberg Literary Archive Foundation. Web. 5 Mar. 2011.

PARENTHETICAL NOTE: (Gissing)

CD-ROM

WORKS CITED ENTRY: "Understanding Macbeth." *Master Dramas.* New York: Educational Media, 2011. CD-ROM.

PARENTHETICAL NOTE: ("Understanding")

E-mail

WORKS CITED ENTRY: Ballard, Morton D. "Rental Cars." Message to Germaine Reinhardt. 21 May 2008. E-mail.

PARENTHETICAL NOTE: (Ballard)

Discussion Group or Blog Posting

WORKS CITED ENTRY: Humphrey, Doug. "US Radar Coverage." Online posting. *Coldwarcomms.* Yahoo! 1 Nov. 2005. Web. 15 Mar. 2008.

PARENTHETICAL NOTE: (Humphrey)

Linked Sources

Sometimes a Google search can help the reader get to the exact source:

WORKS CITED ENTRY: Laskowski, Edward. "BMI: Is It Accurate for Weightlifters?" 15 Nov. 2009. Mayo Foundation for Medical Education and Research. *Google Article Search.* Web. 14 Dec. 2012.

PARENTHETICAL NOTE: (Laskowski)

Visuals

Table, Graph, Chart, or Map

WORKS CITED ENTRY: *Carlino's Sales.* Table. "From Hoboken to Hollywood." *The New Yorker* 25 May 2006: 21. Print.

PARENTHETICAL NOTES: Visuals are numbered and captioned:

George Carlino was one of many writers in the Nineties who abandoned writing highly acclaimed but little-read novels to write lucrative screenplays (see Table 1).

Table 1. George Carlino: From Novels to Screenplays

Year	Novel	Publisher's Advance	Movie Rights
1992	*Jersey Angel*	$10,000	$25,000
1995	*Bronxman*	$15,000	$100,000
1997	*Talk Radio*	$18,000	$750,000
1999	screenplay for *Walker's Point*		$1.2 million

Source of data: *Carlino's Sales,* "From Hoboken to Hollywood, *The New Yorker* 25 May 2006, 21, Print.

Advertisement

General Motors. Advertisement. *Time* 15 Dec. 2008: 12. Print.

Photograph

Include the photographer or original source, title or description, year, and information about the book, newspaper, or online source of the image. Avoid long parenthetical notes by referring to the image within the text and its number:

The most famous photograph of World War II was Joe Rosenthal's shot of the flag raising on Iwo Jima (see Figure 10).

WORKS CITED ENTRY: Joe Rosenthal. *Marines Raising American Flag on Iwo Jima.* 1945. Photograph. *Corbis.* Web. 12 Feb. 2006.

Sample MLA Research Paper

- Five Sources
- Cover Page
- Formal Outline
- Research Paper with Works Cited

Book Excerpt

From: *How to Survive College* by Nancy Hughes, Academic Press, New York City, 2011

HOW TO SURVIVE COLLEGE   176

Today credit card companies bombard incoming freshmen with credit card offers. Card companies operate on campuses, often in student unions and dorm lobbies. Giving out free hats, T-shirts, coffee mugs, and pizza coupons, they encourage students to sign up for cards. Companies generally issue cards to any student over eighteen whether they have jobs or not. Faced with the need for books, clothes, computer supplies, and student fees, many students quickly apply for cards and ring up charges. At Northwestern University nearly 10% of incoming freshmen had maxed out at least one credit card by the end of their first semester.

Actual purchases, however, are often not the culprit. The ability to use a credit card to get cash from an ATM leads many students to live well beyond their means, getting into debt $40 or $60 at a time. Miranda Hayes, who graduated with $7500 in credit card debts, had made only $2,000 in purchases. "I charged a computer my freshman year and all my books," she admits. "The rest was all cash from an ATM that went for movies, beer, pizzas, bus fare, my cell phone, health club dues, and interest."

Magazine Article

From: "University of Wisconsin Takes Up the Issue of Student Credit Card Debt" in *Cardline,* June 11, 2011 volume 4, issue 24, page 1

Cardline June 11, 2011   1

UNIVERSITY OF WISCONSIN TAKES UP THE ISSUE OF STUDENT CREDIT CARD DEBT.

The Board of Regents for the University of Wisconsin System, which operates the state's 13 four-year schools and 14 two-year schools, was expected to discuss credit card solicitation today, a spokesperson for UW–Madison tells *Cardline*. The discussion was promoted by the release in May of a 15-page, UW-commissioned report, "Student Credit Card Debt and Policies on Credit Card Solicitation on the University of Wisconsin," which said that 40% of its students owe credit card balances of $1,000 or more. It's not clear what action the regents, who are meeting at the UW's Milwaukee campus, will take, but three UW campuses have adopted formal policies regarding credit card solicitations and others have informal ones. The report recommends that the regents adopt rules that are consistent system wide. Some UW administrators take a much harsher attitude. They wanted credit card solicitation banned altogether, but the report said such a ban might violate the law. The UW commissioned the report following several national studies, including one by the General Accounting Office. Newspapers also regularly reported on the issue. The report gathered its data through telephone interviews with staff members, student surveys and anecdotal information. It found that between 62% and 71% of students had at least one credit card. A UW Student Spending and Employment Survey found that of those who responded, 40% of students owed credit card debts of $1,000 to $5,000, and 10% owed over $5,000. The high card debt takes a toll on some students. Although the

A Website

From: "Top Ten Student Money Mistakes" by Blythe Terrell on Young Money, updated at http://www.youngmoney.com/money_management/spending/020809_02, and accessed March 21, 2011. Reprinted with permission from YoungMoney.com.

 MAIL   PRINT

➤ careers

➤ consumer issues

➤ credit & debt

➤ entertainment

➤ entrepreneurship

➤ financial aid

➤ investing

➤ lifestyles

➤ money management

➤ technology

➤ travel

➤ wheels

Top Ten Student Money Mistakes
By Blythe Terrell, University of Missouri

For many students, college is the first major landmark on the path to independence. Moving away from home means no more curfews, no asking for permission, and no parents looking over their shoulders. It also means that the liberty-seeking college kid is now free to make his or her own mistakes.

In such an environment, money management often becomes an issue. Knowing how to avoid these problems is the key to beating them. Here are ten common mistakes students make, and how you can avoid them.

1. **Making poor choices about which credit cards to get.** Credit card companies set up booths on college campuses, offering T-shirts and other items to anyone who will sign up for a card. Although the deals can seem fantastic, students must look into the card's repayment terms carefully. "When students get credit cards, two things can happen," said Stephen Ferris, professor of finance at the University of Missouri–Columbia. "One, they don't read the fine print and see what they're paying. And they're paying a lot. Or they use it until it's maxed out." It is absolutely necessary to pay your credit cards on time each month, added Ferris.

2. **Letting friends pressure them into spending money.** College life is full of opportunities to spend money: finals-week smorgasbords, an evening out with friends, road trips, and vacations. Not knowing how to say "no" can cause students to spend money they just do not have. "If you can't afford it, just say no," says David Fingerhut, a financial adviser with Pines Financial in St. Louis.

3. **Not setting up a budget.** If students have a set amount of money, they must plan ahead and know how much they can spend each month. "It has to work on paper before it works in real life," Fingerhut said.

4. **Not seeking out the best bank rates.** Banks offer many different kinds of checking and savings accounts, but some charge fees that others do not. It is essential for students to do research and not simply go with the closest, most accessible bank, Ferris said.

Magazine Article from Online Database

 INFOTRAC COLLEGE EDITION
From Gale Group and Cengage Learning

The New Collegian, Oct 2011 v27 i3 p72(l)

In Bad Faith: Academics, Ethics, and Credit Card Promotions

Full Text: COPYRIGHT 2011 New Collegian Productions, Inc.

Byline: Lisa Hsu

Jessica Jackson earned a 3.8 GPA her freshman year. She also accumulated $3,500 in credit card debt. Like other entering freshmen, she was greeted by smiling sophomores (who were being paid $9.50 an hour) handing out credit card flyers in dorm lobbies, the student union, the auditorium, the bookstore, even classrooms. Attracted by the 5.99% interest rate, generous airline miles, and a discount iPod, she filled out an application online and within weeks was using her card to buy books and pay her cell phone bill. She used her card to buy plane tickets and purchase Christmas presents.

When she started her second semester, she got a shock. Although she paid all her bills on time, her interest rate shot up to 18.5%. A late payment after spring break caused her interest rate to soar to 23% by May.

Jessica Jackson is among the 34% of students at her university with credit card balances exceeding $2,500.

Her parents, both teachers, were troubled by their daughter's mounting debt. They were more troubled when during a campus visit they noticed signs in the student union, bookstore, and food court urging students to "Pay in Plastic."

The Jacksons' anger really took hold when they learned the university was making 1.5% on every dollar students charged on their cards. "It's one thing for a college to encourage affluent alums to donate to the school every time they use a credit card," Derrick Jackson argued in an email to the trustees. "But, it's another," he insisted, "to lure cash-strapped undergraduates with teaser rates, airline miles they can't use, and cheap iPods. I fully understand the university's need to generate revenue. However, the backlash from parents who feel their children have been unfairly manipulated will tarnish the university's image and hinder major fundraising. We trust colleges to educate and protect our children, not exploit them."

Several colleges are reviewing their credit card promotions, requiring companies to fully disclose interest rates, late fees, and limitations to mileage offers.

http://infotrac-college.cengagelearning.com/infomark/27/987/3

Student Notes from Personal Interview

With Maria Valdez, Tulane University, New Orleans, LA. March 15, 2011

Interview

3/15/11

Maria Valdez, Econ prof.

Tulane Univ, New Orleans

College students should be cautious /credit cards. They should follow 3 tips.

1. *Watch out for "teaser rates"—low rates for initial period/3–6 months that go up to 14–21%.*

2. *Watch out for "rewards" like airline miles. Cards often have higher rates. Miles not available peak times like X-mas & Spring break.*

3. *Watch for automatic credit increases → greater debt.*

Quote:

"Institutions that benefit from credit owe their employees and students full disclosure on both the benefits and costs of using credit."

Quote:

"Colleges that ignore the credit card crisis risk alienating their most powerful constituents and supporters, especially students' parents, alumni, and state representatives."

Abusing Plastic:
The College Credit Card Crisis

by
Maria Perez

English 102
Professor Brandeis
10 May 2012

No page
number

Title centered
one third down
from top of
page

Note: If your instructor does not request a separate cover page, the first page of your paper should include the title and your name:

Perez 1

Maria Perez
English 102
Professor Brandeis
10 May 2012

Abusing Plastic:
The College Credit Card Crisis

Perez i

Outline

Thesis statement: Colleges, many of which allow credit card companies to operate on their campuses and sometimes share in the substantial profits, must regulate the way corporations promote their products and educate their students in money management.

I.   Students graduating with substantial debt is nothing new.

II. Freshmen are inundated with credit card offers when they arrive on campus.

III. The traditional credit card market is saturated.

    A. Credit card companies that offered cards to alumni sought a larger customer base by issuing cards to students.

    B. To secure exclusive rights to promote cards on campus, card issuers offered colleges a share of the profits.

(Continued)

IV. Card use by college students has expanded greatly.
   A. The University of Wisconsin reports 40 percent of students owe card balances of $1,000 or more.
   B. One in ten students at Northwestern reached the credit limit on at least one card during the first semester on campus.
V. Students are uninformed consumers and use credit cards recklessly.
   A. Students buy items they cannot afford and yield to peer pressure to spend money.
   B. Students use cash advances to support an unsustainable lifestyle.
   C. Students fail to "read the small print" and do not know what they are paying in interest or understand that mileage offers have restrictions.
VI. Parents are troubled by their children's mounting debts and resent the role colleges play in campus promotions.
VII. The extent of the student credit card crisis is evident on campus.
   A. College newspapers contain ads encouraging students to apply for new cards to pay off debt on other cards.
   B. Campus counseling centers see growing numbers of students seeking debt counseling and advice on bankruptcy.
   C. Colleges are reviewing campus card promotions.
VIII. Teaching young people money management skills is essential to prepare them for issues they will face after graduation. Colleges, too, must avoid the temptation to capitalize on their students and must exercise responsibility in promoting credit cards on campus.

Last name, page number

Perez 1

Title (1" from margin)

Abusing Plastic: The College Credit Card Crisis

Introduction

Students graduating with substantial debt is nothing new. Few students or their parents can afford to pay the full cost of a college education in four years. Even students with scholarships and part-time jobs typically borrow money for books, fees, travel, and incidental living expenses. In recent years students have added to their financial burdens by amassing credit card debts. Colleges, many of which allow credit card companies to operate on their campuses and sometimes share in the substantial profits, must regulate the way corporations promote their products and educate their students in money management.

Thesis statement

Personal example to illustrate issue and create human interest

Jessica Jackson, like many incoming freshmen, was immediately inundated with credit card offers the day she arrived on campus. Sophomores, paid $9.50 an hour to pass out flyers and sign up fellow students, encouraged her to apply online for a credit card that offered her an appealing 5.99% interest rate, generous airline miles, and a discount iPod (Hsu). On other campuses, credit card companies set up booths in dorms, student unions, and college bookstores, offering coffee mugs, T-shirts, pizza coupons, and free cell phones to any student who fills out an application. Banks, which once demanded card applicants have full-time jobs, target college students, assuming they will be able to rely on their parents to pay their bills if needed. Many companies will issue cards to any student over eighteen (Hughes 176).

Paraphrase

Additional examples

The traditional market for credit cards, employed adults with good credit, has been saturated for years, making college students a prime target for companies seeking new customers. In order to secure advantageous arrangements with colleges and universities, some card companies have guaranteed them part of the profits. In the early 1990s, card issuers approached alumni organizations, offering members a Visa or MasterCard featuring the name and image of their alma mater on the card, with a percentage of charges going to the institution. Corporate executives charging $20,000 annually in travel and business expenses might not only demonstrate their school spirit by flashing a credit card bearing their college logo but also donate several hundred dollars a year to their school. Attracted to this new revenue stream, many college administrators were amenable to corporate plans to market cards to their students. By offering a college 1% or 2% on charges, credit card companies can secure exclusive rights to promote their offerings on campus, giving them a captive market of thousands of young (and often naïve) consumers.

Summary of credit card history and search for new customers

Colleges, eager to make the most of this arrangement, not only encourage students to apply for cards but to make ample use of them. At Jessica Jackson's college, signs in the bookstore and student union encourage students to "Pay in Plastic" (Hsu). In collaborating with credit card companies, colleges have also shared in their sometimes misleading promotions.

Students attracted by low rates are typically unaware that these are initial "teaser" rates good for only three to six months, followed by regular rates of over 18%. In addition, a late payment can cost a hefty penalty and push interest rates up to 23% (Hsu). Unaccustomed to using credit cards, many students find it tempting to live beyond their means, unaware that teaser rates will expire and thinking that their interest fees will be offset by discount airline tickets or money-back offers.

Credit card use has expanded greatly on campuses, as have credit card balances. The University of Wisconsin reported in 2008 that "40% of [its] students owe credit card balances of $1,000 or more"("University" 1). At Northwestern University nearly one in ten freshmen had reached the credit limit on at least one credit card during the first semester on campus (Hughes 176). Jessica Jackson, who used her card not only for books and school fees but to pay her cell phone bills and buy Christmas presents, acquired over $3500 in credit card debts her first year. Over a third of her fellow students have credit card balances exceeding $2,500 (Hsu).

Direct quote in quotation marks

Statistical evidence to complement personal examples

Students, according to Stephen Ferris, a finance professor, "don't read the fine print and see what they're paying" and often use a card until it is maxed out (qtd. in Terrell). College students often experience peer pressure, leading them to use credit cards to buy new clothes, electronic gear, DVDs, pizzas, and nights on the town to keep pace with affluent friends. David Fingerhut, a financial advisor, observes that "not knowing how to say 'no' can cause students to spend money they just don't have" (qtd. in Terrell).

Direct quotation taken from source by different author

Direct quotation taken from source by different author

Not only does the easy use of credit cards allow students to make purchases they cannot afford, it leads them to use credit cards to subsidize an economically unsustainable lifestyle. Failing to calculate the full cost of an off-campus apartment or a car tempts students to rely on cash advances to make ends meet:

Actual purchases . . . are not often the culprit. The ability to use a credit card to get cash from an ATM leads students to live well beyond their means, getting into debt $40 or

Block quotation with ellipsis

$60 at a time. Miranda Hayes, who graduated with $7500 in credit card debts, had made only $2,000 in purchases. "I charged a computer my freshman year and all my books," she admits. "The rest was all cash from an ATM that went for movies, beer, pizzas, bus fare, my cell phone, health club dues, and interest." (Hughes 176)

Students who fail to read the small print are often surprised when they learn how much they are paying in interest. The student whose initial interest rate jumps from 5.99% to 23% on a balance of $3,500 faces a $50 increase in monthly interest. Students who assumed that free plane tickets would offset interest charges may discover their miles come with restrictions, making them useless for flights during holidays and spring break.

Many parents are stunned when they realize that their children, in addition to student loans, are now paying over 20% interest on thousands of dollars of credit card debt. Many, like Jessica Jackson's parents, are angered when they also find out that the college charging tens of thousands of dollars a year in tuition is getting paid for every dollar students charge on their cards. Derrick Jackson, troubled by his daughter's mounting debts, told college trustees it was unfair for a school "to lure cash-strapped undergraduates with teaser rates, airline miles they can't use, and cheap iPods" (qtd. in Hsu). He warned that schools could damage their reputation and their ability to obtain donations if parents believe their children have been victimized. "We trust colleges to educate and protect our children," he argued, "not exploit them" (Jackson, qtd. in Hsu).

The extent of the problem is noticeable on many campuses. Student newspapers and campus websites feature ads from credit card companies offering teaser rates for cash advances, encouraging students to pay off high interest credit cards by applying for other credit cards. The crisis counseling centers that traditionally helped students cope with drug abuse or unwanted pregnancies now see a growing number of students seeking debt counseling and advice on bankruptcy.

Newspaper articles and complaints from parents have led colleges to review their policies on credit card solicitations. The University of Wisconsin commissioned a study of student credit card use that revealed that two-thirds of students had at least one credit card, with 40% having balances of $1,000–$5,000. Three university campuses have adopted formal policies regulating credit card solicitations. Some Wisconsin administrators have argued that the state system should ban campus promotions entirely ("University" 1).

In addition to reviewing their own policies, many colleges are seeking to educate students about managing their money. Banning campus promotions and severing ties with credit card companies will not prevent students from getting into debt. As prime customers, college students are barraged with direct mail and online credit card offers. Maria Valdez, a Tulane economics professor, states that students have to recognize that as adults they face responsibilities. In addition to registering for the draft and paying income tax, eighteen-year-olds have to make mature decisions about handling their money and monitoring their use of credit. She suggests that students shop carefully and investigate card company offers. They should read the small print and learn the full interest rate schedule and any limitations on airline miles before applying for a card. Students with cards should

Direct quotation taken from source by different author

Key word in title used for article without an author

Personal interview

Perez 4

also watch out for companies that automatically raise credit limits, which makes it easier for them to get deeper into debt.

Once students select a card, they have to learn how to use it carefully by setting up a budget to limit the amount they will spend each month. College students also have to learn to avoid the temptation to buy items they cannot afford and peer pressure that often leads them to pay with plastic for meals, concert tickets, and road trips.

Just as colleges devote resources to warn students about abusing drugs, they must now work to educate students about the danger of abusing credit cards. Teaching young people sound money management skills is essential because many of the issues they will face leaving college—choosing health-care and retirement plans, applying for car loans and mortgages, and managing investments—require responsibility and critical thinking. Colleges, too, must avoid the easy temptation to capitalize on their students' weaknesses and must exercise responsibility in promoting credit cards on campus. "Colleges that ignore the credit card crisis," argues Maria Valdez, "risk alienating their most powerful constituents and supporters, especially students' parents, alumni, and state representatives."

Conclusion using direct quotation

Works Cited

Heading Centered

Hsu, Lisa. "In Bad Faith: Academics, Ethics, and Credit Card Promotions." *The New Collegian* 27.3 (2011): 72. *InfoTrac College Edition.* Web. 5 May 2011.

Hughes, Nancy. *How to Survive College.* New York: Academic, 2011. Print.

Terrell, Blythe. "Top Ten Student Money Mistakes." *Young Money.* n.d. Web. 21 Mar. 2011.

"University of Wisconsin Takes Up the Issue of Student Credit Card Debt." *Cardline* 4.24 11 June 2011: 1. Print.

Valdez, Maria. Personal interview. 15 Mar. 2011.

First line flush with left margin, then indented

APA Style

Most courses in the social sciences, including anthropology, education, political science, psychology, and sociology, follow the rules for documentation created by the American Psychological Association. For full details, consult the *Publication Manual of the American Psychological Association,* sixth edition.

Strategies for Writing Parenthetical Notes

In APA documentation, parenthetical notes, also called reference citations, are placed after material requiring documentation, and all sources are recorded in a References list at the end of the paper.

1. **Parenthetical notes include author, year of publication, and, for direct quotes, page numbers.** Most sources are identified by the author's name and

(Continued)

the year of publication. Page numbers are usually omitted from paraphrases but are always included in direct quotations. The information may be placed in a single note with a comma between name and year or mentioned in the text:

> Smith (2011) suggested that multiple personality disorder was more common than previously reported.
> It has been suggested that multiple personality disorder is more common than previously believed (Smith, 2011).
> Based on recent studies, Smith (2011) asserts that "multiple personality disorder is more common than previously reported" (p. 321).

2. **Multiple parenthetical notes indicate more than one source.** If two or more sources are cited within a sentence, notes are inserted after the material quoted or paraphrased:

> Johnson (2002) stated that the study "revealed that Chicago schools were adequately staffed" (p. 43), leading Renfro (2003) to reject the teachers' union proposal.

3. **For the first text reference, list up to five authors' names:**

> Johnson, Hyman, Torque, and Kaiser (2011) observed that computers enhance student performance.

Note: With multiple authors in a parenthetical citation, use an ampersand (&):

> (Johnson, Hyman, Torque, & Kaiser, 2011)

4. **For the first reference of a citation with six or more authors, list the first author's name and "et al." (and others):**

> Johnson et al. (2011) examined computer education in Chicago, New York, El Paso, and Philadelphia.

5. **List corporate and group authors in full initially; then abbreviate:**

> Computers are valuable in teaching higher mathematics (Modern Education Council [MEC], 2002). Textbook publishers now include online support for individual tutoring (MEC, 2011).

6. **Assign letters (a, b, c) to indicate use of more than one work by an author with the same year of publication:**

> Kozik studied students in Chicago bilingual classes (2012a) and later reviewed the performance of an English immersion program in San Diego (2012b).

7. **Alphabetize multiple sources and separate with a semicolon:**

> Several reports suggest that noise pollution can directly contribute to hypertension (Jones, 2009; Smith, 2011).

8. **Websites can be mentioned within the text:**

> Chinese educators have attempted to expand Internet access for university students, particularly in the fields of engineering and medicine. Peking University's website (http://www.pku.edu.cn) documents some of their efforts.

Note: APA style dictates there be no period after a URL, so include web addresses in parentheses or recast the sentence to avoid ending a sentence without punctuation.

Strategies for Writing a References Page

List all the sources you have cited on a separate sheet at the end of your paper titled "References" (center the word References and do not italicize it or place it in quotation marks). If you include works you have read for background but not actually cited, title the page "Bibliography."

1. **Arrange the list of works alphabetically by authors' or editors' last names, followed by initials. If no authors are listed, alphabetize by the first significant word of the title. Capitalize only the first word and proper nouns or adjectives in titles. Italicize book and magazine titles; don't use quotation marks for article titles:**

    Jones, W. (2012). *Chicago today*. New York, NY: Putnam.

    A new look for Toronto. (2003, Fall). *Toronto Magazine*, 21.

2. **For sources with more than one author, alphabetize by the first author's last name and list subsequent authors by last names and initials:**

    Zinter, M., & Ames, J. (2002). *First aid*. New York, NY: Dial.

3. **Begin each citation even with the left margin, then indent subsequent lines five spaces. Double-space the entire page. Do not separate entries with additional spaces:**

    Abrams, J. (2002, January 21). Rebuilding America's cities. *Cleveland Plain Dealer*, pp. 1, 7, 8.

    Brown, G. (2003). *The death of the central city: The malling of America*. New York, NY: Macmillan.

4. **If more than one source from a given author is used, list the works in chronological order and repeat the author's name:**

    Brown, G. (2000). *Hope for renewal*. New York, NY: Putnam.

    Brown, G. (2003). *The death of the central city: The malling of America*. New York, NY: Macmillan.

Guidelines for Listing Sources in References and Parenthetical Notes

Books

- Write the author's last name, comma, first and subsequent initials:

  Brown, C. W.

- Place the year of publication in parentheses, followed by a period and one space.

- Italicize the full title of the book. Place a colon between the main heading and any subtitle. Capitalize only the first word in the title and any subtitle and any proper nouns or adjectives within the title:

  Brown, C. W. (2008). *Sharks and lambs: Wall Street in the nineties.*

- Record the city and state of publication and publisher.

  Brown, C. W. (2008). Sharks and lambs: Wall Street in the nineties. New York, NY: Kellogg Press.

Note: Do not shorten or abbreviate words like "University" or "Press."

PARENTHETICAL NOTES:

Brown (2008) stated . . .
(Brown, 2008)
(Brown, 2008, pp. 23–25)

Book with Two to Five Authors

REFERENCES ENTRY:

Smith, D., Johnson, A., & Cook, F. D. (2008). *Writing for television.* New York, NY: Macmillan.

PARENTHETICAL NOTES:

First citation in text:

Smith, Johnson, and Cook (2008) stated . . .

Subsequent citations:

Smith et al. (2008) revealed . . .

First parenthetical note:

(Smith, Johnson, & Cook, 2008)

Subsequent citations:

(Smith et al., 2008)

Book with Corporate Author

REFERENCES ENTRY:

National Broadcasting Company. (2008). *Programming standards.* New York, NY: National Broadcasting Company.

PARENTHETICAL NOTES:

> According to the National Broadcasting Company's *Programming Standards* (2008), "No single executive should be able to cancel a program" (p. 214).
>
> (National Broadcasting Company [NBC], 2008, p. 214)

Book with Unnamed Author

REFERENCES ENTRY:

> *New Yale atlas.* (2012). New York, NY: Random House.

PARENTHETICAL NOTES:

> According to the *New Yale Atlas* (2012) . . . (p. 106).
>
> (*New Yale Atlas,* 2012, p. 106)

Book with Multiple Volumes

REFERENCES ENTRY:

Eisenhower, D. (1960). *Presidential correspondence* (Vol. 2). New York, NY: Dutton Books.

PARENTHETICAL NOTES:

> Eisenhower (1960) predicted . . . (p. 77).
>
> (Eisenhower, 1960, p. 77)

Book with Editor or Editors

REFERENCES ENTRY:

Benson, N. (Ed.). (2012). *The absent parent.* New York, NY: Columbia House.

PARENTHETICAL NOTES:

> According to Benson (2012) . . . (p. 212).
>
> (Benson, 2012, p. 212)

Republished Book

REFERENCES ENTRY:

Smith, J. (2002). *The Jersey devil.* New York, NY: Warner Books. (Original work published 1922)

PARENTHETICAL NOTES:

> Smith (1922/2002) observes . . . (pp. 12–13).
>
> (Smith, 1922/2002, pp. 12–13)

Periodicals

Understanding the DOI System

Increasingly, scholarly articles include a *DOI number*. Developed by international publishers, the *Digital Object Identifier System* provides a common identification for electronic articles. Many articles appearing in print will also include a DOI number, typically placed on the first page near the copyright notice:

Journal of Abnormal Psychology:	Copyright 2011 by the American Psychological Association
Addiction and Depression	0278-8787/0879.00 DOI: 10.8798/ 0044-897.8.090
2011, Vol. 35, No. 3, 434–445	

Self-Medication Among the Unemployed

Randi Shaviz

Marquette University

Include DOI numbers whether the article is retrieved in print or online.

Newspaper Article

REFERENCES ENTRY:

Chavez, M. (2011, August 15). The Hispanic century. *The New York Times,* pp. 2A, 8–9A.

Note: List all page numbers, separated by commas.

PARENTHETICAL NOTES:

Chavez (2007) states . . . (p. 8A)

(Chavez, 2011, p. 8A)

Magazine Article Without DOI

REFERENCES ENTRY:

Janssen, M. (1997, January/February). Iran today. *Foreign Affairs, 64,* 78–88.

PARENTHETICAL NOTES:

Janssen (1997) notes . . . (pp. 80–82)

(Janssen, 1997, pp. 80–82)

Scholarly Article with DOI

REFERENCES ENTRY:

Grant, E. (2002). The Hollywood ten: Fighting the blacklist. *California Film Quarterly, 92,* 112–125. doi:10.1989/9890-7865.24.2.342

PARENTHETICAL NOTES:

Grant (2002) observes . . . (pp. 121–123).

(Grant, 2002, pp. 121–123)

Newspaper or Magazine Article with Unnamed Author

REFERENCES ENTRY:

The legacy of the Gulf War. (2011, October). *American History, 48,* 23–41.

PARENTHETICAL NOTES:

In "The Legacy of the Gulf War" (2011) . . .

("Legacy," 2000, pp. 22–24)

Note: For parenthetical notes, use shortened titles in quotation marks.

Letter to the Editor

REFERENCES ENTRY:

Roper, J. (1997, June 12). [Letter to the editor]. *Chicago Defender,* p. B12.

PARENTHETICAL NOTES:

According to Roper (1997) . . . (p. B12).

(Roper, 1997, p. B12)

Other Print Sources

Encyclopedia Article

REFERENCES ENTRY:

Keller, C. (2003). Lisbon. In J. R. Random (Ed.), *Encyclopedia of Europe* (pp. 200–205). New York, NY: Wiley.

PARENTHETICAL NOTES:

Keller (2003) reports . . . (p. 232).

(Keller, 2003, p. 232)

Encyclopedia Article with Unnamed Author

REFERENCES ENTRY:

Lisbon. (2002). In A. Scholar & B. Scholar (Eds.), *Columbia illustrated encyclopedia* (pp. 155–156). New York, NY: Columbia.

PARENTHETICAL NOTES:

In "Lisbon" (2002) . . . (p. 156).

("Lisbon," 2002, p. 156)

Nonprint Sources

Motion Picture

REFERENCES ENTRY:

De Fina, B. (Producer), & Scorsese, M. (Director). (1995). *Casino* [Motion picture]. United States: Universal Studios.

PARENTHETICAL NOTES:

De Fina and Scorsese (1995) depicts . . .

(De Fina & Scorsese, 1995)

Television Program

REFERENCES ENTRY:
Hong, J. (Writer & Director). (1997). *Women at work* [Television broadcast]. New York, NY: Public Broadcasting System.

PARENTHETICAL NOTES:

According to Hong (1997) . . .

(Hong, 1997)

DVD or Videotape

REFERENCES ENTRY:
Freud, J. (Producer), & Johnson, K. (Director). (2006). *Colonial Williamsburg* [DVD]. New York, NY: American Home Video.

PARENTHETICAL NOTES:

Freud and Johnson (2006) . . .

(Freud & Johnson, 2006)

Speech

REFERENCES ENTRY:
Goode, W. (2011, October). *America in the next century.* Address before the Chicago Press Club, Chicago, IL.

PARENTHETICAL NOTES:

According to Goode (2011) . . .

(Goode, 2011)

Electronic Sources

Web Pages Without DOI

REFERENCES ENTRY:
Regis, T. (2009, January 5). Distance learning [Electronic version]. *Regis.* Retrieved from http://regis.devel.com/home/distlearng/toc.html

Note: Include retrieval dates for sources such as web pages that may change over time.

PARENTHETICAL NOTES:

Regis (2009) suggests . . .

(Regis, 2009)

Work from Library or Personal Subscription Service Such as **InfoTrac, EBSCO,** *and* **LexisNexis**

REFERENCES ENTRY:
Corollo, M. (2008). Mental health in crisis. *Psychology News, 10* (11), 16. Retrieved from InfoTrac database.

PARENTHETICAL NOTE:

Corollo (2008) states

(Corollo, 2008)

Electronic Journal Article Without DOI

REFERENCES ENTRY:

Smith, P. (2009). Help for homeless promised. *Psychology Journal.* 21 (2). 78–92. Retrieved from http://www.psychojournal.org/hts/index.html

PARENTHETICAL NOTES:

According to Smith (2009) . . .

(Smith, 2009)

Electronic Journal Article with DOI

REFERENCES ENTRY:

Jones, M. (2011). Help for the homeless denied. *Social Issues.* 19 (2). 128–145. doi:10.1002/icd.546

Note: If a DOI number is available, do not include the URL or date of retrieval.

PARENTHETICAL NOTES:

According to Jones (2011) . . .

(Jones, 2011)

Online Newspaper Article

REFERENCES ENTRY:

Gulf War syndrome: Diagnostic survey reveals dangerous trend. (2011, March 11). *The New York Times.* Retrieved from http://www.nytimes.com/aponline/ap-gulf.html

PARENTHETICAL NOTES:

In "Gulf War" (2003) . . .

("Gulf War," 2003)

Electronic-only Book

REFERENCES ENTRY:

Weston, T. (2009). *The electronic teacher.* Retrieved from http://www.edserv.edu/index.html

PARENTHETICAL NOTES:

Weston (2009) points out . . .

(Weston, 2009)

E-mail

Because e-mail is not recorded in archives and not available to other researchers, it is mentioned in the text but not included in the list of references. Treat e-mail as a personal communication, as follows:

PARENTHETICAL NOTE:

L. Medhin (personal communication, March 23, 2011) suggested . . .

(L. Medhin, personal communication, March 23, 2011)

Visuals

Visuals, such as charts, tables, diagrams, and photographs, are not listed in references. Number visuals and add a caption crediting the original author or source and copyright holder.

Photograph

Figure 1. *Fire Sweeps Downtown.*

Note. Retrieved from http://www.suntimes.com/images/fire/Mar06/index/html

SAMPLE RESEARCH PAPER WITH VISUALS USING APA STYLE
(with Abstract)

FEEDING FRENZY

Title

Feeding Frenzy:
Journalism and Justice in the Leopold and Loeb Case

Byline

Sean O'Connell
Brooklyn College

Instructor Date

Dr. Abazz
May 10, 2012

FEEDING FRENZY

1

Abstract

Abstract single-spaced in single paragraph block

Current popular opinion suggests that recent high profile legal proceedings have been adversely affected by excessive and sensational media coverage. These cases, many argue, have set dangerous precedents which will cause lasting harm to American justice. The 1924 trial of Leopold and Loeb indicates that this is not a new concern. A careful analysis of the role of journalism in what was called "the crime of the century" reveals the media may have undue influence in individual cases but have little lasting influence on the criminal justice system.

**Feeding Frenzy:
Journalism and Justice in
the Leopold and Loeb Case**

The twentieth century ended with a flurry of highly publicized crimes and trials—the Menendez case, the O. J. Simpson trial, the Jon Benet Ramsey investigation, and the impeachment of President Clinton. In each instance, the media made instant celebrities of suspects and witnesses. Driven by fame or money, even minor figures became household names, publishing books and appearing on talk shows. Commentators continually lamented that justice was being perverted by media attention, that televised trials were turning lawyers into actors and trials into theater. Justice, many argued, was being irrevocably damaged.

An earlier case, however, reveals that this phenomenon is not new. In the spring of 1924 two young men committed a crime that made them nationally known celebrities and sparked a firestorm of media attention, which many at the time insisted "damaged justice forever" (Harrison, 1924, p. 8).

The "Crime of the Century"

On May 21, 1924, Jacob Franks, a wealthy Chicago businessman, received news that his 14-year-old son Bobby had been kidnapped. A letter signed George Johnson demanded $10,000 and gave Franks detailed instructions on how to deliver the ransom. Desperate to save his son, Franks complied with the kidnapper's request, but before he could deliver the money, he learned his son had been found dead. Less than 12 hours after the abduction, a worker discovered the naked body in a ditch on the outskirts of the city (Arkan, 1997).

The killing of Bobby Franks created a national sensation. Rumors circulated that the kidnapper had been a jealous teacher or a disgruntled employee or customer of one of Jacob Franks's enterprises. Because the body had been stripped, many speculated the killer was a sexual pervert (Higdon, 1974).

The press seized upon the story, printing numerous accounts of the police investigation. One newspaper offered readers a cash prize for submitting the best theory of the case and was swamped with thousands of letters (Higdon, 1974). Figures 1 and 2 illustrate typical headlines that appeared after the discovery of Franks's body.

The police soon had a strong lead. A pair of eyeglasses had been discovered near the body. Though common in appearance, the glasses, shown in Figure 3, had a newly patented hinge in the frame. Only three pairs had been sold in the Chicago area. The eyeglasses were quickly traced to a neighbor, 19-year-old Nathan Leopold ("Born Killers," 1998).

Title in all capitals and page number as header on every page.

Full title

Direct quotation with author, year, and page number

Bold subtitles

Numerals for numbers 10 and above

Paraphrase with author and year

Video listed by title and year

FEEDING FRENZY   3

Source information in caption

Figures 1 & 2. *Chicago Daily Tribune* headlines, May 1924
Note. Retrieved from http://homicide.northwestern.edu/documents/5866/19249523trib01.jpg

Nathan Leopold explained he had probably dropped the glasses while leading a birding class a few days earlier. At the time of the crime, he claimed to have been driving with a friend named Richard Loeb and two girls they had picked up in Jackson Park. At first, investigators found Leopold's story believable (Leopold, 1958). Leopold and Loeb seemed unlikely criminals. Like Bobby Franks, they were sons of millionaires; Richard Loeb's father was vice-chairman of Sears & Roebuck. They were gifted students, both having completed college at 18. Leopold spoke numerous languages and had become a nationally recognized ornithologist ("Born Killers," 1998). Brought in for questioning, Richard Loeb initially corroborated Leopold's alibi, claiming they spent May 21st with girls they picked up in Jackson Park (Higdon, 1974).

State's Attorney Robert E. Crowe remained unconvinced and continued his investigation. On May 31st, after a long interrogation, Richard Loeb gave a detailed confession, admitting that he and Nathan Leopold were solely responsible for the murder of Bobby Franks. There was no doubt about their guilt. They led police to where they had disposed of the victim's clothing and the lagoon where they had dumped the typewriter used to write the ransom letter (Arkan, 1997). Satisfied he had an airtight case, Richard E. Crowe announced to the press, "'I have a hanging case'" ("Born Killers," 1998). The stunned Loeb family asked the most famous lawyer of the era, Clarence Darrow, to save their son's life (Leopold, 1958).

FEEDING FRENZY   4

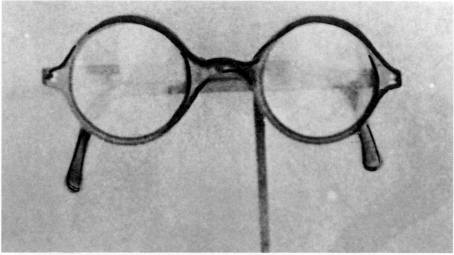

Figure 3. The key piece of evidence, Nathan Leopold's glasses   © Bettman/CORBIS
Note. Retrieved from http://pro.corbis.com/search/search.aspx?&i51208223655

The arrest of two wealthy young men, rumors of homosexuality, and the appearance of Clarence Darrow in the case created a media firestorm. Accustomed to reading stories of hardened gangsters, the public was fascinated by the pair of debonair young men who showed no remorse as they chatted with reporters or posed for photographers (see Figure 4).

The Chicago Press of the 1920s

At the time of the Franks kidnapping, Chicago had six daily newspapers, including two Hearst publications known for sensational headlines (Higdon, 1974). Newspapers of the era were highly competitive. In a personal interview, attorney and journalism professor David Evans (2000) noted, "Newspapers in those years were eager to capitalize on crime, sex, and violence to boost sales and increase their advertising rates based on circulation."

Competition led journalists and newspapers to engage in illegal practices. Reporters, whose salaries and bonuses were tied to sales, impersonated police officers to obtain leads, stole documents, and bribed officials for information (Evans, 2000). Major Chicago dailies engaged in brutal circulation wars, hiring gangsters to terrorize news dealers and newsboys from rival papers. The commuter who stopped at a newstand to purchase a *Herald Examiner* might be beaten by a thug working for *The Chicago Tribune* (Higdon, 1974; Evans, 2000).

Personal interview cited fully in the text but not included on References page

Note for two sources

© Bettman/CORBIS

Figure 4. Under arrest, Richard Loeb and Nathan Leopold pose for photographers, 1924

Note. Retrieved from http://cache.corbis.com/CorbisImage/170/12/22/32/12223236/ U251458INP.jpg

Feeding Frenzy

The Leopold and Loeb case presented the Chicago press with an unparalleled opportunity for sensationalism. For many, the case represented the moral degeneration of American youth. The 1920s was an era of youthful rebellion, marked by flappers, speakeasies, and open discussions of sex. Prohibition was widely violated, leading millions of Americans to associate with bootleggers and fuel the growing criminal empires of gangsters like Al Capone (Bergreen, 1994).

The Chicago papers had given great press coverage to the gangland killings of the era. But unlike the crude turf battles of the "beer wars," the Leopold and Loeb case gave reporters new avenues to exploit. They quickly dubbed the case a "Thrill Killing," a crime motivated by something darker and more sinister than simple greed (Evans, 2000). After Leopold and Loeb were arrested, Chicago papers reported extensively on their privileged status and their total lack of remorse. *The Chicago Daily News* referred to the defendants as "jealous actors" who "taunted" each other as reporters watched ("Leopold and Loeb," 1924, p. 4). Stories commented on the stylish dress and demeanor of the two young men, who smoked cigarettes and gave impromptu press conferences. Stating the crime had been an experiment, Nathan Leopold told *The Chicago Daily News*, ". . . it is as easy to justify such a death as it is to justify an entomologist impaling a beetle on a pin" ("Leopold and Loeb," 1924, p. 4).

These comments and images such as the press photograph shown in Figure 5 inflamed the public. Crowds demanded the young men be hanged. Commentators across the country saw the pair as symbols of a corrupt generation without moral consciousness.

FEEDING FRENZY   6

© Bettmann/CORBIS

Figure 5. Leopold and Loeb laughing during their murder trial

Note. Retrieved from http://cache.corbis.com/CorbisImage/170/12/51/35/12513500/U252138INP.jpg

The "Trial of the Century"

Despite their confessions, Leopold and Loeb pleaded not guilty. Their attorney, Clarence Darrow, an outspoken opponent of the death penalty, took the case to put capital punishment on trial. Sensing the hostile mood of the jury and cognizant of the crowds milling outside the courthouse demanding the killers be put to death, Darrow changed the plea to guilty (Higdon, 1974).

Darrow's Strategy

Convinced that a jury would not only convict his clients but demand the death penalty, Darrow wanted to avoid a trial. By entering a plea of guilty, Darrow would be able to address the judge directly. He believed he would have a better chance to convince a single individual to spare his clients' lives. A jury, Darrow knew, would make a collective decision. A judge, however, would bear individual responsibility for sending two teenagers to the gallows ("Born Killers," 1998).

Darrow did not consider pleading Leopold and Loeb not guilty by reason of insanity, because this would have required a jury trial. He did, however, argue to Judge Caverly that mental illness should be considered a mitigating factor. He argued that Leopold and Loeb should be imprisoned for life rather than executed (Higdon, 1974).

Press Coverage

The hearing before Judge Caverly became a media circus. Each day thousands of people mobbed the courthouse, hoping to obtain a seat in the courtroom. Admiring women sent flowers to Leopold and Loeb. A despondent man offered to be hanged in their place. A young woman offered to perjure herself, claiming to be one of the girls Leopold and Loeb had picked up in Jackson Park. *The Chicago Tribune,* which owned a radio station, briefly urged readers to demand that the hearing be broadcast over the new medium. Reporters stole a medical report from Darrow's office and printed intimate details about the defendants' sex lives (Higdon, 1974).

When Darrow called psychiatrists to testify on behalf of his clients, William Randolph Hearst offered Sigmund Freud an undisclosed sum to travel to Chicago to comment on the defendants' mental state. Freud declined, but less reputable "experts," including phrenologists, offered opinions to the press. Diagrams of Leopold and Loeb's heads appeared in tabloids with arrows pointing to facial features revealing propensities for falsehood and unnatural sexual appetites (Evans, 2000).

Angered by the crime, the public was outraged by the idea that the killers would be let off because they had unhappy childhoods. Widely viewed as spoiled rich kids, Leopold and Loeb received little sympathy in the press. Hundreds of ministers wrote Judge Caverly insisting they should be put to death. Arguing before the judge, State's Attorney Crowe echoed sentiments expressed in dozens of editorials (Evans, 2000). Having called over a hundred witnesses, Crowe felt confident he had made a compelling case for the death penalty.

Darrow's Use of the Press

Sensing that Judge Caverly would be influenced by community opinion, Darrow sought to defuse some of the negative publicity. Numerous reporters had claimed that Darrow was being paid a million dollars, inflaming public resentment against the affluence of his clients ("Born Killers," 1998; Evans, 2000). Darrow encouraged the fathers of Leopold and Loeb to release a statement to the press asserting that his fee would be determined by the Illinois Bar Association and that their goal was only to secure life imprisonment for their sons. Darrow employed primitive sampling techniques to measure the public mood. He directed pollsters to ask randomly selected men in the Loop if they believed Leopold and Loeb should be executed. Before release of the statement, 60% favored the death penalty. After release of the statement, 60% agreed that life imprisonment would be a suitable punishment (Higdon, 1974).

According to Evans (2000), the most significant element of Darrow's strategy was an eloquent 12-hour closing argument against the death penalty. Quoting the Bible, legal scholars, and great works of literature, he delivered a compelling oration. He stressed the youth of the defendants, arguing that in any other case few would see a life sentence for an 18-year-old as lenient. After three weeks of deliberating the case, Judge Caverly shocked the press by sentencing Nathan Leopold and Richard Loeb to life plus 99 years. Despite the severity of the sentence, editorials across the country considered the decision a gross injustice. Edna Harrison (1924) wrote a stinging denunciation of Judge Caverly:

> Nowhere has justice been more blinded than in this city. It is an outrage that perversion, kidnapping, and murder have been rewarded. The science of psychology reduced crime to an ailment and killers to patients. This case has damaged justice forever. (p. 8)

Margin notes:

Note citing two sources

Indented block quotation

FEEDING FRENZY   8

The Lasting Influence

The fact that the "outrage" occurred in 1924 shows the high-profile case made no lasting impact on routine criminal investigations and legal proceedings. Randi Greenwald (2012) has argued that the case of Leopold and Loeb, like the sensational trials of the 1990s, had no lasting effect on justice:

> Thousands of trials, both fair and unfair, followed the Leopold and Loeb case. In most instances media attention has had little impact on judges and juries. The insanity plea is rarely used and rarely successful. Psychiatric arguments about diminished capacity have become routine but have not significantly altered the rate of convictions or the severity of sentences, which have steadily become longer. (pp. 17–18)

The case of Leopold and Loeb indicates clearly that excessive media coverage may alter the outcome of a particular sensational trial but has no significant influence on the criminal justice system.

References

Arkan, J. (1997). *Leopold and Loeb*. Retrieved from http://chicago.crime.com/library/article/trials/c15.html

Bergreen, L. (1994). *Capone: The man and the era*. New York, NY: Touchstone.

Born killers [Television series episode]. (1998). In C. Meindl (Producer), *In search of history*. New York, NY: The History Channel.

Greenwald, R. (2012). The circus trial: Justice and media. *Washington Law Yearbook, 2012*, 12–34. doi:10.0004/4404/87878095

Harrison, E. (1924). *The case of Leopold and Loeb*. Chicago, IL: Dearborn.

Higdon, H. (1974). *The crime of the century*. New York, NY: Putnam.

Leopold, N. (1958). *Life plus 99 years*. Garden City, NY: Doubleday.

Leopold and Loeb. (1924, June 2). *The Chicago Daily News*, pp. 1–4.

[margin notes: Heading centered; Hanging indention for references]

WRITING ACTIVITY

1. Using APA style, develop a References page including five of the following sources. Invent needed details such as dates, page numbers, and web addresses.

   - one of your textbooks
   - an encyclopedia article
   - a *60 Minutes* episode called "Cyber Crime"
   - a *New York Times* editorial
   - your college's home page
   - a scholarly article from an online journal

   (Continued)

- a corporate web page
- the remarks made yesterday by the president on C-SPAN

Develop a parenthetical note for each of the sources you create.

2. Using MLA style, develop a Works Cited page listing five of the following sources. Invent needed details such as dates, page numbers, and web addresses.

- "Mending Wall" by Robert Frost from a book called *100 Poems*
- *Hamlet*
- the Bible
- an interview with Donald Trump published in this month's *New Yorker*
- a translation of Albert Camus's *The Stranger*
- an essay from the Reader portion of this book
- a motion picture
- an online novel

Develop a parenthetical note for each of the sources you create.

RESEARCH PAPER CHECKLIST

Before submitting your research paper, review these questions:

✔ Does your research paper have a clearly stated thesis?
✔ Do you provide sufficient evidence to support your thesis?
✔ Does the paper focus on your ideas and commentary or does it only summarize other sources?
✔ Do you comment on the quantity and quality of the evidence you have found?
✔ Does the opening introduce the subject, present the thesis, or explain your research method?
✔ Does the conclusion end the paper on a strong point?
✔ Does the paper follow the appropriate style for citing sources?
✔ Questions for your instructor:
   - Is my topic acceptable?
   - How many sources do I need?
   - Does my paper need an outline?
   - Which documentation style is required?

For Further Reading

American Chemical Society. *The ACS Style Guide: A Manual for Authors and Editors.*
American Institute of Physics. *AIP Manual of Style.*

American Medical Association. *American Medical Association Manual of Style.*

American Psychological Association. *Publication Manual of the American Psychological Association.*

Council of Science Editors. *Scientific Style and Format: The CBE Manual for Authors, Editors, and Publishers*

Hacker, Diana. *Research and Documentation in the Electronic Age.*

Harvard Law Review. *The Bluebook: A Uniform System of Citation.*

Lester, James D. *Writing Research Papers: A Complete Guide.*

Meyer, Michael. *The Little, Brown Guide to Writing Research Papers.*

Modern Language Association. *MLA Style Manual.*

Turabian, Kate. *A Manual for Writers of Term Papers, Theses, and Dissertations.*

University of Chicago Press. *The Chicago Manual of Style.*

Veit, Richard. *Research: The Student's Guide to Writing Research Papers.*

Walker, Melissa. *Writing Research Papers: A Norton Guide.*

E-Sources

Frequently Asked Questions about the *MLA Handbook*
   http://www.mla.org/style/handbook_faq

Purdue Online Writing Lab: MLA Formatting and Style Guide
   http://owl.english.purdue.edu/owl/resource/557/01/

APA Style Frequently Asked Questions
   http://www.apastyle.org/ learn/faqs/index.aspx

Purdue Online Writing Lab: APA Formatting and Style Guide
   http://owl.english.purdue.edu/owl/resource/560/01/

 Access the English CourseMate for this text at **www.cengagebrain.com** for additional information on writing research papers.

Writing in College

4

The Essay Examination

Vigorous writing is concise.

—William Strunk, Jr.

What Are Essay Exams?

Throughout your college career you will probably face essay examinations. They can be frustrating, especially if you realize afterward how easily you could have improved your grade by studying lecture notes instead of your textbook or by reading the questions more carefully. Writing papers out of class, you have time to select a topic, conduct research, write numerous drafts, and edit. Essay exams force you to truncate the writing process to meet a deadline. Learning to write essay exams can teach you to work under pressure in your profession, when you may have to provide immediate answers to questions or draft statements to manage a crisis with little time for reflection.

Few people feel confident about writing under pressure, but there are strategies that can improve your performance.

The Purpose of Essay Examinations

Instructors use objective tests consisting of multiple choice and true-or-false questions to measure your ability to recall factual information. Essay questions allow instructors to accomplish additional goals:

- measure your understanding of facts by asking you to restate information in your own words
- evaluate your ability to assimilate and analyze material
- analyze your critical thinking skills in diagnosing problems, proposing solutions, comparing situations, outlining causes, evaluating evidence, and predicting outcomes
- determine your ability to apply abstract knowledge to test cases or hypothetical situations

Maria Toutoudaki/jupiterimages

Sam Diephuis/jupiterimages

Strategies for Studying for Essay Examinations

1. **Determine what material the test will cover.** Instructors are often reluctant to answer the direct question, "What's on the test?" But most will respond favorably to two critical questions that you should ask: *What does the examination cover?* and *What is the best way to study?* Asking these questions can help you target your studying and avoid reviewing the wrong material.

2. **Begin studying at once. Don't attempt to cram the night before.** Two hours of studying spread over a week will give you more opportunity to learn and recall information than attempting to absorb the same amount of information in four hours of last-minute cramming.
   - If you delay studying until the night before the examination, you run the risk that an unexpected problem will disrupt your plans and leave you unprepared.
   - Studying in advance gives you the opportunity to ask questions before the examination. If you discover that your instructor defines a term differently than the textbook does, for example, you can ask which one he or she thinks is accurate.

3. **Talk to other students about the upcoming examination.** Discuss possible topics, methods of studying, and lecture notes.

4. **Consider the nature of the discipline.** The kind of response that instructors consider acceptable is determined by the discipline. In the humanities, students may be free to advance highly personal interpretations of a work of art or historical event. Creative essays, provided they are well supported, are highly valued. However, in such fields as law, psychology, sociology, and nursing, students are expected to only advance ideas that follow specific standards and practices and that can be scientifically proved.

5. **Review your syllabus, notes, textbooks, and handouts.** Highlight important passages for easy review just before the exam. Note significant facts, statistics, and quotations that may serve as support for your responses.
   - If you are taking an open-book examination, highlight passages and use labeled bookmarks so you can quickly locate information while writing. Familiarize yourself with the book's table of contents and index.

6. **Recall the types of questions your instructor has asked in class.** The kinds of questions asked to prompt class discussion may provide a clue about the way the instructor may word questions on essay examinations.
   - Does your instructor focus on comparing issues, analyzing problems, debating alternative interpretations or theories?
   - Does he or she concentrate on presenting in-depth analysis of narrow topics or providing a sweeping, inclusive overview of the subject?

7. **Think in terms of the modes.** Most essay questions ask students to *define* elements, *compare* related topics, *explain* a process, or detail *causes* or *effects*.
   - In reviewing your notes and textbook, consider what major items require definition, which subjects are often compared, and what ideas are presented as causes or effects.

8. **Prewrite possible responses.** Select the key issues or topics you expect to appear on the examination and freewrite, cluster, or brainstorm possible essays. List possible thesis statements.

9. **Get as much rest as possible the night before.** Late-night cramming may help you identify facts and figures that appear on multiple-choice tests, but essay questions demand thinking. If you are not rested, you may find yourself unable to quickly analyze issues, generate ideas, make connections, and present your thoughts in an organized fashion.

Strategies for Writing the Essay Examination

1. **Come to the examination prepared to write.** Bring two pens, paper, and, unless prohibited, a dictionary and handbook.

2. **Read the entire exam.** Go over *all* the questions carefully before starting to write. Determine how much each question is worth. Some instructors will indicate the point value of each question.

3. **Budget your time.** Determine how much time you should devote to each question. Give yourself enough time for planning and editing each question.

4. **Answer the easiest questions first while thinking about the more difficult ones.** The easiest questions will take less time to answer and may stimulate ideas that will help you confront more challenging questions.

5. **Read each question twice.** Students often miss points by failing to fully read the question. They react to a word or phrase out of context and energetically begin writing an essay that does not answer the question.

6. **Study the verbs or command words that direct your response.** Most essay questions contain clues to the kind of response the instructor expects.

Question	Desired Response
List reasons for the rise of labor unions in the 1930s.	A series of causes rather than an in-depth analysis of a single factor
Distinguish the differences between ancient Athens and Sparta.	A comparison/contrast essay, highlighting differences

(Continued)

What led to the collapse of the Soviet Union?	A cause-and-effect essay, perhaps related in a narrative or organized by division or classification
Describe three common forms of depression.	Three short definitions or descriptions organized by division
Discuss the effects of global warming on the environment.	An essay consisting of cause and effect, process, description, or division

7. **Study questions that require more than a single response.** Some essay questions contain more than one command and require a two- or three-part response.

Question	Desired Response
Provide a definition of chemical dependency *and explain* why treatment remains problematic.	1. Define term. 2. List causes for problems in treatment.
Select three key economic proposals made by the president in the State of the Union address *and predict how they will affect both the trade deficit and unemployment.*	1. Describe or define three points. 2. Discuss each point, listing effects on trade deficit and unemployment.

8. **Provide a clear thesis statement.** Your response should do more than simply list ideas. A strong thesis statement will give your response direction and can help organize ideas.

   Question:

   How has the concept of separation of church and state affected American society?

   Possible Thesis Statements:

   The separation of church and state has allowed American public schools to accommodate students from diverse religious backgrounds with little of the conflict found in other countries.

   Unlike state-supported religious institutions in other nations, American churches are independent and able to take active roles in criticizing government policies regarding discrimination, capital punishment, US foreign policy, and abortion.

9. **Explain or justify your response to broad questions.** Sometimes instructors ask sweeping questions that cannot be fully addressed with a brief response, such as

   What caused the American Civil War?

If you provide a detailed explanation of slavery, an instructor may assume you believe it to be the sole cause of the war. If you present a list of a dozen reasons, however, an instructor may feel that your response is superficial and lacks substance. You can achieve a higher grade if you justify your answer:

> There were numerous political, social, economic, philosophical, and moral causes of the Civil War. But clearly the most significant and enduring cause for the conflict was the contentious issue of slavery. . . .

> Although most Americans cite slavery as the main reason for the Civil War, it is difficult to isolate a single factor as a cause for the conflict. To understand why the states went to war, one must appreciate the full range of social, economic, commercial, foreign policy, and moral disputes that separated North and South. . . .

10. **Keep an eye on the clock.** Pace yourself. Don't overdo a response simply because you are knowledgeable about the topic. Provide enough information to answer the question, then move on. Save the toughest questions for last.

11. **Keep writing.** If you become blocked or stalled on a question and can't think, move on to other questions or review what you have answered. Often rereading the response to one question will spark ideas that aid in another.

12. **Provide space for revisions.** Write on every other line of the page or leave wide margins. You will not have time to write a full second draft, but you can make neat corrections and slip in ideas if you give yourself space for changes and additions.

Sample Questions and Essays

Read these questions and then examine the responses. How effectively do these students address the questions? Even if you are unsure of the content, you can still evaluate the essay for clarity, organization, and development.

Economics 101 Midterm

Question 1.
During the prosperity caused by government spending during World War II, both workers and business leaders feared a Depression would follow the end of hostilities. Many envisioned millions of jobless veterans camped in abandoned defense plants. Why were these predictions wrong? What led to the economic expansion after 1945?

It was understandable that many Americans, most of whom had a living memory of the Depression of the 1930s, feared the end of wartime spending would lead to massive unemployment and poverty. But these dire predictions failed to consider the political, social, and economic forces that would change the American economy for the rest of the twentieth century.

Introduction

(Continued)

Thesis

Evidence

Evidence

> The doomsayers overlooked two powerful economic forces that would propel post-war prosperity: pent-up consumer demand and personal savings.
>
> During the Second World War nearly every industry focused on military production. Civilian automobile production ceased in 1942. At war's end most Americans were driving cars that were three to six years old. The manufacture of other goods such as washing machines, dishwashers, refrigerators, and radios was curtailed. Clothing, shoes, and tires were rationed. The infant television industry was stalled by the war. At war's end the civilian population and returning veterans needed and wanted to replace worn-out goods. The plants that produced military supplies were rapidly put to use to manufacture a range of consumer products in high demand.
>
> This pent-up demand was coupled with tremendous buying power. With rationed goods, the war workers, many of whom earned substantial overtime pay, had little outlet for spending. Personal savings exploded during the war. Highly publicized bond drives encouraged people to purchase billions of dollars of government bonds to support the war effort. In addition, millions of veterans returned from combat zones where there was no place to spend the money they earned. Many soldiers had saved six months' to a year's salary.
>
> The demand for new goods and services and the ability to pay for them fueled a booming postwar consumer economy.
>
> Other factors, such as the GI Bill, helped finance new homes and businesses. The fact many veterans chose to attend college after the war limited the number of men and women seeking jobs immediately after the war. The Marshall Plan, implemented shortly after the war, created a strong overseas demand for American machinery, vehicles, and other goods.

QUESTIONS FOR REVIEW

1. How effective is the thesis? Should it be placed elsewhere in the essay?
2. Is the thesis clearly supported? Are the details convincing?
3. How effective is the conclusion?

> ### Introduction to Psychology
>
> 2. Distinguish between schizophrenia and multiple personality disorder.
>
> The common confusion of these two psychological disorders stems in part from the name *schizophrenia,* which means "split mind." Many people assume this "split" refers to a Dr. Jekyll and Mr. Hyde duality, a splitting of an individual into two distinct personalities.
>
> But the "split" schizophrenia refers to is a patient's split or disassociation from reality. The schizophrenic can suffer from a number of symptoms affecting thoughts, emotional reactions, behaviors, and relationships. Often schizophrenics display inappropriate reactions—failing to appear moved at a funeral while later becoming tearfully agitated over losing a bus transfer. In broiling summer they may bundle themselves in coats and blankets, claiming to be cold. They may suffer hallucinations, frequently reporting they hear their thoughts spoken out loud or a voice commanding them to do certain things. Schizophrenics may also be paranoid, claiming that the FBI or Martians are controlling their thoughts, spying on them, or attempting to kill them.
>
> *(Continued)*

Schizophrenia is a common mental illness, affecting 1–2 percent of the population. Research has proven a strong link to genetics, since it does run in families. Scientists have identified chemical imbalances in the brains of schizophrenics. Psychologists also believe that social and family factors influence the development of the disease.

Multiple personality disorder has been far less documented since it is believed to be much rarer than schizophrenia and is harder to diagnose. The 1950s movie *The Three Faces of Eve* was based on an actual case of a woman with three distinct personalities. Psychiatrists of that era believed that overwhelming emotional stress or trauma caused people to develop multiple personalities as a defense mechanism. Frequently, one personality will dominate or protect another. Patients often have both male and female personalities. Under hypnosis, patients will alter their behavior, body language, and speech as each personality emerges. In recent years multiple personality disorder has been used as a defense in several high-profile murder cases. Because the condition is rare and research is difficult, the condition is hard to diagnose and study.

The main thing is to realize that schizophrenics do not have more than one personality but are split from reality. Drugs are now available to reduce hallucinations in schizophrenics, but treatments for multiple personality disorder remain experimental.

QUESTIONS FOR REVIEW

1. How effectively does this essay address the question?
2. What is the thesis? Is it clearly stated?
3. Does the student support the thesis with sufficient detail?
4. Does the student adequately address both disorders?
5. Do you sense the student ran out of time?
6. Consult a psychology text or encyclopedia and then evaluate this essay. How accurately does the student define the two disorders? What grade would you give this response?

WRITING ACTIVITY

1. Review essay exams you have taken in the past. How could you have improved your responses? Read the question and write a fresh response within the time limits of the original test.

2. Select one of the following questions and write for fifteen minutes, drawing on your personal experience, reading, and past courses:

   What, in your opinion, is the principal cause for poverty in America?

   How has immigration shaped American society?

   What effects has the Internet had on education?

   Identify the key abilities needed for someone to succeed in your future profession.

   (Continued)

Examine your completed response.
- Is the thesis clearly stated?
- Is the thesis supported by detail?
- Is the response logically organized?
- Are there irrelevant ideas that should be deleted?
- How effective is the conclusion?
- How could you improve your ability to write under pressure?

3. Select a textbook chapter you have recently studied and use one of the questions at the end to prompt a fifteen-minute response. If your book does not offer questions, summarize one or more of the chapter's key points in a short essay without looking at the book.
   - Were you able to develop a thesis and support it with detail?
   - What problems did you encounter in writing?
   - How could you improve your studying?

For Further Reading

Burns, Richard. *Pass Exams and Write Top Essays.*

Galica, Gregory. *The Blue Book: A Student's Guide to Essay Exams.*

Lesyk, Susan Burgess. *The Blue Book: Achieving Success on Essay Exams.*

E-Sources

George Washington University's Academic Success Center: Common Words Used in Essay Questions

  http://gwired.gwu.edu/counsel/asc/SaveYourSemester/ Bigtesttomorrowneedstrategictips/

Study Guides and Strategies: The Essay Exam

  http://www.studygs.net/tsttak4.htm

University of North Carolina–Chapel Hill: Essay Exams

  http://www.unc.edu/depts/wcweb/handouts/essay-exams.html

 Access the English CourseMate for this text at **www.cengagebrain.com** for further information on writing essay examinations.

Writing About Literature

*We need two powers in literature, a power to create and a
power to understand.*

—Northrop Frye

What Is Literature?

Writing about literature—poems, short stories, novels, and plays—can be challenging, especially if you are accustomed to reading only for pleasure or information. Literature courses require you to understand not only what happens in a work but also what it means and how it is stated.

Writers who study literature, like writers in any discipline, use technical terms to discuss their subject. In order to write about a work of literature, it is helpful to understand definitions of key words and concepts.

Major Literary Terms

Characters

protagonist—The main figure, often called the hero, such as Hamlet, Huckleberry Finn, Jay Gatsby.

antagonist—A person or force working against the protagonist, such as an adversary or a hostile environment like the sea or a blizzard.

stock characters—Recurring types—the hard-boiled detective, the innocent child, the vengeful spouse, young lovers.

foils—Minor characters who define the qualities of another figure by comparison. The idealism of a young attorney can be highlighted by surrounding him or her with cynical and uncaring coworkers.

flat characters—Minor characters who are only superficially developed.

Plot

plot—The events that occur in the work. In an adventure or detective novel, the plot dominates the work and is often more important than the characters. In other works, the events are less important than the protagonist's thoughts or feelings. *Julius Caesar* has a strong plot marked by conspiracy, assassination, civil war, and suicides. In contrast, Beckett's *Waiting for Godot* has no discernible plot but a series of interchanges between two characters.

conflict—The struggle or tension that is a key element of the plot. The conflict can be between individuals, an individual and society or nature, or between contrasting forces within a character. Hemingway's *The Old Man and the Sea* pits a character against nature. Charles Jackson's *The Lost Weekend* depicts the internal conflicts faced by an alcoholic.

climax—An event signaling a turning point in the plot, usually when the conflict reaches its greatest intensity. This may be followed by an **anticlimax,** a less dramatic event that occurs after the climax, often providing a final resolution.

setting—The time and place of the work, such as nineteenth-century Paris, Kansas in the Depression, or present-day New York. In some instances setting is simply a backdrop to events that could occur anywhere. In some works, the setting is essential to the characters and action. In *All Quiet on the Western Front,* the First World War engulfs all the characters and shapes the plot. In contrast, the setting of *Who's Afraid of Virginia Woolf?* is relatively incidental to the conflict between spouses.

Theme

genre—A type of literature, such as poetry, fiction, or drama.

theme—The major issue, problem, or controlling idea. *Invisible Man* concerns racism. *Of Mice and Men* reveals the cruelty and insensitivity often shown to the weak and vulnerable. The author's treatment of theme may include political commentary or a call for social reform.

tone—The author's attitude toward events, characters, or plot. The tone of a play, story, or poem can be somber, humorous, sarcastic, or sympathetic.

tragedy—A work of literature in which the protagonist falls from a position of power and respect within a society to destruction, usually marked by exile, death, or suicide. In literature tragedy involves choice, not random disaster. A character killed in an airplane crash is not considered "tragic." Macbeth, however, makes a decision to kill the king and sets into motion the forces that ultimately destroy him. In classic Greek tragedy the heroes often suffer from *hubris,* or pride, which leads them to assume that they can break laws and control events. Often, as in *Oedipus,* the hero learns too late that no mortal can control destiny.

comedy—A work of literature in which the characters, typically a pair of young lovers, overcome obstacles to form a new society, often culminating in a wedding, festivity, or new understanding. Comedies, although they usually have "happy" endings, may not be filled with jokes. Chekhov, for instance, labeled *The Cherry Orchard* and *The Seagull* comedies, even though one play involved a family's being dispossessed and the other involved suicide.

Point of View

point of view—The perspective from which the story is told.

first-person narrator—A narrator who experienced or witnessed the events in the story. The narrator may be the protagonist or a bystander. *Huckleberry*

Finn is narrated by the main character. In contrast, events in *The Great Gatsby* are told not by the protagonist, Jay Gatsby, but by his neighbor, Nick Carroway.

unreliable narrator—A narrator who may have biases or misunderstandings that distort the way readers perceive events. Huckleberry Finn, for example, is unsophisticated and superstitious, and thus often draws erroneous conclusions about what he observes.

third-person narrator—In third person, the narrator may be *omniscient* or all-knowing, entering the minds of several characters, or may have *limited knowledge* of characters and events. Often the third-person narrator may show the inner thoughts and feelings of major characters and only report the actions and dialogue of minor figures.

Technique

exposition—Supplies readers with background information about setting, characters' past lives, or events that occurred before the plot begins.

foreshadowing—Clues or hints of action to follow. Shirley Jackson's "The Lottery," which culminates in a woman being stoned to death, opens with a brief description of small boys piling up stones.

flashback—A scene in a novel, play, story, or poem that returns to earlier events to suggest a character's memory, provide a historical perspective, or clarify the present.

irony—The contrast between anticipated and actual elements. *Verbal* irony consists of remarks in which the spoken words differ from their intended meaning, often for comic or sarcastic effect. An undercover officer arresting a drug dealer might state ironically, "This is your lucky day." In *dramatic* irony there is a discrepancy between what a character believes to be true and what the author or audience knows. In *A Doll's House* Helmer tells his wife that most criminals have mothers who lie, unaware that his wife has been living an elaborate falsehood.

image—A person, object, scene, or situation that creates a strong impression, usually one that relies on the senses. Edgar Allan Poe used images of skulls, bones, tombs, blood, darkness, and death to create sensations of horror and fear.

symbol—A person, object, scene, or situation that represents something else: an idea, quality, or concept. A lion might symbolize courage. Symbols may be obvious or complex. In *Death of a Salesman* Biff Loman steals a fountain pen and a suit, symbols of the success in the business world that has eluded him. For many readers the whale in *Moby Dick* symbolizes nature; for others it represents a destructive obsession.

simile—A comparison of two unlike things using the words *like* or *as:*

The unpaid bills hit him *like a tidal wave.*

The coffee was *as cold as ice.*

metaphor—A direct comparison of two unlike things made without using *like* or *as:*

> He was hit by *a tidal wave of unpaid bills.*
> We drank *ice-cold coffee.*

stanza—A unit of poetry named for the number of lines it contains:

couplet: two lines	sestet: six lines
triplet: three lines	septet: seven lines
quatrain: four lines	octave: eight lines
quintet: five lines	

epiphany—A sudden realization or burst of insight by an author or character.

Strategies for Reading Literature

1. **Survey the work and read available biographical or introductory material.** Many college anthologies include headnotes similar to those in the Reader portion of this book. Examine the biography carefully and review any questions that might appear after the text. Consult an encyclopedia or browse the Web for information about the author or background material about time and setting.
2. **Read the work once to get a first impression.** Allow yourself to read for pleasure. Enjoy the poem or story, noting passages you find interesting, difficult, powerful, or confusing.
3. **Review the overall work and ask questions.**
4. **Identify possible topics for discussion or writing.** Highlight significant passages for easy reference.
5. **Note aspects of the work you find puzzling or confusing.** Sometimes an author will present an image or make a historical reference you do not understand. Characters may use regional or slang expressions you are unfamiliar with. Look up confusing words in a dictionary. Discuss the work with other students who may know the meaning of a word or the significance of a reference or detail. Another reader may have an alternative interpretation that sharpens your analysis of the work.

QUESTIONS FOR LITERARY ANALYSIS

✔ What significance, if any, does the title have? What does it suggest?

✔ What is the time and setting of the story? Is it significant or only incidental?

✔ Who are the principal characters? What motivates their actions and influences their thoughts?

✔ How would you characterize the protagonist? Does he or she have internal or external conflicts? Does the protagonist appear to represent a group of people, a cause, or a set of values? What motivates the protagonist?

✔ How is the plot developed? What is the central conflict? Does the author use devices such as foreshadowing?

✔ Does the writer use imagery and symbols? What are they? What impact do they have?

✔ Who is the narrator? Is the story related in the first or third person? Does the narrator have limited or full knowledge of events and characters? If the story is told in the first person, is the narrator the protagonist, a minor character, or simply a witness?

✔ What seems to be the author's message? Does he or she appear to have a clearly stated opinion about events and characters? Is the author making a social or political statement?

✔ What are the significant themes in the work? If you had to write an essay about it, would you focus on a character, a pattern of imagery, the use of language, or the author's message?

✔ What lasting impression does the work create? What strikes you as being the most significant element of the work—a scene, a symbol, a character, the conflict, the author's message?

Strategies for Writing about Literature

1. **Avoid summarizing the work.** Although most writers analyzing a story, play, or poem will refer to the text, they do more than restate the plot.
   - Assume that everyone you are writing to has read the work. Your job, then, is not to retell the story but to reveal something other readers may have missed.

2. **Ask yourself questions.** One way to avoid writing a summary and identify an effective topic is to pose questions. Ask yourself about a character's behavior, the significance of the ending, or the meaning of a theme or symbol.

3. **Prewrite to explore the topic and develop a thesis.** Use brainstorming, clustering, or freewriting to investigate your topic. As you sketch out ideas, you may have to narrow or expand your approach.

4. **Develop a working thesis.** Your thesis should express a clear opinion about the meaning, structure, or style of the work:

   In *Death of a Salesman* Miller uses Uncle Charlie's relationship with his successful son Bernard to emphasize Willy Loman's failure as a father.

   The Great Gatsby presents a world in which marriage, the stock market, and even the World Series are corrupted by selfish greed.

5. **Support your thesis with evidence from the text.** Works of literature are subject to a variety of interpretations—but they should not be viewed as abstract sculptures that can mean anything you want. Your opinions must be based on evidence presented in the story or poem. If you assert that a

(Continued)

character is mentally ill, you must cite passages where the individual's speech, actions, or thoughts exhibit symptoms of a psychological disorder.

6. **Avoid extensive direct quotes.** Because your readers have read the work, there is no reason to repeat large sections of the text.
   - Use quotations when the author's image or a character's statement is so impressive that a paraphrase would weaken its impact.
   - Abbreviate longer quotations by selecting key words or phrases:

     Montresor leads Fortunato underground to the catacombs of "piled skeletons," guiding him through "low arches" where the narrow chambers are "lined with human remains."

7. **Quote poetry accurately.** When you quote a few lines within a paragraph, use a slash with a space before and after to indicate each original line break:

     Eliot's Prufrock muses at one point, "I should have been a pair of ragged claws / Scuttling across the floors of silent seas."

8. **Write in the present tense.** Although most works are written in past tense, writers usually describe an author's views and a character's action in present tense:

     Shakespeare *presents* his audience with a dramatic dilemma. How *does* an indecisive character like Hamlet *avenge* his father's death? Hamlet *muses* and *ponders* long before taking action to confront the king.

9. **Identify the most effective mode to organize supporting details.** You can structure an analysis by comparing two characters or events, defining a problem the protagonist faces, or discussing the causes or effects of a character's actions.

10. **After writing a first draft, review the work and then examine your thesis and support.**
    - Does your paper have a clear thesis?
    - Do you support the thesis with sufficient evidence from the text?
    - Is the support clearly organized? Would another mode be a better method of structuring the essay?

Writing about Fiction

Read the following story; then review the questions on page 610. Though short and starkly told, with little reference to time and setting, "The Bread" presents a strong plot marked by both a climax and anticlimax.

Wolfgang Borchert (1921–1947) was born in Hamburg, Germany, and worked as an actor and bookseller. During the Second World War he served in the German army in Russia and was wounded. An anti-Nazi, he was twice imprisoned for expressing defeatist views. He captured the despair and deprivation of the war in poems and short stories. Borchert died of a fever contracted during the war the day before the premiere of his play *Outside the Door*.

The Bread

Source: "The Bread" from *The Man Outside* by Wolfgang Borchert. Copyright © 1971 New Directions Publishing Corp., New York and Marion Boyars Publishers, London.

Borchert wrote this story when food was strictly rationed, forcing many families to survive on a few slices of bread a day.

1 Suddenly she woke up. It was half past two. She considered why she had woken up. Oh yes! In the kitchen someone had knocked against a chair. She listened to the kitchen. It was quiet. It was too quiet and as she moved her hand across the bed beside her, she found it empty. That was what had made it so particularly quiet: she missed his breathing. She got up and groped her way through the dark flat to the kitchen. In the kitchen they met. The time was half past two. She saw something white standing on the kitchen cupboard. She put the light on. They stood facing one another in their nightshirts. At night. At half past two. In the kitchen.

2 On the kitchen table lay the bread-plate. She saw that he had cut himself some bread. The knife was still lying beside the plate. And on the cloth there were bread-crumbs. When they went to bed at night, she always made the table-cloth clean. Every night. But now there were crumbs on the cloth. And the knife was lying there. She felt how the cold of the tiles crept slowly up her. And she looked away from the plate.

3 "I thought there was something here," he said and looked round the kitchen.

4 "I heard something, too," she answered and thought that at night, in his nightshirt, he really looked quite old. As old as he was. Sixty-three. During the day he sometimes looked younger. She looks quite old, he thought, in her nightdress she really looks pretty old. But perhaps it's because of her hair. With women at night it's always because of their hair. All at once it makes them so old.

5 "You should have put on your shoes. Barefoot like that on the cold tiles! You'll catch cold."

6 She didn't look at him, because she couldn't bear him to lie. To lie when they had been married thirty-nine years.

7 "I thought there was something here," he said once more and again looked so senselessly from one corner to the other, "I heard something in here. So I thought there'd be something here."

8 "I heard something, too. But it must have been nothing." She took the plate off the table and flicked the crumbs from the table-cloth.

9 "No, it must have been nothing," he echoed uncertainly.

10 She came to his help: "Come on. It must have been outside. Come to bed. You'll catch cold. On the cold tiles."

11   He looked at the window. "Yes, it'll have been outside. I thought it was in here."

12   She raised her hand to the switch. I must now put the light out, or I shall have to look at the plate, she thought. I dare not look at the plate. "Come on," she said and put out the light, "it must have been outside. The gutter always bangs against the wall when there's a wind. I'm sure it was the gutter. It always rattles when there's a wind."

13   They both groped their way along the dark corridor to the bedroom. Their naked feet slapped on the floor.

14   "It is windy," he said, "it's been windy all night."

15   As they lay in bed, she said: "Yes it's been windy all night. It must have been the gutter."

16   "Yes. I thought it was in the kitchen. It must have been the gutter." He said it as though he were already half asleep. But she noticed how false his voice sounded when he lied.

17   "It's cold," she said and yawned softly, "I'll creep under the covers. Good night."

18   "Night," he replied and added: "Yes, it really is pretty cold."

19   Then it was quiet. Many minutes later she heard him softly and cautiously chewing. She breathed deeply and evenly so that he should not notice that she was still awake. But his chewing was so regular that it slowly sent her to sleep.

20   When he came home the next evening, she put four slices of bread in front of him. At other times he had only been able to eat three.

21   "You can safely eat four," she said and moved away from the lamp. "I can't digest this bread properly. Just you eat another one. I don't digest it very well."

22   She saw how he bent deep over the plate. He didn't look up. At that moment she was sorry for him.

23   "You can't eat only two slices," he said to his plate.

24   "Yes, I can. I don't digest this bread properly in the evening. Just eat. Eat it."

25   Only a while later did she sit down at the table under the lamp.

QUESTIONS FOR ANALYSIS

1. Consider the title. How would your reading of the story differ if Borchert had titled it "The Betrayal" or "The Sacrifice"?

2. The author presents no details about time and location. Would they be helpful? Does the author seem to assume his readers understand the significance of a few slices of bread?

3. What characterizes the conflict between the husband and wife?

4. Review the dialogue between the two characters in the kitchen. Why doesn't the wife confront her husband? Why does she go along with his obvious lie?

5. How do you interpret the wife's final gesture?

6. Which event would you label the climax? Which scene represents an anticlimax?

7. What point of view does the author use in telling the story?

STUDENT PAPER

Monica Hernandez   World Literature 202

San Francisco State   Professor Sekulivich

Denial

At first reading Wolfgang Borchert's story about an old couple and a few slices of bread seems trivial, especially when cast against the mass murder and suffering of the Second World War. But by focusing on this small incident, Borchert is able to create a tightly focused drama that explores the toll hunger and deprivation can take on a person's character, morality, and self-respect.

More pointedly, Borchert's story is a study in denial, demonstrating the defense mechanisms people employ to protect themselves from something too painful to acknowledge.

"The Bread" presents a classic case of what current psychologists call "enabling." Awakened by a noise, a woman enters the kitchen and discovers clear evidence that her husband has cut a slice of bread, stealing food from her. Her husband, whom she knows is lying, offers a childishly clumsy explanation, claiming to be investigating a noise in the dark.

Instead of confronting her husband, the wife changes the subject, abruptly scolding him for not wearing shoes. When her husband haltingly explains that he heard a noise, she quickly agrees, enabling his deception. To leave the scene of the crime—the kitchen with its signs of his betrayal—she urges him to come to bed. Even when she hears him chewing the stolen bread, she remains silent.

In helping him lie, in going along and playing dumb, the wife is masking her pain and anger. It is a form of denial, a way of wishing this theft not to be true. This behavior is common in spouses who discover their partners are unfaithful or parents who encounter a child's drug abuse. The wife certainly must feel betrayed on many levels.

First, her husband was stealing food from her. Suffering severe hunger, he evidently did not ask for more bread or even discuss it with her. Instead, he stole. Second, when caught, he did not admit his guilt but lied. She must feel anger at this betrayal and perhaps disgust at his weakness, his inability to control his hunger and his failure to muster the courage to tell the truth and apologize.

The wife's final gesture is a wordless confrontation, letting her husband know that she is aware of his theft. Guilt-stricken, her husband cannot look her in the eye and asserts that she needs to eat more than two slices. The wife lies, claiming to have digestion problems. Her inability to sit at the table, however, reveals the extent of her anger. After decades of life together, the couple can only communicate with shared acts of deception.

Borchert's point is that hunger will drive one to steal from a loved one, to break the trust and love that held a couple together for almost forty years.

QUESTIONS FOR REVIEW AND WRITING

1. What is the student's thesis? Is it clearly stated?

2. Does the student provide enough support from the story?

3. The student introduces a psychological term. Is it suited to this essay? Should it be better explained?

4. Do any passages need expansion? Are there needless details that should be deleted?

5. How would you improve this commentary? Do you have an alternative interpretation of the woman's final gesture?

Writing about Poetry

Poetry is a literary form many students find challenging to analyze. Unlike the sweep of fiction, which offers a movie-like flow of events, a poem usually captures a scene, a moment, or a mood, like a painting or still photograph. Some poems are brief narratives and can be analyzed almost like a short story. Other poems, much like impressionist or abstract paintings, offer images and statements that resist literal interpretations.

Strategies for Writing about Poetry

1. **Read the poem aloud.** Poems rely on subtle relationships between words and meanings. You may find it easier to understand the patterns and language devices the poet uses by hearing the way the poem sounds.

2. **Use peer review.** Ask other students or friends about their understanding or interpretation of a poem, line, or image.

3. **Prewrite by writing a prose summary if possible.** Put the meaning or basic action of the poem in your own words. This may help you identify the literal meaning of the poem as well as topics for writing.

4. **Review the rhyme, meter, and form of the poem.** Notice how the cadence of words affects the poem's meaning.

5. **Look up key words in a dictionary.** Words may have subtle meanings or associations that might be unfamiliar to you. Because poems are brief, almost every word is significant.

Richard Cory

Whenever Richard Cory went down town,
We people on the pavement looked at him:
He was a gentleman from sole to crown,
Clean favored, and imperially slim.

And he was always quietly arrayed,
And he was always human when he talked;
But still he fluttered pulses when he said,
"Good-morning," and he glittered when he walked.

And he was rich—yes, richer than a king—
And admirably schooled in every grace:
In fine, we thought that he was everything
To make us wish that we were in his place.

So on we worked, and waited for the light,
And went without the meat, and cursed the bread;
And Richard Cory, one calm summer night,
Went home and put a bullet through his head.

QUESTIONS FOR ANALYSIS

1. What kind of person is Richard Cory? What attitude does the narrator have toward him?

2. The narrator refers to himself or herself as representing the "people on the pavement." What kind of people would they be?

3. What does this poem say about wealth and envy?

4. What impact does the final line have? What does it leave unanswered or unexplained?

STUDENT PAPER

Michael Knox   Introduction to Literature

One Calm Summer Night: Contrast and Irony in Robinson's "Richard Cory"

"Richard Cory" endures as one of the most memorable and widely anthologized American poems, largely because of its surprise ending. The "lesson" of the poem—that you can't judge a book by its cover—is quite simple but so powerfully stated that it makes a profound impression on most readers. Robinson uses contrast and irony in both content and form to maximize the impact of the unexpected and unexplained suicide of his admired protagonist.

First, there is the ironic contrast of Richard Cory's wealth and his eventual suicide. The title character is handsome, slim, wealthy, elegant, yet "always human." The poem, told from the standpoint of the "people on the pavement," celebrates Richard Cory as someone who embodies everything people admire. Cory, though wealthy and aristocratic, appears modest and graceful. Although poor, the townspeople do not resent Cory's wealth. Like a celebrity, Cory has the power to flutter their pulses by simply acknowledging their presence when he passes them on the street. Working, waiting for the light, living without meat, these common people continue with their pedestrian lives while on a calm summer night the admired Cory shoots himself. Seeing his wealth and grace only from a distance, Cory's poor admirers had no knowledge of his inner life, no hint of the turmoil or depression that led him to commit suicide.

Second, the impact of the poem is heightened by the contrast between syntax and subject matter. In telling the story of a suicide, Robinson writes in the unadorned language of a children's poem. The lines read easily in the simple humdrum pattern and flow of a Mother Goose rhyme. The sing-song effect of the poem makes the violent ending unexpected. In addition, the tone and mood of the poem is largely positive and cheerful. The royal connotations of words describing Cory—"king," "imperially," and "crown"—all contrast with the despair and desperation associated with suicide. All these elements work to create a stunning and memorable ending, making both townspeople and readers perplexed by the mystery of Cory's suicide.

QUESTIONS FOR REVIEW AND WRITING

1. What is the student's thesis?
2. Does the student provide enough detail from the poem to support the thesis?
3. How do you interpret the poem's meaning?
4. Robinson titled the poem with the protagonist's name. Would a more descriptive title give the end away and weaken the impact of the last line?
5. The reasons for Cory's suicide are never explained. What is Robinson's point?
6. How would you improve or expand this student's analysis?

WRITING ACTIVITY

Read the following poem, and then write a short analysis of its meaning, structure, or imagery.

My Life Had Stood—A Loaded Gun—

My Life had stood—a Loaded Gun—
In Corners—till a Day
The Owner passed—identified—
And carried Me away—

And now We roam in Sovereign Woods—
and now We hunt the Doe—
And every time I speak for Him—
The Mountains straight reply—

And do I smile, such cordial light
Upon the Valley glow—
It is as a Vesuvian face
Had let its pleasure through—

And when at Night—Our good Day done—
I guard my Master's Head—
'Tis better than the Eider-Duck's
Deep Pillow—to have shared—

To foe of His—I'm deadly foe—
None stir the second time—
On whom I lay a Yellow Eye—
Or an emphatic Thumb—

Though I than He—may longer live
He longer must—than I—
For I have but the power to kill,
Without—the power to die—

—Emily Dickinson

Source: "My Life Had Stood–A Loaded Gun" by Emily Dickinson. From *The Poems of Emily Dickinson.* Thomas H. Johnson, ed., Cambridge, Mass.: The Belknap Press of Harvard University Press, Copyright © 1951, 1955, 1979, 1983 by the President and Fellows of Harvard College. By permission.

Writing about Drama

Although most plays relate a narrative with a strong emphasis on plot and character development, they differ from stories and novels because the events must be presented through dialogue. If you are unaccustomed to reading plays, you can easily become lost in the interplay among characters.

Strategies for Writing about Drama

1. **Study the set and character descriptions.** Read and review the opening descriptions of each character so you can identify each one.

2. **Review the playwright's biography, other works, or information about the time and place.** If you know something about the writer's concerns or the setting of the play, you may be able to more easily identify key themes or appreciate subtle details.

3. **Visualize the set and actors.** Plays are meant to be seen, not read. Study the set descriptions and imagine what the stage would look like. Is this a living room, warehouse, nightclub, or battlefield? Would it be darkly or brilliantly lit? Does the background suggest a conflict with or between the characters? After reading descriptions of the characters, imagine the actor or actress who might play the part. If you can imagine faces instead of names, you can more easily follow the plot and understand the interplay among characters.

4. **If possible, attend a live performance of a play or watch a filmed version.**

5. **Try to locate films or videotapes of actual stage performances rather than traditional motion pictures.**

6. **Read important lines aloud.** Hearing the words of a protagonist's final speech can bring the text to life and help you appreciate the impact it would have on a live audience.

7. **Study the structure of the play.** Plays are usually divided into acts and scenes, many of which end with an important turn of events, revelation, or conflict. Focus on the way each act ends.

WRITING ACTIVITY

Read this scene from Eugene O'Neill's 1919 play *The Straw* and write a short analysis of one of the following: the conflict between the characters, the exposition of the plot, or the playwright's implied message.

Background: In this scene Dr. Gaynor informs Bill Carmody, a working-class Irishman, that his daughter Eileen has tuberculosis and needs treatment in a sanitarium. Gaynor barely conceals his contempt for Carmody's ignorance and his concern about money.

> **GAYNOR** (*seating himself by the table—gravely*). Your daughter is very seriously ill.

> **CARMODY** (*irritably*). Aw, Doctor, didn't I know you'd be sayin' that, anyway!

> **GAYNOR** (*ignoring this remark—coldly*). Your daughter has tuberculosis of the lungs.

CARMODY (*with puzzled awe*). Too-ber-c'losis?

GAYNOR Consumption, if that makes it plainer to you.

CARMODY (*with dazed terror—after a pause*). Consumption? Eileen? (*With sudden anger.*) What lie is it you're tellin' me?

GAYNOR (*icily*). Look here, Carmody! I'm not here to stand for your insults!

CARMODY (*bewilderingly*). Don't be angry, now, at what I said. Sure I'm out of my wits entirely. Eileen to have the consumption! Ah, Doctor, sure you must be mistaken!

GAYNOR There's no chance for a mistake, I'm sorry to say. Her right lung is badly affected.

CARMODY (*desperately*). It's a bad cold only, maybe.

GAYNOR (*curtly*). Don't talk nonsense. (*Carmody groans. Gaynor continues authoritatively.*) She will have to go to a sanatorium at once. She ought to have been sent to one months ago. The girl's been keeping up on her nerve when she should have been in bed, and it's given the disease a chance to develop. (*Casts a look of indignant scorn at Carmody, who is sitting staring at the floor with an expression of angry stupor on his face.*) It's a wonder to me you didn't see the condition she was in and force her to take care of herself. Why, the girl's nothing but skin and bone!

CARMODY (*with vague fury*). God blast it!

GAYNOR No, your kind never realises things till the crash comes—usually when it's too late. She kept on doing her work, I suppose—taking care of her brothers and sisters, washing, cooking, sweeping, looking after your comfort—worn out—when she should have been in bed—and—(*He gets to his feet with a harsh laugh.*) But what's the use of talking? The damage is done. We've got to set to work to repair it at once. I'll write to-night to Dr. Stanton of the Hill Farm Sanatorium and find out if he has a vacancy. And if luck is with us we can send her there at once. The sooner the better.

CARMODY (*his face growing red with rage*). Is it sendin' Eileen away to a hospital you'd be? (*Exploding.*) Then you'll not! You'll get that notion out of your head damn quick. It's all nonsense you're stuffin' me with, and lies, makin' things out to be the worst in the world. I'll not believe a word of Eileen having the consumption at all. It's doctors' notions to be always lookin' for a sickness that'd kill you. She'll not move a step out of here, and I say so, and I'm her father!

GAYNOR (*who has been staring at him with contempt—coldly angry*). You refuse to let your daughter go to a sanatorium?

CARMODY I do.

GAYNOR (*threateningly*). Then I'll have to report her case to the Society for the Prevention of Tuberculosis of this county, and tell them of your refusal to help her.

CARMODY (*wavering a bit*). Report all you like, and be damned to you!

GAYNOR (*ignoring the interruption—impressively*). A majority of the most influential men of this city are behind the Society. Do you know that? (*Grimly.*) We'll find a way to move you, Carmody, if you try to be stubborn.

(Continued)

CARMODY (*thoroughly frightened, but still protesting*). Ara, Doctor, you don't see the way of it at all. If Eileen goes to the hospital, who's to be takin' care of the others, and mindin' the house when I'm off to work?

GAYNOR You can easily hire some woman.

CARMODY (*at once furious again*). Hire? D'you think I'm a millionaire itself?

GAYNOR (*contemptuously*). That's where the shoe pinches, eh? (*In a rage.*) I'm not going to waste any more words on you, Carmody, but I'm damn well going to see this thing through! You might as well give in first as last.

CARMODY (*wailing*). But where's the money comin' from?

GAYNOR (*brutally*). That's your concern. Don't lie about your poverty. You've a steady well-paid job, and plenty of money to throw away on drunken sprees, I'll bet. The weekly fee at the Hill Farm is only seven dollars. You can easily afford that—the price of a few rounds of drinks.

CARMODY Seven dollars! And I'll have to pay a woman to come in—and the four of the children eatin' their heads off! Glory be to God, I'll not have a penny saved for me old age—and then it's the poor-house!

Source: "The Straw" by Eugene O'Neill. Copyright © 1922 by Jonathan Cape.

LITERARY PAPER CHECKLIST

Before submitting a literary paper, review these points:

✔ Have you selected a work that is appropriate for the assignment?

✔ Does your paper *analyze* or only *summarize* a literary work?

✔ Does your paper focus on a specific element of the work, such as the imagery, structure, character development, or plot—or does it attempt to explain everything the writer presents?

✔ Is the thesis clearly stated and supported by details taken from the text?

✔ Do you avoid quoting passages out of context?

For Further Reading

Barnet, Sylvan. *A Short Guide to Writing about Literature.*

Callaghan, Patsy, and Ann Dobyns. *Literary Conversation: Thinking, Talking, and Writing about Literature.*

Frye, Northrop. *The Educated Imagination.*

Griffith, Kelley. *Writing Essays about Literature: A Guide and Style Sheet.*

Kurata, Marilyn Jane. *Models and Methods for Writing about Literature.*

McMahan, Elizabeth, Robert Funk, and Susan Day. *The Elements of Writing about Literature and Film.*

Meyer, Michael. *Thinking and Writing about Literature.*

Proffitt, Edward. *Reading and Writing about Literature: Fiction, Poetry, Drama, and the Essay.*

E-Sources

Online Writing Lab at Purdue: Writing in Literature
  http://owl.english.purdue.edu/owl/section/4/17/

University of North Carolina—Chapel Hill, Writing Center: Literature (Fiction)
  http://www.unc.edu/depts/wcweb/handouts/literature.html

U.N.C. Writing Center: Poetry Explications
  http://www.unc.edu/depts/wcweb/handouts/poetry-explication.html

U.N.C. Writing Center: Drama
  http://www.unc.edu/depts/wcweb/handouts/drama.html

 Access the English CourseMate for this text at **www.cengagebrain.com** for additional information on writing about literature.

Writing in the
Information Age

5

Image versus reality

Analyzing Visuals

Seeing With a Writer's Eye

We increasingly communicate in images. We are bombarded daily with advertisements on television and online. College textbooks, which thirty years ago consisted of only text, now feature graphs and photographs on nearly every page. Websites, once blocks of words, now include streaming video. Cable news networks provide images of fast-breaking events twenty-four hours a day. The personal computer and desktop publishing enable students and small-business owners to develop sophisticated multimedia presentations rivaling those created by major corporations. Digital cameras allow people to instantly transmit photos and video worldwide.

Images can be used to grab attention, evoke an emotional response, record events, document conditions, record evidence, illustrate an idea or condition, establish a mood, or develop a context for discussion. Images can be presented without comment or woven into the text of a written message.

Photographs, Film, and Video

Photographs, film, and video are compelling. There is an impression that "the camera does not lie." A written description never seems as objective or as accurate as a photograph. The camera, we believe, hides nothing. It tells the whole truth. It leaves nothing out. People writing reports about a car accident can exaggerate or minimize the damage, but a photograph, we assume, provides us with irrefutable evidence. Yet visuals can be highly subjective and often misleading. They require careful analysis to determine their meaning and reliability.

The impression a photograph or video makes is shaped by a number of factors: perspective and contrast, context, timing and duplication, manipulation, and captions.

Perspective and Contrast

How large is a group of a hundred? How tall is a twenty-story building? The impression we get of events, objects, and people depends on perspective, the angle and distance of the camera and the subject. A hundred protesters photographed in close-up will look like an overwhelming force. Fists raised, faces twisted in emotion, lunging toward the camera, they can appear all-powerful and unstoppable. Photographed from a distance, the crowd can seem small against a landscape of multistory buildings or acres of empty pavement. In contrast to large fixed objects, the protest can

Maria Toutoudaki/jupiterimages

Sam Diephuis/jupiterimages

The image as icon. Elvis autographs photographs for fans.

appear futile and weak. If ordinary people going about routine business are shown in the foreground, the protesters, in contrast, may appear abnormal, ephemeral, even pathetic. A twenty-story building in a suburban neighborhood of two-story structures will loom over the landscape. Located in midtown Manhattan, dwarfed by skyscrapers, the same structure will seem undersized, less formidable, even homey in contrast.

An individual can appear large or small, weak or powerful, depending on perspective. Charles Lindbergh is shown on this page in close-up. His face fills the frame. No other people, structures, or objects detract from his larger-than-life presence. In addition, he is photographed wearing his flight helmet and goggles, emblems of his famous 1927 transatlantic flight. His clear eyes look upward as if gazing to the horizon and the future. This photograph depicts a human being as powerful, in command of

Charles Lindbergh, 1927

his environment. It is the type of image seen in movie posters, postage stamps, official portraits, and celebrity stills. Shown in isolation, any subject can appear dominant because there is nothing else to compare it to.

In contrast to Lindbergh's picture, the photograph of James Dean in Times Square is shot at some distance. Unlike Lindbergh, Dean is shown not in isolation but within an environment. Though he is at the center of the photograph, his stature is diminished by the urban landscape. Tall buildings rise above him. The iron fence on the right restricts his freedom of movement. In addition, the environment is hostile—dark, cold, and wet. Dean is hunched forward, his collar turned up against the wind, his hands buried in his pockets against the cold. The picture creates an image of brooding loneliness and alienation, suited to Dean's Hollywood image as a loner and troubled rebel.

The impression created of Lee Harvey Oswald is shaped by perspective. In the press photo taken (on page 626) shortly after his arrest, Oswald looks weak, subdued, cowardly. He is literally cornered, shown off-center at the edge of the frame. Though he is the subject of the photograph, he is markedly smaller in relation to the officers. The angle of the camera distorts the relative sizes of the figures so that

James Dean in Times Square, 1955
Dennis Stock/Magnum Photos

the uniformed men in the foreground are oversized, their power and authority emphasized. The officer's badge appears larger than Oswald's head. The room is blank and featureless. Handcuffed and still disheveled from his arrest, Oswald is depicted as a disarmed menace, an assassin rendered harmless.

Context

Photographs and video images are isolated glimpses of larger events. A camera captures a split second of reality, but it does not reveal what happened before or after the image was taken. The photograph of a baseball player hitting a home run shows a moment of athletic triumph, but it does not reveal the player's batting average or who won the game.

Motion picture and video cameras offer us a window onto the world, bringing world events into our homes—but it is a narrow window. Watching an evening of cable network news creates the illusion that you are being informed about world events. In thirty minutes you see a conflict in the Middle East, a White House spokesperson, a senator commenting on the economy, a high-speed car chase in San Diego. But cable news is highly limited to covering visual stories. More complicated stories may not provide gripping visuals or may require too much explanation to make good television. Stories that break in developed countries within easy reach of media crews receive more coverage than do events that occur in remote areas.

Lee Harvey Oswald under arrest, Dallas, 1963   © AP Photos

Juries have acquitted people caught on videotape buying drugs or engaged in violent assaults. Whereas the public often only sees a dramatic segment, juries are often shown a videotape in its entirety. Defense attorneys place the tape in context by providing additional information about the people and events depicted. By raising doubts, they can persuade a jury to rethink what it has seen, questioning the tape's meaning and reliability.

Visual Connotations

Like words, images have connotations. They create emotional responses. Politicians are interviewed in front of flags and bookshelves to demonstrate patriotism and indicate knowledge. Campaign commercials show candidates with their families, visiting the elderly, shaking hands with firefighters, or visiting veterans to link themselves with positive images. Ads and commercials will use provocative images of sex and violence to arrest people's attention. Book covers and movie posters only vaguely associated with World War II often feature a large swastika because it is a symbol bound to attract attention.

Certain images become icons, symbols of an event, culture, attitude, or value. Reproduced in books, films, on murals, and T-shirts, they serve to communicate a message with a single image. Marilyn Monroe's upswirled skirt symbolizes sex. The photograph of two African American athletes raising gloved fists at the 1968 Olympic Games became an icon of Black Power. The World Trade Center attack has become an international symbol of terrorism.

Patriotic symbols featured in
recruiting ad

© 2002. Paid for by the United States Army/U.S. Army

Osama bin Laden replaces Uncle Sam in political ad

© TimPaine.com, an online public interest journal, a project of
the nonprofit Florence

The image for a recruiting ad (above, left) features a close-up of a soldier in a
beret, with the Lincoln Memorial in the background, an emblem of democracy. The
Pentagon, an actual target in the terrorist attacks of September 11, would no doubt
appear too militaristic. Lincoln, though a wartime leader, is also a symbol of unity,
humanity, and wisdom.

In contrast, an advertisement opposing administration foreign policy (above, right)
uses humor and irony. Osama bin Laden replaces Uncle Sam in a historic recruiting
poster. The irony of the image grabs attention. The accompanying text is also ironic,
urging readers to support what the writers clearly consider the wrong policies.

Both ads appeared in the same issue of *Rolling Stone*.

Timing and Duplication

Timing and duplication can enhance an image's impact and distort perceptions. If
two celebrities meet briefly at a crowded special event and photographs of them shaking hands are widely reproduced over several months, it can create the impression
they are close friends. The two figures become a single image repeatedly imprinted
on the public, few recognizing that they are simply seeing the same moment from
different angles. Stalin, Roosevelt, and Churchill only met on a few occasions during the Second World War, but the continual reproduction of photographs of them
together helped create the image of the Big Three as a solid alliance against Hitler.

Cable news reports of a suicide bombing, a shooting spree, or a car chase will recycle scenes over and over, often creating an exaggerated sense of their significance.

Manipulating Images

Just as painters in a king's court often depicted royalty in flattering poses without blemishes, photographers and filmmakers can use lighting, perspective, and contrast to alter perceptions of reality. Short actors can be made to seem taller on screen by lowering cameras or placing taller people in the background. Makeup and lighting can magnify or diminish facial features, improving someone's appearance. Even candid images can be carefully selected to show a subject in a positive light. Portraits and photographs of Kaiser Wilhelm and Joseph Stalin camouflaged the fact that each man had one arm noticeably shorter than the other. Wishing to project power and authority, each leader wished to disguise his physical disability. Although most Americans knew that President Roosevelt had been stricken with polio, few were aware how severely handicapped he actually was. The media did not release films of him in motion. Photographs and newsreels showed him standing or seated. The

President Wilson and General Pershing. A retoucher has partially erased a figure walking behind the two famous men, altering the perception of a historical event. Frequently, negative or distracting images are removed from pictures to enhance their effect.

© US Army Signal Corps/Time & Life Pictures/Getty Images

fact that he often had to be lifted out of cars or carried up steps was not made public. Although suffering from a painful back injury and Addison's disease, President Kennedy projected an image of youth and vigor by being shown in athletic contexts, playing touch football, swimming, or boating.

Photographs and film can be edited, revised, cut, and altered after the fact. A group photo can be reduced to focus on a single person. People and objects can be added or removed to alter the record of actual events. Leon Trotsky was once a powerful Soviet leader, often photographed standing next to Lenin. Wishing to obliterate his rival's role in the Russian Revolution, Stalin had thousands of pictures retouched to erase Trotsky from history.

Today, with computer technology, images can be digitally removed and inserted. Photographs, motion pictures, and videos now have an increasing power to create their own reality, which may exaggerate, minimize, or distort actual events.

Gender and Cultural Issues

Images, like language, affect our perceptions. Historically, images have reflected prevailing attitudes and biases. Words like *policeman, mankind, mailman,* and the universal use of *he* as a single pronoun gave English a distinct sexist stance. Historically, photographs focused on male activities, actions, and behaviors, with women generally appearing as family members or sex objects. Photographs of minorities often reflected and generated stereotyped views; African Americans were often depicted in subservient, patronizing, or comic roles. Automobile ads often show men standing next to or driving a car, while women are draped across the hood as a kind of ornament. As gender roles change, popular culture and advertising alter our perceptions of men and women.

Social change reflected by a clash of traditional gender images. Makeup and jewelry are decidedly feminine, in stark contrast to the masculine hard hat.

© Vincent Hobbs/Superstock

Perception and Analysis

Our analysis of images is shaped by our perceptions, both personal and cultural. A photograph taken in Iran depicts a male professor lecturing female seminary students from behind a screen (page 630). To Western eyes, this image can seem a shocking example of oppression and exclusion. To many Iranians, however, the image of women studying Islam represents inclusion and empowerment.

In Iran, a male professor lectures female students from behind a screen.

© Lise Sarfati/Magnum Photos

Strategies for Analyzing Visual Images

1. **Examine the image holistically.** What is your initial reaction? Does it convey a message?

2. **Consider the nature of the image.** Is this a professional portrait or a candid press shot? Was this video taken at a prepared ceremony or a spontaneous event? Were people, images, or objects deliberately posed to make a statement?

3. **Examine perspective.** Is the subject depicted in close-up or at a distance? Does the subject appear in control of the environment, or does the background dominate the frame?

4. **Analyze contrasts and contexts.** Is the background supportive, neutral, or hostile to the subject? Does the image depict conflict or harmony?

5. **Examine poses and body language of human figures.** How are human figures depicted? What emotions do they seem to express?

6. **Look for bias.** Do you sense that the photographers were trying to manipulate the people or events depicted, casting them in either a favorable or negative light?

7. **Consider the larger context.** Does the image offer a fair representation of a larger event, or is it an isolated exception?
8. **Review the image for possible manipulation.** Could camera angles or retouching have altered what appears to be a record of actual events?
9. **Consider the story the image seems to tell.** What is the thesis of this image? What visual details or symbols help tell the story?

Captions

Images are frequently accompanied by captions that can shape the way people interpret them. Descriptive or narrative captions place an image in a context, often using verbal connotations to shape perceptions.

For example, the news photograph of a riot in India following the assassination of Indira Gandhi in 1984 (below) could be accompanied by a range of captions:

New Delhi, India, 1984
Police attack demonstrators
Police quell riot
Protesters clash with police following Gandhi assassination
Violence erupts in India following Gandhi assassination
Police restore order following Gandhi assassination

Each caption would prompt readers of a magazine or newspaper to view the image in a different light. Captions, in many cases, can be as powerful as the image they

Jacques Langevin/Sygma/Corbis

Strategies for Analyzing Captions

1. **Examine the photograph before reading the caption.** How do you interpret the image? What can you tell from the setting, perspective, contrast, and visual connotations?

2. **Read the caption carefully.** Does it contain objective information about time, date, and location, or subjective commentary?

3. **Review the use of connotations.** Do the words accompanying the image suggest positive or negative interpretations of what is depicted? Is a small residential building described as a "cottage" or a "shack"? Is a bulldozer "destroying" or "clearing" a forest? Is a politician "waving off journalists leaving a press conference" or "ducking reporters"?

4. **Read the accompanying text.** If the photograph appears in a book, article, or e-mail, read the text to determine whether the author reveals any bias.

5. **Reconsider the validity of the image.** If you detect bias in the caption, consider whether the image has been taken out of context and does not fairly represent what it claims to. Search the Web for other images of the event or situation to discover alternative views of the subject.

---

describe. Captions can turn photojournalism into propaganda or reveal personal and social biases. In the days following Hurricane Katrina, one newspaper ran a photograph of a white couple wading through floodwaters in New Orleans with a caption describing them as carrying supplies they "found" in a convenience store. Other newspapers ran similar photographs of blacks with captions describing them as carrying supplies they "looted."

The power that images have can be illustrated by examining a single photograph. See "The History of an Image" on pages 637–642.

Graphics

Graphics are a visual representation of numbers and facts. Like photographs, they are compelling because they communicate a fact in an instant. But like photographs, they can alter perceptions by use of different perspectives.

For instance, if a company's sales increase 7 percent in a year, it can be accurately demonstrated in a graph:

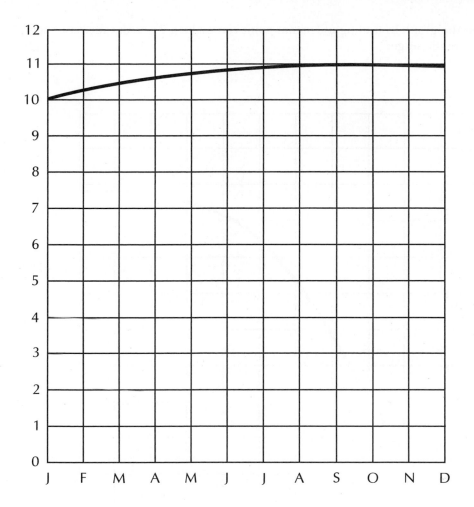

The same 7 percent can look larger by truncating the graph, cutting off the bottom to exaggerate the increase:

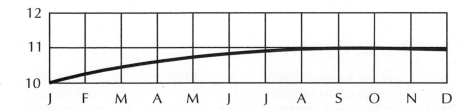

Altering the graph by adding a decimal point can make a 7 percent increase seem like a dramatic surge:

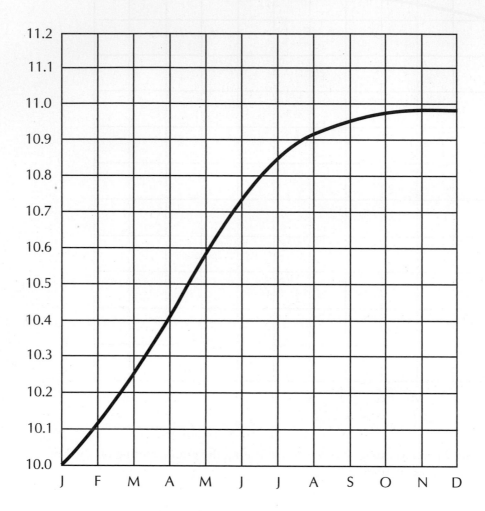

None of these graphs is inaccurate or dishonest, but each alters perceptions for the casual viewer.

An illustration can use a visual illusion to make things seem larger or smaller than they actually are. Suppose a corporation wants to impress investors with the fact that it doubled profits last year from $30 million to $60 million. A simple bar chart demonstrates the difference quite dramatically:

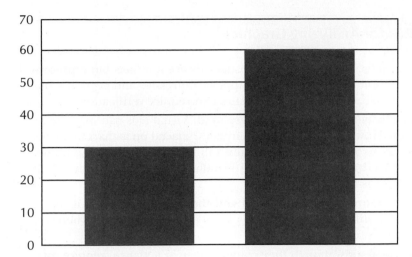

The bar on the right fills twice the space as the bar on the left, accurately showing the relationship between 30 and 60. If the bar, however, is replaced with an image like a money bag, the visual depiction makes an even more dramatic impact:

Unlike the bar which rises vertically in only one direction, the bag of money is enlarged in two directions. The bag representing $60 million is both twice as high and twice as wide as the $30 million bag. If you take the time to look at the numbers on the left side of the chart, you realize the difference is that between 30 and 60. But because the big money bag takes four times, not two times, as much space as the smaller one, it looks four times the size. It would take $120 million to fill this bag. The chart does not lie, the numbers are accurate, but again the visual impression distorts perceptions.

Just as a snapshot captures a brief moment of reality, a visual aid can distort reality by presenting carefully selected data that are accurate but misleading.

Strategies for Analyzing Graphics

1. **Realize that graphs, charts, and other visual aids are not facts but representations of facts.** Detailed graphics can appear impressive and accurate, but their visuals are based on facts and statistics that require verification.

2. **Examine how facts and numbers are displayed.** Visual aids can magnify or minimize facts. How much is $7 million in sales? Placed on a chart that runs from $1 million to $10 million, $7 million will fill 70 percent of the frame. Placed on a chart that runs from $1 to $100 million, the same amount will fill only 7 percent of the frame.

3. **Determine the source of the visual aid and the numbers or facts it represents.** Visual aids, like statistics, can only be objectively evaluated when you understand their source.

4. **Realize that visual aids, though they communicate at a glance, require dual analysis.** First, you must verify whether the numbers depicted are current, accurate, and meaningful. Second, you must determine if the visual aid distorts the facts, presenting them in such a way to prove a preconception.

e-writing

Exploring Visual Images Online

The Web offers a range of sources about analyzing photographs, advertisements, commercials, and film.

1. Using InfoTrac College Edition, available through your English CourseMate at **www.cengagebrain.com,** or one of your library's databases, enter such search terms as *analyzing photographs, image analysis, video analysis, manipulating images,* and *retouching photographs* to learn more about visual images.

2. Enter such terms as *photo analysis, images of women in advertising, political propaganda,* and *graphic design* into a search engine to locate current sites of interest.

E-Sources

Nuovo Contemporary Art: Basic Strategies in Reading Photographs
    http://nuovo.com/southern-images/analyses.html
James Curtis: Making Sense of Documentary Photography
    http://historymatters.gmu.edu/mse/photos/
Paul Martin Lester: Faking Images in Photojournalism
    http://commfaculty.fullerton.edu/lester/writings/faking.html

THE HISTORY OF AN IMAGE

Iwo Jima, February 23, 1945

AP Photo/Joe Rosenthal

If you can get the right moment, the instant, it stays around forever.

—Carl Mydans, *Life* photographer

The photograph of the anonymous Marines lifting in poetic unison the flag on Iwo Jima has been read as the final flowering of the collectivist vision of the New Deal, a group of anonymous men unified in a common purpose to restore the nation's glory, the arching flag.

—Don Graham, *No Name on the Bullet*

Capturing the Moment

The most widely reproduced photograph in history is the flag raising on Iwo Jima taken by Joe Rosenthal. On February 19, 1945, thirty thousand U.S. Marines landed on Iwo Jima, a heavily fortified, Japanese-held island.

THE HISTORY OF AN IMAGE

Joe Rosenthal, AP cameraman
Image by © Bettmann/CORBIS

First flag raised on Iwo Jima
AP Photo/Louis R. Lowery

The battle lasted thirty-six days and claimed six thousand American lives. On February 23, 1945, Marines raised a flag atop Mount Suribachi, the highest point on the island. The sight of this flag inspired the men fighting on the beaches. Later that day, it was decided to replace this flag with a larger one.

Joe Rosenthal, an AP photographer, accompanied several Marines and military cameramen to the summit. Rosenthal was getting into position when the Marines began to raise the flag. He quickly swung his camera around and snapped a picture. Unsure whether he had taken a usable photo, he asked the Marines to gather around the flagpole for a group picture.

The Making of an Icon

Rosenthal's film was flown to Guam, where a technician spotted the dramatic picture of the flag raising, cropped off the edges to center the image, and wired it to the United States. Within days the picture appeared on the front pages of hundreds of newspapers. President Roosevelt was impressed by the photograph and ordered millions of copies to boost morale and promote

THE HISTORY OF AN IMAGE

Marines pose for Rosenthal's camera

© Bettman/CORBIS

the sale of war bonds. The image appeared on stamps and posters and was recreated in statues.

Confusion and Controversy

The image was so dramatic that it raised doubts. It seemed too perfect to be an action photo of an actual event. A reporter asked Rosenthal, who had no idea the flag raising had become a national sensation, whether he had posed the shot. Thinking the reporter was referring to his group picture (above), he said yes. A radio program then reported the famous photo was posed, starting a long-standing rumor that the image was just a piece of wartime propaganda. For fifty years, Rosenthal repeatedly insisted it was a genuine photograph of a real event.

Historians still debate the validity of the image. Most agree that the photograph, taken by accident, depicts a genuine event, the raising of the second flag on Iwo Jima. It was not the flag that inspired the Marines fighting on the beaches but a replacement that few noticed at the time. There was no question about the bravery and sacrifice of the Marines in the photograph. Of the six flag raisers, three died on Iwo Jima.

THE HISTORY OF AN IMAGE

"Now All Together" War Loan Poster, 1945
Image by © Swim Ink 2, LLC/CORBIS

Flag-raising statue unveiled in Times
Square, May 1945
© Bettmann/CORBIS

Marine Corps War Memorial, dedicated 1954   Image by © William Manning/CORBIS

THE HISTORY OF AN IMAGE

Marines re-enact Iwo Jima flag raising, Doss, Texas, 2005
Image by © Bob Daemmrich/Corbis

Marines re-create flag raising during Hollywood Christmas Parade, 2004
Image by © Fred Prouser/Reuters/Corbis

The flag raising inspired the USMC memorial and led to many reen-actments in subsequent years.

The Other Flag Raising

Throughout the cold war, textbooks in the United States featured Rosenthal's photograph as a symbol of victory at the end of World War II. Soviet textbooks ran Yevgeny Khaldei's photograph of a Russian soldier raising the Red flag over the Reichstag after the fall of Berlin (next page).

Images snapped in 1/400th of a second can define a war, a nation, and an ideology.

THE HISTORY OF AN IMAGE

Soviet flag raising over Berlin, May 1945

Image by © Yevgeny Khaldei/CORBIS

Soviet photographer Yevgeny Khaldei compares flag raisings, Moscow, 1996

Image by © Peter Turnley/CORBIS

Writing with Visuals

Visual images—photographs, diagrams, charts, maps, drawings, and graphs—can enhance written documents. Pictures can bring a description to life, dramatize a situation, and document an event. Graphs and charts help readers visualize and comprehend data and statistics. Images create immediate impressions that can attract attention, establish a context, and shape reader expectations.

Visuals must be used carefully. Like the words you choose, images must suit the writing context and not detract from the goal of the document. Visuals that are effective in one document may be inappropriate in another.

Visuals and the Writing Context

The Internet and digital photography make it very easy to download images or incorporate your own photographs into documents. Effective visuals can add depth and rigor to your writing. Inappropriate visuals, however, can distract readers and weaken a document by making it appear amateurish and unprofessional. Before including visuals in a paper, it is important to consider the writing context or genre.

- *What is your goal—to inform, persuade, refute an argument, or motivate people to take action?* What visuals, if any, will support your purpose?

- *Who are your readers? What are their needs, attitudes, values, and concerns?* Will they respond favorably to your visuals? Images that some people find amusing may be offensive to others. Will they understand how the images support your text or the meaning of your graphs or charts?

- *What is the discipline or situation?* Engineers, contractors, and architects will demand far more precise plans or drawings of a proposed building than the general public will. Historians and political scientists scrutinize photographs of historical events for signs of bias. Journalists may question the sources of your images. Professors in subjects that stress the written word, such as philosophy and literature, may view visual images as unnecessary and distracting.

- *What is the nature of the document?* An ad for a sports car or a fund-raising e-mail for a charity has to communicate at a glance with a striking and memorable image. A formal research paper or business report may be expected to follow specific guidelines and standards in presenting visuals. Review sample documents to determine which, if any, visuals are considered appropriate.

Maria Toutoudaki/jupiterimages

Sam Diephuis/jupiterimages

The Role of Visuals

Visuals serve specific purposes. **Design features,** such as photographs, decorative borders, stylistic lettering, logos, and symbols, can identify a subject, idea, or organization, set a tone or mood, and prepare readers to view information in a specific context. A website titled "Famous African Americans," featuring images of W. E. B. Dubois, Martin Luther King, and Thurgood Marshall, instantly creates a different impression and set of expectations than one displaying pictures of Oprah, Beyoncé, and Chris Rock. A brochure about homelessness, containing pictures of church volunteers distributing food baskets, immediately announces a different purpose and approach than one showing activists marching on city hall. Macy's uses a changing series of colorful images from its stores on its consumer website to sell products to the general public. The same company features a stock chart, news links, and the cover of its annual report on its investors web page to establish a formal, businesslike image.

- Design features are essential in web pages, posters, brochures, ads, newsletters, promotional material, and product packaging.
- Design features in college papers and formal business reports, which are expected to communicate through substance rather than image, are generally limited to text decisions, such as fonts, spacing, and margins. Decorative borders and elaborate logos are avoided.
- Design features should match the tone and style of the document's level of diction and connotation.

General illustrations and attention-getters, such as a striking image, graph, or photograph, can serve to attract attention and illustrate an idea. They often appear without captions in popular magazines, promotional literature, and websites. The student paper "Why They Hate Us" (pages 432–434) uses a photograph of flag burning to identify the topic. The paper itself does not refer to the image explicitly. It serves only to attract attention and reinforce the title.

- Illustrations and attention-getters have to be chosen carefully to elicit the response you want. Avoid images that may be controversial, offensive, or confusing.
- If you present illustrations without captions, make sure that the images create the impression you intend. Captions can guide how readers see the image.
- Attention-getters are rarely used in formal academic papers or business reports. Often only used as cover art for major documents, they are generally conservative in nature. A one-hundred-page proposal to rehabilitate a college stadium might display a photograph of the existing building or an architect's drawing of the completed restoration on its cover.

Specific illustrations document a specific event or illustrate a particular example. A homeowner filing a flood insurance claim could include a photograph (top on the next page) to document the extent of the damage. A city engineering report might use an aerial photograph of a neighborhood (bottom on the next page) to demonstrate the extent of flood damage.

New Orleans, September 6, 2005
© BARBARA DAVIDSON/Dallas Morning News/Corbis

The photograph on page 350 illustrates a specific step in a process. Graphs, bar charts, and pie charts can highlight important facts and numbers that may be hard to appreciate when expressed in text alone.

- Specific illustrations are generally consecutively numbered and captioned. Formal reports may only number exhibits or label images with factual details, such as time, place, and location. Informal documents, such as promotional brochures, might use subjective captions to create positive or negative impressions.
- Specific illustrations are referred to by number or caption to connect them to the text:

  Last year sales fell dramatically in all sectors (Figure 6).

  Kuwait's oil exports increased greatly last year (see World Oil Exports, 2012).

New Orleans, September 4, 2005
Image by © David J. Phillip/Pool/Reuters/Corbis

- Specific illustrations should clearly represent what is stated in the text. Avoid images that may be controversial, distracting, or subject to varying interpretations. Graphs and charts should be suited to the audience. A report on climate change prepared by scientists at the Environmental Protection Agency may contain complex diagrams that would not be suitable for a newsmagazine or high school textbook.

- Exact details about the time, date, and location of a photograph may be critical. For engineers investigating the failure of the levees in New Orleans, photographs of floodwaters moving through a neighborhood may be useless unless investigators can establish a timeline of events.

- It is important to explain the source of images to establish credibility. A report about UFOs that includes images of strange objects flying over a city would gain authority if the pictures came from NASA or the United States Air Force.

- Documents using specific illustrations often have to follow professional formats of captioning, lettering, or documentation. Many disciplines have style manuals dictating how illustrations should appear in documents. If no manual exists, follow examples found in professional journals and official reports.

The kind of visuals you include in a document or presentation depends on your purpose. An ad, website, or newsletter might contain only visual elements to create eye appeal and establish a style or tone for the message. A biology research paper may contain only specific visuals, such as charts and microscopic photographs of cells. A sales brochure for a luxury car, however, might use a striking

The Louisiana Superdome, September 1, 2005
Image by © Michael Ainsworth/Dallas Morning News/Corbis

general illustration on the cover to grab attention, design features to establish and reinforce a mood of style and class, and specific illustrations of leather seats, wood paneling, and a high performance engine to emphasize particular features.

Types of Visuals

Photographs

Photographs can be compelling support, provided they suit the document's context. The picture of the hurricane victims at the Superdome (p. 646) captures the human drama of an actual event. It would make a powerful image for a fund-raising brochure, a Red Cross website, an article in *Time* or *Newsweek,* or a book cover. It would not be suited for a report arguing that the government responded appropriately to the disaster or for most kinds of academic papers.

Photographs can highlight a specific person, object, or location or provide readers with the big picture. Photographs can capture events as they happen or preserve images carefully posed for the camera.

For all their power, photographs have limitations. They can overemphasize minor events. A dramatic news photo of a demonstration that results in a dozen arrests and a few injuries may be splashed across the front pages of newspapers, while a riot that killed hundreds goes unnoticed because no cameras recorded the events.

Strategies for Using Photographs

1. **Select photographs from reliable sources.** Books, newsmagazines, newspapers, news services, and stock photo websites provide visuals suited for academic and professional writing. Stock photo services often include specific details about photographs, including date, location, and event. *Avoid using visuals that cannot be verified.*

2. **Include photographs that serve specific purposes.** Avoid including images that do not serve to set a tone, illustrate a general idea, attract attention, or document a particular point. You may find interesting and striking images, but if they do not clearly relate to your subject, they will confuse or distract readers.

3. **Let the context of the document guide your selection.** Keep your goal, readers, and discipline in mind when you include images.

4. **Avoid cluttering a document with too many images.** Do not let photographs overwhelm or distract from the text. Images should support the writing. You can integrate specific illustrations within the text and supply additional images in an appendix or supporting website.

(Continued)

5. **Link specific illustrations to text.** To prevent confusion, direct readers to look at specific images by referring to them in the text by figure number, caption, or page number.

6. **Include sources of photographs.** Photographs will have greater impact if sources, dates, and locations are offered in captions or a reference page. Readers may question the validity of images if they are presented without sources.

7. **Obtain permission before posting photographs online or using them in documents that are mailed or widely distributed.** Fair use allows students to include images in academic papers read by a single professor or shown to a single class. You must obtain permission to use photographs that will appear in printed documents or websites.

Tables, Graphs, and Charts

Tables, graphs, and charts express numbers, facts, or statistics in visual form. They can be used to dramatize facts or simply to help people comprehend and remember data. **Tables** present numbers in columns for easy reading and reference. Important tables, such as delivery schedules or price lists, can be placed on a separate page in large type so that they can be detached, scanned, or copied for readers to use as reference tools.

QUARTERLY SALES FIGURES (IN MILLIONS)		
	CD	DVD
New York	2.5	1.3
Chicago	1.2	1.2
Los Angeles	3.0	2.5

Line graphs show changing numbers over time. They can help readers review and appreciate the rise and fall of sales, prices, cases of flu, homicides, or the earth's temperature over days, weeks, months, or years. Time lines should be clearly presented.

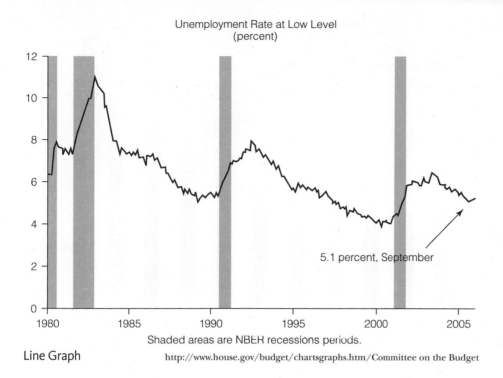

Unemployment Rate at Low Level
(percent)

Shaded areas are NBER recessions periods.

Line Graph   http://www.house.gov/budget/chartsgraphs.htm/Committee on the Budget

Line graphs that include anomalies might need explanations or a footnote to ex-plain a dramatic change that might be misunderstood. A graph showing homicides in Manhattan might have to explain that figures for 2001 include the 2,752 victims of the World Trade Center attack.

Bar charts represent data visually by using bars or columns to show differ-ences in values with different heights of bars. Like line graphs, they can show changes over time or comparisons between different topics. A bar chart about high school graduation rates could reflect a ten-year period of a single city or last year's statistics for ten different cities. Bars or columns can be coded to show subdivisions.

Pie charts show percentages of a whole by slicing a circle into shaded or col-ored sections. A pie chart could categorize immigrants by their nation of origin, a company's sales by product, or an investor's portfolio by stock type. Because pie charts represent a breakdown of a single subject at one time, more than one chart has to be used to compare different subjects or demonstrate a change over time.

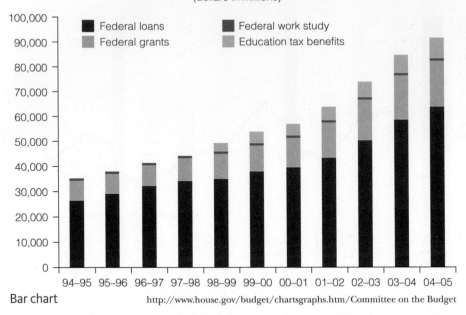

Bar chart

http://www.house.gov/budget/chartsgraphs.htm/Committee on the Budget

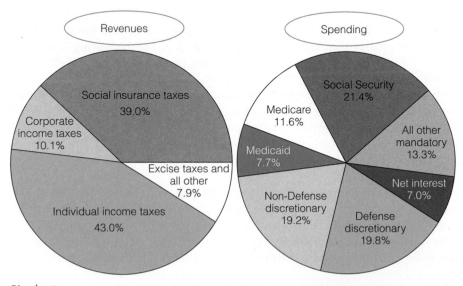

Pie chart

http://www.house.gov/budget/chartsgraphs.htm/Committee on the Budget

Strategies for Using Tables, Graphs, and Charts

1. **Select tables, graphs, and charts from reliable sources.** Visuals are based on numbers. Statistics can be taken out of context, misinterpreted, or distorted. Use visuals from major news services, government agencies, and nonpartisan organizations.

2. **Use visuals your readers will be able to understand and refer to.** Avoid including overly detailed or complex charts or graphs that require specialized knowledge or training. You may use simplified visuals in the main document for general readers and present more complex visuals in an appendix or supporting website for readers requiring greater detail.

3. **Present tables, charts, and graphs in a readable format.** Avoid shrinking visuals to a size that makes them difficult to see. To prevent large-scale charts and graphs from interrupting text, consider placing them in an appendix.

4. **Include sources.** Readers will only accept visuals as accurate if they know where they came from. You can note a graph's source, date, and other important information in a caption or source list.

5. **Link specific illustrations to text.** To prevent confusion, direct readers to look at specific images by referring to them in the text by number, caption, or page number.

6. **Analyze visuals for bias.** Truncated and two-dimensional graphs (see pages 632–635) can be used to distort, inflate, and dramatize numbers. Avoid using or creating graphs and charts that try to maximize or minimize numbers.

Captions

Captions that accompany visuals can present objective identifications or make subjective statements, guiding reader interpretations.

The photograph of the hurricane victims outside the Superdome (p. 646) could be accompanied by an objective description that simply labels the image:

> *Superdome, New Orleans, September 1, 2005*
> *Hurricane Katrina victims outside the Louisiana Superdome*

Subjective captions present readers with an implication of the photograph's meaning:

> *Five days after Hurricane Katrina, victims await rescue.*
> *Minority victims crowd outside Superdome.*

Captions like these contain descriptive or narrative elements suggesting a delayed or racially biased response to the disaster.

Strategies for Writing Captions

1. **Use captions for specific illustrations to connect images to the text.**
2. **Make sure captions connect to the text.** Avoid mentioning names, places, or events in the caption that are not explained in the text.
3. **Identify people in photographs from left to right.**
4. **Make sure the tone, style, and wording of captions suit the writing context.** A sales brochure may use colorful language to create favorable impressions of a chart or photograph. Use objective, neutral language in college papers and professional documents.

A chart showing a 9 percent increase in a company's sales can be labeled with an objective caption:

> *Ford sales, 2012*
> *Ford sales rise 9 percent in 2012.*

Subjective captions use connotations to maximize or minimize numbers:

> *Ford sales soar 9 percent in 2012.*
> *Ford sales rise less than 10 percent in 2012.*

Understanding Fair Use

Nearly all visual aids you may find in print or online are copyrighted and cannot be reproduced or distributed without permission. The concept of fair use allows students to include a photograph or chart in a research paper as long as the source is identified. However, the same image cannot be used in a website, brochure, ad, packaging, mass e-mail, T-shirt, or poster without permission.

Stock photo and clip art services offer images in the public domain and are therefore available for wider use.

Strategies for Using Visuals in College Writing

1. **Review the assignment to see whether visuals will enhance your paper.** A research paper in biology, engineering, business, or economics might demand extensive use of visual aids. In other courses, visuals may be nonessential but helpful. In a literature or political science course, visuals may be irrelevant.
2. **Select visuals that support specific points in your paper.** Limit use of attention-getters and general illustrations.

3. **Let your thesis guide your use of visuals.** Visuals should provide illustrations that explain or provide evidence for important points in your paper. Do not include photographs just because they are striking or interesting. Like quotations, visuals should directly support your thesis.

4. **Consider your method of development.** A narrative paper may benefit from a time line or line graph. Comparisons can be illustrated with tables and bar charts. Diagrams, photographs, and maps can explain a process.

5. **Use objective captions and references to link visuals to your text.** Freestanding images can be distracting or confusing. Consecutively number each image and use parenthetical notes to link them to your text:

> Between 1986 and 2005 the price of oil fluctuated greatly (Figure 12).

6. **Select appropriate sizes.** Simple charts and photographs may be shrunk to the size of an oversized postage stamp and wrapped with text to create a readable text. Detailed photographs, maps, and intricate charts may require a full page to be readable.

7. **Don't allow visuals to overwhelm the text.** If you have a large number of images, especially ones requiring a full page, consider placing some or all of them in an appendix.

8. **Document sources of visuals or information you use to create visuals.** Like quotations, visuals from other sources should be documented. If you create your own graphs or charts, indicate the source for the numbers or statistics they represent. Captions should list sources (see photographs in Chapter 27).

9. **Budget your time carefully.** Locating or creating visuals can be time-consuming. Determine whether your time would be better spent revising and editing your paper.

e-writing

Exploring Images Online

Explore the Web to learn more about using visuals in writing.

1. Using a search engine, enter such terms as *using visuals, locating photographs, designing tables and charts, writing with visuals,* or *using visuals in college writing* to locate current sites of interest.

2. Search websites of newsmagazines, such as *Time* and *Newsweek,* and cable news channels, such as CNN and FOX, to see how they use visuals in news stories. Can you detect biases in either the images that are selected or their captions?

E-Sources

Stock Photo Services

http://www.FotoSearch.com

http://www.corbisimages.com

http://www.photolibrary.com

Business and Professional Writing

*You won't work in a vacuum: You'll work with and through
other people, and you'll have to communicate with them.
Without the ability to inform, you will not be successful.*

—Thomas Pearsall and Donald Cunningham

What Is Business and Professional Writing?

Writing at work is very different from writing in college. Although executives, managers, scientists, and professionals follow the basic rules of English grammar, there are significant differences between academic and business writing.

- **Business writing occurs in a specific context.** The tone, style, diction, and format of business and professional documents are shaped by the history of the organization, the discipline, the reader, the extended audience, and the topic. The writing style suited for an ad agency might be considered unprofessional in a law firm.
  - When you write, consider the nature of your career, the image and history of the organization, your superiors' concerns, and the needs and expectations of your readers.
- **Business writing addresses specific readers.** In college you write for professors who are expected to be objective readers, evaluating your work on the basis of its presentation rather than its point of view. Outside the classroom, you will write to people with fixed attitudes and opinions. Instead of asking for a grade, you will be asking readers to buy your product, give you a job, approve your loan, or accept your side in an argument.
- **Business writing emphasizes results.** College writing demonstrates skills. Your professors are less interested in your opinions and more concerned about the way you develop and support your thesis. In an algebra class, for instance, the numbers are abstract. Getting the right answer is less important than demonstrating the ability to solve problems. In business and industry, ideas and answers mean money.
- **Business writing is sensitive to legal implications.** Letters, e-mail, reports, and contracts can become legal documents. Writers must be careful to avoid making statements they cannot support. A poorly worded phrase, even a grammatical or typographical error, can place writers in legal jeopardy, exposing them to litigation.
- **Business writing is carefully designed.** Business documents are carefully designed to follow professional standards and match an organization's image. Writers

Maria Toutoudaki/jupiterimages

Sam Diephuis/jupiterimages

656 | 29 BUSINESS AND PROFESSIONAL WRITING

must consider how the document will look. Law firms, banks, government agencies, and accounting firms will use traditional letterheads, margins, and fonts. Ad agencies, rock radio stations, and hair salons may use colorful designs to attract attention and project a unique image. In addition, business writers use bold headings, white space, and bulleted points to highlight important ideas and help readers follow their train of thought.

- **Business writing represents the views of others.** In college your papers are individual creations and can express personal views, but in your career you will most likely work as a representative of a corporation, organization, partnership, or agency.

  - Never write anything to clients that would be unacceptable to your employer.

  - Avoid making promises or commitments unless you know that your organization or employer will honor them.

  - Never use official stationery for personal letters.

E-mail

Many people write and answer e-mail without pausing to think, producing a stream of tangled ideas, missing details, grammatical errors, and inappropriate comments. E-mail, like any kind of writing, takes thought and planning to be effective.

Strategies for Writing E-mail

1. **Realize that e-mail is *real mail*.** E-mail can be stored, distributed, and printed. Unlike a note or memo that can be retrieved or corrected, e-mail, once sent, becomes permanent. *Never send e-mail when you are tired or angry. Avoid sending messages you will later regret.*

2. **Follow the prewriting, drafting, revising, and editing strategies you would use in writing a paper document.** E-mail should have a clear purpose and an easy-to-follow organization. *Plan before you write.*

3. **Understand what messages *should not* be expressed in e-mail.** E-mail is appropriate for short, informative messages. Do not attempt to send a fifteen-page report by e-mail, though it might be sent as an attachment. Do not send personal or sensitive information by e-mail without permission.

4. **Respond to e-mail carefully.** Often e-mail messages list multiple readers. Before sending a reply, determine whether you want everyone or just a few people to see your response.

5. **Make sure you use the correct e-mail address.** E-mail addresses can be complicated and oddly spelled. Often names are shortened or reversed. Donald Peterson might appear as "donald.peterson," "dpeterson," or "petersond." *Double-check addresses.*

6. **Clearly label your e-mail in the subject line.** Spam—unwanted e-mail messages— uses misleading headings such as "Following your request" or "next week's

conference" to grab attention. To prevent your e-mail from being overlooked or deleted before it is read, use specific identifying details in the subject such as "April 19th health insurance reminder" or "Smithkin Supplies Annual Audit."

7. **Include your reader's full name and the date in your inside address.**

8. **Keep e-mail direct and concise.** People expect e-mail to be brief and easy to read. Avoid complicated sentences and long paragraphs. Use short paragraphs and bulleted or numbered points to increase readability.

9. **End the e-mail with a clear summary, request, or direction.**
   - Summarize important points.
   - If you are asking for information or help, clearly state what you need, when you need it, and how you can be reached.
   - If you want readers to take action, provide clear instructions.

10. **Ask readers for an acknowledgment if you want to make sure they received your message.**

11. **Make sure your name and other pertinent information appear on attachments.**

12. **Review, edit, and double-check e-mail before sending.** Check spelling, addresses, names, prices, or figures for accuracy. Read e-mail aloud to catch missing words, illogical statements, confusing sentences, or awkward phrases.

13. **Save or print hard copies of important e-mail for future reference.**

Sample E-mail

Subject: Expense Account Reports
From: John Rio
Date: January 30, 2013
To: Sales Staff

To all sales staff:

As of March 1, 2013, Pacific Mutual will no longer provide sales representatives with company cars or expense accounts. Instead, sales representatives will be given a flat monthly grant to cover office, travel, and vehicle expenses.

Inside Sales Reps:	$250 per month
District Sales Reps:	$500 per month
Regional Sales Reps:	$750 per month

This policy affects only regular monthly expenses. Pacific Mutual will continue to pay all expenses for those attending regional and national sales conventions.

   If you have any questions about the new policy, please contact me at Ext. 7689.

Regards,
John Rio

Résumés and Cover Letters

The first business documents you will probably write are a résumé and cover letter. Before undertaking this often frustrating task, it is important to understand what a résumé is.

- **A résumé is a ten-second advertisement.** Research has revealed that the average executive spends about ten seconds skimming a résumé before rejecting it or setting it aside for further review. *A résumé is not a list of every job you have had or a description of your ultimate goal in life; it is an ad presenting facts and accomplishments relevant to a specific position.*

- **The goal of a résumé is to secure an interview, not a job.** Few, if any applicants, are hired solely on the basis of a one- or two-page document. The goal of a résumé is simply to generate enough interest in the applicant to prompt the employer to schedule an interview. Present only the highlights of your career and education.

- **Applicants usually benefit from having more than one résumé.** Just as companies design different advertisements to market the same product to different consumers, you may have three or four résumés. An accounting major may have one résumé emphasizing auditing expertise and another stressing tax experience. Because they are read quickly, résumés targeted to a single job are more effective than general statements.

Strategies for Writing Résumés

1. **Understand that there are few absolute rules in writing effective résumés—only guidelines.** You may have heard that a résumé must be only one page, that it is useless to list hobbies, or that you should never mention your age. Because there is such a range of jobs and applicants, there are instances in which breaking the rules may be the only effective way of getting attention. An actor's résumé is usually accompanied by a photograph. A restaurant manager once secured an interview by designing a résumé in the form of a menu.

2. **Focus your résumé by carefully reading the want ad or job description.** Note the key requirements employers seek, and highlight those skills. Pay attention to key words and phrases and determine whether you can repeat them in your résumé.

3. **Include your full name, address, telephone number with area code, or e-mail address.** If you are in the process of moving, you can list two addresses.

4. **Provide a clear, objective statement describing the job you seek.** Avoid using general statements, such as "a position making use of my skills and abilities," or one that lists too many job titles: "Sales Manager/Marketing Manager/Advertising Director." Broad objectives make applicants appear indecisive or desperate. It is better to have specific statements:

   A position in publishing design making use of my experience in graphics Assistant Sales Manager

5. **Use a short *summary* or *overview* statement to encapsulate key elements in your background.** A short paragraph describing your background, goals, and

skills can personalize a résumé. It can encourage the reader to view your experience in a certain light, showing how seemingly unrelated jobs or education would be relevant to the job you seek, as shown in the following examples:

Textbook Sales
Ten years experience in textbook sales. Increased territory 25 percent in eighteen months. Introduced online marketing. Reduced service budget 18 percent in first six months. Received extensive sales training as agent for New York Life.

Security Consultant
- FBI agent 1995–2005
- Conducted computer fraud investigations for Banker's Life, General Motors Credit Corporation, Miller Brewing, and Westwood Industries.
- Trained New York City detectives in online investigative methods.

You may find it easier to write the summary last, after you have identified your key strengths.

6. **Open your résumé with your strongest and most recent credentials.** If you have professional experience, you may find it more effective to highlight your recent job than to emphasize a new degree. If you are unsure which area to highlight, prepare two résumés, one emphasizing experience and the other stressing education. Use both résumés, selecting the version that best matches a particular job. Before applying for a larger set of positions, send out a small number of résumés to identify which version produces the better results.

7. **Arrange education and experience chronologically, beginning with the most recent.**

8. **If you are a recent graduate with little professional experience, list significant courses, awards, grade point averages, and honors.** If you have worked as an intern or completed clinical work, place this under the heading Experience rather than Education:

EXPERIENCE   WESTERN SOFTWARE, San Diego, CA
Intern in marketing program directly assisting two managers in introducing new consumer products.
- Wrote two sales brochures for national distribution.
- Edited text of promotional video.
- Attended national sales seminars.

9. **Stress individual accomplishments.** Briefly list dates of employment, title, and general job description; then provide examples of specific skills and experiences. Use action verbs to give your résumé a sense of action:

2008–Present   Sales Manager in Miami's third largest bookstore; responsible for hiring, training, purchasing, and promotions.
- Lowered employee turnover 25 percent in first year.
- Redesigned promotions to increase point-of-purchase stationery supplies from $25,000 to $87,500 in first year.
- Organized book-signing receptions, drawing national media coverage.

(Continued)

10. **List training seminars, volunteer work, hobbies, and military service only if directly related to the position.** A résumé is a fact sheet listing your key skills and experiences. Secondary information can be included in a cover letter or mentioned at a job interview.

Student Résumé Including Previous Experience

MARIA SANCHEZ
1732 St. Charles Avenue
New Orleans, LA 70130
(504) 455-5767
sanchezm@delgado.edu

Goal	OBJECTIVE	Management position in retail printing with opportunities for advancement
Overview blends education and previous experience	OVERVIEW	Five years experience in retail sales management. Fully familiar with state-of-the-art printing equipment and methods. Proven ability to lower overhead and build customer relations. ■ Certified to service all Xerox copiers.
Most recent credential	EDUCATION	DELGADO COMMUNITY COLLEGE, New Orleans, LA Associate Degree, Printing and Publishing, 2013 Completed courses in graphic design, editing, high speed printing, and equipment repair. ■ Attended Quadgraphics seminar. ■ Assisted in design and publication of college newspaper.
Corporate training		XEROX, New Orleans, LA Completed service training program, 2010.
	EXPERIENCE	FAST-PRINT, New Orleans, LA
Current student job	2010–	**Retail Sales** Work twenty hours a week assisting manager in counter sales, customer relations, printing, and inventory.
Previous job description emphasizing skills related to desired job	2005–2010	CRESCENT CITY MUSIC, New Orleans, LA **Manager** directly responsible for retail record outlet with annual gross sales of $1.8 million. ■ Reduced operating costs 15% first year. ■ Hired and trained sales staff. ■ Prepared all financial statements. ■ Developed advertising plan generating 35% increase in sales in first month.
	HONORS	Dean's List 2011, 2012, 2013

References and Transcript Available

Cover Letters

Cover letters can be as important as the résumés they introduce. Résumés submitted without letters are often dismissed by employers, who assume that applicants who do not take the time to address them personally are not serious. Résumés tend to be rather cold lists of facts; cover letters allow applicants to present themselves in a more personalized way. The letter also allows applicants to counter possible employer objections by explaining a job change, a period of unemployment, or a lack of formal education.

Strategies for Writing Cover Letters

In most instances, cover letters are short sales letters using standard business letter formats.

1. **Avoid beginning a cover letter with a simple announcement:**

   Dear Sir or Madam:

   This letter is to apply for the job of controller advertised in the *San Francisco Chronicle* last week. . . .

2. **Open letters on a strong point emphasizing skills or experiences:**

   Dear Sir or Madam:

   In the last two years I opened fifty-eight new accounts, increasing sales by nearly $800,000.

3. **Use the letter to include information not listed on the résumé.** Volunteer work, high school experiences, or travel that might not be suited to a résumé can appear in the letter—if they are career related.

4. **Refer to the résumé, indicating how it documents your skills and abilities.**

5. **End the letter with a brief summary of notable skills and experiences and a request for an interview.** To be more assertive, state that you will call the employer in two or three days to schedule an appointment.

Letter Responding to Job Announcement

MARIA SANCHEZ
1732 St. Charles Avenue
New Orleans, LA 70130
(504) 455-5767
sanchezm@delgado.edu

May 24, 2013

Bayou Printing
1500 Magazine Street
New Orleans, LA 70130

Identifies position

RE: Manager position description e-mailed to Delgado Placement Office on May 18, 2013

Dear Sir or Madam:

Opens with strong point
Refers to résumé

This month I will be graduating from Delgado Community College with an associate degree in printing and publishing. As my résumé shows, I have been trained in state-of-the-art publishing and equipment repair. I received additional training in printing at Quadgraphics and Xerox.

Explains relevance of previous experience

Before choosing printing and publishing as a career, I managed one of New Orleans's high-volume record stores. I hired, trained, and supervised thirty employees. In addition to decreasing turnover, I lowered overhead and increased sales.

Close and request for interview

Given my training in state-of-the-art publishing and my extensive background in retail sales, I think I would be an effective store manager. I would appreciate the opportunity to meet with you to discuss my abilities at your convenience. I can be reached at (504) 455-5767.

Sincerely yours,

Maria Sanchez

Putting Your Résumé to Work

Like any advertisement, a résumé is only effective if it reaches the appropriate reader. Don't limit your job search to obvious sources such as the want ads or Internet listings. Talk with instructors in your major courses, contact local recruiters and employment agencies, and investigate professional organizations for networking leads.

Business and Professional Reports

Business and professional reports differ from academic research papers in purpose and format. Scholarly writing stresses intellectual growth and reflection. A research paper may discuss background details in depth, explore alternative theories, and speculate about the significance of people, historical events, scientific discoveries, or works of art. Documentation is important to distinguish the writer's ideas from outside sources.

In contrast, business writing is result-oriented. Although it may stem from scholarly research, the information is presented to guide actions and decisions. The thesis or recommendation is clearly stated. Although acknowledging sources is important, less attention is paid to formal academic documentation.

- **Business reports emphasize results rather than reflection.** The thesis or main idea is often stated at the very opening of the report with little or no introduction.

- **Business reports are terse but thorough.** Academic writers may insert interesting asides or references because their goal is to teach. Business writers, however, focus on specific tasks and restrict their commentary to practical details.

- **Business reports use subheadings.** Unlike research papers, which are generally double-spaced and presented with few internal subtitles, business reports contain subheadings for easy reading. Because they may be presented to professionals seeking specific information, business reports serve as reference material. Readers may not be interested in reading the entire report but only in locating specific facts or numbers.

- **Business reports may follow industry or corporate formats.** In academics, nearly all research papers follow common standards. English students use the Modern Language Association (MLA) style. Psychology and sociology students follow standards set by the American Psychological Association (APA). But in many jobs, you will be expected to follow formats used in a particular industry, corporation, or division.

  - If you are unsure what a report should look like, request samples to use as models.

  - Before turning in a fifty-page proposal only to discover you have used an incorrect format, show a rough draft to your supervisor.

  - Ask experienced employees for advice and samples of their work.

- **Business reports use informal documentation.** Scientific research reports will include a works cited page, whereas most managers use simple parenthetical notes. Business writers frequently paraphrase the work of others without formal footnotes. Although readers may not evaluate your use of documentation, it is important to identify those sources that support your point of view.

- **Business reports are usually written for multiple readers.** Reports are often submitted to boards, committees, employees, regulators, or shareholders. They may have to address the needs and concerns of dozens of experts in different fields. They may be distributed by mail, reviewed by the media, or posted on the Internet. The extended audience is very important. Consider how your comments might be viewed out of context. Avoid making statements that may appear unprofessional or insensitive to others.

- **Business reports are often the product of collaborative writing.** In many instances you will have to work with others to produce a report. See "Strategies for Collaborative Writing" (pages 670–671).

Sample Business Report

RECOMMENDATIONS FOR CONTRACTORS FOR BID
CONSIDERATION FOR RENOVATION OF HISPANIC CULTURAL CENTER

Prepared by
Kim Gonzalez
Selena Dunn
Abraham Perez

Renovation Committee
Hispanic Cultural Center
El Paso, Texas

April 2012

RECOMMENDATIONS FOR CONTRACTORS FOR BID CONSIDERATION
FOR RENOVATION OF HISPANIC CULTURAL CENTER

I. Recommendation of Three Contractors and Summary

The Renovation Committee recommends that the Hispanic Cultural Center approach three contractors for possible bid consideration. The Renovation Committee unanimously rated these firms in order of preference:

1. Felber & Riley
2. Montano Builders
3. Ortega Design

II. Background

In 2011 the Hispanic Cultural Center, a 503(c) nonprofit organization, purchased the former First Methodist Church located at 2727 West Elm Street, El Paso, Texas. The property consists of a 125-year-old church with 25,000 square feet of usable space and an attached two-story, 12,550–square-foot addition constructed in 1910.

The mission of the Hispanic Cultural Center is to operate a facility housing a theater for plays and concerts, a library and cultural center, an art gallery, meeting and banquet rooms, and storage.

The current building provides ample space for storage and meetings and serves as an acceptable venue for artistic performances. However, the lack of a modern kitchen and bar service limit banquet operations, a prime income source for the center. Renovation is necessary to increase attendance at concerts, improve banquet and bar income, create an art gallery, and attract patrons and visitors. In addition, the buildings do not contain the wheelchair ramps and elevators needed to meet ADA (Americans with Disabilities Act) requirements.

III. Charge to the Renovation Committee

Following several board meetings and discussions with city and local business leaders, the directors of the Hispanic Cultural Center created the Renovation Committee to begin selecting architectural firms and contractors to initiate a bidding process for renovation.

Due to the large number of firms suggested by the directors, it was determined that the Renovation Committee should review all suggested firms and present to the board a list of no less than three firms for the board to consider. In soliciting information from contractors it was made clear by the committee that these inquiries were for research purposes only and that any offers or requests for bids, reviews, and proposals would have to be approved by the full board of directors.

IV. Evaluation Methods

The Renovation Committee collected the names of eleven building firms suggested by directors at the January and February board meetings:

Architects 2000	Montano Builders
Arco Builders	Odway & Schmitt
Diaz & Wilson	Pfeiffer & DuChamp
Felber & Riley	Ortega Design
Gulf Coast Construction	Rodriguez Design
Lone Star Builders	

In selecting firms for recommendation, the Renovation Committee was guided by directives approved by the board of directors in a motion at the February meeting:

> Recommended firms should be experienced in renovation of structures similar to the existing church, understand the unique needs of a cultural center, and demonstrate experience in working with nonprofit organizations.

Members strongly advocated selecting a minority-owned firm.

Given the large number of firms, the committee decided to break the selection process into two phases:

Phase One

1. Contact all named firms by telephone to solicit brochures and lists of recent projects.
2. Review firms based on board of directors' criteria and select six firms for further review.

Phase Two

1. Conduct in-depth interviews with principals of each firm and examine corporate profiles.
2. Select three firms to recommend to the Board of Directors for discussion.

V. Phase One: Screening

All firms were contacted for telephone interviews during the second week of March. Two firms—Lone Star Builders and Pfeiffer & DuChamp—are involved in the airport expansion and are not seeking new clients for two years.

The Renovation Committee reviewed brochures and other documents from the remaining nine firms. Further telephone requests for information were made in the last week of March. After examining the nine firms, six were selected:

Architects 2000	Montano Builders
Arco Builders	Ortega Design
Felber & Riley	Rodriguez Design

VI. Phase Two: Recommendations

The Renovation Committee requested further documentation from the six firms and scheduled interviews for the first week of April. In one instance a conference telephone interview was conducted because the principal partners were at a convention in Atlanta.

After conducting the interviews, the Renovation Committee met twice to evaluate the six firms. Architects 2000 and Arco Builders were eliminated because their experience is limited to new residential construction. Rodriguez Design is highly experienced in commercial renovations but has never designed a cultural facility or restored a historic building.

The Renovation Committee identified three finalists, and based on further discussions, the contractors are listed in order of preference:

1. **Felber & Riley**

   This firm has extensive experience in renovating century-old structures, including several churches. They are accustomed to working with nonprofit and cultural institutions.

   Felber & Riley's renovation projects include St. John's Church, the Montez Art Gallery in Fort Worth, and the Jewish Community Center in Austin. Although not certified as a minority contractor, the firm employs several Hispanics in key positions. Mr. Hector Diaz, who helped transform a turn-of-the-century high school into the Montez Art Gallery, has agreed to work with the Hispanic Cultural Center. The firm's experience in redesigning existing structures to serve as cultural venues distinguishes it from the competition.

   The Renovation Committee highly recommends Felber & Riley for consideration.

2. **Montano Builders**

   This firm is a certified minority contractor with extensive experience in new construction. Recent projects include a number of strip malls and warehouses. Montano Builders has served as a subcontractor on three major renovation projects for the City of El Paso, including the Zoo Administration Building and Symphony Hall. The firm has not worked with nonprofit organizations and has no experience in designing cultural facilities.

3. **Ortega Design**

   This fifty-year-old firm is a certified minority contractor with a national reputation for church renovation. It has rebuilt and restored churches in Austin, Dallas, San Diego, Fort Worth, New Orleans, and Kansas City. The Ortega team includes woodworkers from Germany, stained glass makers from Italy, and masons from Mexico. The firm specializes in restoring old churches to their original specifications rather than converting these structures to serve other purposes. Though highly recommended by community leaders, the firm's expertise lies outside the needs of the Hispanic Cultural Center.

VII. Final Considerations

The Renovation Committee limited its search to the eleven firms suggested by the Board of Directors and strongly suggests further investigations be carried out to locate other qualified firms to insure a favorable bid process.

Strategies for Successful Business and Professional Writing

1. **Establish a clear goal for each document.**
2. **Address the needs and concerns of both immediate and extended readers.**
3. **Make sure your writing does not conflict with the policy or image of the organization you represent.**
4. **Review your document for legal liability.** Avoid making commitments or promises you cannot keep.
5. **Conform to the standards used in your organization or industry.**
6. **Use peer review to evaluate documents before submission or publication.**
7. **Test-market documents before mass distribution.** After peer review, submit copies to a limited audience and evaluate the response before sending the document to every reader.

For Further Reading

Baugh, Sue L., Maridell Fryar, and David A. Thomas. *Handbook for Business Writing.*

Beatty, Richard. *The Perfect Cover Letter.*

Bell, Arthur. *Complete Business Writer's Manual: Model Letters, Memos, Reports, and Presentations for Every Occasion.*

Brock, Susan L., and Beverly Manber. *Writing Business Proposals and Reports: Strategies for Success.*

Brown, Leland. *Effective Business Report Writing.*

Clover, Vernon. *Business Research Methods.*

Frailey, L. E., Susan Mamchak, and Steven Mamchak. *Handbook of Business Letters.*

Griffin, Jack. *The Complete Handbook of Model Business Letters.*

Hansen, Katherine. *Dynamic Cover Letters for New Graduates.*

Kupsh, Joyce. *How to Create High-Impact Business Reports.*

Ryan, Robert. *Winning Resumes.*

Tepper, Ron. *Power Resumes.*

e-writing

Exploring Business and Professional Writing Online

You can use the Web to learn more about business and professional writing.

1. Using a search engine, enter such terms as *writing e-mail, tips on writing e-mail, resumes, cover letters,* or *writing business reports* to locate current sites of interest.

2. Using InfoTrac College Edition, available through your English CourseMate at **www.cengagebrain.com**, or one of your library's databases, locate online articles from professional journals to examine how the writing context differs from one discipline to another.

E-Sources

Online Writing Lab at Purdue: Workplace Writers
> **http://owl.english.purdue.edu/owl/resource/681/01/**

Kaitlin Duck Sherwood: A Beginner's Guide to Effective E-mail
> **http://www.webfoot.com/advice/email.top.html**

About.com: Writing Résumés
> **http://jobsearch.about.com/od/resumes/Resumes.htm**

Access the English CourseMate for this text at **www.cengagebrain.com** for additional information on business and professional writing.

Special Writing Contexts

What Are Special Writing Contexts?

College courses and your future career may place you in special writing contexts. Instead of working alone to prepare an assignment for an individual instructor, you may have to collaborate with others or broadcast a message to a mass audience.

Collaborative Writing

We think of writing as a solitary activity, but many professions require people to work with others to produce a single document. Two business partners may cowrite a sales brochure. A committee investigating a problem or proposing a solution usually issues a single document.

Whether people are writing alone or in a group, the basic process is the same. The completed document must address the issue, meet the needs of the readers, and respect the conventions of the discourse community, discipline, or situation. To be effective, writing groups must achieve the "Three Cs" of group dynamics: *cohesion, cooperation,* and *compromise.* Members of a group must be able to meet, communicate, and work together, and must be willing to accept the views and criticism of others. Members must understand that not all of their ideas will be represented in the final product and that their opinions will not always prevail.

Strategies for Collaborative Writing

1. **Establish cohesion by stressing the common goal, intended readers, and the needs of the discourse community.**
2. **Keep the group focused on the task by creating a time line containing deadlines for each stage of the writing process.** Make sure your group allows time for revision and editing.
3. **Use prewriting strategies to develop topics and explore ideas.** Members can take time to individually freewrite, brainstorm, or cluster ideas and then participate in group prewriting.
4. **Designate one member to serve as moderator or recorder to document progress and keep discussions on target.**

5. **Avoid topics that are too controversial, require too much research, or cannot be adequately explored in the allotted time.** If members of your group have strikingly different opinions and you find time being consumed by arguments and debates, suggest the group select a topic that will prompt cooperation and compromise.

6. **Make meetings productive by setting goals and assigning tasks.** Meetings can become repetitions of previous discussions.
   - Keep the group on track by opening each meeting with a brief summary of what has been accomplished and a list of what has to be achieved in the current meeting.
   - Summarize points that have been agreed to; then announce tasks for the next meeting.
   - Make sure each member is assigned work and knows what is expected at the next meeting.

7. **Avoid personalizing disagreements.** It is important to discuss opposing viewpoints in neutral terms. Avoid attaching ideas to individuals, which leads to *us*-against-*them* conflicts.

8. **Experiment with different writing methods.** There are a number of ways groups can produce writing:
   - *Individual drafting.* If the writing is short and not too complex, ask each member to prepare a draft and bring copies to the next meeting. Members can then select the best version and suggest alterations, adding items from other drafts.
   - *Parallel drafting.* For longer documents or those that include specialized information, divide the paper into sections, assigning each one to a different group member.
   - *Team drafting.* Assign two or more writers to the document or each section. A lead writer begins the first draft, then passes the writing onto subsequent authors when he or she gets stuck or lacks knowledge or data to continue. Drafts are then reviewed by the group.

9. **Take advantage of technology.** Use telephone conferences and Internet chat rooms for long-distance meetings. Use e-mail to distribute drafts so that members can read and post comments.

Online Writing Groups

Many college students and professionals use the Internet to expedite the writing process, posting drafts for others to read, criticize, and revise. Online writing groups allow writers to elicit responses from people who cannot meet in person. A marketing executive developing a promotional brochure can easily solicit responses from sales representatives across the country. In addition, online writing groups allow members to respond to a posted draft at their convenience. Students who find it difficult to voice comments in class may feel more comfortable expressing their opinions in writing. Because writing requires more concentration than talking, online writing groups can prompt more thoughtful responses about a draft than a discussion can. Members can easily make revisions and suggest alternative versions.

Strategies for Working in Online Writing Groups

1. **Allow time for members to respond.** Unlike those meeting in person, members of online writing groups respond individually. Don't post the draft of an essay at midnight and expect to receive feedback the next morning. Budget your time carefully.

2. **Label your documents and restate goals.** If members receive a number of assignments or documents, they can easily become confused. They will be in a better position to respond to your work if you remind them of the assignment or the purpose of your document.

3. **Proofread your document before posting.** Errors in spelling and punctuation, though minor, are distracting. The better edited your writing is, the more likely it is that readers will be able to respond to the content and analyze your ideas.

4. **Direct responses by asking questions.** Simply posting an essay or letter can generate scattered or otherwise unhelpful commentary that may not enhance the revision process. Provide readers with questions about specific problems or shortcomings you detect in your draft. Encourage them to make suggestions and possible revisions.

5. **Use alternative communications.** Posting and reading e-mail can lead to static exchanges. The work of online writing groups can benefit from personal meetings, chat room conferences, and telephone calls.

6. **Print and save hard copies of posted drafts.** Hard copies allow you to preserve different versions of documents and work while away from your computer.

7. **Observe standards of *netiquette*.** When you send e-mail or post messages, follow these basic guidelines for electronic messages:
   - *Write responsibly.* Think before you send anyone anything that you might later regret. Consider your professional role and potential extended audiences
   - *Keep subject lines brief.* The subject line of your e-mail serves as a title. It should be short and clearly identify the purpose of the message.

- *Keep line length short.* Many monitors display only forty characters in a line. State messages concisely in short paragraphs using tightly worded sentences. Use attachments to transmit longer, more complex documents.
- *Follow standard capitalization rules.* Use lowercase and capital letters as you would in a print document.
- *Proofread your messages.* Review the spelling and grammar of e-mail with the same rigor you would apply to a standard letter or research paper.
- *Respect copyrights.* Do not electronically distribute copyrighted material, including e-mail from others, without permission. Document use of outside sources.
- *Sign and date your e-mail.* Include your name, affiliation, and e-mail address at the end of your message. *Always include the date for future reference.*

Writing as a Representative of Others

Outside the classroom, you often write as a representative of other people. Your work will not be viewed as a personal creation or an individual opinion, but as the expression of a company, union, board, agency, or institution.

When you write as a representative, avoid making statements that contradict the mission or philosophy of the organization. Never write anything that might place the organization in jeopardy, expose it to liability, or provoke needless criticism. Keep in mind that whatever you write will be seen as an expression of the corporation, agency, club, or organization. Business letters, reports, newsletters, advertisements, and e-mails are assumed to state the views and values of the group, not of an individual member or employee. Expressing personal opinions that conflict with corporate practices or administrative policy can jeopardize your position.

Strategies for Writing as a Representative

1. **Remember that you are writing as a representative of the group, not as an individual.** Keep the values, beliefs, policies, and attitudes of the group in mind as you write. Do not make any statements in official correspondence you will not be able to explain or defend to other members of the group.

2. **Clearly distinguish personal opinion from passages expressing ideas of the group.** If you insert personal views in a business letter, clearly label them and indicate to your reader that your views do not reflect those of the group.

(Continued)

3. **Never use official letterhead for personal communications.** Never write anything on office stationery that you would not want your supervisor or manager to read.

4. **Never make profane or even humorous comments that will compromise your professional position.** Even if you are sending an e-mail to your best friend, be aware that others may read it out of context and draw negative conclusions about your performance or professionalism. Whatever you write should reflect the image you wish to project in your career.

5. **Model your writing style on existing documents.** Large organizations provide employees with style manuals containing samples of letters and reports. If official guidelines do not exist, ask your supervisor or fellow employees for examples of what they consider good writing.

Broadcasting to Mass Audiences

In many instances you will write something to be distributed to a mass audience—an ad, a website, a sales brochure, or a newsletter. The more people you plan to reach with your document, the more challenging your task becomes. If you make an error or omit a detail in a memo directed to three or four people, you can easily correct yourself by making a few telephone calls. But if you have already mailed five thousand letters or received ten thousand hits on a website containing misinformation, any attempt to correct the error will be time-consuming and costly.

In addition, the wider the audience you attempt to reach, the more important it is to measure your readers' perceptual world, particularly their existing knowledge and attitudes. A sales letter directed to urban professionals may alienate rural consumers. A fund-raising brochure that succeeds with Catholics may fail to impress non-Catholics. Consider *all* your readers.

Strategies for Writing to Mass Audiences

1. **Arouse attention.** People are flooded with e-mail, letters, and reports. Don't assume readers will appreciate the importance of your message.
   - Announce the significance of your document at the outset. Tell readers *why* the text is worth reading.
   - If appropriate, use bold headlines, larger font sizes, italics, and underlining to highlight points.

- Consider including visual aids that can communicate at a glance—diagrams, graphs, cartoons, and photographs. Images should both illustrate your ideas and match the tone and style of the document.

2. **Define your goal clearly.** Whatever document you address to a mass audience must be clearly stated. Most readers will skim rather than read mass-distributed items. *Reader attention is limited.*
   - Avoid attempting to express too much information in a single document.
   - Make sure your goal is clearly stated at the beginning or end. Do not bury important ideas in the middle of the text.

3. **Keep your document as brief as possible.** Although you must provide support for your ideas, realize that readers respond poorly to long documents.
   - Delete minor details.
   - Use an appendix and attachments for lengthy detail so the primary document can serve as a readable preface or brief overview.

4. **Direct readers to take specific action.** If you wish readers to respond in a certain way or if you desire to motivate them to take action, provide clear directions.
   - What is it that you want people to do after reading this document?
   - Provide instructions, as well as pertinent information—names, dates, and addresses.

5. **Use peer review and focus groups.** Give copies of your document to half a dozen or more people who represent your mass audience and ask for their reactions.
   - Direct people to read the document once; then ask questions to test their ability to recall information.
   - Ask readers to identify strong and weak points.
   - Ask readers to summarize the document's main ideas in their own words. If they can only repeat statements drawn from the text, they may have not fully understood or incorporated the content.

6. **Test-market your writing.** Before sending a fund-raising e-mail to ten thousand people, send out five hundred to test the results. If your message generates a desired response, continue distribution. If the e-mail fails to produce results, use focus groups and peer review to guide revisions or a change in tactics.

7. **Consider using alternative versions.** There is no reason why you must use only one version of a sales letter, e-mail, or handbill. Different people respond to different ideas, words, and images. Instead of attempting to develop a master document to serve everyone, consider developing multiple versions using varying texts, styles, and images.
   - The basic message must be the same if you want people to have a common response. Make sure all facts such as names, dates, prices, and addresses are accurate.
   - Track the success rate of each type. If you find that more people respond to a particular version, you might discard others.

Writing to Multiple Readers

In college, most of your papers are directed to a single instructor. In seminars, graduate school, and most organizations you will have a group of readers, many with specific needs and concerns. Although you will, in most cases, be expected to distribute the same report to each member, you can personalize the document to communicate more effectively with a diverse audience.

Strategies for Writing to Multiple Readers

1. **Include a detailed table of contents and index.** Readers lose patience if they have to page through a report to search for information. Detailed tables of contents and indexes can make your document easy to read, making it a resource people can use as a reference.

2. **Attach a cover letter or note.** You can reach different people by attaching letters directing them to specific pages and adding comments unsuited for the basic text:

   > Dear Ms. O'Neill:
   >
   > Here is the proposal for next year's Chicago Convention.
   > In response to your concern about additional meeting rooms,
   > I suggest renting a second ballroom. (See diagrams of the Hyatt on page 12.)
   > If you have any questions, feel free to call me at extension 7403.
   >
   > Warm regards,
   > Sidney Falco

3. **Mark copies for specific readers.** You can aid readers, especially those pressed for time, by highlighting or underlining text, inserting bookmarks, or using Post-it notes.

4. **Motivate people to read your document.**
   - Send notes, e-mail, or voice mail to alert readers when to expect your document and why it is important.
   - Use attention-getting ideas or facts to arouse interest.

Giving Oral and Multimedia Presentations

Many college courses and your career will require you to make oral or multimedia presentations. In some instances, this will be simply an introduction to or a brief overview of a document. In other instances, it may be a complete alternative to a written report.

Writing and public speaking call on very different skills. An oral presentation occurs in a specific location at a specific time. Environmental factors, such as noise and seating arrangements, affect how messages are received. Listeners, unlike readers, are part of an audience. Their reactions are often shaped by the responses of the people around them. Readers can study a document at their own pace, taking as long as they wish to read and reread. They can skim over familiar information to concentrate on new or difficult material. Listeners, however, receive the message at the same rate and cannot alter the flow of information. Studies reveal that even the most attentive listeners retain much less than do readers.

Strategies for Giving Oral and Multimedia Presentations

1. **Study the environment.** The more you know about the time, place, and conditions of your presentation, the more comfortable and effective you will be.
   - If you are unfamiliar with the location, visit it beforehand if you can. If you cannot survey the site in person, ask what kind of room it is—a seminar room, an auditorium, a lounge? What kind of seating arrangement will be used for the speech? Does it lend itself to a formal or informal presentation? What kind of presentation aids, such as a computer and projector, chalkboard, whiteboard, or microphone, will be available?
   - Find out, if you can, how many people are expected. Meeting with three or four people around a coffee table calls for a different presentation style than addressing two hundred from a podium.

2. **Learn as much as you can about your audience.** A speech is a public event, an interpersonal exchange. People expect a certain formality or distance in a written document but anticipate that a speaker will connect with them personally. Learn as much as you can about your listeners and their perceptual world so you can tailor your presentation to address their needs, answer their concerns, and confront their objections.
   - If possible, meet or call people you expect to attend the presentation and ask about their interests or opinions.
   - Go to the meeting early and introduce yourself to people. Ask about their backgrounds, ideas, and reactions to your subject.

3. **Isolate the key points of your document.** Listeners are unable to grasp the range of details usually presented in written form. Highlight and number the key points of your paper, emphasizing your thesis, the most important evidence, and actions you wish the audience to take.

4. **Prepare a range of presentations.** If you are not sure how long your presentation should be, ask. If you are given thirty minutes, prepare a thirty-minute, a twenty-minute, and a ten-minute version.

5. **Do not *read* your speech.** The worst thing a speaker can do is to read a speech. Reading a written document—except for key quotes—has a deadly effect on listeners. Written language, no matter how clear and eloquent on paper, is

(Continued)

often difficult to present orally or to remember. Spoken English, even in formal circumstances, is usually simpler and delivered in shorter sentences.

- Do not attempt to memorize your speech—*talk* to your audience, using a few notes as reminders.
- Practice your delivery, especially the pronunciation of difficult words or phrases.

6. **Maintain eye contact.** The most important skill effective speakers develop is maintaining eye contact with listeners. If looking at people makes you nervous, look above their heads, moving your eyes about the room as you speak.

7. **Use visual aids.** People retain more information if they receive it in more than one medium. Even motivated listeners will recall only about a third of what they hear. A simple outline, a list of talking points, a diagram, or the table of contents of your report can help people follow your presentation.

- If giving a speech makes you nervous, a visual can reduce stress because people will be viewing the picture or chart instead of looking in your direction.
- Keep handouts, transparencies, and PowerPoint images simple and direct. Avoid distracting artwork. Emphasize key words that appear in the text of your presentation.

8. **Provide distinct transitions between main points.** In writing, you can use visual indicators such as paragraph or page breaks, titles, or chapters to signal transitions between ideas.

- Listeners have only a flow of words, which can easily become confusing. Give your audience clear signals of when your presentation changes course.
- Numbering points makes your speech easier to follow and remember. If you tell people there are five points to consider and they can only recall three, they will realize they have lost something and are more likely to ask questions or refer to your document.

9. **Encourage listeners to write.** One way of getting people to become active listeners is to encourage them to take notes.

10. **If you plan to take questions, mention it at the outset.** Let listeners know you will be taking questions rather than asking at the end, "Are there any questions?" If listeners do not know beforehand that they can ask questions, they may fail to pay attention during your talk. Not knowing they will be able to ask for clarification, they may dismiss ideas they find difficult or confusing.

11. **Motivate listeners to read your document.** Unless your document is a brief letter or memo, no oral presentation is likely to communicate the complete message. Urge your audience to read the paper or report.

- Challenge your audience with an interesting fact, question, or statistic, alerting them that more information is contained in the report.

- Pose questions and concerns shared by the listeners and tell them the answers are in the document.
- Direct them to look at specific pages of special importance.

12. **Do not waste the audience's time.** Listeners grow impatient with speakers who arrive late or unprepared. Although it is useful to pause between main points to give people an opportunity to absorb ideas, avoid long moments of silence. If you have misplaced or forgotten something, do not take time to search for it. Instead, move to the next point.

- Anticipate problems and prepare alternative presentations. Don't assume people will bring their reports to the meeting. Consider how you will proceed if a DVD player is not available, the bulb burns out on the overhead projector, or the computer won't open your presentation files. Be flexible and ready to adapt to last-minute changes.

Compiling a Writing Portfolio

Many composition courses require students to present a writing portfolio as a final assignment. A writer's portfolio, much like an artist's portfolio, is a collection of documents. Instructors generally assign two types of portfolios—a **representative portfolio** that offers examples of your best writing or a **self-assessment portfolio** that also includes a reflective autobiographical essay that traces your development as a writer over the course.

Representative Portfolios

Some instructors will simply ask you to resubmit three or four revised essays demonstrating your best work. Other instructors require that the portfolio include specific assignments, such as a personal essay, an analytical essay, or a documented argumentative paper. A representative portfolio gives you a chance to select, revise, and polish previous assignments for reconsideration to determine your final grade.

Self-Assessment Portfolios

Other instructors require that in addition to a collection of revised essays, your portfolio contain prewriting notes, outlines, and first drafts to demonstrate your skills in each step of the writing process. Usually the portfolio includes a **reflective essay,** a first-person account detailing your development as a writer, outlining your strengths and weaknesses, and explaining what you have learned.

Sample Portfolio

Table of Contents

A 2- to 5-page Reflective Essay

Two or more essays with prewriting notes, outlines, first drafts, and final draft.

Final drafts of specific essays required by the instructor

One or more optional pieces

Strategies for Creating a Portfolio

1. **Study the portfolio assignment carefully to make sure you include everything that is required.**

2. **Select previous assignments that reflect your best work.** Before revising any essays, review the assignment with the following questions and carefully read any instructor's comments.

   Does each paper have a clear thesis?
   Do you include adequate supporting detail?
   Is each paper clearly organized?
   Are introductions and conclusions effective?
   Are there errors in spelling, punctuation, and mechanics that require editing?
   Do you properly document outside sources?
   Can you improve the style and readability of your paper by using different words, deleting awkward phrases, and stating ideas more clearly?

3. **Review your writing experiences in a reflective essay prompted by these questions:**

   What were your past writing experiences?
   What were your strengths and weaknesses at the beginning of the course?
   What specific writing skills have you learned—thesis development, organization, sentence structure?
   How did your writing change throughout the course—which assignments were the most challenging?
   What have you learned as a writer?
   How will what you have learned help you write in other courses and your future career?

e-writing

Exploring Special Writing Contexts Online

You can gather additional insights into special writing contexts by exploring the Web. Academic and professional organizations, research institutions, and technical journals provide current advice on writing in special situations.

1. Using InfoTrac College Edition, available through your English CourseMate at **www.cengagebrain.com**, or one of your library's databases, search for current articles about collaborative writing, writing online, giving oral presentations, e-mail, and business writing.

2. Conduct a Web search using such terms as *collaborative writing, writing to mass audiences, giving oral presentations, writing online, online writing groups, writing e-mail, using PowerPoint, netiquette, writing to multiple readers,* and *writing portfolios* to locate current sites of interest.

3. Review e-mails you have sent and received for netiquette. Do you detect different standards for online communications? Do you need to change your style of online writing?

E-Sources

Collaborative Writing

> **http://www.stanford.edu/group/collaborate/**

Creating Multimedia Presentations

> **http://www.adobe.com/designcenter/acrobat/articles/acr7it_cibexcerpts/Lesson12.pdf**

Sample Writing Portfolio Assignment

> **http://apps.carleton.edu/campus/writingprogram/carletonwritingprogram/portfolio_requirements/**

 Access the English CourseMate for this text at **www.cengagebrain.com** for further information about special writing contexts.

CREDITS

Adler, Mortimer, "How to Mark a Book," reprinted with the permission of Simon & Schuster Inc., from *How to Read a Book* by Mortimer J. Adler and Charles Van Doren. Copyright © 1940 by Mortimer J. Adler. Copyright renewed © 1967 by Mortimer J. Adler. Copyright © 1972 by Mortimer J. Adler and Charles van Doren. All rights reserved.

Austin, James, "Four Kinds of Chance." From Austin, James H., *Chase, Chance and Creativity: The Lucky Art of Novelty,* excerpt from pages 70–77: "Four Kinds of Chance", © 2003 Massachusetts Institute of Technology, by permission of The MIT Press.

Barrett, Paul M., "American Islam," from *American Islam: The Struggle for the Soul of a Religion* by Paul M. Barrett. Copyright © 2007 by Paul M. Barrett. Reprinted by permission of Farrar, Straus and Giroux, LLC., and the Stuart Krichevsky Literary Agency, Inc.

Begley, Sharon, "What's in a Word?" from *Newsweek,* July 20, 2009, p. 31. Copyright © 2009 The Newsweek/Daily Beast Company LLC. All rights reserved. Used by permission and protected by the Copyright Laws of the United States. The printing, copying, redistribution, or retransmission of the Material without express written permission is prohibited.

Borchert, Wolfgang, "The Bread." Translated by David Porter, from *The Man Outside,* copyright © 1971 by New Directions Publishing Corp., New York and Marion Boyars Publishers, London.

Brooks, John, "The Effects of the Telephone," from *Telephone: The First Hundred Years,* pp. 8–9. Copyright © 1975, 1976 by John Brooks. Reprinted by permission of HarperCollins-Publishers, Inc. and Harold Ober Associates Incorporated.

Brown, Carolyn M., "Attacking Student Loan Debt" from *Black Enterprise,* October 2010, pp. 73(2). Reprinted by permission from Earl G. Graves Publishing Company, Inc.

Brown, Lee P., "Two Takes: Drugs Are a Major Social Problem, We Cannot Legalize Them" from *U.S. News & World Report,* July 25, 2008. Reprinted with permission from Wright's Media.

Budish, Armond, "Fender Benders: Do's and Don't's" from *Family Circle,* July 19, 1994. Copyright © 1994 by Armond D. Budish. Reprinted with permission from Armond Budish.

Capote, Truman, "Out There" from *In Cold Blood* by Truman Capote. Copyright © 1965 by Truman Capote and renewed 1993 by Alan U. Schwartz. Used by permission of Random House, Inc. and Hamish Hamilton/Penguin Books Ltd.

Carson, Rachel, "A Fable for Tomorrow" from *Silent Spring* by Rachel Carson. Copyright © 1962 by Rachel L. Carson. Copyright © renewed 1990 by Roger Christie. Reprinted by permission of Houghton Mifflin Harcourt Publishing Company and Frances Collin, Trustee. All rights reserved. Any electronic copying or distribution of this text is expressly forbidden.

Catton, Bruce, "Grant and Lee," from *The American Story* by Earll Schenk Miers. Reprinted with permission from the U.S. Capital Historical Society.

Dickinson, Emily, "My Life Had Stood—A Loaded Gun." Reprinted by permission of the publishers and the Trustees of Amherst College from *The Poems of Emily Dickinson,* Thomas H. Johnson, ed., Cambridge, Mass.: The Belknap Press of Harvard University Press, Copyright © 1951, 1955, 1979, 1983 by the President and Fellows of Harvard College.

Ramon "Tianguis" Perez (© 1991 Arte Público Press–University of Houston).

Prager, Emily, "Our Barbies, Ourselves." Copyright © 1991 by Emily Prager, used with permission of The Wylie Agency, LLC.

Quart, Alissa, "Listening to Madness." *Newsweek,* May 18, 2009, p. 54. Copyright © 2009 The Newsweek/Daily Beast Company LLC. All rights reserved. Used by permission and protected by the Copyright Laws of the United States. The printing, copying, redistribution, or retransmission of the Material without express written permission is prohibited.

Quindlen, Anna, "Homeless," copyright © 1987 by Anna Quindlen, from *Living Out Loud* by Anna Quindlen. Used by permission of Random House, Inc. and International Creative Management.

Quinn, Jane Bryant, "The Case for Walking Away" copyright © 2009 by Jane Bryant Quinn. Originally published in *Newsweek*. Reprinted by permission of the author.

Rodriguez, Joe, "Mexicans Deserve More Than La Mordida," from Knight–Ridder/Tribune Services, April 1, 1997. Copyright © 1997, KRT. Distributed by McClatchy-Tribune Information Services.

Rosenberg, Don, "What Is Depression?" Reprinted by permission of the author.

Ross, Sherwood, "Nuclear Power Not Clean, Green or Safe." Reprinted with permission from Sherwood Ross.

Sherry, Mary, "In Praise of the 'F' Word." From *Newsweek,* May 6, 1991. Reprinted with permission from Mary Sherry.

Simpson, Eileen, "Dyslexia," from *Reversals* by Eileen Simpson. Copyright © 1979, 1991 by Eileen Simpson. Reprinted by permission of Georges Borchardt, Inc., on behalf of the Estate of Eileen Simpson.

Terrell, Blythe, "Top Ten Student Money Mistakes." From http://www.youngmoney.com/money_management/spending/020809_02 and accessed March 21, 2005. Reprinted with permission from Young Money.com

Tuan, Yi–Fu, "Chinese Place, American Space." Reprinted with permission from Yi-Fu Tuan.

Urrea, Luis Alberto, "Border Story" from *Across the Wire: Life and Hard Times* by Luis Alberto Urrea, copyright © 1993 by Luis Alberto Urrea. Photographs © 1993 by John Leuders–Booth. Used by permission of Doubleday, a division of Random House, Inc. and Thomas S. Hart Enterprises on behalf of the author. For online information about other Random House, Inc. books and authors, see the Internet Web Site at http://www.randomhouse.com.

Viorst, Judith, "Friends, Good Friends, and Such Good Friends." Copyright © 1977 by Judith Viorst. Originally appeared in *Redbook*. Reprinted by permission of Lescher & Lescher Ltd. All rights reserved.

Williams, Armstrong, "Hyphenated Americans." From www.armstrong–williams.com, Nov. 7, 2000. Reprinted with permission from Mr. Armstrong Williams.

INDEX

Bold page numbers indicate material in photographs and drawings.